SEMANTIC COMPUTING

World Scientific Encyclopedia with Semantic Computing and Robotic Intelligence

ISSN: 2529-7686

Published

Vol. 1 *Semantic Computing*
        edited by Phillip C.-Y. Sheu

World Scientific Encyclopedia with Semantic Computing and Robotic Intelligence – Vol. 1

SEMANTIC COMPUTING

Editor

Phillip C-Y Sheu

University of California, Irvine

World Scientific

NEW JERSEY · LONDON · SINGAPORE · BEIJING · SHANGHAI · HONG KONG · TAIPEI · CHENNAI · TOKYO

Published by

World Scientific Publishing Co. Pte. Ltd.

5 Toh Tuck Link, Singapore 596224

USA office: 27 Warren Street, Suite 401-402, Hackensack, NJ 07601

UK office: 57 Shelton Street, Covent Garden, London WC2H 9HE

Library of Congress Cataloging-in-Publication Data

Names: Sheu, Phillip C.-Y., editor.

Title: Semantic computing / editor, Phillip C-Y Sheu, University of California, Irvine.

Other titles: Semantic computing (World Scientific (Firm))

Description: Hackensack, New Jersey : World Scientific, 2017. |
  Series: World Scientific encyclopedia with semantic computing and robotic intelligence ; vol. 1 |
  Includes bibliographical references and index.

Identifiers: LCCN 2017032765| ISBN 9789813227910 (hardcover : alk. paper) |
  ISBN 9813227915 (hardcover : alk. paper)

Subjects: LCSH: Semantic computing.

Classification: LCC QA76.5913 .S46 2017 | DDC 006--dc23

LC record available at https://lccn.loc.gov/2017032765

British Library Cataloguing-in-Publication Data

A catalogue record for this book is available from the British Library.

Desk Editor: Catherine Domingo Ong

Typeset by Stallion Press

Email: enquiries@stallionpress.com

Foreword

The line between computer science and robotics is continuing to be softened. On one hand computers are continuing to be humanized and a large number of cyber-physical systems are being developed to act upon the physical world. On the other hand, the robotic community is working on future robots that are versatile computing machines with very sophisticated intelligence compatible to human brain.

As a branch of computer science, semantic computing (SC) addresses the derivation, description, integration, and use of semantics ("meaning", "context", "intention") for all types of resource including data, document, tool, device, process and people. It considers a typical, but not exclusive, semantic system architecture to consist of five layers:

- **(Layer 1) Semantic Analysis**, that analyzes and converts signals such as pixels and words (content) to meanings (semantics);
- **(Layer 2) Semantic Data Integration**, that integrates data and their semantics from different sources within a unified model;
- **(Layer 3) Semantic Services**, that utilize the content and semantics as the source of knowledge and information for building new applications - which may in turn be available as services for building more complex applications;
- **(Layer 4) Semantic Service Integration**, that integrates services and their semantics from different sources within a unified model; and
- **(Layer 5) Semantic Interface**, that realize the user intentions to be described in natural language, or express in some other natural ways.

A traditional robot often works with a confined context. If we take the Internet (including IoT) as the context and consider the advances in clouding computing and mobile computing, it is realistic to expect that future robots are connected to the world of knowledge, so as to interact with humans intelligently as a collaborative partner to solve general as well as domain specific problems. We call such intelligence robotic intelligence.

It is for this reason that a marriage between Semantic Computing and Robotic Intelligence is natural. Accordingly, we name this encyclopedia the Encyclopedia with Semantic Computing and Robotic Intelligence (ESCRI). We expect the marriage of the two, together with other enabling technologies (such as machine vision, big data, cloud computing, mobile computing, VR, IoT, etc.), could synergize more significant contributions to achieve the ultimate goal of Artificial Intelligence.

We believe that while the current society is information centric, the future will be *knowledge centric*. The challenge is how to structure, deliver, share and make use of the large amounts of knowledge effectively and productively. The concept of this encyclopedia may constantly evolve to meet the challenge. Incorporating the recent technological advances in semantic computing and robotic intelligence, the encyclopedia has a long term goal of building a new model of reference that delivers quality knowledge to both professionals and laymen alike.

I would like to thank members of the editorial board for their kind support, and thank Dr. K. K. Phua, Dr. Yan Ng, Ms. Catherine Ong and Mr. Mun Kit Chew of World Scientific Publishing for helping me to launch this important journal.

Phillip Sheu
Editor-in-Chief
University of California, Irvine

v

CONTENTS

Foreword   v

Part 1: Understanding Semantics   1

Open information extraction   3
    D.-T. Vo and E. Bagheri

Methods and resources for computing semantic relatedness   9
    Y. Feng and E. Bagheri

Semantic summarization of web news   15
    F. Amato, V. Moscato, A. Picariello, G. Sperlí, A. D'Acierno and A. Penta

Event identification in social networks   21
    F. Zarrinkalam and E. Bagheri

Community detection in social networks   29
    H. Fani and E. Bagheri

High-level surveillance event detection   37
    F. Persia and D. D'Auria

Part 2: Data Science   43

Selected topics in statistical computing   45
    S. B. Chatla, C.-H. Chen and G. Shmueli

Bayesian networks: Theory, applications and sensitivity issues   63
    R. S. Kenett

GLiM: Generalized linear models   77
    J. R. Barr and S. Zacks

OLAP and machine learning   85
    J. Jin

Survival analysis via Cox proportional hazards additive models   91
    L. Bai and D. Gillen

Deep learning   103
    X. Hao and G. Zhang

Two-stage and sequential sampling for estimation and testing
with prescribed precision   111
    S. Zacks

Business process mining   117
    A. Pourmasoumi and E. Bagheri

The information quality framework for evaluating data science programs   125
    S. Y. Coleman and R. S. Kenett

(Continued)

Part 3: Data Integration   139

Enriching semantic search with preference and quality scores   141
    M. Missikoff, A. Formica, E. Pourabbas and F. Taglino

Multilingual semantic dictionaries for natural language
processing: The case of BabelNet   149
    C. D. Bovi and R. Navigli

Model-based documentation   165
    F. Farazi, C. Chapman, P. Raju and W. Byrne

Entity linking for tweets   171
    P. Basile and A. Caputo

Enabling semantic technologies using multimedia ontology   181
    A. M. Rinaldi

Part 4: Applications   189

Semantic software engineering   191
    T. Wang, A. Kitazawa and P. Sheu

A multimedia semantic framework for image understanding and retrieval   197
    A. Penta

Use of semantics in robotics — improving doctors' performance using a
cricothyrotomy simulator   209
    D. D'Auria and F. Persia

Semantic localization   215
    S. Ma and Q. Liu

Use of semantics in bio-informatics   223
    C. C. N. Wang and J. J. P. Tsai

Actionable intelligence and online learning for semantic computing   231
    C. Tekin and M. van der Schaar

Subject Index   239

Author Index   241

Part 1

Understanding Semantics

Open information extraction

Duc-Thuan Vo* and Ebrahim Bagheri[†]

Laboratory for Systems, Software and Semantics (LS³)
Ryerson University, Toronto, ON, Canada
*thuanvd@ryerson.ca
†bagheri@ryerson.ca

Open information extraction (Open IE) systems aim to obtain relation tuples with highly scalable extraction in portable across domain by identifying a variety of relation phrases and their arguments in arbitrary sentences. The first generation of Open IE learns linear chain models based on unlexicalized features such as Part-of-Speech (POS) or shallow tags to label the intermediate words between pair of potential arguments for identifying extractable relations. Open IE currently is developed in the second generation that is able to extract instances of the most frequently observed relation types such as Verb, Noun and Prep, Verb and Prep, and Infinitive with deep linguistic analysis. They expose simple yet principled ways in which verbs express relationships in linguistics such as verb phrase-based extraction or clause-based extraction. They obtain a significantly higher performance over previous systems in the first generation. In this paper, we describe an overview of two Open IE generations including strengths, weaknesses and application areas.

Keywords: Open information extraction; natural language processing; verb phrase-based extraction; clause-based extraction.

1. Information Extraction and Open Information Extraction

Information Extraction (IE) is growing as one of the active research areas in artificial intelligence for enabling computers to read and comprehend unstructured textual content.[1] IE systems aim to distill semantic relations which present relevant segments of information on entities and relationships between them from large numbers of textual documents. The main objective of IE is to extract and represent information in a tuple of two entities and a relationship between them. For instance, given the sentence *"Barack Obama is the President of the United States"*, they venture to extract the relation tuple President of (Barack Obama, the United States) automatically. The identified relations can be used for enhancing machine reading by building knowledge bases in Resource Description Framework (RDF) or ontology forms. Most IE systems[2–5] focus on extracting tuples from domain-specific corpora and rely on some form of pattern-matching technique. Therefore, the performance of these systems is heavily dependent on considerable domain specific knowledge. Several methods employ advanced pattern matching techniques in order to extract relation tuples from knowledge bases by learning patterns based on labeled training examples that serve as initial seeds.

Many of the current IE systems are limited in terms of scalability and portability across domains while in most corpora likes news, blog, email, encyclopedia, the extractors need to be able to extract relation tuples from across different domains. Therefore, there has been move towards next generation IE systems that can be highly scalable on large Web corpora. Etzioni *et al.*[1] have introduced one of the pioneering Open IE systems called TextRunner.[6] This system tackles an unbounded number of relations and eschews domain-specific training data, and scales linearly. This system does not presuppose a predefined set of relations and is targeted at all relations that can be extracted. Open IE is currently being developed in its second generation in systems such as ReVerb,[7] OLLIE,[7] and ClausIE,[8] which extend from previous Open IE systems such as TextRunner,[6] StatSnowBall,[9] and WOE.[10] Figure 1 summarizes the differences of traditional IE systems and the new IE systems which are called Open IE.[1,11]

2. First Open IE Generation

In the first generation, Open IE systems aimed at constructing a general model that could express a relation based on unlexicalized features such as POS or shallow tags, e.g., a description of a verb in its surrounding context or the presence of capitalization and punctuation. While traditional IE requires relations to be specified in their input, Open IE systems use their relation-independent model as self-training to learn relations and entities in the corpora. TextRunner is one of the first Open IE systems. It applied a Naive Bayes model with POS and Chunking features that trained tuples using examples heuristically generated from the Penn Treebank. Subsequent work showed that a linear-chain Conditional Random Field (CRF)[1,6] or Markov Logic Network[9] can be used for identifying extractable relations. Several Open IE systems have been proposed in the first generation, including TextRunner, WOE, and StatSnowBall that typically

Bill Gates, Microsoft co-founder, stepped down as **CEO** in January 2000. **Gates** was included in the **Forbes wealthiest list** since 1987 and **was the wealthiest** from 1995 to 2007...

It was announced that **IBM** would buy **Ciao** for an undisclosed amount. The **CEO, MacLorrance** has occupied the **corner office of the Hopkinton**, company

The **company's storage business** is also threatened by new, born-on-the **Web could providers** like **Dropbox** and **Box**, and ...

IE →

Co-founder(Bill Gates, Microsoft)
Director-of (MacLorrance, Ciao)
Employee-of (MacLorrance, Ciao)
...

Open IE →

(Bill Gate, be, Microsoft co-founder)
(Bill Gates, stepped down as, CEO)
(Bill Gates, was included in, the Forbes wealthiest list)
(Bill Gates, was, the wealthiest)
(IBM, would buy, Ciao)
(MacLorrance, has occupied, the corner office of the Hopkinton)
...

	IE	Open IE
Input	Sentences + Labeled relations	Sentences
Relation	Specified relations in advance	Free discovery
Extractor	Specified relations	Independent-relations

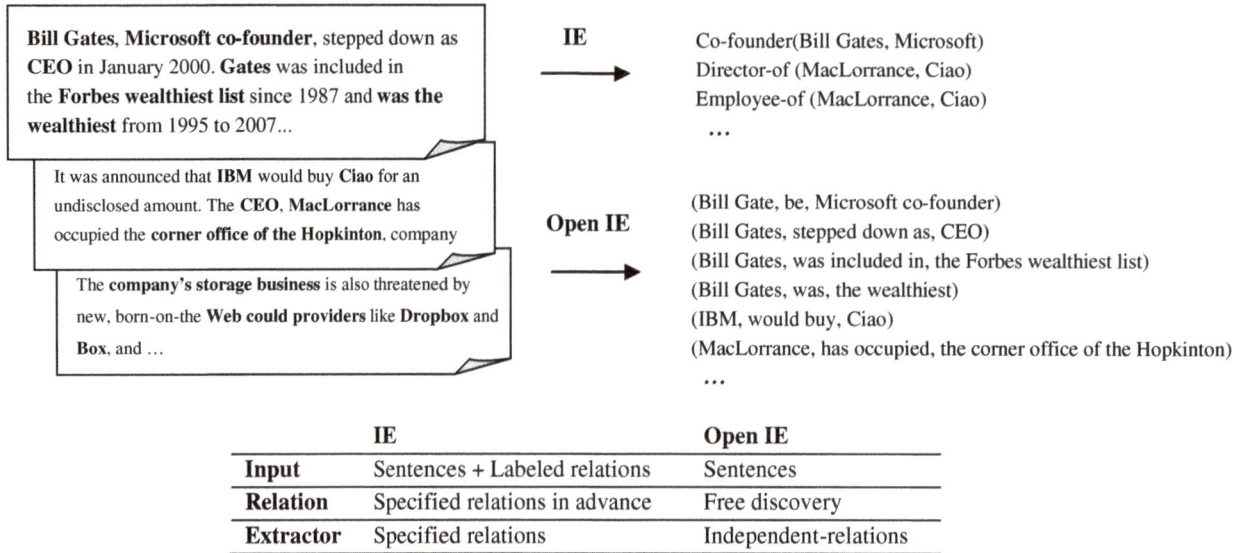

Fig. 1. IE versus Open IE.

consist of the following three stages: (1) Intermediate levels of analysis and (2) Learning models and (3) Presentation, which we elaborate in the following:

Intermediate levels of analysis

In this stage, Natural Language Processing (NLP) techniques such as named entity recognition (NER), POS and Phrase-chunking are used. The input sequence of words are taken as input and each word in the sequence is labeled with its part of speech, e.g., noun, verb, adjective by a POS tagger. A set of nonoverlapping phrases in the sentence is divided based on POS tags by a phrase chunked. Named entities in the sentence are located and categorized by NER. Some systems such as TextRunner, WOE used KNnext[8] work directly with the output of the syntactic and dependency parsers as shown in Fig. 2. They define a method to identify useful proposition components of the parse trees. As a result, a parser will return a parsing tree including the POS of each word, the presence of phrases, grammatical structures and semantic roles for the input sentence. The structure and annotation will be essential

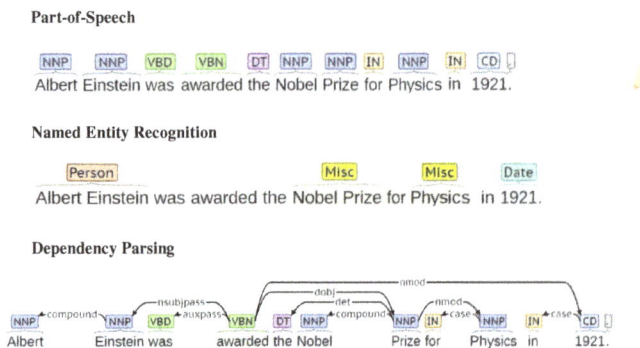

for determining the relationship between entities for learning models of the next stage.

Learning models

An Open IE would learn a general model that depicts how a relation could be expressed in a particular language. A linear-chain model such as CRF can then be applied to a sequence which is labeled with POS tags, word segments, semantic roles, named entities, and traditional forms of relation extraction from the first stage. The system will train a learning model given a set of input observations to maximize the conditional probability of a finite set of labels. TextRunner and WOE^{pos} use CRFs to learn whether sequences of tokens are part of a relation. When identifying entities, the system determines a maximum number of words and their surrounding pair of entities which could be considered as possible evidence of a relation. Figure 3 shows entity pairs "Albert Einstein" and "the Nobel Prize" with the relationship "was awarded" serving to anchor the entities. On the other hand, WOE^{parse} learns relations generated from corePath, a form of shortest path where a relation could exist, by computing the normalized logarithmic frequency as the probability that a relation could be found. For instance, the shortest

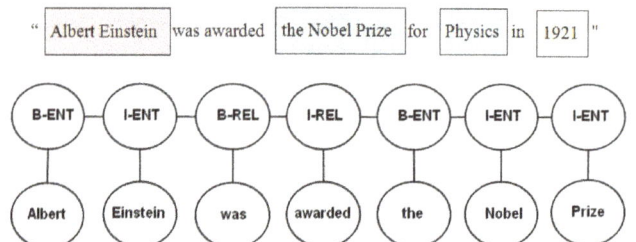

Part-of-Speech

NNP NNP VBD VBN DT NNP NNP IN NNP IN CD
Albert Einstein was awarded the Nobel Prize for Physics in 1921.

Named Entity Recognition

Person   Misc   Misc   Date
Albert Einstein was awarded the Nobel Prize for Physics in 1921.

Dependency Parsing

NNP NNP VBD VBN DT NNP NNP IN NNP IN CD
Albert Einstein was awarded the Nobel Prize for Physics in 1921.

Fig. 2. POS, NER and DP analysis in the sentence "Albert Einstein was awarded the Nobel Prize for Physics in 1921".

"Albert Einstein | was awarded | the Nobel Prize | for | Physics | in | 1921"

B-ENT — I-ENT — B-REL — I-REL — B-ENT — I-ENT — I-ENT

Albert | Einstein | was | awarded | the | Nobel | Prize

Fig. 3. A CRF is used to identify the relationship "was awarded" between "Albert Einstein" and "the Nobel Prize".

path "Albert Einstein" $\xrightarrow{nsubjpass}$ "was awarded" $\xleftarrow{dobj}$ "the Nobel Prize" presents the relationship between "Albert Einstein" and "the Nobel Prize" could be learned from the patterns "E1" $\xrightarrow{nsubjpass}$ "V" $\xleftarrow{dobj}$ "E2" in the training data.

Presentation

In this stage, Open IE systems provide a presentation of the extracted relation triples. The sentences of the input will be presented in the form of instances of a set of relations after being labeled by the learning models. TextRunner and WOE take sentences in a corpus and quickly extract textual triples that are present in each sentence. The form of relation triples contain three textual components where the first and third denote pairs of entity arguments and the second denotes the relationship between them as (Arg1, Rel, Arg2). Figure 4 shows the differences of presentations between traditional IE and Open IE.

Additionally, with large scale and heterogeneous corpora such as the Web, Open IE systems also need to address the disambiguation of entities, e.g., same entities may be referred to by a variety of names (Obama or Barack Obama or B. H. Obama) or the same string (Michael) may refer to different entities. Open IE systems try to compute the probability that two strings denote synonymous pairs of entities based on a highly scalable and unsupervised analysis of tuples. TextRunner applies the Resolver system[12] while WOE uses the infoboxes from Wikipedia for classifying entities in the relation triples.

2.1. *Advantages and disadvantages*

Open IE systems need to be highly scalable and perform extractions on huge Web corpora such as news, blog, emails, and encyclopedias. TextRunner was tested on a collection of over 120 million Web pages and extracted over 500 million triples. This system also had a collaboration with Google on running over one billion public Web pages with noticeable precision and recall on this large-scale corpus.

First generation Open IE systems can suffer from problems such as extracting incoherent and uninformative relations. Incoherent extractions are circumstances when the system extracts relation phrases that present a meaningless interpretation of the content.[6,13] For example, TextRunner and WOE would extract a triple such as (Peter, thought, his career as a scientist) from the sentence *"Peter thought that John began his career as a scientist"*, which is clearly incoherent because "Peter" could not be taken as the first argument for relation "began" with the second argument "his

---

Sentence: *"Apple Inc. is headquartered in California"*
Traditional IE: Headquarters(Apple Inc., California)
Open IE: (Apple Inc., is headquartered in, California)

Fig. 4. Traditional IE and Open IE extractions.

career as a scientist". The second problem, uninformative extractions, occurs when Open IE systems miss critical information of a relation. Uninformative extraction is a type of error relating to light verb construction[14,23] due to multi-word predicates being composed of a verb and an additional noun. For example, given the sentence *"Al-Qaeda claimed responsibility for the 9/11 attacks"*, Open IE systems such as TextRunner return the uninformative relation (Al-Qaeda, claimed, responsibility) instead of (Al-Qaeda, claimed responsibility for, the 9/11 attack).

3. Second Open IE Generation

In the second generation, Open IE systems focus on addressing the problem of incoherent and uninformative relations. In some cases, TextRunner and WOE do not extract the full relation between two noun phrases, and only extract a portion of the relation which is ambiguous. For instance, where it should extract the relation "is author of", it only extracts "is" as the relation in the sentence *"William Shakespeare is author of Romeo and Juliet"*. Similar to first generation systems, Open IE systems in the second generation have also applied NLP techniques in the intermediate level analysis of the input and the output is processed in a similar vein to the first generation. They take a sentence as input and perform POS tagging, syntactic chunking and dependency parsing and then return a set of relation triples. However, in the intermediate level analysis process, Open IE systems in the second generation focus deeply on a thorough linguistic analysis of sentences. They expose simple yet principled ways in which verbs express relationships in linguistics. Based on these linguistic relations, they obtain a significantly higher performance over previous systems in the first generation. Several Open IE systems have been proposed after TextRunner and WOE, including ReVerb, OLLIE, Christensen *et al.*,[15] ClausIE, Vo and Bagheri[16] with two extraction paradigms, namely verb-based relation extraction and clause-based relation extraction.

3.1. *Verb phrase-based relation extraction*

ReVerb is one of the first systems that extracts verb phrase-based relations. This system builds a set of syntactic and lexical constraints to identify relations based on verb phrases then finds a pair of arguments for each identified relation phrase. ReVerb extracts relations by giving first priority to verbs. Then the system extracts all arguments around verb phrases that help the system to avoid common errors such as incoherent or uninformative extractions made by previous systems in the first generation. ReVerb considers three grammatical structures mediated by verbs for identifying extractable relations. In each sentence, if the phrase matches one of the three grammatical structures, it will be considered as a relation. Figure 5 depicts three grammatical structures in ReVerb. Give a sentence *"Albert Einstein was awarded the*

$V \mid VP \mid VW^*P$
V = verb particle? adv?
W = (noun | adj | adv | pron | det)
P = (prep | particle | inf. marker)

Fig. 5. Three grammatical structures in ReVerb.[7]

Nobel Prize." for each verb V (awarded) in sentence S, it will find the longest sequence of words $(V \mid VP \mid VW * P)$ such that (1) it starts with V, (2) it satisfies the syntactic constraint, and (3) it satisfies the lexical constraint. As result, $(V \mid VP \mid VW * P)$ identifies "was awarded" as a relation. For each identified relation phrase R, it will find the nearest noun phrase X to the left of R, which is "Albert Einstein" in this case. Then it will find the nearest noun phrase Y to the right of R, which is "the Nobel Prize" in S.

Some limitations in ReVerb prevent the system from extracting all of the available information in a sentence, e.g., the system could not extract the relation between "Bill Gates" and "Microsoft" in the sentence "*Microsoft co-founder Bill Gates spoke at . . .*" shown in Fig. 6. This is due to the fact that ReVerb ignores the context of the relation by only considering verbs, which could lead to false and/or incomplete relations. Mausam *et al.*[3] have presented OLLIE, as an extended ReVerb system, which stands for Open Language Learning for IE. OLLIE performs deep analysis on the identified verb-phrase relation then the system extracts all relations mediated by verbs, nouns, adjectives, and others. For instance, in Fig. 6 ReVerb only detects the verb-phrase to identify the relation. However, OLLIE analyzes not only the verbs but also the noun and adverb that the system could determine. As in the earlier sentence, the relations ("Bill Gates","co-founder of", "Microsoft") is extracted by OLLIE but will not be extracted using ReVerb.

OLLIE has addressed the problem in ReVerb by adding two new elements namely "*AttributedTo*" and "*ClauseModifier*" to relation tuples when extracting all relations mediated by noun, adjective, and others. "AttributeTo" is used for deterring additional information and "ClauseModifier" is used for adding conditional information as seen in sentences 2 and 3 in Fig. 6. OLLIE produces high yield by extracting

---

1. "*Microsoft co-founder Bill Gates spoke at ... *"
   OLLIE: ("Bill Gates","be co-founder of", "Microsoft")
2. "*Early astronomers believed that the earth is the center of the universe.*"
   ReVerb: ("the earth","be the center of", "the universe")
   OLLIE: ("the earth","be the center of", "the universe")
   AttributeTo believe; Early astronomers
3. "*If he wins five key states, Romney will be elected President.*"
   ReVerb:("Romney", "will be elected", "President")
   OLLIE: ("Romney", "will be elected", "President")
   ClausalModifier if; he wins five key states

Fig. 6. ReVerb extraction versus OLLIE extraction.[3]

---

relations not only mediated by verbs but also mediated by nouns, and adjectives. OLLIE follows ReVerb to identify potential relations based on verb-mediated relations. The system applies bootstrapping to learn other relation patterns using its similarity relations found by ReVerb. In each pattern the system uses dependency path to connect a relation and its corresponding arguments for extracting relations mediated by noun, adjective and others. After identifying the general patterns, the system applies them to the corpus to obtain new tuples. Therefore, OLLIE extracts a higher number of relations from the same sentence compared to ReVerb.

3.2. *Clause-based relation extraction*

A more recent Open IE system named ClausIE presented by Corro and Gemulla[8] uses clause structures to extract relations and their arguments from natural language text. Different from verb-phrase based relation extraction, this work applies clause types in sentences to separate useful pieces. ClausIE uses dependency parsing and a set of rules for domain-independent lexica to detect clauses without any requirement for training data. ClausIE exploits grammar clause structure of the English language for detecting clauses and all of its constituents in sentence. As a result, ClausIE obtains high-precision extraction of relations and also it can be flexibly customized to adapt to the underlying application domain. Another Open IE system, presented by Vo and Bagheri,[16] uses clause-based approach inspired by the work presented in Corro and Gemulla[8] for open IE. This work proposes a reformulation of the parsing trees that will help the system identify discrete relations that are not found in ClausIE, and reduces the number of erroneous relation extractions, e.g., ClausIE incorrectly identifies 'there' as a subject of a relation in the sentence: "*In today's meeting, there were four CEOs*", which is avoided in the work by Vo and Bagheri.

Particularly, in these systems a clause can consist of different components such as subject (S), verb (V), indirect object (O), direct object (O), complement (C), and/or one or more adverbials (A). As illustrated in Table 1, a clause can be categorized into different types based on its constituent components. Both of these systems obtain and exploit clauses for relation extraction in the following manner:

Step 1. Determining the set of clauses. This step seeks to identify the clauses in the input sentence by obtaining the head words of all the constituents of every clause. The mapping of syntactic and dependency parsing are utilized to identify various clause constituents. Subsequently, a clause is constructed for every subject dependency, dependent constitutes of the subject, and the governor of the verb.

Step 2. Identifying clause types. When a clause is obtained, it needs to be associated with one of the main clause types as shown in Table 1. In lieu of the previous assertions, these

Table 1. Clause types.[8,17]

Clause types	Sentences	Patterns	Derived clauses
SV	Albert Einstein died in Princeton in 1955.	SV	(Albert Einstein, died)
		SVA	(Albert Einstein, died in, Princeton)
		SVA	(Albert Einstein, died in, 1955)
		SVAA	(Albert Einstein, died in, 1955, [in] Princeton)
SVA	Albert Einstein remained in Princeton until his death.	SVA	(Albert Einstein, remained in, Princeton)
		SVAA	(Albert Einstein, remained in, Princeton, until his death)
SVC	Albert Einstein is a scientist of the 20th century.	SVC	(Albert Einstein, is, a scientist)
		SVCA	(Albert Einstein, is, a scientist, of the 20 the century)
SVO	Albert Einstein has won the Nobel Prize in 1921.	SVO	(Albert Einstein, has won, the Nobel Prize)
		SVOA	(Albert Einstein, has won, the Nobel Prize, in 1921)
SVOO	RSAS gave Albert Einstein the Nobel Prize.	SVOO	(RSAS, gave, Albert Einstein, the Nobel Prize)
SVOA	The doorman showed Albert Einstein to his office.	SVOA	(The doorman, showed, Albert Einstein, to his office)
SVOC	Albert Einstein declared the meeting open.	SVOC	(Albert Einstein, declared, the meeting, open)

Notes: S: Subject, V: Verb, A: Adverbial, C: Complement, O: Object.

systems use a decision tree to identify the different clause types. In this process, the system marks all optional adverbials after the clause types have been identified.

Step 3. Extracting relations. The systems extract relations from a clause based on the patterns of the clause type as illustrated in Table 1. Assuming that a pattern consists of a subject, a relation and one or more arguments, it is reasonable to presume that the most reasonable choice is to generate *n*-ary propositions that consist of all the constituents of the clause along with some arguments. To generate a proposition as a triple relation (Arg1, Rel, Arg2), it is essential to determine which part of each constituent would be considered as the subject, the relation and the remaining arguments. These systems identify the subject of each clause and then use it to construct the proposition. To accomplish this, they map the subject of the clause to the subject of a proposition relation. This is followed by applying the patterns of the clause types in an effort to generate propositions on this basis. For instance, for the clause type SV in Table 1, the subject presentation "Albert Einstein" of the clause is used to construct the proposition with the following potential patterns: SV, SVA, and SVAA. Dependency parsing is used to forge a connection between the different parts of the pattern. As a final step, *n*-ary facts are extracted by placing the subject first followed by the verb or the verb with its constituents. This is followed by the extraction of all the constituents following the verb in the order in which they appear. As a result, these systems link all arguments in the propositions in order to extract triple relations.

3.3. *Advantages and disadvantages*

The key differentiating characteristic of these systems is a linguistic analysis that guides the design of the constraints in ReVerb and features analysis in OLLIE. These systems address incoherent and uninformative extractions which occur in the first generation by identifying a more meaningful relation phrase. OLLIE expands the syntactic scope of Reverb by identifying relations mediated by nouns and adjectives around verb phrase. Both ReVerb and OLLIE outperform the previous systems in the first Open IE generation. Another approach in the second generation, clause-based relation extraction, uses dependency parsing and a set of rules for domain-independent lexica to detect clauses for extracting relations without raining data. They exploit grammar clauses of the English language to detect clauses and all of their constituents in a sentence. As a result, systems such as ClausIE obtain high-precision extractions and can also be flexibly customized to adapt to the underlying application domain.

In the second Open IE generation, binary extractions have been identified in ReVerb and OLLIE, but not all relationships are binary. Events can have time and location and may take several arguments (e.g., "*Albert Einstein was awarded the Nobel Prize for Physics in 1921.*"). It would be essential to extend Open IE to handle *n*-ary and even nested extractions.

4. Application Areas

There are several areas where Open IE systems can be applied:

First, the ultimate objectives of Open IE systems are to enable the extraction of knowledge that can be represented in structured form and in human readable format. The extracted knowledge can be then used to answer questions.[16,18] For instance, TextRunner can support user input queries such as "(?, kill, bacteria)" or "(Barack Obama, ?, U.S)" similar to Question Answering systems. By replacing the question mark in the triple, questions such as "what kills bacteria" and "what are the relationships between Barack Obama and U.S" will be developed and can be answered.

Second, Open IE could be integrated and applied in many higher levels of NLP tasks such as text similarity or text summarization.[19–21] Relation tuples from Open IE systems could be used to infer or measure the redundancy between sentences based on the facts extracted from the input corpora.

Finally, Open IE can enable the automated learning and population of an upper level ontology due to its ability in the scalable extraction of information across domains.[22] For instance, Open IE systems can enable the learning of a new biomedical ontology by automatically reading and processing published papers in the literature on this topic.

References

[1] O. Etzioni, M. Banko, S. Soderland and D. S. Weld, Open information extraction from the web, *Commun. ACM*, **51**(12) (2008).

[2] R. Bunescu and R. J. Mooney, Subsequence kernels for relation extraction, *Proc. NIPS* (2005).

[3] Mausam, M. Schmitz, R. Bart and S. Soderland, Open language learning for information extraction, *Proc. EMNLP* (2012).

[4] D. T. Vo and E. Bagheri, Relation extraction using clause patterns and self-training, *Proc. CICLing* (2016).

[5] G. Zhou, L. Qian and J. Fan, Tree kernel based semantic relation extraction with rich syntactic and semantic information, *Inform. Sci.* **180** (2010).

[6] M. Banko, M. J. Cafarella, S. Soderland, M. Broadhead and O. Etzioni, Open information extraction from the Web, *Proc. IJCAI* (2007).

[7] A. Fader, S. Soderland and O. Etzioni, Identifying relations for open information extraction, *Proc. EMNLP* (2011).

[8] L. D. Corro and R. Gemulla, ClausIE: Clause-based open information extraction, *Proc. WWW* (2013).

[9] J. Zhu, Z. Nie, X. Liu, B. Zhang and J. R. Wen, StatSnowball: A statistical approach to extracting entity relationships, *Proc. WWW* (2009).

[10] F. Wu and D. S Weld, Open information extraction using wikipedia, *Proc. ACL* (2010).

[11] B. V. Durme and L. K. Schubert, Open knowledge extraction using compositional language processing, *Proc. STEP* (2008).

[12] A. Yates and O. Etzioni, Unsupervised resolution of objects and relations on the web, *Proc. HLT-NAACL* (2007).

[13] O. Etzioni, A. Fader, J. Christensen and S. Soderland, Mausam, Open information extraction: The second generation, *Proc. IJCAI* (2012).

[14] S. Stevenson, A. Fazly and R. North, Statistical measures of the semi-productivity of light verb constructions, *2nd ACL Workshop on Multiword Expressions* (2004), pp. 1–8.

[15] J. Christensen, Mausam, S. Soderland and O. Etzioni, An analysis of open information extraction based on semantic role labeling, *Proc. KCAP* (2011).

[16] D. T. Vo and E. Bagheri, Clause-based open information extraction with grammatical structure reformation, *Proc. CICLing* (2016).

[17] R. Quirk, S. Greenbaum, G. Leech and J. Svartvik, *A Comprehensive Grammar of the English Language* (Longman 1985).

[18] S. Reddy, M. Lapata and M. Steedman, Large-scale semantic parsing without question-answer pairs, *Trans. Assoc. Comput. Linguist.* **2**, 377 (2014).

[19] J. Christensen, Mausam, S. Soderland and O. Etzioni, Towards coherent multi-document summarization, *Proc. NAACL* (2013).

[20] J. Christensen, S. Soderland and G. Bansal, Mausam, Hierarchical summarization: Scaling up multi-document summarization, *Proc. ACL* (2014).

[21] O. Levy and Y. Goldberg, Dependency-based word embeddings, *Proc. ACL* (2014).

[22] S. Soderland, J. Gilmer, R. Bart, O. Etzioni and D. S. Weld, Open information extraction to KBP relation in 3 hours, *Proc. KBP* (2013).

[23] D. J. Allerton, Stretched verb constructions in english, *Routledge Studies in Germanic Linguistics*, (Routledge Taylor and Francis, New York, 2002).

[24] H. Bast and E. Haussmann, More informative open information extraction via simple inference, *Proc. ECIR* (2014).

[25] P. Pantel and M. Pennacchiotti, Espresso: Leveraging generic patterns for automatically harvesting semantic relations, *Proc. COLING* (2006).

[26] G. Stanovsky and I. Dagan, Mausam, Open IE as an intermediate structure for semantic tasks, *Proc. ACL* (2015).

[27] X. Yao and B. V. Durme, Information extraction over structured data: Question answering with freebase, *Proc. ACL* (2014).

Methods and resources for computing semantic relatedness

Yue Feng* and Ebrahim Bagheri†

Ryerson University
Toronto, Ontario, Canada
*yue.feng@ryerson.ca
†ebrahim.bagheri@ryerson.ca

Semantic relatedness (SR) is defined as a measurement that quantitatively identifies some form of lexical or functional association between two words or concepts based on the contextual or semantic similarity of those two words regardless of their syntactical differences. Section 1 of the entry outlines the working definition of SR and its applications and challenges. Section 2 identifies the knowledge resources that are popular among SR methods. Section 3 reviews the primary measurements used to calculate SR. Section 4 reviews the evaluation methodology which includes gold standard dataset and methods. Finally, Sec. 5 introduces further reading.

In order to develop appropriate SR methods, there are three key aspects that need to be examined: (1) the knowledge resources that are used as the source for extracting SR; (2) the methods that are used to quantify SR based on the adopted knowledge resource; and (3) the datasets and methods that are used for evaluating SR techniques. The first aspect involves the selection of knowledge bases such as WordNet or Wikipedia. Each knowledge base has its merits and downsides which can directly affect the accuracy and the coverage of the SR method. The second aspect relies on different methods for utilizing the beforehand selected knowledge resources, for example, methods that depend on the path between two words, or a vector representation of the word. As for the third aspect, the evaluation for SR methods consists of two aspects, namely (1) the datasets that are used and (2) the various performance measurement methods.

SR measures are increasingly applied in information retrieval to provide semantics between query and documents to reveal relatedness between non-syntactically-related content. Researchers have already applied many different information and knowledge sources in order to compute SR between two words. Empirical research has already shown that results of many of these SR techniques have reasonable correlation with human subjects interpretation of relatedness between two words.

Keywords: Semantic relatedness; information retrieval; similarity; natural language processing.

1. Overview of Semantic Relatedness

It is effortless for humans to determine the relatedness between two words based on the past experience that humans have in using and encountering related words in similar contexts. For example, as human beings, we know *car* and *drive* are highly related, while there is little connection between *car* and *notebook*. While the process of deciding semantic relatedness (SR) between two words is straightforward for humans, it is often challenging for machines to make a decision without having access to contextual knowledge surrounding each word. Formally, SR is defined as some form of lexical or functional association between two words rather than just lexical relations such as synonymy and hyponymy.[1]

1.1. Applications

Semantic relatedness is widely used in many practical applications, especially in natural language processing (NLP) such as word sense disambiguation,[2] information retrieval,[3] spelling correction[1] and document summarization, where it is used to quantify the relations between words or between words and documents.[4] SR is extremely useful in information retrieval techniques in terms of the retrieval process where it allows for the identification of semantic-related but lexically-dissimilar content.[1] Other more specialized domains such as biomedical informatics and geoinformatics have also taken advantages of SR techniques to measure the relationships between bioentities[5] and geographic concepts,[6] respectively.

1.2. Challenges

Developing SR methods is a formidable task which requires solutions for various challenges. Two primary challenges are encountered with the underlying knowledge resources and formalization of the relatedness measures respectively.

(1) Knowledge resources challenges: Knowledge resources provide descriptions for each word and its relations. Knowledge resources can be structured or unstructured, linguistically constructed by human subjects or collaboratively constructed through encyclopedia or web-based.

It is challenging to clean and process the large set of knowledge resources and represent each word with its extracted descriptions which requires considerable computation power.

(2) Formalization challenges: Designing algorithms to compute SR between words is also challenging since efficiency and accuracy are two important factors to be considered.

2. Knowledge Resources

In the world of SR techniques, the term knowledge resources refers to the source of information where the descriptions and relations of words are generated from. Five knowledge resources that are popular adopted literature are introduced below.

2.1. *WordNet*

WordNet is an English lexical database which is systematically developed by expert linguists. It is considered the most reliable knowledge resource due to the reason that it has been curated through a well-reviewed and controlled process. WordNet provides descriptions for English words and expresses various meanings for a word which is polysemy according to different contexts. Expert linguists defined relations and synsets in WordNet which are two of the main parts where the relations express the relations between two or more words such as hypernymy, antonymy and hyponymy, and synsets are a set of synonymous words. Moreover, a short piece of text called gloss is attached to describe members of each synset.

WordNet has been widely applied in researches for computing the degree of SR. For example, Rada *et al.*[7] constructed a word graph whose nodes are Wordnet synsets and edges are associated relations. Then SR is represented as the shortest path between two nodes. Glosses defined in Wordnet have also been explored to compute SR. For instance, Lesk[8] introduced his method in 1986 that is counting the word overlap between two glosses where the higher count of overlap indicates higher SR between the two words.

A German version of Wordnet has also been constructed named GermaNet. GermaNet shares all the features from Wordnet except it does not include glosses, therefore, approaches based on glosses are not directly applicable on GermaNet. However, Gurevych[9] has proposed an approach to solve the problem by generating pseudo-glosses for a target word where the pseudo-glosses are the set of words that are in close relations to the target word in the relationship hierarchy.

2.2. *Wikipedia*

Wikipedia provides peer-review and content moderation processes to ensure reliable information. The information in Wikipedia is presented as a collection of articles where each article is focused on one specific concept. Besides articles, Wikipedia contains hyperlinks between articles, categories and disambiguation pages.

Some researchers have benefited from the textual content of Wikipedia articles. For example, a widely-used SR technique called explicit semantic analysis (ESA)[10] treats a target word as a concept and uses its corresponding Wikipedia article as the knowledge resource to describe the target word; therefore, each word is represented as a vector of words from the associated Wikipedia article and the weights are the TF-IDF values of the words. Then cosine similarity method is applied on two vectors for two words respectively to calculate SR. Besides exploring the article contents, hyperlinks between Wikipedia articles can also be used to establish relationships between two words. Milne and Witten[11] and Milne[12] represented each word as a weighted vector of links obtained through the number of links on the corresponding Wikipedia article and the probability of the links occurrences. In their work, they have proved that processing only links on Wikipedia is more efficient and can achieve comparable results with ESA. The Wikipedia category system has also been exploited for the task of SR. For instance, WikiRelate[13] expressed the idea that SR between two words is dependent on the relatedness of their categories, therefore, they represented each word with their related category.

2.3. *Wiktionary*

Wiktionary is designed as a lexical companion to Wikipedia which is a multilingual, Web-based dictionary. Similar to Wordnet, Wiktionary includes words, lexical relations between words and glosses. Researchers have taken advantages of the large number of words in Wiktionary to create high dimensional concept vectors. For example, Zesch *et al.*[14] constructed a concept vector for each word where the value of the term is the TF-IDF score in the corresponding Wiktionary entry. Then the SR is calculated based on the cosine similarity of the two concept vectors. Also, given the fact that Wiktionary consists of lexical-semantic relations embedded in the structure of each Wiktionary entry, researchers have also considered Wiktionary as a knowledge resource for computing SR. For instance, Krizhanovsky and Lin[15] built a graph from Wiktionary where nodes are the words and the edges are the lexical-semantic relations between pairs of words. Then they applied path-based method on the graph to find SR between words. Similar to Wordnet, the glosses provided by Wiktionary are explored. Meyer and Gurevych[16] performed sense disambiguation process based on word overlaps between glosses.

2.4. *Web search engines*

Given Web search engines provide access to over 45 billion web pages on the World Wide Web, their results have been used as a knowledge source for SR. For a given search query, search engines will return a collection of useful information including rich snippets that are short pieces of text each containing a set of terms describing the result page, Web page URIs, user-specified metadata and descriptive page titles. Works based on search engines snippets include the method from Spanakis *et al.*[17] in which they extracted lexico-synactic patterns from snippets with the assumption that related words should have similar patterns. Duan and Zeng[18] computed the SR based on the co-occurrences of the two words and occurrences of each word from the snippets returned by the search engine. Also there are some works that rely on the content of the retrieved pages. For example, Sahami and Heilman[19] enhanced the snippets by including the top-*k* words with the highest TF-IDF value from each of the returned page to represent a target word.

2.5. *Semantic web*

Some researchers have exploited the Semantic Web and the Web of Data. The data on the Web of Data is structured so that it can be interlinked. Also, the collection of Semantic Web technologies such as RDF, and OWL among others allows for running queries. REWOrD[20] is one of the earlier works in this area. In this work, each target word is represented as a vector where each element is generated from RDF predicates and their informativeness scores. The predicates are obtained from DBpedia triples where they correspond to each word and the informativenss scores are computed based on predicate frequency and inverse triple frequency. After that, the cosine similarity method is applied on the vectors to generate the SR between two words. The semantic relations defined by the Web ontology language (OWL) have also been explored, for example, In Karanastasi and Christodoulakiss model,[21] three facts that are (1) the number of common properties and the inverseOf properties that the two concepts share; (2) the path distance between two concepts common subsumer; and (3) the count of the common nouns and synonyms from the concepts description are combined to compute SR.

3. Semantic Relatedness Methods

Many SR methods have been developed by manipulating the information extracted from the selected knowledge resources. Some methods use the relationships between each word from the knowledge resource to create a graph and apply these relations to indicate SR, while other methods directly use content provided by the knowledge resource to represent each concept as a vector and apply vector similarity methods to compute the SR. Moreover, there have been works on temporal modeling for building SR techniques.

3.1. *Resnik*

Resnik[22] proposed his model in 1995. The idea is that the more information two words share, the higher their SR will

be. Therefore, the IS-A hierarchy is adopted to find the lowest common subsumer of two words in a taxonomy, then the information content value is calculated as the SR score.

3.2. *WikiRelate!*

Strube and Ponzetto[13] created a graph based on the information extracted from Wikipedia where nodes are Wikipedia articles, and the edges are the links between the articles. Then the shortest path is selected between two words which are Wikipedia articles to determine the SR score.

3.3. *Hughes and Ramage*

Hughes and Ramage[23] construct a graph from WordNet where the nodes are Synsets, TokenPOS and Tokens, and the edges are the relations defined in WordNet between these nodes. The conditional probability from one node to another is caluclated beforehand, then the authors apply Random Walk algorithm on the graph to create a stationary distribution for each target word by starting the walk on the target word node. Finally, SR is computed by comparing the similarity between the stationary distributions obtained for two words.

3.4. *ESA*

Gabrilovich adn Markovitch[10] have proposed the ESA technique in 2007 by considering Wikipedia as its knowledge resource. In their approach, a semantic mapper is built to represent a target word as a vector of Wikipedia concepts where the weights are the TF-IDF values of the words in the underlying articles. Then the SR is computed by calculating the similarity between two vectors represented for the two words respectively.

3.5. *Lesk*

Lesk[8] takes advantage of the glosses defined for each word from WordNet. Specifically, SR is determined by counting the number of words overlap between two glosses obtained for the two words. The higher the count of overlap, the more related the two words are.

3.6. *Sahami and Heilman*

Sahami and Heilman[19] benefit from the results returned by a Web search engine. By querying the target word, they enrich the short snippets by including the top words ranked based on the TF-IDF values from each returned page. Then the vector is used to compute the degree of SR between two words.

3.7. *WLM*

Milne[11] intends to reduce the computation costs of the ESA approach, therefore, a more efficient model is built by considering links found within corresponding Wikipedia articles where the basic assumption is the more links two articles share, the more they are related. So a word is represented as a vector of links. Finally, SR is computed by comparing the similarity between the link vectors.

3.8. *TSA*

Radinsky *et al.*[24] propose a temporal semantic analysis method based on the idea that enormous information can be revealed by studying the similarity of word usage patterns over time. Therefore, in their model, a word is represented as a weighted vector of concept time series obtained from a historical archive such as NY Times archive. Then SR is found by comparing the similarity between two time series.

4. Evaluation

In order to evaluate a SR method, researchers have adopted various goldstandard datasets and strategies for comparative analysis. In this section, we introduce the common datasets and metrics researchers have used.

4.1. *Datasets*

The gold standard datasets are often constructed by collecting subjective opinion of humans in terms of the SR between words. The main purpose of creating a SR dataset is to assign a degree of SR between a set of word pairs so they can be used as a gold standard benchmark for evaluating different SR methods. The datasets that have been used and cited in literatures are mainly in English and German languages. Below are four popular English datasets.

4.1.1. *RG-65*

The Rubenstein–Goodenough (RG-65)[25] is created by collecting human judgments from 51 subjects, the similarity between each word pair is equal to the average of the scores given by the subjects. The RG-65 dataset includes 65 noun pairs, and the similarity of each word pair is scored on a scale between 0 to 4 where higher score indicates higher similarity. The RG-65 dataset has been used as gold standard in many researches such as Strube and Ponzetto.[13]

4.1.2. *MC-30*

Miller–Charles (MC-30)[26] is a subset of the original RG-65 dataset that contains 30 noun pairs. The MC-30 dataset is additionally verified and evaluated by another 38 subjects and it is widely adopted in many works such as in Refs. 11 and 17.

4.1.3. *Fin-353*

Finkelstein *et al.*[27] introduced a dataset that contains 353 word pairs where 30 word pairs are obtained from the MC-30 dataset. The dataset is divided into two parts where the first part contains 153 word pairs obtained from 13 subjects and the second part contains 200 word pairs that are judged from 16 subjects. In some literature, the first set is used for training and the second is used for evaluation. The use of Fin-353 dataset can be found in Ref. 28 among others.

4.1.4. *YP-130*

Yang Powers (YP-130) is a dataset designed especially for evaluating a SR methods ability to assign the relatedness between verbs. The YP-130 contains 130 verb pairs.

There are also some datasets in German language. For instance, Gurevych dataset (Gur-65)[9] is the German translation of the English RG-65 dataset, Gurevych dataset (Gur-30) is a subset of the Gur-65 dataset, which is associated with the English MC-30 dataset. Gurevych dataset (Gur-350)[29] consists of 350 word pairs which includes nouns, verbs and adjectives judged by eight human subjects. The Zesch–Gurvych (ZG-222) dataset[29] contains 222 domain specific word pairs that were evaluated by 21 subjects which includes nouns, verbs and adjectives.

4.2. *Methods*

There are two typical ways to evaluate a SR method that are (1) calculating the degree of correlation with human judgments and (2) measuring performance in application-specific tasks.

4.2.1. *Correlation with human judgments*

Calculating the correlation between the output of a SR method and the score obtained from a gold standard dataset is one of the main techniques for evaluating a semantic method. Either the absolute values from a semantic method and the relatedness values from the gold standard are used, or the rankings produced by the relatedness method with the rankings in the gold standard are compared. Comparing the correlation between rankings is more popularly adopted in literature due to the reason it is less sensitive to the actual relatedness values. Pearson product-moment correlation coefficient[31] and Spearmans rank correlation coefficient[30] are two most popular coefficient to calculate the correlation between a SR method and the human judgments.

4.2.2. *Application-specific tasks*

Instead of directly comparing the output from a SR method with the gold standard dataset, a SR method can be embedded into an application-specific task, and the performance of the application can be the indicator of the performance of the SR method. The underlying hypothesis of this evaluation is that the more accurate a SR method is, the better the performance of the application task.

Various application-specific tasks have been used to evaluate the SR method. For instance, Sahami and Heilman[19] evaluated their work through the task of search query suggestion; Patwardhan and Pedersen[2] used their SR method in the word sense disambiguation application as the target evaluation application; while Gracia and Mena[32] deployed their method in the ontology matching task.

References

[1] I. A. Budan and H. Graeme, Evaluating wordnet-based measures of semantic distance, *Comput. Linguist.* **32**(1), 13 (2006).

[2] S. Patwardhan, S. Banerjee and T. Pedersen, SenseRelate: TargetWord: A generalized framework for word sense disambiguation, *Proc. ACL 2005 on Interactive Poster and Demonstration Sessions, Association for Computational Linguistics* (2005).

[3] L. Finkelstein *et al.*, Placing search in context: The concept revisited, *Proc. 10th Int. Conf. World Wide Web*, ACM (2001).

[4] C. W. Leong and R. Mihalcea, Measuring the semantic relatedness between words and images, *Proc. Ninth Int. Conf. Computational Semantics, Association for Computational Linguistics* (2011).

[5] M. E. Renda *et al.*, *Information Technology in Bio- and Medical Informatics*.

[6] B. Hecht *et al.*, Explanatory semantic relatedness and explicit spatialization for exploratory search, *Proc. 35th Int. ACM SIGIR Conf. Research and Development in Information Retrieval*, ACM (2012).

[7] R. Rada *et al.*, Development and application of a metric on semantic nets, *IEEE Trans. Syst. Man Cybern.* **19**(1), 17 (1989).

[8] M. Lesk, Automatic sense disambiguation using machine readable dictionaries: How to tell a pine cone from an ice cream cone, *Proc. 5th Ann. Int. Conf. Systems Documentation*, ACM (1986).

[9] I. Gurevych, Using the structure of a conceptual network in computing semantic relatedness, *Natural Language Processing IJCNLP 2005* (Springer Berlin Heidelberg, 2005), pp. 767–778.

[10] E. Gabrilovich and S. Markovitch, Computing semantic relatedness using wikipedia-based explicit semantic analysis, *IJCAI*, Vol. 7 (2007).

[11] I. Witten and D. Milne, An effective, low-cost measure of semantic relatedness obtained from Wikipedia links, *Proc. AAAI Workshop on Wikipedia and Artificial Intelligence: An Evolving Synergy*, AAAI Press, Chicago, USA (2008).

[12] D. Milne, Computing semantic relatedness using wikipedia link structure, *Proc. New Zealand Computer Science Research Student Conference* (2007).

[13] M. Strube and S. P. Ponzetto, WikiRelate! Computing semantic relatedness using Wikipedia, *AAAI*, Vol. 6 (2006).

[14] T. Zesch, C. Mller and I. Gurevych, Using wiktionary for computing semantic relatedness, AAAI, Vol. 8.

[15] A. A. Krizhanovsky and L. Feiyu, Related terms search based on wordnet/wiktionary and its application in ontology matching, arXiv:0907.2209.

[16] C. M. Meyer and I. Gurevych, To Exhibit is not to Loiter: A Multilingual, Sense-Disambiguated Wiktionary for Measuring Verb Similarity, COLING 2012 (2008).

[17] G. Spanakis, G. Siolas and A. Stafylopatis, A hybrid web-based measure for computing semantic relatedness between words, *21st Int. Conf. Tools with Artificial Intelligence, 2009. ICTAI'09*, IEEE (2009).

[18] J. Duan and J. Zeng, Computing semantic relatedness based on search result analysis, *Proc. The 2012 IEEE/WIC/ACM Int. Joint Conf. Web Intelligence and Intelligent Agent Technology* Vol. 3, IEEE Computer Society (2012).

[19] M. Sahami and T. D. Heilman, A web-based kernel function for measuring the similarity of short text snippets, *Proc. 15th Int. Conf. World Wide Web*, ACM (2006).

[20] G. Pirr, REWOrD: Semantic relatedness in the web of data, *AAAI* (2012).

[21] A. Karanastasi and S. Christodoulakis, The OntoNL semantic relatedness measure for OWL ontologies, *2nd Int. Conf. Digital Information Management, 2007. ICDIM'07*, Vol. 1. IEEE (2007).

[22] P. Resnik, Using information content to evaluate semantic similarity in a taxonomy, arXiv:cmp-lg/9511007.

[23] T. Hughes and D. Ramage, Lexical Semantic Relatedness with Random Graph Walks. EMNLP-CoNLL (2007).

[24] K. Radinsky *et al.*, A word at a time: Computing word relatedness using temporal semantic analysis, *Proc. 20th Int. Conf. World Wide Web*, ACM (2011).

[25] H. Rubenstein and J. B. Goodenough, Contextual correlates of synonymy, *Commun. ACM* **8**(10), 627 (1965).

[26] G. A. Miller and W. G. Charles, Contextual correlates of semantic similarity, *Lang. Cogn. Process.* **6**(1), 1 (1991).

[27] E. Agirre *et al.*, A study on similarity and relatedness using distributional and wordnet-based approaches, *Proc. Human Language Technologies: The 2009 Annual Conf. North American Chapter of the Association for Computational Linguistics, Association for Computational Linguistics* (2009).

[28] C. Fellbaum, *WordNet* (Blackwell Publishing Ltd, 1998).

[29] T. Zesch and I. Gurevych, Automatically creating datasets for measures of semantic relatedness, *Proc. Workshop on Linguistic Distances, Association for Computational Linguistics* (2006).

[30] J. H. Zar, Spearman rank correlation, *Encyclopedia of Biostatistics* (1998).

[31] J. Benesty *et al.*, Pearson correlation coefficient, *Noise Reduction in Speech Processing* (Springer Berlin Heidelberg, 2009), pp. 1–4.

[32] J. Gracia and E. Mena, Web-based measure of semantic relatedness, *Web Information Systems Engineering-WISE 2008* (Springer Berlin Heidelberg, 2008), pp. 136–150.

Semantic summarization of web news

Flora Amato*, Vincenzo Moscato[†], Antonio Picariello[‡] and Giancarlo Sperlí[§]

Dipartimento di Ingegneria Elettrica e Tecnologie dell'Informazione
University of Naples, Naples Italy
*flora.amato@unina.it
[†]vmoscato@unina.it
[‡]antonio.picariello@unina.it
[§]giancarlo.sperli@unina.it

Antonio D'Acierno
ISA - CNR, Avellino, Italy
dacierno.a@isa.cnr.it

Antonio Penta
United Technology Research Center Ireland (UTRC-1)
pentaa@utrc.utc.com

In this paper, we present a general framework for retrieving relevant information from news papers that exploits a novel summarization algorithm based on a deep semantic analysis of texts. In particular, we extract from each Web document a set of triples (subject, predicate, object) that are then used to build a summary through an unsupervised clustering algorithm exploiting the notion of semantic similarity. Finally, we leverage the centroids of clusters to determine the most significant summary sentences using some heuristics. Several experiments are carried out using the standard DUC methodology and ROUGE software and show how the proposed method outperforms several summarizer systems in terms of recall and readability.

Keywords: Web summarization; information extraction; text mining.

1. Introduction

The exponential growth of the Web has made the search and track of information apparently easier and faster, but the huge information overload requires algorithms and tools allowing for a fast and easy access to the specific *desired* information. In other words, from one hand information is available to everybody, from the other hand, the vast quantity of information is itself the reason of the difficulty to retrieve data, thus creating the well known problem of discriminating between "useful" and "useless" information.

This new situation requires to investigate new ways to handle and process information, that has to be delivered in a rather small space, retrieved in a short time, and represented as accurately as possible.

Due to the 80% of data in information generation process is contained in *natural-language* texts, the searching of suitable and efficient *summarization* techniques has become a hot research topic. Moreover, summarization, especially text summarization from web sources, may be considered as the process of "distilling" the most important information from a variety of logically related sources, such as the ones returned from classic search engines, in order to produce a short, concise and grammatically meaningful version of information spread out in pages and pages of texts.

We can consider as an example a typical workflow related to a news reporter that has just been informed of a plane crash in Milan and that would quickly like to gather more details about this event. We suppose that the following textual information on the accident, extracted from some web sites already reporting the news, are publicly available:

"A Rockwell Commander 112 airplane crashed into the upper floors of the Pirelli Tower in Milan, Italy. Police and ambulances are at the scene. The president, Marcello Pera, just moments ago was informed about the incident in Milan, he said at his afternoon press briefing". "It was the second time since the Sept 11 terror attacks on New York and Washington that a plane has struck a high-rise building. Many people were on the streets as they left work for the evening at the time of the crash. Ambulances streamed into the area and pedestrians peered upward at the sky. The clock fell to the floor. The interior minister had informed the senate president, Marcello Pera, that the crash didn't appear to be a terror attack."

The paper is organized as follows. Section 2 provide an overview of literature on multiple document summarizer systems. In Sec. 3, we discuss a general model, that is useful to solve the problem of automatic summarization and then we illustrate the instance of the model used for our aims. Section 4 presents the summarization framework developed to test the theoretical model. Finally, in Sec. 5 we provide the experimental evaluation performed to test the effectiveness of the system and its performances.

2. Related Works

Summarization has been studied for a long time in the scientific community: as a matter of fact, the automatic document summarization has been actively researched since the original work by Luhn[1] from both Computational Linguistics and Information Retrieval points of view.[2]

Automatic summarizer systems are classified by a number of different criteria.[3–5]

The first important categorization distinguishes between *abstraction* or *extraction*-based summaries. An extraction-based summary involves the selection of text fragments from the source document while an abstraction-based summary involves the sentences' compression and reformulation. Although an abstractive summary could be more concise, it requires deep natural language processing techniques while extractive summaries are more feasible and became the *de facto* standard in document summarization.[6] Another key distinction is between summarization of *single* or *multiple* documents. The latter case brings about more challenges, as summarization systems have to take into account different aspects such as the diversity and the similarity of the different sources and the order of the extracted information.

Our research contributions lie in the area of multi-document summarization: thus, in this context, it is important to compare our approach with the existing related work on the base of: (i) how to define the information value of a text fragment, (ii) how to extract a meaningful part of it and (iii) how to combine different sources.

To extract the most significant part of a text, the majority of the proposed techniques follows the *bag of words* approach, which is based on the observation that words occurring frequently or rarely in a set of documents have to be considered with a higher probability for human summaries.[8]

In such systems, another important issue is *"to determine not only what information can be included in the summary, but also how important this information is"*;[7] thus, the *relevance* of the information changes depending on what information has already been included in the summary. To reach this goal, several systems and techniques have been proposed in the most recent literature.

Wang *et al.*[9] uses a probabilistic model, computing the words' relevance through a regression model based on several word features, such as frequency and dispersion. The words with the highest scores are selected for the final summary. In addition, in order to smooth the phenomenon of redundancy, a cross-sentence word overlap value is computed to discard sentences having the same semantic content.

In Ref. 10, key-phrases are extracted from the narrative paragraphs using classifiers that learn the significance of each kind of sentences. Finally, a summary is generated by a sentence extraction algorithm. Another interesting approach is proposed by Ref. 11, where the goal is to analyze text and retrieve relevant information in the form of a semantic graph based on subject-verb-object triples extracted from sentences.

A general framework able to combine sentence-level structure information and semantic similarity is presented in Ref. 6. Finally, in Ref. 12 the authors propose an extractive summarization of ontology based on a notion of RDF sentence as the basic unit of summarization. The summarization is obtained by extracting a set of salient RDF sentences according to a re-ranking strategy. Ontologies are also used to support the summarization: for instance,[13] describe how they use Yago ontology to support entity recognition and disambiguation.

3. A Model for Automatic Multi-Document Summarization

3.1. *Basic elements of the model*

Our idea is inspired by the text summarization models based on *Maximum Coverage Problem*,[14,15] but differently from them we design a methodology that combines both the syntactic and the semantic structure of a text. In particular, in the proposed model, the documents are segmented into several linguistic units (named as *summarizable sentences*). Our main goal is to *cover* as many conceptual units as possible using only a small number of sentences.

Definition 1 (Summarizable sentence and semantic atoms). A *Summarizable Sentence* σ defined over a document D is a couple:

$$\sigma = \langle s, \{t_1, t_2, \dots, t_m\} \rangle, \tag{1}$$

s being a sentence belonging to D and $\{t_1, t_2, \dots, t_m\}$ being a set of atomic or structured information that expresses in some way the semantic content related to s.

We provide the example sentences in Table 1 to better explain the introduced definitions.

Document	Sentence	Text of Sentence
1	1(a)	People and ambulances were at the scene.
	1(b)	Many cars were on the street.
	1(c)	A person died in the building.
2	2(a)	Marcello Pera denied the terror attack
	2(b)	A man was killed in the crash.
	2(c)	The president declared an emergency.

Definition 2 (Summarization algorithm). Let $\mathcal{D}$ be a set of documents, a *Summarization Algorithm* is formed by a sequence of two functions ϕ and χ. The semantic partitioning function (ϕ) partitions $\mathcal{D}$ in K sets $\mathcal{P}_1, \ldots, \mathcal{P}_K$ of summarizable sentences having similar semantics in terms of semantic atoms and returns for each set the related *information score* by opportunely combining the score of each semantic atom:

$$\phi : \mathcal{D} \to \mathcal{S}^* = \{\langle \mathcal{P}_1, \hat{w}_1 \rangle, \ldots, \langle \mathcal{P}_K, \hat{w}_K \rangle\} \quad (2)$$

s. t. $\mathcal{P}_i \cap \mathcal{P}_j = \emptyset, \forall i \neq j$.

The *Sequential Sentence Selection* function (χ):

$$\chi : \mathcal{S}^* \to \mathcal{S} \quad (3)$$

selects a set of the sentences $\mathcal{S}$ from original documents containing the semantics of most important clustered information sets in such a way that:

(1) $|\mathcal{S}| \leq L$,
(2) $\forall \mathcal{P}_k, \hat{w}_k \geq \iota, \nexists t_j, t_j \in_\sigma \mathcal{S}^* : \text{sim}(t_i, t_j) \geq \gamma, t_i \in_\sigma \mathcal{S}$.

ι and γ being two opposite thresholds. With abuse of notation, we use the symbol $\in_\sigma$ to indicate that a semantic atom comes from a sentence belonging to the set of summarizable sentences $\mathcal{S}$.

Now, we are going to explain the following points of our model are: (i) how to represent and extract semantic atoms of a document, (ii) how to evaluate the similarity between two semantic atoms, (iii) how to calculate a score for each semantic atom, and finally, (iv) how to define suitable semantic partitioning and sentence selection functions.

3.2. *Extracting semantic atoms from a text*

We adopted the principles behind the RDF framework used in the Semantic Web community to semantically describe web resources. The idea is based on representing data in terms of a triple $\langle$*subject, verb, object*$\rangle$, attaching to each element of triples the tokens extracted by processing the document.

The triples are extracted from each sentence in the documents as by applying a set of rules on the *parse tree* structure computed on each sentence. In our rules, subjects and objects are nouns or chunks while the verbs are reported in the infinitive form.[a] It is worth to be noted that in the case of long sentences more triples may be associated to a sentence. The rules are obtained by defining a set of patterns for subject, verb and object which includes not only part of speech features but also parse tree structures. In particular, we start from the patterns described in Ref. 16 in order to include

not only relations but also subjects and objects and we add to the pattern expressions features related to the sentence linguistic structure (parse tree).

3.3. *Semantic similarity function*

In our model, we decided to compare two semantic atoms based on the similarity measure obtained by the comparison of the elements hosted by a summarization triple, namely subject, predicate, and object. In particular, let us consider two sentences and assume to extract from them two triples t_1 and t_2; we define as similarity between two t_1 and t_2 the function:

$$\text{sim}(t_1, t_2) = F_{\text{agr}}(F^{\text{sim}}(\text{sub}_1, \text{sub}_2), F^{\text{sim}}(\text{pred}_1, \text{pred}_2),$$
$$F^{\text{sim}}(\text{obj}_1, \text{obj}_2)) \quad (4)$$

The function F^{sim} is used to obtain the similarity among values of the semantic atoms, while F_{agr} is an aggregation function. In particular, we use the Wu and Palmer similarity[17] for computing the similarity among elements of our triples. This similarity is based on the *Wordnet Knowledge Base*, that lets us compare triples based on their semantic content.

3.4. *Semantic atom score*

Several metrics (*frequency-based*, *based on frequency and position*, *query-based*) were studied and applied proving the capability to get meaningful results on certain types of documents as described in Ref. 4. We developed the following method that combines the values of *frequency* and *position* with a value of *source preference*[b]: (i) A value of reputation (r) is assigned to each semantic atom obtained from the value of reputation of the related source to which the information element belongs, (ii) The frequency (Fr) is calculated through the occurrences of the semantic atom $t =$ (subject, predicate and object) across the document set (Fr $= \frac{\text{count}(t)}{\mathcal{N}}$), (iii) A score ($\rho$) is assigned depending on the position of the sentence, to which a semantic atom is associated in the original document. We assume this relationship to be $\rho = \frac{1}{\text{pos}}$, pos being the related position.

The final score for our semantic atom is thus obtained combining frequency, position and reputation as: $\omega(t) = \beta_1 \cdot r + \beta_2 \cdot \text{Fr} + \beta_3 \cdot \rho$, being $\sum_{i=1}^3 \beta_i = 1$ and $\beta_i \in \mathbb{R}$. In turn, the information score for a set of summarizable sentences ($\mathcal{P}$) is defined as the average value of the information scores of all the semantic atoms belonging to $\mathcal{P}$: $\hat{\omega}(\mathcal{P}) = \frac{1}{|\mathcal{P}|} \cdot \sum_{t_i \in \mathcal{P}} (\omega(t_i))$.

3.5. *The semantic partitioning function*

In our context, the clusters have different shapes and they are characterized from density-connected points; thus, we

---

[a]We do not consider any other grammatical units for a sentence such as adjective, preposition and so on. This is because we are not interested in detecting the sentiment or opinion in the text or to provide just triples themselves as final summarization results to the user, but we exploit them like "pointers" to original sentences that are the real components of our summaries.

[b]A value given by the user through a qualitative feedback that is assumed to be the *value of reputation* of each sources.

decided to use in our experiments the *OPTICS* algorithm,[18] that is based on a *density-based* cluster approach. In our context, the clustering procedure is applied on semantic atoms, thus we can use as distance $d(t_i, t_j)$ the value of $1 - \text{sim}(t_i, t_j)$.

Cluster	$\hat{\omega}$	ω	DI	PI	SI	Sentence
1	0.25	0.3	1	12	a	The ambulance arrived on the scene.
1	0.25	0.2	2	14	b	The cars were on the street.
2	0.15	0.2	1	3	c	A man was killed in the crash
2	0.15	0.1	3	2	d	He ended in the crash
3	0.15	0.2	2	15	e	He declared an emergency
3	0.15	0.1	4	10	f	The chief asked help

In this way, we will have clusters where the sentences that are semantically more similar are grouped together. Now, we have to describe how we choose the sentences from the clusters by minimizing the information score and the text redundancy.

3.6. *Sentence selection function and summary ordering*

In this section, we discuss how we choose the sentences from the clusters by maximizing the information score and minimizing text redundancy, following the general approach described in the basic model. First, we order the clusters according to their scores, then we use the threshold ι_1 to select the most important ones with respect to the length restrictions. After this stage, we select the sentence that has the most representative semantic atoms, minimizing, at the same time, the redundancy. As several sentences may have multiple semantic atoms, we need to eliminate the possibility that the same sentence can be reported in the summary several times, because its semantic atoms are spread all over the clusters. We penalize the average score of each cluster if we have already considered it during our summary building process; we also check if the clusters contain any other useful information by comparing their comulative average score with the threshold ι_2.

Once the optimal summary has been determined, the sentences are ordered maximizing the partial ordering of sentences within the single documents.

4. Proposal Framework

We propose a framework, called *iWin*, composed by the following steps: (i) *Web Search*: in this phase several web pages are retrieved and stored into a local repository, using the available API of the most common search engines, *Text Extractor*: allows to extract related textual sentences of the

documents are extracted parsing the HTML pages, *NLP and triplets extraction*: several NLP algorithms split the extracted text into sentences and identifies the functional elements (subject, verb and object) of each sentence and the related form thus extracting the related triple, *Clustering*: performs the clustering of the triples using *OPTICS* algorithm, *Sentence Selection*: On the base of the generated clusters, the most representative sentences are selected using a maximum coverage sentence selection greedy algorithm and *Summary building*: generates the summary related to the search keywords and user preferences.

5. Experimental Process

In this section, we provide a comparison between iWIN and other existing automatic summarizer systems using the ROUGE evaluation software.[c] The provided evaluation is based on ground truth summaries produced by human experts, using recall-based metrics as the summary needs to contain the most important concepts coming from the considered documents. Two fundamental problems have been addressed: (i) the choice of the documents data set; (ii) the selection of existing tools to be compared with iWIN.

Concerning the data set, our experiments have been performed on four different data corpora used in the text-summarization field.[d] With regard to summarizer systems, we have selected the following applications: (i) **Copernic Summarizer**[22]; (ii) **Intellexer Summarizer Pro**[21]; (iii) **Great Summary**[20]; (iv) **Tools4Noobs Summarizer**[21]; (v) **Text Compactor**.[19]

For each of the four chosen topics, three summaries of different lengths (15%, 25% and 35%) have been generated both by the current system and by the other tools. Figures 2–4 show the comparison between our system and the others with respect to the ground truth using the average recall values of ROUGE-2 and ROUGE-SU4.

5.1. *Considerations on the efficiency of our approach*

We have measured the running times (on a machine equipped with Intel core i5 cpu M 430 at 2.27 GHz and with 4 GB of

---

[c]*Recall-Oriented Understudy for Gisting Evaluation*, http://haydn.isi.edu/ ROUGE/.

[d]The first contains nine newspaper articles about the air accident which happened in Milan the 18th April 2002, when a little airplane crashed to the Pirelli skyscraper; there are also three ideal summaries generated by humans (15%, 25% and 35% of the original documents' length). The second data corpus is composed of four papers about a bomb explosion in a Moscow building, which caused many dead and injured; three human generated summaries (15%, 25% and 35% of the original documents' length) are also available. A document set containing three papers about Al-Qaida with summaries whose length are 15%, 25% and 35% of the original documents' length is the third data set we used in our experiments. While the fourth data corpus (Turkey) is a document about the problems related to Turkey's entry into the European Community with available summaries with a number of sentences equal to the 15%, 25% and 35% of the original document length.

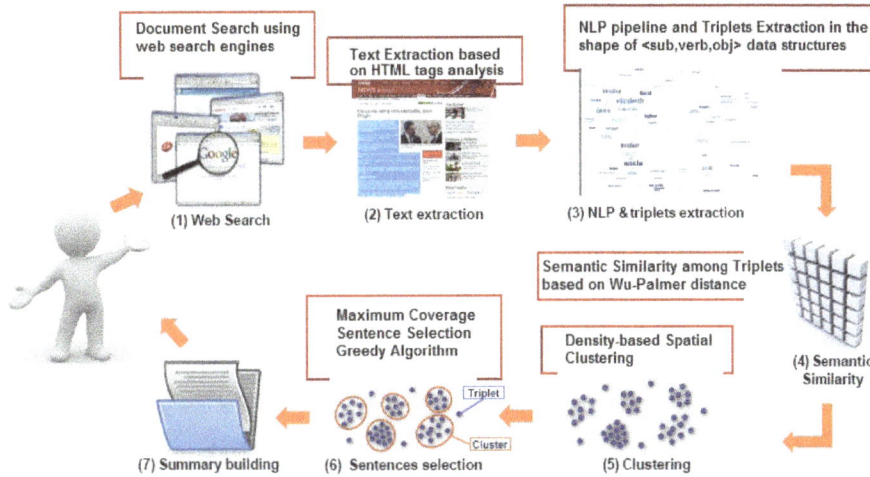

Fig. 1. The summarization process.

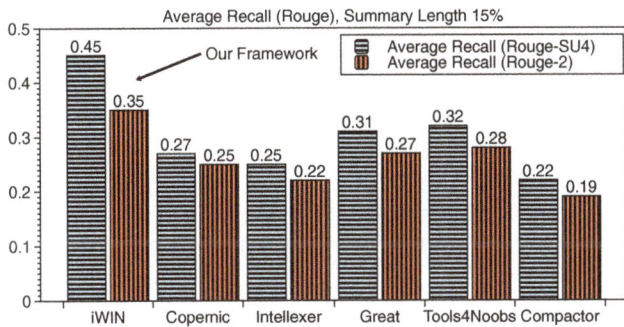

Fig. 2. ROUGE values, length = 15%.

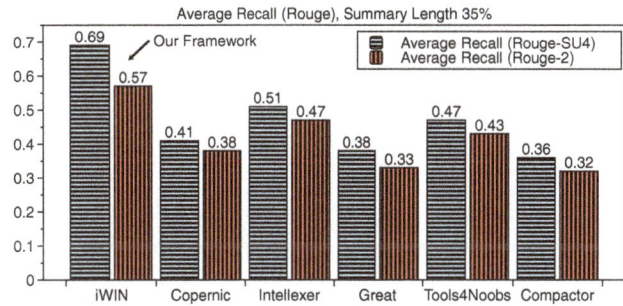

Fig. 4. ROUGE values, length = 35%.

DDR3 ram) for each summary building phase in relation to the number of input sentences; the most critical step, that can constitute a bottleneck for the system, is the semantic distances' computation. In order to have an idea of iWIN efficiency performances with respect to some of the analyzed commercial systems, we also computed running times for the Copernic and Intellexer summarizers. In particular, for a dataset of 10,000 input sentences, we observe an execution time of few seconds for Copernic, 30 s for Intellexer while our framework takes 500 s. We can point out that the average

quality of produced summary is better than commercial systems, but the efficiency of our system at the moment represents a bottleneck of its application in the case of great number of input sentences. We observed that, to reach performances of commercial systems, iWIN elaboration can be significantly improved by caching similarity values between terms that have to be computed more times and using concurrent computation threads for subjects, verbs and objects. Moreover, distances matrix can be opportunely stored and accessed by a proper indexing strategy.

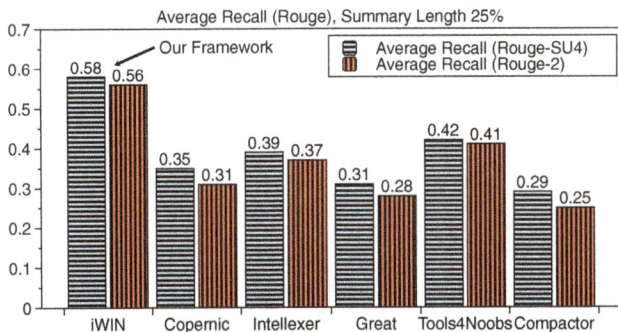

Fig. 3. ROUGE values, length = 25%.

References

[1] H. P. Luhn, The automatic creation of literature abstracts, *IBM J. Res. Dev.*, **159** (1958).

[2] R. McDonald, A study of global inference algorithms in multi-document summarization, *Proc. 29th Eur. Conf. IR Res.* (2007), pp. 557–564.

[3] U. Hahn and I. Mani, The challenges of automatic summarization, *Computer* **29** (2000).

[4] R. McDonald and V. Hristidis, A survey of text summarization techniques, *Mining Text Data*, **43** (2012).

[5] V. Gupta and S. Gurpreet, A survey of text summarization extractive techniques, *J. Emerg. Technol. Web Intell.* **258** (2010).

[6]D. Wang and T. Li, Weighted consensus multi-document summarization, *Inform. Process. Manag.* **513** (2012).

[7]H. Van Halteren and S. Teufel, Examining the consensus between human summaries: Initial experiments with factoid analysis, *Proc. HLT-NAACL 03 on Text summarization workshop*, Vol. 5 (2003), pp. 57–64.

[8]L. Vanderwende, H. Suzuki, C. Brockett and A. Nenkova, Beyond SumBasic: Task-focused summarization with sentence simplification and lexical expansion, *Inf. Process. Manage.* **1606** (2007).

[9]M. Wang, X. Wang, C. Li and Z. Zhang, Multi-document summarization based on word feature mining, *Proc. 2008 Int. Conf. Computer Science and Software Engineering* Vol. 01, (2008), pp. 743–746.

[10]M. Wang, X. Wang, C. Li and Z. Zhang, World wide web site summarization, *Web Intell. Agent Syst.* **39** (2004).

[11]D. Rusu, B. Fortuna, M. Grobelnik and D. Mladenic, Semantic Graphs derived from triplets with application in document summarization, *Informatica (Slovenia)*, **357** (2009).

[12]X. Zhang, G. Cheng and Y. Qu, Ontology summarization based on rdf sentence graph, *Proc. WWW Conf.* (2007), pp. 322–334.

[13]E. Baralis, L. Cagliero, S. Jabeen, A. Fiori and S. Shah, Multi-document summarization based on the Yago ontology, *Expert Syst. Appl.* **6976** (2013).

[14]H. Takamura and M. Okumura, Text summarization model based on maximum coverage problem and its variant, *Proc. 12th Conf. European Chapter of the AC* (2009), pp. 781–789.

[15]D. Gillick and B. Favre, A scalable global model for summarization, *Proc. Workshop on Integer Linear Programming for Natural Language Processing* (2009), pp. 10–18.

[16]O. Etzioni, A. Fader, J. Christensen, S. Soderland and M. Mausam, Open information extraction: The second generation, *IJCAI.* (2011), pp. 3–10.

[17]Z. Wu and M. Palmer, Verb semantics and lexical selection, *32nd Annual Meeting of the Association for Computational Linguistics* (1994), pp. 133–138.

[18]M. Ankerst, M. M. Breunig, H. Kriegel and J. Sander, OPTICS: Ordering points to identify the clustering structure, *Proc 1999 ACM SIGMOD Int. Conf. Management of data* (1999), pp. 49–60.

[19]Copernic, http://www.copernic.com/data/pdf/summarization-white-paper-eng.pdf.

[20]GreatSummary, http://www.greatsummary.com/.

[21]Tool4Noobs, http://summarizer.intellexer.com/.

[22]Copernic, https://www.copernic.com/en/products/summarizer/.

Event identification in social networks

Fattane Zarrinkalam*,[†,‡] and Ebrahim Bagheri*

*Laboratory for Systems, Software and Semantics (LS3)
Ryerson University, Toronto, Canada

[†]Department of Computer Engineering, Ferdowsi University of Mashhad
Mashhad, Iran
[‡]fattane.zarrinkalam@gmail.com

Social networks enable users to freely communicate with each other and share their recent news, ongoing activities or views about different topics. As a result, they can be seen as a potentially viable source of information to understand the current emerging topics/events. The ability to model emerging topics is a substantial step to monitor and summarize the information originating from social sources. Applying traditional methods for event detection which are often proposed for processing large, formal and structured documents, are less effective, due to the short length, noisiness and informality of the social posts. Recent event detection techniques address these challenges by exploiting the opportunities behind abundant information available in social networks. This article provides an overview of the state of the art in event detection from social networks.

Keywords: Event detection; social network analysis; topic detection and tracking.

1. Overview

With the emergence and the growing popularity of social networks such as Twitter and Facebook, many users extensively use these platforms to express their feelings and views about a wide variety of social events/topics as they happen, in real time, even before they are released in traditional news outlets.[1] This large amount of data produced by various social media services has recently attracted many researchers to analyze social posts to understand the current emerging topics/events. The ability to identify emerging topics is a substantial step towards monitoring and summarizing the information on social media and provides the potential for understanding and describing real-world events and improving the quality of higher level applications in the fields of traditional news detection, computational journalism[2] and urban monitoring,[3] among others.

information, because the information that the users publish on Twitter are more publicly accessible compared to other social networks.

To address the task of detecting topics from social media streams, a stream is considered to be made of posts which are generated by users in social network (e.g., tweets in the case of Twitter). Each post, in addition to its text formed by a sequence of words/terms, includes a user id and a timestamp. Additionally, a time interval of interest and a desired update rate is provided. The expected output of topic detection algorithms is the detection of emerging topics/events. In TDT, a topic is "a seminal event or activity, along with all directly related to events and activities."[4] where event refers to a specific thing that happens at a certain time and place.[9–11] A topic can be represented either through the clustering of documents in the collection or by a set of most important terms or keywords that are selected.

1.1. Problem definition

The task of topic detection and tracking (TDT) to provide the means for news monitoring from multiple sources in order to keep users updated about news and developments. One of the first forums was the TDT Forum, held within TREC.[4] There has been a significant interest in TDT in the past for static documents in traditional media.[5–8] However, recently the focus has moved to Social Network data sources. Most of these works use Twitter as their source of

1.2. Challenges

The works proposed within the scope of the TDT have proven to be relatively well-established for topic detection in traditional textual corpora such as news articles.[11] However, applying traditional methods for event detection in the social media context poses unique challenges due to the distinctive features of textual data in social media[12] such as Time Sensitivity, Short Length, Unstructured Phrases, and Abundant Information.

[‡]Corresponding author.

- **Time sensitivity.** Different from traditional textual data, the text in social media has real-time nature. Besides communicating and sharing ideas with each other, users in social networks may publish their feelings and views about a wide variety of recent events several times daily.[7,13,14] Users may want to communicate instantly with friends about "What they are doing (Twitter)" or "What is on their mind" (Facebook).

- **Short length.** Most of social media platforms restrict the length of posts. For example, Twitter allows users to post tweets that are no longer than 140 characters. Similarly, Picasa comments are limited to 512 characters, and personal status messages on Windows Live Messenger are restricted to 128 characters. Unlike standard text with lots of words and their resulting statistics, short messages consist of few phrases or sentences. They cannot provide sufficient context information for effective similarity measure, the basis of many text processing methods.[12,29,57]

- **Unstructured phrases.** In contrast with well-written, structured, and edited news releases, social posts might include large amounts of meaningless messages, polluted and informal content, irregular, and abbreviated words, large number of spelling and grammatical errors, and improper sentence structures and mixed languages. In addition, in social networks, the distribution of content quality has high variance: from very high-quality items to low-quality, sometimes abusive content, which negatively affect the performance of the detection algorithms.[61,12]

- **Abundant information.** In addition to the content itself, social media in general exhibit a rich variety of information sharing tools. For example, Twitter allows users to utilize the "#" symbol, called hashtag, to mark keywords or topics in a Tweet; an image is usually associated with multiple labels which are characterized by different regions in the image; users are able to build connection with others (link information). Previous text analytics sources most often appear as <user, content> structure, while the text analytics in social media is able to derive data from various aspects, which include user, content, link, tag, timestamps and others.[62–64]

In the following, we explain different methodologies that have been proposed in the state of the art to tackle challenges in social networks.

2. Background Literature

According to the availability of the information about events, event detection algorithms can be classified into specified and unspecified techniques.[13] The specified techniques rely on specific information and features that are known about the event, such as a venue, time, type, and description. On the other hand, when there are no prior information available about the event, unspecified event detection technique rely on the social media streams to detect the occurrence of a real-world event.

2.1. *Specified event detection*

Specified event detection aims at identifying known social events which are partially or fully specified with its content or metadata information such as location, time, and venue. For example, Sakaki et al.[14] have focused on monitoring tweets posted recently by users to detect earthquake or rainbow. They have used three types of features: the number of words (statistical), the keywords in a tweet message, and the words surrounding users queries (contextual), to train a classifier and classify tweets into positive or negative cases. To identify the location of the event a probabilistic spatiotemporal model is also built. They have evaluated their proposed approach in an earthquake-reporting system in Japan. The authors have found that the statistical features provided the best results, while a small improvement in performance has been achieved by the combination of the three features.

Popescu and Pennacchiotti[15] have proposed a framework to identify controversial events. This framework is based on the notion of a Twitter snapshot which consists of a target entity, a given period, and a set of tweets about the entity from the target period. Given a set of Twitter snapshots, the authors first assign a controversy score to each snapshot and then rank the snapshots according to the controversy score by considering a large number of features, such as linguistic, structural, sentiment, controversy and external features in their model. The authors have concluded that Hashtags are important semantic features to identify the topic of a tweet. Further, they have found that linguistic, structural, and sentiment features provide considerable effects for controversy detection.

Benson et al.[16] have proposed a model to identify a comprehensive list of musical events from Twitter based on artist–venue pairs. Their model is based on a conditional random field (CRF) to extract the artist name and location of the event. The input features to CRF model include word shape; a set of regular expressions for common emoticons, time references, and venue types; a bag of words for artist names extracted from external source (e.g., Wikipedia); and a bag of words for city venue names. Lee and Sumiya[17] have proposed a geosocial local event detection system, to identify local festivals. They have collected Twitter geotagged data for a specific region and used k-means algorithm applied to the geographical coordinates of the collected data to divide them into several regions of interest (ROI). The authors have found that an increased user activity, i.e., moving inside or coming to an ROI, combined with an increased number of tweets provides strong indicator of local festivals.

Becker et al.[18] have used a combination of simple rules and query building strategies to identify planned events from Twitter. They have identified tweets related to an event by utilizing simple query building strategies that derive queries from the structured description of the event and its associated aspects (e.g., time and venue). To provide high-precision tweets, they have asked an annotator to label the results returned by each strategy, then they have employed term-frequency analysis and co-location techniques to improve recall to identify descriptive event terms and phrases, which are then used recursively to define new queries. Similarly, Becker et al.[19] have proposed centrality-based approaches to extract high-quality, relevant, and useful related tweets to an event. Their approach is based on the idea that the most topically central messages in a cluster are more likely to reflect key aspects of the event than other less central cluster messages.

2.2. *Unspecified event detection*

The real-time nature of social posts reflect events as they happen about emerging events, breaking news, and general topics that attract the attention of a large number of users. Therefore, these posts are useful for unknown event detection. Three main approaches have been studied in the literature for this purpose: topic-modeling, document-clustering and feature-clustering approaches[1]:

2.2.1. *Topic modeling methods*

Topic modeling methods such as LDA assume that a document is a mixture of topics and implicitly use co-occurrence patterns of terms to extract sets of correlated terms as topics of a text corpus.[20] More recent approaches have extended LDA to provide support for temporality including the recent topics over time (ToT) model,[21] which simultaneously captures term co-occurrences and locality of those patterns over time and is hence able to discover more event-specific topics.

The majority of existing topic models including LDA and TOT, focus on regular documents, such as research papers, consisting of a relatively small number of long and high quality documents. However, social posts are shorter and noisier than traditional documents. Users in social networks are not professional writers and use very diverse vocabulary, and there are many abbreviations and typos. Moreover, the online social media websites have a social network full of context information, such as user features and user-generated labels, which have been normally ignored by the existing topic models. As a result, they may not perform so well on social posts and might suffer from the sparsity problem.[22–25] To address this problem, some works aggregate multiple short texts to create a single document and discover the topics by running LDA over this document.[25–27] For instance, Hong and Davison,[30] have combined all the tweets from each user as one document and apply LDA to extract the document topic mixture, which represents the user interest. However, in social networks a small number of users usually account for a significant portion of the content. This makes the aggregation process less effective.

There are some recent works that deal with the sparsity problem by applying some restrictions to simplify the conventional topic models or develop novel topic models for short texts. For example, Zhao et al.[28] have proposed the Twitter-LDA model. It assumes that a single tweet contains only one topic, which differs from the standard LDA model. Diao et al.[29] have proposed biterm topic model (BTM), a novel topic model for short texts, by learning the topics by directly modeling the generation of word co-occurrence patterns (i.e., biterms) in the whole corpus. BTM is extended by Yan et al.[57] by incorporating the burstiness of biterms as prior knowledge for bursty topic modeling and proposed a new probabilistic model named bursty biterm topic model (BBTM) to discover bursty topics in microblogs.

It should be noted that applying such restrictions and the fact that the number of topics in LDA is assumed to be fixed can be considered strong assumptions for social network content because of the dynamic nature of social networks.

2.2.2. *Document clustering methods*

Document-clustering methods extract topics by clustering related documents and consider each resulting cluster as a topic. They mostly represent textual content of each document as a bag of words or *n*-grams using TF/IDF weighting schema and utilize cosine similarity measures to compute the co-occurrence of their words/*n*-grams.[31,32] Document-clustering methods suffer from cluster fragmentation problems and since the similarity of two documents may be sensitive to noise, they perform much better on long and formal documents than social posts which are short, noisy and informal.[33] To address this problem, some works, in addition to textual information, take into account other rich attributes of social posts such as timestamps, publisher, location and hashtags.[33,35,36] These works typically differ in that they use different information and different measures to compute the semantic distance between documents.

For example, Dong et al.[34] have proposed a wavelet-based scheme to compute the pairwise similarity of tweets based on temporal, spatial, and textual features of tweets. Fang et al.[35] have clustered tweets by taking into consideration multi-relations between tweets measured using different features such as textual data, hashtags and timestamp. Petrovic et al.[31] have proposed a method to detect new events from a stream of Twitter posts. To make event detection feasible on web-scale corpora, the authors have proposed a constant time and space approach based on an adapted variant of locality sensitive hashing methods. The authors have found that ranking according to the number of users is better than ranking according to the number of tweets and considering entropy of the message reduces the amount of spam messages in the output. Becker et al.[39] have first proposed a method to identify real-world events using an a classical incremental clustering algorithm. Then, they have classified the clusters content into real-world events or nonevents. These nonevents includes Twitter-centric topics, which are trending activities in Twitter that do not reflect any real-world occurrences. They have trained the classifier on the variety of features including temporal, social, topical, and Twitter-centric features to decide whether the cluster (and its associated messages) contains real-world event.

In the context of breaking news detection from Twitter, Sankaranarayanan et al.[37] have proposed TwitterStand which is a news processing system for Twitter to capture tweets related to late breaking news that takes into account both textual similarity and temporal proximity. They have used a naive Bayes classifier to separate news from irrelevant information and an online clustering algorithm based on weighted term vector to cluster news. Further, they have used hashtags to reduce clustering errors. Similarly, Phuvipadawat and Murata[38] have presented a method for breaking news detection in Twitter. They first sample tweets using predefined search queries, and then group them together to form a news story. Similarity between posts is based on tf-idf with an increased weight for proper noun terms, hashtags, and usernames. They use a weighted combination of number of followers (reliability) and the number of retweeted messages (popularity) with a time adjustment for the freshness of the message to rank each cluster. New messages are included in a cluster if they are similar to the first post and to the top-k terms in that cluster.

2.2.3. Feature clustering methods

Feature clustering methods try to extract features of topics from documents. Opics are then detected by clustering features based on their semantic relatedness. As one of the earlier work that focused on Twitter data, Cataldi et al.[40] have constructed a co-occurrence graph of emerging terms selected based on both the frequency of their occurrence and the importance of the users. The authors have applied a graph-based method in order to extract emerging topics. Similarly, Long et al.[41] have constructed a co-occurrence graph by extracting topical words from daily posts. To extract events during a time period, they have applied a top-down hierarchical clustering algorithm over the co-occurrence graph. After detecting events in different time periods, they track changes of events in consecutive time periods and summarize an event by finding the most relevant posts to that event. The algorithm by Sayyadi et al.[42] builds a term co-occurrence graph, whose nodes are clustered using a community detection algorithm based on betweenness centrality. Additionally, topic description is enriched with the documents that are most relevant to the identified terms. Graphs of short phrases, rather than of single terms, connected by edges representing lexical inclusion or similarity have also been used.

There are also some works that utilize signal processing techniques for event detection from social networks. For instance, Weng and Lee[43] have used wavelet analysis to discover events in Twitter streams. First, they have selected bursty words by representing each word as a frequency-based signal and measuring the bursty energy of each word using autocorrelation. Then, they build a graph whose nodes are

bursty words and edges are cross-correlation between each pair of bursty words and used graph-partitioning techniques to discover events. Similarly, Cordeiro[44] has used wavelet analysis for event detection from Twitter. This author has constructed a wavelet signal for each hashtag, instead of words, over time by counting the hashtag mentions in each interval. Then, he has applied the continuous wavelet transformation to get a time-frequency representation of each signal and used peal analysis and local maxima detection techniques to detect an event within a given time interval. He et al.[6] have used Discrete Fourier Transform to classify the signal for each term based on its power and periodicity. Depending on the identified class, the distribution of appearance of a term in time is modeled using one or more Gaussians, and the KL-divergence between the distributions is then used to determine clusters.

In general, most of these works are based on terms and compute similarity between pairs of terms based on their co-occurrence patterns. Petkos et al.[45] have argued that the algorithms that are only based on pairwise co-occurrence patterns cannot distinguish between topics which are specific to a given corpus. Therefore, they have proposed a soft frequent pattern mining approach to detect finer grained topics. Zarrinkalam et al.[46] have inferred fine grained users' topics of interest by viewing each topic as a conjunction of several concepts, instead of terms, and benefit from a graph clustering algorithms to extract temporally related concepts in a given time period. Further, they compute inter-concept similarity by customizing the concepts co-occurrences within a single tweet to an increased, yet semantic preserving context.

3. Application Areas

There are a set of interesting applications of event/topic detection systems and methods. Health monitoring and management is an application in which the detection of events plays an important role. For example, Culotta[49] have explored the possibility of tracking influenza by analyzing Twitter data. They have proposed an approach to predict influenza-like illnesses rates in a population to identify influenza-related messages and compare a number of regression models to correlate these messages with U.S. Centers for disease control and prevention (CDC) statistics. Similarly, Aramaki et al.[52] have identified flu outbreaks by analyzing tweets about Influenza. Their results are similar to Google-trends based flu outbreak detection especially in the early stages of the outbreak

Paul and Dredze[50] have proposed a new topic model for Twitter, named ailment topic aspect model (ATAM), that associates symptoms, treatments and general words with diseases. It produces more detailed ailment symptoms and tracks disease rates consistent with published government statistics (influenza surveillance) despite the lack of supervised influenza training data. In Ref. 51, the authors have used Twitter to identify posts which are about health issues and they have investigated what types of links the users consult for publishing health related information.

Natural events detection (Disasters) is another application for the automatic detection of events from social network. For example, Sakaki *et al.*[14] have proposed an algorithm to monitor the real-time interaction of events, such as earthquakes in Twitter. Their approach can detect an earthquake with high probability by monitoring tweets and detects earthquakes promptly and sends e-mails to registered users. The response time of the system is shown to be quite fast, similar to the Japan Meteorological Agency. Cheong and Cheong[53] have analyzed the tweets during Australian floods of 2011 to identify active players and their effectiveness in disseminating critical information. As their secondary goal, they have identified the most important users among Australian floods to be: local authorities (Queensland Police Services), political personalities (Premier, Prime Minister, Opposition Leader and Member of Parliament), social media volunteers, traditional media reporters, and people from not for profit, humanitarian, and community associations. In Ref. 54, the authors have applied visual analytics approach to a set of georeferenced Tweets to detect flood events in Germany providing visual information on the map. Their results confirmed the potential of Twitter as a distributed "social sensor". To overcome some caveats in interpreting immediate results, they have explored incorporating evidence from other data sources.

Some applications with marketing purpose have also utilized event detection methods. For example, Medvent *et al.*[55] have focused on detecting events related to three major brands including Google, Microsoft and Apple. Examples of such events are the release of a new product like the new iPad or Microsoft Security Essential software. In order to achieve the desired outcome, the authors study the sentiment of the tweets. Si *et al.*[56] have proposed a continuous Dirichlet Process Mixture model for Twitter sentiment, to help predict the stock market. They extract the sentiment of each tweet based on its opinion words distribution to build a sentiment time series. Then, they regress the stock index and the Twitter sentiment time series to predict the market.

There are also some works that model user's interests over detected events from social networks. For example, Zarrinkalam *et al.*[47] have proposed a graph-based link prediction schema to model a user's interest profile over a set of topics/events present in Twitter in a specified time interval. They have considered both explicit and implicit interests of the user. Their approach is independent of the underlying topic detection method, therefore, they have adopted two types of topic extraction methods: feature clustering and LDA approaches. Fani *et al.*[48] have proposed a graph-based framework that utilizes multivariate time series analysis to tackle the problem of detecting time-sensitive topic-based communities of user who have similar temporal tendency with regards to topics of interests in Twitter. To discover topics of interest from Twitter, they have utilized an LDA-based topic model that jointly captures word co-occurrences and locality of those patterns over time.

4. Conclusion and Future Directions

Due to the fast-growing and availability of social network data, many researchers has recently become attracted to event detection from social networks. Event detection aims at finding real-world occurrences that unfold over space and time. The problem of event detection from social networks has faced different challenges due to the short length, noisiness and informality of the social posts. In this paper, we presented an overview of the recent techniques to address this problem. These techniques are classified according to the type of target event into specified or unspecified event detection. Further, we provided some potential applications in which event detection techniques are utilized.

While there are many works related to event detection from social networks, one challenge that has to be addressed in this research area is the lack of public datasets. Privacy issues along with Social Network companies' terms of use hinder the availability of shared data. This obstacle is of great significance since it relates to the repeatability of experiments and comparison between approaches. As a result, most of the current approaches have focused on a single data source, specially the Twitter platform because of the usability and accessibility of the Twitter API. However, being dependent on a single data source entails many risks. Therefore, one future direction can be monitoring and analyzing the events and activities from different social network services simultaneously. As an example, Kaleel[58] have followed this idea and utilized Twitter posts and Facebook messages for event detection. They have used LSH to classify messages. The proposed algorithm first independently identifies new events (first stories) from both sources (Twitter, Facebook) and then hashes them into clusters.

As another future direction, there is no method in the field of event detection from social networks which is able to automatically answer the following questions for each detected event: what, when, where, and by whom. Therefore, improving current methods to address these questions can be a new future direction. As a social post is often associated with spatial and temporal information, it is possible to detect when and where an event happens.

Several further directions can be explored to achieve efficient and reliable event detection systems such as: investigating how to model the social streams together with other data sources, like news streams to better detect and represent events,[60] designing better feature extraction and query generation techniques, designing more accurate filtering and detection algorithms as well as techniques to support multiple languages.[59]

References

[1] L. M. Aiello, G. Petkos, C. Martin and D. Corney, Sensing trending topics in twitter, *IEEE Trans. Multimedia* **15**(6) 1268.

[2] S. Cohen, J. T. Hamilton and F. Turner, Computational journalism, *Comm. ACM* **54**, 66 (2011).

[3] D. Quercia, J. Ellis, L. Capra and J. Crowcroft, Tracking "Gross Community Happiness" from Tweets, in *CSCW: ACM Conf. Computer Supported Cooperative Work*, New York, NY, USA, (2012), pp. 965–968.

[4] J. Fiscus and G. Duddington, Topic detection and tracking overview, *Topic Detection and Tracking: Event-Based Information Organization* (2002), pp. 17–31.

[5] J. Kleinberg, Bursty and hierarchical structure in streams, *Proc. Eighth ACM SIGKDD International Conf. Knowledge Discovery and Data Mining, KDD '02*, ACM, New York, NY (2002), pp. 91–101.

[6] Q. He, K. Chang and E.-P. Lim. Analyzing feature trajectories for event detection, *Proc. 30th Annual Int. ACM SIGIR Conf. Research and Development in Information Retrieval, SIGIR '07*, ACM, New York, NY (2007), pp. 207–214.

[7] X. Wang, C. Zhai, X. Hu and R. Sproat, Mining correAn event extraction model based on timelinelated bursty topic patterns from coordinated text streams, *Proc. 13th ACM SIGKDD International Conf. Knowledge Discovery and Data Mining, KDD '07*, ACM, New York, NY (2007), pp. 784–793.

[8] S. Goorha and L. Ungar, Discovery of significant emerging trends, *Proc. 16th ACM SIGKDD Int. Conf. Knowledge Discovery and Data Mining, KDD '10*, ACM, New York, NY (2010), pp. 57–64.

[9] R. Troncy, B. Malocha and A. T. S. Fialho, Linking events with media, *Proc. 6th Int. Conf. Semantic Systems, I-SEMANTICS '10*, ACM, New York, NY (2010), pp. 42:1–42:4.

[10] L. Xie, H. Sundaram and M. Campbell, Event mining in multimedia stream, *Proc. IEEE* **96**(4), 623 (2008).

[11] J. Allan, J. Carbonell, G. Doddington, J. Yamron and Y. Yang, Topic detection and tracking pilot study final report, *Proc. DARPA Broadcast News Transcription and Understanding Workshop*, Lansdowne, VA (1998), pp. 194–218.

[12] X. Hu and H. Liu, Text analytics in social media, *Mining Text Data* (Springer US, 2012), pp. 385–414.

[13] F. Atefeh and W. Khreich, A survey of techniques for event detection in Twitter, *Comput. Intell.* **31**(1), 132 (2015).

[14] T. Sakaki, M. Okazaki and Y. Matsuo, Earthquake shakes Twitter users: Real-time event detection by social sensors, *Proc. 19th WWW* (2010).

[15] A.-M. Popescu and M. Pennacchiotti, Detecting controversial events from twitter, *Proc. CIKM '10 Proc. 19th ACM Int. Conf. Information and Knowledge Management* (2010), pp. 1873–1876.

[16] E. Benson, A. Haghighi and R. Barzilay, Event discovery in social media feeds, *Proc. HLT '11 Proc. 49th Annual Meeting of the Association for Computational Linguistics: Human Language Technologies*, Vol. 1 (2011), pp. 389–398.

[17] R. Lee and K. Sumiya, Measuring geographical regularities of crowd behaviors for Twitter-based geosocial event detection, *Proc. 2nd ACM SIGSPATIAL Int. Workshop on Location Based Social Networks, LBSN '10*, ACM, New York, NY (2010), pp. 1–10.

[18] H. Becker, F. Chen, D. Iter, M. Naaman and L. Gravano, Automatic identification and presentation of Twitter content for planned events, *Int. AAAI Conf. Weblogs and Social Media* (Barcelona, Spain, 2011).

[19] H. Becker, M. Naaman and L. Gravano, Selecting quality Twitter content for events, *Int. AAAI Conf. Weblogs and Social Media* (Barcelona, Spain, 2011).

[20] D. Blei, Probabilistic topic models, *Commun. ACM* **55**(4), 77 (2012).

[21] X. Wang and A. McCallum, Topics over time: A non-Markov continuous-time model of topical trends, *Proc. 12th ACM SIGKDD Int. Conf. Knowledge Discovery and Data Mining* (2006), pp. 424–433.

[22] M. Michelson and S. A. Macskassy, Discovering users' topics of interest on twitter: A first look, *4th Workshop on Analytics for Noisy Unstructured Text Data (AND'10)* (2010), pp. 73–80.

[23] B. Sriram, D. Fuhry, E. Demir, H. Ferhatosmanoglu and M. Demirbas, Short text classification in twitter to improve information filtering, *33rd Int. ACM SIGIR Conf. Research and Development in Information Retrieval* (2010), pp. 841–842.

[24] C. Xueqi, Y. Xiaohui, L. Yanyan and G. Jiafeng, BTM: Topic modeling over short texts, *IEEE Trans. Knowl. Data Eng.* **26**(12), 2928 (2014).

[25] R. Mehrotra, S. Sanner, W. Buntine and L. Xie, Improving lda topic models for microblogs via tweet pooling and automatic labeling, *36th Int. ACM SIGIR Conf. Research and Development in Information Retrieval* (2013).

[26] J. Weng, E. P. Lim, J, Jiang and Q. He, TwitterRank: Finding topic-sensitive influential twitterers, *3rd ACM Int. Conf. Web Search and Data Mining (WSDM '10)* (2010), pp. 261–270.

[27] N. F. N. Rajani, K. McArdle and J. Baldridge, Extracting topics based on authors, recipients and content in microblogs, *37th Int. ACM SIGIR Conf. Research & Development in Information Retrieval* (2014), pp. 1171–1174.

[28] W. X. Zhao, J. Jiang, J. Weng, J. He, E.-P. Lim, H. Yan and X. Li, Comparing twitter and traditional media using topic models, *33rd European Conf. Advances in Information Retrieval* (2011), pp. 338–349.

[29] Q. Diao, J. Jiang, F. Zhu and E. Lim, Finding bursty topics from microblogs, *50th Annual Meeting of the Association for Computational Linguistics: Human Language Technologies* (ACL HLT, 2012), pp. 536–544.

[30] L. Hong and B. Davison, Empirical study of topic modeling in Twitter, *1st ACM Workshop on Social Media Analytics* (2010).

[31] S. Petrović, M. Osborne and V. Lavrenko, Streaming first story detection with application to Twitter, *Proc. HLT: Ann. Conf. North American Chapter of the Association for Computational Linguistics* (2010), pp. 181–189.

[32] G. Ifrim, B. Shi and I. Brigadir, Event detection in twitter using aggressive filtering and hierarchical tweet clustering, *SNOW-DC@WWW* (2014), pp. 33–40.

[33] G. P. C. Fung, J. X. Yu, P. S. Yu and H. Lu, Parameter free bursty events detection in text streams, *Proc. 31st Int. Conf. Very Large Data Bases, VLDB '05* (2005), pp. 181–192.

[34] X. Dong, D. Mavroeidis, F. Calabrese and P. Frossard, Multiscale event detection in social media, *CoRR abs/1406.7842* (2014).

[35] Y. Fang, H. Zhang, Y. Ye and X. Li, Detecting hot topics from Twitter: A multiview approach, *J. Inform. Sci.* **40**(5), 578 (2014).

[36] S-H. Yang, A. Kolcz, A. Schlaikjer and P. Gupta, Large-scale high-precision topic modeling on twitter, *Proc. 20th ACM SIGKDD Int. Conf. Knowledge Discovery and Data Mining* (2014), pp. 1907–1916.

[37] J. Sankaranarayanan, H. Samet, B. E. Teitler, M. D. Lieberman and J. Sperling, Twitterstand: News in tweets, *Proc. 17th ACM*

SIGSPATIAL Int. Conf. Advances in Geographic Information Systems (2009), pp. 42–51.

[38]S. Phuvipadawat and T. Murata, Breaking news detection and tracking in Twitter, *IEEE/WIC/ACM Int. Conf. Web Intelligence and Intelligent Agent Technology (WI-IAT)*, Vol. 3, Toronto, ON (2014), pp. 120–123.

[39]H. Becker, M. Naaman and L. Gravano, Beyond trending topics: Real-world event identification on Twitter, ICWSM (Barcelona, Spain, 2011).

[40]M. Cataldi, L. D. Caro and C. Schifanella, Emerging topic detection on twitter based on temporal and social terms evaluation, *10th Int. Workshop on Multimedia Data Mining, MDMKDD '10* (USA, 2010), pp. 4:1–4:10.

[41]R. Long, H. Wang, Y. Chen, O. Jin and Y. Yu, Towards effective event detection, tracking and summarization on microblog data, *Web-Age Information Management*, Vol. 6897 (2011), pp. 652–663.

[42]H. Sayyadi, M. Hurst and A. Maykov, Event detection and tracking in social streams, *Proc. ICWSM 2009* (USA, 2009).

[43]J. Weng and F. Lee, Event detection in Twitter, *5th Int. AAAI Conf. Weblogs and Social Media* (2011), pp. 401–408.

[44]M. Cordeiro, Twitter event detection: Combining wavelet analysis and topic inference summarization, *Doctoral Symp. Informatics Engineering* (2012).

[45]G. Petkos, S. Papadopoulos, L. M. Aiello, R. Skraba and Y. Kompatsiaris, A soft frequent pattern mining approach for textual topic detection, *4th Int. Conf. Web Intelligence, Mining and Semantics (WIMS14)* (2014), pp. 25:1–25:10.

[46]F. Zarrinkalam, H. Fani, E. Bagheri, M. Kahani and W. Du, Semantics-enabled user interest detection from twitter, *IEEE/WIC/ACM Web Intell. Conf.* (2015).

[47]F. Zarrinkalam, H. Fani, E. Bagheri and M. Kahani, Inferring implicit topical interests on twitter, *38th European Conf. IR Research, ECIR 2016*, Padua, Italy, March 20–23 (2016), pp. 479–491.

[48]H. Fani, F. Zarrinkalam, E. Bagheri and W. Du, Time-sensitive topic-based communities on twitter, *29th Canadian Conf. Artificial Intelligence, Canadian AI* 2016, Victoria, BC, Canada, May 31–June 3 (2016), pp. 192–204.

[49]A. Culotta, Towards detecting influenza epidemics by analyzing twitter messages, *KDD Workshop on Social Media Analytics* (2010), pp. 115–122.

[50]J. M. Paul and M. Dredze, A model for mining public health topics from twitter, Technical Report, Johns Hopkins University (2011).

[51]E. V. D. Goot, H. Tanev and J. Linge, Combining twitter and media reports on public health events in medisys, *Proc. 22nd Int.*

Conf. World Wide Web Companion, International World Wide Web Conf. Steering Committee (2013), pp. 703–705.

[52]E. Aramaki, S. Maskawa and M. Morita, Twitter catches the flu: Detecting influenza epidemics using Twitter, *Proc. Conf. Empirical Methods in Natural Language Processing* (2011), pp. 1568–1576.

[53]F. Cheong and C. Cheong, Social media data mining: A social network analysis of tweets during the 2010–2011 australian floods, *PACIS*, July (2011), pp. 1–16.

[54]G. Fuchs, N. Andrienko, G. Andrienko, S. Bothe and H. Stange, Tracing the German centennial flood in the stream of tweets: First lessons learned, *Proc. Second ACM SIGSPATIAL Int. Workshop on Crowdsourced and Volunteered Geographic Information* (ACM, New York, NY, USA, 2013), pp. 31–38.

[55]E. Medvet and A. Bartoli, Brand-related events detection, classification and summarization on twitter, *IEEE/WIC/ACM Int. Conf. Web Intelligence and Intelligent Agent Technology* (2012), pp. 297–302.

[56]J. Si, A. Mukherjee, B. Liu, Q. Li, H. Li and X. Deng, Exploiting topic based twitter sentiment for stock prediction, *ACL* (2) (2013), pp. 24–29.

[57]X. Yan, J. Guo, Y. Lan, J. Xu and X. Cheng, A probabilistic model for bursty topic discovery in microblogs, *AAAI Conf. Artificial Intelligence* (2015), pp. 353–359.

[58]S. B. Kaleel, Event detection and trending in multiple social networking sites, *Proc. 16th Communications & Networking Symp. Society for Computer Simulation International* (2013).

[59]G. Lejeune, R. Brixtel, A. Doucet and N. Lucas, Multilingual event extraction for epidemic detection, *Artif. Intell. Med.* **65**(2), 131 (2015).

[60]W. Gao, P. Li and K. Darwish, Joint topic modeling for event summarization across news and social media streams, *Proc. 21st ACM Int. Conf. Information and Knowledge Management, CIKM '12* (New York, NY, USA, ACM, 2012), pp. 1173–1182.

[61]P. Ferragina and U. Scaiella, Fast and accurate annotation of short texts with wikipedia pages, *J. IEEE Softw.* **29**(1), 70 (2012).

[62]S. Yang, A. Kolcz, A. Schlaikjer and P. Gupta, Large-scale high-precision topic modeling on twitter, *Proc. 20th ACM SIGKDD Int. Conf. Knowledge Discovery and Data Mining* (2014), pp. 1907–1916.

[63]D. Duan, Y. Li, R. Li, R. Zhang, X. Gu and K. Wen, LIMTopic: A framework of incorporating link based importance into topic modeling, *IEEE Trans. Knowl. Data Eng.* (2013), 2493–2506.

[64]M. JafariAsbagh, E. Ferrara, O. Varol, F. Menczer and A. Flammini, Clustering memes in social media streams, *Soc. Netw. Anal. Min.* (2014).

Community detection in social networks

Hossein Fani[*,†,‡] and Ebrahim Bagheri[*]

Laboratory for Systems, Software, and Semantics (LS3)
Ryerson University, Toronto, ON, Canada

†*University of New Brunswick, Fredericton, NB, Canada*
‡hosseinfani@gmail.com

Online social networks have become a fundamental part of the global online experience. They facilitate different modes of communication and social interactions, enabling individuals to play social roles that they regularly undertake in real social settings. In spite of the heterogeneity of the users and interactions, these networks exhibit common properties. For instance, individuals tend to associate with others who share similar interests, a tendency often known as homophily, leading to the formation of *communities*. This entry aims to provide an overview of the definitions for an online community and review different community detection methods in social networks. Finding communities are beneficial since they provide summarization of network structure, highlighting the main properties of the network. Moreover, it has applications in sociology, biology, marketing and computer science which help scientists identify and extract actionable insight.

Keywords: Social network; community detection; topic modeling; link analysis.

1. Introduction

A social network is a net structure made up of social actors, mainly human individuals, and ties between them. Online social networks (OSN) are online platforms that provide social actors, i.e., users, in spatially disperse locations to build social relations. Online social networks facilitate different modes of communication and present diverse types of social interactions. They not only allow individual users to be connected and share content, but also provide the means for active engagement, which enables users to play social roles that they regularly undertake in real social settings. Such features have made OSNs a fundamental part of the global online experience, having pulled ahead of email.[1] Given individuals mimic their real world ties and acquaintances in their online social preferences,[2] the tremendous amount of information offered by OSNs can be mined through social network analysis (SNA) to help sociometrists, sociologists, and decision makers from many application areas with the identification of actionable insight.[3,4] For instance, despite the heterogeneity of user bases, and the variety of interactions, most of these networks exhibit common properties, including the small-world and scale-free properties.[5,6] In addition, some users in the networks are better connected to each other than to the rest. In other words, individuals tend to associate with others who share similar interests in order to communicate news, opinions or other information of interest, as opposed to establishing sporadic connections; a tendency termed homophily as a result of which *communities* emerge on social networks.[7]

Communities also occur in many other networked systems from biology to computer science to economics, and politics, among others. Communities identify proteins that have the same function within the cell in protein networks,[8] web pages about similar topics in the World Wide Web (WWW),[9] functional modules such as cycles and pathways in metabolic networks,[10] and compartments in food webs.[11]

The purpose of this entry is to provide an overview of the definition of community and review the different community detection methods in social networks. It is not an exhaustive survey of community detection algorithms. Rather, it aims at providing a systematic view of the fundamental principles.

2. Definition

The word community refers to a social context. People naturally tend to form groups, within their work environment, family, or friends. A *community* is a group of users who share similar interests, consume similar content or interact with each other more than other users in the network. Communities are either *explicit* or *latent*. Explicit communities are known in advance and users deliberately participate in managing explicit communities, i.e., users create, destroy, subscribe to, and unsubscribe from them. For instance, Google's social network platform, Google+[a], has *Circles* that allows users to put different people in specific groups. In contrast, in this entry, communities are meant to be latent. Members of latent communities do not tend to show explicit membership and their similarity of interest lies within their social interactions.

---

[a]plus.google.com

No universally accepted quantitative definition of the community has been formulated yet in the literature. The notion of *similarity* based on which users are grouped into communities has been addressed differently in social network analysis. In fact, similarity often depends on the specific system at hand or application one has in mind, no matter whether they are explicit connections. The similarity between pairs of users may be with respect to some reference property, based on part of the social network or the whole. Nonetheless, a required property of a community is *cohesiveness*. The more users gather into groups such that they are intra-group close (internal cohesion) and inter-group loose (external incoherence), the more the group would be considered as a community.

Moreover, in *partitioned* communities, each user is a member of one and only one community. However, in real networks users may belong to more than one community. In this case, one speaks of *overlapping* communities where each user, being associated with a *mixture*, contributes partially to several or all communities in the network.

3. Application

Communities provide summarization of network structure, highlighting the main properties of the network at a macro level; hence, they give insights into the dynamics and the overall status of the network. Community detection finds application in areas as diverse as sociology, biology, marketing and computer science. In sociology, it helps with understanding the formation of action groups in the real world such as clubs and committees.[12] Computer scientists study how information is disseminated in the network through communities. For instance, community drives to connect like-minded people and encourages them to share more content. Further, grouping like-minded users who are also spatially near to each other may improve the performance of internet service providers in that each community of users could be served by a dedicated mirror server.[13] In marketing, companies can use communities to design targeted marketing as the 2010 Edelman Trust Barometer Report[b] found, 44% of users react to online advertisements if other users in their peer group have already done so. Also, communities are employed to discover previously unknown interests of users, alias implicit interest detection, which can potentially useful in recommender systems to set up efficient recommendations.[12]

In a very recent concrete application, Customer Relationship Management (CRM) systems are empowered to tap into the power of social intelligence by looking at the collective behavior of users within communities in order to enhance client satisfaction and experience. As an example, customers often post their opinions, suggestions, criticisms or support requests through online social networks such as Twitter[c] or Facebook.[d] Customer service representatives would quickly identify the mindset of the customer that has called into the call center by a series of short questions. For such cases, appropriate techniques are required that would look at publicly available social and local customer data to understand their background so as to efficiently address their needs and work towards their satisfaction. Important data such as the list of influential users within the community, the position of a given user in relation to influential users, the impact of users' opinions on the community, customer's social behavioral patterns, and emergence of social movement patterns are of interest in order to customize the customer care experience for individual customers.[14]

4. Detection

Given a social network, at least two different questions may be raised about communities: (i) how to identify all communities, and (ii) given a user in the social network, what is the best community for the given user if such a community exists. This entry addresses proposed approaches solving the former problem, known as community detection; also called community discovery or mining. The latter problem, known as community identification, is relevant but not aimed here.

The problem of community detection is not well-defined since its main element of the problem, the concept of community, is not meticulously formulated. Some ambiguities are hidden and there are often many true answers to them. Therefore, there are plenty of methods in the literature and researchers do not try to ground the problem on a shared definition.

4.1. *History*

Probably the earliest account of research on community detection dates back to 1927. At the time, Stuart Rice studied the voting themes of people in small legislative bodies (less than 30 individuals). He looked for *blocs* based on the degree of agreement in casting votes within members of a group, called Index of Cohesion, and between any two distinct groups, named Index of Likeness.[15] Later, in 1941, Davis *et al.*[16] did a social anthropological study on the social activities of a small city and surrounding county of Mississippi over 18 months. They introduced the concept of *caste* to the earlier studies of community stratification by social class. They showed that there is a system of colored caste which parsed a community through rigid social ranks. The general approach was to partition the nodes of a network into discrete subgroup positions (communities) according to some *equivalence* definition. Meantime, George Homans showed that

[b]www.edelman.co.uk/trustbarometer/files/edelmantrust-barometer-2010.pdf

[c]twitter.com

[d]www.facebook.com

social groups could be detected by reordering the rows and the columns of the matrix describing social ties until they form a block-diagonal shape.[17] This procedure is now standard and mainly addressed as *blockmodel* analysis in social network analysis. Next analysis of community structure was carried out by Weiss and Jacobson in 1955,[18] who searched for work groups within bureaucratic organizations based on attitude and patterns of interactions. The authors collected the matrix of working relationships between members of an agency by means of private interviews. Each worker had been asked to list her workers along with frequency, reason, subject, and the importance of her contacts with them. In addition to matrix's rows and columns reordering, work groups were separated by removing the persons working with people of different groups, i.e. *liaison* person. This concept of liaison has been received the name *betweenness* and is at the root of several modern algorithms of community detection.

4.2. *Contemporaries*

Existing community detection approaches can be broadly classified into two categories: *link-based* and *content-based* approaches. Link-based approaches, also known as topology-based, see a social network as a graph, whose nodes are users and edges indicate explicit user relationships. On the other hand, content-based approaches mainly focus on the information content of the users in the social network to detect communities. Also called topic-based, the goal of these approaches is to detect communities formed toward the topics extracted from users' information contents. Hybrid approaches incorporate both topological and topical information to find more meaningful communities with higher quality. Recently, researchers have performed a longitudinal study on the community detection task in which the social network is monitored at regular time intervals over a period of time.[19,20] Time dimension opens up a new *temporal* version of community detections. The following sections include the details of some of the seminal works in each category.

4.2.1. *Link analysis*

Birds of a feather, flock together. People tend to bond with similar others. The structures of ties in a network of any type, from friendship to work to information exchange, and other types of relationship are grounds on this tendency. Therefore, links between users can be considered as important clues for inferring their interest similarity and subsequently finding communities. This observation which became the earliest reference guideline at the basis of most community definitions was studied thoroughly long after its usage by McPherson *et al.*[7] as the homophily principle: 'Similarity breeds connection'.

In link-based community detection methods, the social network is modeled by a graph with nodes representing social actors and edges representing relationships or interactions. Required cohesiveness property of communities, here, is reduced to *connectedness* which means that connections within each community are dense and connections among different communities are relatively sparse. Respectively, primitive graph structures such as components and cliques are considered as promising communities.[21] However, more meaningful communities can be detected based on graph partitioning (clustering) approaches, which try to minimize the number of edges between communities so that the nodes inside one community have more intra-connections than inter-connections with other communities. Most approaches are based on iterative bisection: continuously dividing one group into two groups, while the number of communities which should be in a network is unknown. With this respect, Girvan–Newman approach has been used the most in link-based community detection.[22] It partitions the graph by removing edges with high betweenness. The edge betweenness is the number of the shortest paths that include an edge in a graph. In the proposed approach, the connectedness of the communities to be extracted is measured using modularity (Sec. 5). Other graph partitioning approaches include max-flow min-cut theory,[23] the spectral bisection method,[24] Kernighan–Lin partition,[25] and minimizing conductance cut.[26]

Link-based community detection can be viewed as a data mining/machine learning clustering, an unsupervised classification of users in a social network in which the proximity of data points is based on the topology of links. Then, unsupervised learning which encompasses many other techniques such as k means, mixture models, and hierarchical clustering can be applied to detect communities.

4.2.2. *Content analysis*

On the one hand, in spite of the fact that link-based techniques are intuitive and grounded on sociological homophily principle, they fall short in identifying communities of users that share similar conceptual interests due to two reasons, among others. Firstly, many of the social connections are not based on users' interest similarity but other factors such as friendship and kinship that do not necessarily reflect inter-user interest similarity. Secondly, many users who have similar interests do not share connections with each other.[27] On the other hand, with the ever growing of online social networks, a lot of user-generated content, known as social content, is available on the networks, besides the links among users. Users maintain profile pages, write comments, share articles, tag photos and videos, and post their status updates. Therefore, researchers have explored the possibility of utilizing the topical similarity of social content to detect communities. They have proposed content- or topic-based community detection methods, irrespective of the social network structure, to detect like-minded communities of users.[28]

Most of the works in content-based community detection have focused on probabilistic models of textual content for detecting communities. For example, Abdelbary et al.[29] have identified users' topics of interest and extracted topical communities using Gaussian Restricted Boltzmann Machines. Yin et al.[30] have integrated community discovery with topic modeling in a unified generative model to detect communities of users who are coherent in both structural relationships and latent topics. In their framework, a community can be formed around multiple topics and a topic can be shared among multiple communities. Sachan et al.[12] have proposed probabilistic schemes that incorporate users' posts, social connections, and interaction types to discover latent user communities in Twitter. In their work, they have considered three types of interactions: a conventional tweet, a reply tweet, and a retweet. Other authors have also proposed variations of Latent Dirichlet Allocation (LDA), for example, Author-Topic model[31] and Community-User-Topic model,[32] to identify communities.

Another stream of work models the content-based community detection problem into a graph clustering problem. These works are based on a similarity metric which is able to compute the similarity of users based on their common topics of interest and a clustering algorithm to extract groups of users (latent communities) who have similar interests. For example, Liu et al.[33] have proposed a clustering algorithm based on topic-distance between users to detect content-based communities in a social tagging network. In this work, LDA is used to extract hidden topics in tags. Peng et al.[34] have proposed a hierarchical clustering algorithm to detect latent communities from tweets. They have used predefined categories in SINA Weibo and have calculated the pairwise similarity of users based on their degree of interest in each category.

Like link-based methods, content-based community detection methods can be turned into data clustering in which communities are sets of points. The points, representing users, are close to each other inside versus outside the community with respect to a measure of distance or similarity defined for each pair of users. In this sense, *closeness* is the required cohesiveness property of the communities.

4.2.3. *Link jointly with content*

Content-based methods are designed for regular documents and might suffer from short, noisy, and informal social contents of some social networks such as Twitter or the like microblogging services. In such cases, the social content alone is not the reliable information to extract true communities.[35] Presumably, enriching social contents with social structure, i.e. links, does help with finding more meaningful communities. Several approaches have been proposed to combine link and content information for community detection. They have achieved better performance, as revealed in studies such as Ref. 36 and 37. Most of these approaches devise an integrated generative model for both link and content through shared latent variables for community memberships.

Erosheva et al.[38] introduce Link-LDA, an overlapping community detection to group scientific articles based on their abstract (content) and reference (link) parts. In their generative model, an article is assumed to be a couple model for the abstract and the reference parts each of which is characterized by LDA. They adopt the same bag-of-words assumption used in abstract part for the reference part as well, named bag-of-references. Thus, articles that are similar in the abstract and the references tend to share the same topics. As opposed to Link-LDA in which the citation links are treated words, Nallapti et al.[39] suggest to explicitly model the topical relationship between the text of the citing and cited document. They propose Pairwise-Link-LDA to model the link existence between pairs of documents and have obtained better quality of topics by employing this additional information. Other approaches that utilize LDA to join link and content are Refs. 40 and 41. In addition to probabilistic generative models, there are other approaches such as matrix factorization and kernel fusion for spectral clustering that combine link and content information for community detection.[42,43]

4.2.4. *Overlapping communities*

The common approach to the problem of community detection is to partition the network into disjoint communities of members. Such approaches ignore the possibility that an individual may belong to two or more communities. However, many real social networks have communities with overlaps.[44] For example, a person can belong to more than one social group such as family groups and friend groups. Increasingly, researchers have begun to explore new methods which allow communities to overlap, namely *overlapping* communities. Overlapping communities introduces a further variable, the membership of users in different communities, called *covers*. Since there is an enormous number of possible covers in overlapping communities comparing to standard partitions, detecting such communities is expensive.

Some overlapping community detection algorithms utilize the structural information of users in the network to divide users of the network into different communities. The dominant algorithm in this trend is based on clique percolation theory.[45] However, LFM and OCG are based on local optimization of a fitness function over user's out/in links.[46,47] Furthermore, some fuzzy community detection algorithms calculate the possibility of each node belonging to each community, such as SSDE and IBFO.[48,49] Almost all algorithms need prior information to detect overlapping communities. For example, LFM needs a parameter to control the size of communities. There are, also, some probabilistic approaches in which communities are latent variables with distributions on the entire user space such as Ref. 50.

Recent studies, however, have focused on links. Initially suggested by Ahn *et al.*,[51] link clustering finds communities of links rather than communities of users. The underlying assumption is that while users can have many different relationships, the relationships within groups are structurally similar. By partitioning the links into non-overlapping groups, each user can participate in multiple communities by inheriting the community assignment of its links. Link clustering approach significantly speeds up the discovering of overlapping communities.

4.2.5. *Temporal analysis*

The above methods do not incorporate temporal aspects of users' interests and undermine the fact that users of communities would ideally show similar contribution or interest patterns for similar topics throughout the time. The work by Hu *et al.*[19] is one of the few that considers the notion of temporality. The authors propose a unified probabilistic generative model, namely GrosToT, to extract temporal topics and analyze topics' temporal dynamics in different communities. Fani *et al.*[20] follow the same underlying hypothesis related to topics and temporality to find time-sensitive communities. They use time series analysis to model user's temporal dynamics. While GrosToT is primarily dependent on a variant of LDA for topic detection, the unique way of user representation in Ref. 20 provides the flexibility of being agnostic to any underlying topic detection method.

5. Quality Measure

The standard procedure for evaluating results of a community detection algorithm is assessing the similarity between the results and the ground truth that is known for benchmark datasets. These benchmarks are typically small real-world social networks or synthetic ones. Similarity measures can be divided into two categories: measures based on pair counting and measures based on information theory. A thorough introduction of similarity measures for communities has been given in Ref. 52. The first type of measures based on pair counting depends on the number of pairs of vertices which are classified in the same (different) communities in the ground truth and the result produced by the community detection method. The *Rand index* is the ratio of the number of user pairs correctly classified in both the ground truth and the result, either in the same or in different communities, over the total number of pairs.[53] The *Jaccard index* is the ratio of the number of user pairs classified in the same community in both ground truth and the result, over the number of user pairs which are classified in the same community of result *or* ground truth. Both the Rand and the Jaccard index are adjusted for random grouping, in that a null model is

introduced. The normal value of the index is subtracted from the expectation value of the index in the null model, and the result is normalized to [0, 1], yielding 0 for independent partitions and 1 for identical partitions. The second type of similarity measures models the problem of comparing communities as a problem of message decoding in information theory. The idea is that, if the output communities are similar to the ground truth, one needs very little information to infer the result given the ground truth. The extra (less) information can be used as a measure of (dis)similarity. The *normalized mutual information* is currently very often used in this type of evaluation.[54] The normalized mutual information reaches 1 if the result and the ground truth are identical, whereas it has an expected value of 0 if they are independent. These measures have been recently extended to the case of overlapping communities such as the work by Lancichinetti *et al.*[55]

Ground truth is not available in most cases of the real-world applications and there is no well-defined criterion for evaluating the resulting communities. In such cases, quality functions are defined as a quantitative measure to assess the communities. The most popular quality function is the *modularity* introduced by Newman and Girvan.[22] It is based on the idea that a random network is not expected to have a modular structure. The communities are going to emerge as the network deviate from a random network. Therefore, the more density of links exists in the actual community with compare to the expected density when the users were connected randomly, the more modular a community is. Simply, modularity of a community is the number of links within communities minus expected number of such links. Evidently, the expected link density depends on the chosen null model. One simple null model would be a network with the same number of links as the actual network and links are placed between any pair of users with the uniform probability. However, this null model yields a Poissonian degree distribution which is not a true descriptor of real networks. With respect to the modularity, high values imply *good* partitions. So, a community with maximum modularity in a network should be the near best one. This ignites a class of community detection which is based on modularity maximization. While the application of modularity has been questioned,[4] it continues to be the most popular and widely accepted measure of the fitness of communities.

As another quality function, the conductance of the community was chosen by Leskovec *et al.*[26] The conductance of a community is the ratio between the cut size of the community and the minimum between the total degree of the community and that of the rest of the network. So, if the community is much smaller than the whole network, the conductance equals the ratio between the cut size and the total degree of the community. A *good* community is characterized by a low cut size and a large internal density of links which result in low values of the conductance. For each real network, Leskovec *et al.* have carried out a systematic analysis on the quality of communities that have various sizes. They derived the network community profile plot (NCPP), showing the minimum conductance score among subgraphs of a given size as a function of the size. They found that communities are well defined only when they are fairly small in size. Such small communities are weakly connected to the rest of the network, often by a single edge (in this case, they are called whiskers), and form the periphery of the network. The fact that the best communities appear to have a characteristic size of about 100 users is consistent with Dunbar conjecture that 150 is the upper size limit for a working human community.[56]

6. Future Direction

No doubt community detection has matured and social network analysts have achieved an in-depth knowledge of the communities, their emergence and evolution, in real social networks, but interesting challenges still yet to be addressed. As hinted in the introduction (Sec. 1), the quest for a single *correct* definition of network communities and a single *accurate* community detection method seem to be futile which is not necessarily a problem. Years of endeavors have resulted in many methods for finding communities based on a variety of principles. The picture that is emerging is that the choice of community detection algorithm depends on the properties of the network under study. In many ways, the problem of community detection has a parallel in the more mature topic of clustering in computer science, where a variety of methods exist, each one with standard applications and known issues. As a consequence, one challenge for the task of community detection is about distinguishing between existing ones. One way is to compare algorithms on real networks where network's metadata is available. In the case of social networks, for example, we can use demographic and geographic information of users. One example of such a metadata-based evaluation has been done in Ref. 57, but a standard framework for evaluation has yet to be emerged.

Moreover, networks are dynamic with a time stamp associated with links, users, and the social contents. As seen, almost all measures and methods ignore temporal information. It is also inefficient to apply such community detection algorithms and measures to static snapshots of the social network in each time interval. In order to truly capture the properties of a social network, the methods have to analyze data in their full complexity fueled with time dimension. This trend has slowly started.[19,20] What makes the problem more complex is the fact that online social network data arrive in a streaming fashion, esp. the social contents. The states of the network need to be updated in an efficient way *on the fly*, in order to avoid a bottleneck in the processing pipeline. To date, only a small number of work has approached this problem directly.[58]

The last area is the computational complexity in which the current methods will need dramatic enhancement,

particularly with the ever-increasing size of current online social networks. As an example, Facebook has close to one billion active users who collectively spend twenty thousand years online in one day sharing information. Meanwhile, there are also 340 million tweets sent out by Twitter users. A community detection algorithm needs to be efficient and scalable, taking practical amount of time to finish when applied on such large-scale networks. Many existing methods are only applicable to small networks. Providing fast and scalable versions of community detection methods is one proposed direction worthy of significant future efforts. One solution to deal with large-scale networks is the sampling. The goal is to reduce the number of users and/or links while keeping the underlying network structure. Network sampling is done in the preprocessing step and is independent of the subsequent steps in community detection algorithms. Hence, it provides performance improvement to all community detection algorithms. Although sampling seems to be straightforward and easy to implement, it has a direct impact on the results of community detection, in terms of both accuracy and efficiency. It has been shown that naively sampled users or links by uniform distribution will bring bias into the output sampled network, which will affect the results negatively.[59] One of the challenges going forward in social network analysis will be to provide sampling methods and, particularly, to take sampling into account in the overall performance analysis of community detection methods.

References

[1] F. Benevenuto *et al.*, Characterizing user behavior in online social networks, *Proc. 9th ACM SIGCOMM Conf. Internet Measurement Conf.* (ACM, 2009).

[2] P. Mateos, Demographic, ethnic, and socioeconomic community structure in social networks, *Encyclopedia of Social Network Analysis and Mining* (Springer New York, 2014), pp. 342–346.

[3] R. Claxton, J. Reades and B. Anderson, On the value of digital traces for commercial strategy and public policy: Telecommunications data as a case study, World Economic Forum Global Information Technology Report, 2012-Living in a Hyperconnected World, World Economic Forum, (pp. 105–112)

[4] A. Stevenson and J. Hamill, Social media monitoring: A practical case example of city destinations, *Social Media in Travel, Tourism and Hospitality* (Ashgate, Farnham, 2012), pp. 293–312.

[5] D. J. Watts and S. H. Strogatz, Collective dynamics of 'small-world' networks, *Nature* **393**, 440 (1998).

[6] A. L. Barabasi and R. Albert, Emergence of scaling in random networks, *Science* **286**, 509 (1999).

[7] M. McPherson, L. Smith-Lovin and J. M. Cook, Birds of a feather: Homophily in social networks, *Ann. Rev. Sociol.* **415** (2001).

[8] J. Chen and B. Yuan, Detecting functional modules in the yeast protein–protein interaction network, *Bioinformatics* **22**, 2283 (2006).

[9] Y. Dourisboure, F. Geraci and M. Pellegrini, Extraction and classification of dense communities in the web, *Proc. 16th Int. Conf. World Wide Web* (ACM, 2007).

[10] R. Guimera and L. A. N. Amaral, Functional cartography of complex metabolic networks, *Nature* **433**, 895 (2005).

[11] A. Krause *et al.*, Compartments revealed in food-web structure, *Nature* **426**, 282 (2003).

[12] M. Sachan, D. Contractor, T. A. Faruquie and L. V. Subramaniam, Using content and interactions for discovering communities in social networks, *21st Int. Conf. World Wide Web (WWW'12)*, (2012), pp. 331–340.

[13] B. Krishnamurthy and J. Wang, On network-aware clustering of web clients, *ACM SIGCOMM Computer Commun. Rev.* **30**, 97 (2000).

[14] Y. Richter, E. Yom-Tov and N. Slonim, Predicting customer churn in mobile networks through analysis of social groups, SDM, *SIAM* (2010), pp. 732–741.

[15] S. A. Rice, The identification of blocs in small political bodies, *Am. Political Sci. Rev.* **21**, 619 (1927).

[16] A. Davis *et al.*, *Deep South: A Sociological Anthropological Study of Caste and Class* (University of Chicago Press, 1941).

[17] G. C. Homans, The Human Croup (1950).

[18] R. S. Weiss and E. Jacobson, A method for the analysis of the structure of complex organizations, *Am. Sociol. Rev.* **20**, 661 (1955).

[19] Z. Hu, Y. Junjie and B. Cui, User Group Oriented Temporal Dynamics Exploration, AAAI (2014).

[20] H. Fani *et al.*, Time-sensitive topic-based communities on twitter, *Canadian Conf. Artificial Intelligence*. Springer International Publishing (2016).

[21] S. Fortunato, Community detection in graphs, *Phys. Rep.* **486**, 75 (2010).

[22] M. Girvan and M. E. J. Newman, Community structure in social and biological networks, *Proc. Nat. Acad. Sci.* **99**, 7821 (2002).

[23] L. R. Ford and D. R. Fulkerson, Maximal flow through a network, *Can. J. Math.* **8**, 399 (1956).

[24] A. Pothen, H. D. Simon and K.-P. Liou, Partitioning sparse matrices with eigenvectors of graphs, *SIAM J. Matrix Anal. Appl.* **11**, 430 (1990).

[25] B. W. Kernighan and L. Shen, An efficient heuristic procedure for partitioning graphs, *Bell System Tech. J.* **49**, 291 (1970).

[26] J. Leskovec, J. Kleinberg and C. Faloutsos, Graphs over time: Densification laws, shrinking diameters and possible explanations, *Proc. Eleventh ACM SIGKDD Int. Conf. Knowledge Discovery in Data Mining* (ACM, 2005).

[27] Q. Deng, Z. Li, X. Zhang and J. Xia, Interaction-based social relationship type identification in microblog, *Int. Workshop on Behavior and Social Informatics and Computing* (2013), pp. 151–164.

[28] N. Natarajan, P. Sen and V. Chaoji, Community detection in content-sharing social networks, *IEEE/ACM Int. Conf. Advances in Social Networks Analysis and Mining* (2013), pp. 82–89.

[29] H. A. Abdelbary, A. M. ElKorany and R. Bahgat, Utilizing deep learning for content-based community detection, *Science and Information Conf.* (2014), pp. 777–784.

[30] Z. Yin, L. Cao, Q. Gu and J. Han, Latent community topic analysis: Integration of community discovery with topic modeling, *J. ACM Trans. Intell. Syst. Technol. (TIST)* **3**(4) (2012).

[31] M. Rosen-Zvi, T. Griffiths, M. Steyvers and P. Smyth, The author-topic model for authors and documents, *20th Conf. Uncertainty in Artificial Intelligence* (2004), pp. 487–494.

[32] D. Zhou, E. Manavoglu, J. Li, C. L. Giles and H. Zha, Probabilistic models for discovering e-communities, *15th Int. Conf. World Wide Web* (2006), pp. 173–182.

[33] H. Liu, H. Chen, M. Lin and Y. Wu, Community detection based on topic distance in social tagging networks, TELKOMNIKA *Indonesian J. Electr. Eng.* **12**(5), 4038.

[34] D. Peng, X. Lei and T. Huang, DICH: A framework for discovering implicit communities hidden in tweets, *J. World Wide Web* (2014).

[35] T. Yang *et al.*, Combining link and content for community detection: A discriminative approach, *Proc. 15th ACM SIGKDD Int. Conf. Knowledge Discovery and Data Mining* (ACM, 2009).

[36] D. Cohn and T. Hofmann, The missing link — a probabilistic model of document content and hypertext connectivity, NIPS (2001).

[37] L. Getoor, N. Friedman, D. Koller and B. Taskar, Learning probabilistic models of link structure, *J. MLR* **3** (2002).

[38] E. Erosheva, S. Fienberg and J. Lafferty, Mixed membership models of scientific publications, *Proc. Natl. Acad. Sci.* 101 (2004).

[39] R. M. Nallapati, A. Ahmed, E. P. Xing and W. W. Cohen, Joint latent topic models for text and citations, KDD (2008).

[40] L. Dietz, S. Bickel and T. Scheffer, Unsupervised prediction of citation influences, In ICML (2007).

[41] A. Gruber, M. Rosen-Zvi and Y. Weiss, Latent topic models for hypertext, UAI (2008).

[42] S. Zhu, K. Yu, Y. Chi and Y. Gong, Combining content and link for classification using matrix factorization, SIGIR (2007).

[43] S. Yu, B. D. Moor and Y. Moreau, Clustering by heterogeneous data fusion: Framework and applications, NIPS workshop (2009).

[44] J. Xie, S. Kelley and B. K. Szymanski, Overlapping community detection in networks: The state of the art and comparative study, *ACM Comput. Surv.* **45** (2013), doi: 10.1145/2501654.2501657.

[45] G. Palla, I. Derényi, I. Farkas and T. Vicsek, Uncovering the overlapping community structure of complex networks in nature and society, *Nature* **435**, 814 (2005).

[46] A. Lancichinetti, S. Fortunato and J. Kertész, Detecting the overlapping and hierarchical community structure in complex networks, *New J. Phys.* **11**, 033015 (2009), doi: 10.1088/1367-2630/11/3/033015.

[47] E. Becker, B. Robisson, C. E. Chapple, A. Guénoche and C. Brun, Multifunctional proteins revealed by overlapping clustering in protein interaction network, *Bioinformatics* **28**, 84 (2012).

[48] M. Magdon-Ismail and J. Purnell, SSDE-Cluster: Fast overlapping clustering of networks using sampled spectral distance embedding and gmms, *Proc. 3rd Int. Conf. Social Computing (SocialCom/ PASSAT)*, Boston, MA, USA. NJ, USA: IEEE Press (2011), pp. 756–759, 10.1109/PASSAT/SocialCom.2011.237.

[49] X. Lei, S. Wu, L. Ge and A. Zhang, Clustering and overlapping modules detection in PPI network based on IBFO, *Proteomics* **13**, 278 (2013).

[50] W. Ren *et al.*, Simple probabilistic algorithm for detecting community structure, *Phys. Rev. E* **79**, 036111 (2009).

[51] Y.-Y. Ahn, J. P. Bagrow and S. Lehmann, Link communities reveal multiscale complexity in networks, *Nature* **466**, 761 (2010).

[52] M. Meilă, Comparing clusterings — an information based distance, *J. Multivariate Anal.* **98**, 873 (2007).

[53] W. M. Rand, Objective criteria for the evaluation of clustering methods, *J. Am. Stat. Assoc.* **66**, 846 (1971).

[54] L. Danon *et al.*, Comparing community structure identification, *J. Stat. Mech., Theory Exp.* **09**, P09008 (2005).

[55] A. Lancichinetti, S. Fortunato and J. Kertész, Detecting the overlapping and hierarchical community structure in complex networks, *New J. Phys.* **11**, 033015 (2009).

[56] R. Dunbar, *Grooming, Gossip, and the Evolution of Language* (Harvard University Press, Cambridge, USA, 1998).

[57] Y. Y. Ahn, J. P. Bagrow and S. Lehmann, Link communities reveal multi-scale complexity in networks, *Nature* (2010).

[58] C. C. Aggarwal, Y. Zhao and S. Y. Philip, On clustering graph streams, SDM (SIAM, 2010), pp. 478–489.

[59] Y. Ruan *et al.*, Community discovery: Simple and scalable approaches, *User Community Discovery* (Springer International Publishing, 2015), pp. 23–54.

High-level surveillance event detection

Fabio Persia[*,‡] and Daniela D'Auria[†,§]

*Faculty of Computer Science, Free University of Bozen-Bolzano,
Piazza Domenicani 3, Bozen-Bolzano, 39100, Italy

†Department of Electrical Engineering and Information Technology,
University of Naples Federico II,
Via Claudio 21, Naples, 80125, Italy

‡fabio.persia@unibz.it
§daniela.dauria4@unina.it

Security has been raised at major public buildings in the most famous and crowded cities all over the world following the terrorist attacks of the last years, the latest one at the Promenade des Anglais in Nice. For that reason, video surveillance systems have become more and more essential for detecting and hopefully even prevent dangerous events in public areas. In this work, we present an overview of the evolution of high-level surveillance event detection systems along with a prototype for anomaly detection in video surveillance context. The whole process is described, starting from the video frames captured by sensors/cameras till at the end some well-known reasoning algorithms for finding potentially dangerous activities are applied.

Keywords: Video surveillance; anomaly detection; event detection.

1. Problem Description

In latest years, modern world's needs of safety caused a speed spreading of video surveillance systems; these systems are collocated especially in the most crowded places. The main purpose of a video surveillance system is to create some automatic tools, which can extend the faculties of human perception, allowing collection and real-time analysis of data coming from lots of electronic "viewers" (sensors, cameras, etc...).

One of the main limits of modern security systems is that most of them have been designed for specific functionalities and contexts: they generally use an only kind of sensors (such as cameras, motes, scanners) which cannot notice all the possible important phenomena connected to the observation context. A second and not negligible limit is that the "semantics" of the phenomena (events) that such systems can notice is quite limited and, as well, these systems are not very flexible when we want to introduce new events to be identified. For example, a typical video surveillance system at the entrance of a tunnel uses a set of cameras monitoring train transit and the possible presence of objects in the scene. When a person transits on the tracks, we want the system automatically to identify the anomalous event and to signal it to a keeper. The commonest "Image Processing" algorithms (that can be directly implemented on a camera processor or can be stored on a dedicated server that can process information sent by a camera) can quite precisely identify the changes between a frame and the next one and, in this way, discover the potential presence of anomalies (train transit, presence of a person,...) in the scene. In the scene analysis, a system does not consider all the environmental parameters, such as brightness, temperature and so on, and how these parameters can modify the surveys (the identification of a small object in the scene is more complex in the night); as well, this system cannot identify semantic higher level events (such as a package left near a track) with the same precision and reliability. Similarly, a traditional video surveillance system can discover, in a bank, the presence of objects near the safe, but cannot automatically notify an event interesting for the context, such as a "bank robbery" (every time that an object is near the safe, an alarm should be generated: in this way, nevertheless, false alarms could be generated also when the bank clerk goes into the safe room to take some money).

In the end, we want a modern video surveillance system to attain the following points: it is to integrate heterogeneous information coming from different kinds of sensors, to be flexible in capability to discover all possible events that can happen in the monitored environment and to be adaptable to the context features of the observed scene. From a technological point of view, the main requirements of this kind of systems are: heterogeneity of the adopted surveying systems, heterogeneity of noticed data and of those to be processed, wiring of devices and communication with servers dedicated to processing. However, the design and development of a complete framework addressing all the issues listed above is unfortunately a very challenging task.

In this work, we present a prototype of framework for anomaly detection in video surveillance context. The whole process is described: thus, we start from the video frames captured by sensors/cameras and then, after several steps, we apply some well-known reasoning algorithms[1,2] for finding high-level *unexplained* activities in time-stamped observation data.

The remainder of the paper is organized as follows. Section 2 deals with the evolution of video surveillance systems up to the proposed general method (third generation surveillance systems (3GSD)), while Sec. 3 describes in detail a possible implementation of a prototype attaining to the general method. Eventually, Sec. 4 discusses some conclusions and possible future improvements.

2. Method

The video surveillance systems proposed in literature can be classified into three categories (or generations[3]), from a technological point of view. The three proposed generations, in fact, have followed the evolution of the communication techniques of the image processing and of the data storing and they have been evolving with the same rapidity as these techniques.

First generation surveillance systems (1GSS) extend human perception capability from a spatial point of view: a set of cameras (*sensor layer*) are used to capture visual signals from different positions set in a monitored environment. Such signals are then sent and visualized by operators, after an analogical transmission, in an only location (control room). 1GSS most considerable disadvantages are due to the operators' short duration of attention, which is responsible for a high rate of missed recording of important events.[4]

From the early 80's, because of the increasing interest of research in video processing and in order to improve the basic technologies in this area, scientists obtained a sensible improvement in camera resolution and, at the same time, a reduction of hardware (computers, memories, ...) costs. Most of the researches made during second generation surveillance system (2GSS) period have improved the development of automatic techniques called *automated event*

detection. These techniques have made monitoring of very large areas easier, because they act as pre-filters of defined events. Nevertheless, the 2GSS systems are characterized by a good level of digitalization about signal transmission and processing, in the sense that systems include digital components in some parts of their architecture.

The main goal of 3GSS is to obtain, to manage and to efficiently transmit real time noticed video events, from a large set of sensors, through a *full digital* approach; this approach uses digital components in all layers of the system architecture, from *sensor layer* till visual and codified presentation of information to operators.[3] In a 3GSS system, cameras communicate with some processing and transmission devices: in this way *intelligent cameras* are built. A network layer, whose principal component is an *intelligent hub*, has the purpose to assemble data coming from different cameras. So, we can say that the automatic video surveillance system goal is to act as a *pre-filter* for human validation of suspicious events. Such *pre-filtering* is generally based on video processing and gives some important parameters for object localization and for tracking of their trajectories, while they are in the monitored environment. Figure 1 shows a schematization of a 3GSS video surveillance system logical architecture, which can be assumed as general method to be applied for building effective and efficient video surveillance systems.

The *sensor layer* is composed of one or more fixed or mobile cameras: their purpose is to collect images, to be sent to the *image processing* system (IPS).

Images captured by cameras are stored in a specific video database (*VideoRepository*),[13,14] then, they are sent in input to IPS system, that processes them. Such module extracts low-level information (such as the presence of new objects in the scene, their position, and so on. ..) through *image processing* algorithms; it also converts this information into a format conformable to a syntax used by higher layers.

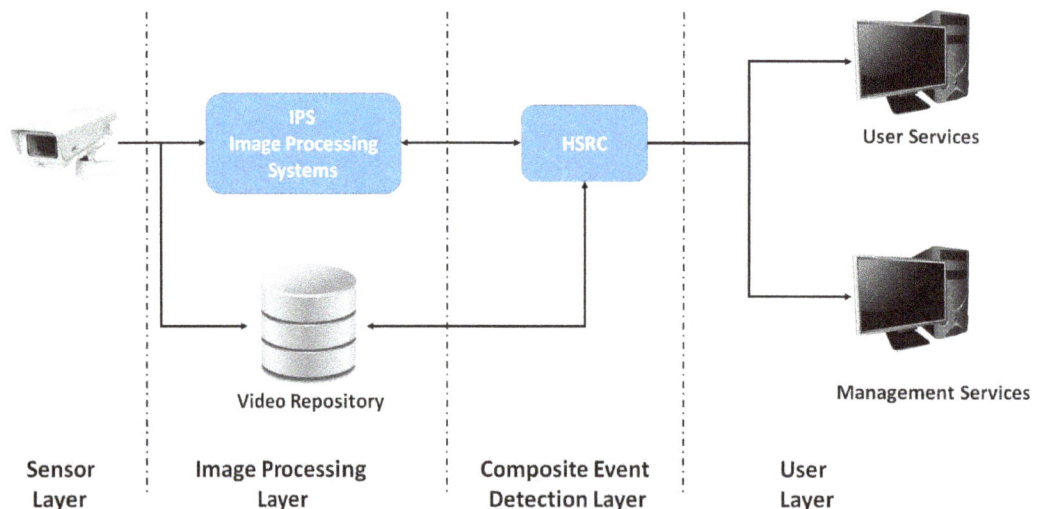

Fig. 1. Video surveillance system architecture.

Then, an event description language (EDL) has been defined on the basis of image processing algorithms; through this language, it is possible to formalize a complex event in a strict way. The data organized in this way, is stored in a specific area of Database (*Data Collection*).

A post-processing framework, called high semantic reasoning center (HSRC) is the part of the system responsible for complex events' occurrences surveying, through the processing of low-level data made available by IPS. We can classify the following components:

- *Event Repository*: It is the part of Database in which predicates and complex events' definitions are stored; as well, information about event occurrence surveying in the video are stored in it, too.
- *Data Collection*: It is the part of Database that collects the output of the IPS framework, organized according to EDL language syntax.
- *Agent Based Processor* (*ABP*): Its main aims are to capture the interesting event definition, composed of the Event Repository, to catch the observation, that is, the video description in terms of predicates, from Data Collection, and to verify the event occurrence during the observation.
- *Subvideo Extractor*: When an event is detected, this framework extracts from the video the interesting frame sequence and saves it in the Video Repository as a new file; in this way, the sequence is made available for *on-line* and *off-line* visualizations.
- *Query Builder*: The framework assigned to client service creation organizes parameters which the attitude of ABP processor bases on. Management services are built on language capability and on algorithms ability available in IPS.

The system presents a set of services to final clients through *user-friendly* interfaces. Such services can be classified into two different categories:

(1) *Management services*: The system manager can define new kinds of primitive and complex events and can extend the image processing algorithm suite of the IPS framework.

(2) *Client services*: The client can specify the working system parameters, based for example on the alert mode. He can visualize *on-line* and *off-line* Video sequences corresponding to alarms detected by the system; he can also visualize whole stored videos and make some statistics on detected event occurrences.

In the last years, many framework have been developed to identify anomalies or suspicious events in video sequences. In Ref. 10, the authors present a framework for detecting complex events through inferencing process based on Markov logic networks (MLNs) and rule-based event models. Another approach has been employed by Zin *et al.*[11] which propose an integrated framework for detecting suspicious behaviors in video surveillance systems exploiting multiple background modeling techniques, high-level motion feature extraction methods and embedded Markov chain models. Moreover, Helmer and Persia[12] propose a framework for high-level surveillance event detection exploiting a language based on relational algebra extended by intervals.

3. The Proposed Implementation

In this section, we describe the prototype designed and developed for finding anomalous activities in video surveillance context attaining to the general method shown in Sec. 2. The architecture of the proposed prototype (Fig. 2) consists of the following layers: an *Image Processing Library*, a *Video Labeler*, an *Activity Detection Engine* and the unexplained activities problem (UAP) *Engine*, implementing the algorithms for video anomaly detection. In particular, the *Image Processing Library* analyzes the video captured by sensors/cameras and returns the low level annotations for each video frame as output; the *Video Labeler* fills the semantic gap between the low level annotations captured for each frame and the high level annotations, representing high level events

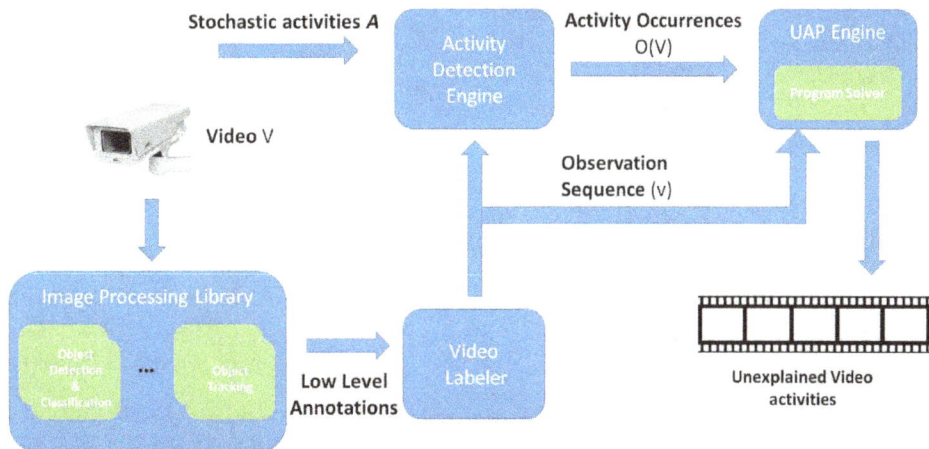

Fig. 2. The prototype architecture.

Fig. 3. A video frame from ITEA-CANDELA dataset.

that can be associated to the video frames; then, we used an *Activity Detection Engine* to find activity occurrences matching the well-known models, that can be classified into *good* and *bad* ones: thus, such a module takes as inputs the *high level annotations* previously caught by the *Video Labeler* and the stochastic activity models; eventually, the *Unexplained Activity Problem (UAP) Engine* described in Refs. 1 and 2 takes as input the activity occurrences previously found with the associated probabilities and the high level annotations and discovers the *Unexplained Video Activities*.

3.1. *The image processing library*

The image processing library used in our prototype implementation is the reading people tracker (RPT),[5] that achieves a good accuracy in object detection and tracking. RPT takes the frame sequence of the video as input and returns an XML file describing the low level annotations caught in each frame, according to a standard schema defined in an *XML Schema*. We have only made some few updates to the RPT's source code, in order to be able to get more easily the type of each object detected in a frame (person, package, car). For instance, Fig. 4 shows the low level annotations associated to the frame number 18 (Fig. 3) of a video belonging to the *ITEA-CANDELA* dataset,[a] which has been used to carry out some preliminary experiments. As we can see in Fig. 4, the RPT correctly identifies two objects (represented by the XML elements called *track*) into the frame shown in Fig. 3: the former, identified by *ID* = 5, is a person (*type* = 5), while the latter, identified by *ID* = 100, is a package (*type* = 6). The XML attribute *type* of the element *track* denotes the type of the detected object.

[a]http://www.multitel.be/~va/candela/abandon.html.

3.2. *The video labeler*

As we mentioned above, the *Video Labeler* fills the semantic gap between the low level annotations captured for each frame and the high level annotations. So, through the Video Labeler, some high level events, called *action symbols*, with the related *timestamps* are detected; thus, the output of the Video Labeler is the list of *action symbols* related to the considered video source. The Video Labeler has been implemented in *Java* programming language: it uses the *DOM libraries* to parse the XML file containing the output of the *Image Processing Library*. The Video Library defines the rules that have to be checked to verify the presence of each interested *high level atomic event* in the video. So, a Java method for each action symbol we want to detect, containing the related rules, has been defined. There are listed below some examples of rules defined to detect some *atomic events* (action symbols) in a video belonging to the *ITEA-CANDELA* dataset.

Action Symbol *A*: A person *P* goes into the central zone with the package

- There are at least two objects in the current frame;
- at least one of the objects is a person;
- at least one of the objects is a package;
- the person identified appears on the scene for the first time;
- the distance between the person's barycenter and the package one is smaller than a specific distance threshold.

Action Symbol *B*: A person *P* drops off the package

- There are at least two objects in the current frame;
- at least one of the objects is a person;
- at least one of the objects is a package;
- the person was previously holding a package;

```
177  <frame xmlns="http://www.cvg.cs.reading.ac.uk/ADVISOR/people"
178          xmlns:xsi="http://www.w3.org/2001/XMLSchema-instance"
179              xsi:schemaLocation="http://www.cvg.reading.ac.uk/ADVISOR
180                  http://www.cvg.cs.reading.ac.uk/~nts/ADVISOR/people_tracker-multi.xsd"
181                      id="18" pc_name="fabio-desktop" num_cameras="1">
182      <camera id="2002" time="3600">
183          <mobile id="5" start_time="3400">
184              <track id="5" type="5">
185                  <info2d xmin="314" xmax="357" ymin="126" ymax="277" xcog="335" ycog="195" />
186                  <info3d x="0" y="0" z="0" width="0" height="0" />
187                  <occlusion left="0" right="0" bottom="0" top="0" />
188              </track>
189              <track id="100" type="6">
190                  <info2d xmin="314" xmax="357" ymin="126" ymax="277" xcog="333" ycog="197" />
191                  <info3d x="0" y="0" z="0" width="0" height="0" />
192                  <occlusion left="0" right="0" bottom="0" top="0" />
193              </track>
194          </mobile>
195      </camera>
196  </frame>
```

Fig. 4. The related low level annotations.

- the distance between the person's barycenter and the package one is smaller than a specific distance threshold.

Action Symbol C: A person *P* goes into the central zone

- There is at least one object in the current frame;
- at least one of the objects is a person;
- the person identified appears on the scene for the first time;
- if there are also some packages on the scene, their distances are greater than a specific distance threshold.

Action Symbol D: A person *P* picks up the package

- There are at least two objects in the current frame;
- at least one of the objects is a person;
- at least one of the objects is a package;
- the distance between the person's barycenter and the package one is smaller than a specific distance threshold;
- the person was not previously holding a package.

Action Symbol E: A person *P1* gives the package to another person *P2*

- There are at least three objects in the current frame;
- at least two of the objects are persons;
- at least one of the objects is a package;
- P1 was previously holding a package;
- in the current frame, both the distances of P1 and P2's barycenters from the package are smaller than a specific distance threshold;
- in the next frames, P1's distance from the package is greater than the threshold, while P2's one is smaller (it means that P2 has got the package and P1 is not holding it anymore)

Action Symbol F: A person *P* goes out of the central zone with the package

- This symbol is detected when a person holding a package does not appear anymore on the scene for a specified time to live (TTL).

3.3. *The activity detection engine*

An *Activity Detection Engine* is able to find activity occurrences matching the well-known models: thus, such a module takes as inputs the list of *action symbols* previously caught by the *Video Labeler* and the *stochastic activity models*, and finally returns the list of the discovered activity occurrences with the related probabilities. To reach this goal, a specific software called temporal multi-activity graph index creation (*tMAGIC*), which is the implementation of a theoretical model presented in Ref. 6 has been used.

As a matter of fact, the[6] approach addresses the problem of efficiently detecting occurrences of high-level activities from such interleaved data streams. In this approach, there has been proposed a temporal probabilistic graph so that the elapsed time between observations also plays a role in defining whether a sequence of observations constitutes an activity. First, a data structure called *temporal multiactivity graph* to store multiple activities that need to be concurrently monitored has been proposed. Then, an index called tMAGIC has been defined. It basically exploits the data structure just described to examine and link observations as they occur. There are also some defined algorithms for insertion and bulk insertion into the tMAGIC index showing that this can be efficiently accomplished. In this approach, the algorithms are basically defined to solve two problems: the *evidence problem* that tries to find all occurrences of an activity (with probability over a threshold) within a given sequence of observations, and the *identification problem* that tries to find the activity that best matches a sequence of observations. Some methods of reducing complexity and pruning strategies have been introduced to make the problem, which is intrinsically exponential, linear to the number of observations. It is demonstrated that *tMAGIC* has time and space complexity linear to the size of the input, and can efficiently retrieve instances of the monitored activities. Moreover, this activity detection engine has been also exploited in other works belonging to different contexts, such as in Refs. 7–9.

3.4. *The UAP engine*

The UAP *Engine* takes as input the *activity occurrences* previously found by the *Activity Detection Engine* with the associated probabilities and the list of the detected *action symbols* and finally discovers the *Unexplained Video Activities*, that are subsequences of the video source which are not sufficiently explained with a certain confidence by the activity models and that could thus be potentially dangerous. Such module is based on the concept of *possible worlds*, has been developed in Java programming language and provides the implementations of the theoretical algorithms FindTUA, FindPUA.[1,2]

4. Conclusion and Future Work

This work presented on overview of the evolution of high-level surveillance event detection systems along with a possible implementation of a prototype attaining to the general method. More specifically, we started from describing how the video frames are captured by sensors/cameras and thus analyzed, then we showed the different steps applied in order to finally discover some high-level activities which are not sufficiently explained by the well-known activity models and that could be potentially dangerous in the video surveillance context.

Future work will be devoted to compare this framework with other ones which can be built for instance by replacing the components used at each layer with others either already well-known in literature or specifically designed and developed following innovative approaches. For instance, we planned to also try to use another *Image Processing Library* which would hopefully improve the overall effectiveness of the framework and allow the whole process to work as much as possible automatically. Moreover, we can try to exploit a different *UAP Engine* for discovering unexplained activities in video surveillance context, which would be no longer based on the concept of *possible worlds*, but on *game theory*.

References

[1] M. Albanese, C. Molinaro, F. Persia, A. Picariello and V. S. Subrahmanian, Discovering the top-k unexplained sequences in time-stamped observation data, *IEEE Trans. Knowl. Data Eng. (TKDE)* **26**(3) 577 (2014).

[2] M. Albanese, C. Molinaro, F. Persia, A. Picariello and V. S. Subrahmanian, Finding unexplained activities in video, *Int. Joint Conf. Artificial Intelligence (IJCAI)* (2011), pp. 1628–1634.

[3] J. K. Petersen, *Understanding Surveillance Technologies* (CRC Press, Boca Raton, FL, 2001).

[4] C. Regazzoni and V. Ramesh, Scanning the Issue/Technology Special Issue on Video Communications, Processing, and Understanding for Third Generation Surveillance Systems, *Proc. IEEE, University of Genoa, Siemens Corporate Research*, University of Udine (2001).

[5] N. T. Siebel and S. Maybank, Fusion of multiple tracking algorithms for robust people tracking, *Proc. ECCV02* (2002), pp. 373–387.

[6] M. Albanese, A. Pugliese and V. S. Subrahmanian, Fast activity detection: Indexing for temporal stochastic automaton based activity models, *IEEE Trans. Knowl. Data Eng. (TKDE)* **25**(2) 360 (2013).

[7] F. Persia and D. D'Auria, An application for finding expected activities in medial context scientific databases, SEBD (2014), pp.77–88.

[8] D. D'Auria and F. Persia, Automatic evaluation of medical doctors' performances while using a cricothyrotomy simulator, IRI (2014), pp. 514–519.

[9] D. D'Auria and F. Persia, Discovering Expected Activities in Medical Context Scientific Databases, DATA (2014), pp. 446–453.

[10] I. Onal, K. Kardas, Y. Rezaeitabar, U. Bayram, M. Bal, I. Ulusoy and N. K. Cicekli, A framework for detecting complex events in surveillance videos, *2013 IEEE Int. Conf. Multimedia and Expo Workshops (ICMEW)*, pp. 1–6.

[11] T. T. Zin, P. Tin, H. Hama and T. Toriu, An integrated framework for detecting suspicious behaviors in video surveillance, *Proc. SPIE 9026, Video Surveillance and Transportation Imaging Applications* 2014, 902614 (March 5, 2014); doi:10.1117/12.2041232.

[12] S. Helmer and F. Persia, High-level surveillance event detection using an interval-based query language, *IEEE 10th Int. Conf. Semantic Computing (ICSC'16)* (2016), pp. 39–46.

[13] V. Moscato, A. Picariello, F. Persia and A. Penta, A system for automatic image categorization, *IEEE 3rd Int. Conf. Semantic Computing (ICSC'09)* (2009), pp. 624–629.

[14] V. Moscato, F. Persia, A. Picariello and A. Penta, iwin: A summarizer system based on a semantic analysis of web documents, *IEEE 6th Int. Conf. Semantic Computing (ICSC'12)* (2012), pp.162–169.

Part 2

Data Science

Selected topics in statistical computing

Suneel Babu Chatla[*,‡], Chun-Houh Chen[†] and Galit Shmueli[*]

Institute of Service Science, National Tsing Hua University,
Hsinchu 30013, Taiwan R.O.C.

†*Institute of Statistical Science, Academia Sinica, Taipei 11529, Taiwan R.O.C.*
‡suneel.chatla@iss.nthu.edu.tw

The field of computational statistics refers to statistical methods or tools that are computationally intensive. Due to the recent advances in computing power, some of these methods have become prominent and central to modern data analysis. In this paper, we focus on several of the main methods including density estimation, kernel smoothing, smoothing splines, and additive models. While the field of computational statistics includes many more methods, this paper serves as a brief introduction to selected popular topics.

Keywords: Histogram; kernel density; local regression; additive models; splines; MCMC; Bootstrap.

1. Introduction

- "Let the data speak for themselves"

In 1962, John Tukey[76] published a paper on "the future of data analysis", which turns out to be extraordinarily clairvoyant. Specifically, he accorded algorithmic models the same foundation status as algebraic models that statisticians had favored at that time. More than three decades later, in 1998 Jerome Friedman delivered a keynote speech[23] in which he stressed the role of data driven or algorithmic models in the next revolution of statistical computing. In response, the field of statistics has seen tremendous growth in research areas related to computational statistics.

According to the current Wikipedia entry on "Computational Statistics"[a]: "Computational statistics or statistical computing refers to the interface between statistics and computer science. It is the area of computational science (or scientific computing) specific to the mathematical science of statistics." Two well known examples of statistical computing methods are the bootstrap and Markov Chain Monte Carlo (MCMC). These methods are prohibitive with insufficient computing power. While the bootstrap has gained significant popularity both in academic research and in practical applications its feasibility still relies on efficient computing. Similarly, MCMC, which is at the core of Bayesian analysis, is computationally very demanding. A third method which has also become prominent in both academia and practice is nonparametric estimation. Today, nonparametric models are popular data analytic tools due to their flexibility despite being very computationally intensive, and even prohibitively intensive with large datasets.

In this paper, we provide summarized expositions for some of these important methods. The choice of methods highlights major computational methods for estimation and for inference. We do not aim to provide a comprehensive review of each of these methods, but rather a brief introduction. However, we compiled a list of references for readers interested in further information on any of these methods. For each of the methods, we provide the statistical definition and properties, as well as a brief illustration using an example dataset.

In addition to the aforementioned topics, the 21st century has witnessed tremendous growth in statistical computational methods such as functional data analysis, lasso, and machine learning methods such as random forests, neural networks, deep learning and support vector machines. Although most of these methods have roots in the machine learning field, they have become popular in the field of statistics as well. The recent book by Ref. 15 describes many of these topics.

The paper is organized as follows. In Sec. 1, we open with nonparametric density estimation. Sections 2 and 3 discuss smoothing methods and their extensions. Specifically, Sec. 2 focuses on kernel smoothing while Sec. 3 introduces spline smoothing. Section 4 covers additive models, and Sec. 5 introduces MCMC methods. The final Sec. 6 is dedicated to the two most popular resampling methods: the bootstrap and jackknife.

2. Density Estimation

A basic characteristic describing the behavior of any random variable X is its probability density function. Knowledge of

---

[a]https://en.wikipedia.org/wiki/Computational_statistics, accessed August 24, 2016.

the density function is useful in many aspects. By looking at the density function chart, we can get a clear picture of whether the distribution is skewed, multi-modal, etc. In the simple case of a continuous random variable X over an interval $X \in (a, b)$, the density is defined as

$$P(a < X < b) = \int_a^b f(x)dx.$$

In most practical studies, the density of X is not directly available. Instead, we are given a set of n observations $x_1, \ldots, x_n$ that we assume are iid realizations of the random variable. We then aim to estimate the density on the basis of these observations. There are two basic estimation approaches: the parametric approach, which consists of representing the density with a finite set of parameters, and the nonparametric approach, which does not restrict the possible form of the density function by assuming it belongs to a pre-specified family of density functions.

In parametric estimation, only the parameters are unknown. Hence, the density estimation problem is equivalent to estimating the parameters. However, in the nonparametric approach, one must estimate the entire distribution. This is because we make no assumptions about the density function.

2.1. *Histogram*

The oldest and most widely used density estimator is the histogram. Detailed discussions are found in Refs. 65 and 34. Using the definition of derivatives, we can write the density in the following form:

$$f(x) \equiv \frac{d}{dx} F(x) \equiv \lim_{h \to 0} \frac{F(x+h) - F(x)}{h}, \qquad (1)$$

where $F(x)$ is the cumulative distribution function of the random variable X. A natural finite sample analog of Eq. (1) is to divide the real line into K equi-sized bins with small bin width h and replace $F(x)$ with the empirical cumulative distribution function

$$\hat{F}(x) = \frac{\#\{x_i \le x\}}{n}.$$

This leads to the empirical density function estimator

$$\hat{f}(x) = \frac{(\#\{x_i \le b_{j+1}\} - \#\{x_i \le b_j\})/n}{h}, \qquad x \in (b_j, b_{j+1}],$$

where $(b_j, b_{j+1}]$ defines the boundaries of the jth bin and $h = b_{j+1} - b_j$. If we define $n_j = \#\{x_i \le b_{j+1}\} - \#\{x_i \le b_j\}$ then

$$\hat{f}(x) = \frac{n_j}{nh}. \qquad (2)$$

The same histogram estimate can also be obtained using maximum likelihood estimation methods. Here, we try to find a density $\hat{f}$ maximizing the likelihood in the observations

$$\prod_{i=1}^n \hat{f}(x_i). \qquad (3)$$

Since the above likelihood (or its logarithm) cannot be maximized directly, penalized maximum likelihood estimation can be used to obtain the histogram estimate.

Next, we proceed to calculate the bias, variance and MSE of the histogram estimator. These properties give us an idea of the accuracy and precision of the estimator. If we define

$$B_j = [x_0 + (j-1)h, x_0 + jh), \quad j \in \mathbb{Z},$$

with x_0 being the origin of the histogram, then the histogram estimator can be formally written as

$$\hat{f}_h(x) = (nh)^{-1} \sum_{i=1}^n \sum_j I(X_i \in B_j)I(x \in B_j). \qquad (4)$$

We now define the bias of the histogram estimator. Assume that the origin of the histogram x_0 is zero and $x \in B_j$. Since X_i are identically distributed

$$\begin{aligned}
E(\hat{f}_h(x)) &= (nh)^{-1} \sum_{i=1}^n E[I(X_i \in B_j)] \\
&= (nh)^{-1} nE[I(X \in B_j)] \\
&= h^{-1} \int_{(j-1)h}^{jh} f(u)du.
\end{aligned}$$

This last term is not equal to $f(x)$ unless $f(x)$ is constant in B_j. For simplicity, assume $f(x) = a + cx, x \in B_j$ and $a, c \in \mathbb{R}$. Therefore,

$$\begin{aligned}
\text{Bias}(\hat{f}_h(x)) &= E[\hat{f}_h(x)] - f(x) \\
&= h^{-1} \int_{B_j} (f(u) - f(x))du \\
&= h^{-1} \int_{B_j} (a + cu - a - cx)du \\
&= h^{-1} hc \left(\left(j - \frac{1}{2} \right)h - x \right) \\
&= c \left(\left(j - \frac{1}{2} \right)h - x \right).
\end{aligned}$$

Instead of slope c we may write the first derivative of the density at the midpoint $(j - \frac{1}{2})h$ of the bin B_j

$$\begin{aligned}
\text{Bias}(\hat{f}_h(x)) &= f'\left(\left(j - \frac{1}{2} \right)h \right)\left(\left(j - \frac{1}{2} \right)h - x \right) \\
&= O(1)O(h) \\
&= O(h), \quad h \to 0.
\end{aligned}$$

When f is not linear, a Taylor expansion of f to the first-order reduces the problem to the linear case. Hence, the bias of the histogram is given by

$$\begin{aligned}
\text{Bias}(\hat{f}_h(x)) = \left(\left(j - \frac{1}{2} \right)h - x \right)f'\left(\left(j - \frac{1}{2} \right)h \right) \\
+ o(h), \quad h \to 0. \qquad (5)
\end{aligned}$$

Similarly, the variance for the histogram estimator can be calculated as

$$\text{Var}(\hat{f}_h(x)) = \text{Var}\left((nh)^{-1} \sum_{i=1}^{n} I(X_i \in B_j)\right)$$

$$= (nh)^{-2} \sum_{i=1}^{n} \text{Var}[I(X_i \in B_j)]$$

$$= n^{-1}h^{-2}\text{Var}[I(X \in B_j)]$$

$$= n^{-1}h^{-2}\left(\int_{B_j} f(u)du\right)\left(1 - \int_{B_j} f(u)du\right)$$

$$= (nh)^{-1}\left(h^{-1}\int_{B_j} f(u)du\right)(1 - O(h))$$

$$= (nh)^{-1}(f(x) + o(1)), \quad h \to 0, nh \to \infty.$$

Bin width choice is crucial in constructing a histogram. As illustrated in Fig. 1, bin width choice affects the bias-variance trade-off. The top three represent histograms for a normal random sample but with three different bin sizes. Similarly, the bottom three histograms are from another normal sample. From the plot, it can be seen that the histograms with larger bin width have smaller variability but larger bias and vice versa. Hence, we need to strike a balance between bias and variance to come up with a good histogram estimator.

We observe that the variance of the histogram is proportional to $f(x)$ and decreases as nh increases. This contradicts with the fact that the bias of the histogram decreases as h decreases. To find a compromise, we consider the mean squared error (MSE):

$$\text{MSE}(\hat{f}_h(x)) = \text{Var}(\hat{f}_h(x)) + (\text{Bias}(\hat{f}_h(x)))^2$$

$$= \frac{1}{nh}f(x) + ((j - 1/2)h - x)^2 f'((j - 1/2)h)^2$$

$$+ o(h) + o\left(\frac{1}{nh}\right).$$

In order for the histogram estimator to be consistent, the MSE should converge to zero asymptotically. This means that the bin width should get smaller with the number of observations per bin n_j getting larger as $n \to \infty$. Thus, under $nh \to \infty$, $h \to 0$, the histogram estimator is consistent; $\hat{f}_h(x) \xrightarrow{P} f(x)$.

Implementing the MSE using the formula is difficult in practice because of the unknown density involved. In addition, it should be calculated for each and every point. Instead of looking at the estimate at one particular point, it might be worth calculating a measure of goodness of fit for the entire histogram. For this reason, the mean integrated squared error

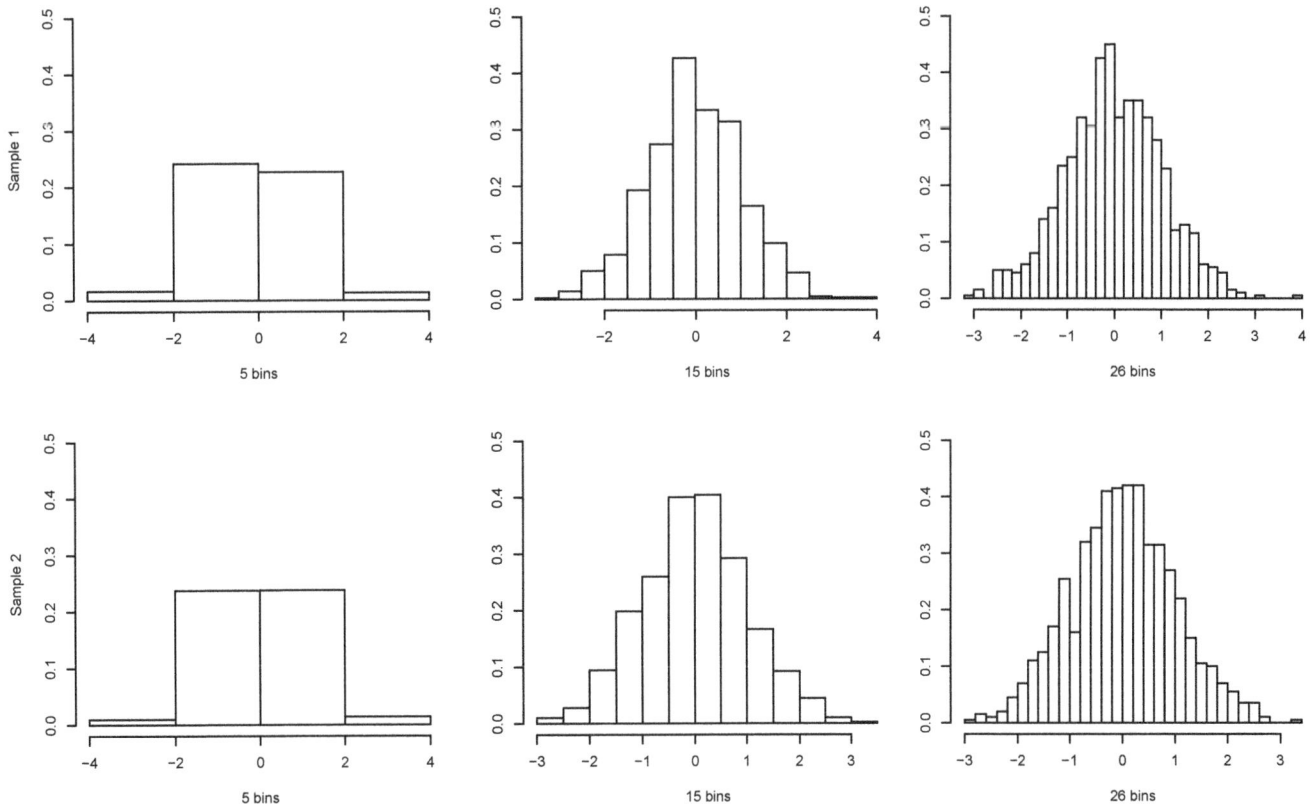

Fig. 1. Histograms for two randomly simulated normal samples with five bins (left), 15 bins (middle), and 26 bins (right).

(MISE) is used. It is defined as:

$$\text{MISE}(\hat{f}_h(x)) = E\left[\int_{-\infty}^{\infty} (\hat{f} - f)^2(x)dx\right]$$

$$= \int_{-\infty}^{\infty} \text{MSE}(\hat{f}_h(x))dx$$

$$= (nh)^{-1} + h^2/12\|f'\|_2^2 + o(h^2) + o((nh)^{-1}).$$

Note that $\|f'\|_2^2$ (dx is omitted in shorthand notation) is the square of the L_2 norm of f' which describes how smooth the density function f is. The common approach for minimizing MISE is to minimize it as a function of h without higher order terms (Asymptotic MISE, or AMISE). The minimizer (h_0), called an *optimal bandwidth*, can be obtained by differentiating AMISE with respect to h.

$$h_0 = \left(\frac{6}{n\|f'\|_2^2}\right). \tag{6}$$

Hence, we see that for minimizing AMISE we should theoretically choose $h_0 \sim n^{-1/3}$, which if we substitute in the MISE formula, would give the best convergence rate $O(n^{-2/3})$ for a sufficiently large n. Again, the solution of Eq. (6) does not help much as it involves f' which is still unknown. However, this problem can be overcome by using any reference distribution (e.g., Gaussian). This method is often called the "plug-in" method.

2.2. *Kernel density estimation*

The idea of the kernel estimator was introduced by Ref. 57. Using the definition of the probability density, suppose X has density f. Then

$$f(x) = \lim_{h \to 0} \frac{1}{2h} P(x - h < X < x + h).$$

For any given h, we can estimate the probability $P(x - h < X < x + h)$ by the proportion of the observations falling in the interval $(x - h, x + h)$. Thus, a naive estimator $\hat{f}$ of the density is given by

$$\hat{f}(x) = \frac{1}{2hn} \sum_{i=1}^{n} I_{(x-h,x+h)}(X_i).$$

To express the estimator more formally, we define the weight function w by

$$w(x) = \begin{cases} \dfrac{1}{2} & \text{if } |x| < 1 \\ 0 & \text{otherwise.} \end{cases}$$

Then, it is easy to see that the above naive estimator can be written as

$$\hat{f}(x) = \frac{1}{n} \sum_{i=1}^{n} \frac{1}{h} w\left(\frac{x - X_i}{h}\right). \tag{7}$$

However, the naive estimator is not wholly satisfactory because $\hat{f}(x)$ is of a "stepwise" nature and not differentiable everywhere. We therefore generalize the naive estimator to overcome some of these difficulties by replacing the weight function w with a kernel function K which satisfies the conditions

$$\int K(t)dt = 1, \int tK(t)dt = 0, \quad \text{and} \quad \int t^2 K(t)dt = k_2 \neq 0.$$

Usually, but not always, K will be a symmetric probability density function. Now the kernel density estimator becomes

$$\hat{f}(x) = \frac{1}{nh} \sum_{i=1}^{n} K\left(\frac{x - X_i}{h}\right).$$

From the kernel density definition, it can be observed that

- Kernel functions are symmetric around 0 and can be integrated to 1
- Since the kernel is a density function, the kernel estimator is a density too: $\int K(x)dx = 1$ implies $\int \hat{f}_h(x)dx = 1$.
- The property of smoothness of kernels is inherited by $\hat{f}_h(x)$. If K is n times continuously differentiable, then $\hat{f}_h(x)$ is also n times continuously differentiable.
- Unlike histograms, kernel estimates do not depend on the choice of origin.
- Usually kernels are positive to assure that $\hat{f}_h(x)$ is a density. There are reasons to consider negative kernels but then $\hat{f}_h(x)$ may be sometimes negative.

We next consider the bias of the kernel estimator:

$$\text{Bias}[\hat{f}_h(x)] = E[\hat{f}_h(x)] - f(x)$$

$$= \int K(s)f(x + sh)ds - f(x)$$

$$= \int K(s)\left[f(x) + shf'(x) + \frac{h^2 s^2}{2}f''(x)\right.$$

$$\left. + o(h^2)\right]ds - f(x)$$

$$= \frac{h^2}{2}f''(x)k_2 + o(h^2), \quad h \to 0.$$

For the proof see Ref. 53. We see that the bias is quadratic in h. Hence, we must choose small h to reduce the bias. Similarly, the variance for the kernel estimator can be written as

$$\text{var}(\hat{f}_h(x)) = n^{-2}\text{var}\left(\sum_{i=1}^{n} K_h(x - X_i)\right)$$

$$= n^{-1}\text{var}[K_h(x - X)]$$

$$= (nh)^{-1}f(x)\int K^2 + o((nh)^{-1}), \quad nh \to \infty.$$

Similar to the histogram case, we observe a bias-variance trade-off. The variance is nearly proportional to $(nh)^{-1}$, which requires choosing h large for minimizing variance. However, this contradicts with the aim of decreasing bias by choosing small h. From a smoothing perspective, smaller

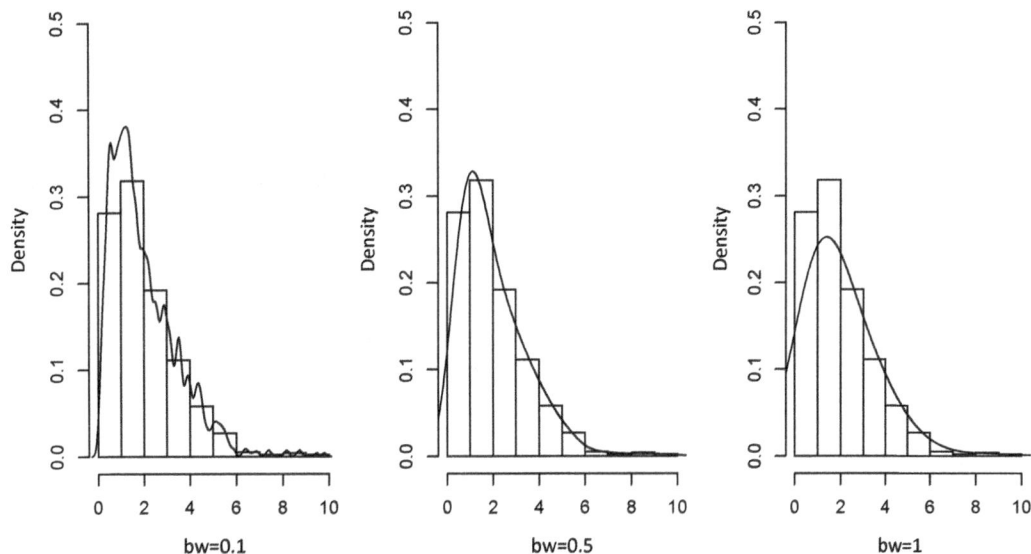

Fig. 2. Kernel densities with three bandwidth choices (0.1, 0.5, and 1) for a sample from an exponential distribution.

bandwidth results in under-smoothing and larger bandwidth results in over-smoothing. From the illustration in Fig. 2, we see that when the bandwidth is too small (left) the kernel estimator under-smoothes the true density and when the bandwidth is large (right) the kernel estimator over-smoothes the underlying density. Therefore, we consider MISE or MSE of h as a compromise.

$$\text{MSE}[\hat{f}_h(x)] = \frac{1}{nh}f(x)\int K^2 + \frac{h^4}{4}(f''(x)k_2)^2 + o((nh)^{-1})$$
$$+ o(h^4), h \to 0, nh \to \infty.$$

Note that $\text{MSE}[\hat{f}_h(x)]$ converges to zero, if $h \to 0$ and $nh \to \infty$. Thus, the kernel density estimator is consistent, that is $\hat{f}_h(x) \xrightarrow{p} f(x)$. On the whole, the variance term in MSE penalizes under smoothing and the bias term penalizes over smoothing.

Further, the asymptotic optimal bandwidth can be obtained by differentiating MSE with respect to h and equating it to zero:

$$h_0 = \left(\frac{\int K^2}{(f''(x))^2 k_2^2 n}\right)^{1/5}.$$

It can be further verified that if we substitute this bandwidth in the MISE formula then

$$\text{MISE}(\hat{f}_{h_0}) = \frac{5}{4}\left(\int K^2\right)^{4/5} k_2^{2/5}\left(\int f''(x)^2\right)^{1/5} n^{-4/5}$$
$$= \frac{5}{4}C(K)\left(\int f''(x)^2\right)^{1/5} n^{-4/5},$$

where $C(K) = \left(\int K^2\right)^{4/5} k_2^{2/5}$. From the above formula, it can be observed that we should choose a kernel K with a small value of $C(K)$, when all other things are equal. The problem of minimizing $C(K)$ can be reduced to that of minimizing $\int K^2$ by allowing suitable rescaled version of kernels. In a different context, Ref. 38 showed that this problem can be solved by setting K to be a *Epanechnikov kernel*[17] (see Table 1.2).

We define the efficiency of any symmetric kernel K by comparing it to the Epanechnikov kernel:

$$\text{eff}(K) = C(K_e)/C(K)^{5/4}$$
$$= \frac{3}{5\sqrt{5}}k_2^{-1/2}\int K^{2^{-1}}.$$

The reason for the power $5/4$ in the above equation is that for large n, the MISE will be the same, whether we use n observations with kernel K or $n\,\text{eff}(K)$ observations and the kernel K_e.[72] Some kernels and their efficiencies are given in Table 1.2.

The top four kernels are particular cases of the following family:

$$K(x;p) = \{2^{2p+1}B(p+1,p+1)\}^{-1}(1-x^2)^p I_{\{|x|<1\}},$$

where $B(\cdot,\cdot)$ is the beta function. These kernels are symmetric beta densities on the interval $[-1,1]$. For $p = 0$, the expression gives rise to a rectangular density, $p = 1$ to Epanechnikov, and $p = 2$ and $p = 3$ are bivariate and trivariate kernels, respectively. The standard normal density is obtained as the limiting case $p \to \infty$.

Similar to the histogram scenario, the problem of choosing the bandwidth (smoothing parameter) is of crucial importance to density estimation. A natural method for choosing the bandwidth is to plot several curves and choose the estimate that is most desirable. For many applications,

Table 1. Definitions of some kernels and their efficiencies.

Kernel	$K(t)$	Efficiency
Rectangular	$\begin{cases} \dfrac{1}{2} & \text{for } \lvert t \rvert \leq 1, \\ 0 & \text{otherwise.} \end{cases}$	0.9295
Epanechnikov	$\begin{cases} \dfrac{3}{4}\left(1 - \dfrac{1}{5}t^2\right)\big/ \sqrt{5} & \text{for } \lvert t \rvert \leq 5, \\ 0 & \text{otherwise.} \end{cases}$	1
Biweight	$\begin{cases} \dfrac{15}{16}(1 - t^2)^2 & \text{for } \lvert t \rvert \leq 1, \\ 0 & \text{otherwise.} \end{cases}$	0.9939
Triweight	$\begin{cases} \dfrac{35}{32}(1 - t^2)^3 & \text{for } \lvert t \rvert \leq 1, \\ 0 & \text{otherwise.} \end{cases}$	0.987
Triangular	$\begin{cases} 1 - \lvert t \rvert & \text{for } \lvert t \rvert \leq 1, \\ 0 & \text{otherwise.} \end{cases}$	0.9859
Gaussian	$\dfrac{1}{\sqrt{2\pi}} e^{-(1/2)t^2}$	0.9512

this approach is satisfactory. However, there is a need for data-driven and automatic procedures that are practical and have fast convergence rates. The problem of bandwidth selection has stimulated much research in kernel density estimation. The main approaches include cross-validation (CV) and "plug-in" methods (see the review paper by Ref. 39).

As an example, consider least squares CV, which was suggested by Refs. 58 and 3 — see also Refs. 4, 32 and 69. Given any estimator $\hat{f}$ of a density f, the integrated squared error can be written as

$$\int (\hat{f} - f)^2 = \int \hat{f}^2 - 2 \int \hat{f} f + \int f^2.$$

Since the last term ($\int f^2$) does not involve f', the updated quantity $R(\hat{f})$ of the above equation, is

$$R(\hat{f}) = \int \hat{f}^2 - 2 \int \hat{f} f.$$

The basic principle of least squares CV is to construct an estimate of $R(\hat{f})$ from the data themselves and then to minimize this estimate over h to give the choice of window width. The term $\int \hat{f}^2$ can be found from the estimate $\hat{f}$. Further, if we define $\hat{f}_{-i}$ as the density estimate constructed from all the data points except X_i, then $\int \hat{f} f$ can be computed using

$$\hat{f}_{-i}(x) = (n - 1)^{-1} h^{-1} \sum_{j \neq i} K h^{-1}(x - X_j).$$

Now we define the required quantity without any unknown terms f, as

$$M_0(h) = \int \hat{f}^2 - 2n^{-1} \sum_i \hat{f}_{-i}(X_i).$$

The score M_0 depends only on data and the idea of least squares CV is to minimize the score over h. There also exists a computationally simple approach to estimate M_0 — Ref. 69 provided the large sample properties for this estimator. Thus, asymptotically, least squares CV achieves the best possible choice of smoothing parameter, in the sense of minimizing the integrated squared error. For further details, see Ref. 63.

Another possible approach related to "plug-in" estimators is to use a standard family of distributions as a reference for the value $\int f''(x)^2 dx$ which is the only unknown in the optimal bandwidth formula h_{opt}. For example, if we consider the normal distribution with variance σ^2, then

$$\int f''(x)^2 dx = \sigma^{-5} \int \phi''(x)^2 dx = \frac{3}{8}\pi^{-1/2}\sigma^{-5} \approx 0.212\sigma^{-5}.$$

If a Gaussian kernel is used, then the optimal bandwidth is

$$\begin{aligned} h_{\text{opt}} &= (4\pi)^{-1/10} \frac{3}{8} \pi^{-1/2} \sigma n^{-1/5} \\ &= \left(\frac{4}{3}\right)^{1/5} \sigma n^{-1/5} \\ &= 1.06 \sigma n^{-1/5}. \end{aligned}$$

A quick way of choosing the bandwidth is therefore estimating σ from the data and substituting it in the above formula. While this works well if the normal distribution is a reasonable approximation, it may oversmooth if the population is multimodal. Better results can be obtained using a robust measure of spread such as the interquartile (R) range, which in this example yields $h_{\text{opt}} = 0.79 R n^{-1/5}$. Similarly, one can improve this further by taking the minimum of the standard deviation and the interquartile range divided by 1.34. For most applications, these bandwidths are easy to evaluate and serve as a good starting value.

Although the underlying idea is very simple and the first paper was published long ago, the kernel approach did not make much progress until recently, with advances in computing power. At present, without an efficient algorithm, the calculation of a kernel density for moderately large datasets can become prohibitive. The direct use of the above formulas for computations is very inefficient. Researchers developed fast and efficient Fourier transformation methods to calculate the estimate using the fact that the kernel estimate can be written as a convolution of data and the kernel function.[43]

3. Kernel Smoothing

The problem of smoothing sequences of observations is important in many branches of science and it is demonstrated by the number of different fields in which smoothing methods have been applied. Early contributions were made in fields as diverse as astronomy, actuarial science, and economics. Despite their long history, local regression methods have received little attention in the statistics literature until the late

1970s. Initial work includes the mathematical development of Refs. 67, 40 and 68, and the LOWESS procedure of Ref. 9. Recent work on local regression includes Refs. 19, 20 and 36.

The local linear regression method was developed largely as an extension of parametric regression methods and accompanied by an elegant finite sample theory of linear estimation methods that build on theoretical results for parametric regression. It is a method for curve estimation by fitting locally weighted least squares regression. One extension of local linear regression, called local polynomial regression, is discussed in Ref. 59 and in the monograph by Ref. 21.

Assume that $(X_1, Y_1), \ldots, (X_n, Y_n)$ are iid observations with conditional mean and conditional variance denoted respectively by

$$m(x) = E(Y|X = x) \quad \text{and} \quad \sigma^2(x) = \text{Var}(Y|X = x). \quad (8)$$

Many important applications involve estimation of the regression function $m(x)$ or its νth derivative $m^{(\nu)}(x)$. The performance of an estimator $\hat{m}_\nu(x)$ of $m^{(\nu)}(x)$ is assessed via its MSE or MISE defined in previous sections. While the MSE criterion is used when the main objective is to estimate the function at the point x, the MISE criterion is used when the main goal is to recover the whole curve.

3.1. *Nadaraya–Watson estimator*

If we do not assume a specific form for the regression function $m(x)$, then a data point remote from x carries little information about the value of $m(x)$. In such a case, an intuitive estimator of the conditional mean function is the running locally weighted average. If we consider a kernel K with bandwidth h as the weight function, the Nadaraya–Watson kernel regression estimator is given by

$$\hat{m}_h(x) = \frac{\sum_{i=1}^n K_h(X_i - x)Y_i}{\sum_{i=1}^n K_h(X_i - x)}, \quad (9)$$

where $K_h(\cdot) = K(\cdot/h)/h$. For more details see Refs. 50, 80 and 33.

3.2. *Gasser–Müller estimator*

Assume that the data have already been sorted according to the X variable. Reference 24 proposed the following estimator:

$$\hat{m}_h(x) = \sum_{i=1}^n \int_{s_{i-1}}^{s_i} K_h(u - x)du Y_i, \quad (10)$$

with $s_i = (X_i + X_{i+1})/2, X_0 = -\infty$ and $X_{n+1} = +\infty$. The weights in Eq. (10) add up to 1, so there is no need for a denominator as in the Nadaraya–Watson estimator. Although it was originally developed for equispaced designs, the Gasser–Müller estimator can also be used for non-equispaced designs. For the asymptotic properties please refer to Refs. 44 and 8.

3.3. *Local linear estimator*

This estimator assumes that locally the regression function m can be approximated by

$$m(z) \approx \sum_{j=0}^p \frac{m^{(j)}(x)}{j!}(z - x)^j \equiv \sum_{j=0}^p \beta_j(z - x)^j, \quad (11)$$

for z in a neighborhood of x, by using a Taylor's expansion. Using a local least squares formulation, the model coefficients can be estimated by minimizing the following function:

$$\sum_{i=1}^n \left\{ Y_i - \sum_{j=0}^p \beta_j(X_i - x)^j \right\}^2 K_h(X_i - x), \quad (12)$$

where $K(\cdot)$ is a kernel function with bandwidth h. If we let $\hat{\beta}_j$ $(j = 0, \ldots, p)$ be equal to the estimates obtained from minimizing Eq. (12), then the estimator for the regression functions are obtained as

$$\hat{m}_\nu(x) = \nu! \hat{\beta}_\nu. \quad (13)$$

When $p = 1$, the estimator $\hat{m}_0(x)$ is termed a *local linear smoother* or *local linear estimator* with the following explicit expression:

$$\hat{m}_0(x) = \frac{\sum_1^n w_i Y_i}{\sum_1^n w_i},$$
$$w_i = K_h(X_i - x)\{S_{n,2} - (X_i - x)S_{n,1}\}, \quad (14)$$

where $S_{n,j} = \sum_1^n K_h(X_i - x)(X_i - x)^j$. When $p = 0$, the local linear estimator equals to the Nadaraya–Watson estimator. Also, both Nadaraya–Watson and Gasser–Müller estimators are of the type of local least squares estimator with weights $w_i = K_h(X_i - x)$ and $w_i = \int_{s_{i-1}}^{s_i} K_h(u - x)du$, respectively. The asymptotic results are provided in Table 2.3, which is taken from Ref. 19.

To illustrate both Nadaraya–Watson and local linear fit on data, we considered an example of a dataset on trees.[2,60] This dataset includes measurements of the girth, height, and volume of timber in 31 felled back cherry trees. The smooth fit results are described in Fig. 3. The fit results are produced using the *KernSmooth*[79] package in R-Software.[73] In the right panel of Fig. 3, we see that for a larger bandwidth, as expected, Nadaraya–Watson fits a global constant model while the local linear fits a linear model. Further, from the left

Table 2. Comparison of asymptotic properties of local estimators.

Method	Bias	Variance
Nadaraya–Watson	$\left(m''(x) + \frac{2m'(x)f'(x)}{f(x)}\right)b_n$	V_n
Gasser–Müller	$m''(x)b_n$	$1.5V_n$
Local linear	$m''(x)b_n$	V_n

Note: Here, $b_n = \frac{1}{2}\int_{-\infty}^{\infty} u^2 K(u)du h^2$ and $V_n = \frac{\sigma^2(x)}{f(x)nh}\int_{-\infty}^{\infty} K^2(u)du$.

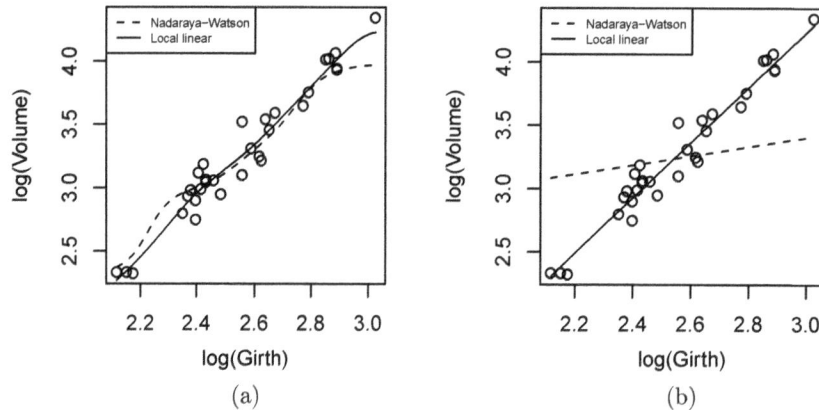

Fig. 3. Comparison of local linear fit versus Nadaraya–Watson fit for a model of (log) volume as a function of (log) girth, with choice of two bandwidths: 0.1 (a) and 0.5 (b).

panel, where we used a reasonable bandwidth, the Nadara–Watson estimator has more bias than the local linear fit.

In comparison with the local linear fit, the Nadaraya–Watson estimator locally uses one parameter less without reducing the asymptotic variance. It suffers from large bias, particularly in the region where the derivative of the regression function or design density is large. Also it does not adapt to nonuniform designs. In addition, it was shown that the Nadaraya–Watson estimator has zero minimax efficiency — for details see Ref. 19. Based on the definition of minimax efficiency, a 90% efficient estimator uses only 90% of the data. Which means that the Nadaraya–Watson does not use all the available data. In contrast, the Gasser–Müller estimator corrects the bias of the Nadaraya–Watson estimator but at the expense of increasing variability for random designs. Further, both the Nadaraya–Watson and Gasser–Müller estimator have a large order of bias when estimating a curve at the boundary region. Comparisons between local linear and local constant (Nadaraya–Watson) fit were discussed in detail by Refs. 8, 19 and 36.

3.4. *Computational considerations*

Recent proposals for fast implementations of nonparametric curve estimators include the binning methods and the updating methods. Reference 22 gave careful speed comparisons of these two fast implementations and direct naive implementations under a variety of settings and using various machines and software. Both fast methods turned out to be much faster with negligible differences in accuracy.

While the key idea of the binning method is to bin the data and compute the required quantities based on the binned data, the key idea of the updating method involves updating the quantities previously computed. It has been reported that for practical purposes neither method dominates the other.

4. Smoothing Using Splines

Similar to local linear estimators, another family of methods that provide flexible data modeling is spline

methods. These methods involve fitting piecewise polynomials or splines to allow the regression function to have discontinuities at certain locations which are called "knots".[18,78,30]

4.1. *Polynomial spline*

Suppose that we want to approximate the unknown regression function m by a cubic spline function, that is, a piecewise polynomial with continuous first two derivatives. Let $t_1, \ldots, t_J$ be a fixed knot sequence such that $-\infty < t_1 < \cdots < t_J < +\infty$. Then the cubic spline functions are twice continuously differentiable functions s such that restrictions of s to each of the intervals $(-\infty, t_1], [t_1, t_2], \ldots, [t_{J-1}, t_J]$, $[t_J, +\infty)$ is a cubic polynomial. The collection of all these cubic spline functions forms a $(J + 4)$-dimensional linear space. There exist two popular cubic spline bases for this linear space:

Power basis: $1, x, x^2, x^3, (x - t_j)_+^3, (j = 1, \ldots, J)$;
B-spline basis: The ith B-spline of degree $p = 3$, written as $N_{i,p}(u)$, is defined recursively as:

$$N_{i,0}(u) = \begin{cases} 1 & \text{if } u_i \leq u \leq u_{i=1} \\ 0 & \text{otherwise.} \end{cases}$$

$$N_{i,p}(u) = \frac{u - u_i}{u_{i+p} - u_i} N_i, p - 1(u) + \frac{u_{i+p+1} - u}{u_{i+p+1} - ui + 1} N_{i+1,p-1}(u).$$

The above is usually referred to as the *Cox-de Boor recursion formula*.

The B-spline basis is typically numerically more stable because the multiple correlation among the basis functions is smaller, but the power spline basis has the advantage that it provides easier interpretation of the knots so that deleting a particular basis function is the same as deleting that particular knot. The direct estimation of the regression function m depends on the choice of knot locations and the number of knots. There exist some methods based on the knot-deletion idea. For full details please see Refs. 41 and 42.

4.2. *Smoothing spline*

Consider the following objective function

$$\sum_{i=1}^{n} \{Y_i - m(X_i)\}^2. \tag{15}$$

Minimizing this function gives the best possible estimate for the unknown regression function. The major problem with the above objective function is that any function m that interpolates the data satisfies it, thereby leading to overfitting. To avoid this, a penalty for the overparametrization is imposed on the function. A convenient way for introducing such a penalty is via the roughness penalty approach. The following function is minimized:

$$\sum_{i=1}^{n} \{Y_i - m(X_i)\}^2 + \lambda \int \{m''(x)\}^2 dx, \tag{16}$$

where $\lambda > 0$ is a smoothing parameter. The first term penalizes the lack of fit, which is in some sense modeling bias. The second term denotes the roughness penalty which is related to overparametrization. It is evident that $\lambda = 0$ yields interpolation (oversmoothing) and $\lambda = \infty$ yields linear regression (undersmoothing). Hence, the estimator obtained from the objective function $\hat{m}_\lambda$, which also depends on the smoothing parameter, is called the *smoothing spline estimator*. For local properties of this estimator, please refer to Ref. 51.

It is well known that the solution to the minimization of (16) is a cubic spline on the interval $[X_{(1)}, X_{(n)}]$ and it is unique in this data range. Moreover, the estimator is a linear smoother with weights that do not depend on the response $\{Y_i\}$.[33] The connections between kernel regression, which we discussed in the previous section, and smoothing splines have been critically studied by Refs. 62 and 64.

The smoothing parameter λ can be chosen by minimizing the CV[71,1] or generalized cross validation (GCV)[77,11] criteria. Both quantities are consistent estimates of the MISE of $\hat{m}_\lambda$. For other methods and details please see Ref. 78. Further, for computational issues please refer to Refs. 78 and 18.

5. Additive Models

While the smoothing methods discussed in the previous section are mostly univariate, the additive model is a widely used multivariate smoothing technique. An additive model is defined as

$$Y = \alpha + \sum_{j=1}^{p} f_j(X_j) + \epsilon, \tag{17}$$

where the errors ϵ are independent of the X_js and have mean $E(\epsilon) = 0$ and variance $\text{var}(\epsilon) = \sigma^2$. The f_j are arbitrary univariate functions, one for each predictor. Since each variable is represented separately, the model retains the interpretative ease of a linear model.

The most general method for estimating additive models allows us to estimate each function by an arbitrary smoother. Some possible candidates are smoothing splines and kernel smoothers. The backfitting algorithm is a general purpose algorithm that enables one to fit additive models with any kind of smoothing functions although for specific smoothing functions such as smoothing splines or penalized splines there exist separate estimation methods based on least squares. The backfitting algorithm is an iterative algorithm and consists of the following steps:

(i) Initialize: $\alpha = \text{ave}(y_i), f_j = f_j^0, j = 1, \ldots, p$
(ii) Cycle: for $j = 1, \ldots, p$ repeat $f_j = S_j(y - \alpha - \sum_{k \neq j} f_k | x_j)$.
(iii) Continue (ii) until the individual functions do not change.

The term $S_j(y|x_j)$ denotes a smooth of the response y against the predictor x_j. The motivation for the backfitting algorithm can be understood using conditional expectation. If the additive model is correct then for any k, $E(Y - \alpha - \sum_{j \neq k} f_j(X_j)|X_k) = f_k(X_k)$. This suggests the appropriateness of the backfitting algorithm for computing all the f_j.

Reference 70 showed in the context of regression splines — OLS estimation of spline models — that the additive model has the desirable property of reducing a full p-dimensional nonparametric regression problem to one that can be fitted with the same asymptotic efficiency as a univariate problem. Due to lack of explicit expressions, the earlier research by Ref. 5 studied only the bivariate additive model in detail and showed that both the convergence of the algorithm and uniqueness of its solution depend on the behavior of the product of the two smoothers matrices. Later, Refs. 52 and 45 extended the convergence theory to p-dimensions. For more details, please see Refs. 5, 45 and 52.

We can write all the estimating equations in a compact form:

$$\begin{pmatrix} I & S_1 & S_1 & \cdots & S_1 \\ S_2 & I & S_2 & \cdots & S_2 \\ \vdots & \vdots & \vdots & \ddots & \vdots \\ S_p & S_p & S_p & \cdots & I \end{pmatrix} \begin{pmatrix} f_1 \\ f_2 \\ \vdots \\ f_p \end{pmatrix} = \begin{pmatrix} S_1 y \\ S_2 y \\ \vdots \\ S_p y \end{pmatrix}$$

$$\hat{P}f = \hat{Q}y.$$

Backfitting is a Gauss–Seidel procedure for solving the above system. While one could directly use QR decomposition without any iterations to solve the entire system, the computational complexity prohibits doing so. The difficulty is that QR require $O\{(np)^3\}$ operations while the backfitting involves only $O(np)$ operations, which is much cheaper. For more details, see Ref. 37.

We return to the trees dataset that we considered in the last section, and fit an additive model with both height and girth as predictors to model volume. The fitted model is

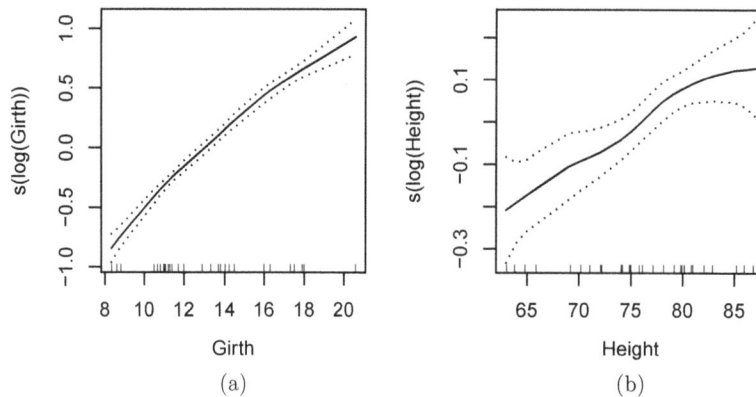

Fig. 4.   Estimated functions for girth (a) and height (b) using smoothing splines.

log(Volume) $\sim$ log(Height) + log(Girth). We used the gam[35] package in R-software. The fitted functions are shown in Fig. 4.

The backfitting method is very generic in the sense that it can handle any type of smoothing function. However, there exists another method specific to penalized splines, which has become quite popular. This method uses penalized splines by estimating the model using penalized regression methods. In Eq. (16), because m is linear in parameters β, the penalty can always be written as a quadratic form in β:

$$\int \{m''(x)\}^2 dx = \beta^T S \beta,$$

where S is the matrix of known coefficients. Therefore, the penalized regression spline fitting problem is to minimize

$$\|y - X\beta\|^2 + \lambda\beta^T S\beta, \tag{18}$$

with respect to β. It is straightforward to see that the solution is a least squares type of estimator and depends on the smoothing parameter λ:

$$\hat{\beta} = (X^T X + \lambda S)^{-1} X^T y. \tag{19}$$

Penalized likelihood maximization can only estimate model coefficients β given the smoothing parameter λ. There exist two basic useful estimation approaches: when the scale parameter in the model is known, one can use Mallow's C_p criterion; when the scale parameter is unknown, one can use GCV. Furthermore, for models such as generalized linear models which are estimated iteratively, numerically there exist two different ways of estimating the smoothing parameter:

Outer iteration: The score can be minimized directly. This means that the penalized regression must be evaluated for each trial set of smoothing parameters.
Performance iteration: The score can be minimized and the smoothing parameter selected for each working penalized linear model. This method is computationally efficient.

Performance iteration was originally proposed by Ref. 31. It usually converges, and requires only a reliable and efficient

method for score minimization. However, it also has some issues related to convergence. In contrast, the outer method suffers from none of the disadvantages that performance iteration has but it is more computationally costly. For more details, please see Ref. 81.

The recent work by Ref. 83 showcases the successful application of additive models on large datasets and uses performance iteration with block QR updating. This indicates the feasibility of applying these computationally intensive and useful models for big data. The routines are available in the R-package $mgcv$.[82]

6. Markov Chain and Monte Carlo

The MCMC methodology provides enormous scope for realistic and complex statistical modeling. The idea is to perform Monte Carlo integration using Markov chains. Bayesian statisticians, and sometimes also frequentists, need to integrate over possibly high-dimensional probability distributions to draw inference about model parameters or to generate predictions. For a brief history and overview please refer to Refs. 28 and 29.

6.1. *Markov chains*

Consider a sequence of random variables, $\{X_0, X_1, X_2, \ldots\}$, such that at each time $t \geq 0$, the next state X_{t+1} is sampled from a conditional distribution $P(X_{t+1}|X_t)$, which depends only on the current state of the chain X_t. That is, given the current state X_t, the next state X_{t+1} does not depend on the past states — this is called the memory-less property. This sequence is called a Markov chain.

The joint distribution of a Markov chain is determined by two components:

The marginal distribution of X_0, called the initial distribution.
The conditional density $p(\cdot|\cdot)$, called the transitional kernel of the chain.

It is assumed that the chain is time-homogeneous, which means that the probability $P(\cdot|\cdot)$ does not depend on time t. The set in which X_t takes values is called the *state space* of the Markov chain and it can be countably finite or infinite.

Under some regularity conditions, the chain will gradually forget its initial state and converge to a unique stationary (invariant) distribution, say $\pi(\cdot)$, which does not depend on t and X_0. To converge to a stationary distribution, the chain needs to satisfy three important properties. First, it has to be *irreducible*, which means that from all starting points the Markov chain can reach any nonempty set with positive probability in some iterations. Second, the chain needs to be *aperiodic*, which means that it should not oscillate between any two points in a periodic manner. Third, the chain must be *positive recurrent* as defined next.

Definition 1 (Ref. 49). (i) Markov chain X is called irreducible if for all i, j, there exists $t > 0$ such that $P_{i,j}(t) = P[X_t = j | X_0 = i] > 0$.

(ii) Let τ_{ii} be the time of the first return to state i, ($\tau_{ii} = min\{t > 0 : X_t = i | X_0 = i\}$). An irreducible chain X is recurrent if $P[\tau_{ii} < \infty] = 1$ for some i. Otherwise, X is transient. Another equivalent condition for recurrence is

$$\sum_t P_{ij}(t) = \infty,$$

for all i, j.

(iii) An irreducible recurrent chain X is called positive recurrent if $E[\tau_{ii}] < \infty$ for some i. Otherwise, it is called null-recurrent. Another equivalent condition for positive recurrence is the existence of a stationary probability distribution for X, that is there exists $\pi(\cdot)$ such that

$$\sum_i \pi(i) P_{ij}(t) = \pi(j) \tag{20}$$

for all j and $t \geq 0$.

(iv) An irreducible chain X is called aperiodic if for some i, the greatest common divider is $\{t > 0 : P_{ii}(t) > 0\} = 1$.

In MCMC, since we already have a target distribution $\pi(\cdot)$, then X will be positive recurrent if we can demonstrate irreducibility.

After a sufficiently long burn-in of, say, m iterations, points $\{X_t; t = m + 1, \ldots, n\}$ will be the dependent sample approximately from $\pi(\cdot)$. We can now use the output from the Markov chain to estimate the required quantities. For example, we estimate $E[f(X)]$, where X has distribution $\pi(\cdot)$ as follows:

$$\bar{f} = \frac{1}{n-m} \sum_{t=m+1}^{n} f(X_t).$$

This quantity is called an *ergodic average* and its convergence to the required expectation is ensured by the ergodic theorem.[56,49]

Theorem 2. *If X is positive recurrent and aperiodic then its stationary distribution $\pi(\cdot)$ is the unique probability distribution satisfying Eq. (20). We then say that X is ergodic and the following consequences hold:*

(i) $P_{ij}(t) \to \pi(j)$ as $t \to \infty$ for all i, j.
(ii) (*Ergodic theorem*) *If $E[|f(X)|] < \infty$, then*

$$P(\bar{f} \to E[f(X)]) = 1,$$

where $E[f(X)] = \sum_i f(i)\pi(i)$, the expectation of $f(X)$ with respect to $\pi(\cdot)$.

Most of the Markov chains procedures in MCMC are reversible which means that they are positive recurrent with stationary distribution $\pi(\cdot)$, and $\pi(i)P_{ij} = \pi(j)P_{ji}$.

Further, we say that X is geometrically ergodic, if it is ergodic (positive recurrent and aperiodic) and there exists $0 \leq \lambda < 1$ and a function $V(\cdot) > 1$ such that

$$\sum_j |P_{ij}(t) - \pi(j)| \leq V(i)\lambda^t, \tag{21}$$

for all i. The smallest λ for which there exists a function satisfying the above equation is called the rate of convergence. As a consequence to the geometric convergence, the central limit theorem can be used for ergodic averages, that is

$$N^{1/2}(\bar{f} - E[f(X)]) \to N(0, \sigma^2),$$

for some positive constant σ, as $N \to \infty$, with the convergence in distribution. For an extensive treatment of geometric convergence and central limit theorems for Markov chains, please refer to Ref. 48.

6.2. *The Gibbs sampler and Metropolis–Hastings algorithm*

Many MCMC algorithms are hybrids or generalizations of the two simplest methods: the Gibbs sampler and the Metropolis-Hastings algorithm. We therefore describe each of these two methods next.

6.2.1. *Gibbs sampler*

The Gibbs sampler enjoyed an initial surge of popularity starting with the paper of Ref. 27 (in a study of image processing models), while the roots of this method can be traced back to Ref. 47. The Gibbs sampler is a technique for indirectly generating random variables from a (marginal) distribution, without calculating the joint density. With the help of techniques like these we are able to avoid difficult calculations, replacing them with a sequence of easier calculations.

Let $\pi(x) = \pi(x_1, \ldots, x_k), x \in \mathbb{R}^n$ denote a joint density, and let $\pi(x_i | x_{-i})$ denote the induced full conditional densities for each of the components x_i, given values of other components $x_{-i} = (x_j; j \neq i), i = 1, \ldots, k, 1 < k \leq n$. Now the Gibbs sampler proceeds as follows. First, choose arbitrary starting values $x^0 = (x_1^0, \ldots, x_k^0)$. Then, successively make random drawings from the full conditional distributions $\pi(x_i | x_{-i})$, $i = 1, \ldots, k$ as follows[66]:

$$x_1^1 \text{ from } \pi(x_1 | x_{-1}^0),$$
$$x_2^1 \text{ from } \pi(x_2 | x_1^1, x_3^0, \ldots, x_k^0),$$
$$x_3^1 \text{ from } \pi(x_3 | x_1^1, x_2^1, x_4^0, \ldots, x_k^0),$$
$$\vdots$$
$$x_k^1 \text{ from } \pi(x_k | x_{-k}^1)$$

This completes a transition from $x^0 = (x_1^0, \ldots, x_k^0)$ to $x^1 = (x_1^1, \ldots, x_k^1)$. Each complete cycle through the conditional distributions produces a sequence $x^0, x^1, \ldots, x^t, \ldots$ which is a realization of the Markov chain, with transition probability from x^t to x^{t+1} given by

$$\text{TP}(x^t, x^{t+1}) = \prod_{l=1}^{k} \pi(x_l^{t+1} | x_j^t, j > l, x_j^{t+1}, j < l). \quad (22)$$

Thus, the key feature of this algorithm is to only sample from the full conditional distributions which are often easier to evaluate rather than the joint density. For more details, see Ref. 6.

6.2.2. *Metropolis–Hastings algorithm*

The Metropolis–Hastings (MH) algorithm was developed by Ref. 47. This algorithm is extremely versatile and produces the Gibbs sampler as a special case.[25]

To construct a Markov chain $X_1, X_2, \ldots, X_t, \ldots$ with state space χ and equilibrium distribution $\pi(x)$, the M–H algorithm constructs the transition probability from $X_t = x$ to the next realized state X_{t+1} as follows. Let $q(x, x')$ denote a candidate generating density such that $X_t = x, x'$ drawn from $q(x, x')$ is considered as a proposed possible value for X_{t+1}. With some probability $\alpha(x, x')$, we accept $X_{t+1} = x'$; otherwise, we reject the value generated from $q(x, x')$ and set $X_{t+1} = x$. This construction defines a Markov chain with transition probabilities given as

$$p(x, x') = \begin{cases} q(x, x') \alpha(x, x') & \text{if } x' \neq x \\ 1 - \sum_{x''} q(x, x'') \alpha(x, x'') & \text{if } x' = x. \end{cases}$$

Next, we choose

$$\alpha(x, x') = \begin{cases} \min\left\{ \dfrac{\pi(x') q(x', x)}{\pi(x) q(x, x')}, 1 \right\} & \text{if } \pi(x) q(x, x') > 0, \\ 1 & \text{if } \pi(x) q(x, x') = 0. \end{cases}$$

The choice of the arbitrary $q(x, x')$ to be irreducible and aperiodic is a sufficient condition for $\pi(x)$ to be the equilibrium distribution of the constructed chain.

It can be observed that different choices of $q(x, x')$ will lead to different specific algorithms. For $q(x, x') = q(x', x)$,

we have $\alpha(x, x') = \min\{\pi(x')/\pi(x), 1\}$, which is the well-known Metropolis algorithm.[47] For $q(x, x') = q(x' - x)$, the chain is driven by a random walk process. For more choices and their consequences please refer to Ref. 74. Similarly for applications of the MH algorithm and for more details see Ref. 7.

6.3. *MCMC issues*

There is a great deal of theory about the convergence properties of MCMC. However, it has not been found to be very useful in practice for determining the convergence information. A critical issue for the users of MCMC is how to determine when to stop the algorithm. Sometimes a Markov chain can appear to have converged to the equilibrium distribution when it has not. This can happen due to the prolonged transition times between state space or due to the multimodality nature of the equilibrium distribution. This phenomenon is often called *pseudo convergence* or *multimodality*.

The phenomenon of pseudo convergence has led many MCMC users to embrace the idea of comparing multiple runs of the sampler started at multiple points instead of the usual single run. It is believed that if the multiple runs converge to the same equilibrium distribution then everything is fine with the chain. However, this approach does not alleviate all the problems. Many times running multiple chains leads to avoiding running the sampler long enough to detect if there are any problems, such as bugs in the code, etc. Those who have used MCMC in complicated problems are probably familiar with stories about last minute problems after running the chain for several weeks. In the following, we describe the two popular MCMC diagnostic methods.

Reference 26 proposed a convergence diagnostic method which is commonly known as "Gelman–Rubin" diagnostic method. It consists of the following two steps. First, obtain an an overdispersed estimate of the target distribution and from it generate the starting points for the desired number of independent chains (say 10). Second, run the Gibbs sampler and re-estimate the target distribution of the required scalar quantity as a conservative Student distribution, the scale parameter of which involves both the between-chain variance and within-chain variance. Now the convergence is monitored by estimating the factor by which the scale parameter might shrink if sampling were continued indefinitely, namely

$$\sqrt{\hat{R}} = \sqrt{\left(\frac{n-1}{n} + \frac{m+1}{mn} \frac{B}{W} \right) \frac{df}{df - 2}},$$

where B is the variance between the means from the m parallel chains, W is the within-chain variances, df is the degrees of freedom of the approximating density, and n is number of observations that are used to re-estimate the target density. The authors recommend an iterative process of running additional iterations of the parallel chains and redoing step 2 until the shrink factors for all the quantities of interest are near 1. Though created for the Gibbs sampler, the method by Ref. 26 may be applied to the output of any MCMC algorithm. It emphasizes the reduction of bias in estimation. There also exist a number of criticisms for Ref. 26 method. It relies heavily on the user's ability to find a starting distribution which is highly overdispersed with the target distribution. This means that the user should have some prior knowledge on the target distribution. Although the approach is essentially univariate the authors suggested using −2 times log posterior density as a way of summarizing the convergence of a joint density.

Similarly, Ref. 55 proposed a diagnostic method which is intended both to detect convergence to the stationary distribution and to provide a way of bounding the variance estimates of the quantiles of functions of parameters. The user must first run a single chain Gibbs sampler with the minimum number of iterations that would be needed to obtain the desired precision of estimation if the samples were independent. The approach is based on the two-state Markov chain theory, as well as the standard sample size formulas that involves formulas of binomial variance. For more details, please refer to Ref. 55. Critics point out that the method can produce variable estimates of the required number of iterations needed given different initial chains for the same problem and that it

is univariate rather than giving information about the full joint posterior distribution.

There are more methods available to provide the convergence diagnostics for MCMC although not as popular as these. For a discussion about other methods refer to Ref. 10.

Continuing our illustrations using the trees data, we fit the same model that we used in Sec. 4 using MCMC methods. We used the *MCMCpack*[46] package in R. For the sake of illustration, we considered three chains and 600 observations per chain. Among 600 only 100 observations are considered for the burnin. The summary results are described as follows.

```
Iterations = 101:600
Thinning interval = 1
Number of chains = 3
Sample size per chain = 500
```

1. Empirical mean and standard deviation for each variable, plus standard error of the mean:

	Mean	SD	Naive SE	Time-series SE
(Intercept)	-6.640053	0.837601	2.163e-02	2.147e-02
log(Girth)	1.983349	0.078237	2.020e-03	2.017e-03
log(Height)	1.118669	0.213692	5.518e-03	5.512e-03
sigma2	0.007139	0.002037	5.259e-05	6.265e-05

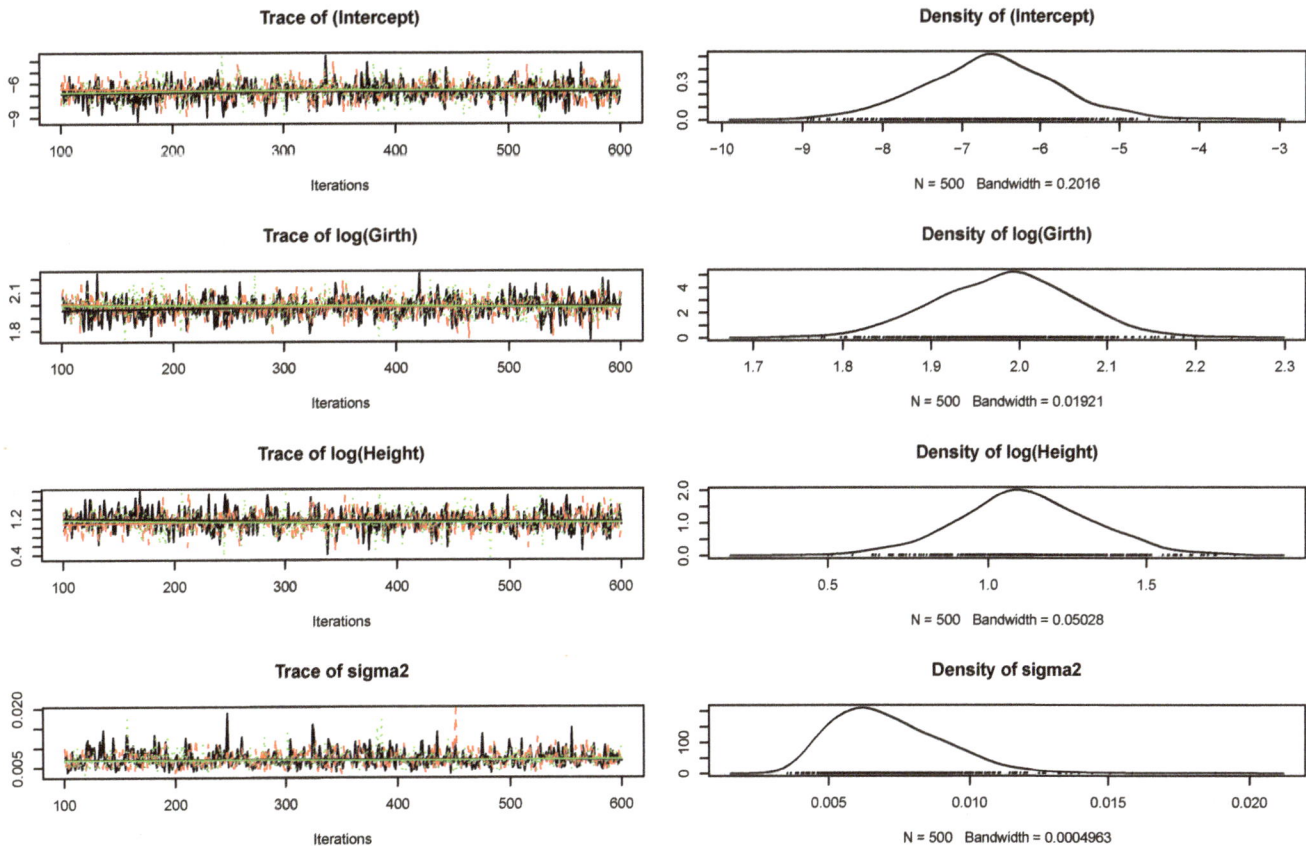

Fig. 5. MCMC trace plots with three chains for each parameter in the estimated model.

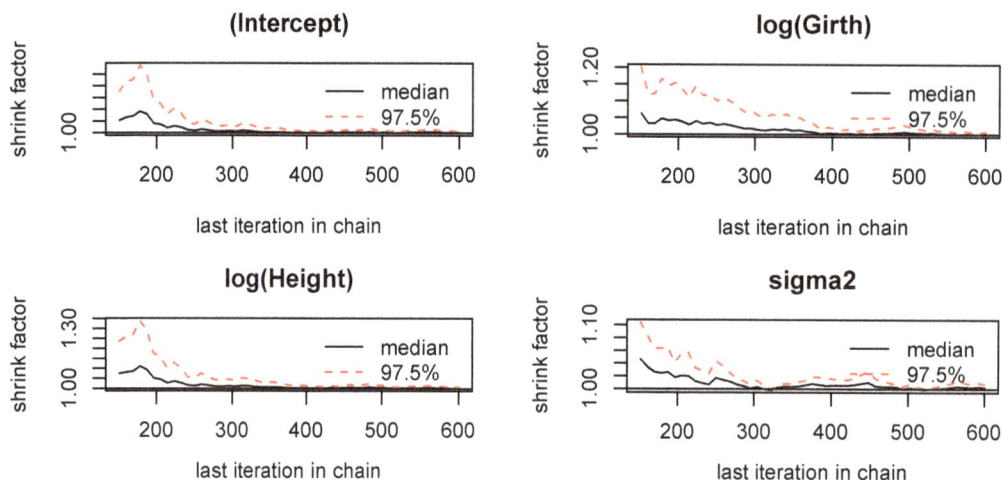

Fig. 6. Gelman–Rubin diagnostics for each model parameter, using the results from three chains.

2. Quantiles for each variable:

```
               2.5%       25%       50%       75%      97.5%
(Intercept) -8.307100 -7.185067 -6.643978 -6.084797 -4.96591
log(Girth)   1.832276  1.929704  1.986649  2.036207  2.13400
log(Height)  0.681964  0.981868  1.116321  1.256287  1.53511
sigma2       0.004133  0.005643  0.006824  0.008352  0.01161
```

Further, the trace plots for the each parameter are displayed in Fig. 5. From the plots, it can be observed that the chains are very mixed which gives an indication of convergence of MCMC.

Because we used three chains, we can use the Gelman–Rubin convergence diagnostic method and check whether the shrinkage factor is close to 1 or not, which indicates the convergence of three chains to the same equilibrium distribution. The results are shown in Fig. 6. From the plots, we see that for all the parameters, the shrink factor and its 97.5% value are very close to 1, which confirms that the three chains converged to the same equilibrium distribution.

7. Resampling Methods

Resampling methods are statistical procedures that involve repeated sampling of the data. They replace theoretical derivations required for applying traditional methods in statistical analysis by repeatedly resampling the original data and making inference from the resamples. Due to the advances in computing power these methods have become prominent and particularly well appreciated by applied statisticians. The jacknife and bootstrap are the most popular data-resampling methods used in statistical analysis. For a comprehensive treatment of these methods, see Refs. 14 and 61. In the following, we describe the Jackknife and bootstrap methods.

7.1. *The jackknife*

Quenouille[54] introduced a method, later named the jackknife, to estimate the bias of an estimator by deleting one data point each time from the original dataset and recalculating the estimator based on the rest of the data. Let $T_n = T_n(X_1, \ldots, X_n)$ be an estimator of an unknown parameter θ. The bias of T_n is defined as

$$\text{bias}(T_n) = E(T_n) - \theta.$$

Let $T_{n-1,i} = T_{n-1}(X_1, \ldots, X_{i-1}, X_{i+1}, \ldots, X_n)$ be the given statistic but based on $n - 1$ observations $X_1, \ldots, X_{i-1},$ $X_{i+1}, \ldots, X_n, i = 1, \ldots, n$. Quenouille's jackknife bias estimator is

$$b_{\text{JACK}} = (n - 1)(\tilde{T}_n - T_n), \tag{23}$$

where $\tilde{T}_n = n^{-1} \sum_{i=1}^n T_{n-1,i}$. This leads to a bias reduced jackknife estimator of θ,

$$T_{\text{JACK}} = T_n - b_{\text{JACK}} = nT_n - (n - 1)\tilde{T}_n. \tag{24}$$

The jackknife estimators b_{JACK} and T_{JACK} can be heuristically justified as follows. Suppose that

$$\text{bias}(T_n) = \frac{a}{n} + \frac{b}{n^2} + O\left(\frac{1}{n^3}\right), \tag{25}$$

where a and b are unknown but do not depend on n. Since $T_{n-1,i}, i = 1, \ldots, n$, are identically distributed,

$$\text{bias}(T_{n-1,i}) = \frac{a}{n - 1} + \frac{b}{(n - 1)^2} + O\left(\frac{1}{(n - 1)^3}\right), \tag{26}$$

and bias$(\tilde{T}_n)$ has the same expression. Therefore,

$$E(b_{\text{JACK}}) = (n-1)[\text{bias}(\tilde{T}_n) - \text{bias}(T_n)]$$

$$= (n-1)\left[\left(\frac{1}{n-1} - \frac{1}{n}\right)a\right.$$

$$\left. + \left(\frac{1}{(n-1)^2} - \frac{1}{n^2}\right)b + O\left(\frac{1}{n^3}\right)\right]$$

$$= \frac{a}{n} + \frac{(2n-1)b}{n^2(n-1)} + O\left(\frac{1}{n^2}\right),$$

which means that as an estimator of the bias of T_n, b_{JACK} is correct up to the order of n^{-2}. It follows that

$$\text{bias}(T_{\text{JACK}}) = \text{bias}(T_n) - E(b_{\text{JACK}})$$

$$= -\frac{b}{n(n-1)} + O\left(\frac{1}{n^2}\right),$$

that is, the bias of T_{JACK} is of order n^{-2}. The jackknife produces a bias reduced estimator by removing the first-order term in bias(T_n).

The jackknife has become a more valuable tool since Ref. 75 found that the jackknife can also be used to construct variance estimators. It is less dependent on model assumptions and does not need any theoretical formula as required by the traditional approach. Although it was prohibitive in the old days due to its computational costs, today it is certainly a popular tool in data analysis.

7.2. The bootstrap

The bootstrap[13] is conceptually the simplest of all resampling methods. Let $X_1, \ldots, X_n$ denote the dataset of n independent and identically distributed (iid) observations from an unknown distribution F which is estimated by $\hat{F}$, and let $T_n = T_n(X_1, \ldots, X_n)$ be a given statistic. Then, the variance of T_n is

$$\text{var}(T_n) = \int \left[T_n(x) - \int T_n(y)d\Pi_{i=1}^n F(y_i)\right]^2 d\Pi_{i=1}^n F(x_i),$$

$$(27)$$

where $x = (x_1, \ldots, x_n)$ and $y = (y_1, \ldots, y_n)$. Substituting $\hat{F}$ for F, we obtain the bootstrap variance estimator

$$\nu_{\text{BOOT}} = \int \left[T_n(x) - \int T_n(y)d\Pi_{i=1}^n \hat{F}(y_i)\right]^2 d\Pi_{i=1}^n \hat{F}(x_i)$$

$$= \text{var}_*[T_n(X_1^*, \ldots, X_n^*)|X_1, \ldots, X_n],$$

where $\{X_1^*, \ldots, X_n^*\}$ is an iid sample from $\hat{F}$ and is called a bootstrap sample. var$_*[X_1, \ldots, X_n]$ denotes the conditional variance for the given $X_1, \ldots, X_n$. The variance cannot be used directly for practical applications when ν_{BOOT} is not an explicit function of $X_1, \ldots, X_n$. Monte Carlo methods can be used to evaluate this expression when F is known. That is, we repeatedly draw new datasets from F and then use the sample variance of the values T_n computed from new datasets as a

numeric approximation to var(T_n). Since $\hat{F}$ is a known distribution, this idea can be further extended. That is, we can draw $\{X_{1b}^*, \ldots, X_{nb}^*\}, b = 1\ldots, B$, independently from $\hat{F}$, conditioned on $X_1, \ldots, X_n$. Let $T_{n,b}^* = T_n(X_{1b}*, \ldots, X_{nb}*)$ then we approximate ν_{BOOT} using the following approximation:

$$\nu_{\text{BOOT}}^{(B)} = \frac{1}{B}\sum_{b=1}^B \left(T_{n,b}^* - \frac{1}{B}\sum_{l=1}^B T_{n,l}^*\right)^2. \quad (28)$$

From the law of large numbers, $\nu_{\text{BOOT}} = \lim_{B\to\infty} \nu_{\text{BOOT}}^{(B)}$ almost surely. Both ν_{BOOT} and its Monte Carlo approximations $\nu_{\text{BOOT}}^{(B)}$ are called bootstrap estimators. While $\nu_{\text{BOOT}}^{(B)}$ is more useful for practical applications, ν_{BOOT} is convenient for theoretical derivations. The distribution $\hat{F}$ used to generate the bootstrap datasets can be any estimator (parametric or nonparametric) of F based on $X_1, \ldots, X_n$. A simple nonparametric estimator of F is the empirical distribution. While we have considered the bootstrap variance estimator here, the bootstrap method can be used for more general problems such as inference for regression parameters, hypothesis testing etc. For further discussion of the bootstrap, see Ref. 16.

Next, we consider the bias and variance of the bootstrap estimator. Efron[13] applied the delta method to approximate the bootstrap bias and variance. Let $\{X_1^*, \ldots, X_n^*\}$ be a bootstrap sample from the empirical distribution F_n. Define

$$P_i^* = (\text{the number of } X_j^* = X_i, j = 1, \ldots, n)/n$$

and

$$P^* = (P_1^*, \ldots, P_n^*)'.$$

Given $X_1, \ldots, X_n$, the variable nP^* is distributed as a multinomial variable with parameters n and $P_0 = (1, \ldots, 1)'/n$. Then

$$E_*P^* = P^0 \quad \text{and} \quad \text{var}_*(P^*) = n^{-2}\left(I - \frac{1}{n}11'\right)$$

where I is the identity matrix, 1 is a column vector of 1's, and E_* and var$_*$ are the bootstrap expectation and variance, respectively.

Now, define a bootstrap estimator of the moment of a random variable $R_n(X_1, \ldots, X_n, F)$. The properties of bootstrap estimators enable us to substitute the population quantities with the empirical quantities $R_n(X_1^*, \ldots, X_n^*, F_n) = R_n(P^*)$. If we expand this around P^0 using a multivariate Taylor expansion, we get the desired approximations for the bootstrap bias and variance:

$$b_{\text{BOOT}} = E_*R_n(P^*) \approx R_n(P^0) + \frac{1}{2n^2}tr(V),$$

$$\nu_{\text{BOOT}} = \text{var}_*R_n(P^*) \approx \frac{1}{n^2}U'U,$$

where $U = \Delta R_n(P^0)$ and $V = \Delta^2 R_n(P^0)$.

7.3. *Comparing the jackknife and the bootstrap*

In general, the jackknife will be easier to compute if n is less than, say, the 100 or 200 replicates used by the bootstrap for standard error estimation. However, by looking only at the n jackknife samples, the jackknife uses only limited information about the statistic, which means it might be less efficient than the bootstrap. In fact, it turns out that the jackknife can be viewed as a linear approximation to the bootstrap.[14] Hence, if the statistics, are linear then both estimators agree. However, for nonlinear statistics, there is a loss of information. Practically speaking, the accuracy of the jackknife estimate of standard error depends on how close the estimate is to linearity. Also, while it is not obvious how to estimate the entire sampling distribution of T_n by jackknifing, the bootstrap can be readily used to obtain a distribution estimator for T_n.

In considering the merits or demerits of the bootstrap, it is to be noted that the general formulas for estimating standard errors that involve the observed Fisher information matrix are essentially bootstrap estimates carried out in a parametric framework. While the use of the Fisher information matrix involves parametric assumptions, the bootstrap is free of those. The data analyst is free to obtain standard errors for enormously complicated estimators subject only to the constraints of computer time. In addition, if needed, one could obtain more smoothed bootstrap estimates by convoluting the nonparametric bootstrap with the parametric bootstrap, a parametric bootstrap involves generating samples based on the estimated parameters while nonparametric bootstrap involves generating samples based on available data alone.

To provide a simple illustration, we again consider the trees data and fit an ordinary regression model with the formula mentioned in Sec. 4. To conduct a bootstrap analysis on the regression parameters, we resampled the data with replacement 100 times (bootstrap replications) and fit the same model to each sample. We calculated the mean and standard deviation for each regression coefficient, which are analogous to the OLS coefficient and standard error. We performed the same for the jackknife estimators. The results are produced in Table 6.3. From the results, it can be seen that the jackknife is

off due to the small sample size. However, the bootstrap results are much closer to the values from OLS.

8. Conclusion

The area and methods of computational statistics have been evolving rapidly. Existing statistical software such as R already have efficient routines to implement and evaluate these methods. In addition, there exists literature on parallelizing these methods to make them even more efficient, for details, please see Ref. 83.

While some of the existing methods are still prohibitive even with moderately large data — such as the local linear estimator — implementations using more resourceful environments such as servers or clouds make such methods feasible even with big data. For an example, see Ref. 84 where they used a server (32GB RAM) to estimate their proposed model on the real data which did not take more than 34 s. Otherwise, it would have taken more time. This illustrates the helpfulness of the computing power while estimating these computationally intensive methods.

To the best of our knowledge, there exist multiple algorithms or R-packages to implement all the methods discussed here. However, it should be noted that not every method is computationally efficient. For example, Ref. 12 reported that within R software there are 20 packages that implement density estimation. Further, they found that two packages (*KernSmooth, ASH*) are very fast, accurate and also well-maintained. Hence, the user should be wise enough to choose efficient implementations when dealing with larger datasets.

Lastly, as we mentioned before, we are able to cover only a few of the modern statistical computing methods. For an expanded exposition of computational methods especially for inference, see Ref. 15.

Acknowledgment

The first and third authors were supported in part by grant 105-2410-H-007-034-MY3 from the Ministry of Science and Technology in Taiwan.

Table 3. Comparison of the bootstrap, jackknife, and parametric method (OLS) in a regression setting.

	OLS	Bootstrap	Jackknife
(Intercept)	−6.63	−6.65	−6.63
	(0.80)	(0.73)	(0.15)
log(Height)	1.12	1.12	1.11
	(0.20)	(0.19)	(0.04)
log(Girth)	1.98	1.99	1.98
	(0.08)	(0.07)	(0.01)
Observations	31		
Samples		100	31

References

[1] D. M. Allen, The relationship between variable selection and data agumentation and a method for prediction, *Technometrics* **16**(1), 125 (1974).

[2] A. C. Atkinson, *Plots, Transformations, and Regression: An Introduction to Graphical Methods of Diagnostic Regression Analysis* (Clarendon Press, 1985).

[3] A. W. Bowman, An alternative method of cross-validation for the smoothing of density estimates, *Biometrika* **71**(2), 353 (1984).

[4] A. W. Bowman, P. Hall and D. M. Titterington, Cross-validation in nonparametric estimation of probabilities and probability densities, *Biometrika* **71**(2), 341 (1984).

[5]A. Buja, T. Hastie and R. Tibshirani, Linear smoothers and additive models, *Ann. Stat.* 453 (1989).

[6]G. Casella and E. I. George, Explaining the gibbs sampler, *Am. Stat.* **46**(3), 167 (1992).

[7]S. Chib and E. Greenberg, Understanding the metropolis-hastings algorithm, *Am. Stat.* **49**(4), 327 (1995).

[8]C.-K. Chu and J. S. Marron, Choosing a kernel regression estimator, *Stat. Sci.* 404 (1991).

[9]W. S. Cleveland, Robust locally weighted regression and smoothing scatterplots, *J. Am. Stat. Assoc.* **74**(368), 829 (1979).

[10]M. K. Cowles and B. P. Carlin, Markov chain monte carlo convergence diagnostics: A comparative review, *J. Am. Stat. Assoc.* **91**(434), 883 (1996).

[11]P. Craven and G. Wahba, Smoothing noisy data with spline functions, *Num. Math.* **31**(4), 377 (1978).

[12]H. Deng and H. Wickham, Density estimation in r, (2011).

[13]B. Efron, *Bootstrap Methods: Another Look at the Jackknife*, Breakthroughs in Statistics, (Springer, 1992), pp. 569–593.

[14]B. Efron and B. Efron, *The Jackknife, the Bootstrap and Other Resampling Plans*, Vol. 38, SIAM (1982).

[15]B. Efron and T. Hastie, *Computer Age Statistical Inference*, Vol. 5 (Cambridge University Press, 2016).

[16]B. Efron and R. J. Tibshirani, *An Introduction to The Bootstrap* (CRC press, 1994).

[17]V. A. Epanechnikov, Nonparametric estimation of a multidimensional probability density, *Teor. Veroyatn. Primen.* **14**(1), 156 (1969).

[18]R. L. Eubank, Spline smoothing and nonparametric regression. no. 04; QA278. 2, E8. (1988).

[19]J. Fan, Design-adaptive nonparametric regression, *J. Am. Stat. Assoc.* **87**(420), 998 (1992).

[20]J. Fan, Local linear regression smoothers and their minimax efficiencies, *Ann. Stat.* 196 (1993).

[21]J. Fan and I. Gijbels, *Local Polynomial Modelling and its Applications: Monographs on Statistics and Applied Probability 66*, Vol. 66 (CRC Press, 1996).

[22]J. Fan and J. S. Marron, Fast implementations of nonparametric curve estimators, *J. Comput. Graph. Stat.* **3**(1), 35 (1994).

[23]J. H. Friedman, Data mining and statistics: What's the connection? *Comput. Sci. Stat.* **29**(1), 3 (1998).

[24]T. Gasser and H.-G. Müller, Kernel estimation of regression functions, *Smoothing Techniques for Curve Estimation* (Springer, 1979), pp. 23–68.

[25]A. Gelman, Iterative and non-iterative simulation algorithms, *Comput. Sci. Stat.* **433** (1993).

[26]A. Gelman and D. B. Rubin, Inference from iterative simulation using multiple sequences, *Stat. Sci.* 457 (1992).

[27]S. Geman and D. Geman, Stochastic relaxation, gibbs distributions, and the bayesian restoration of images, *IEEE Trans. Pattern Anal. Mach. Intell.* (6), 721 (1984).

[28]C. Geyer, Introduction to markov chain monte carlo, *Handbook of Markov Chain Monte Carlo* (2011), pp. 3–48.

[29]W. R. Gilks, *Markov Chain Monte Carlo* (Wiley Online Library).

[30]P. J. Green and B. W. Silverman, *Nonparametric Regression and Generalized Linear Models*, Vol. 58, Monographs on Statistics and Applied Probability (1994).

[31]C. Gu, Cross-validating non-gaussian data, *J. Comput. Graph. Stat.* **1**(2), 169 (1992).

[32]P. Hall, Large sample optimality of least squares cross-validation in density estimation, *Ann. Stat.* 1156 (1983).

[33]W. Hardle, *Applied Nonparametric Regression* (Cambridge, UK, 1990).

[34]W. Härdle, *Smoothing Techniques: With Implementation in s* (Springer Science & Business Media, 2012).

[35]T. Hastie, Gam: generalized additive models. r package version 1.06. 2 (2011).

[36]T. Hastie and C. Loader, Local regression: Automatic kernel carpentry, *Stat. Sci.* **120** (1993).

[37]T. J. Hastie and R. J. Tibshirani, *Generalized Additive Models*, Vol. 43 (CRC Press, 1990).

[38]J. L. Hodges Jr and E. L. Lehmann, The efficiency of some nonparametric competitors of the t-test, *Ann. Math. Stat.* 324 (1956).

[39]M. C. Jones, J. S. Marron and S. J. Sheather, A brief survey of bandwidth selection for density estimation, *J. Am. Stat. Assoc.* **91**(433), 401 (1996).

[40]V. Ya Katkovnik, Linear and nonlinear methods of nonparametric regression analysis, *Sov. Autom. Control* **5**, 25 (1979).

[41]C. Kooperberg and C. J. Stone, A study of logspline density estimation, *Comput. Stat. Data Anal.* **12**(3), 327 (1991).

[42]C. Kooperberg, C. J. Stone and Y. K. Truong, Hazard regression, *J. Am. Stat. Assoc.* **90**(429), 78 (1995).

[43]C. Loader, *Local Regression and Likelihood* (Springer Science & Business Media, 2006).

[44]Y. P. Mack and H.-G. Müller, Derivative estimation in nonparametric regression with random predictor variable, *Sankhyā: Indian J. Stat. A* 59 (1989).

[45]E. Mammen, O. Linton, J. Nielsen *et al.*, The existence and asymptotic properties of a backfitting projection algorithm under weak conditions, *Ann. Stat.* **27**(5), 1443 (1999).

[46]A. D. Martin, K. M. Quinn, J. H. Park *et al.*, Mcmcpack: Markov chain monte carlo in r, *J. Stat. Softw.* **42**(9), 1 (2011).

[47]N. Metropolis, A. W. Rosenbluth, M. N. Rosenbluth, A. H. Teller and E. Teller, Equation of state calculations by fast computing machines, *J. Chem. Phys.* **21**(6), 1087 (1953).

[48]S. P. Meyn and R. L. Tweedie, Stability of markovian processes ii: Continuous-time processes and sampled chains, *Adv. Appl. Probab.* 487 (1993).

[49]P. Mykland, L. Tierney and B. Yu, Regeneration in markov chain samplers, *J. Am. Stat. Assoc.* **90**(429), 233 (1995).

[50]E. A. Nadaraya, On estimating regression, *Theory Probab. Appl.* **9**(1), 141 (1964).

[51]D. Nychka, Splines as local smoothers, *Ann. Stat.* 1175 (1995).

[52]J. D. Opsomer, Asymptotic properties of backfitting estimators, *J. Multivariate Anal.* **73**(2), 166 (2000).

[53]E. Purzen, On estimation of a probability density and mode, *Ann. Math. Stat.* **39**, 1065 (1962).

[54]M. H. Quenouille, Approximate tests of correlation in time-series 3, *Math. Proc. Cambr. Philos. Soc.* **45**, 483 (1949).

[55]A. E. Raftery, S. Lewis *et al.*, How many iterations in the gibbs sampler, *Bayesian Stat.* **4**(2), 763 (1992).

[56]G. O. Roberts, Markov chain concepts related to sampling algorithms, *Markov Chain Monte Carlo in Practice*, Vol. **57** (1996).

[57]M. Rosenblatt *et al.*, Remarks on some nonparametric estimates of a density function, *Ann. Math. Stat.* **27**(3), 832 (1956).

[58]M. Rudemo, Empirical choice of histograms and kernel density estimators, *Scand. J. Stat.* 65 (1982).

[59]D. Ruppert and M. P. Wand, Multivariate locally weighted least squares regression, *Ann. Stat.* 1346 (1994).

[60]T. A. T. A. Ryan, B. L. Joiner and B. F. Ryan, *Minitab Student Handbook* (1976).

[61] J. Shao and D. Tu, *The Jackknife and Bootstrap* (Springer Science & Business Media, 2012).

[62] B. W. Silverman, Spline smoothing: the equivalent variable kernel method, *Ann. Stat.* 898 (1984).

[63] B. W. Silverman, *Density Estimation for Statistics and Data Analysis*, Vol. 26 (CRC press, 1986).

[64] B. W. Silverman, Some aspects of the spline smoothing approach to non-parametric regression curve fitting, *J. R. Stat. Soc. B (Methodol.)* 1 (1985).

[65] J. S. Simonoff, *Smoothing Methods in Statistics* (Springer Science & Business Media, 2012).

[66] A. F. M. Smith and G. O. Roberts, Bayesian computation via the gibbs sampler and related markov chain monte carlo methods, *J. R. Stat. Soc. B (Methodol.)* 3 (1993).

[67] C. J. Stone, Consistent nonparametric regression, *Ann. Stat.* 595 (1977).

[68] C. J. Stone, Optimal rates of convergence for nonparametric estimators, *Ann. Stat.* 1348 (1980).

[69] C. J. Stone, An asymptotically optimal window selection rule for kernel density estimates, *Ann. Stat.* 1285 (1984).

[70] C. J. Stone, Additive regression and other nonparametric models, *Ann. Stat.* 689 (1985).

[71] M. Stone, Cross-validatory choice and assessment of statistical predictions, *J. R. Stat. Soc. B (Methodol.)* 111 (1974).

[72] A. Stuart, M. G. Kendall *et al.*, *The Advanced Theory of Statistics*, Vol. 2 (Charles Griffin, 1973).

[73] R. C. Team *et al.*, R: A language and environment for statistical computing (2013).

[74] L. Tierney, Markov chains for exploring posterior distributions, *Ann. Stat.* 1701 (1994).

[75] J. W. Tukey, Bias and confidence in not-quite large samples, *Ann. Math. Stat.*, Vol. 29, Inst Mathematical Statistics IMS Business OFFICE-SUITE 7, 3401 INVESTMENT BLVD, Hayward, CA 94545 (1958), pp. 614–614.

[76] J. W. Tukey, The future of data analysis, *Ann. Math. Stat.* **33**(1), 1 (1962).

[77] G. Wahba, Practical approximate solutions to linear operator equations when the data are noisy, *SIAM J. Numer. Anal.* **14**(4), 651 (1977).

[78] G. Wahba and Y. Wang, When is the optimal regularization parameter insensitive to the choice of the loss function? *Commun. Stat.-Theory Methods* **19**(5), 1685 (1990).

[79] M. P. Wand and B. D. Ripley, Kernsmooth: Functions for kernel smoothing for wand and jones (1995). r package version 2.23-15 (2015).

[80] G. S. Watson, Smooth regression analysis, *Sankhyā: The Indian J. Stat. A* **359** (1964).

[81] S. Wood, *Generalized Additive Models: An Introduction with r* (CRC press, 2006).

[82] S. N. Wood, *mgcv: Gams and Generalized Ridge Regression for r*, R news **1**(2), 20 (2001).

[83] S. N. Wood, Y. Goude and S. Shaw, Generalized additive models for large data sets, *J. R. Stat. Soc. C (Appl. Stat.)* **64**(1), 139 (2015).

[84] X. Zhang, B. U. Park and J.-L. Wang, Time-varying additive models for longitudinal data, *J. Am. Stat. Assoc.* **108**(503), 983 (2013).

Bayesian networks: Theory, applications and sensitivity issues

Ron S. Kenett

KPA Ltd., Raanana, Israel

University of Turin, Turin, Italy

ron@kpa-group.com

This chapter is about an important tool in the data science workbench, Bayesian networks (BNs). Data science is about generating information from a given data set using applications of statistical methods. The quality of the information derived from data analysis is dependent on various dimensions, including the communication of results, the ability to translate results into actionable tasks and the capability to integrate various data sources [R. S. Kenett and G. Shmueli, On information quality, *J. R. Stat. Soc. A* **177**(1), 3 (2014).] This paper demonstrates, with three examples, how the application of BNs provides a high level of information quality. It expands the treatment of BNs as a statistical tool and provides a wider scope of statistical analysis that matches current trends in data science. For more examples on deriving high information quality with BNs see [R. S. Kenett and G. Shmueli, *Information Quality: The Potential of Data and Analytics to Generate Knowledge* (John Wiley and Sons, 2016), www.wiley.com/go/information_quality.] The three examples used in the chapter are complementary in scope. The first example is based on expert opinion assessments of risks in the operation of health care monitoring systems in a hospital environment. The second example is from the monitoring of an open source community and is a data rich application that combines expert opinion, social network analysis and continuous operational variables. The third example is totally data driven and is based on an extensive customer satisfaction survey of airline customers. The first section is an introduction to BNs, Sec. 2 provides a theoretical background on BN. Examples are provided in Sec. 3. Section 4 discusses sensitivity analysis of BNs, Sec. 5 lists a range of software applications implementing BNs. Section 6 concludes the chapter.

Keywords: Graphical models; Bayesian networks; expert opinion; big data; causality models.

1. Bayesian Networks Overview

Bayesian networks (BNs) implement a graphical model structure known as a directed acyclic graph (DAG) that is popular in statistics, machine learning and artificial intelligence. BN enable an effective representation and computation of the joint probability distribution (JPD) over a set of random variables.[40] The structure of a DAG is defined by two sets: the set of nodes and the set of directed arcs. The nodes represent random variables and are drawn as circles labeled by the variables names. The arcs represent links among the variables and are represented by arrows between nodes. In particular, an arc from node X_i to node X_j represents a relation between the corresponding variables. Thus, an arrow indicates that a value taken by variable X_j depends on the value taken by variable X_i. This property is used to reduce the number of parameters that are required to characterize the JPD of the variables. This reduction provides an efficient way to compute the posterior probabilities given the evidence present in the data.[4,22,32,41,44] In addition to the DAG structure, which is often considered as the "qualitative" part of the model, a BN includes "quantitative" parameters. These parameters are described by applying the Markov property, where the conditional probability distribution (CPD) at each node depends only on its parents. For discrete random variables, this conditional probability is represented by a table, listing the local probability that a child node takes on each of the feasible values — for each combination of values of its parents. The joint distribution of a collection of variables is determined uniquely by these local conditional probability tables (CPT). In learning the network structure, one can include *white lists* of forced causality links imposed by expert opinion and *black lists* of links that are not to be included in the network. For examples of BN application to study management efficiency, web site usability, operational risks, biotechnology, customer satisfaction surveys, healthcare systems and testing of web services see, respectively.[2,24–27,31,42] For examples of applications of BN to education, banking, forensic and official statistics see Refs. 10 and 34, 43, 46, 47. The next section provides theoretical details on how BNs are learned and what are their properties.

2. Theoretical Aspects of Bayesian Networks

2.1. *Parameter learning*

To fully specify a BN, and thus represent the JPDs, it is necessary to specify for each node X the probability distribution for X conditional upon X's parents. The distribution of X, conditional upon its parents, may have any form with or without constraints.

These conditional distributions include parameters which are often unknown and must be estimated from data, for example using maximum likelihood. Direct maximization of the likelihood (or of the posterior probability) is usually based on the expectation–maximization (EM) algorithm which alternates computing expected values of the unobserved variables conditional on observed data, with maximizing the complete likelihood assuming that previously computed expected values are correct. Under mild regularity conditions, this process converges to maximum likelihood (or maximum posterior) values of parameters.[19]

A Bayesian approach treats parameters as additional unobserved variables and computes a full posterior distribution over all nodes conditional upon observed data, and then integrates out the parameters. This, however, can be expensive and leads to large dimension models, and in practice classical parameter-setting approaches are more common.[37]

2.2. Structure learning

BNs can be specified by expert knowledge (using white lists and black lists) or learned from data, or in combinations of both. The parameters of the local distributions are learned from data, priors elicited from experts, or both. Learning the graph structure of a BN requires a scoring function and a search strategy. Common scoring functions include the posterior probability of the structure given the training data, the Bayesian information criteria (BIC) or Akaike information criteria (AIC). When fitting models, adding parameters increases the likelihood, which may result in over-fitting. Both BIC and AIC resolve this problem by introducing a penalty term for the number of parameters in the model with the penalty term being larger in BIC than in AIC. The time requirement of an exhaustive search, returning back a structure that maximizes the score, is super-exponential in the number of variables. A local search strategy makes incremental changes aimed at improving the score of the structure. A global search algorithm like Markov Chain Monte Carlo (MCMC) can avoid getting trapped in local minima. A partial list of structure learning algorithms includes Hill-Climbing with score functions BIC and AIC Grow-Shrink, Incremental Association, Fast Incremental Association, Interleaved Incremental association, hybrid algorithms and Phase Restricted Maximization. For more on BN structure learning, see Ref. 36.

2.3. Causality and Bayesian networks

Causality analysis has been studied from two main different points of view, the "probabilistic" view and the "mechanistic" view. Under the probabilistic view, the causal effect of an intervention is judged by comparing the evolution of the system when the intervention is present and when it is not present. The mechanistic point of view focuses on understanding the mechanisms determining how specific effects come about. The interventionist and mechanistic viewpoints are not mutually exclusive. For examples, when studying biological systems, scientists carry out experiments where they intervene on the system by adding a substance or by knocking out genes. However, the effect of a drug product on the human body cannot be decided only in the laboratory. A mechanistic understanding based on pharmacometrics models is a preliminary condition for determining if a certain medicinal treatment should be studied in order to elucidate biological mechanisms used to intervene and either prevent or cure a disease. The concept of potential outcomes is present in the work of randomized experiments by Fisher and Neyman in the 1920s and was extended by Rubin in the 1970s to non-randomized studies and different modes of inference.[35] In their work, causal effects are viewed as comparisons of potential outcomes, each corresponding to a level of the treatment and each observable, had the treatment taken on the corresponding level with at most one outcome actually observed, the one corresponding to the treatment level realized. In addition, the assignment mechanism needs to be explicitly defined as a probability model for how units receive the different treatment levels. With this perspective, a causal inference problem is viewed as a problem of missing data, where the assignment mechanism is explicitly modeled as a process for revealing the observed data. The assumptions on the assignment mechanism are crucial for identifying and deriving methods to estimate causal effects.[16]

Imai *et al.*[21] studied how to design randomized experiments to identify causal mechanisms. They study designs that are useful in situations where researchers can directly manipulate the intermediate variable that lies on the causal path from the treatment to the outcome. Such a variable is often referred to as a 'mediator'. Under the parallel design, each subject is randomly assigned to one of the two experiments. In one experiment, only the treatment variable is randomized whereas in the other, both the treatment and the mediator are randomized. Under the crossover design, each experimental unit is sequentially assigned to two experiments where the first assignment is conducted randomly and the subsequent assignment is determined without randomization on the basis of the treatment and mediator values in the previous experiment. They propose designs that permit the use of indirect and subtle manipulation. Under the parallel encouragement design, experimental subjects who are assigned to the second experiment are randomly encouraged to take (rather than assigned to) certain values of the mediator after the treatment has been randomized. Similarly, the crossover encouragement design employs randomized encouragement rather than direct manipulation in the second experiment. These two designs generalize the classical parallel and crossover designs in clinical trials, allowing for imperfect manipulation, thus providing informative inferences about causal mechanisms by focusing on a subset of the population.

Causal Bayesian networks are BNs where the effect of any intervention can be defined by a 'do' operator that separates intervention from conditioning. The basic idea is that intervention breaks the influence of a confounder so that one can make a true causal assessment. The established counterfactual definitions of direct and indirect effects depend on an ability to manipulate mediators. A BN graphical representations, based on local independence graphs and dynamic path analysis, can be used to provide an overview of dynamic relations.[1] As an alternative approach, the econometric approach develops explicit models of outcomes, where the causes of effects are investigated and the mechanisms governing the choice of treatment are analyzed. In such investigations, counterfactuals are studied (Counterfactuals are possible outcomes in different hypothetical states of the world). The study of causality in studies of economic policies involves: (a) defining counterfactuals, (b) identifying causal models from idealized data of population distributions and (c) identifying causal models from actual data, where sampling variability is an issue.[20] Pearl developed BNs as the method of choice for reasoning in artificial intelligence and expert systems, replacing earlier *ad hoc* rule-based systems. His extensive work covers topics such as: causal calculus, counterfactuals, Do calculus, transportability, missingness graphs, causal mediation, graph mutilation and external validity.[38] In a heated head to head debate between probabilistic and mechanistic view, Pearl has taken strong standings against the probabilistic view, see for example the paper by Baker[3] and discussion by Pearl.[39] The work of Aalen *et al.*[1] and Imai *et al.*[21] show how these approaches can be used in complementary ways. For more examples of BN applications, see Fenton and Neil.[12–14] The next section provides three BN application examples.

3. Bayesian Network Case Studies

This section presents the applications of BNs to three diverse case studies. The first case study is based on an expert assessment of risks in monitoring of patients in a hospital, the second example is based on an analysis of an open source community and involves social network analysis (SNA) and data related to the development of software code. The third used case is derived from a large survey of customers of an airline company.

3.1. *Patient monitoring in a hospital*

Modern medical devices incorporate alarms that trigger visual and audio alerts. Alarm-related adverse incidents can lead to patient harm and represent a key patient safety issue. Clinical alarms handling procedures in the monitoring of hospitalized patients is a complex and critical task. This involves both addressing the response to alarms and the proper setting of control limits. Critical alarm hazards include (1) Failure of staff to be informed of a valid alarm on time and take appropriate action and (2) Alarm Fatigue, when staff is overwhelmed, distracted and desensitized. Prevention to avoid harm to patients requires scrutinizing how alarms are initiated, communicated and responded to.

To assess the conditions of alarm monitoring in a specific hospital, once can conduct a mapping of current alarms and their impact on patient safety using a methodology developed by ECRI.[11] This is performed using a spreadsheet documenting any or all alarm signals that a team identifies as potentially important (e.g., high priority) for management. Figure 1 is an example of such a worksheet. It is designed to assess the decision processes related to alarms by comparing potentially important signals in such a way that the most important become more obvious.

Care area	Alarm load	Obstacles to effective alarm communication or response	Alarm signal	Device/system	Medical opinion of alarm importance	Risk to patient from alarm malfunction or delayed caregiver response	Contribution to alarm load/fatigue
ICU	moderate	low	low alarm volume	physiologic monitor	high	high	low
ICU	moderate	low	bradycardia	physiologic monitor	high	high	low
ICU	moderate	low	tachicardia	physiologic monitor	moderate	moderate	moderate
ICU	high	low	leads off	physiologic monitor	high	moderate	moderate
ICU	moderate	low	low oxygen saturation	physiologic monitor	high	high	moderate
ICU	moderate	low	low BP	physiologic monitor	high	high	moderate
ICU	moderate	low	high BP	physiologic monitor	moderate	moderate	moderate
RECOVERY	high	low	low alarm volume	physiologic monitor	high	high	low
RECOVERY	high	low	bradycardia	physiologic monitor	high	moderate	high
RECOVERY	high	low	tachicardia	physiologic monitor	moderate	moderate	high
RECOVERY	high	low	leads off	physiologic monitor	high	moderate	high
RECOVERY	moderate	low	low oxygen saturation	physiologic monitor	high	high	moderate
RECOVERY	moderate	low	low BP	physiologic monitor	high	high	moderate
RECOVERY	moderate	low	high BP	physiologic monitor	moderate	moderate	moderate
Med-surg dep	high	high	low alarm volume	physiologic monitor	high	high	low
Med-surg dep	high	high	bradycardia	physiologic monitor	high	moderate	high
Med-surg dep	high	high	tachicardia	physiologic monitor	moderate	moderate	high
Med-surg dep	high	high	leads off	physiologic monitor	high	moderate	high
Med-surg dep	moderate	high	low oxygen saturation	physiologic monitor	high	high	high
Med-surg dep	moderate	high	low BP	physiologic monitor	high	high	high
Med-surg dep	moderate	high	high BP	physiologic monitor	moderate	moderate	high

Fig. 1. Spreadsheet for alarm monitoring risks.

Filling in the spreadsheet requires entering ratings derived from experts, other tools (e.g., Nursing Staff Survey) as well as from other sources (e.g., input from medical staff). The first column in Fig. 1, specifies the care area. In the figure, one can see information related to the intensive care unit (ICU), the recovery room and the surgery department. The second column reflects the alarm lad intensity. The third column shows us an assessment of obstacles to effective alarm communication or response. The next column lists the different types of alarm signals from a specific device. In Fig. 1, we see only the part related to a physiology monitor. The last three columns correspond to a medical opinion of alarm importance, the risk to patient from an alarm malfunction or delay, and the contribution of the alarm to load and fatigue of the medical staff.

We show next how data from such a clinical alarm hazard spreadsheet can be analyzed with a BN that links care area, device, alarm signal, risks to patients and load on staff.

The software we will use in the analysis is GeNie version 2.0 from the university of Pittsburgh (http://genie.sis.pitt.edu). Figure 2 shows the GeNie data entry screen corresponding to the data shown in Fig. 1. The low, medium and high levels in Fig. 1 are represented here as s1, s2 and s3. Figure 3 shows the BNs derived from the data in Fig. 2.

Figure 4 shows a diagnostic analysis where we condition the BN on high level of fatigue. We can now see what conditions are the main contributor to this hazardous condition. Specifically, one can see that the percentage of surgery department increased from 33% to 42% and high load from 36% to 43%.

Figure 5 is an example of predictive analysis where the BN is conditioned on ICU and bradycardia. We see that the contribution of an alarm indicates a slower than normal heart rate (bradycardia) in ICU, if not treated properly, increases the potential high level harm to patients from 39% to 52%, a very dramatic increase. In parallel, we see that the impact of this condition on light load to staff increased from 30% to 49% and the option of low level of obstacles to communicate the alarm increased from 55% to 78%.

In other words, the bradycardia alarm in ICU does not increase fatigue, is very effectively communicated with a low level of obstruction and is considered higher than average alarm in terms if impact on patient safety. This analysis relies on expert opinion assessments and does not consider unobservable latent variables.

In this case study, the data was derived from expert opinion assessment of seven types of alarms from a patient monitoring device placed in three care delivery areas. The alarms are evaluated on various criteria such as contribution to staff fatigue, risk to patient from malfunction, obstacles to communicate alarms etc. This assessment is feeding a spreadsheet which is then analyzed using a BN. The analysis provides both diagnostic and predictive capabilities that supports various improvement initiatives aimed at improving monitoring effectiveness.

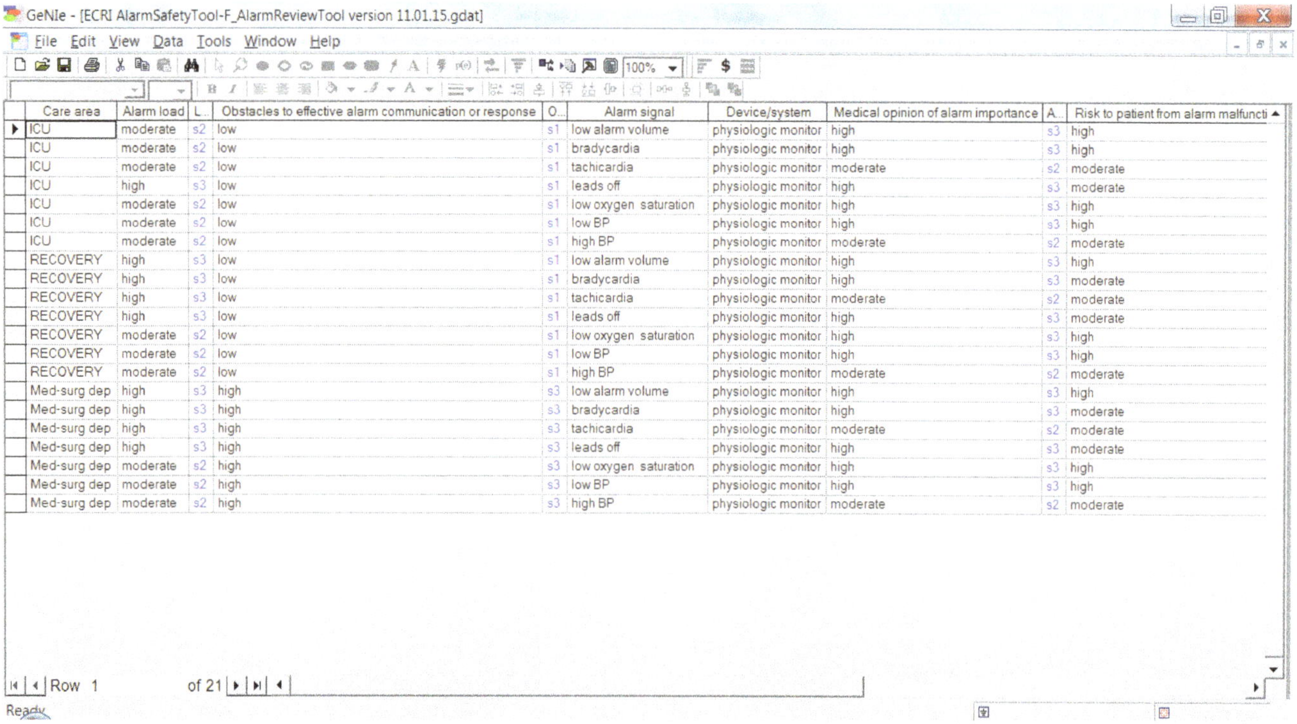

Fig. 2. Data entry of GeNie software Version 2.0.

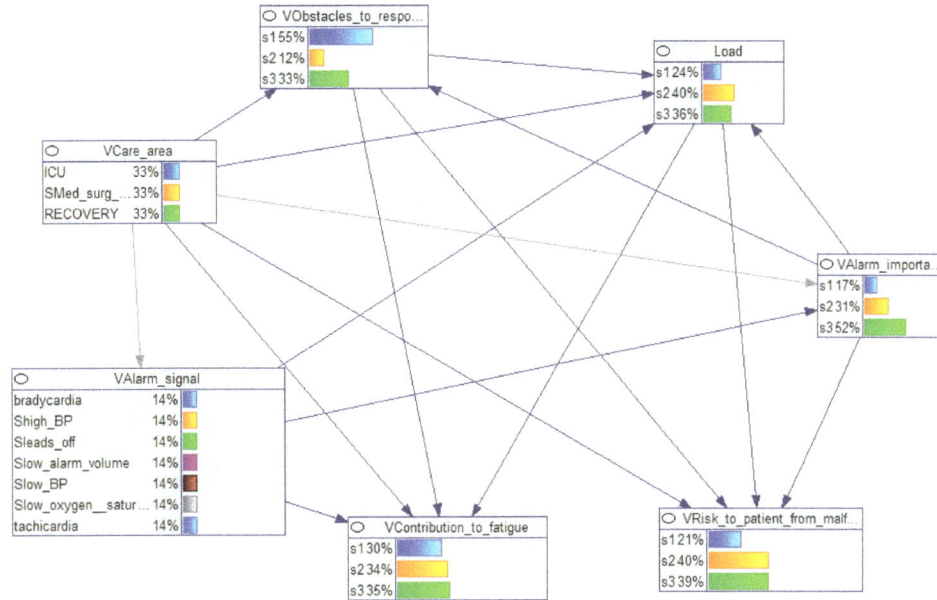

Fig. 3. BN of data collected in spreadsheet presented in Fig. 1.

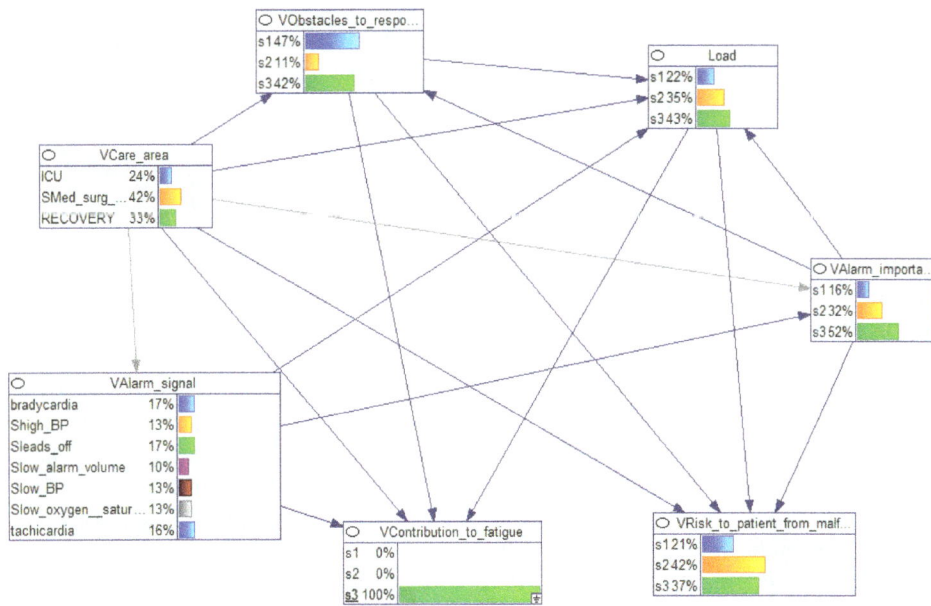

Fig. 4. BN conditioned on high contributors to fatigue (diagnostic analysis).

3.2. *Risk management of open source software*

The second example is based on data collected from a community developing open source software (OSS). Risk management is a necessary and challenging task for organizations that adopt OSS in their products and in their software development process.[33] Risk management in OSS adoption can benefit from data that is available publicly about the adopted OSS components, as well as data that describes the behavior of OSS communities. This use case is derived from the RISCOSS project (www.riscoss.eu), a platform and related assessment methodology for managing risks in OSS adoption.[15]

As a specific example, we aim at understanding the roles of various members in the OSS community and the relationships between them by the analysis of the mailing lists or forums of the community. The analysis should provide us

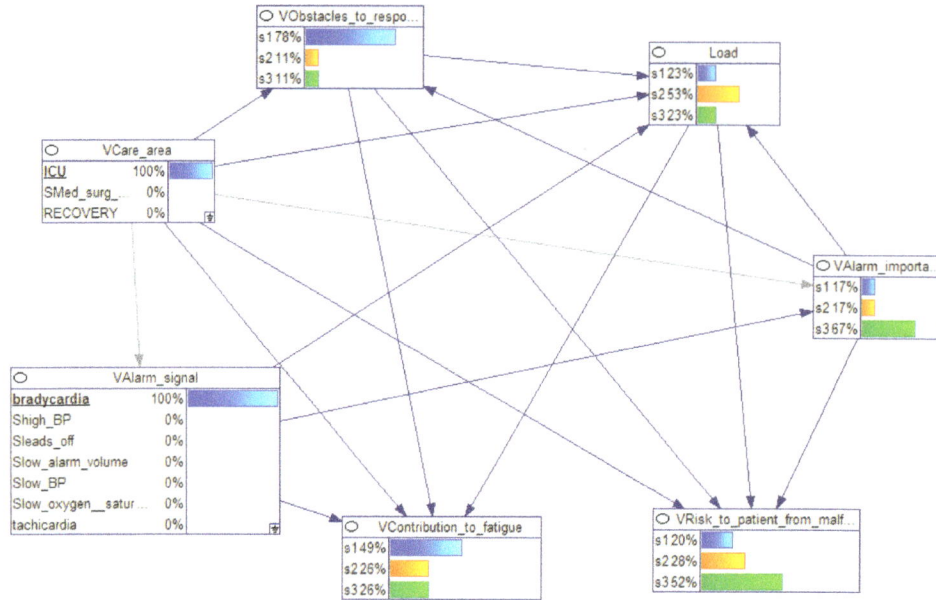

Fig. 5. BN conditioned on ICU and bradycardia (predictive analysis).

information on dimensions such as timeliness of an OSS community that can be measured by its capacity of following a roadmap or to release fixes and evolutions of the software in time. The methods illustrated here are based on data coming from the XWiki OSS community (http://www.xwiki.org), an Open Source platform for developing collaborative applications and managing knowledge using the wiki metaphor. XWiki was originally written in 2003 and released at the beginning of 2004; since then, a growing community of users and contributors started to gather around it. The data consists of: user and developer mailing lists archives, IRC chat archives, code commits and code review comments, and information about bugs and releases. The community is around 650,000 lines of code, around 95 contributors responsible for around 29,000 commits and with more than 200.000 messages, and 10.000 issues reported since 2004.

Specifically, we apply a SNA of the interactions between members of the OSS community. Highlighting actors of importance to the network is a common task of SNA. Centrality measures are ways of representing this importance in a quantifiable way. A node (or actor)'s importance is considered to be the extent of the involvement in a network, and this can be measured in several ways. Centrality measures are usually applied to undirected networks, with indices for directed graphs termed prestige measures. The degree centrality is the simplest way to quantify a node's importance which is used to consider the number of nodes it is connected to, with high numbers interpreted to be of higher importance. Therefore, the degree of a node provides local information of its importance. For a review of SNA see Ref. 45.

As an example of an SNA, we analyze the data from XWiki community over five years using data preprocessing

of the IRC chat archives so extracting the dynamics of the XWiki community over time. Some of the challenges included a chat format change towards the end of 2010 and ambiguous names of a unique user (e.g., Vincent, VincentM, Vinny, Vinz). Eventually names were fixed manually. Figure 6 represents the visual rendering of the dynamics, over time, of the community in terms of intensity and kind of relationships between the different groups of actors (mainly contributors and manager of the community), that can be captured by community metrics such as degree of centrality. The analysis has been performed using NodeXL (http://nodexl.codeplex.com) a tool and a set of operations for SNA. The NodeXL-Network Overview, Discovery and Exploration add-in for Excel adds network analysis and visualization features to the spreadsheet. The core of NodeXL is a special Excel workbook template that structures data for network analysis and visualization. Six main worksheets currently form the template. There are worksheets for "Edges", "Vertices", and "Images" in addition to worksheets for "Clusters," mappings of nodes to clusters ("Cluster Vertices"), and a global overview of the network's metrics. NodeXL workflow typically moves from data import through steps such as import data, clean the data, calculate graph metrics, create clusters, create sub-graph images, prepare edge lists, expand worksheet with graphing attributes, and show graph such as the graphs in Fig. 6.

Each of the social networks presented in Fig. 6 is characterized by a range of measures such as the degree of centrality of the various community groups. The dynamics of a social network is reflected by a changing value of such measures, over time. We call these, and other measures derived from the OSS community, risk drivers. These risk

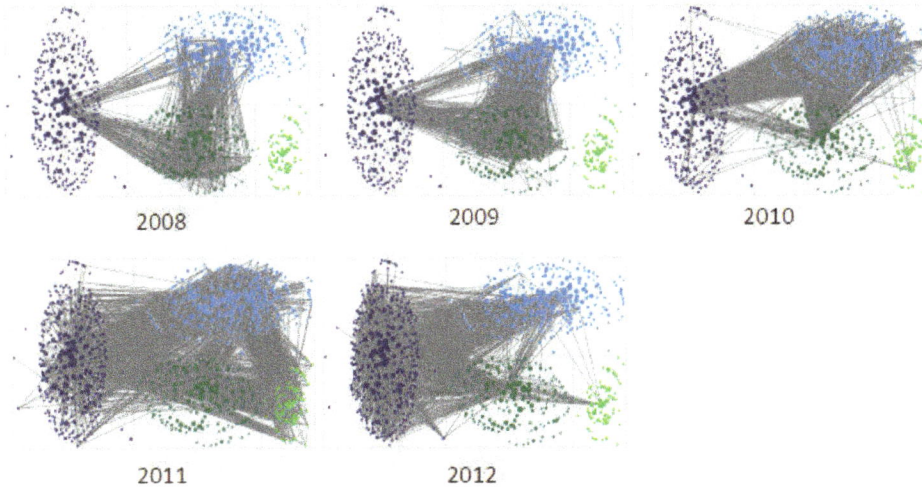

Fig. 6. SNA of the XWiki OSS community chats.

drivers form the raw data used in the risk assessment, in this case of adopting the XWiki OSS. This data can be aggregated continuously using specialized data collectors.

The data sources used in this analysis consisted of:

(1) Mailing lists archives:
- XWiki users mailing list: http://lists.xwiki.org/piper-mail/users
- XWiki devs mailing list: http://lists.xwiki.org/piper-mail/devs

(2) IRC chat archives: http://dev.xwiki.org/xwiki/bin/view/IRC/WebHome

(3) Commits (via git): https://github.com/xwiki

(4) Code review comments available on GitHub

(5) Everything about bugs and releases: http://jira.xwiki.org

From this data and SNA measures, one derives risk drivers that are determining risk indicators. Examples of risk indicators include Timeliness (is the community responsive to open issues), Activeness (what is the profile and number of active members) and Forking (is the community likely to split). These risk indicators are representing an interpretation of risk drivers values by OSS experts. To link risk drivers to risk indicators, the RISCOSS project developed a methodology based on workshops where experts are asked to rate alternative scenarios. An example of such scenarios is presented in Fig. 7.

The risk drivers are set at various levels and the expert is asked to evaluate the scenario in terms of the risk indicator. As an example, in scenario 30 of Fig. 7, the scenario consists of two forums posts per day, 11 messages per thread, a low amount of daily mails and a small community with a high proportion of developers, a med size number of testers and companies using the OSS. These conditions were determined as signifying low Activeness by the expert who did the rating. After running about 50 such scenarios, one obtains data that can be analyzed with BN, like in the alarm monitoring use case. Such an analysis is shown in Fig. 8.

The BN linking of risk drivers to risk indicators is providing a framework for ongoing risk management of the OSS community. It provides a tool for exploring the impact of specific behavior of the OSS community and evaluate risk mitigation strategies. For more on such models, see Ref. 15.

A	B	C	D	E	F	AI	AJ	AK	AL	AM	AN
Risk Driver	State 1	State 2	State 3	State 4	State 5	29	30	31	32	33	34
Forum posts per day	0	1	4	9	12	10	2	6	6	7	11
Forum messages per thread	0	1	4	9	19	14	11	9	19	16	4
Mail per day	low	medium	high			medium	low	low	high	medium	high
Overall community size	small	medium	high			low	low	low	medium	medium	medium
Number of developers involved	small	medium	high			high	high	high	high	high	medium
Number of testers (individuals providing feedback)	small	medium	high			high	medium	high	high	low	medium
Number of companies using the software	small	medium	high			low	medium	medium	medium	medium	low
Companies supporting the project (adding to code)	small	medium	high			high	high	low	high	low	medium
Activeness	1	2	3	4	5	4	1	3	4	4	5

Fig. 7. Alternative scenarios for linking risk drivers to the Activeness risk indicator.

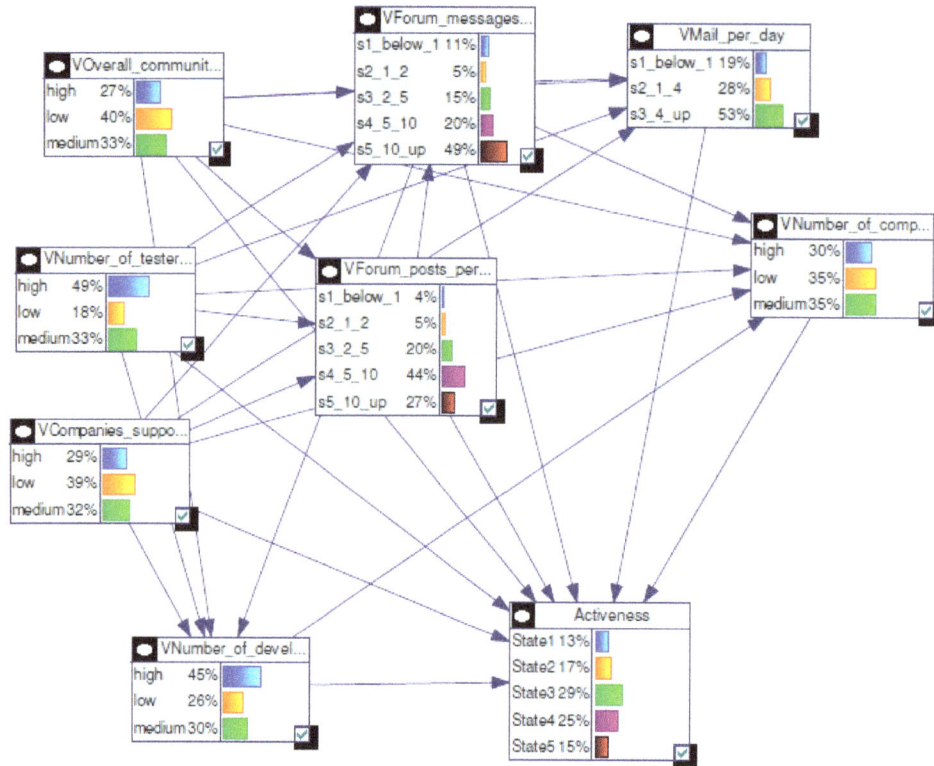

Fig. 8. BN linking risk drivers to risk indicators.

3.3. *Satisfaction survey from an airline company*

The third case study is about a customer satisfaction survey presented in Ref. 8. The example consists of a typical customer satisfaction questionnaire directed at passengers of an airline company to evaluate their experience. The questionnaire contains questions (items) on passengers' satisfaction from their overall experience and from six service elements (departure, booking, check-in, cabin environment, cabin crew, meal). The evaluation of each item is based on a four-point scale (from 1= extremely dissatisfied to 4 = extremely satisfied). Additional information on passengers was also collected such as gender, age, nationality and the purpose of the trip. The data consists of responses in $n = 9720$ valid questionnaires. The goal of the analysis is to evaluate these six dimensions and the level of satisfaction from the overall experience, taking into account the interdependencies between the degree of satisfaction from different aspects of the service. Clearly, these cannot be assumed to be independent of each other, and therefore a BN analysis presents a particularly well-suited tool for this kind of analysis. For more examples of BN applications to customer survey analysis see Refs. 5 and 27. Figure 9 is a BN of this data constructed using the Hill-Climbing algorithm with score functions AIC. The proportion of customers expressing very high overall satisfaction (a rating of "4") is 33%.

In Fig. 10, one sees the conditioning of the BN on extremely dissatisfied customer (left) and extremely satisfied customers (right).

The examples in Fig. 10 show how a BN provides an efficient profiling of very satisfied and very unsatisfied customers. This diagnostic information is a crucial input to initiatives aimed at improving customer satisfaction. Contrasting very satisfied with very unsatisfied customers is typically an effective way to generate insights for achieving this goal. Like in the previous two examples, the BN considered here is focused on observable data. This can be expanded by including modeling and latent variable effects. For an example of latent variables in the analysis of a customer satisfaction survey, see Ref. 17. For more considerations on how to determine causality, see Sec. 2.

4. Sensitivity Analysis of Bayesians Networks

The three examples presented above shop how a BN can be used as a decision support tool for determining which predictor variables are important on the basis of their effect on target variables. In such an analysis, choosing an adequate BN structure is a critical task. In practice, there are several algorithms available for determining the BN structure, each on with its specific characteristics. For example, the

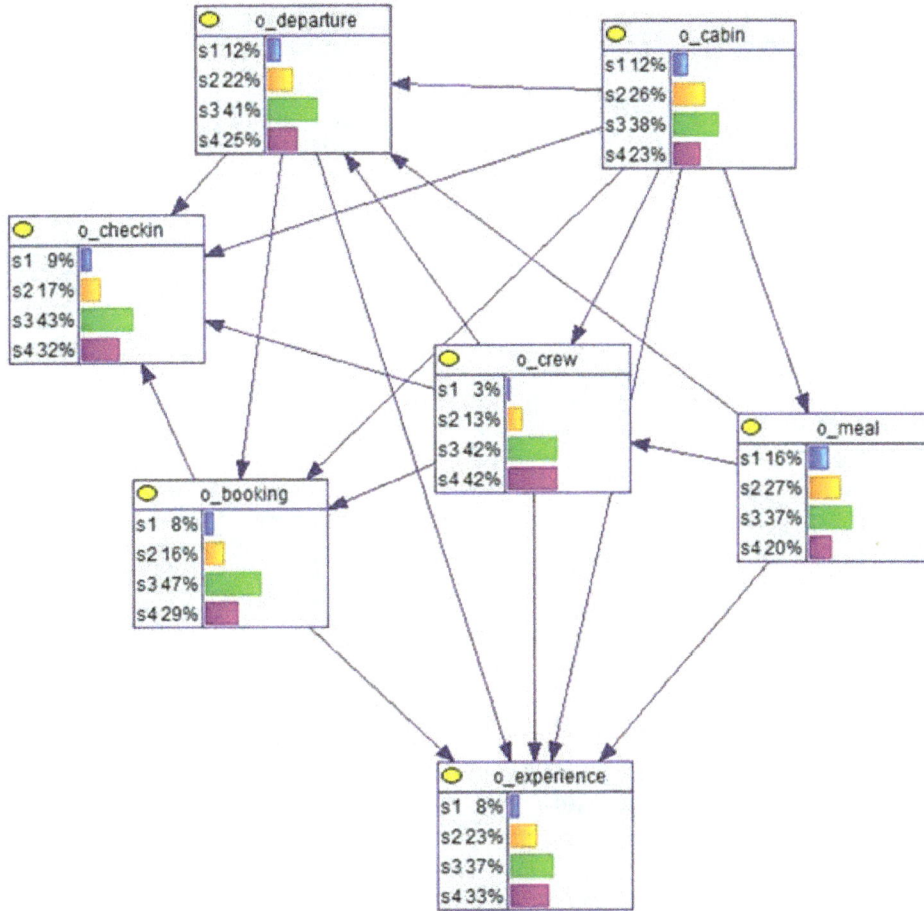

Fig. 9. BN of airline passenger customer satisfaction survey.

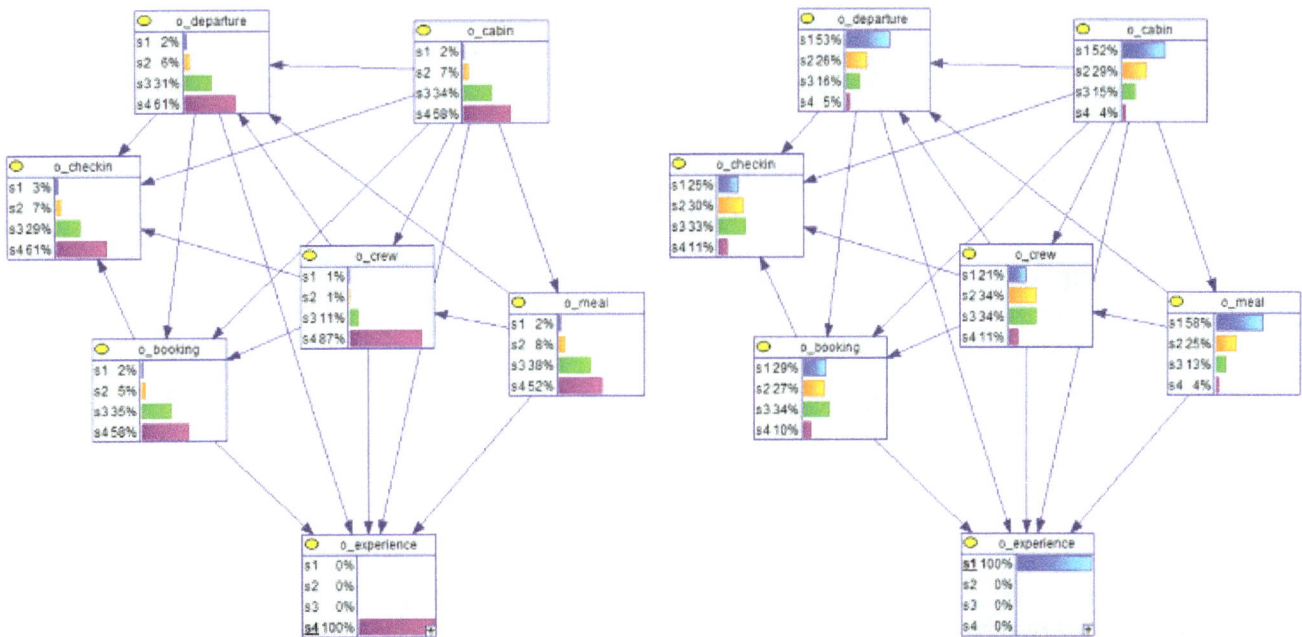

Fig. 10. BN conditioned on extremely dissatisfied customer (left) and extremely satisfied customers (right).

Table 1. BN with proportion of occurrence of each are in the bootstrap replicates.

	hc-bic	hc-aic	tabu-bic	tabu-aic	gs	iamb	fiamb	intamb	mmhc-bic	mmhc-aic	rsmax	tot
Booking Checkin	1.0	1.0	1.0	1.0	1.0	0.5	0.5	0.5	1.0	1.0	1.0	9.5
Cabin crew	1.0	1.0	1.0	1.0	0.0	0.0	0.0	0.0	1.0	1.0	0.0	6.0
Cabin departure	1.0	1.0	1.0	1.0	1.0	1.0	0.0	1.0	1.0	1.0	0.0	9.0
Cabin experience	1.0	1.0	1.0	1.0	0.0	1.0	1.0	1.0	1.0	1.0	0.0	9.0
Cabin meal	1.0	1.0	1.0	1.0	1.0	1.0	1.0	1.0	1.0	1.0	1.0	11.0
Crew booking	1.0	1.0	1.0	1.0	0.0	0.0	0.0	0.0	1.0	1.0	0.0	6.0
Crew departure	1.0	1.0	1.0	1.0	0.0	0.0	1.0	0.0	1.0	1.0	0.0	7.0
Crew experience	1.0	1.0	1.0	1.0	0.0	1.0	1.0	1.0	1.0	1.0	0.0	9.0
Departure booking	1.0	1.0	1.0	1.0	0.0	0.0	0.0	0.0	1.0	1.0	0.0	6.0
Departure checkin	1.0	1.0	1.0	1.0	1.0	0.0	0.0	0.0	1.0	1.0	0.0	7.0
Departure experience	1.0	1.0	1.0	1.0	0.0	1.0	1.0	1.0	1.0	1.0	0.0	9.0
Meal crew	1.0	1.0	1.0	1.0	0.0	0.0	0.0	0.0	1.0	1.0	1.0	7.0
Cabin booking	0.0	1.0	0.0	1.0	0.0	0.0	0.0	0.0	0.0	1.0	0.0	3.0
Crew checkin	0.0	1.0	0.0	1.0	1.0	0.0	0.0	0.0	0.0	1.0	0.0	4.0
Meal departure	0.0	1.0	0.0	1.0	0.0	0.0	0.0	0.0	0.0	1.0	0.0	3.0
Meal experience	0.0	1.0	0.0	1.0	0.0	1.0	1.0	1.0	0.0	1.0	0.0	6.0
Booking departure	0.0	0.0	0.0	0.0	1.0	1.0	1.0	1.0	0.0	0.0	1.0	5.0
Crew meal	0.0	0.0	0.0	0.0	1.0	1.0	1.0	1.0	0.0	0.0	0.0	4.0
Departure meal	0.0	0.0	0.0	0.0	1.0	0.0	0.0	0.0	0.0	0.0	1.0	2.0
Checkin booking	0.0	0.0	0.0	0.0	0.0	0.5	0.5	0.5	0.0	0.0	0.0	1.5
Checkin departure	0.0	0.0	0.0	0.0	0.0	1.0	1.0	1.0	0.0	0.0	1.0	4.0
Booking experience	0.0	0.0	0.0	0.0	0.0	0.0	1.0	1.0	0.0	0.0	0.0	2.0
Checkin experience	0.0	0.0	0.0	0.0	0.0	0.0	1.0	1.0	0.0	0.0	0.0	2.0
Checkin crew	0.0	0.0	0.0	0.0	0.0	0.0	0.0	0.0	0.0	0.0	1.0	1.0
Departure cabin	0.0	0.0	0.0	0.0	0.0	0.0	0.0	0.0	0.0	0.0	1.0	1.0

R package *bnlearn* includes eleven algorithms: two-scored based learning algorithms (Hill-Climbing with score functions BIC and AIC and TABU with score functions BIC and AIC), five constraint-based learning algorithms (Grow-Shrink, Incremental Association, Fast Incremental Association, Interleaved Incremental association, Max-min Parents and Children), and two hybrid algorithms (MMHC with score functions BIC and AIC, Phase Restricted Maximization). In this section, we present an approach for performing a sensitivity analysis of BN, across various structure learning algorithms, in order to assess the robustness of the specific BN, one plans to use. Following the application of different learning algorithms to set up a BN structure, some arcs in the network are recurrently present and some are not. As a basis for designing a robust BN, one can compute how often an arc is present, across various algorithms, with respect to the total number of networks examined.

Table 1 shows the impact of the 11 learning algorithms implemented in the *bnlearn* R application. The last column represents the total number of arcs across the 11 algorithms. The robust structure is defined by arcs that appear in a majority of learned networks. For these variables, the link connection does not depend on the learning algorithm and the derived prediction and is therefore considered robust. For more on this topic and related sensitivity analysis issues, see Ref. 8.

After selection of a robust network, one can perform what-if sensitivity scenario analysis. These scenarios are computer experiments on a BN performed by conditioning on specific variable combinations and predicting the target variables using empirically estimated network. We can then analyze the effect of variable combinations on target distributions using the type of conditioning demonstrated in Sec. 4. The next section provides an annotated listing of various software products implementing BNs.

5. Software for Bayesian Network Applications

(i) Graphical Network Interface (GeNIe) is the graphical interface to Structural Modeling, Inference, and Learning Engine (SMILE), a fully portable Bayesian inference engine developed by the Decision Systems Laboratory of the University of Pittsburgh and thoroughly field tested since 1998. Up to version 2.0 GeNIe could be freely downloaded from http://genie.sis.pitt.edu with no restrictions on applications or otherwise. Version 2.1 is now available from http://www.bayesfusion.com/ with commercial and academic versions, user guides and related documentation.

(ii) Hugin (http://www.hugin.com) is a commercial software which provides a variety of products for both research and nonacademic use. The HUGIN Decision Engine (HDE) implements state-of-the-art algorithms for BNs and influence diagrams such as object-oriented modeling, learning from data with both continuous and discrete variables, value of information analysis, sensitivity analysis and data conflict analysis.

(iii) IBM SPSS Modeller (http://www-01.ibm.com/software/analytics/spss) is a general application for analytics that has incorporated the Hugin tool for running BNs (http://www.ibm.com/developerworks/library/wa-bayes1). IBM SPSS is not free software.

(iv) The R bnlearn package is powerful and free. Compared with other available BN software programs, it is able to perform both constrained-based and score-based methods. It implements five constraint-based learning algorithms (Grow-Shrink, Incremental Association, Fast Incremental Association, Interleaved Incremental association, Max–min Parents and Children), two scored-based learning algorithms (Hill-Climbing, TABU) and two hybrid algorithms (MMHC, Phase Restricted Maximization).

(v) Bayesia (http://www.bayesia.com) developed proprietary technology for BN analysis. In collaboration with research labs and big research projects, the company develops innovative technology solutions. Its products include (1) BayesiaLab, a BN publishing and automatic learning program which represents expert knowledge and allows one to find it among a mass of data, (2) Bayesia Market Simulator, a market simulation software package which can be used to compare the influence of a set of competing offers in relation to a defined population, (3) Bayesia Engines, a library of software components through which can integrate modeling and the use of BNs and (4) Bayesia Graph Layout Engine, a library of software components used to integrate the automatic position of graphs in specific application.

(vi) Inatas (www.inatas.com) provides the Inatas System Modeller software package for both research and commercial use. The software permits the generation of networks from data and/or expert knowledge. It also permits the generation of ensemble models and the introduction of decision theoretic elements for decision support or, through the use of a real time data feed API, system automation. A cloud-based service with GUI is in development.

(vii) SamIam (http://reasoning.cs.ucla.edu/samiam) is a comprehensive tool for modeling and reasoning with BNs, developed in Java by the Automated Reasoning Group at UCLA. Samiam includes two main components: a graphical user interface and a reasoning engine. The graphical interface lets users develop BN models and save them in a variety of formats. The reasoning engine supports many tasks including: classical inference; parameter estimation; time-space tradeoffs; sensitivity analysis; and explanation-generation based on MAP and MPE.

(viii) BNT (https://code.google.com/p/bnt) supports many types of CPDs (nodes), decision and utility nodes, static and dynamic BNs and many different inference algorithms and methods for parameter learning. The source code is extensively documented, object-oriented, and free, making it an excellent tool for teaching, research and rapid prototyping.

(ix) Agenarisk (http://www.agenarisk.com/) is able to handle continuous nodes without the need for static discretization. It enables decision-makers to measure and compare different risks in a way that is repeatable and auditable and is ideal for risk scenario planning.

6. Discussion

This chapter presents several examples of BNs in order to illustrate their wide range of relevance, from expert opinion-based data to big data applications. In all these cases, BNs has helped enhance the quality of information derived from an analysis of the available data sets. In Secs. 1 and 2, we describe various technical aspects of BNs, including estimation of distributions and algorithms for learning the BN structure. In learning the network structure, one can include *white lists* of forced causality links imposed by expert opinion and *black lists* of links that are not to be included in the network, again using inputs from content experts. This essential feature permits an effective dialogue with content experts who can impact the model used for data analysis. We also briefly discuss statistical inference of causality links, a very active area of research. In general, BNs provide a very effective descriptive causality analysis, with a natural graphical display. A comprehensive approach to BNs, with application sports, medicine and risks is provided by the Bayes knowledge project (http://bayes-knowledge.com/). Additional example of applications of BNs in the context of the quality of the generated information are included in Refs. 23 and 29.

References

[1] O. Aalen, K. Røysland and JM. Gran, Causality, mediation and time: A dynamic viewpoint, *J. R. Stat. Soc. A*, **175**(4), 831 (2012).

[2] X. Bai, R. S. Kenett and W. Yu, Risk Assessment and adaptive group testing of semantic web services, *Int. J. Softw. Eng. Knowl. Eng.* **22**(5), 595 (2012).

[3] S. Baker, Causal inference, probability theory, and graphical insights, *Stat. Med.* **2**(25), 4319 (2013).

[4] I. Ben Gal, Bayesian networks, in *Encyclopedia of Statistics in Quality and Reliability*, eds. F. Ruggeri, R. S. Kenett and F. Faltin (Wiley, UK, 2007).

[5] A. C. Constantinou, N. Fenton, W. Marsh and L. Radlinski, From complex questionnaire and interviewing data to intelligent Bayesian network models for medical decision support, *Artif. Intell. Med.* **67**, 75 (2016).

[6] G. F. Cooper, The computational complexity of probabilistic inference using Bayesian belief networks, *Artif. Intell.* **42**, 393 (1990).

[7] C. Cornalba, R. S. Kenett and P. Giudici, Sensitivity Analysis of Bayesian Networks with Stochastic Emulators, *ENBIS-DEINDE Proc.* University of Torino, Torino, Italy (2007).

[8] F. Cugnata, R. S. Kenett and S. Salini, Bayesian networks in survey data: Robustness and sensitivity issues, *J. Qual. Technol.* **48**, 253 (2016).

[9] L. DallaValle, Official statistics data integration using vines and non parametric. Bayesian belief nets, *Qual. Technol. Quant. Manage.* **11**(1), 111 (2014).

[10] M. Di Zio, G. Sacco, M. Scanu and P. Vicard, Multivariate techniques for imputation based on Bayesian networks, *Neural Netw. World* **4**, 303 (2005).

[11] ECRI, *The Alarm Safety Handbook Strategies, Tools, and Guidance* (ECRI Institute, Plymouth Meeting, Pennsylvania, USA, 2014).

[12] N. E. Fenton and M. Neil, The use of Bayes and causal modelling in decision making, uncertainty and risk, *UPGRADE, Eur. J. Inf. Prof. CEPIS (Council of European Professional Informatics Societies)*, **12**(5), 10 (2011).

[13] N. E. Fenton and M. Neil, *Risk Assessment and Decision Analysis with Bayesian Networks* (CRC Press, 2012), http://www.bayesianrisk.com.

[14] N. E. Fenton and M. Neil, Decision support software for probabilistic risk assessment using Bayesian networks, *IEEE Softw.* **31**(2), 21 (2014).

[15] X. Franch, R. S. Kenett, A. Susi, N. Galanis, R. Glott and F. Mancinelli, Community data for OSS adoption risk management, in *The Art and Science of Analyzing Software Data*, eds. C. Bird, T. Menzies and T. Zimmermann (Morgan Kaufmann, 2016).

[16] B. Frosini, Causality and causal models: A conceptual perspective, *Int. Stat. Rev.* **74**, 305 (2006).

[17] M. Gasparini, F. Pellerey and M. Proietti, Bayesian hierarchical models to analyze customer satisfaction data for quality improvement: A case study, *Appl. Stoch. Model Bus. Ind.* **28**, 571 (2012).

[18] A. Harel, R. S. Kenett and F. Ruggeri, Modeling web usability diagnostics on the basis of usage statistics, in *Statistical Methods in eCommerce Research*, eds. W. Jank and G. Shmueli (John Wiley & Sons, New Jersey, USA, 2009).

[19] D. Heckerman, A tutorial on learning with Bayesian networks, Microsoft research technical report MSR-TR-95-06, Revised November 1996, from http://research.microsoft.com.

[20] J. Heckman, Econometric causality. *Int. Stat. Rev.* **76**, 1 (2008).

[21] K. Imai, D. Tingley and T. Yamamoto, Experimental designs for identifying causal mechanisms, *J. R. Stat. Soc. A* **176**(1), 5 (2013).

[22] F. V. Jensen, *Bayesian Networks and Decision Graphs* (Springer, 2001).

[23] R. S. Kenett, On generating high infoQ with Bayesian networks, *Qual. Technol. Quant. Manag.* **13**(3), (2016), http://dx.doi.org/10.1080/16843703.2016.11891.

[24] R. Kenett, A. De Frenne, X Tort-Martorell and C. McCollin, The statistical efficiency conjecture, in *Applying Statistical Methods in Business and Industry — The State of the Art*, eds. T. Greenfield, S. Coleman and R. Montgomery (John Wiley & Sons, Chichester, UK, 2008).

[25] R. S. Kenett, Risk analysis in drug Manufacturing and Healthcare, in *Statistical Methods in Healthcare*, eds. F. Faltin, R. S. Kenett and F. Ruggeri (John Wiley & Sons, 2012).

[26] R. S. Kenett and Y. Raanan, *Operational Risk Management: A Practical Approach to Intelligent Data Analysis* (John Wiley & Sons, Chichester, UK, 2010).

[27] R. S. Kenett and S. Salini, *Modern Analysis of Customer Satisfaction Surveys: With Applications Using R* (John Wiley & Sons, Chichester, UK, 2011).

[28] R. S. Kenett and G. Shmueli, On information quality, *J. R. Stat. Soc. A* **177**(1), 3 (2014).

[29] R. S. Kenett and G. Shmueli, *Information Quality: The Potential of Data and Analytics to Generate Knowledge* (John Wiley & Sons, 2016). www.wiley.com/go/information_quality.

[30] R. S. Kenett and S. Zacks, *Modern Industrial Statistics: With Applications Using R, MINITAB and JMP*, 2nd edn (John Wiley & Sons, Chichester, UK, 2014).

[31] R. S. Kenett, A. Harel and F. Ruggeri, Controlling the usability of web services, *Int. J. Softw. Eng. Knowl. Eng.* **19**(5), 627 (2009).

[32] T. Koski and J. Noble, *Bayesian Networks — An Introduction* (John Wiley & Sons, Chichester, UK, 2009).

[33] J. Li, R. Conradi, O. Slyngstad, M. Torchiano, M. Morisio and C. Bunse, A state-of-the-practice survey of risk management in development with off-the-shelf software components, *IEEE Trans. Softw. Eng.* **34**(2), 271 (2008).

[34] D. Marella and P. Vicard, Object-oriented Bayesian networks for modelling the respondent measurement error, *Commun. Stat. — Theory Methods* **42**(19), 3463 (2013).

[35] F. Mealli, B. Pacini and D. B. Rubin, Statistical inference for causal effects, in *Modern Analysis of Customer Satisfaction Surveys: with Applications using R*, eds. R. S. Kenett and S. Salini (John Wiley and Sons, Chichester, UK, 2012).

[36] F. Musella, A PC algorithm variation for ordinal variables, *Comput. Stat.* **28**(6), 2749 (2013).

[37] E. R. Neapolitan, *Learning Bayesian Networks* (Prentice Hall, 2003).

[38] J. Pearl, *Probabilistic Reasoning in Intelligent Systems: Networks of Plausible Inference* (Morgan Kaufmann, 1988).

[39] J. Pearl, Comment on causal inference, probability theory, and graphical insights (by Stuart G. Baker). UCLA Cognitive Systems Laboratory, *Stat. Med.* **32**(25), 4331 (2013).

[40] J. Pearl, Bayesian networks: A model of self-activated memory for evidential reasoning (UCLA Technical Report CSD-850017). *Proc. 7th Conf. Cognitive Science Society* (University of California, Irvine, CA), pp. 329–334.

[41] J. Pearl, *Causality: Models, Reasoning, and Inference*, 2nd edn. (Cambridge University Press, UK, 2009).

[42] J. Peterson and R. S. Kenett, Modelling opportunities for statisticians supporting quality by design efforts for pharmaceutical development and manufacturing, *Biopharmaceut. Rep.* **18**(2), 6 (2011).

[43] L. D. Pietro, R. G. Mugion, F. Musella, M. F. Renzi and P. Vicard, Reconciling internal and external performance in a holistic approach: A Bayesian network model in higher education, *Expert Syst. Appl.* **42**(5), 2691 (2015).

[44] O. Pourret, P. Naïm and B. Marcot, *Bayesian Networks: A Practical Guide to Applications* (John Wiley & Sons, Chichester, UK, 2008).

[45]M. Salter-Townshend, A. White, I. Gollini, T. B. Murphy, Review of statistical network analysis: Models, algorithms, and software, *Stat. Anal. Data Min.* **5**(4), 243 (2012).

[46]C. Tarantola, P. Vicard and I. Ntzoufras, Monitoring and improving Greek banking services Using Bayesian networks: An analysis of mystery shopping data, *Expert Syst. Appl.* **39**(11), 10103 (2012).

[47]P. Vicard, A. P. Dawid, J. Mortera and S. L. Lauritzen, Estimation of mutation rates from paternity casework, *Forensic Sci. Int. Genet.* **2**, 9 (2008).

motivated by the George Box maxim that all models are wrong but some are useful, and so the practitioner is guided by the data to help approximate the unknown (and unknowable) distribution as best as possible, based on the data and whatever assumptions made about the mechanism generating it.

2. Least-Squares Estimation

A generic *linear model* is one having the form

$$Y = X\beta + \epsilon, \tag{9}$$

where Y is N-dimensional column vector, X is a N-by-p rank-p matrix with $N > p$, β a p-dimensional column vector, and ϵ N-dimensional column vector. Furthermore, Y is an observable vector, the matrix X has known values, β is a vector of unknown and unobservable parameters, and ϵ is a vector of unobservable 'noise'. Further, the standard linear model assumes that $(\epsilon_1, \ldots, \epsilon_N)^{tr}$ has the N-dimensional normal distribution with mean 0 and variance matrix $\sigma^2 I_N$, where $\sigma^2 > 0$ and I_N is an N-by-N identity matrix. To relate the standard linear model with GLiM, we notice that because the mean of $\epsilon = 0$ $E(Y) = X\beta$ and so the model may be viewed as one relating the mean $E(Y)$ with the covariates via a linear combination of the parameters $E(Y) = X\beta$ with (presumably) the error vector ϵ being swept aside.

We give here a brief presentation of *least-squares estimation* (*LSE*) for linear models. For further reading see Ref. 2 or some of the other references listed below.

First, consider the simplest form of linear model, *simple linear regression*, $E\{Y\} = \beta_0 + \beta_1 x$, $-\infty < x < \infty$. Given a set of N linearly dependent observations $\{(x_i, Y_i), i = 1, 2, \ldots, n\}$, such that x_i, $i = 1, \ldots, n$, are fixed (not random) and $Y_i = \beta_0 + \beta_1 x_i + \epsilon_i, i = 1, \ldots, N$, where $\{\epsilon_i, i = 1, \ldots, N\}$ are random variables satisfying the conditions

(i) $E\{\epsilon_i\} = 0$, $i = 1, \ldots, n$, and
(ii) $\text{var}\{\epsilon_i\} = \sigma^2$, $i = 1, \ldots, n$,
(iii) $\text{cov}(\epsilon_i, \epsilon_j) = 0$, $1 \le i < j \le n$,

The estimators of (β_0, β_1) which minimize the sum of squares of deviations

$$Q = \sum_{i=1}^{n} (Y_i - \beta_0 - \beta_1 x_i)^2, \tag{10}$$

are called *least-squares estimators* (*LSE*). The minimum is calculated using standard calculus technique by solving $\nabla(Q(\beta_0, \beta_1) = 0$, where ∇ is the gradient of Q with respect to β_0 and β_1. The solutions $(\hat{\beta}_0, \hat{\beta}_1)$ are the least square estimators, given by

$$\hat{\beta}_0 = \frac{1}{n} \sum_{i=1}^{n} (Y_i - \hat{\beta}_1 x_i), \tag{11}$$

and

$$\hat{\beta}_1 = \frac{\sum_{i=1}^{n} Y_i(x_i - \bar{x})}{\sum_{i=1}^{n} (x_i - \bar{x})^2}, \tag{12}$$

and where $\bar{x} = \frac{1}{n} \sum_{i=1}^{n} x_i$ is the sample mean. These least-square estimators can be generalized to cases where $\{\epsilon_i, i = 1, \ldots, n\}$ are correlated and have different variances. This will be shown later.

The variance and covariance of the above LSE are

$$\text{var}\{\hat{\beta}_1\} = \sigma^2 \sum_{i=1}^{n} (x_i - \bar{x}^2)^{-1}, \tag{13}$$

$$\text{var}\{\hat{\beta}_0\} = \sigma^2 \left(\frac{1}{n} + \bar{x}^2 \left(\sum_{i=1}^{n} (x_i - \bar{x})^2 \right)^{-1} \right), \tag{14}$$

$$\text{cov}(\hat{\beta}_0, \hat{\beta}_1) = -\sigma^2 \bar{x} \left(\sum_{i=1}^{n} (x_i - \bar{x})^2 \right)^{-1}. \tag{15}$$

A linear regression on several variables, *multiple linear regression*, is a model

$$Y = \sum_{j=0}^{k} \beta_j x_j + \epsilon, \tag{16}$$

identical to (9). The data set comprises of $\{(Y_i, x_i^t), i = 1, \ldots, n\}$, where $\mathbf{x}_i^t = (x_{i0}, x_{i1}, \ldots, x_{ip})$. If the 'y-intercept' is different than 0, $x_{i0} = 1$, for all $i = 1, \ldots, n$.

It will not hurt repeating; the linear model can be written as

$$Y = X\beta + \epsilon, \tag{17}$$

where Y is an n-dimensional column vector, X is a full rank matrix of N rows and $p = k + 1$ columns, where $N > p$. $\boldsymbol{\beta}$ is a p-dimensional column vector, and ϵ is an N-dimensional column vector. As mentioned earlier assume that $E(\epsilon) = 0$, and $\text{var}(\epsilon) = \sigma^2 \mathbf{I}$, where $\mathbf{I}$ is an n by n identity matrix.

Let Ξ denote the p-dimensional subspace spanned by the column vectors of X. The reader can readily prove that the orthogonal projection of Y on Ξ is

$$X\hat{\boldsymbol{\beta}} = X(X'X)^{-1}X'Y. \tag{18}$$

$X'(= X^{tr})$ denotes the *transposed* matrix. $\hat{\boldsymbol{\beta}}$ is the least-squares estimate (LSE) of the vector of unknown parameters $\boldsymbol{\beta}$ and this vector is given by

$$\hat{\boldsymbol{\beta}} = (X'X)^{-1}X'Y. \tag{19}$$

LSE is an unbiased estimate since

$$\mathbf{E}\{\hat{\boldsymbol{\beta}}\} = \beta. \tag{20}$$

The *variance–covariance* of matrix of $\hat{\beta}$ is

$$\text{var}(\hat{\beta}) = \sigma^2 (X'X)^{-1}. \tag{21}$$

The results written above for simple linear regression are special cases of (14) and (15).

3. Maximum Likelihood Estimation

Applications of classical statistical theory posits that a parametric family of distributions $\mathcal{F}_\theta \theta \in \Theta \subset \mathbb{R}^p$, is assumed to represent a phenomenon, with the specific value of the parameter θ is otherwise unknown, in fact, not even directly observable. Variants of the *likelihood principle* occupy much of classical statistics with working assumption that all the information about the unknown parameter lies squarely within the likelihood function of a sample. We introduce and delineate some of those issues below.

Let $\{X_1, \ldots, X_n\}$ be i.i.d. random variables having a common pmf or p.d.f. $f(x; \theta)$. Suppose that the parameter θ belongs to a parametric-space Θ. The *likelihood function of* θ, where $\Theta \subset \mathbb{R}^p$, is defined as

$$L(\theta; X_1, \ldots, X_n) = \prod_{i=1}^{i=n} f(X_i; \theta), \theta \in \Theta. \quad (22)$$

An estimator of θ, $\widehat{\theta}(X_1, \ldots, X_n)$ is called *maximum likelihood estimator* (MLE), if

$$\widehat{\theta}(X_1, \ldots, X_n) = \arg\max_{\theta \in \Theta} L(\theta; X_1, \ldots, X_n). \quad (23)$$

Let ∇_θ denote a gradient vector. If the pmf or p.d.f. f is second-order continuously differentiable, then the MLE of θ can be determined by the root θ of the equation

$$\sum_{i=1}^{n} \nabla_\theta \log(f(X_i; \theta)) = \mathbf{0}. \quad (24)$$

The variance–covariance matrix of the gradient vector $\nabla_\theta \log(f(X_i; \theta))$, if exists, is called the *Fisher information matrix*, $I(\theta)$, with (i, j)-entry $E(\frac{\partial}{\partial \theta_i} \log f(X; \theta) \frac{\partial}{\partial \theta_j} \log f(X; \theta))$.

Under stringent regularity conditions, see Ref. 1, one can prove that the variance–covariance matrix of the MLE of θ is the inverse of $I(\theta)$.

4. About a Linear Model

Ever since Francis Galton's *REGRESSION TOWARDS MEDIOCRITY* (1886), regression, in all its variants has, and still is the most popular of all statistical methods. Although the generic OLS was described previously, a good model is hard to develop. A few issues with a linear model are

  (i) The data, especially the output, the 'Y' column, is discrete (not continuous).
 (ii) Too much noise or not enough information. Lack of meaningful correlation between inputs and outputs.
(iii) The complexity is too high ('too many variables').
 (iv) Columns are correlated, or nearly so.
  (v) Too many outliers skewing, or "leveraging" the model one way or another.
 (vi) Too many variables compared to the number of examples.

Various tools exist to address the items above. Items (i) and (ii) may rule out altogether the linear model approach. Items (iii) and (iv) are addressed by reducing feature space by heuristic means; a class of methods which includes the art of combining multiple variables/features into fewer ones, or the mathematically- defensible class of methods for variable selection, e.g., via try-and-true methods like the *F*-test, and threshold values for the AIC, VIF, etc.

A significant advantage of linear model is that it is interpretable. A model, especially a normalized model, i.e., one with column having zero mean and unit variance, is easy to interpret, and lends itself to sensitivity analysis.

A good linear model is one satisfying the general principle of *parsimony*, in that it is *lean* on variables and, more importantly, the model tests well against the *out-of-sample* data in the sense that the metrics, like *R-squared*, used to assess model goodness experience little degradation.

5. The Logit

A common 2-class classification paradigm is one where data consists of pairs (X, y) where X is a vector of features, $X = (x_1, \ldots, x_p)$ and y is a binary (0–1) response. Sifting through the literature one encounters several popular approaches to model this paradigm including *support-vector machines, decision trees, boosting* and *neural nets*. However, if the modeling choice emphasizes interpretability, the logistic regression (Logit) approach is a natural choice. The logistic regression is without a doubt the most popular of all the GLiM models and so we will devote considerable space to discuss various aspects of Logit.

5.1. *Logit: A special case*

We demonstrate the estimation approach with the binomial case that we discussed in the introduction. Consider an experiment in which we collected data at N different x values. For each value of x, we performed m Bernoulli trials. Consequently, the data consists of the set $D = \{(x_i, \widehat{p}_i), i = 1, \ldots, N\}$, where $\widehat{p}_i$ is the ratio of successes at level x_i.

The GLiM equation which in the binomial context is better known as Logit is

$$\log\left(\frac{\widehat{p}_i}{1 - \widehat{p}_i}\right) = \beta_0 + \beta_1 x_i, \quad (25)$$

where $0 < \widehat{p} < 1$, and $i = 1, \ldots, N$. The objective is to estimate the regression coefficients β_0, β_1, with which we can predict the probability of success $p(x)$ in future trials, at a new level x.

One approach to estimate the coefficients is the method of least-squares estimate. In this approach, we define $Y_i = \log(\frac{\widehat{p}_i}{1 - \widehat{p}_i})$, and compute $\widehat{\beta}_0$ and $\widehat{\beta}_1$ according to (18) and (19).

Another approach is to apply the maximum likelihood method, which in large samples yields more efficient estimators.

It is not difficult to show that solving (25) for $p(x_i)$, we get

$$p(x_i) = \frac{e^{\beta_0 + \beta_1 x_i}}{1 + e^{\beta_0 + \beta_1 x_i}}. \tag{26}$$

Accordingly, the likelihood function is

$$L(\beta_0, \beta_1; D)$$
$$= \prod_{i=1}^{i=n} \left(\frac{e^{\beta_0 + \beta_1 x_i}}{1 + e^{\beta_0 + \beta_1 x_i}} \right)^{S_i} \left(\frac{1 - e^{\beta_0 + \beta_1 x_i}}{(1 + e^{\beta_0 + \beta_1 x_i}}) \right)^{m - S_i} \tag{27}$$

where $S_i = m\widehat{p}_i$, $i = 1, \ldots, n.$, the number of 1s in the ith replication of the experiment (at level x_i), and often suppressing D.

Equivalently,

$$L(\beta_0, \beta_1) = \exp \left\{ \sum_{i=1}^n (\beta_0 + \beta_1 x_i) S_i \right\} \prod_{i=1}^n (1 + e^{\beta_0 + \beta_1 x_i})^{-m}. \tag{28}$$

The log-likelihood function is

$$\log L(\beta_0, \beta_1) = \sum_{i=1}^n (\beta_0 + \beta_1 x_i) S_i - m$$
$$\times \sum_{i=1}^n \log(1 + e^{\beta_0 + \beta_1 x_i}). \tag{29}$$

The partial derivatives of the log-likelihood are

$$\frac{\partial}{\partial \beta_0} \log L(\beta_0, \beta_1) = \sum_{i=1}^n S_i - m \sum_{i=1}^n \frac{e^{\beta_0 + \beta_1 x_i}}{1 + e^{\beta_0 + \beta_1 x_i}}$$
$$\frac{\partial}{\partial \beta_1} \log L(\beta_0, \beta_1) = \sum_{i=1}^n x_i S_i - m \sum_{i=1}^n x_i \frac{e^{\beta_0 + \beta_1 x_i}}{1 + e^{\beta_0 + \beta_1 x_i}}. \tag{30}$$

The MLE of β_0 and β_1 are the roots of the equations

$$\sum_{i=1}^n \frac{e^{\beta_0 + \beta_1 x_i}}{1 + e^{\beta_0 + \beta_1 x_i}} = \sum_{i=1}^n \widehat{p}_i$$
$$\sum_{i=1}^n x_i \frac{e^{\beta_0 + \beta_1 x_i}}{1 + e^{\beta_0 + \beta_1 x_i}} = \sum_{i=1}^n x_i \widehat{p}_i. \tag{31}$$

The solution of these nonlinear equations for the MLE, can be done numerically by, e.g., the *Newton–Raphson method*, using the LSE as initial values.

5.2. *The logit: Generics*

A dependency between input vector $X = (1, x_1, \ldots, x_p)$ and a binary response y is given via the *logit equation*

$$\log \left(\frac{p(X)}{1 - p(X)} \right) = \beta_0 + x_1 \beta_1 + \cdots + x_p \beta_p. \tag{32}$$

The value $p(X)$ is the probability of 1 with input X and the parameter vector $(\beta_0, \ldots, \beta_p)$ is unobservable. Unlike linear regression where a jointly Gaussian distribution of (X, Y) ensure $E(Y|X = x)$ is a linear function of x, there is no simple analogy, or even a meaningful interpretation for $E(Y|X = x)$ in case Y is $B(1, p)$, — in fact, it is even meaningless to talk about the joint distribution of (Y, X). The likelihood of the observed data $(y_1, \ldots, y_N)$ is

$$L(y_1, \ldots, y_N) = \prod_{j=1}^N p(X)_j^y (1 - p(X))^{1 - y_j}$$
$$= p(X)^{\sum_{j=1}^N y_j} (1 - p(X))^{N - \sum_{j=1}^N y_j}. \tag{33}$$

The log-likelihood can be re-written as

$$l = \log(L)$$
$$= \log(p(X)) \sum_{j=1}^N y_j + \log(1 - p(X)) \left(N - \sum_{j=1}^N y_j \right)$$
$$= \log \frac{p(X)}{1 - p(X)} \sum_{j=1}^N y_j + N \log(1 - p(X)) \tag{34}$$

The term $\log \frac{p(X)}{1 - p(X)}$ is called *log-odds ratio* which takes real values $\in (-\infty, +\infty)$ and, according to (32) is modeled as a linear function of the feature vector $X = (1, x_1, \ldots, x_p)$,

$$\log \frac{p(X)}{1 - p(X)} = X'\beta.$$

Solving for $p(X)$, we get

$$p(\beta; X) = \frac{\exp(X'\beta)}{1 + X'\beta} \tag{35}$$

Plugging back into (34) we get

$$L(\beta; y_1 \ldots y_N) = \left(\frac{\exp(X'\beta)}{1 + X'\beta} \right)^{\sum_{j=1}^N y_j}$$
$$\times \left(1 - \frac{\exp(X'\beta)}{1 + X'\beta} \right)^{N - \sum_{j=1}^N y_j} \tag{36}$$

The MLE $\widehat{\beta}$ is

$$\widehat{\beta} = \arg \max_{\beta \in \mathbb{R}^{p+1}} L(\beta; y_1 \ldots y_N). \tag{37}$$

The solution is approximated via a numerical algorithm like the one described at the bottom of 4.1.

5.3. *Logit: A simple example*

Consider a generic paradigm that related exposure to pathogen to a disease. Exposure does not guarantee getting sick, and since there is no additional information about individuals, an aggregated data suffice.

x	Y	Total
1	0	10
0	1	40
0	0	45
1	1	5

where $x = 1$ or 0, depending whether subject is exposed or not, and $Y = 1$ or 0, depending if subject is sick or not. The likelihood function for the 100 data points is

$$L(\beta_0, \beta_1)$$

$$= \prod_{j=1}^{100} \left(\frac{\exp(\beta_0 + \beta_1 X_j)}{1 + \exp(\beta_0 + \beta_1 X_j)} \right)^{Y_j}$$

$$\times \left(\frac{1}{1 + \exp(\beta_0 + \beta_1 X_j)} \right)^{1-Y_j}$$

$$= \left(\frac{\exp(\beta_0 + \beta_1 X_j)}{1 + \exp(\beta_0 + \beta_1 X_j)} \right)^{45} \left(\frac{1}{1 + \exp(\beta_0 + \beta_1 X_j)} \right)^{55}.$$

The MLE estimate results in the model (for example, using R function "glm" with the optional parameter family = "binomial")

$$\mathbf{Pr}(Y = 1|X = x) = \frac{\exp(-0.1178 - 0.5754x)}{1 + \exp(-0.1178 - 0.5754)}. \quad (38)$$

For low exposure

$$\mathbf{Pr}(Y = 1|X = 0) = \frac{\exp(-0.1178 - 0.5754 \times 0)}{1 + \exp(-0.1178 - 0.5754 \times 0)}$$

$$\approx 0.4706,$$

and for high exposure

$$\mathbf{Pr}(Y = 1|X = 1) = \frac{\exp(-0.1178 - 5754 \times 1)}{1 + \exp(-01178 - 0.5754 \times 1)}$$

$$\approx 0.3333.$$

In other words, contraction risk, although not negligible, is rather low (33%.)

6. Poisson Regression

In the Poisson settings, with unconditional probability mass function is

$$\mathbf{Pr}(Y = k) = \exp(-\lambda)\frac{\lambda^k}{k!}, \quad (39)$$

the GLiM model stipulates a linear relationship between $\log(\lambda)$ and the covariates $X = (x_1, \ldots, x_p)$.

The Poisson data is a set of ordered pairs $(X^{(j)}, Y^{(j)})$, $j = 1, \ldots, N$ with $Y^{(j)} \geq 0$ and $X^{(j)} = (x_1^{(j)}, \ldots, x_N^{(j)})$. At a level $X^{(j)}$, we have $Y(X^{(j)}) \sim \text{Poisson}(\lambda(X^{(j)}))$. The Poisson parameter λ varies as a function of the level X, and the GLiM model stipulates that the conditional mean $\log(E(Y|X))$ is related via $\log(\lambda(X)) = \beta_0 + \beta'X$, where $X' = (x_1, \ldots, x_p)$

and $\beta' = (\beta_1, \ldots, \beta_p)$. The data is a set of ordered pairs (X_j, y_j), $j = 1, \ldots, N$, where X_j is p-dimensional vector and Y_j is a non-negative integer. The log-likelihood of Poisson

$$l(\lambda_1, \ldots, \lambda_N; X_1, \ldots,_N)$$

$$= \log \left(\prod_{j=1}^{N} \exp(-\lambda_j) \frac{\lambda_j^{Y_j}}{Y_j!} \right)$$

$$= \sum_{j=1}^{N} (-\lambda_j + \log(\lambda_j)Y_j - \log(Y_j!))$$

Substitute $\lambda = \beta_0 + \beta'X$ we get,

$$l(\beta; X) = -\sum_{j=1}^{N} (\exp(\beta'X_j) - (\beta'X_j)Y_j + \log(Y_j!)). \quad (40)$$

The MLE $\hat{\beta} = \arg \max_\beta l(\beta; X)$ can be approximated using standard approximation techniques.

With the no-frills R function $glm(\log(\lambda)1 + var1 + var2 +$ (more variables), family = poisson (link = log)) one obtains an estimate for the logarithm of the unknown mean λ. The caveat is that, although data may appear to fit the Poisson model, it may exhibit an annoying feature of 'over (or under) dispersion', in the sense that the empirical mean (estimate for λ) is significantly smaller (or bigger) that the empirical variance (also λ.) This is rather bad because in the Poisson model, the mean equals to the variance. In that event *negative binomial* regression may be preferred.

6.1. *A poisson example*

As an example, consider the count data for some (made up, unimportant) inputs x_1 and x_2, response Y, summarized in the following table, where the total represents the number of patterns.

x_1	x_2	Y	Total
1	1	0	5
1	2	0	2
1	2	1	1
2	2	0	1
2	2	1	3
2	2	2	2
2	3	2	3
2	4	2	2
2	4	3	2
2	4	4	1
3	1	1	1
3	1	2	2
3	2	2	4
3	3	3	4
3	4	3	5
3	6	4	1
3	7	4	4
4	1	2	5
4	4	4	4
4	4	5	1
5	6	5	1

The GLiM model equation at level (x_1, x_2) is $\log(\lambda(x_1, x_2) = -0.8336 + 0.3653 \times x_1 + 0.1829 \times x_2$, from which we can predict for any level of x_1 and x_2. For example, for levels $(x_1, x_2) = (8, 2)$,

$$\lambda(8, 2) = \exp(-0.8336 + 0.3653 \times 8 + 0.1829 \times 2)$$

$$\approx 11.65.$$

7. Final Notes

As noted above, GLiM, with all its variants is the most popular and arguably the most useful of all statistical modeling techniques. The popularity of this class of models stems from its apparent simplicity and utility as a basis for further analysis. For reference purpose, we suggest further examination of the following sub-topics.

1. Sometime instead of Logit, Probit analysis is used where the Probit model is $\Phi(p) = \beta_0 + \beta_1 x_1 + \cdots + \beta_p x_p$, where $\Phi(\zeta)$ is the ζ quantile of the standard normal distribution.

2. Equality of the mean and the variance of a Poisson distribution imply that data that fails to exhibit 'near' equality of the two parameters may not be suitable for a Poisson regression model. In that case, the *Negative Binomial*, the one modeling the number of trials to kth success, in independent Bernoulli trials, may be a more apt choice.

3. Linear models, GLiM with the identity link function come with multiple varieties and flavors, each with its own techniques and idiosyncratic pecularities. We will only mention a few. At times, data does not support that the variance is independent from one observation to the next. This phenomenon is called *heteroscedasticity*. In other words, $\text{cov}(\epsilon_i, \epsilon_j) \neq 0$, $i \neq j$. If so, then the *weighted least square model* (*WLS*) applies, where $Y = X\beta + \epsilon$, where $\epsilon \sim N(0, \Sigma)$, for some symmetric p-by-p matrix Σ. The

difficulty in building WLS models stems from the need to estimate the $\frac{N^2}{2}$ terms ($\text{cov}(Y_i, Y_j, 1 \leq i \leq j \leq N)$ with merely N observed values. It is common to estimate Σ based on experience.

4. *Multinomial regression.* Binomial regression (Logit) can be extended to more than a binary classification, m classes, $m > 2$. The standard setup is to regress the log-odds-ratio of each class and some pivot class, say class m. For p variables, the model is based on observed $(1, x_1, \ldots, x_p)$ and so the complexity of the model is $(p + 1) \times (m - 1)$, roughly the number of classes times dimension of the input space. Consequently, models with large number of classes tend to diminish in predictability.

Because of the limited scope of this survey paper, we will not go into fine details to analyze quality of the estimate. The reader may consult with the bibliography.

References

[1] S. Zacks, *Examples and Problems in Mathematical Statistics* (Wiley, New York, 2014).

[2] G. A. F. Seber, *Linear Regression Analysis* (Wiley, New York, 1977).

[3] A. Agresti, *Foundations of Linear and Generalized Linear models*, (Wiley Series in Probability and Statistics (Wiley New York, 2015).

[4] A. J. Dobson and A. Barnett, *An Introduction to Generalized Linear Models*, 3rd edn. (Chapman & Hall, 2008).

[5] J. J. Faraway, *Linear Models with R*, 2nd edn. (Chapman & Hall, 2014).

[6] P. McCullagh and J. A. Nelder, *Generalized Linear Models*, 2nd edn. (Chapman & Hall, 1989).

[7] C. E. McCulloch and S. R. Searle, *Generalized, Linear, and Mixed Models* (2008).

[8] R. H. Myers and D. C. Montgomery, *Generalized Linear Models: With Applications in Engineering and the Sciences* (2010).

OLAP and machine learning

Jennifer Jin

Department of Electrical Engineering and Computer Science
University of California-Irvine, 5200 Engineering Hall
Irvine, CA 92697, USA
jenniyk2@uci.edu

The objective of this tutorial is to present an overview of machine learning (ML) methods. This paper outlines different types of ML as well as techniques for each kind. It covers popular applications for different types of ML. On-Line Analytic Processing (OLAP) enables users of multidimensional databases to create online comparative summaries of data. This paper goes over commercial OLAP software available as well as OLAP techniques such as "slice and dice" and "drill down and roll up." It discusses various techniques and metrics used to evaluate how accurate a ML algorithm is.

Keywords: OLAP; machine learning; classification; clustering; regression; associativity; neural network.

1. Problem Statement

Machine learning (ML) is one of the fastest growing fields in computer science right now. With the data continuously growing, there is a need for the theory to process it and turn it into knowledge. In many different aspects of life, there are many applications where data is continuously generated and collected. More people have been finding new ways to make use of this growing data and turn it into something useful. ML plays a big role in this process. The volume of digital data accessible to researchers and knowledge workers has grown immensely in recent years. As the amount of data grows, it is becoming critical to provide users with flexible and effective tools to retrieve, evaluate, and understand large information sets.

With datasets growing every year, it is not only the number of observations but also the number of observed attributes that are growing immensely. The data has more structure and includes images, video, audio, documents, web pages, click logs, graphs on top of numbers and character strings.

With data so complex and voluminous, there is a need to be able to explain it in terms of a relatively simple model with a small number of factors and their interaction. With so many different types of ML techniques, there is a necessity to figure out which techniques and algorithms are the most ideal for each application. Also, with massive amounts of multidimensional databases available, there is a need to create online summaries of data so the user can view and explore data just by clicking, dragging and dropping.

2. On-Line Analytic Processing

On-Line Analytic Processing (OLAP) refers to technology that lets users of multidimensional databases generate online comparative summaries of data. OLAP services can be incorporated into corporate database systems and they permit analysts and managers to observe the performance of the business. The concluding result of OLAP techniques can be very simple or more complex.[1,2]

There are numerous commercial OLAP software available. IBM provides business intelligence and enterprise planning solutions for many Global 3500 companies. IBM Cognos 8 Business Intelligence (BI) gives companies the capability to rapidly analyze complex data from any viewpoint and present it in ways that are easy to understand. Users can explore multidimensional data by clicking and dragging. Data relationships can be viewed and analyzed in graphic displays that can be easily changed and customized. IBM Cognos 8 BI gives users the ability to explore large complex data sets with drag-and-drop techniques, drilling down through levels of detail to view information from many angles. IBM offers greater functionality for slicing and dicing data, ranking, sorting forecasting and nesting information to get a better sense of causes, effects and trends.[3]

InetSoft offers dashboards, reporting and visual analysis software that can access OLAP data sources and cubes. InetSoft's BI software provides data block foundation for real-time data mashup and presents information through interactive dashboards, enterprise reporting, scorecards, and exception alerts. It includes analytics software, refined reporting capabilities and direct access to almost any data source. For enterprise reporting, there are production reports with embedded business logic and parametrization, interactive reports and in-report exploration, and ad hoc reporting wizards and free form editing.[4]

Oracle OLAP is a multidimensional analytic engine embedded in Oracle Database 11 g. Oracle OLAP cubes provide calculations using simple SQL queries. This query performance may be leveraged transparently when using OLAP

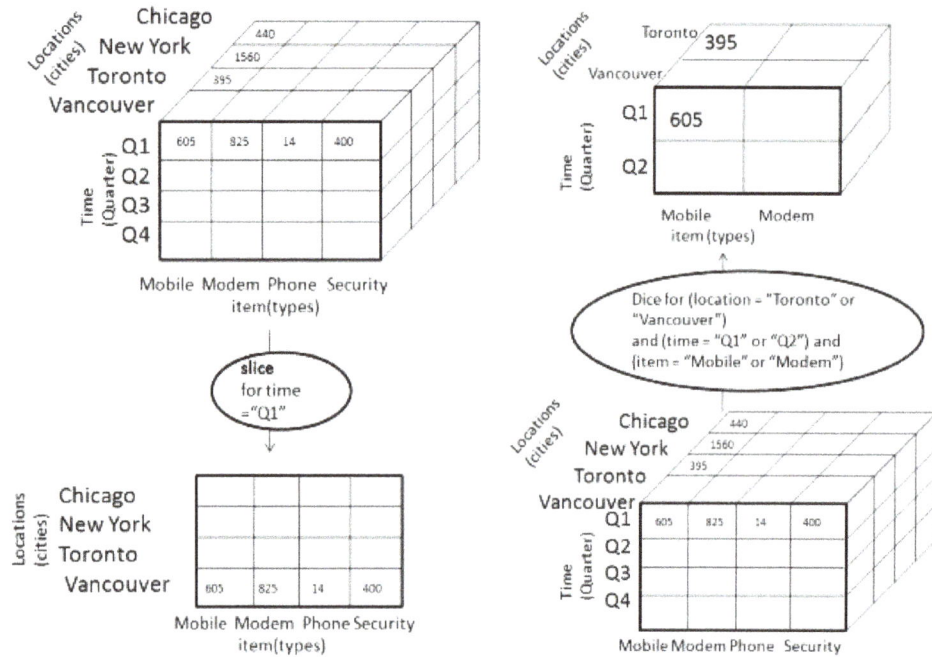

Fig. 1. Slice and dice operation OLAP.[9]

cubes as materialized views. Because Oracle OLAP is embedded in Oracle Database 11 g, it permits centralized management of data and business rules in a secure, scalable and enterprise-ready platform. This tool enables users to easily produce analytic measures, including time-series calculations, financial models, forecasts, allocations and regressions.[5]

OLAP data sources are able to be connected just as other external data sources. It is compatible with databases that are created with Microsoft SQL Server OLAP Services version 7.0, Microsoft SQL Server Analysis Services version 2000, and Microsoft SQL Server Analysis Services version 2005, the Microsoft OLAP server products. Excel can also work with third-party OLAP products that are compatible with OLE-DB for OLAP. It is also possible to generate an offline cube file with a subset of the data from an OLAP server database.[6]

It is easy to express a multidimensional model with innovative analytic designs with OLAP. Using SQL, it can effectively provide rich analytics to any reporting and analysis tool. It clearly progresses summary queries against tables using cube-based materialized views. OLAP data can be combined with any other data in the database such as spatial, data mining, XML and documents.[7] An OLAP cube is a specifically intended database that is enhanced for reporting. OLAP cubes are designed for productivity in data retrieval unlike other databases designed for online transaction processing. While other databases treat all data into the database similarly, OLAP cubes categorize data into dimensions and measures.[8]

"Slice and Dice" is a process initiated by the user for navigating. This is done by calling for page displays interactively, through the specification of slices via rotations

and drill down/up. The most used operations are slice and dice, drill down, roll up, and pivot.

Slice is when a rectangular subset of a cube is picked by selecting a single value for one of its dimensions. This provides a new sub-cube with one less dimension. As shown in Fig. 1, slice is performed for the dimension "time" using the criterion time = "Q1" and forms a new subcube by picking one or more dimensions. The dice operation provides a sub cube by selecting two or more dimensions from a given cube and offers a new subcube. Consider Fig. 1 that shows the dice operation. The dice operation on the cube based on the following selection criteria contains three dimensions-location, time and item.[9]

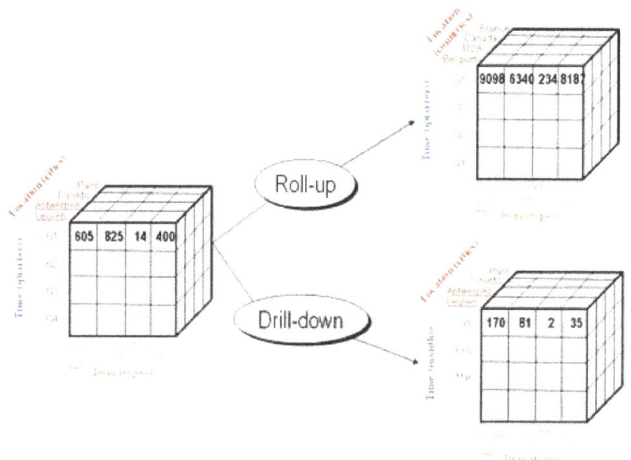

Fig. 2. OLAP cubes roll-up and drill-down.[10]

Drill Down/Roll Up shown in Fig. 2 allows the user to navigate among levels of data ranging from the most summarized (up) to the most detailed (down). Roll-up involves summarizing the data along a dimension. The summarization rule might be computing totals along a hierarchy or a applying a set of formulas such as "profit = sales − expenses".[10]

Finally, a cube and the dimensions are input to the data mining model that was just built. After the dicing is done using the dimensions given, the updated cube is returned as the result. The updated cube then can be used as an input to another operation.

3. Machine Learning

A computer program is said to learn some task from experience if its performance at the task improves with experience, according to some performance measure. ML involves the study of algorithms that can extract information automatically (i.e., without on-line human guidance). It is certainly the case that some of these procedures include ideas derived directly from, or inspired by, classical statistics, but they do not have to be.

The conventional ML with observations, i.e., datasets, takes two stages; learning stage and evaluation stage, as shown in Fig. 3.

A training set is a set of observations used for the learning purpose. The learning stage is performed by running a ML method such as *regression, classification, clustering,* and *association*. The result of the learning stage is a knowledge model which captures a set of rules and patterns derived from the training set. The learned model is used to evaluate a given observation in a test set, and the evaluation can be in various forms such as prediction, diagnosis, and recommendation.

Cluster analysis divides data into groups that are meaningful, useful, or both. The clusters should capture the natural structure of the data.[11] For example, a large number of grocery stores could be grouped into clusters based on their physical location. A clustering algorithm would calculate the distance between these stores and divide them into k clusters.

Classification is the task of assigning objects to one of several predefined categories. For example, using classification algorithms, one can detect if an email is spam or not based on the message header and content.[11] Each email would be classified as either "spam" or "non-spam." Regression is a statistical measure that tries to decide the strength of the relationship between one dependent variable and a series of other changing variables (known as independent variables).[12] For example, regression can helps home buyers to value assets and understand the relationships between variables with housing price being the dependent variable and independent variables such as lot size, year built and last sold price. Association analysis is valuable for learning interesting relationships hidden in large data sets. The uncovered relationships can be accessible in the form of association rules or sets of frequent items.[11] For example, there is a large amount of customer purchase data at the checkout counters of grocery stores. Each transaction contains a set of items bought together by a given customer. Using an association algorithm, one could learn which items are bought together frequently.

There are two types of learning-supervised and unsupervised. In supervised learning, the output datasets used to train the machine are provided and get the desired outputs. In unsupervised learning, no datasets are provided, instead the data is clustered into different classes.

For example, let us say we have a basket full of different fruits. With supervised learning, one would already know that there are apples, bananas, cherries and grapes from previous work. The colors and shapes would already be known based on trained data. With unsupervised learning, the types of fruits are now known. The fruits would be divided into similar physical characters, not knowing how many different types of fruits there are because there is no model based on trained data.

3.1. *Supervised learning*

With supervised learning, one is given a data set and already know what the correct output should be, having the idea that there is an association between the input and the output. Supervised learning problems include regression and classification problems. With regression, the user is trying to guess the results within a continuous output. This means he or she is trying to plot the input variables to some continuous function. With classification, he or she is trying to guess results in a discrete output.

Training data includes both the input and the desired results. For some cases, the correct results are identified and are given the input to the model during the learning process. For the creation of a good training, validation and test sets are critical. These approaches are usually fast and precise and have to be able to generalize to give the precise results when new data are given the input without knowing the target.

3.1.1. *Regression*

Regression is a statistical technique to determine the linear relationship between two or more variables. Regression is mainly used for prediction and causal inference. It includes numerous methods for modeling and analyzing many variables. It is a relationship between one numerical dependent variable and one or more numerical or categorical independent

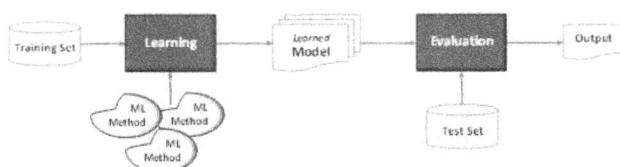

Fig. 3. Process for conventional ML.

(explanatory) variable(s) using equation to set up relationship. Regression model could be simple or multiple depending on the number of explanatory variables.

The model could result in a linear relationship or non-linear relationship. Regression analysis predicts new values based on the past, inference, computes the new values for a dependent variable based on the values of one or more measured attributes.

For example, a real estate firm may apply regression on a database of house sales for a period. The feature set for house sales may include size of each house, year built, number of bedrooms, number of bathrooms, number of stories and school district. The variable in this case could be the value of houses. The regression on the sales database with the feature set produces a distribution of houses over the features of houses and their values. Utilizing the regression result, a price of a new house on the market can be predicted.

3.1.2. *Classification*

Classification is the problem of finding which category a new observation belongs to. This is determined based on a training set of data encompassing observations whose category membership is known. Classification forecasts categorical class labels. Some applications include credit approval, target marketing, medical diagnosis, treatment effectiveness analysis and stock market.

Classification includes two steps: model construction and model usage. The first step describes a set of predetermined classes. The model is represented as classification rules, decision trees or mathematical formulae. Model usage is for classifying future or unknown objects. The known label of test sample is compared with the classified result from the model.

3.1.3. *Artificial neural network*

An Artificial Neural Network (ANN) is an information processing model that is inspired by the way biological nervous systems like brain process information. The main element of this paradigm is the new structure of the information processing system. It contains a large number of highly interconnected processing elements working in union to solve specific problems. ANNs learn by example just like people do. An ANN is configured for a specific application like pattern recognition or data classification, through a learning process. Learning in biological systems encompasses modifications to the synaptic connections that occur between the neurons. This is the case for ANNs as well. A classic application of ANN is the handwriting recognition problem where ANN is used for recognizing the pattern of hand writings.

3.2. *Unsupervised learning*

The difference between supervised and unsupervised learning is that with unsupervised learning there is no feedback based on the prediction results. It is not just about clustering. Unsupervised learning includes clustering and association rule learning.

The model does not come with the correct results during the training. It can be used to cluster the input data in classes based on their statistical properties only. The labeling can be performed even if the labels are only accessible for a small number of objects, representative of the desired classes.

3.2.1. *Clustering*

Clustering is a grouping of a data set into subsets called clusters so that the data in each subset share some mutual characteristics. It is the process of clustering physical or abstract objects into classes of alike objects. A cluster is a subset of objects such that the distance between any two objects in the cluster is less than the distance between any object in the cluster and any object not located within. An effective clustering method will result in high quality clusters in which the intra-class similarity is high and the inter-class similarity is low. However, objective evaluation is problematic because it is usually done by human inspection.

A partitional clustering is a partition of the set of data objects into nonoverlapping subsets such that each data object is in exactly one subset. A hierarchical clustering is a set of nested clusters that are ordered as a tree. Each node (cluster) in the tree (except for the leaf node) is the union of its children (subclusters), and the root of the tree is the cluster containing all the objects.[11]

As an example, consider a supermarket chain which has a number of branch stores in California. Each store carries a number of different product models. *K*-means clustering can be applied to define clusters of stores which carry similar product types as shown in Fig. 4. Each type of the circle represents a cluster of similar stores which might be distributed on different regions.

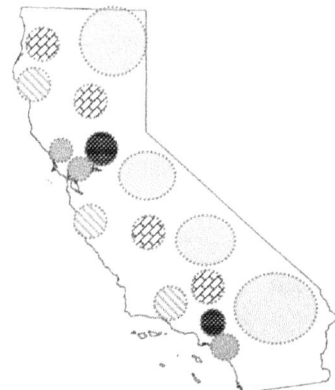

Fig. 4. Cluster of stores in California.

Table 1. An example of market basket transactions.

TID	Items
1	{Bread, Milk}
2	{Bread, Diapers, Beer, Eggs}
3	{Milk, Diapers, Beer, Cola}
4	{Bread, Milk, Diapers, Beer}
5	{Bread, Milk, Diapers, Cola}

3.2.2. *Association*

Association rule learning is a method for discovering interesting relations between variables in large databases. It is intended to identify strong rules discovered in databases using different measures of interestingness. In general, association rule mining can be viewed as a two-step process. The first step includes finding all frequent item sets and the second step is to generate strong association rules from the frequent item sets. Each frequent item set will occur at least as frequently as a predetermined minimum support count. The association rules must satisfy minimum support and minimum confidence.

Market basket analysis is a classic example of association rule learning. In order for a store manager to learn the buying habits of his or her customers, shopping transactions are analyzed. Through the analysis, one can find out which groups or sets of items customers are likely to purchase together in a given trip to the store. As shown in Table 1, each transaction has a unique ID with a list of items bought together. Using association rule learning, one can find out {Diapers} → {Beer}. The rules could suggest that a strong relationship exists between the sale of diapers and beer because many customers who buy diapers also buy beer.[11] Retailers can use this type of rules to help them identify new opportunities for cross selling their products to the customers.

4. Evaluation

There are various techniques and metrics used to evaluate how accurate an algorithm is. These can be used to derive a conclusion about a ML model. Some aspects to consider are accuracy, comprehensibility and conciseness. Based on which ML method is being evaluated, there could be more appropriate evaluation methods.

4.1. *Classification accuracy*

During development, and in testing before deploying a classifier in the wild, one needs to be able to quantify the performance of the classifier. How accurate is the classifier? The accuracy of a classifier on a given test set is the percentage of test set tuples that are correctly classified by the classifier, also referred to as recognition rate and error rate (or misclassification rate) is the opposite of accuracy. While it is

useful to generate the simple accuracy of a model, sometimes one needs more. When is the model wrong? One needs to consider false positives versus false negatives. Confusion Matrix is a device used to illustrate how a model is performing in terms of false positives and false negatives. It gives one more information than a single accuracy figure and allows one to think about the cost of mistakes. It can be extended to any number of classes. Other accuracy measures include model accuracy, misclassification rate, sensitivity (true positive rate) and specificity (true negative rate).[13]

4.2. *ROC curves*

Receive Operating Characteristics (ROC) was developed in the 1950s for signal detection theory to analyze noisy signals. It characterizes the trade-off between positive hits and false alarms. ROC curve plots true positives on the *y*-axis against false positives on the *x*-axis. Performance of each classifier represented as a point on the ORC curve changes the threshold of algorithm, sampling distribution or cost matrix changes the location of the point.[13]

4.3. *Precision/recall*

Precision (also called positive predictive value) is the fraction of retrieved instances that are relevant, while recall (also known as sensitivity) is the fraction of relevant instances that are retrieved. Both precision and recall are therefore based on an understanding and measure of relevance. A precision/recall curve plots the precision versus recall (TP-rate) as a threshold on the confidence of an instance being positive is varied. PR curves show the fraction of predictions that are false positives and are well suited for tasks with lots of negative instances. On the other hand, ROC curves are insensitive to changes in class distribution (ROC curve does not change if the proportion is positive and negative instances in the test set are varied). They can identify optimal classification thresholds for tasks with differential misclassification costs. They both allow predictive performance to be assessed at various levels of confidence, assume binary classification tasks and sometimes summarized by calculating area under the curve.[13]

Other than these methods recent studies have studied different evaluation methods. Mousavizadegan and Mohabatkar[14] compare five different ML algorithms frequently used for classification of biological data were used and their performance was evaluated were based on accuracy, sensitivity, specificity and Matthew's correlation coefficient.

Japkowicz and Shah[15] discuss some of the confusion matrix-based measures (accuracy, precision, recall or sensitivity, and false alarm rate) as well as ROC analysis; several error estimation or resampling techniques belonging to the cross-validation family as well as bootstrapping are involved in the context of the second subtask.

In the study by Bal *et al.*,[16] synthetic data with different number of records have been produced to reflect the probabilities on the ALARM network. The accuracy of 11 ML methods for the inference mechanism of medical decision support system is compared on various data sets.

Schlemmer *et al.*[17] evaluate several ML algorithms in the context of long-term prediction of cardiac diseases. Results from applying K Nearest Neighbors Classifiers (KNN), Support Vector Machines (SVMs) and Random Forests (RFs) to data from a cardiological long-term study suggests that multivariate methods can significantly improve classification results.

Low *et al.*[18] extend the GraphLab framework to the substantially more challenging distributed setting while preserving strong data consistency guarantees. They develop graph-based extensions to pipelined locking and data versioning as well as introduce fault tolerance to the GraphLab abstraction. Finally, they evaluate their distributed implementation of the GraphLab abstraction on a large Amazon EC2 deployment and show 1–2 orders of magnitude performance gains over Hadoop-based implementations.

Shashidhara *et al.*[19] compare two selected ML algorithms on data sets of different sizes deployed on different platforms like Weka, Scikit-Learn and Apache Spark. They are evaluated based on Training time, Accuracy and Root mean squared error.

Soysal and Schmidt[20] employ three supervised ML algorithms, Bayesian Networks, Decision Trees and Multilayer Perceptrons for the flow-based classification of six different types of Internet traffic including Peer-to-Peer (P2P) and content delivery traffic. The dependency of the traffic classification performance on the amount and composition of training data is investigated followed by experiments that show that ML algorithms such as Bayesian Networks and Decision Trees are suitable for Internet traffic flow classification at a high speed, and prove to be robust with respect to applications that dynamically change their source ports.

Mcfee and Lanckriet[21] study metric learning as a problem of information retrieval. They present a general metric learning algorithm, based on the structural SVM framework, to learn a metric such that rankings of data induced by distance from a query can be optimized against various ranking measures, such as AUC, Precision-at-k, MRR, MAP or NDCG. They demonstrate experimental results on standard classification data sets, and a large-scale online dating recommendation problem.

References

[1] T. Hill and P. Lewicki, *Statistics: Methods and Applications: A Comprehensive Reference for Science, Industry, and Data Mining*, December (2005).

[2] Mangisengi, A. Min Tjoa and R. Wagner, Metadata management concept for multidimensional OLAP data based on object-oriented concepts, *Proc. WISE 2000* (2000), pp. 358–365.

[3] IBM Analytics. 2016, OLAP Aug. 4, 2016, <http://www-01.ibm.com/software/analytics/cognos/olap.html>.

[4] InetSoft. 2016, Style Intelligence — Business Intelligence Software, Aug. 4, 2016, <http://www.inetsoft.com/products/StyleIntelligence/>.

[5] Oracle Database, 2016. Oracle OLAP. Aug. 4, 2016, <http://www.oracle.com/technetwork/database/options/olap/index.html>.

[6] Microsoft Business Intelligence, 2016. SQL Server 2012. Aug. 4, 2016, <http://www.microsoft.com/sqlserver/en/us/solutions-technologies/business-intelligence/analysis.aspx>.

[7] Oracle Database, 2016. Oracle OLAP. Aug. 4, 2016, <http://www.oracle.com/technetwork/database/options/olap/index.html>.

[8] C. J. Date, *An Introduction to Database Systems*, 8th edn. (Addison-Wesley, 2004).

[9] Tutorial Points. Data Warehousing- OLAP, <http://www.tutorialspoint.com/dwh/dwh_olap.htm>.

[10] Y. M. Choi, Web-enabled OLAP tutorial, Drexel University. <http://www.cis.drexel.edu/faculty/song/courses/info%20607/tutorial_OLAP/operations.htm>.

[11] P. Tan, M. Stteinbach and V. Kumar, *Introduction to Data Mining* (2006).

[12] Investopedia. 2016. Regression. Aug. 4. 2016, <http://www.investopedia.com/terms/r/regression.asp>.

[13] C. D. Page, Evaluating machine learning methods, CS 760: Machine Learning PPT (2016).

[14] M. Mousavizadegan and H. Mohabatkar, An evaluation on different machine learning algorithms for classification and prediction of antifungal peptides, *Med. Chem.* (2016).

[15] N. Japkowicz and M. Shah, Performance evaluation in machine learning, *Machine Learning in Radiation Oncology: Theory and Applications*, I. El Naqa *et al.* (eds.), Chap. 4 (Springer International Publishing, Switzerland, 2015), pp. 41–56.

[16] M. Bal, M. F. Amasyali, H. Sever, G. Kose and A. Demirhan, Performance evaluation of the machine learning algorithms used in inference mechanism of a medical decision support system, *Sci. World J.* **2014**, 15, Article ID 137896.

[17] A. Schlemmer, H. Zwirnmann, M. Zabel, U. Parlitz and S. Luther, Evaluation of machine learning methods for the long-term prediction of cardiac diseases, *8th Conf. European Study Group on Cardiovascular Oscillations (ESGCO)*, May 25–28 (2014).

[18] Y. Low, D. Bickson, J. Gonzalez, C. Guestrin, A. Kyrola and J. M. Hellerstein, Distributed GraphLab: A framework for machine learning and data mining in the cloud, *The 38th Int. Conf. Very Large Data Bases*, August 27th–31st 2012, Istanbul, Turkey (2012).

[19] B. M. Shashidhara, S. Jain, V. D. Rao, N. Patil and G. S. Raghavendra, Evaluation of machine learning frameworks on bank marketing and Higgs datasets, *Second Int. Conf. Advances in Computing and Communication Engineering* (2015).

[20] M. Soysal and E. G. Schmidt, Machine learning algorithms for accurate flow-based network traffic classification: Evaluation and comparison, *Int. J. Perform. Eval.* **67**(6), 451 (2010).

[21] B. McFee and G. Lanckriet, Metric learning to rank, *Proc. 27th Int. Conf. Machine Learning*, Haifa, Israel (2010).

Survival analysis via Cox proportional hazards additive models

Lu Bai* and Daniel Gillen[†]

*Department of Statistics, University of California,
Irvine, California 92617, USA
[†]dgillen@uci.edu

The Cox proportional hazards model is commonly used to examine the covariate-adjusted association between a predictor of interest and the risk of mortality for censored survival data. However, it assumes a parametric relationship between covariates and mortality risk though a linear predictor. Generalized additive models (GAMs) provide a flexible extension of the usual linear model and are capable of capturing nonlinear effects of predictors while retaining additivity between the predictor effects. In this paper, we provide a review of GAMs and incorporate bivariate additive modeling into the Cox model for censored survival data with applications to estimating geolocation effects on survival in spatial epidemiologic studies.

Keywords: Survival analysis; Cox proportional hazard model; smoothing; GAM; additive model.

1. Introduction

Survival analysis is a collection of statistical methods for the analysis of the time from a specified origin until the occurrence of a well-defined event, commonly referred to as the survival or failure time. Examples include the time to death since disease diagnosis, the time to divorce since marriage, lifetime of industrial components or unemployment duration. It is often the case that some observations are *right-censored*, implying that followup of subjects may end prior to the occurrence of the event of interest. Multiple reasons for censoring exist. For example, in clinical studies reasons may include a subject prematurely withdrawing consent from the study or study termination prior to the occurrence of the event. It is well known that, in the presence of censoring, standard statistical methods for analyzing continuous times yield inefficient (at best) and biased (at worst) estimates of covariate effects on survival. To address these issues, survival analysis methods consist of a class of procedures for analyzing covariate effects on the time-to-event in the presence of censoring. The Cox proportional hazards model[1] has become ubiquitous in statistical applications since it provides interpretable estimates of covariate effects on right-censored observations without the assumption of a full probability distribution on the event time.

The Cox model identifies the impact of multiple predictors on survival by relating the hazard function to a linear predictor of covariates in a multiplicative fashion. However, the effect of some covariates on the hazard function may best be represented by a complex pattern rather than linear simple linear term. One example is the effect of geospatial location on the risk of death among ovarian cancer patients within the California Ovarian Cancer Study.[3] Briefly, the California Ovarian Cancer Study is a retrospective population-based study designed to analyze the effect of geographic variation on advanced-stage invasive epithelial ovarian cancer mortality.

Cases were obtained from the California Cancer Registry. All participants were reported with International Federation of Gynecology and Obstetrics (FIGO) stage III/IV disease during the time period ranging from 1/1/1996 through 12/31/2006. The primary outcome of interest is represented by patient survival time, defined as the time from diagnosis to the time of death. Patients that were not observed to expire over the course of followup are right-censored and contribute partial information to the outcome, represented as the last known time of survival prior to being censored. The study recorded multiple known factors previously shown to be associated with patient survival including demographic characteristics (age, race, insurance type and socioeconomic status score), tumor characteristics (FIGO stage, grade, histology and tumor size) and utilized health care delivery system characteristics (whether the hospital where treatment was received treats more than 20 cases per year and whether the treatment received was adherent to National Comprehensive Cancer Network treatment guidelines for advanced-stage ovarian cancer). The primary goal of the study is to examine whether geolocation has an independent effect on patient survival time after adjustment for the above recorded known correlates of mortality in ovarian cancer patients, and to quantify how the adjusted survival rate changes over different geolocations across California. Ultimately, the adjusted geospatial effect reflects the effect of underlying spatially-varying factors that are not adjusted in the model, which may be related to general health disparities including health care resource utilization, environmental exposures, and lifestyle choices among others.

As previously noted, the spatial effect considered in the California ovarian cancer data is likely to be complex and the assumption of linearity of the effect or a nonlinear effect with a specific functional form would likely lead to bias in estimated spatial associations. As such it is necessary to nonparametrically smooth the effect of geospatial location on the risk of mortality. Generalized additive models[4,5] (GAMs) were originally proposed by Hastie and Tibshirani[4] to capture the nonlinear pattern of the relationship between predictors and dependent variables. Moreover, the impact of different predictors can be incorporated additively in GAMs so that the adjusted impact of a single predictor does not depend on the values of the other predictors in the model. For survival analysis, the Cox proportional hazards additive model can be used to apply these additive modeling techniques within the context of a semi-parametric censored data model. In the context of the California Ovarian Cancer Study, a bivariate smoother can be employed to estimate the complex pattern of the effect of geolocation parameters, and by adding up the spatial effects and linear effects of other covariates, the Cox additive model provides a unified statistical framework that allows for the adjustment of covariates when evaluating spatial variability in a flexible way.

The remainder of the paper is organized as follows. A brief review of survival analysis and the semi-parametric Cox proportional hazards model for the analysis of censored time-to-event data is provided in Sec. 2. In Sec. 3, we review two of the most commonly employed methods for statistical smoothing of a response variable: local-averaging smoother and smoothing splines. In Sec. 4, we provide a review of GAMs along with an overview of the backfitting algorithm for estimating parameters in GAMs for a univariate outcome with probability distribution belonging to the exponential family. Additive modeling for censored survival data within Cox's proportional hazards model is introduced in Sec. 5, followed by an example of the spatial analysis of the California Ovarian Cancer Study in Sec. 6. A brief discussion of the reviewed methods is provided in Sec. 7.

2. Cox Proportional Hazards Regression for Survival Analysis

2.1. *The survival and hazard functions*

Let T'_i and C_i denote the *true* time-to-event and censoring time for observation i, respectively, $i = 1, \ldots, N$. Only one of T'_i or C_i is observed for each observation, and hence we define $T_i = \min(T'_i, C_i)$ to be the *observed* time for observation i. Further, define δ_i to be the event indicator for observation i such that $\delta_i = 1$ if $T_i \le C_i$ and $\delta_i = 0$ if $T_i > C_i$.

Let $f(t)$ and $F(t)$ denote the probability density function (pdf) and cumulative distribution function (cdf) for T', respectively (omitting the observation index i for brevity). Then, the survival function $S(t)$ is defined as the probability that the true time-to-event is longer than t. That is, the survival function is defined as

$$S(t) = \Pr\{T' > t\} = 1 - \Pr\{T' <= t\}$$
$$= 1 - F(t) = \int_t^\infty f(s)ds. \qquad (1)$$

The hazard function, $\lambda(t)$, is defined as the instantaneous rate of failure at time t given survival up to time t. Thus, the hazard function is given by

$$\lambda(t) = \lim_{\Delta t \to 0^+} \frac{\Pr\{t \le T' < t + \Delta t | T' \ge t\}}{\Delta t}. \qquad (2)$$

It is easy to see that the hazard function can be written in terms of the pdf and survival distribution by noting that

$$\begin{aligned} \lambda(t) &= \lim_{\Delta t \to 0^+} \frac{\Pr\{t \le T' < t + \Delta t | T' \ge t\}}{\Delta t} \\ &= \lim_{\Delta t \to 0^+} \frac{\Pr\{t \le T' < t + \Delta t, T' \ge t\}/\Pr\{T' \ge t\}}{\Delta t} \\ &= \lim_{\Delta t \to 0^+} \frac{\Pr\{t \le T' < t + \Delta t\}}{\Delta t} \bigg/ \Pr\{T' \ge t\} = \frac{f(t)}{S(t)}. \end{aligned}$$
$$(3)$$

Further, noting that $f(t)$ is the negative derivative of $S(t)$, i.e.,

$$\lambda(t) = -\frac{d}{dt}\log(S(t)), \qquad (4)$$

and we also have that

$$S(t) = \exp\left\{-\int_0^t \lambda(s)ds\right\}. \qquad (5)$$

The above relationship gives rise to the cumulative hazard function, $\Lambda(t)$, defined as

$$\Lambda(t) = \int_0^t \lambda(s)ds, \qquad (6)$$

and hence the relationship,

$$S(t) = \exp\left\{-\Lambda(t)\right\}. \qquad (7)$$

Thus, both the hazard function and survival can be used to fully characterize the distribution of the survival time, T'.

In many cases, it is justifiable to assume that the true failure time T'_i and censoring time C_i for observation i are independent. In this case, the likelihood function incorporated both censored and fully observed survival times obtained as

$$L = \prod_{i=1}^N [f(T_i)]^{\delta_i}[S(T_i)]^{1-\delta_i}. \qquad (8)$$

Thus, the above likelihood function reduces to the usual likelihood function for independent data when all observations have fully observed survival times (i.e., $\delta_i = 1$ for $i = 1, \ldots, N$), but allows for partial contributions up to the censoring times for those individuals that were censored prior to failure.

Given the above specification of the likelihood function in the presence of censoring, it is relatively straightforward to obtain maximum likelihood estimates when one is willing to assume a parametric probability model for the true survival times. For example, the simplest survival model assumes survival times follow the exponential distribution which is characterized by a constant hazard function $\lambda(t) = \lambda$ for $t > 0$. Using the relationship between the survival function and the hazard function, the corresponding survival function for the exponential distribution is then given by

$$S(t) = \exp\{-\lambda t\}. \tag{9}$$

In this case, covariate effects on the survival distribution can easily be incorporated into the model by writing the hazard function as a linear combination of the covariates and unknown parameters of the covariate:

$$\log(\lambda) = \beta_0 + \beta_1 X^{(1)} + \cdots + \beta_d X^{(d)}. \tag{10}$$

Given the above model specification, the parameter β_j represents the difference in the log-hazard comparing subpopulations differing in X^j by 1-unit that are similar with respect to all other adjustment covariates. Alternatively, e^{β_j} represents the ratio of hazard functions comparing subpopulations differing in X^j by 1-unit that are similar with respect to all other adjustment covariates. Because this ratio is constant with respect to time (recall that $\lambda(t) = \lambda$ for $t > 0$), the above model is said to belong to the family of proportional hazards survival models.

2.2. Cox proportional hazards model

The assumption of a mis-specified parametric survival distribution can lead to biased and/or inefficient estimates of covariate effects on survival, as is true with mis-specified parametric models for uncensored data. This lack of robustness in parametric models motivated the use of semi-parametric regression models in the context of censored survival data. Indeed, the most widely used regression model for relating covariates to censored survival times is the semi-parametric Cox proportional hazards model.[1,2] Briefly, let $X = [X^{(1)}, \ldots, X^{(d)}]^T$ be a $d \times 1$ vector of covariates to be related to survival. The Cox proportional hazard assumes

$$\lambda(t) = \lambda_0(t) \exp\{X^T \beta\}, \tag{11}$$

where $\lambda(t)$ represents the hazard at time t, $\lambda_0(t)$ is a non-specified baseline hazard (i.e., the hazard for observations with covariate value $X = 0$), and β is a $d \times 1$ vector of regression coefficients associated with covariate vector X. As with the exponential survival model previously presented, the Cox model specification provided in Eq. (11) is also a member of the family of proportional hazards survival models. This is easily seen by noting that the ratio of hazard functions comparing subpopulations differing in, say $X^{(j)}$, by 1-unit but similar with respect to all other covariate values is constant as a function of time, and is given by e^{β_j}, $j = 1, \ldots, d$.

While the exponential model and the Cox model are both members of the family of proportional hazards survival models, there is a key distinction between the two approaches. This distinction comes in the form of the specification of the baseline hazard function, $\lambda_0(t)$. While the baseline

hazard function is assumed to be constant and hence can be estimated via a single parameter using maximum likelihood estimation in the exponential survival model, estimation of β in the Cox model can be carried out with no assumptions regarding the baseline hazard function. Because of this, the Cox proportional hazards is termed a *semi-parametric*, as the baseline hazard may be infinitely dimensional yet the relative covariate effects are specified by a finite number of parameters (i.e., $\beta_1, \ldots, \beta_d$).

The desire to estimate the regression coefficient vector β in the Cox model without any assumptions on the baseline hazard function implies that estimation cannot be carried out via usual maximum likelihood. Instead, Cox[2] proposed and justified under the assumption of independence between censoring and failure times that estimation of β be carried out by maximizing the *partial likelihood*. Following Cox's construction of the partial likelihood, suppose that one and only one observation (with covariate $X_i = x_i$) fails at time $T_i = t_i$, then the partial likelihood contribution for observation i is given by the probability that an observation with covariate value $X = x_i$ fails at time $T = t_i$ given that some observation failed at time $T = t_i$. More specifically, letting $R_i \equiv \{j | t_j \leq t_i\}$ denote the *risk set* or set of all sampling units not censored or observed to fail by time t_i, the contribution of observation i to the partial likelihood is given by

$$
\begin{aligned}
\mathrm{PL}_i &= \Pr\{\text{observation with } x_i \text{ fails at } t_i \\
&\quad |\text{some observation failed at } t_i\} \\
&= \frac{\Pr\{\text{observation with } x_i \text{ fails at } t\}}{\Pr\{\text{some observation in } R_i \text{ failed at } t\}} \\
&= \frac{\lambda_i(t_i)(\Delta t)}{\sum_{j \in R_i} \lambda_j(t_i)(\Delta t)} \\
&= \frac{\lambda_0(t_i) \exp\{x_i^T \beta\}}{\sum_{j \in R_i} \lambda_0(t_i) \exp\{x_j^T \beta\}} \quad \text{(from (11))} \\
&= \frac{\exp\{x_i^T \beta\}}{\sum_{j \in R_i} \exp\{x_j^T \beta\}} \tag{12}
\end{aligned}
$$

Under this specification, only observations with observed failure times contribute terms to the partial likelihood. However, the partial likelihood still incorporates information from right-censored observations by considering the probability that any observation that is still at risk at time $T = t_i$ (whether eventually censored or not) fails at time $T = t_i$. Perhaps more importantly, it can be seen from the specification of PL_i that the partial likelihood does not depend upon the baseline hazard function, and hence there is no need to assume any parametric form for the baseline hazard function. Supposing no tied failure times, the partial likelihood is defined as

$$\mathrm{PL} = \prod_{i \in D} \mathrm{PL}_i, \tag{13}$$

where D denotes the set of indices of the failures. Although the partial likelihood does not correspond to a fully parametric likelihood, it has been shown that many of the asymptotic properties of traditional maximum likelihood methods including analogous asymptotic distributions of the Wald, score, and likelihood ratio test hold for partial maximum likelihood estimators.[2,6]

It should be noted that the above derivation of the partial likelihood assumed that no two observations were observed to have the same failure time. In the event of tied failure times, there are two ways to calculate the partial likelihood. As an illustration, suppose two observations, subjects 1 and 2, both have a recorded failure time of t. The *exact* partial likelihood[7,8] assumes that survival times are truly continuous in nature, and hence the probability of two subjects having the exact same survival time is zero. In this case, these two subjects have the same recorded survival time because the system of measurement used for recording time does not yield sufficient accuracy to distinguish between the times (e.g., death times may be measured in days as opposed to seconds). Without any knowledge of the true ordering of the survival times of the two subjects, it is necessary to take into account all possible ordering of the ties when calculating the denominator in (13). If one assumes that subject 2 failed before subject 1, then the risk set of subject 2 would include subject 1 while the risk set of subject 1 would not include subject 2. Similarly, if subject 1 failed before subject 2, then subject 1 would be included in the risk set of subject 2. Notationally, let D denote the set of indices of the *distinct* failure times, then the exact partial likelihood taking into account all possible orderings of tied failure times is given by

$$\mathrm{PL}_M = \prod_{i \in D} \left\{ \prod_{j \in F_i} e^{X_j^T \beta} \sum_{P \in Q_i} \prod_{r=1}^{d_i} \left[\sum_{l \in R(i,P,r)} e^{X_l^T \beta} \right]^{-1} \right\}, \quad (14)$$

where F_i denotes the set of failures at time t_i, d_i is the number of elements in F_i, Q_i is the set of $d_i!$ possible permutations of the corresponding observations in F_i, $P = (p_1, \ldots, p_{d_i})$ is an element of Q_i, and $R(i, P, r)$ is the risk set R_i excluding the elements $p_1, \ldots, p_{r-1}$.

An alternative approach to handling tied failure times in the partial likelihood is to assume that time is truly discrete (e.g., the number of visits prior to testing positive for a particular illness) so that there is no true ordering of any tied observations.[1] As before suppose two observations, subjects 1 and 2, both failed at time t. Under the *discrete* method, the partial likelihood contribution for this failure time is constructed as the probability that the two subjects both failed at time t given that two failures were observed at time t. Notationally, the partial likelihood assuming discrete ties is given by

$$\mathrm{PL}_D = \prod_{i \in D} \frac{\prod_{j \in F_i} e^{X_j^T \beta}}{\sum_{l \in R_{d_i}} \prod_{j \in l} e^{X_j^T \beta}}, \quad (15)$$

where R_{d_i} is the collection of all sets of d_i labels chosen from the risk set R_i without replacement, and l is an element of R_{d_i}.

Both the exact and discrete methods are computationally complex when maximizing the partial likelihood in the presence of many tied failure times. As such, approximations to the partial likelihood are often used. The first approximation due to Breslow[9] modifies the partial likelihood as follows:

$$\mathrm{PL}_B = \prod_{i \in D} \frac{\prod_{j \in F_i} e^{X_j^T \beta}}{\left[\sum_{l \in R_i} e^{X_l^T \beta} \right]^{d_i}}. \quad (16)$$

In the Breslow approximation, the denominator of the partial likelihood is inflated as it assumes that all tied observations are in the risk set without taking into account that one event may have occurred before another. Noting that the Breslow approximation can lead to bias in coefficient estimates when survival data contain many tied events, Efron proposed an alternative approximation[10] as follows:

$$\mathrm{PL}_E = \prod_{i \in D} \frac{\prod_{j \in F_i} e^{\eta_j}}{\prod_{j=1}^{d_i} \left[\sum_{l \in R_i} e^{\eta_l} - \sum_{l \in F_i} e^{\eta_l} (j-1)/d_i \right]}. \quad (17)$$

As can be seen, Efron's approximation uses an average of the risk of the tied failures when considering ties in the risk set. While still resulting in some bias when multiple ties are present, the Efron approximation tends to perform better than the Breslow approximation and is generally recommended when the exact or discrete partial likelihood cannot be computed due to computational constraints.

3. Smoothing Methods

To this point, the Cox proportional hazards model presented above assumed a parametric relationship between covariates and the response as defined in the linear predictor. In order to relax the parametric assumptions on these associations, smoothing may be utilized. However, before introducing smoothing in the context of a regression model, we first present a basic background on the most common types of smoothers that are utilized by analysts.

A smoother is a tool for summarizing the trend of a response measurement, Y, as a function of one or more predictors, $X \in \mathbb{R}^d$, where d denotes the number of predictors. The high flexibility of a smoother produces an estimate of the trend that is less variable than Y itself and hence must be weighed against potential increases in bias due to model overfitting. In the context of a linear smoother, we consider a continuous response modeled with a smooth function of covariates so that

$$Y = f(X^{(1)}, \ldots, X^{(d)}) + \epsilon, \quad (18)$$

where ϵ denotes a random error term such that $E[\epsilon] = 0$ and $var(\epsilon) = \sigma^2$ (the assumption of constant variance can be relaxed when we discuss weighted smoothers). Here $f(\cdot)$ denotes the smoothing function, and the goal is to estimate

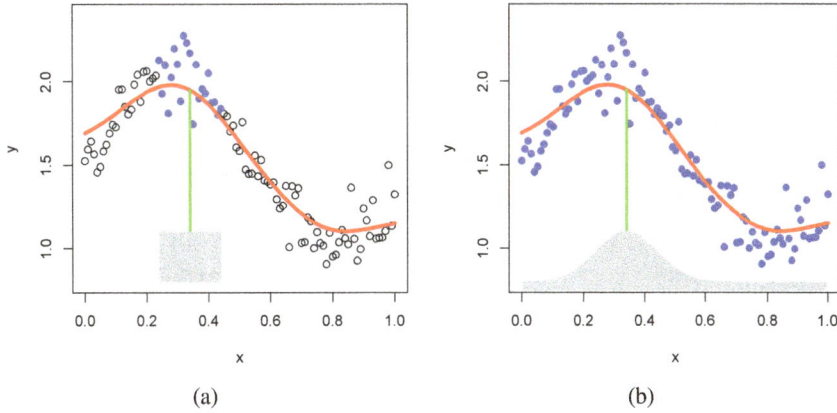

(b)

Fig. 1. (Color online) Kernel representation. (a) K-nearest neighbor smoother kernel; (b) Gaussian kernel. Black dots: observed data; Red line: estimated curve; Green line: vertical line indicating the target location; Blue dots: points used for local smoothing at the target location; Gray box: shape of weight function when estimating the smooth function at the target location.

$f(\cdot)$ based upon observed data $[(Y_1, X_1), \ldots, (Y_N, X_N)]$ where Y_i is the univariate response for observation i and X_i is the $d \times 1$ vector of observed covariates for observation i, $i = 1, \ldots, N$. An important property of the smoother is that it does not assume a rigid form for the smooth function.

In this section, we review two commonly employed choices of smoothing methods. Local-averaging smoothers and regression splines are the mostly commonly used techniques in the context of regression modeling and are implemented in most standard statistical software packages.

3.1. *Local-averaging smoother*

Perhaps, the most intuitive of all smoothing techniques, local-averaging smoothers use the weighted average of observations across the neighborhood of the prediction point as an estimate. For example, K-nearest-neighbor methods use the average value of the response within a specified neighborhood as an estimate, given by

$$\hat{f}(X_0) = \frac{1}{k} \sum_{X_i \in N_k(X_0)} Y_i, \qquad (19)$$

where the neighborhood $N_k(X_0)$ is defined by the k closest points to X_0 in the data. Thus, k is a smoothing parameter determine the amount of smoothing to be performed. The K-nearest neighbor estimator can be written as a weighted summation of the observations:

$$\hat{f}(X_0) = \sum_{i=1}^{N} K_k(X_0, X_i) Y_i, \qquad (20)$$

where the function

$$K_k(X_0, X) = \begin{cases} 1/k & \text{if} \quad X_i \in N_k(X_0) \\ 0 & \text{otherwise} \end{cases} \qquad (21)$$

assigns weights to each observation Y_i. The weight function is dependent on the target location X_0 and choice of smoothing

parameter, k. The left plot in Fig. 1 illustrates the effect of the weighting function when estimating the smoothed mean of the response at a particular location.

In later work, extensions of the kernel smoother[11,12] were suggested wherein the weights assigned to observations are based on a kernel function, $K_{h_\lambda}(X_0, X)$, of the form

$$K_{h_\lambda}(X_0, X) = D\left(\frac{||X - X_0||}{h_\lambda(X_0)}\right), \qquad (22)$$

where $X, X_0 \in \mathbb{R}^d$ are two vectors of covariates, and $|| \cdot ||$ defines the Euclidean distance between them. Here, $h_\lambda(X_0)$ is a *smoothing parameter* determining the kernel radius of the smoothing neighborhood and hence partly determining the level of resulting smoothing. Finally, the *kernel* function $D(\cdot)$ is a positive valued function, with values decreasing as the distance between X and X_0 increases. Popular choices of kernel functions include:

- The tri-cube kernel: $D(x) = (1 - |x|^3)^3$
- The Gaussian kernel: $D(x) = e^{\{-\frac{x^2}{2}\}}$.

After specification of $h_\lambda(X_0)$ and $D(\cdot)$, the smooth function at X_0 can be estimated using a kernel-weighted average given by

$$\hat{f}(X_0) = \frac{\sum_{i=1}^{N} K_{h_\lambda}(X_0, X_i) Y_i}{\sum_{i=1}^{N} K_{h_\lambda}(X_0, X_i)}.$$

The left plot in Fig. 1 illustrates the smoothing performed by a Gaussian kernel representation.

The kernel estimates described above can suffer from bias at the boundary and where observed locations are not evenly spaced. Therefore, instead of taking a weighted average of observations as kernel smoothers do, locally-weighted scatterplot smoothers (LOESS)[13] fit a weighted linear or polynomial regression model over the observations as an estimate. For any given point X_0, the smooth function can be estimated by a polynomial function of X_0, i.e.,

$$\hat{f}(X_0) = P^p_{\beta(X_0)}(X_0)$$
$$= \sum_{j_1+j_2+\cdots+j_d \leq p} \beta_{j_1 j_2 \cdots j_d}(X_0)(X_0^{(1)})^{j_1} \cdots (X_0^{(d)})^{j_d},$$

where $P^p_{\beta(X_0)}(X_0)$ is a p degree polynomial function of $X_0 = [X_0^{(1)}, \ldots, X_0^{(d)}]^T \in \mathbb{R}^d$ and $\beta(X_0)$ is a set of model coefficients $\beta(X_0) = \{\beta_{j_1 j_2 \cdots j_d}(X_0), j_1 + j_2 + \cdots + j_d \leq p\}$ to be estimated. The coefficients are obtained by solving a weighted least squares problem of the form

$$\min_{\beta(X_0)} \sum_{i=1}^{N} K_{h_\lambda}(X_0, X_i)(Y_i - P^p_{\beta(X_0)}(X_i)).$$

Building on previous work, the weights used in local regression can be assigned using the kernel function. Most commonly, the tri-cube weighting function is used to provide weights for LOESS method.

LOESS requires a choice of span, or window size, w for the weighting function. The span size w is the proportion of the total number of observations that are contained in each neighborhood. Suppose the sample size of the study is N, then for each point, LOESS will choose the $[wN]$ observed points with smallest Euclidean distance from the target point as the neighborhood. Then, the tri-cube weighting function for one observation X_0 will be

$$w(X_0) = \left(1 - \left(\frac{\|X - X_0\|}{h_w(X_0)}\right)^3\right)^3,$$

where $h_w(X_0)$ is the longest Euclidean distance among the distances from neighborhood points to X_0, and the choice of neighborhood points are related to the span size w. In the assignment of weights, observations with covariate value X_0 receive the highest weight, 1, and observation of the longest distance in the neighborhood receive the lowest weight, 0.

3.2. *Smoothing splines*

In contrast to the kernel smoothers discussed above, smoothing splines represent the smooth function as an element in the space spanned by a set of basis functions conditional on a collection of specified knots that partition the domain of the predictor space into disjoint intervals. If $b_i(X)$ is the ith basis function, then the smooth function $f(X)$ is assumed to have a representation given by

$$f(X) = \sum_{i=1}^{q} b_i(X)\beta_i. \tag{23}$$

$f(X)$ in Eq. (18) is specified as a linear model and can thus be estimated using least squares.

Suppose X in Eq. (18) is one-dimensional, with K inner knots $k_1 < k_2 < \cdots < k_K$, the domain of X can be separated into $K + 1$ intervals. A piecewise polynomial function $f(X)$ can be obtained by joining separate polynomial functions in all intervals together. For example, X ranges from 0 to 1, and two knots are put at $k_1 = 1/3$ and $k_2 = 2/3$. The top left plot in Fig. 2 shows a piecewise linear function fit. For piecewise linear polynomial, let $k_0 = 0$ and $k_3 = 1$, then 2 basis functions are used for $j = 0, 1, 2$: $b_{1j}(x) = I_{[k_j \leq x < k_{j+1}]}$ and $b_{2j}(x) = xI_{[k_j \leq x < k_{j+1}]}$, so six basis functions are used in total and six parameters are estimated in the model. To fit a piecewise cubic polynomial as shown in the bottom left plot in Fig. 2, two more basis function are needed for each $j = 0, 1, 2$: $b_{3j}(x) = x^2 I_{[k_j \leq x < k_{j+1}]}$ and $b_{4j}(x) = x^3 I_{[k_j \leq x < k_{j+1}]}$, resulting in 12 basis functions and parameters to be estimated.

The curve in the top right plot in Fig. 2 is fitted by incorporating continuity restrictions to piecewise linear polynomials. The continuity restrictions require $f(k_j^-) = f(k_j^+)$, $j = 1, 2$, which leads to two constraint conditions to piecewise linear polynomials, so there will be four free parameters in the model. Four basis functions can be used for fitting the continuous linear polynomial function: $b_1(x) = 1$; $b_2(x) = x$; $b_3(x) = (x - k_1)_+$ and $b_4(x) = (x - k_2)_+$, where r_+ denotes the positive part, i.e., $r_+ = r$ if $r > 0$, otherwise $r_+ = 0$.

An example of a cubic spline is shown in the bottom right plot of Fig. 2, which increases the order of continuity to 2 based on piecewise cubic polynomials. Not only is the fitted function continuous, but it is also smooth to the human eye as the first- and second-order derivatives of the cubic spline are continuous at the specified knot points. The basis functions for a cubic spline are:

- $b_1(x) = 1$; $b_2(x) = x$; $b_3(x) = x^2$; $b_4(x) = x^3$;
- $b_{j+4} = (x - k_j)_+$, for $j = 1, \ldots, K$,

with number of parameters of $K + 4 = 4 \times (K + 1) - 3 \times K$.

Cubic splines tend to behave erratically near the boundaries of the observed covariate support due to the nature of polynomial fit. To address this, the natural cubic spline adds two more constraints enforcing linearity at the boundaries, resulting in $K + 2$ basis functions[14]:

- $b_1(x) = 1$; $b_2(x) = x$;
- $b_{j+2}(x) = d_j(x) - d_{j-1}(x)$, for $j = 1, \ldots, K$, where

$$d_j(x) = \frac{(x - k_j)_+^3 - (x - k_{K+1})_+^3}{k_K - k_j}, \tag{24}$$

and k_0, k_{K+1} are boundary knots.

As an alternative to standard least squares estimation, coefficients for basis functions can be estimated based on a penalized least-squares criterion.[15] This approach is often preferred as it avoids the problem of knot selection by selecting a maximal set of knots, and the complexity of the fit is controlled by regularization.[18]

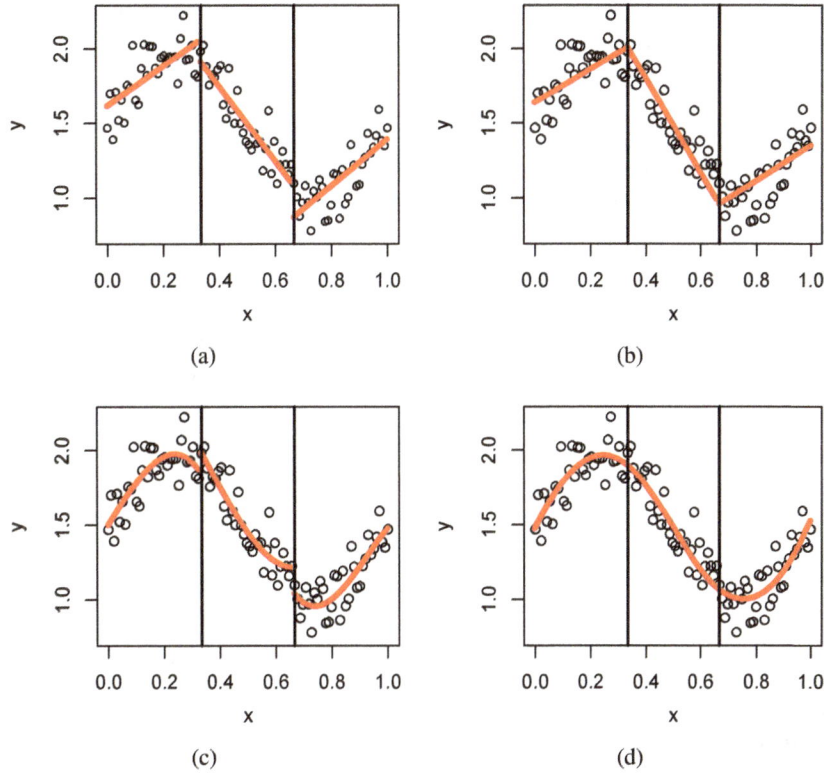

Fig. 2. (Color online) Examples of smooth function representations: (a) piecewise linear polynomial; (b) continuous linear polynomial; (c) piecewise cubic polynomial; (d) cubic splines (continuous second derivative). Black lines indicate positions of two knots. Red lines are estimated smooth functions.

Suppose one desires a smooth function is with respect to a univariate predictor. Then, the estimated smooth function is obtained by minimizing

$$\sum_{i=1}^{N} [y_i - f(x_i)]^2 + \lambda \int f''(x)^2 dx, \qquad (25)$$

where λ is a tuneable parameter that controls the penalty afforded to high volatility in $f(x)$, thereby balancing the conflicting goals of fitting the observed data well and producing a smooth estimate. It has been shown that[16] Eq. (25) can be written as

$$||Y - B\beta||^2 + \lambda\beta^T S\beta, \qquad (26)$$

where B is a design matrix containing specified basis functions, β is a vector of coefficients corresponding to the basis functions, and S is a positive definite penalty matrix. The solution to minimizing Eq. (26) is then given by

$$\hat{\beta} = (B^T B + \lambda S)^{-1} B^T Y. \qquad (27)$$

The estimate from this penalized least squares procedures hence shrinks the least square estimates towards the linear predictor,[14] and λ controls the extent of shrinkage.

4. Generalized Additive Models

To this point, we have assumed that the model includes only one univariate smoother. GAMs extend the previous approaches by allowing for multiple smoothers in a regression model to reflect the additive effects of covariates in different smooth terms. In this section, we introduce the general form of a GAM as well as the fitting algorithm used to implement the model.

4.1. *Model specification*

Assume the probability distribution of response Y belongs to the exponential family and hence Y has density function of the form

$$p_Y(y; \theta; \phi) = \exp\left\{\frac{y\theta - b(\theta)}{a(\phi)} + c(y, \phi)\right\}. \qquad (28)$$

In the above density, θ is termed the canonical or natural parameter, and ϕ generally represents a nuisance parameter that characterizes the dispersion of response Y. Denoting the expectation and variance of Y as μ and V, it is easily shown that μ are V are related to θ by $\mu = b'(\theta)$, and $V = b''(\theta)a(\phi)$.

Generalized linear models (GLMs)[19] relate μ to d covariates $X^{(1)}, \ldots, X^{(d)}$ by considering a mean model of the form

$$g(\mu) = \eta = \beta_0 + \beta_1 X^{(1)} + \cdots + \beta_d X^{(d)}, \qquad (29)$$

where η represents the linear predictor or systematic component of the model and $g(\cdot)$ is termed the link function, linking the mean response to the linear predictor. β_i, $i = 1, \ldots, d$ represents the coefficient associated with $X^{(i)}$, reflecting the relationship between the outcome and the corresponding covariate.

GAMs provide an extension of GLMs by replacing the parametric linear predictor with an additive predictor that incorporates non-parametric smoothing terms. In the absence of interaction effects among the covariates, the GAM assumes that

$$g(\mu) = \eta = \beta_0 + \sum_{j=0}^{d} s_j(X^{(j)}), \qquad (30)$$

where η is the additive predictor, and $s_j(\cdot)$ is a smooth term for covariate $X^{(j)}$, which can be estimated by any of the smoothing methods discussed in Sec. 3. In the trivial case, $s_j()$ can also be a linear function reducing the model to the usual GLM. For identifiability, we constrain the model so that $\sum_{i=1}^{N} s_j(X_i^{(j)}) = 0$ for each covariate $X^{(j)}, j = 1, \ldots, d$, with i representing the ith observation, $i = 1, \ldots, N$.

For ease of exposition, we will focus on the model specification provided in Eq. (30) to illustrate the fitting procedure for a GAM in the following sections. While this specification excludes potential interaction terms among the covariates, it should be noted that an interaction effect among two or more covariates can be included in a single smoothing term, thus maintaining the basic structure of the model. However, in practice, since the smooth term is to be nonparametrically estimated via a defined smoothing technique one must consider the increased variance that is likely to result when smoothing over multiple covariate interactions. Of course, the tolerance for variance inflation, and ultimate performance of the model, will depend upon the size of data used for model fitting, but in general it is commonly suggested that no more than three covariates should be included in a single smooth term.

4.2. *Backfitting algorithm to estimate the additive effects*

In this section, we illustrate the backfitting algorithm to simultaneously estimate multiple smoothing functions. Starting from the simplest case and omitting the observation index for clarity, we begin by assuming that response Y follows the Gaussian distribution (a member of the exponential family of distributions) and that the model utilizes the identity link function. Under this specification, the mean model is given by

$$E[Y] = \mu = \beta_0 + \sum_{j=0}^{d} s_j(X^{(j)}). \qquad (31)$$

For some s_j, $j = 1, \ldots, d$, if β_0 and $s_{j'}$ for $j' \neq j$ are all known, then s_j can be estimated by regressing the univariate *partial residual*, $R_j \equiv Y - \beta_0 - \sum_{j' \neq j} s_{j'}(X^{(j')})$, on the specified smoother for X_j. Motivated by this, the

backfitting procedure estimates $s_j, j = 1, \ldots, d$ with following steps:

(i) Initialize $\hat{\beta}_0 = E[Y] = \mu$ and $\hat{s}_1 = \cdots = \hat{s}_d = 0$;
(ii) for $j = 1, \ldots, d$:

(a) Calculate the partial residual:

$$R_j = Y - \hat{\beta}_0 - \sum_{j' \neq j} \hat{s}_{j'}(X^{(j')}); \qquad (32)$$

(b) Update $\hat{s}_j$ by regressing partial residual R_j on the smoother for X_j;
(c) Center the $\hat{s}_j$ obtained from last step at zero.
(d) For each observation, compute fitted value $\hat{Y}_i = \hat{\beta}_0 + \sum_{j=0}^{d} \hat{s}_j(X_i^{(j)})$, $i = 1, \ldots, N$.

(iii) Repeat (ii) until: The change in $\sum_{i=1}^{N} (Y_i - \hat{Y}_i)^2$ from the past iteration to the current iteration is less than a defined convergence criteria.

Breiman and Freidman[20] have shown that with the above backfitting algorithm, the prediction for $E[Y]$ is unique and is therefore the best additive approximation. For each smooth term, the uniqueness cannot be guaranteed for all classes of smoothers. However, it has been shown that uniqueness is guaranteed for two of the most commonly used smoothers in the context of GAMs: cubic spline and kernel smoothers as discussed in Sec. 3.

4.3. *Local scoring procedure*

By way of introduction, we first illustrated the backfitting algorithm for the case of a Gaussian distributed response with identity link function. We now consider the more general case of model (30) by assuming that the probability distribution of the response belongs to the exponential family with arbitrary link function. In this case, modeling fitting implements a *local scoring* procedure[4] that focuses on the local score function rather than the Fisher score function that is commonly used when estimating standard GLMs.

To motivate the local scoring procedure, let l denote the log-likelihood function based upon the response and covariates for observation i, $i = 1, \ldots, N$. For a GLM, estimation of η_i via Fisher scoring maximizes the log-likelihood function l. However, for a general response this procedure does not force the estimate of η_i to be smooth. For example, in the case of a logistic regression model for a binary outcome, Fisher scoring yields $\hat{\eta}_i = +\infty$ if $Y_i = 1$ and $\hat{\eta}_i = -\infty$ if $Y_i = 0$. To address this concern in the context of a GAM where smoothness of η_i is required, local scoring instead estimates η_i by maximizing the expected log-likelihood function fo the ith observation:

$$E(l(\hat{\eta}_i, Y)) = \max_{\eta_i} E(l(\eta_i, Y)), \qquad (33)$$

where the expectation is taken over the joint distribution of X and Y. Let η denote the additive predictor for one observation, then under standard regularity conditions (namely the ability to interchange integration and differentiation), we obtain

$$E[dl/d\eta]_{\hat{\eta}} = 0. \tag{34}$$

While there is no general closed-form solution to (34), a first-order Taylor series expansion leads to an iterative estimating procedure given by

$$\eta^{\text{new}} = \eta^{\text{old}} - E[dl/d\eta]_{\eta^{\text{old}}}/E[d^2l/d\eta^2]_{\eta^{\text{old}}}, \tag{35}$$

which is equivalent to

$$\eta^{\text{new}} = E\left[\eta - \frac{dl/d\eta}{E[d^2l/d\eta^2]}\right]_{\eta^{\text{old}}}. \tag{36}$$

When the distribution of the response belongs to the exponential family, the first and second derivatives of the expected log-likelihood are given by

$$\frac{dl}{d\eta} = (Y - \mu)V^{-1}\left(\frac{d\mu}{d\eta}\right), \tag{37}$$

and

$$\frac{d^2l}{d\eta^2} = (Y - \mu)V^{-1}\left(\frac{d}{d\eta}\right)\left[V^{-1}\left(\frac{d\mu}{d\eta}\right)\right] - \left(\frac{d\mu}{d\eta}\right)^2 V^{-1}. \tag{38}$$

Then, taking the expectation (conditional on X) of Eq. (38), we obtain

$$E\left[\left(\frac{d^2l}{d\eta^2}\right)\bigg|X\right] = -\left(\frac{d\mu}{d\eta}\right)^2 V^{-1}. \tag{39}$$

Hence, η is updated by

$$\eta^{\text{new}} = E\left[\eta + (Y - \mu)\left(\frac{d\eta}{d\mu}\right)\right]\bigg|_{\eta^{\text{old}},\mu^{\text{old}}}. \tag{40}$$

Further, letting Y_w^{old} denote the working response computed in terms of η^{old} and μ^{old} and given by

$$Y_w^{\text{old}} = \eta + (Y - \mu)\left(\frac{d\eta}{d\mu}\right)\bigg|_{\eta^{\text{old}},\mu^{\text{old}}}, \tag{41}$$

we obtain from Eqs. (30), (40) and (41),

$$E[Y_w^{\text{old}}] = \beta_0^{\text{new}} + \sum_{j=1}^{d} s_j^{\text{new}}. \tag{42}$$

As such, the coefficient vector β_0^{new} and s_j^{new} must be estimated in order to obtain an updated value of η^{new} in Eq. (40). This is achieved via the backfitting algorithm shown in Sec. 4.2. Specifically, we begin by defining W as

$$W = (d\mu/d\eta)^2 V^{-1}|_{\eta^{\text{old}},\mu^{\text{old}}} \tag{43}$$

and initializing $s = 0$. The backfitting procedure is used to iteratively update each smooth term by regressing the partial residual on the smoother for X_j with weight W defined in Eq. (43) until a specified convergence criteria is met.

Putting the above together, the overall algorithm for fitting a GAM is as follows:

(i) Initialize $\beta_0 = E[Y]$ and $s_j = 0, j = 1, \dots, d$.
(ii) Loop:

    (a) Based on the current estimates of β_0 and $s_j, j = 1, \dots, d$, calculate η^{old} as well as the working response Y_w^{old} and corresponding weights W using Eq. (30), Eqs. (41) and (43), respectively.

    (b) Update β_0 and $s_j, j = 1, \dots, d$ via the backfitting algorithm.

(iii) Repeat 1 and 2 until convergence.

While the backfitting algorithm is a relatively efficient method to estimate additive effects, convergence can be slow if the covariates included in the linear predictor are correlated.[21] To eliminate most of the problems associated with slow fitting due to multicollinearity when more than one smooth term is included in the linear predictor, it is beneficial for all of the linear terms in the model to be fitted together, treating them as a single term in the iterative procedure above. Moreover, it can be additionally beneficial to decompose each smooth term into a parametric (linear) and nonparametric (smooth) component such that

$$s_j(X^{(j)}) = \beta_j X_j + s_j'(X^{(j)}), \tag{44}$$

where $s_j'(X_j)$ represents the nonparametric component, and the linear coefficient β_j is fitted together with the remaining parametric linear terms in the model.

4.4. *Standard errors and degrees of freedom*

If no smooth terms are included in the specification of a GAM, the model reduces to a standard GLM where the covariance matrix for the estimated model parameters (obtained via maximum likelihood) is given by the inverse of the Fisher information matrix. However, when smooth terms are present in the GAM, variance estimation requires computation of the *operation matrix* G_j for each smooth term s_j, such that $s_j = G_j z$, where z is the working response from the last iteration of the fitting algorithm described above and is asymptotically distributed as a Gaussian random variable. From this, the covariance matrix for the estimated s_j is given by $G_j \text{Cov}(z)G_j^T$, which can be estimated by $\hat{\phi}G_j W^{-1}G_j^T$, where W is a diagonal matrix with elements defined by the weights used in the last iteration of the fitting algorithm.

The operation matrix, G_j, tends to be computationally expensive to obtain for nonparametric or semi-parametric smoothing procedures, and hence approximations are often used when estimating $G_j Cov(z)G_j^T$. One approach is to approximate $\hat{\phi}G_j W^{-1}G_j^T$ by $\hat{\phi}G_j W^{-1}$, which is generally conservative for nonprojection smoothers.[21] In this case, G_j can be orthogonally decomposed into $G_j = H_j + N_j$, where H_j

can be obtained as the design matrix corresponding to the parametric portion of Eq. (44), and N_j corresponds to the nonparametric portion. Thus, the variance of the estimated smooth term can be approximated via a decomposition of two variance components: (1) the variance from the parametric portion of Eq. (44) which captures the correlation of all parametric terms that are fitted together, and (2) the variance from the nonparametric portion of Eq. (44) reflecting the marginal information obtained in the smoothing terms.

The degrees of freedom df_j of each smoother can be approximated by $tr(G_j) - 1$, and the degrees of freedom of the model can be obtained by summation[21] of $df_j, j = 1, \ldots, d$.

5. Cox Proportional Hazards Additive Models

In this section, we consider the use of GAM methods as discussed in Sec. 4 to the analysis right-censored survival data that were introduced in Sec. 2. Let t denote survival time and X be a $d \times 1$ vector of d adjustment covariates. The Cox proportional hazards additive model to analyze the nonlinear effect of covariates incorporates smoothers into the Cox proportional hazards model as

$$\lambda(t) = \lambda_0(t) \exp\{\eta\} \tag{45}$$

with

$$\eta = \sum_{j=0}^{d} f_j(X^{(j)}), \tag{46}$$

where $\lambda(t)$ represents the hazard at time t and $\lambda_0(t)$ represents the baseline hazard function. $f_j(X^{(j)})$ represents the effect of covariate X^j on the hazard, which is a nonlinear function of X_j. We separate $f_j(X^{(j)})$ into two parts (for further details see Sec. 4.1):

$$f_j(X_j) = \beta_j X^{(j)} + s_j(X^{(j)}), \tag{47}$$

where the parametric part, $\beta_j X^{(j)}$, will be estimated jointly with the parametric terms corresponding to other adjusted variables included in the model, and the nonparametric part, $s_j(X^{(j)})$, will be estimated using a smoother. To ensure identifiability, we constrain the model so that the summation of the nonparametric part over all observations is 0. Let $\beta = [\beta_1, \ldots, \beta_d]^T$ denote the vector of coefficients reflecting the first-order relationship between the hazard and the corresponding covariates. Then, the model becomes

$$\eta = X\beta + \sum_{j=1}^{d} s_j(X^{(j)}). \tag{48}$$

Let t_i, δ_i, X_i denote the observed time, censoring status, and covariates for subject i. With $\eta_i = X_i^T \beta + \sum_{j=1}^{d} s_j(X_i^j)$, the partial likelihood is

$$PL = \prod_{i \in D} \frac{e^{\eta_i}}{\sum_{j \in R_i} e^{\eta_i}}, \tag{49}$$

where D is the set of indices of observed events and $R_i = \{j : t_j \geq t_i\}$ denotes the risk set just prior to time t_i. In the event of tied failure times, the partial likelihood can be approximated using methods introduced in Sec. 2.

Let l denote the log partial likelihood function for the data. To estimate the parameters of the model, we seek to maximize the expected local log-likelihood function:

$$\hat{\eta}_i = \max_{\eta_i} E(l(\eta(X_i, s_i), t_i, \delta_i)), \tag{50}$$

where η_i can be obtained by an iteration procedure given by

$$\eta_i^{\text{new}} = E\left[\eta - \frac{dl/d\eta}{E[d^2l/d\eta^2]}\right]_{\eta_i^{\text{old}}}. \tag{51}$$

The first and second derivatives of the log partial likelihood are computed as

$$\frac{dl}{d\eta_i} = \delta_i - \sum_{j \in C_i} \frac{e^{\eta_i}}{\sum_{k \in R_j} e^{\eta_k}}, \tag{52}$$

and

$$\frac{d^2l}{d\eta_i^2} = -\sum_{j \in C_i} \frac{e^{\eta_i}}{\sum_{k \in R_j} e^{\eta_k}} + \sum_{j \in C_i} \frac{e^{2\eta_i}}{\left(\sum_{k \in R_j} e^{\eta_k}\right)^2}, \tag{53}$$

where $C_i = j : i \in R_j$ is the sets of subjects whose risk sets contain i.

The Cox model is a semi-parametric model without any specification for the distribution of the survival times, so it is not possible to calculate a close form for the expectation of the second derivatives of the log partial likelihood as required in Eq. (51). As such, before updating η, a GAM model can be fitted using the second derivatives as responses to estimate the expectation of the second derivatives of log partial likelihood. To this end, by Eq. (51), with an estimate η^{old}, the new estimate for η can be obtained using the following two steps:

(i) Estimate $E[d^2l/d\eta^2]$ by fitting a GAM using $d^2l/d\eta^2$ as responses, including the linear predictor of X and specified smoothing term(s).
(ii) Estimate η^{new} using the backfitting algorithm described in Sec. 4.2 with $-1/\hat{E}[d^2l/d\eta^2]$ as weights and $\eta^{\text{old}} - [dl/d\eta]_{\eta^{\text{old}}}/\hat{E}[d^2l/d\eta^2]$ as responses.

6. Application Example

Recall the California Ovarian cancer study introduced in Sec. 1. In this section, we consider the use of the Cox proportional hazards additive model for estimating the adjusted spatial effect on survival hazard. In this study, $N = 11,765$ patients are distributed on the California map with location coordinates u and v. The function $\lambda(t)$ is modeled by Eq. (45) with

$$\eta = X\beta + \beta_u u + \beta_v v + s(u, v), \tag{54}$$

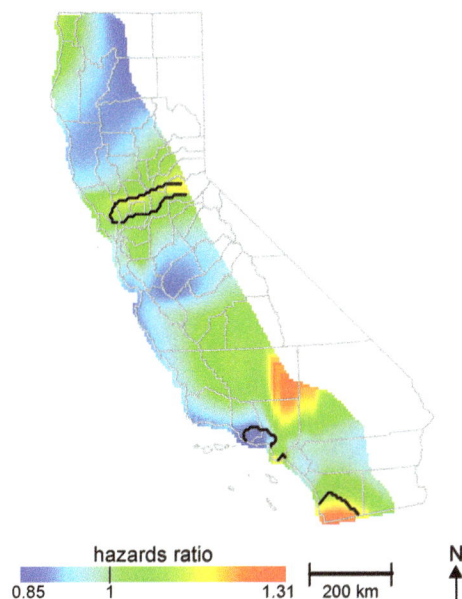

Fig. 3. Heatmap of the hazards ratio compared to the median hazard for California Ovarian cancer patients. Areas circled by black lines have significantly hazard compared to the median hazard across the state.

where X is the design matrix with columns containing the adjustment covariates, and β is a vector of coefficients reflecting the impact of the corresponding covariates. $\beta_u u + \beta_v v + s(u, v)$ is the adjusted spatial effect on survival, where the parametric portion $\beta_u u + \beta_v v$ reflects the first-order spatial effect and is fitted jointly along with the other adjustment variables, X_i. The nonparametric portion is fitted using a bivariate LOESS smoother as discussed in Sec. 3.1.

We generate a prediction grid for the state of California excluding areas with sparse population density and estimate spatial effects of each grid point on the relative risk of death. 95% confidence interval bands, relying on asymptotic normality of the estimated log-hazard ratio and standard error obtained from the GAM fit, are calculated for each point. A heatmap of the hazard ratios comparing the hazard of each location to the median hazard across the state displayed in Fig. 3, where areas with confidence intervals excluding 1 are circled. Areas around Sacramento and San Diego circled by black lines have significantly higher hazard compared to the median hazard, and the hazard is significantly lower in circled areas around Los Angeles.

7. Discussion

Cox's proportional hazards model is a useful tool for evaluating the impact of explanatory variables on survival times for right-censored survival data. By incorporating additive modeling techniques into the Cox model, the proportional

hazards additive model provides greater flexibility for exploring the nonlinear relationship of covariates on the risk of event without *a priori* knowledge of the nonlinear pattern. If all the smoothing functions in the additive model are represented by basis functions, then the additive predictor can be written as a linear combination of basis functions. In this case, the additive model are recast as a parametric penalized GLM or Cox model, and can be evaluated using all properties of the framework of GLMs or Cox regression.[18]

References

[1] D. Cox, Regression models and life-tables, *J. R. Stat. Soc. B (Methodol.)* **34**, 187 (1972).

[2] D. Cox, Partial likelihood, *Biometrika* **62**, 269 (1975).

[3] R. E. Bristow, J. Chang, A. Ziogas, H. Anton-Culver and V. M. Vieira, Spatial analysis of adherence to treatment guidelines for advanced-stage ovarian cancer and the impact of race and socioeconomic status, *Gynecol. Oncol.* **134**, 60 (2014).

[4] T. Hastie and R. Tibshirani, Generalized additive model, *Stat. Sci.* **1**, 297 (1986).

[5] T. Hastie and R. Tibshirani, *Generalized Additive Models* (Chapman and Hall, New York, 1990).

[6] P. Andersen and R. Gill, Cox's regression model for counting process: A large sample study, *Ann. Stat.* **10**, 1100 (1982).

[7] R. Peto, Contribution to the discussion of 'regression modes and life-tables' by dr cox, *J. R. Stat. Soc. B* **34**, 205 (1972).

[8] J. Kalbeisch and R. Prentice, Marginal likelihoods based on cox's regression and life model, *Biometrika* **60**, 267 (1973).

[9] N. Breslow, Covariance analysis of censored survival data, *Biometrics* **30**, 89 (1974).

[10] B. Efron, The efficiency of cox's likelihood function for censored data, *J. Am. Stat. Assoc.* **72**, 557 (1977).

[11] E. A. Nadaraya, On estimating regression, *Theor. Prob. Appl.* **9**, 141 (1964).

[12] M. B. Priestley and M. T. Chao, Non-parametric function fitting, *J. R. Stat. Soc. B* **34**, 385 (1972).

[13] W. S. Cleveland, Robust locally weighted regression and smoothing scatterplots, *J. Am. Stat. Assoc.* **74**, 829 (1979).

[14] T. Hastie, R. Tibshirani and J. Friedman, *The Elements of Statistical Learning*, 2nd edn. Springer Series in Statistics (2001).

[15] C. Rreinsch, Smoothing by spline functions, *Numer. Mathe.* **10**, 177 (1967).

[16] P. Lancaster and K. Salkauskas, *Curve and Surface Fitting.* (Elsevier Science and Technology Books, 1986).

[17] C, De Boor, *A Practical Guide to Splines* (Springer-Verlag, 1978).

[18] S. N. Wood, *Generalized Additive Models* (Chapman and Hall: London, 2006).

[19] J. Nelder and R. Wedderburn, Generalized linear models, *J. R. Stat. Soc. A (General)* **135**, 370 (1972).

[20] L. Breiman and J. Freidman, Estimating optimal transformations for multiple regression and correlation, *J. Ame. Stat. Assoc.* **80**, 580 (1985).

[21] J. M. Chambers and T. J. Hastie, *Statistical Models in S* (Chapman and Hall/CRC, 1992), pp. 300–304.

Deep learning

Xing Hao[*,‡] and Guigang Zhang[†]

University of California, Irvine, Irvine, California, USA
†Institute of Automation, Chinese Academy of Sciences
Beijing, P. R. China
‡xingh2@uci.edu

Artificial intelligence is one of the most beautiful dreams of mankind. Although computer technology has made considerable progress, so far, there is no computer showing intelligence like human beings. The emergence of deep learning gives people a glimmer of hope. So, what is learning deep? Why is it so important? How does it work? And what are the existing achievements and difficulties? This paper provides an overview of deep learning which will answer these questions.

Keywords: Deep learning; neural networks; training.

1. Introduction

Artificial Intelligence (AI) is one of the most beautiful dreams of mankind. In Turing's 1950 paper, he proposed the idea of Turing test, that a human being should be unable to distinguish the machine from another human being by using the replies to questions put to both. This no doubt presented a high expectation for AI. But after the development for the past half century, AI is still far from this expectation.

However, since 2006, the field of machine learning has achieved breakthrough progress. The Turing test is no longer unattainable. And it not only depends on the parallel processing ability of the cloud computing of big data, but also depends on a new technique, deep learning.

Before we dive into deep learning, let us look back the history of AI and how deep learning appears. Early AI can solve very complex mathematical problems that can be described by a list of formal, mathematical rules like playing chess, but the real challenge is to solve problems which humans can solve intuitively, such as image or speech recognition.

To solve these more intuitive problems, only logical reasoning is not enough. Scientists started to believe that we must try to make the machine learn knowledge. Machine learning is to design and analyze algorithms which can let the computer automatically learn knowledge. Machine learning algorithms automatically analyze and extract the patterns obtained from data, and use patterns of data to make predictions.

From the perspective of the hierarchical model, the development of machine learning has gone through two major steps since the late 1980s: shallow learning and deep learning.

In the late 1980's, the invention of Back Propagation (BP) algorithm for artificial neural network set off a wave of machine learning based on statistical models. It was found that the use of BP algorithm allows an artificial neural network model to learn patterns from a lot of training data, and make predictions based on those patterns. This method beats previous systems in many ways. In 1990's, a variety of shallow machine learning models have been proposed. These models showed great success in both theoretical analysis and applications.

Although machine learning has been developed for decades, there are still a lot of problems which have not been solved well such as image recognition, speech recognition, natural language understanding, weather prediction, gene expression, content recommendation, and so on.

To make a better prediction, we need to extract features of data correctly. So the accuracy of the feature extracting has played a very critical role in machine learning. However, this was generally done manually at that time. However, manual selection of features is a very laborious, heuristic method, and it requires a lot of time. Since manual selection of features is not very good, can we automatically learn features of data? The answer is yes, and the solution is deep learning.

In 2006, an paper by Geoffrey Hinton[1] opened the gate of deep learning in academia and industry. There are two main messages in the paper: an artificial neural network with more hidden layers has better learning ability; the difficulty in training Deep Neural Networks (DNNs) can be overcome by layer-wise pre-training.

Since then, the research of deep learning has continued to heat up. Today, Google, Microsoft, and other well-known high-tech companies with large data are eager to put resources to deep learning study, because they believe that more complex and powerful models can reveal the wealth of information with the huge amounts of data, and make accurate predictions for future or unknown events.

Different from shallow machine learning, deep learning uses a cascade of layers of nonlinear processing units for feature extraction and transformation. It allows computers to learn from a hierarchical representation of the data where higher level features are derived from lower level features.

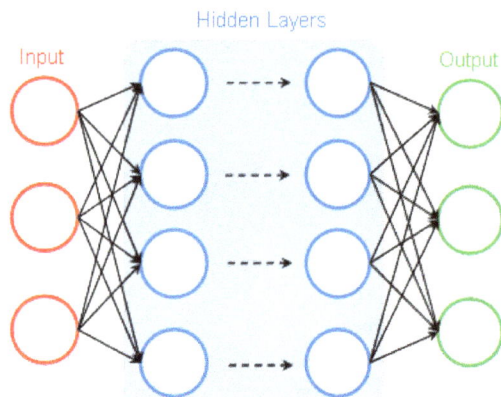

Fig. 1. A simple example of deep neural network.

Figure 1 gives a simple example of deep neural network, in which the inputs of deep learning algorithms are transformed through several hidden layers and the outputs are derived from the computation of the hidden layers.

In the rest of this paper, we will review the work related to deep learning. As the first step, we will talk about the architectures in Sec. 2 and the training algorithms in Sec. 3. Following them, we will talk about the possible applications of deep learning in Sec. 4, which is then followed by a discussion of the most popular deep learning frameworks in Sec. 5, the existing difficulties of deep learning study in Sec. 6, and the future of deep learning in Sec. 7.

2. Deep Learning Architectures

The research of deep learning attempts to model large-scale data by multiple processing layers with complex structures. Thus, unlike the architectures of shallow machine learning, deep learning architectures are composed of multiple non-linear transformations.

Among all the deep learning architectures, Convolutional Neural Networks (CNNs), Recurrent Neural Network (RNN), and Deep Belief Networks (DBF) are the highlights of the history of deep learning.

Besides CNN, RNN, and DBN, other deep learning architectures include: Deep Stacking Networks (DSN)[2] which is mainly used for classification and regression of images and language[3,4]; Deep coding network (DPCN),[5,6] a predictive coding scheme which predicts the representation of the layer by using a top-down approach; and so on.

2.1. Convolutional neural network

CNN is a type of feed-forward artificial neural network which uses convolution in at least one of their layers. It was inspired by biological neural networks. CNN combines artificial neural networks and discrete convolution for image processing which can be used to automatically extract features. Thus, it is particularly designed for recognizing two-dimensional data, such

as images and videos. Images can be directly used as the input of the network, which avoids the complex feature extraction and data reconstruction process in traditional image recognition algorithms.

In 1980, Kunihiko Fukushima proposed a neural network model for a mechanism of visual pattern recognition — "neocognitron",[7] which is the predecessor of CNN. In 1990s, LeCun et al.[8] established the modern CNN structure. They designed a multi-layer artificial neural network, named LeNet-5, which can be used to classify handwritten numbers.

After that, researchers tried different ways[8–14] to train multi-layer neural networks, and applied them to various scenarios. CNN can effectively extract the features of an image, which makes CNN can recognize images with very few preprocessing steps. However, while the breadth and depth of a network increases, the performance of CNN algorithms was limited by computing resources.

After 2006, efficient GPUs became generalized computing devices, which made training larger networks possible. Thus, several models[15–17] have been proposed to train deep CNNs more efficiently. Among them, the most famous one is AlexNet[18] proposed by Krizhevsky et al. which achieved a major breakthrough in the image recognition task.

Today, CNN is used in many areas including image and video understanding.[18–22]

CNNs are modeled as collections of neuron units which are connected in an acyclic graph. Figure 2 shows an example of a CNN with two hidden layers. Each layer of this network takes the outputs of the previous layer as the inputs. Therefore, cycles are not allowed in the CNN architecture. Typically, the neuron units between adjacent two layers are fully-connected, but neurons within the same layer share no connection.

Take image recognition as an example, where CNN arranges its neurons in three dimensions (width, height, depth). The input of CNN is an image, so its width and height are the dimensions of the image, and the depth is 3 (Red, Green, Blue channels). The output of the CNN is a single vector of class scores, arranged along the depth dimension. Between input and output, three main types of layers are used

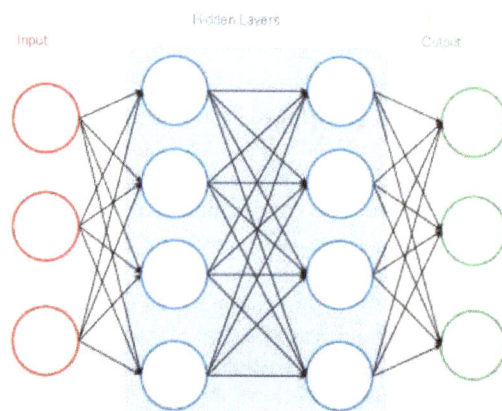

Fig. 2. CNN.

to build CNN architectures including the convolutional layer, the pooling layer, and the fully-connected layer. And there is also a loss function (e.g., SVM/Softmax) in the last layer. Sometimes, other types of layer are used to improve the performance of CNN such as drop out layer which is used to control the size of CNN.

To extract the right patterns from data, we need to train a network. The training process is to update the weights in a network to minimize the error generated from the network. We will introduce some training algorithms in Sec. 3.

A direction for the development of CNN is that there are more and more layers. ResNet,[23] which is the champion of ILSVRC 2015, has 152 layers, which is 20 times more than AlexNet.[18] By increasing the depth, the network can extract better features. However, doing so also increases the overall complexity of the network, so the network becomes more difficult to optimize, and easy to over fitting.

2.2. *Recurrent neural network*

RNNs aim to process sequential data. In the traditional feed forward neural network model, like CNNs, data flows from the input layer to the hidden layer and then the output layer. There is no connection between neurons in the same layer. Some problems cannot be fully handled by this kind of neural network. This architecture cannot solve the problem where the input data have relationships with each other. For example, we need the previous word in a sentence to predict the next one, because the words in the same sentence are not independent.

In RNNs, the current output and previous output are relevant. To be more specific, the output of the previous step is stored and used to calculate the current output, that is, the input of the network contains both the data from the input layer and the output of the hidden layers from the previous step. This makes them applicable to tasks such as handwriting recognition[24] and speech recognition.[25,26] The architecture of RNN is shown in Fig. 3.

In Fig. 3, except the data flow from the input x to the hidden layer s and from the hidden layer s to the output y, which is the same in CNN, there is also data transferring among neurons in the same hidden layer. A RNN can be unfolded into an acyclic neural network, as shown in Fig. 3. For example, a RNN of a five-word sentence can be unfolded to a five-layer neural network with each layer representing a word.

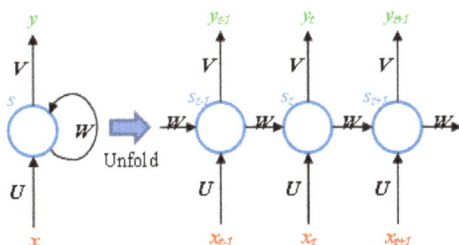

Fig. 3. RNN.

In Fig. 3, t represents the number of steps. For example, x_1 and y_1 is the input and output of step 1, where x_1 might be the first word in one sentence, and y_1 is the predicted next word. s_t, which is the state of step t, can be calculated using the input of step t x_t and the state of the hidden layer in previous step s_{t-1} by the formula:

$$s_t = f(U^*x_t + W^*s_{t-1}), \qquad (1)$$

where f is normally nonlinear activation function. s_t can also be viewed as the memory units in hidden layers which can be used to store the information from the previous steps.

In CNN, the parameters of different layers are different. However, in RNN, each layer shares the parameters U, V, and W. That means each step in RNN is doing the same thing, just with different inputs. This greatly reduces the requirement to learn the parameters of the network.

Over the years, researchers have proposed many sophisticated RNNs to deal with the shortcomings of the regular RNN model including Simple RNNs,[27] Deep Bidirectional RNNs,[28] Echo State Networks,[29] Long short-term memory (LSTM),[25] and so on.

In 2012, Google Voice transcription is first used in Android speech recognition. The using of RNN, especially the LSTM, rapidly improved the performance. Compared with RNN, LSTM has additional recurrent connections and memory unit, which can remember the data they have processed.

There are some differences between RNN and CNN. First, the parameter W, U, V are shared for an unfolded RNN. Second, the output of each step depends on not only the current input, but also a number of previous steps of the network. So people use another algorithm to train RNN which is called Backpropagation Through Time (BPTT). We will introduce this algorithm in Sec. 3.

2.3. *Deep belief network*

As the complexity of learning process increase, deep learning will need more time on training. In this case, we usually can not achieve acceptable results. One solution for this problem is DBN. DBNs was proposed by Geoffrey Hinton in 2006.[1] It not only can be used to recognize and classify data, but also can generate data.

DBN consists of multi-layers of neurons. These neurons are divided into hidden units and visible units. Visible units are used to receive data, while hidden units are used to extract features, so they are also called feature detectors. A DBN is composed of multiple layers of Restricted Boltzmann Machines (RBM). The training of the DBN is processed layer by layer. In each layer, the input data is used to calculate the hidden units, and then the hidden units are given to the next layer as the input data. Figure 4 shows an example of DBN and restricted Boltzmann machine.

Different with CNN, to obtain generative weights, the initial pre-training of DBN occurs in an unsupervised greedy

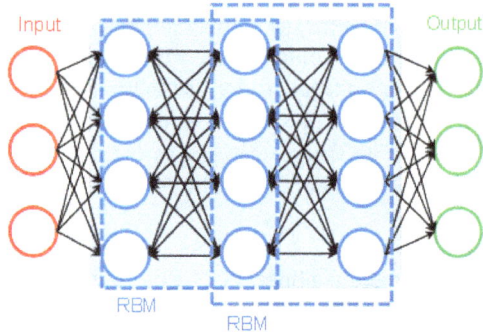

Fig. 4. DBNs.

layer-by-layer manner. The training process of DBN includes two main steps:

Step 1. Pre-train: Train RBM separately in an unsupervised way. Ensure that when feature vectors are mapped to a different space, information is preserved as much as possible. We will introduce this algorithm later in Sec. 3;

Step 2. Fine-Tuning: Using the error from the output layer to update the weights in DBN. This process is supervised training similar to training CNN.

Compared to traditional neural networks, DBN can be trained layer by layer. This significantly reduces the resource needed to train the network.

3. Training Algorithms

As mentioned in Sec. 2, we need to train or teach a deep learning model before we can use it to do classification or prediction. Training of a machine learning model can be summarized to several categories, including supervised learning, unsupervised learning, semi-supervised learning, and reinforcement learning.

In this section, we will discuss the first two categories which are widely used in training deep models.

3.1. *Supervised learning*

A supervised learning algorithm analyzes the training data and produces an inferred function, which can be used for mapping new examples. In supervised learning, each training data is a pair consisting of an input object and a desired output value. That means we must have told the network the answer to our question at some point.

Supervised learning is normally used to do data classification and prediction.

3.1.1. *Backpropagation*

The BP algorithm is used in many machine learning scenarios to train learning models. It was originally introduced in the

1970's, but its importance was not fully noticed until David Rumelhart's work in 1986.[30] They described several neural networks where BP works far faster than earlier approaches. Today, the BP algorithm is the most widely used algorithm of unsupervised learning for neural networks.

As we mentioned in Sec. 2, the output of a neural network can be considered as a function of input and parameters or weights:

$$\text{Output} = f(\text{input}, \text{parameters}). \qquad (2)$$

Using this function, we can compute the error of the network ε, which is the difference between the output of the network and the label of the input. So the error can also be represented by a function of the input and parameters of the network. To reduce the error, we can use the partial derivation of ε respect to *parameters* w to update w:

$$w - c * \partial\varepsilon/\partial w \rightarrow w, \qquad (3)$$

where c is the size of the update step, which will determine how many steps we need before reaching the minimum of the function.

The BP algorithm is shown in Table 1.

3.1.2. *Backpropagation through time*

Backpropagation Through Time (BPTT) is a supervised learning algorithm to train RNN. It is similar to the BP algorithm, except that the weights U, V, and W in RNN are shared by each step as shown in Fig. 3.

BPTT begins by unfolding a RNN through time as shown in Fig. 3. When the network is unfolded through time, the network has been unfolded to a depth of $k = 3$. Training then proceeds in a manner similar to training a feed-forward neural network with BP, except that we need to sum up the contributions of each time step to the gradient.

So the BPTT algorithm can be written as Table 2.

3.2. *Unsupervised learning*

In unsupervised learning, we give our algorithms a large amounts of unlabeled data to learn a good feature representation of the input.

Unsupervised learning is often used to do data clustering and encoding.

Table 1. Backpropagation algorithm.

Backpropagation
Initial random weights
Do until stopping criteria is met:
For each input (x, y):
Do a feed-forward pass to compute activations at all hidden layers, then at the output layer obtain an output y'
Measure the deviation of y' from the target y
Backpropagate the error through the net and perform weight updates

Table 2. BPTT algorithm.

Backpropagation Through Time
Initial random weights
Unfold the network
Do until stopping criteria is met:
x = the zero-magnitude vector
for t from 0 to $n-1$:
Set the network inputs to x, $a[t]$, $a[t+1]$,...
Do a feed-forward pass to compute activations at all hidden layers, then at the output layer obtain an output y'
Measure the deviation of y' from the target y
Backpropagate the error through the net and perform weight updates
Average the weights in each step, so that the parameter is identical
$x = f(x)$

3.2.1. *Autoencoder*

Autoencode[31] is one of the most widely used unsupervised learning algorithms for deep neural networks. Autoencoder is simply a compression encoder, which is to transform things by changing the input to an output which is the same as the input. That is to find a function that enables the *function (input) = input*, which is called the identity function. Figure 5 shows the schematic structure of autoencoder.

The network does not learn the function between the input object and output value, but instead it learns its own internal data structure and characteristics (and therefore, the hidden layer becomes a feature detector). Usually, the number of hidden units is less than the number of input/output layer, forcing a network to learn only the most important features and achieve dimensional reduction.

We want to learn some small nodes in the medium-scale conceptual level data to produce a compressed representation, which somehow captures the core features of the input.

The training algorithm for an autoencoder is summarized in Table 3.

3.2.2. *Training restricted boltzmann machine*

Actually, when RBM is unfolded, it is similar to autoencoder, as shown in Fig. 6. The training of RBM is also similar to

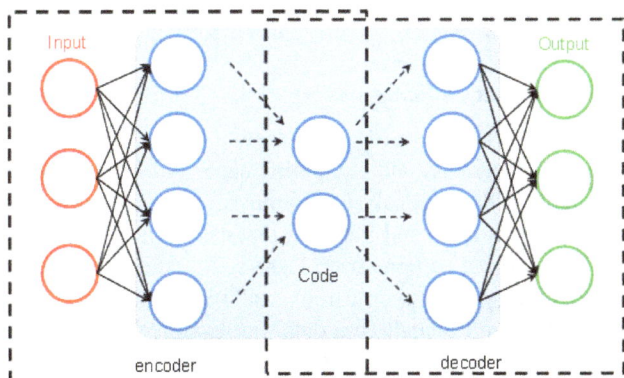

Fig. 5. Schematic structure of autoencoder.

Table 3. Autoencoder.

Autoencoder
Initial random weights
Do until stopping criteria is met:
For each input x:
Do a feed-forward pass to compute activations at all hidden layers, then at the output layer obtain an output x'
Measure the deviation of x' from the input x
Backpropagate the error through the net and perform weight updates

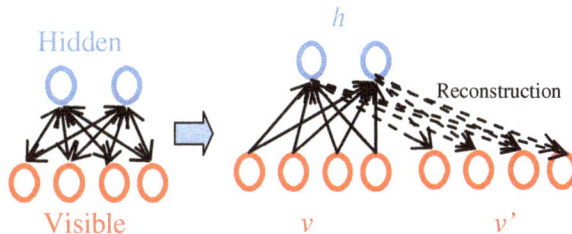

Fig. 6. Unfold RBM.

Table 4. RBM.

Restricted Boltzmann Machine
Initial random weights
Do until stopping criteria is met:
For each input vector $X = \{x_1, x_2, ...\}$:
Calculate h_j using X, and denote positive $(w_{ij}) = x_i * h_j$
Reconstruct X', and denote negative $(w_{ij}) = h_j * x_i$
Perform weight updates: $w_{ij} = w_{ij} + \alpha*(\text{positive }(w_{ij}) - \text{negative }(w_{ij}))$

training of autoencoder. We first calculate the value of hidden units h using the vector from the visible units v and then reconstruct the visible units v'. Using the difference between v and v', we can update the weights between the visible and hidden units.

The detailed algorithm for training RBM is shown in Table 4.

When RBMs are put together layer by layer where the visible units of the upper layer are the hidden units of the bottom layer, they form DBN, as mentioned in Sec. 2.

4. Applications

Deep learning has been applied to solve different kinds of problems. In this section, we summarize some of the application examples.

4.1. *Image understanding*

The most influential breakthrough of computer vision occurred in 2012 when Hinton's team used deep learning to win the ImageNet image classification champion.[18] Their results generated a great deal of shock in the field of computer vision and opened a gate to deep learning. In ImageNet ILSVRC 2013 competition, all the top 20 teams used deep learning technology. Among them the winner was Rob Fergus of New York University (Rob Fergus). Their model is called Clarifai.[32] In ILSVRC 2014 the winner, GoogLeNet,[2] reduced the error rate to 6.656%.

Object detection is more difficult than object classification. An image may include a number of objects belonging to different classes and object detection is to determine the location and type of each object. In ImageNet ILSVRC 2013, the organizer added the object detection tasks which were required to detect objects belonging to 200 class in 40,000 images. The winners used manual design features, and the mean Averaged Precision (mAP) was only 22.581%. In ILSVRC 2014, deep learning increased the number to 43.933%. More influential work that employed deep learning to machine vision includes RCNN,[9] VGG,[33] Overfeat,[34] network in network,[35] and spatial pyramid pooling in deep CNN.[36]

Another important breakthrough in deep learning on object recognition is facial recognition. The biggest challenge of facial recognition is to distinguish between intra-class variation due to different lights, gestures and expressions, and extra-class variations caused by different identities. Since distribution of these two variations is nonlinear and highly complex, traditional linear models cannot distinguish them effectively. Deep learning aims to obtain new features representations by multiple layers of nonlinear transformation. These new features have to remove as much as possible intra-class variations, while retaining the extra-class variations. In IEEE CVPR 2014, DeepID[37] and DeepFace[38] used face recognition as the supervisory signal and achieved 97.45% and 97.35% recognition rate on the Labeled Faces in the Wild (LFW) face database.

4.2. *Speech understanding*

Automatic Speech Recognition (ASR), aimed to enable natural human–machine interaction, has been an intensive research area for decades. There are many commercial systems for speech recognition such as AT&T Watson,[39] Microsoft Speech Server,[40] Google Speech API,[41] and Nuance Recognizer.[42]

Since its launch in 2009, Google Voice[43] has used the Gaussian Mixture Model (GMM) acoustic model for 30+ years. Sophisticated techniques like adapting the models to the speaker's voice have augmented this relatively simple modeling method. Then around 2012, DNNs revolutionized the field of speech recognition. These multi-layer networks can distinguish sounds better than GMMs by training differentiating phonetic units instead of modeling each one independently. Technologies have improved rapidly with RNNs, and especially LSTM RNNs, that were first launched in Android's speech recognizer in May 2012. Compared to DNNs, LSTM RNNs have additional recurrent connections

and memory cells allowing them to "remember" the data they have seen so far.

4.3. *Video understanding*

Deep learning for the classification of video applications is still in its infancy. Deep learning models obtained from ImageNet can be used to describe static image features of videos, while the difficulty is how to describe dynamic characteristics. The most direct approach is to consider video as three-dimensional images, and directly use a convolution neural network.[44] But this idea apparently did not take into account the differences of the time dimension and the space dimension. Another simple but more effective idea is to pre-calculate the spatial statistics of optical flows or other dynamic features as the input of convolution.[45] Recently, Long Short-Term Memory (LSTM)[46] attracted widespread attention, which is a special type of RNNs to model the variable-range dependencies entailed in the task of video understanding.

Lots of time, we can find some objects especially some high speed moving objects in a video, but it is very difficult to know what they are. The main reason is that we can only crawl very little information when finding an object. And so, we need to develop some new methods to recognize these targets. Deep learning may do this work well in the future.

4.4. *Nature language processing*

In addition to voice and image, another application of deep learning is Natural Language Processing (NLP). The first NLP application using neural networks is the language model. In 2003, Yoshua Bengio[47] proposed to map a word to a vector apace using embedding, and then used a nonlinear neural network to represent the *N*-Gram model. Today, deep learning has been used in many NLP applications such as text generation and translation.

Overall, the progress of deep learning made on NLP is not as impressive as on voice or image. Compared to voice and image, language is the only artificial signal that is produced and processed by the human brain. So we believe there is still much to explore for NLP using deep learning.

4.5. *Big data and data mining*

Big Data generally refers to data that exceeds the typical storage, processing, and computing capacity of conventional databases and data analysis techniques. As a resource, Big Data requires tools and methods that can be applied to analyze and extract patterns from large-scale data.

In industry, most people think shallow machine learning is more effective to handle big data. For example, in many big data applications, the simplest linear model has been widely used. But recently the progress of deep learning prompted us to rethink this idea. In the case of big data, perhaps only more complex models or models with high expression ability can fully exploit the wealth of information hidden in the vast amounts of data. Maybe we can learn more valuable information and knowledge using deep learning.

The shallow model has an important feature — extract patterns or features from sample data by experience, and the shallow model is mainly responsible for classification or prediction. So the quality of extracted patterns becomes a bottleneck in the overall system performance. Thus, generally more effort of a development team is devoted to discover better patterns. To find a good pattern requires developers to have a deep understanding of the problem. Thus, artificially designing sample patterns may not be a good approach.

On the other hand, deep learning aims to learn more useful features from big data via constructing deep models with multiple hidden layers and training vast amounts of data. Different from shallow machine learning, deep learning emphasizes the depth of the model and the importance of training, so that it can improve the accuracy of classification or prediction by extracting more appropriate features. Deep learning uses training of big data to learn features, which has a better ability to express the features of rich information. So, in the next few years, we may see more and more big-data applications using deep learning instead of a linear shallow model.

5. Deep Learning Frameworks

There are many open source deep learning frameworks for startups in this area.

Convolutional Architecture for Fast Feature Embedding (Caffe)[48] was developed by the Berkeley Vision and Learning Center, started in late 2013. It is the most popular toolkit in computer vision, with many extensions being actively added. However, its support for RNN and other deep models is poor.

Tensorflow[49] was developed by Google. It has an ideal RNN API and implementation. Tensorflow supports heterogeneous distributed computing, and can run on different platforms, from mobile phones, a single CPU/GPU to distributed systems with hundreds of GPUs. However, Tensorflow has a major weakness in terms of modeling flexibility. Every computational flow has to be constructed as a static graph. That makes some computations difficult.

CNTK[50] was developed by Microsoft which was firstly only used for the Cortana personal assistant and Skype Translator services, and was released in April 2015. It is better known in the speech community than in the general deep learning community.

Theano[51] was born in Montreal Polytechnic. Many deep learning packages were derived from Theano including Blocks and Keras. Theano's symbolic API supports looping control, which makes implementing RNNs easy and efficient.

Torch[52] has existed for more than 10 years. It is implemented on LuaJIT, which has better speed compared to C++, C# and Java. The only problem is that Lua is not a mainstream programming language.

In addition to these well-known projects, there are many other deep learning frameworks such as Brainstorm[53] which can be used to handle super-deep neural networks with hundreds of hidden layers; Deeplearning4j[54] which is a deep learning framework for Java; MXnet[55] which emphasizes the efficiency of memory usage; and so on.

6. The Difficulties of Deep Learning

Although deep learning has made significant progress and been used in many applications in the last few decades, there are still some difficulties that we need to consider and solve in the future.

Since the deep model is nonconvex, theoretical research in this area may be difficult. Recently, Mallat did quantitative analysis for deep networks using wavelet,[56] which may be an important direction.

Since theoretical analysis is difficult for current deep models, finding a new model which has the same strong learning ability as the existing models and at the same time is easier to analyze will be an important problem for deep learning. Another question is how to design a unified model that can handle different types of data such as language, speech and image.

References

[1] G. E. Hinton, Learning multiple layers of representation, *Trends Cogn. Sci.* **11**, 428 (2007).

[2] L. Deng and D. Yu, Deep convex net: A scalable architecture for speech pattern classification, *Proc. Interspeech* (2011).

[3] L. Deng, X. He and J. Gao, May. Deep stacking networks for information retrieval, *IEEE Int. Conf. Acoustics, Speech and Signal Processing* (2013), pp. 3153–3157.

[4] J. Li, H. Chang and J. Yang, Sparse deep stacking network for image classification, arXiv:1501.00777.

[5] R. Chalasani and J. C. Principe, Deep predictive coding networks, arXiv:1301.3541.

[6] S. Zhou, S. Zhang and J. Wang, August. Deep sparse coding network for image classification, *Proc. 7th ACM Int. Conf. Internet Multimedia Computing and Service* (2015), p. 24.

[7] K. Fukushima, Neocognitron: A self-organizing neural network model for a mechanism of pattern recognition unaffected by shift, position, *Biol. Cybern.* **36**, 193 (1980).

[8] Y. LeCun, L. Bottou, Y. Bengio and P. Haffner, Gradient-based learning applied to document recognition, *Proc. of the IEEE* **86**, 2278 (1998).

[9] L. E. Atlas, T. Homma and R. J. Marks II, An artificial neural network for spatio-temporal bipolar patterns: Application to phoneme classification, *Proc. Neural Information Processing Systems* (1988), p. 31.

[10] S. Behnke, *Hierarchical Neural Networks for Image Interpretation*, Vol. 2766 (Springer Science & Business Media, 2003).

[11] P. Y. Simard, D. Steinkraus and J. C. Platt, Best practices for convolutional neural networks applied to visual document analysis, in *ICDAR* Vol. 3, (2003), pp. 958–962.

[12] D. Graupe, R. W. Liu and G. S. Moschytz, Applications of neural networks to medical signal processing, *Proc. 27th IEEE Conf. Decision and Control* (1988), pp. 343–347.

[13] D. Graupe, B. Vern, G. Gruener, A. Field and Q. Huang, Decomposition of surface EMG signals into single fiber action potentials by means of neural networks, *Proc. IEEE Int. Symp. Circuits and Systems* (1989), pp. 1008–1011.

[14] Q. Huang, D. Graupe, Y. F. Huang and R. Liu, Identification of firing patterns of neuronal signals, *Proc. 28th IEEE Conf. on Decision and Control* (1989), pp. 266–271.

[15] K. Chellapilla, S. Puri and P. Simard, High performance convolutional neural networks for document processing, *Proc. 10th Int. Workshop on Frontiers in Handwriting Recognition* (2006).

[16] D. Strigl, K. Kofler and S. Podlipnig, Performance and scalability of GPU-based convolutional neural networks, in *PDP* (2010), pp. 317–324.

[17] D. C. Ciresan, U. Meier, J. Masci, L. Maria Gambardella and J. Schmidhuber, J., Flexible, high performance convolutional neural networks for image classification, *Proc. Int. Joint Conf. Artificial Intelligence* (2011), p. 1237.

[18] A. Krizhevsky, I. Sutskever and G. E. Hinton, Imagenet classification with deep convolutional neural networks, *Advances in Neural Information Processing Systems*, (2012), pp. 1097–1105.

[19] C. Szegedy, D. Erhan and A. T. Toshev, Object detection using deep neural networks, U.S. Patent 9,275,308. 2016.

[20] G. Hinton, L. Deng, D. Yu, G. E. Dahl, A. R. Mohamed, N. Jaitly, A. Senior, V. Vanhoucke, P. Nguyen, T. N. Sainath and B. Kingsbury, Deep neural networks for acoustic modeling in speech recognition: The shared views of four research groups, *IEEE Signal Process. Mag.* **29**, 82 (2012).

[21] C. Szegedy, W. Liu, Y. Jia, P. Sermanet, S. Reed, D. Anguelov, D. Erhan, V. Vanhoucke and A. Rabinovich, Going deeper with convolutions, *Proc. IEEE Conf. Computer Vision and Pattern Recognition* (2015), pp. 1–9.

[22] A. Karpathy, G. Toderici, S. Shetty, T. Leung, R. Sukthankar and L. Fei-Fei, Large-scale video classification with convolutional neural networks, *Proc. IEEE Conf. Computer Vision and Pattern Recognition* (2014), pp. 1725–1732.

[23] K. He, X. Zhang, S. Ren and J. Sun, Deep residual learning for image recognition, arXiv:1512.03385.

[24] A. Graves, M. Liwicki, S. Fernández, R. Bertolami, H. Bunke and J. Schmidhuber, A novel connectionist system for unconstrained handwriting recognition, *IEEE Trans. Pattern Anal. Mach. Intell.* **31**, 855 (2009).

[25] S. Hochreiter and J. Schmidhuber, Long short-term memory, *Neural Comput.* **9**, 1735 (1997).

[26] A. Graves and N. Jaitly, Towards end-to-end speech recognition with recurrent neural networks, *ICML* Vol. 14, (2014), pp. 1764–1772.

[27] J. L. Elman, Finding structure in time, *Cogn. Sci.* **14**, 179 (1990).

[28] M. Schuster and K. K. Paliwal, Bidirectional recurrent neural networks, *IEEE Trans. Signal Process.* **45**, 2673 (1997).

[29] H. Jaeger, The "echo state" approach to analysing and training recurrent neural networks-with an erratum note. Bonn, Germany: German National Research Center for Information Technology GMD Technical Report **148**, 34(2001).

[30] D. E. Rumelhart, G. E. Hinton and R. J. Williams, Learning representations by back-propagating errors, *Cogn. Model.* **5**, 1 (1998).

[31] P. Vincent, H. Larochelle, Y. Bengio and P. A. Manzagol, Extracting and composing robust features with denoising autoencoders, *Proc. 25th Int. Conf. Machine learning* (2008), pp. 1096–1103.

[32] Clarifai: http://www.clarifai.com/.

[33] K. Simonyan and A. Zisserman, Very deep convolutional networks for large-scale image recognition, arXiv:1409.1556.

[34] P. Sermanet, D. Eigen, X. Zhang, M. Mathieu, R. Fergus and Y. LeCun, Overfeat: Integrated recognition, localization and detection using convolutional networks, arXiv:1312.6229.

[35] M. Lin, Q. Chen and S. Yan, Network in network, arXiv:1312.4400.

[36] K. He, X. Zhang, S. Ren and J. Sun, Spatial pyramid pooling in deep convolutional networks for visual recognition, *Eur. Conf. Computer Vision* (2014), pp. 346–361.

[37] Y. Sun, X. Wang and X. Tang, Deep learning face representation from predicting 10,000 classes, *Proc. IEEE Conf. Computer Vision and Pattern Recognition* (2014), pp. 1891–1898.

[38] Y. Taigman, M. Yang, M. A. Ranzato and L. Wolf, Deepface: Closing the gap to human-level performance in face verification, *Proc. IEEE Conf. Computer Vision and Pattern Recognition* (2014), pp. 1701–1708.

[39] V. Goffin, C. Allauzen, E. Bocchieri, D. Hakkani-Tür, A. Ljolje, S. Parthasarathy, M. G. Rahim, G. Riccardi and M. Saraclar, The AT&T WATSON Speech Recognizer, *ICASSP* (1), (2005), pp. 1033–1036.

[40] A. Dunn, *Pro Microsoft Speech Server 2007: Developing Speech Enabled Applications with. NET* (Apress, 2007).

[41] J. Adorf, Web Speech API, KTH Royal Institute of Technology, (2013).

[42] Nuance Communication Inc.: Speech recognition solutions. http://www.nuance.com/for-individuals/by-solution/speech-recognition/index.htm.

[43] Google Voice: https://www.google.com/googlevoice/about.html.

[44] S. Ji, W. Xu, M. Yang and K. Yu, 3D convolutional neural networks for human action recognition, *IEEE Trans. Pattern Anal. Mach. Intell.* **35**, 221 (2013).

[45] K. Simonyan and A. Zisserman, Two-stream convolutional networks for action recognition in videos, *Advances in Neural Information Processing Systems*, (2014), pp. 568–576.

[46] J. Donahue, L. Anne Hendricks, S. Guadarrama, M. Rohrbach, S. Venugopalan, K. Saenko and T. Darrell, Long-term recurrent convolutional networks for visual recognition and description, *Proc. IEEE Conf. Computer Vision and Pattern Recognition* (2015), pp. 2625–2634.

[47] Y. Bengio, R. Ducharme, P. Vincent and C. Jauvin, A neural probabilistic language model, *J. Mach. Learn. Res.* **3**, 1137 (2003).

[48] Caffe: http://caffe.berkeleyvision.org/.

[49] Tensorflow: http://tensorflow.org/.

[50] CNTK: https://www.cntk.ai/.

[51] Theano: https://github.com/Theano/Theano.

[52] Torch: http://torch.ch/.

[53] Brainstorm: https://github.com/IDSIA/brainstorm.

[54] Deeplearning4j: http://deeplearning4j.org.

[55] MXnet: https://github.com/dmlc/mxnet.

[56] J. Bruna and S. Mallat, Invariant scattering convolution networks, *IEEE Trans. Pattern Anal. Mach. Intell.* **35**, 872 (2013).

[57] R. Girshick, J. Donahue, T. Darrell and J. Malik, Rich feature hierarchies for accurate object detection and semantic segmentation, *Proc. IEEE Conf. Computer Vision and Pattern recognition* (2014), pp. 580–587.

Two-stage and sequential sampling for estimation and testing with prescribed precision

Shelemyahu Zacks

Emeritus, State University of New York

Binghamton, New York

shzacks@outlook.com

Statistical data analysis includes several phases. First, there is the phase of data collection. Second, there is the phase of analysis and inference. The two phases are interconnected. There are two types of data analysis. One type is called parametric and the other type is nonparametric. In the present paper, we discuss parametric inference. In parametric inference, we model the results of a given experiment as realization of random variables having a particular distribution, which is specified by its parameters. A random sample is a sequence of independent and identically distributed (i.i.d.) random variables. Statistics are functions of the data in the sample, which do not involve unknown parameters. A statistical inference is based on statistics of a given sample. We discuss two kinds of parametric inference. Estimating the values of parameters, or testing hypotheses concerning the parameters in either kind of inference, we are concerned with the accuracy and precision of the results. In estimation of parameters, the results are precise if, with high probability, they belong to a specified neighborhoods of the parameters. In testing hypotheses, one has to decide which one of two or several hypotheses should be accepted. Hypotheses which are not accepted are rejected. We distinguish between two types of errors. Type I error is the one committed by rejecting a correct hypothesis. Type II is that of accepting a wrong hypothesis. It is desired that both types of errors will occur simultaneously with small probabilities. Both precision in estimation or small error probabilities in testing depend on the statistics used (estimators or test functions) and on the sample size. In this paper, we present sampling procedures that attain the desired objectives. In Sec. 2, we discuss estimation of the parameters of a binomial distribution. In Sec. 3, more general results about estimation of expected values are presented. In Sec. 4, we discuss the Wald Sequential Probability Ratio Test (SPRT), which has optimal properties for testing two simple hypotheses.

Keywords: Precision of estimation; sequential probability ratio test.

1. Estimating the Binomial Parameters

Consider a sequence of independent binary random variables, $\{J_1, J_2, \ldots\}$ where the probabilities $p = P\{J_i = 1\}$ are the same for all $J_i, i = 1, 2, \ldots$ Such random variables can represent success or failure of independent experiments, having equal success probabilities. These experiments are called *Bernoulli trials*. Let $S_n = \sum_{i=1}^{n} J_i$ be the number of successes among n Bernoulli trials. The distribution of S_n is called the *binomial distribution*. The *probability mass function* (p.m.s.) of this distribution is

$$b(j; n, p) = \binom{n}{j} p^j (1-p)^{n-j}, \quad j = 0, \ldots, n. \quad (1)$$

The *cumulative binomial distribution*, (c.d.f.) is

$$B(j; n, p) = \sum_{i=1}^{j} b(i; n, p). \quad (2)$$

(n, p) are the binomial parameters. In the following sections, we discuss the problem of estimating the binomial parameters with a prescribed precision.

1.1. *Estimating the parameter p.*

Given the result S_n of n Bernoulli trials, with a known n, the likelihood function of p is

$$L(p, S_n) = c p^{S_n} (1-p)^{n-S_n} \quad (3)$$

for any $c > 0$. The *maximum likelihood estimator* (MLE) of p is the value of p maximizing the likelihood function. This estimator is the sample mean $\bar{X}_n = S_n/n$. Notice that the sample mean in the binomial case is the proportion of successes (of ones) in the sample, to be denoted by $\hat{p}_n$.

This estimator by itself is insufficient, since it is important to assess its precision. One measurement of precision is the *standard error*, which is the estimator of its standard deviation, namely

$$\text{S.E.}\{\hat{p}_n\} = \left(\frac{\hat{p}_n(1-\hat{p}_n)}{n} \right)^{1/2}. \quad (4)$$

A confidence interval for p, with level of confidence $1 - \alpha$, is an interval $(L_\alpha(\hat{p}_n), U_\alpha(\hat{p}_n))$ such that

$$P_p\{p \in (L_\alpha(\hat{p}_n), U_\alpha \hat{p}_n)\} \geq 1 - \alpha \quad (5)$$

for all $0 < p < 1$. Exact formulas of the limits of the confidence interval are (see p. 131 in Ref. 11)

$$L_\alpha(\widehat{p}_n) = \frac{\widehat{p}_n}{\widehat{p}_n + (1 - \widehat{p}_n + 1/n)F_1}, \quad (6)$$

and

$$U_\alpha(\widehat{p}_n) = \frac{(\widehat{p}_n + 1/n)F_2}{1 - \widehat{p}_n + (\widehat{p}_n + 1/n)F_2}, \quad (7)$$

where $F_1 = F_{1-\alpha/2}[2(n - S_n + 1), 2S_n]$, and $F_2 = F_{1-\alpha/2} \times [2(S_n + 1), 2(n - S_n)]$.

Generally, $F_p[k_1, k_2]$ denotes the pth quantile of the F-distribution, with k_1 and k_2 degrees of freedom. For example, when $n = 30$ and $S_{30} = 8$, and $\alpha = 0.05$, the confidence interval for p is $(0.123, 0.459)$. This may not be acceptable if we desire to estimate p more precisely.

2. Large Sample Approximation

To achieve high precision, one needs large samples. By the *central limit theorem*, (CLT), the MLE $\widehat{p}_n$ is asymptotically normal, i.e., the distribution of $\widehat{p}_n$ is approximated for large n by the normal distribution $N(\mu, \sigma^2)$ with mean $\mu = p$ and variance $\sigma^2 = p(1 - p)/n$.

In large samples situation, one can use the approximation

$$L_\alpha(\widehat{p}_n) = \widehat{p}_n - z_{1-\alpha/2}(\widehat{p}_n(1 - \widehat{p}_n)/n)^{1/2}, \quad (8)$$

and

$$U_\alpha(\widehat{p}_n) = \widehat{p}_n + z_{1-\alpha/2}(\widehat{p}_n(1 - \widehat{p}_n)/n)^{1/2}, \quad (9)$$

where $z_{1-\alpha/2} = \Phi^{-1}(1 - \alpha/2)$ is the $(1 - \alpha/2)-$ quantile of the standard normal distribution. An important question is, how large should the sample size be, so that the width of the approximate confidence interval should not exceed 2δ. Notice that $0 < \widehat{p}_n(1 - \widehat{p}_n) \leq \frac{1}{4}$. Hence, if $n > z_{1-\alpha/2}^2/4\delta^2$ the width of the approximate confidence interval would be smaller than 2δ. This result is independent of p and might therefore be too large.

3. Sequential Sampling

From the equation

$$z_{1-\alpha/2}(\widehat{p}_n(1 - \widehat{p}_n)/n)^{1/2} = \delta, \quad (10)$$

we obtain the stopping variable,

$$N = \min\{n \geq m : n \geq \chi_{1-\alpha}^2 \widehat{p}_n(1 - \widehat{p}_n)/\delta^2\}, \quad (11)$$

where $\chi_{1-\alpha}^2 = z_{1-\alpha/2}^2$ is the quantile of the chi-squared distribution with one degree of freedom. This stopping variable suggests a *sequential* sampling procedure, based on the stopping variable (11). In such a sequential procedure, one takes first a pilot sample of size m, and continues sampling,

Table 1.

p	$\widehat{E}\{N\}$	$(\widehat{\text{Var}}\{N\})^{1/2}$
0.1	3460.89	159.9391
0.2	6142.94	112.8656
0.3	8070.05	84.4160
0.4	9224.96	35.2377
0.5	9603.03	1.8338

one trial at a time, until (11) is satisfied. The resulting stopping time is a random variable.

Notice that a reasonable value of δ should be smaller than $\min(\widehat{p}_n, 1 - \widehat{p}_n)/3$. For example, if $\delta = 0.01$, $\widehat{p}_n = 0.5$, $\alpha = 0.05$, and $m = 100$, we get from (1) the required sample size $N \geq 9535$. For values of $\widehat{p}_n$ smaller than 0.5, smaller values of N will be obtained.

It is important to investigate the distribution of this stopping variable. In the following table, we present simulation estimates of the expected value and standard deviation of N. In these simulations, we used 100 replicas, $m = 100$, $\alpha = 0.05$, and $\delta = 0.01$.

$\widehat{E}$ and $\widehat{\text{Var}}$ indicate simulation estimates of the expected value and variance of N. Obviously, if the required precision is relaxed, the expected value of N would be smaller. For example, for the parameters of Table 1, if $\delta = 0.05$ one obtains for $p = 0.1$, $\widehat{E}\{N\} = 134.19$ and $(\widehat{\text{Var}}\{N\})^{1/2} = 27.3588$.

The exact distribution of the stopping variable N can be derived in a manner as in the paper of Ref. 22. In that paper, a sequential procedure was studied for the estimation of the log-odds, $\rho = \log(p/(1 - p))$.

3.1. *Estimating the parameter n*

There are applications in which the parameter n, which is the number trials in an experiment, is unknown and should be estimated. Examples of such applications are found in ecology, in clinical trials, in software reliability and other areas of research. Much research has been done in the past on estimating n. A few references are: (see Ref. 9,7,2,12,13 and 15).

The estimation problem is difficult if the parameter p is unknown. Neither one of the above referenced papers studied the precision problem. To explain the problem in this context, suppose that in n Bernoulli trials X successes are observed. When p is known, the estimator $\widehat{N} = X/p$ is unbiased, since $E\{X\} = np$. The variance of this unbiased estimator is $V\{\widehat{N}\} = n(1 - p)/p$. Thus, the S.E. of $\widehat{N}$ might be too large. For example, suppose that $n = 100$ (unknown), $p = 0.3$ and $X = 27$, then $\widehat{N} = 90$ and the confidence interval is $(46.53, 133.47)$.

Our inference about n is quite imprecise, with high probability, it could be anywhere between 47 and 133. Precision can be obtained if the binomial experiment can be replicated independently with the same parameters (n, p). The question is, how many replications are required in order to achieve a reasonable precision. De and Zacks[6] studied the problem of how many replications should be done, when p is known, in order to estimate n with a fixed-width confidence interval 2δ.

3.2. *Two-stage and sequential sampling for estimating n*

The following is a two-stage procedure for estimating n.

Stage I. Stage I is a pilot study with initially k replications. Thus, let $X_1, \ldots, X_k$ be k independent and identically distributed (i.i.d.) random variables from $B(n, p)$. Let $S_k = \sum_{i=1}^{k} X_i$. An unbiased estimator of n is

$$\widehat{N}_k = \frac{S_k}{kp} \tag{12}$$

with standard error

$$\text{S.E.}\{\widehat{N}_k\} = \left(\frac{S_k(1-p)}{kp^2}\right)^{1/2}. \tag{13}$$

Accordingly, we consider the stopping variable

$$K = \left\lfloor \frac{\chi_{1-\alpha}^2 S_k(1-p)}{\delta^2 kp^2} \right\rfloor + 1 \tag{14}$$

where $\lfloor x \rfloor$ designates the largest integer smaller than x. If $K \leq k$, stop sampling and estimate n by $\widehat{N}_k$. Otherwise, proceed to Stage II.

Stage II: Let $K^* = K - k$. Sample additional independent K^* random variables from $B(n, p)$. Let S_{K*} be the sum of these stage II observations. Estimate n by

$$\widehat{N}_K = \left\lfloor \frac{S_k + S_{K*}}{Kp} \right\rfloor + 1. \tag{15}$$

The sequential procedure starts also with an initial sample of size k and then proceeds sampling one by one, changing the values of k and S_k after each observation and stopping when

$$k \geq \frac{\chi_{1-\alpha}^2 S_k(1-p)}{\delta^2 kp^2}. \tag{16}$$

The total sample size at stopping is denoted by K_S. The estimator of n after stopping is

$$\widehat{N}_{K_S} = \left\lfloor \frac{S_{K_S}}{pK_S} \right\rfloor + 1. \tag{17}$$

The formulas of the exact distributions of K and $\widehat{N}_K$ and those of K_S and $\widehat{N}_{K_S}$ are given in the paper of De and Zacks.[6] In Table A.1 of Appendix A, we present some numerical results for the case $k = 30, \alpha = 0.1$, and $n = 100$.

We see in Table A.1 that the two-stage and the sequential procedures yield similar values of $E\{K\}$, but the standard deviation of the K_S in the sequential procedure is substantially smaller than that of the two-stage sampling.

4. Two-Stage and Sequential Fixed Width-Confidence Intervals for the Mean

4.1. *The Chow–Robbins procedure*

Chow and Robbins[3] considered sequential procedures which yield fixed-width confidence intervals for the mean $\mu = E\{X\}$, for any sequence of i.i.d. random variables, which satisfy the CLT for random stopping time N. See also the important theorem of Ref. 1, which requires that the sequence of the X's will be uniformly continuous in probability (or tight).

For a given such sequence of i.i.d. random variables, let $\bar{X}_n = \sum_{i=1}^{n} X_i/n$ be the sample mean and $S_n^2 = \frac{1}{n} \times \sum_{i=1}^{n} (X_i - \bar{X}_n)^2$ the sample variance. The Chow-Robbins stopping variable is

$$N = \min\{n \geq n_0 : n \geq a_n S_n^2/\delta^2\}, \tag{18}$$

where $a_n \searrow \chi_{1-\alpha}^2$, almost surely $n \nearrow \infty$. Let $\sigma^2 = V\{X\}$, and $n^0(\delta, \sigma) = \chi_{1-\alpha}^2 \sigma^2/\delta^2$. Chow and Robbins proved that if $\sigma^2 < \infty$ then

  (i) $P_\sigma\{N < \infty\} = 1$,
  (ii) $E_\sigma\{N\} \leq n_0 + 1 + n^0(\delta, \sigma)$,
  (iii) $E_\sigma\{N^2\} \leq (n_0 + 1 + n^0(\delta, \sigma))^2 - 2$,
  (iv) $N \nearrow \infty$, as $\delta \to 0$,
  (v) $N/n^0(\delta, \sigma) \to 1, a.s.$
  (vi) $\lim_{\delta \to 0} E_\sigma\{N\}/n^0(\delta, \sigma) = 1$,
  (vii) $\lim_{\delta \to 0} P\{\bar{X}_N - \delta < \mu < \bar{X}_N + \delta\} = 1 - \alpha$. Property (vi) is called "asymptotic efficiency" and property (vii) is called "asymptotic consistency".

Notice that stopping variables (11) and (16) are special cases of (18).

4.2. *The normal case*

We start with a few technical details. A random variable X has a normal distribution, $N(\mu, \sigma)$, if its density (p.d.f.) is

$$f(x; \mu, \sigma) = \frac{1}{\sqrt{2\pi}\sigma} e^{-\frac{1}{2}(\frac{x-\mu}{\sigma})^2},$$

$-\infty < x < \infty$, and the parameters are $-\infty < \mu < \infty; 0 < \sigma < \infty$.

For review, see Chap. 3 in Ref. 11. For this distribution, $\mu = E\{X\}$ and $\sigma^2 = V\{X\}$. The standard normal distribution is $N(0, 1)$, whose c.d.f. is (the standard normal integral)

$$\Phi(z) = \frac{1}{\sqrt{2\pi}} \int_{-\infty}^{z} e^{-y^2/2} dy, -\infty < z < \infty.$$

Given a sample of i.i.d. random variables from $N(\mu, \sigma)$, the distribution of the sample variance $S_n^2 = \frac{1}{n-1} \times \sum_{i=1}^{n} (X_i - \bar{X}_n)^2$ is that of $\sigma^2 \chi^2[n-1]/(n-1)$, where $\chi^2[k]$ denotes a random variable having a chi-squared distribution, with k degrees of freedom. The statistic $t = N(0, 1)/\sqrt{\chi^2[k]}$ has a (Student) t-distribution with k degrees of freedom.

4.3. *The stein two-stage sampling*

Dantzig[4] proved that in the normal case, if σ is unknown, there exists no fixed-width confidence interval for μ, based on a single sample of size n (For a proof, see p. 539 in Ref. 19. Stein[15,16] showed that, in order to construct a fixed-width confidence interval of size 2δ, one has to apply the following two-stage sampling procedure:

Stage I: take an initial sample of size $m \geq 3$, and compute the (sufficient) statistics $(\overline{X}_m, S_m^2)$. Compute the stopping variable

$$N_m = \max\{\lfloor t_{1-\alpha/2}^2[m-1]S_m^2/\delta^2\rfloor + 1, m\}. \tag{19}$$

If $N_m = m$ stop sampling; else, go to Stage II.

Stage II: Sample additionally, $N_m^* = N_m - m$ independent random variables from $N(\mu, \sigma)$ and compute the grand mean

$$\overline{X}_{N_m} = (m\overline{X}_m + N_m^*\overline{X}_{N_m^*})/N_m. \tag{20}$$

The desired confidence interval is $(\overline{X}_{N_m} - \delta, \overline{X}_{N_m} + \delta)$.

For a proof that $P_\sigma\{\overline{X}_{N_m} - \delta < \mu < \overline{X}_{N_m} + \delta\} \geq 1 - \alpha, 0 < \sigma < \infty$, see pp. 16 and 17 of Ref. 20. It is shown there also that if $m = 2k + 1$, then

$$E\{N_m\} = m + \sum_{j=0}^{\infty} P(k-1, \lambda_k(m+j)), \tag{21}$$

where

$$\lambda_k = k\delta^2/(\sigma^2 F_{1-\alpha}[1, 2k]). \tag{22}$$

Here, $P(k, \eta)$ denotes the c.d.f. of the Poisson distribution, whose p.m.f. is $p(k, \eta) = e^{-\eta}\frac{\eta^k}{k!}, k = 0, 1, \ldots$
As before, let

$$n^0(\delta, \sigma) = \chi_{1-\alpha}^2\sigma^2/\delta^2. \tag{23}$$

A two-stage procedure is called asymptotically efficient if

$$\lim_{\delta \to 0} E_\sigma\{N_m\}/n^0(\delta, \sigma) = 1. \tag{24}$$

The Stein procedure is not asymptotically efficient. Ghosh and Mukhopadhyay[8] modified Stein's procedure to attain asymptotic efficiency.

4.4. *Sequential sampling*

Ray[14] suggested a sequential procedure based on (22), in which the sample variance S_n^2 is substituted for σ^2. We will consider this procedure in which we start initially with $n = 2m + 1$ observations and then, in each stage we observe two more observations. Thus, $m = 1, 2, \ldots$ The stopping variable is

$$N^* = \min\{n = 2m + 1 : n \geq \chi_{1-\alpha}^2 S_n^2/\delta^2\}. \tag{25}$$

Notice that in the present case, for the normal distribution,

$$S_n^2 =_d \frac{\sigma^2}{2m}\chi^2[2m] =_d \frac{\sigma^2}{m}G(1, m) \tag{26}$$

Table 2.

δ	$E\{N^*\}$	CP
1.25	7.018	0.999
1.00	7.211	0.992
0.90	7.478	0.985
0.75	8.439	0.965
0.60	10.957	0.938
0.50	14.706	0.923
0.25	60.161	0.938

Here$=_d$ denotes equality in distribution, i.e., the random variables in the two sides of the equation have the same distribution. Furthermore, $\frac{\sigma^2}{m}G(1, m)$ is distributed like the sum of m independent exponentially distributed random variables, having a expected value equal to $\frac{\sigma^2}{m}$. The Poisson process is a jump process, whose jumps occur at random times $0 < \tau_1 < \tau_2 < \cdots$ and the times between consecutive jumps, $T_i = \tau_i - \tau_{i-1}$, are independent exponentially distributed random variables. See p. 47 in Ref. 10 for the properties of the Poisson process. Let $N^* = 2M^* + 1$. The distribution of M^* is the same as the distribution of the first time a Poisson process $M(t)$, with intensity $\lambda = 1/\sigma^2$, crosses the boundary

$$B(t) = \frac{1}{4}[(1 + 8t\chi_{1-\alpha}^2/\delta^2)^{1/2} - 1]. \tag{27}$$

For details see pp. 38–40 in Ref. 20. In Table 2, we present the expected value of N^* and the coverage probability (CP), of the interval $(\overline{X}_{N^*} - \delta, \overline{X}_{N^*} + \delta)$, for $\alpha = 0.05, \sigma = 1$ and initial sample $n = 7$.

5. The Wald sequential probability ratio test (SPRT)

Consider the problem of testing two simple hypotheses

H_0: The p.d.f. (p.m.f.) of X is f_0 against H_1: The p.d.f. (p.m.f.) of X is f_1. Let $X_1, \ldots, X_n$ be a random sample from one of these two distributions we have to decide which hypothesis can be accepted. Let α denote the probability of rejecting H_0 when it is true and let β denote the probability of rejecting H_1 when it is true. α is called the size of the test, and $1 - \beta$ is the power of the test. According to Neyman–Pearson Lemma (see p. 248 in Ref. 21) the most powerful test of size α is the likelihood ratio test, which rejects H_0 if $\Pi_{i=1}^n f_1(X_i)/f_0(X_i)$ is sufficiently large. More specifically, let $S_n = \sum_{i=1}^n \log\frac{f_1(X_i)}{f_0(X_i)}$, $n \geq 1$.

The SPRT is a sequential test specified by two bounds $b < 0 < a$, and a stopping variable

$$N = \min\{n \geq 1 : S_n < b \text{ or } S_n > a\}. \tag{28}$$

After stopping, H_0 is accepted if $S_n < b$; otherwise H_0 is rejected.

We can prove (see p. 286 in Ref. 20) that

$$P_j\{N < \infty\} = 1, \quad j = 0, 1. \tag{29}$$

The probabilities of Types I and II errors depend on the bounds (b, a). Generally, it is complicated to find the exact values of α and β associated with given (b, a). Wald[17] suggested to use the boundary values $b^* = \log(\beta/(1 - \alpha))$ and $a^* = \log((1 - \beta)/\alpha)$. If we denote by α' and β' the error probabilities associated with (b^*, a^*) then one can prove (see p. 288 in Ref. 20) that $\alpha' + \beta' \leq \alpha + \beta$.

The expected stopping time under the corresponding hypotheses are denoted by $E_0\{N\}$ and by $E_1\{N\}$. Wald approximated these expectations by neglecting the remainders over the boundaries. His approximations are

$$E_0\{N\} \approx \frac{(1 - \alpha) \log\left(\frac{\beta}{1-\alpha}\right) + \alpha \log\left(\frac{1-\beta}{\alpha}\right)}{-I(f_0, f_1)} \tag{30}$$

and

$$E_1\{N\} \approx \frac{(1 - \beta) \log\left(\frac{1-\beta}{\alpha}\right) + \beta \log\left(\frac{\beta}{1-\alpha}\right)}{I(f_1, f_0)}, \tag{31}$$

where $I(f, g) = E_f\{\log(\frac{f}{g})\}$ is the Kullback–Leibler Divergence, or the information for discriminating between f and g. (see p. 210 of Ref. 21). One can show that $I(f, g) \geq 0$. We need a formula for the probability of accepting H_0 after stopping, $\pi = P_0\{S_N \leq \log(\frac{1-\beta}{\alpha})\}$. For this purpose, we

apply the Wald fundamental identity (Martingale equation) namely,

$$E_\theta\{e^{tS_N}(M_\theta(t))^{-N}\} = 1, \theta = 0, 1; \{t : M_\theta(t) < \infty\}, \tag{32}$$

where $M_\theta(t)$ is the moment generating function of $R = \log\left(\frac{f_1(X)}{f_0(X)}\right)$.

We solve for $t_0, \neq 0$, the equation $M_\theta(t_0) = 1$, then,

$$E_\theta\{e^{t_0 S_N}\} = 1, \quad \theta = 0, 1 \tag{33}$$

For $\theta = 0$, $P_0\{S_N \geq \log\left(\frac{1-\beta}{\alpha}\right)\} = 1 - \pi$, and $P_0\{S_N \leq \log\left(\frac{\beta}{1-\alpha}\right)\} = \pi$. Thus, from Wald Martingale equation, we get the approximation

$$\pi e^{t_0 \log((1-\beta)/\alpha)} + (1 - \pi)e^{t_0 \log(\beta/(1-\alpha))} \approx 1, \tag{34}$$

or

$$\pi \approx \frac{1 - e^{t_0 \log(\beta/(1-\alpha))}}{e^{t_0 \log((1-\beta)/\alpha)} - e^{t_0 \log(\beta/(1-\alpha))}}$$

$$= \frac{((1 - \beta)/\alpha)^{t_0} - 1}{((1 - \beta)/\alpha)^{t_0} - (\beta/(1 - \alpha))^{t_0}}. \tag{35}$$

Wald and Wolfowitz[18] proved that the SPRT is optimal in the following sense. Suppose that an SPRT has error probabilities α and β and expected sample size $E_\theta\{N\}$.

Let s be any sampling procedure for testing H_θ, $\theta = 0, 1$, having error probabilities $\alpha(s)$ and $\beta(s)$ and expected sample size $E_\theta\{N(s)\}$. Then, $\alpha(s) \leq \alpha$, and $\beta(s) \leq \beta$ implies that $E_\theta\{N\} \leq E_\theta\{N(s)\}$.

Appendix A.

Table A.1.

δ	p	$E\{K\}$	$SD\{K\}$	$E\{\widehat{N}_K\}$	$CP\{\widehat{N}_K\}$	$E\{K_S\}$	$SD\{K_S\}$	$E\{\widehat{N}_{K_S}\}$	$CP\{\widehat{N}_{K_S}\}$
1	0.1	2435.49	133.37	100.50	0.8995	2435.19	14.87	100.49	0.8998
	0.3	631.79	17.61	100.50	0.9000	631.74	3.84	100.49	0.9017
	0.6	180.85	2.70	100.50	0.9005	180.85	1.14	100.49	0.8994
2	0.1	609.25	33.35	100.48	0.8996	609.09	7.39	100.48	0.9039
	0.3	158.32	4.41	100.48	0.9003	158.25	1.94	100.46	0.9012
	0.6	45.59	0.73	100.47	0.9010	45.57	0.63	100.47	0.9057

Notes: SD denotes the standard deviation and CP denotes the coverage probability of the confidence interval.

References

[1] F. J. Anscomb, Large sample theory for sequential estimation, *Proc. Camb. Philos. Soc.* **48**, 600 (1952).

[2] S. Blumenthal and R. C. Dahiya, Estimating the Binomial parameter n, *J. Am. Stat. Assoc.* **76**, 903 (1981).

[3] Y. S. Chow and H. Robbins, On the asymptotic theory of fixed-width sequential confidence intervals for the mean, *Ann. Math. Stat.* **36**, 457 (1965).

[4] G. E. Dantzig, On the nonexistence of tests of "Student's" hypothesis having power functions independent of σ^2, *Ann. Math. Stat.* **11**, 186 (1940).

[5] A DasGupta and H. Rubin, Estimation of the binomial parameter when both n,p are unknown, *J. Stat. Plan. Inference*, **130**, 391 (2005).

[6] S. K. De and S. Zacks, Two-Stage and Sequential Estimation of the Parameter N of Binomial Distribution When p Is Known. *Sequential Anal.* **35**, 440 (2016).

[7]D. Feldman and M. Cox, Estimation of the parameter *n* in the binomial distribution, *J. Am. Stat. Assoc.* **63**, 150 (1968).

[8]M. Ghosh and N. Mukhopadhyay, Consistency and asymptotic efficiency of two-stage and sequential estimation procedures, *Sankyha A* **43**, 220 (1981).

[9]J. B. S. Haldane, The fitting of binomial distributions, *Ann. Eugenics* **11**, 179 (1941).

[10]E. P. C. Kao, *Introduction to Stochastic Processes* (Duxbury, New York, 1997).

[11]R. S. Kenett and S. Zacks, *Modern Industrial Statistics: With Applications in R, MINITAB and JMP*, 2nd edn. (Wiley, New York, 2014).

[12]I. Olkin, A. J. Petkau and J. V. Zidek, A comparison of the n estimators for the binomial distributions, *J. Am. Stat. Assoc.* **76**, 637 (1981).

[13]A. Raftery, Inference on the binomial N parameter: A hierarchical Bayes approach, *Biometrika* **75**, 223 (1988).

[14]W. D. Ray, Sequential confidence intervals for the mean of a normal population with unknown variance, *J. R. Stat. Soc. B* **19**, 133 (1957).

[15]C. Stein, A two sample test for a linear hypothesis when power is independent of variance, *Ann. Math. Stat.* **16**, 243 (1945).

[16]C. Stein, Some problems in sequential estimation (abstract) *Econometrika*, **17**, 77 (1949).

[17]A. Wald, *Sequential Analysis* (Wiley, New York, 1947).

[18]A. Wald and J. Wolfowitz, Optimum character of sequential probability ratio test, *Ann. Math. Stat.* **19**, 326 (1948).

[19]S. Zacks, *The Theory of Statistical Inference* (Wiley, New York, 1971).

[20]S. Zacks, *Stage-Wise Adaptive Designs* (Wiley, New York, 2009).

[21]S. Zacks, *Examples and Problems in Mathematical Statistics* (Wiley, New York, 2014).

[22]S. Zacks and N. Mukhopadhyay, Distributions of sequential and two-stage stopping times for fixed-width confidence intervals in Bernulli trials: Applications in reliability, *Sequential Anal.* **26**, 425 (2007).

Business process mining

Asef Pourmasoumi* and Ebrahim Bagheri[†]

Department of Electrical and Computer Engineering
Ryerson University, Canada

Laboratory for Systems, Software and Semantics (LS3)
87 Gerrard St East, Toronto, ON, M5B 1G9, Canada
*a.pourmasoumi@ryerson.ca
[†]bagheri@ryerson.ca

One of the most valuable assets of an organization is its organizational data. The analysis and mining of this potential hidden treasure can lead to much added-value for the organization. Process mining is an emerging area that can be useful in helping organizations understand the status quo, check for compliance and plan for improving their processes. The aim of process mining is to extract knowledge from event logs of today's organizational information systems. Process mining includes three main types: discovering process models from event logs, conformance checking and organizational mining. In this paper, we briefly introduce process mining and review some of its most important techniques. Also, we investigate some of the applications of process mining in industry and present some of the most important challenges that are faced in this area.

Keywords: Business process mining; process discovery; conformance checking; organizational mining; process improvement.

1. Introduction

Most organizations spend a lot of resources for implementing, analyzing and managing their business process models. Hence, tools or techniques that can help managers reach these goals are desirable. Process mining is a new research agenda, which helps managers gain more insight about their organization's processes. The main goal of process mining is to extract process-centric knowledge from event logs of existing information system of organizations. Process mining can be considered to be the X-ray machine, which shows the reality that occurs within the organization. In many cases, the process that is executed in an organization can have many differences with the process that is expected to be running. This can be because of several reasons such as management changes, infractions and so on. Process mining extracts valuable knowledge for managers and brings transparency for them by analyzing event logs that are stored in the database of information systems of organizations.

Process mining is a bridge between data mining and process modeling/analysis. Process mining and data mining have many commonalities. Most of data mining techniques such as classification, clustering, and sequence mining can be used in process mining as well. For example, extracting the bottlenecks of a process, improving a process, detecting the deviations in a process, analyzing the performance of a process, identifying the best and worst employee involved in a process are the types of objectives that require data mining techniques applied on business processes. The main

difference is that data mining is data-oriented while process mining is process-oriented. Process mining techniques include three main classes: (i) process discovery (automated discovery of process model from event log), (ii) conformance checking (detecting deviations by comparing process model and the corresponding event log), (iii) organizational mining (including several techniques such as social network analysis, prediction and recommendation systems).

Process mining techniques often work with event logs as input. Each event data to be usable should have at least three properties: (i) data should have timestamps, (ii) activity labels should be present and (iii) case id of each record should be specified (case id is the id of each process instance). Therefore, there is need to standardize the logging format of event logs. The *"IEEE Task Force on Process Mining"* has developed an xml-based XES[a] logging format. The XES is supported by OpenXES library and many tools such as ProM, Disco, and XESame.

In 2012, the "IEEE Task Force on process mining" also presented a manifesto for process mining, which is translated to more than ten languages.[1] In this manifesto, process mining is introduced and the most challenges and future works of this domain is specified.

1.1. *Quality measures in process mining*

Before discussing any process mining approach, it is better to talk about the quality measures in process mining. The most useful quality criteria are as follows[1]:

---

[a]www.xes-standard.org.

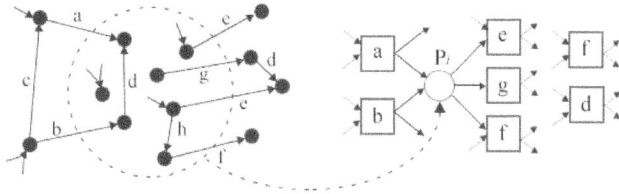

Fig. 1. Mapping of a region into a place.

(a) Fitness: This criteria indicates how much a discovered process model is in accordance with a corresponding event log. A common way for calculating fitness is replaying all traces on the process model and calculating the number of cases that trace cannot be replayed on the process model. The process model that has too much fitness, might suffer from the *overfitting* problem.

(b) Simplicity: The more the discovered model is simple, the more desirable it would be. Various ways of computing simplicity based on the number of activities and relations can be found in Ref. 2.

(c) Precision: A model is precise if it does not allow for too much unobserved behavior in event logs. For example, in "flower model", all traces of any event log set (which have the same set of activities) can be replayed (Fig. 1). Such models can lack precision and hence suffer from an *underfitting* problem.

(d) Generalization: This criteria is used for avoiding the overfitting problem. A model should have a minimum generalization and not be restricted to the behavior that is seen in the logs. Because we should always consider that the event logs might be incomplete.

In many cases, these criteria are competing with each other and increasing one may decrease another (e.g., a model that has high fitness might have low generalization). So, process mining algorithms should balance between these quality dimensions.

2. What is Process Mining?

2.1. *Process discovery*

The first main type and one of the most challenging tasks of process mining is process discovery. A process discovery technique takes an event log of an information system as input and generates a model without using any *a priori* information.[2] Process discovery can be investigated from various perspectives, e.g., the control-flow perspective, the organizational perspective, the case perspective and the time perspective. The control-flow perspective focuses on the control-flow of process models such as extracting activity orders in terms of a modeling language (e.g., BPMN,[3] Petri net,[4] EPCs[5] and UML activity diagram[6]). The organizational or resource perspective focuses on organizational resource (e.g., human, monetary, raw materials and capital) information that can be extracted from event logs. In the case view, we attend to various properties of cases (e.g., count of cases).

The time view is related with timing and frequency of events. Process discovery through each of these perspectives can give different valuable insight to managers. In the following, we introduce a classification of process discovery approaches.

2.1.1. *Region-based process mining*

The Alpha algorithm is one of the simplest and practical discovery approaches that produces a Petri net explaining the process behavior recorded in event logs.[7] The idea of the Alpha algorithm is simple and used by many process mining algorithms. The α-algorithm scans the event log for particular patterns. For example, if in the event logs, activity a is always followed by b but b is never followed by a, then it is assumed that there is a causal dependency between a and b.[8] There are four relations in α-algorithm that we briefly explained it:

- Direct succession: $a > b$ if for some case a is directly followed by b,
- Causality: $a \rightarrow b$ if $a > b$ and not $b > a$,
- Parallel: $a \| b$ if $a > b$ and $b > a$,
- Choice: $a \# b$ if not $a > b$ and not $b > a$

Event logs should be scanned for extracting these relations. The result can be shown as footprint matrix as shown in Fig. 2. Suppose that L_1 is a simple log describing the history of seven cases:

$$L_1 = [\langle a, b, d, e \rangle^2, \langle a, d, b, e \rangle^2, \langle a, c, e \rangle^3].$$

Each trace in L_1 corresponds to a possible execution in Petri net process model of Fig. 3. Scanning L_1 led to footprint matrix of Fig. 2. Using the footprint matrix, the particular patterns as shown in Fig. 4 can be discovered easily. The detailed algorithm can be found in Ref. 8.

Although α-algorithm can discover a large class of process models, there are several limitations. In the face of one-length loop, two-length loop, invisible tasks, duplicated tasks,

	a	b	c	d	e
a	#	$\rightarrow$	$\rightarrow$	$\rightarrow$	#
b	$\leftarrow$	#	#	$\|$	$\rightarrow$
c	$\leftarrow$	#	#	#	$\rightarrow$
d	$\leftarrow$	$\|$	#	#	$\rightarrow$
e	#	$\leftarrow$	$\leftarrow$	$\leftarrow$	#

Fig. 2. Footprint matrix of L_1.

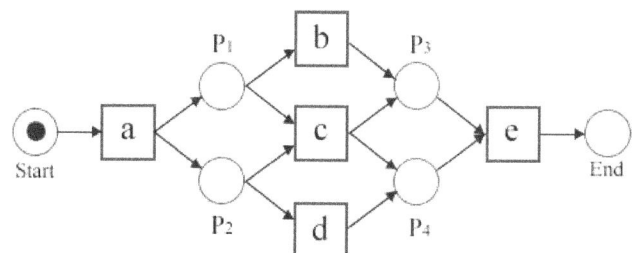

Fig. 3. Discovered process model for event logs. $L_1 = [\langle a, b, d, e \rangle^2, \langle a, d, b, e \rangle^2, \langle a, c, e \rangle^3]$.

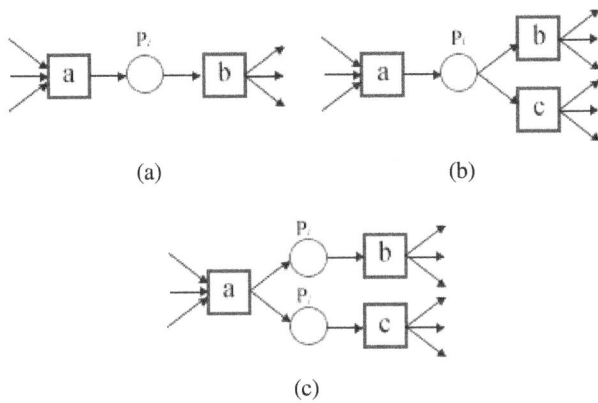

Fig. 4. Some of the most widely used. (a) Sequence pattern $a \rightarrow b$, (b) XOR-split pattern $a \rightarrow b$, $a \rightarrow c$, $b \# c$ and (c) AND-split pattern $a \rightarrow b$, $a \rightarrow c$, $b \| c$.

and nonfree choice constructs, the α-algorithm cannot work properly. Hence, several extensions of the α-algorithm like as α^+-algorithm,[9]α^{++}-algorithm[10] is proposed to overcome these problems. However, for real-life event data more advanced algorithms are needed to better balance between different discovery quality measures.

2.1.2. *Region-based process mining*

Region-based process mining approaches are highly based on the *theory of regions*.[11] The theory of regions makes a link between transition systems and Petri nets through the so-called *Net synthesis*. The main idea of theory of regions is that a state-based model such as transition system can be transformed into a Petri net. In Ref. 2, several functions for converting event logs to a transition system is introduced. There two main region-based process mining types: (a) state-based regions,[11] (b) language-based regions.[12] In state-based region process discovery, a region is defined as set of states such that all activities in the transition system "agree" on the region.[2] Based on each region, all activities can be classified into entering the region, leaving the region, and noncrossing. After extracting regions based on these simple rules, each minimal region corresponds to a place in Petri net model. In Fig. 5, an example region and its corresponding place is shown. In this region, activities a and b enter to region and activities e, g and f exit the region. Also, activities d and h do not cross the region. This region can be mapped into a place P_i such as one is show in Fig. 5. In similar vein, all regions

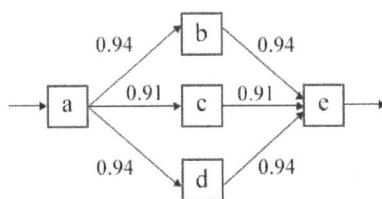

Fig. 5. Dependency graph.

extracted and a corresponding place for each of them is created.

The second main type of region based process mining is language-based.[12] Similar to state-based algorithms, the aim of this type is to determine Petri net places; however, these models use some specific pre-defined *"language"* instead of a transition system as input. The basic idea of language-based approaches is based on the fact that removing place P_i will not remove any behavior, but adding place P_i may remove some possible behaviors in the Petri net.[2] So, adding a place to a Petri net may restrict the corresponding behavior in the event log. Based on this simple idea, language-based approaches try to add various places as long as the behaviors seen in the logs are not limited. This problem can be modeled in terms of an inequation system. The main obstacle of this category is that linear inequation systems have many solutions and they need to consider the log to be complete. There are some newer approaches for solving these problems such as.[13]

2.1.3. *Heuristic mining*

Heuristic mining algorithms use *casual nets* representation. A causal net is a graph whose nodes are activities and arcs are causal dependencies. Each activity has a set of possible input bindings and a set of possible output bindings. In heuristic mining, the frequencies of events and sequences is considered.[14,15] In fact, heuristic mining aims to remove infrequent paths. For this purpose, at first, similar to footprint matrix in the α-algorithm, a dependency matrix is calculated. A dependency matrix, shows the frequency of *directly follows* relation (i.e., $|a > b|$ is the number of times that a is directly followed by b) in the event logs. Using the dependency matrix, the so-called *dependency graph* is created (Fig. 5). The dependency graph shows the arcs that meet certain *thresholds*. The main drawback of this presentation approach is that it cannot show the routing logic of business process correctly. For example, in Fig. 5, the exact relation type between b, c and d is not clear. However, it can show the main stream of process.[14] After extracting dependency graph, it should be converted to casual nets. The detailed algorithm can be found in Refs. 14 and 15.

2.1.4. *Evolutionary process mining*

Evolutionary process mining is a subcategory of the larger category of search based process mining.[16] Similar to other applications of evolutionary approaches in other domains, evolutionary process mining techniques use iterative procedure, are nondeterministic and have four main steps[2]:

(i) Initialization: In this step, the initial population including a set of individual process models is generated randomly. These process models are generated using

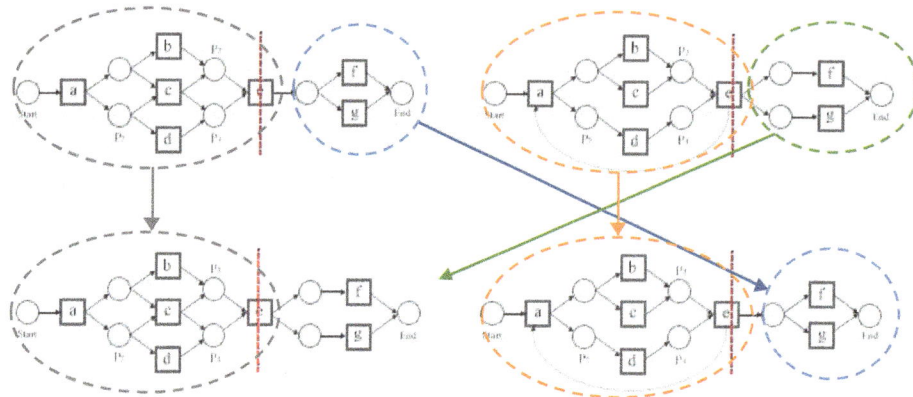

Fig. 6. (Color online) An example of genetic process mining.

activities that exist in the event logs, however they might have little compliance with the seen behavior in the event logs, due to the random generation procedure.

(ii) Selection: In this step, the best generated individuals should be selected based on a fitness function for mutation (regenerate step). The fitness function calculates the quality of the discovered process according to existing event logs based on process discovery quality criteria.[1] The best individuals are selected based on the highest fitness score.

(iii) Regenerate: After selecting the best individuals, new generation of individuals is created using two operators: *crossover* and *mutation*. Using crossover operator (the red dotted line in Fig. 6), individuals are separated into children. Next, these children are modified using mutation to generate the next generation. The new generation would be considered as the initial population and the algorithm iterates as long as the termination constraint is not satisfied.

(iv) Termination: The algorithm will terminate when the newly generated individuals reach a minimum fitness score. These individuals will be returned as the discovered process model.

In Fig. 6, an example of procedure of genetic process mining is shown. There are two individual process models which using *crossover*, each of them are splitted into two sub-processes. Then, using *mutation* the first child of the first process model is composed with the second child of the second process model and second child of the first process is composed with the first child of the second process.

The main drawback of genetic process mining approaches is their time complexity and their uncertainty.[16]

2.2. *Conformance checking*

The second major type of process mining is conformance checking.[2] Conformance checking is used for deviation detection, prediction, decision making and recommendation systems. In conformance checking, an event log is compared with its existing corresponding process model and it reveals

that if process model conforms to reality and vice versa. For example, in educational systems, using conformance checking it can check which students do not select their courses according to their educational chart and have deviations. As another example, in the banking domain, it can check which cases do not follow the process model and why it happens? Scanning event logs using conformance checking techniques increases transparency and leads to fraud detection[17] and is very useful tool for auditors. Conformance checking also used for evaluating process discovery approaches from a *fitness* point of view.

One of the most widely used methods for conformance checking is replaying all cases of event log using a token on its corresponding process model.[17,18] Based on this method, the *fitness* of the event log in light of the process model is calculated (the fitness is most relevant measure from the four quality criteria for calculating conformance). In Ref. 2, fitness is defined as "the proportion of behavior in the event log possible according to the model". Token-replay based techniques are simple and can be implemented efficiently.[2]

The main drawback of token-replay based methods is that those cases that do not fit the process model would be ignored totally. So, in this situation, the result might be biased and diagnostics would be decreased. Furthermore, token-replay based methods are only Petri-net specific. There are another class of methods for conformance checking such as *alignment*-based techniques.[2] Alignment-based approaches have been developed to overcome these problems. In these approaches, a table mapping between each trace and process model is created.[19] These mappings are called alignment or optimal alignment. Using alignment-based approaches, each case can be analyzed separately and the results can be aggregated at the process model level.[2] More details on alignment-based approaches can be found in Refs. 19–21.

2.3. *Organizational mining*

Organizational mining is the third type of process mining activity, which brings more insight for organizations and can led to added value. Using organizational mining, the bottlenecks of processes is analyzed and new improvements are proposed. The most widely used technique for this purpose is social network analysis.[8] The resources are represented by nodes and the relations by links. The thickness of a link shows the amount of relationships between two nodes.[8] Also, the nodes or links may have weight which show their importance. So far, many metrics for analyzing social networks have been proposed such as *closeness*, *betweenness*, *centrality*, and *shortest distance* among others.[2]

Another application of organizational mining is extracting organizational structures or organizational charts. In reality, in many cases the discovered organizational chart from event logs differ from existing organizational structure on the documents. Based on the discovered chart, the senior manager can make decisions, e.g., change the physical location of the employee based on their real connections. For more details on organizational mining see Ref. 22.

One main aspect of organizational mining is cross-organizational mining.[1] In cross-organizational mining more than one organization is involved. Actually, the cross-organizations collaborations is usually in two modes. First, different organizations work with each other on the same instance of a process. For example, for building a house several organization such as municipality, insurance, power authority and others might be involved. In this case, the organizations act like puzzle pieces.[1] In the second type, several organizations share a common infrastructure and execute the same process model. The example of this case is cloud based software services. A famous example is *Salesforce.com*, which manages and supports the sales of processes for many organizations.[2]

3. Applications of Process Mining

Process mining has been used in several domains such as healthcare, financial (specially banking domain), production, e-commerce, logistics, monitoring, e-government, insurance, among others. Here, we have presented two important applications of process mining in today's life: healthcare and e-commerce. In the following, we give an example of application of process mining in these domains.

3.1. *Process mining in healthcare*

One of the most important challenges in healthcare is rising costs of healthcare. Based on OECD health statistics 2015, average per capita health spending across OECD countries has been on an upward trend.[b] So, there is urgent need for decreasing these costs. One ideal solution is focusing on the complex time-consuming treatment processes such as cancer or surgery treatment processes.[24,25] Traditional approaches for improving and redesigning such process models is

conducting interviews and field studies. Analyzing process models in this way is too costly and time consuming. Moreover, depending on the person being interviewed and depending on the interviewer, it can be subjective. Furthermore, in some cases, there might be organizational resistances and many stakeholders may not tend to decrease costs or have any changes in the process models. So in this case, we need to capture the reality from existing information systems. Process mining tools can give objective suggestions for reducing the treatment processing time of patients.

For further information, you can refer to Ref. 26. Man *et al.* published an interesting book about applications of process mining in the healthcare domain and the challenges that exist in this regards.[26]

3.2. *Process mining in e-commerce*

E-commerce has significant portion of business in today's world. The most worthy thing in e-commerce is data. As more data is available, further analysis can be done and more and more customers will be attracted. For example, Amazon as one of the biggest marketplace seller uses process mining for analyzing the online purchase process of customers. Combining process mining algorithms with natural language processing methods such as sentiment analysis can give clear insight into each user's behavior and led to accurate recommendations. Suppose a customer who wants to purchase a camera. Certainly, the customer investigates and compares various brands and models to make the most optimal decision and finally decide to purchase a camera of model X. In the meantime, the customer would read other user's comments (feedbacks). Having clicking/scrolling data of different customers that purchased camera of model X, using process discovery techniques the seller can discover the path that most of the customers follow to purchase camera of model X. Based on the discovered path, the seller can make some decisions to change this path to decrease the time to decision of customers and also selling more camera of model X.

3.3. *Other applications of process mining*

Process mining has also seen widely increasing applications in banking/financial domain.[27] Todays, large number of banks and financial institutes use process mining techniques in threefolds: (i) improving their own inter-organizational processes, (ii) in order to increase income and attract more customers, (iii) auditing financial accounts.[28]

Process mining has also been used successfully in the insurance domain. In Ref. 29, a case study of applications of process mining in one of the largest insurance companies in Australia (Suncorp) is reported. This paper reported new insight of the way insurance claims has being processed at Suncorp.

Process mining also has been used in many *municipalities*,[30] *hardware manufacturers* like as ASML,[31] *educational*

---

[b]https://www.oecd.org.

organizations such as universities, (e.g., TU/e employed process mining to analyze the educational behaviors of the students), *transportation* industry, *cloud computing* based industry such as Salesforce.com and others.

4. Challenges

Despite the many capabilities and applications of process mining techniques, there are still important challenges that should be addressed.[1,2] The most important challenge of process mining is data. There are several concerns about event data; (a) data usually are *object-oriented*, not *process-oriented* (there is need for nontrivial efforts to convert object-oriented event data to process-oriented data); (b) event data might be *incomplete*; (c) data might be distributed over several sources with different terminology, (d) in most of situations there is need to do data cleansing on processes, (e) different levels of *timestamps* ranging from milliseconds to coarse format, e.g., 23-08-2016 might exist, and (f) the activities names may differ in different data sources.

Another important concern about processes is *concept drift*.[32] Here, concept drift means that a process might change during analysis. There are several reasons that can lead to these changes. The data can change because of business conditions. For example, in some periods of the year like such as Christmas time or before the opening of schools, store sales change considerably, or in some days such as Sundays there is less need for the presence of employees. Hence, it is important to select appropriate range of data. Sometimes, event data changes due to the changes in process models or event in information systems. For example, a new manager may want to make some changes in running processes. So, there will be a concept drift between data related to old process and the newer process. In Ref. 33, four types of concept drift have been introduced: sudden drifts, gradual drifts, recurring drifts and incremental drifts. In a sudden drift, the whole process will suddenly change from start to end (e.g., due to management changes the whole process changes). In gradual drift, the process model changes for the nonuniform interval of time. For example, according to requests from different stockholders or even the employee, the process changes gradually over time. Recurring drifts refers to cyclical changes that are caused by business conditions (e.g., as changes in store sales in certain period of time). In incremental drift, a process will change in a gradual fashion.

Considering concept drift is important issue in dealing with real processes logs. In the recent years, several papers have been published in this domain.[32,34,35] In Ref. 36 a review on concept drift in process mining is presented.

The different level of granularity of event logs is another important issue that should be considered. For example, in the health care domain, hospital information systems (HIS) cover wide range of treatment processes; from the simple outpatient to complex surgical or cancer treatment procedures.[26]

5. Process Mining Tools

There are several free open source and commercial software for process mining. ProM[c] is the most widely used and complete open-source process mining platform.[37] ProM is multi-perspective and includes several modules for process discovery, conformance checking and organizational mining. Most of the process discovery and conformance checking algorithms is implemented in ProM and can be accessed freely. There are also some other noncommercial process mining tools such as RapidProM[d] (combination of Rapid-Miner with some process mining plug-ins from ProM),[38] PMLAB[e] (a script-based process mining tool which support variety of process discovery techniques, specially region-based approaches), CoBeFra[f] (a framework for conformance checking), PLG[g] (a platform for generating random process models and corresponding event logs)[38] and PVLG (a tool for generating process variants).[39]

There are also several commercial process mining software such as Disco,[h] Celonis,[i] Minit,[j] myInvenio,[k] QPR Process Analyzer,[l] Rialto,[m] SNP,[n] Interstage Business Process Manager Analytics (Fujitsu) etc. In Ref. 2, a comprehensive classification of these products based on the different criteria (e.g., openness, formalness of discovered process, input types, output types, and types of deployments) is presented. Moreover, an analysis of strengths and weaknesses of these tools is presented.

5.1. *Conclusion & future directions*

We have briefly review the state of the art in process mining. We introduced the main works in process mining and presented well known approaches and tools. Furthermore, we introduced some open problems and challenges in this field. Handling incomplete, noisy, object-oriented event data in proposing different process mining algorithms should be considered.

With increasing amount of data in today's databases, there is need for techniques that can handle such big data. There are some works on distributed systems for handling and processing event logs.[40,41] However, there is yet need for more work for developing process mining algorithms based on big data infrastructures.

---

[c]http://www.promtools.org.
[d]www.rapidprom.org.
[e]https://www.cs.upc.edu/~jcarmona/PMLAB/.
[f]http://www.processmining.be/cobefra.
[g]http://plg.processmining.it/.
[h]www.fluxicon.com.
[i]www.celonis.de.
[j]http://www.minitlabs.com.
[k]https://www.my-invenio.com.
[l]http://www.qpr.com/products/qpr-processanalyzer.
[m]www.exeura.eu.
[n]www.snp-bpa.com.

Online process mining is another research direction that allows for the real-time processing of event and process data. Along with the increase in the quality of process mining techniques, the time complexity of these algorithms should also be considered.

Analyzing cross-organizational mining is also an attractive research area. In cross-organizational mining, there are more challenges compared to single organizational mining, because each organization has its own organizational culture and its own process structure and infrastructure. Mining process models through the event logs of different information systems can be challenging.

References

[1] F. Daniel, K. Barkaoui and S. Dustdar (eds.), IEEE task force on process mining, process mining manifesto, *Business Process Management Workshops*, Lecture Notes in Business Information Processing, Vol. 99 (Springer, Berlin, 2012), pp. 169–194.

[2] W. M. P. van der Aalst, *Process Mining — Data Science in Action*, Second Edition (Springer, 2016), pp. 3–452.

[3] S. White, *Introduction to BPMN* (BPMI, New York, NY, 2004).

[4] K. Salimifard and M. Wright, Petri net-based modelling of workflow systems: An overview, *Eur. J. Oper. Res.* **134**, 664 (2001).

[5] W. M. P. van der Aalst, Formalization and verification of event driven process chains, *Inf. Softw. Technol.* **41**(10), 639 (1999).

[6] M. Dumas and A. T. Hofstede, UML activity diagrams as a workflow specification language, *Proc. Int. Conf. Unified Modeling Language* (UML), (2001), pp. 86–90.

[7] W. M. P. van der Aalst, A. J. M. M. Weijters and L. Maruster, Workflow mining: Discovering process models from event logs, *IEEE Trans. Knowl. Data Eng.* **16**(9), 1128 (2004).

[8] W. M. P. van der Aalst and M. Song, Mining social networks: Uncovering interaction patterns in business processes, *Business Process Management 2004 LNCS*, eds. J. Diesel, B. Pernici and M. Weske, Vol. 3080 (Springer, Heidelberg, 2004), pp. 244–260.

[9] A. K. Alves de Medeiros, W. M. P. van der Aalst and A. J. M. M. Weijters, Workflow mining: Current status and future directions, *On the Move to Meaningful Internet Systems 2003: CoopIS, DOA, and ODBASE*, Vol. 2888, Lecture Notes in Computer Science (Springer, Berlin, 2003), pp. 389–406.

[10] L. Wen, W. M. P. van der Aalst, J. Wang and J. Sun, Mining process models with non-free-choice constructs, *Data Min. Knowl. Discov.* **15**(2), 145 (2007).

[11] B. F. van Dongen, N. Busi, G. M. Pinna and W. M. P. van der Aalst, An iterative algorithm for applying the theory of regions in process mining, eds. W. Reisig, K. van Hee and K. Wolf, *Proc. Workshop on Formal Approaches to Business Processes and Web Services (FABPWS'07)*, (Publishing House of University of Podlasie, Siedlce, 2007), pp. 36–55.

[12] R. Bergenthum, J. Diesel, R. Lorenz and S. Mauser, Process mining based on religions of languages, *International Conference on Business Process Management (BPM 2007)*, G. Alonso, P. Dadam and M. Rosemann, Lecture Notes in Computer Science, Vol. 4714 (Springer, Berlin, 2007), pp. 375–383.

[13] S. J. van Zelst, B. F. van Dongen and W. M. P. van der Aalst, Filter Techniques for Region-Based Process Discovery, Technical Report 15-4, BPM Center.org (2015).

[14] A. J. M. M. Weijters and J. T. S. Ribeiro, Flexible Heuristics Miner (FHM), BETA Working Paper Series, WP 334, Eindhoven University of Technology, Eindhoven (2010).

[15] A. J. M. M. Weijters and W. M. P. van der Aalst, Rediscovering workflow models from event-based data using little thumb, *Integrated Computer-Aided Eng.* **10**(2), 151 (2003).

[16] A. K. A de Medeiros, A. J. M. M. Weijters and W. M. P. van der Aalst, Genetic process mining: An experimental evaluation, *Data Min. Knowl. Discov.* **14**(2), 245 (2007).

[17] A. Rozinat and W. M. P. van der Aalst, Conformance checking of processes based on monitoring real behavior, *Inf. Syst.* **33**(1), 64 (2008).

[18] A. Rozinat, Process Mining: Conformance and Extension. Ph.D. thesis, Eindhoven University of Technology, November (2010).

[19] M. de Leoni, F. M. Maggi and W. M. van der Aalst, An alignment-based framework to check the conformance of declarative process models and to preprocess event-log data, *Inf. Syst.* (2015).

[20] A. Adriansyah, Aligning observed and modeled behavior, Ph.D. thesis, Eindhoven University of Technology, April (2014).

[21] A. Adriansyah, J. Munoz-Gama, J. Carmona, B. F. van Dongen and W. M. P. van der Aalst, Measuring precision of modeled behavior, *Inf. Syst. e-Bus. Manage.* **13**(1), 37 (2015).

[22] M. Song and W. M. P. van der Aalst, Towards comprehensive support for organizational mining, *Decis. Support Syst.* **46**(1), 300 (2008).

[23] A. Pourmasoumi, M. Kahani and E. Bagheri, Mining variable fragments from process event logs, *Inf. Syst. Front.* (2016).

[24] H. Berthold, J. Cardoso, P. Cunha, R. Mans, S. Quaglini and W. M. P. van der Aalst, A framework for next generation e-health systems and services, AMCIS (2015).

[25] M. Rovani, F. M. Maggi, M. de Leoni and W. M. P. van der Aalst, Declarative process mining in healthcare, *Expert Syst. Appl.* **42**, 9236 (2015).

[26] R. Mans, W. M. P. van der Aalst and R. J. B. Vanwersch, *Process Mining in Healthcare — Evaluating and Exploiting Operational Healthcare Processes* (Springer Briefs in Business Process Management, Springer, 2015), pp. 1–91.

[27] N. Gehrke and N. Mueller-Wickop, Basic principles of financial process mining: A journey through financial data in accounting information systems, *Proc. Sixteenth Americas Conference on Information Systems*, Lima, Peru (2010).

[28] M. Jans, M. Alles and M. Vasarhelyi, The case for process mining in auditing: Sources of value added and areas of application, *Int. J. Account. Inf. Syst.* **14**, 1 (2013).

[29] S. Suriadi, M. T. Wynn, C. Ouyang, A. H. ter Hofstede and N. van Dijk, Understanding process behaviours in a large insurance company in Australia: A case study, *25th Int. Conf. Advanced Information Systems Engineering, CAiSE 2013*, Valencia, Spain (2013), pp. 449–464.

[30] F. Gottschalk, T. A. C. Wagemakers, M. H. Jansen-Vullers, W. M. P. van der Aalst and M. La Rosa, Configurable Process Models: Experiences from a Municipality Case Study, CAiSE (2009), pp. 486–500.

[31] A. Rozinat, I. S. M. de Jong, C. W. Günther and W. M. P. van der Aalst, Process mining applied to the test process of wafer scanners in ASML, *IEEE Trans. Syst. Man, and Cybern. C* **39**(4), 474 (2009).

[32] R. P. J. C. Bose, W. M. P. van der Aalst, I. Zliobaite and M. Pechenizkiy, Dealing with concept drift in process mining, (accepted to) *IEEE Trans. Neur. Net. Learn. Syst.*

[33]V. Mittal and I. Kashyap, Online methods of learning in occurrence of concept drift, *Int. J. Comput. Appl.* (2015).

[34]B. Hompes, J. C. A. M. Buijs, W. M. P. van der Aalst, P. Dixit and H. Buurman, Detecting Change in Processes Using Comparative Trace Clustering, SIMPDA (2015), pp. 95–108.

[35]A. Maaradji, M. Dumas, M. La Rosa and A. Ostovar, Fast and accurate business process drift detection, *Business Process Management* (Springer, 2015), pp. 406–422.

[36]N. A. Dumasia and A. Shah, Review paper on concept drift in process mining, *Int. Res. J. Eng. Technol.* (IRJET) (2016).

[37]H. M. W. Verbeek, J. C. A. M. Buijs, B. F. van Dongen and W. M. P. van der Aalst, XES, XESame, and ProM 6, *Information System Evolution*, Vol. 72 (Springer, 2011), pp. 60–75.

[38]R. Mans, W. M. P. van der Aalst and E. Verbeek, Supporting process mining workflows with RapidProM, *Business Process Management Demo Sessions (BPMD 2014)*, eds. L. Limonad and B. Weber, Vol. 1295, CEUR Workshop Proc. CEUR-WS.org (2014), pp. 56–60.

[39]A. Burattin and A. Sperduti, PLG: A framework for the generation of business process models and their execution logs, *Business Process Management Workshops* (Springer, 2010), pp. 214–219.

[40][POU15] A. Pourmasoumi, M. Kahani, E. Bagheri and M. Asadi, On Business Process Variants Generation, CAiSE FORUM (2015).

[41]M. Leemans and W. M. P. van der Aalst, Process mining in software systems: Discovering real-life business transactions and process models from distributed systems, MoDELS (2015), pp. 44–53.

[42]W. M. P. van der Aalst, Distributed Process Discovery and Conformance Checking, FASE (2012), pp. 1–25.

The information quality framework for evaluating data science programs

Shirley Y. Coleman

ISRU, Newcastle University, UK

shirley.coleman@newcastle.ac.uk

Ron S. Kenett

KPA, Israel and University of Turin, Italy

ron@kpa-group.com

Designing a new Analytics programF requires not only identifying needed courses, but also tying the courses together into a cohesive curriculum with an overriding theme. Such a theme helps to determine the proper sequencing of courses and create a coherent linkage between different courses often taught by faculty staff from different domains. It is common to see a program with some courses taught by computer science faculty, other courses taught by faculty and staff from the statistics department, and others from operations research, economics, information systems, marketing or other disciplines. Applying an overriding theme not only helps students organize their learning and course planning, but it also helps the teaching faculty in designing their materials and choosing terminology. The InfoQ framework introduced by Kenett and Shmueli provides a theme that focuses the attention of faculty and students on the important question of the value of data and its analysis with flexibility that accommodates a wide range of data analysis topics. In this chapter, we review a number of programs focused on analytics and data science content from an InfoQ perspective. Our goal is to show, with examples, how the InfoQ dimensions are addressed in existing programs and help identify best practices for designing and improving such programs. We base our assessment on information derived from the program's web site.

Keywords: Decision science; information quality; educational framework.

1. Introduction

The last several years have seen an incredible growth in the number of courses and new programs in "Data Science", "Business Analytics", "Predictive Analytics", "Big Data Analytics", and related titles. Different programs have a different emphasis depending on whether they are housed in a business school, a computer science department, or a cross-departmental program. What is however common to all of them, is their focus on data (structured and unstructured), and specifically, on data analysis.

Many Statistics and Operations Research programs and departments have been restructuring, revising, and rebranding their courses and programs to match the high demand for people skilled in data analysis.

Designing a new analytics program requires not only identifying needed courses, but also tying the courses together into a cohesive curriculum with an overriding theme. Such a theme helps determine the proper sequencing of courses and create a coherent linkage between different courses often taught by faculty from different domains. It is common to see a program with some courses taught by computer science faculty, other courses taught by faculty from the statistics department, and others from operations research, economics, information systems, marketing or other disciplines. Applying an overriding theme not only helps students organize their learning and course planning, but it also helps the teaching faculty in designing their materials and choosing terminology. A theme like this also helps in designing courses to be co-taught by faculty with different backgrounds and expertise.

The InfoQ framework introduced in Ref. 1 provides a theme that focuses the attention of faculty and students on the important question of the value of data and its analysis with flexibility that accommodates a wide range of data analysis topics.

By adopting an InfoQ framework, the instructor and students focus on the goals of a study, the data used in the analysis, the analysis methods, and the utility measures learned in a certain course. This focus helps compare and contrast knowledge provided across courses, creating richness and cohesion. The eight InfoQ dimensions can be used in structuring any empirical data analysis course — be it predictive analytics, econometrics, optimization, advanced regression analysis, database management, or any other course that touches on data and data analysis.

In this chapter, we review a number of programs focused on analytics and data science content from an InfoQ perspective. Our goal is to show, with examples, how the InfoQ dimensions are addressed in existing programs and help identify best practices for designing and improving such programs. We base our assessment on information derived from the program's web site. The next section provides a review of the InfoQ dimensions. Following sections provide a review of a number of data science programs offered in Europe. This is followed by an integrated analysis of these findings. A final section concludes the chapter with a summary and points deserving further consideration.

2.   Introduction to Information Quality

The concept of information quality (InfoQ) is defined as the potential of a dataset to achieve a specific (scientific or practical) goal using a given empirical analysis method (Ref. 1). InfoQ is different from data quality and analysis quality, but is dependent on these components and on the relationship between them. InfoQ is derived from the utility of applying an analysis (f) to a data set (X) for a given purpose (g). Formally, the concept of InfoQ is defined as:

$$\text{InfoQ}(f, X, U, g) = U(f(X|g)).$$

InfoQ is therefore affected by the quality of its components g ("quality of goal definition"), X ("data quality"), f ("analysis quality"), and U ("utility measure") as well as by the relationships between X, f, g and U. Expanding on the four InfoQ components provides some additional insights.

Analysis Goal (g): Data analysis is used for various purposes. Three general classes of goals are causal explanations, predictions, and descriptions. Causal explanation includes questions such as "Which factors cause the outcome?" Prediction goals include forecasting future values of a time series and predicting the output value of new observations given a set of input variables. Descriptive goals include quantifying and testing for population effects using data summaries, graphical visualizations, statistical models, and statistical tests.

Data (X): The term "data" includes any type of data to which empirical analysis can be applied. Data can arise from different collection tools such as surveys, laboratory tests, field and computer experiments, simulations, web searches, observational studies and more. "Data" can be univariate or multivariate and of any size. It can contain semantic, unstructured information in the form of text or images with or without a dynamic time dimension. Data is the foundation of any application of empirical analysis.

Data Analysis Method (f): The term data analysis refers to statistical analysis and data mining. This includes statistical models and methods (parametric, semi-parametric, nonparametric), data mining algorithms, and graphical methods. Operations research methods, such as simplex optimization, where problems are modeled and parametrized, fall into this category as well.

Utility (U): The extent to which the analysis goal is achieved is typically measured by some performance measure or "utility". For example, in studies with a predictive goal, a popular performance measure is predictive accuracy. In descriptive studies, common utility measures are goodness-of-fit measures. In explanatory models, statistical power and strength-of-fit measures are common utility measures.

Eight dimensions are used to deconstruct InfoQ and thereby provide an approach for assessing it. These are: Data Resolution, Data Structure, Data Integration, Temporal Relevance, Chronology of Data and Goal, Generalizability, Operationalization and Communication. We proceed with a description of these dimensions.

(i) *Data Resolution*: Data resolution refers to the measurement scale and aggregation level of X. The measurement scale of the data needs to be carefully evaluated in terms of its suitability to the goal, the analysis methods to be used, and the required resolution of U. Given the original recorded scale, the researcher should evaluate its adequacy. It is usually easy to produce a more aggregated scale (e.g., two income categories instead of ten), but not a finer scale. Data might be recorded by multiple instruments or by multiple sources. To choose among the multiple measurements, supplemental information about the reliability and precision of the measuring devices or data sources is useful. A finer measurement scale is often associated with more noise; hence the choice of scale can affect the empirical analysis directly. The data aggregation level must also be evaluated in relation to the goal.

(ii) *Data Structure*: Data structure relates to the type of data analyzed and data characteristics such as corrupted and missing values due to the study design or data collection mechanism. Data types include structured numerical data in different forms (e.g., cross-sectional, time series, network data) as well as unstructured, nonnumerical data (e.g., text, text with hyperlinks, audio, video, and semantic data). The InfoQ level of a certain data type depends on the goal at hand.

(iii) *Data Integration*: With the variety of data source and data types, there is often a need to integrate multiple sources and/or types. Often, the integration of multiple data types creates new knowledge regarding the goal at hand, thereby increasing InfoQ. For example, in online auction research, the integration of temporal bid sequences with cross-sectional auction and seller information leads to more precise predictions of final prices as well as to an ability to quantify the effects of different factors on the price process.

(iv) *Temporal Relevance*: The process of deriving knowledge from data can be put on a time line that includes the data collection, data analysis, and study deployment periods as well as the temporal gaps between the data collection, the data analysis, and the study deployment stages. These different durations and gaps can each affect InfoQ. The data collection duration can increase or decrease InfoQ, depending on the study goal, e.g., studying longitudinal effects versus a cross-sectional goal. Similarly, if the collection period includes uncontrollable transitions, this can be useful or disruptive, depending on the study goal.

(v) *Chronology of Data and Goal*: The choice of variables to collect, the temporal relationship between them, and their meaning in the context of the goal at hand also affects InfoQ. For example, in the context of online auctions, classic auction theory dictates that the number of bidders is an important driver of auction price. Models based on this theory are useful for explaining the effect of the number of bidders on price. However, for the purpose of predicting the price of ongoing online auctions, where the number of bidders is unknown until the auction ends, the variable "number of bidders", even if available in the data, is useless. Hence, the level of InfoQ contained in "number of bidders" for models of auction price depends on the goal at hand.

(vi) *Generalizability*: The utility of $f(X|g)$ is dependent on the ability to generalize f to the appropriate population. There are two types of generalization, statistical and scientific generalizability. Statistical generalizability refers to inferring from a sample to a target population. Scientific generalizability refers to applying a model based on a particular target population to other populations. This can mean either generalizing an estimated population pattern/model f to other populations, or applying f estimated from one population to predict individual observations in other populations using domain specific knowledge.

(vii) *Operationalization*: Operationalization relates to both construct operationalization and action operationalization. Constructs are abstractions that describe a phenomenon of theoretical interest. Measurable data is an operationalization of underlying constructs. The relationship between the underlying construct and its operationalization can vary, and its level relative to the goal is another important aspect of InfoQ. The role of construct operationalization depends on the goal, and especially on abstractions whether the goal is explanatory, predictive, or descriptive. In explanatory models, based on underlying causal theories, multiple operationalization might be acceptable for representing the construct of interest. As long as the data is assumed to measure the construct, the variable is considered adequate. In contrast, in a predictive task, where the goal is to create sufficiently accurate predictions of a certain measurable variable, the choice of operationalized variable is critical. Action operationalization is characterizing the practical implications of the information provided.

(viii) *Communication*: Effective communication of the analysis and its utility directly impacts InfoQ. There are plenty of examples where miscommunication of valid results has led to disasters, such as the NASA shuttle Challenger disaster (Ref. 2). Communication media are visual, textual, and verbal in the form of presentations and reports. Within research environments, communication focuses on written publications and conference presentations. Research mentoring and the refereeing process are aimed at improving communication and InfoQ within the research community.

3. Application of InfoQ to Data Science Programs

The eight InfoQ dimensions provide a framework that will enable the Data Science programs (DSPs) to be assessed from their websites in more detail than would be afforded by a casual read through. Each dimension implies relevant questions that should be asked. Examples of these questions are now given and it should be noted that a similar process of extracting questions based on InfoQ dimensions can be formulated for many other tasks. Some of the InfoQ dimensions give rise to questions that are more appropriate than others although all of the dimensions have something to offer. For a general set of questions to help review papers and technical reports using InfoQ dimensions see Refs. 3 and 4.

InfoQ depends on the goal set for the task and an appraisal of DSP can have a number of goals: for program directors to find a DSP to emulate as an exemplar; for potential students to choose a DSP to study. Students may be full time employees looking for a part time course, or may be employees wanting to change career or to enlarge their career options, or graduates wanting to continue their education. These are different stakeholders each having their own goal in appraising the programs. Other stakeholders include: funders, employers, the business community and the world at large. For this exercise, the goal is to appraise the InfoQ of DSPs with a view to finding a DSK to emulate as an exemplar. The utility of the various stakeholders obviously differs. Employers will look to hire employees which can provide added value in the short term. The DSK participant might rate high in his utility definition potential contacts and employability networks.

The DSPs have different aspects including content, mode of study, focus (employability, education as an end point, education as a route to PhD), cost, location, staffing, mode of delivery, reputation and status. These aspects are related to the goal of the DSP which may be to provide education, career development, access (thereby influencing cost and location), a revenue stream for the provider or a reputation boost. The classic components of problem analysis all need to be taken into consideration when appraising the DSP. Kepner and Tregoe (http://www.kepner-tregoe.com/), for example, focus on what, where, who and when in their problem analysis worksheets. Such questions are addressed in the different InfoQ dimension questions.

InfoQ also depends on data. There are many levels of research that can be carried out to explore the nature of a DSP ranging from appraising website information, studying staff profiles and publications, reviewing assessment material, examining employability figures and student feedback. For this exercise, the "data" used will be high level website information revealing details about the nature of the DSP. It is not the websites that are being appraised but the DSP behind the websites. We also do not consider any matching of the DSP to the profile of prospective students. To achieve this requires data on past students. A nice example, in the context of massive online open courses (MOOC) is provided in Ref. 5.

Recalling the four components of InfoQ, the following specific questions, organized by InfoQ dimension, provide the analytical method to be applied to the DSP as presented in its website and are offered as a suitable means of fulfilling the goal of appraising the quality of the DSP with a view to finding a DSP to emulate as an exemplar. Our adopted goal will be the same regardless of the goal of the DSP. The utility of the process and the findings are left to the opinion of the reader.

3.1. *Data resolution*

Data resolution refers to the measurement scale and aggregation level of the data. The measurement scale of the data should be carefully evaluated in terms of its suitability to the stated goal, the analysis methods used, and the required resolution of the research utility. A DSP program should provide students with tools and methods for understanding the appropriate data resolution for meeting specific goals. Questions related to this dimension include:

— Is the course content up to date regarding data collection tools and methods?
— Does the course have the flexibility to embrace changes and external influences?

A low rating on data resolution can be indicative of low trust in the usefulness of the DSP.

3.2. *Data structure*

Data structure relates to the type(s) of data and data characteristics such as corrupted and missing values due to the DSP design or data collection mechanism. Data types include structured numerical data in different forms (e.g., cross-sectional, time series, network data) as well as unstructured, nonnumerical data (e.g., text, text with hyperlinks, audio, video, and semantic data). The InfoQ level of a certain data type depends on the goal at hand. Questions related to this dimension include:

— Does the DSP offer good coverage of various data types (semantic, imaging, audio, social networks)?
— Are there any missing areas of content?
— Is there provision to fill gaps in knowledge and ensure all attendees can understand and benefit from the DSP?

— Is a good variety of teaching methods offered?
— Are different learning styles catered for?

A low rating on data structure can be indicative of poor coverage and/or a poor level of attention to the requirements of the different students.

3.3. *Data integration*

There is a wide variety of course structures and teaching methods available today. DSPs can sometimes integrate methods and content from multiple sources and/or types to create new ways of imparting knowledge. Such integration can increase InfoQ, but in other cases, it can reduce InfoQ, e.g., by putting some types of students off. Questions related to this dimension include:

— Are the DSP methods integrated from multiple sources? If so, what is the credibility of each source?
— How is the integration done? Are there linking issues that lead to dropping crucial information?
— Does the integration add value in terms of the DSP goals?
— Does the integration cause any exclusivity?

A low rating on data integration can be indicative of missed potential in utilizing the vast range of teaching resources available. For example, a DSP can incorporate use of MOOCS, online material such as webinars and discussion forums.

3.4. *Temporal relevance*

The process of deriving knowledge can be put on a time line that includes the orientation, central learning, and results' usage periods. The different durations and gaps between these three stages can each affect InfoQ. The orientation period duration can increase or decrease InfoQ, depending on the DSP goal, e.g., if the DSP goal is to educate then a strong orientation focus will ensure everyone is on board and no-one becomes disenchanted, whereas if the goal is to build a strong reputation too long an introduction period may be deemed to lower the intellectual level achieved. Similarly, if the introductory period includes options, this can be useful or disruptive, depending on the DSP goal. Questions related to this dimension include:

— Is there adequate time for orientation at the start of the program to bring everyone to the same starting level?
— Is there adequate time at the end of the DSP for implementation and practice?
— Is the allocation of time at each stage of the DSP appropriate?
— Does the DSP cater for people at different stages of their career?
— Does the DSP cater for people at different life stages?

A low rating on temporal relevance can be indicative of a DSP with low suitability to prospective students due to not accommodating different needs such as child care commitments. This can happen with courses that are based on an out of date model.

3.5. *Chronology of data and goal*

The content and goal of the DSP and the temporal relationship between them affects InfoQ. Questions related to this dimension include:

— Are the methods taught in the DSP suitable for use in the market place?
— Will students be able to function and excel in the workplace after studying the DSP?
— Are the IT methods used in sync with those available in business?
— Are topics covered in the DSP timely and relevant?

A low rating on chronology of data and goal can be indicative of low relevance of a DSP due to misaligned timing. A high level course that was designed to further research into new ideas but which pays no attention to applications becomes irrelevant if its results are to be used by the current generation of data scientists.

3.6. *Generalizability*

The ability to generalize the DSP learning to the appropriate environment is an important feature of the InfoQ of the DSP. Two types of generalizability are statistical generalizability and scientific generalizability. Statistical generalizability refers to inferring from a sample to a target population. Scientific generalizability refers to applying a model based on a particular target population to other populations. This can mean generalizing a methodology to other situations. Generalizability is related to the concepts of reproducibility, repeatability and replicability. Reproducibility is the ability to replicate the scientific conclusions and insights, while repeatability is the ability to replicate the exact same numerical results. Replicability (used mainly in biostatistics) refers to replicating results under different conditions, i.e., it is related to scientific generalization. Questions related to this dimension include:

— Does the DSP give examples in a wide range of contexts?
— Does the DSP facilitate application of methods taught to different situations, environments and circumstances?

A low rating on generalizability reflects a DSP with relatively low impact. Pearl in Ref. 6 states that "Science is about generalization, and generalization requires transportability. Conclusions that are obtained in a laboratory setting are transported and applied elsewhere, in an environment that differs in many aspects from that of the laboratory." Reference 7 used the term specific objectivity to describe that case essential to measurement in which "comparisons between

individuals become independent of which particular instruments — tests or items or other stimuli — have been used. Symmetrically, it is thought to be possible to compare stimuli belonging to the same class — measuring the same thing — independent of which particular individuals, within a class considered, were instrumental for comparison. "The term general objectivity is reserved for the case in which absolute measures (i.e., amounts) are independent of which instrument (within a class considered) is employed, and no other object is required. By "absolute" we mean the measure "is not dependent on, or without reference to, anything else; not relative". In reviewing a DSP, one should assess the contribution of the DSP also in terms of its generalization.

3.7. *Operationalization*

Two types of operationalization are considered: Construct operationalization and action operationalization. Constructs are abstractions that describe a phenomenon of theoretical interest. Measurable activities such as group projects, exams, reports, business collaboration within the DSP are an operationalization of underlying constructs based around the complexities of data science and its importance in the modern, globalized world. The relationship between the underlying construct and its operationalization can vary, and its level relative to the DSP goal is another important aspect of InfoQ. As long as the DSP outputs are assumed to measure the construct, the activity is considered adequate. Action operationalizing outputs refers to three questions posed in Ref. 8: (i) What do you want to accomplish? (ii) By what method will you accomplish it? And (iii) How will you know when you have accomplished it?

Questions that reflect the strength of construct operationalization:

— Are the methods studied in the DSP likely to be of interest in themselves, or is it their underlying construct?
— What are the justifications for the choice of DSP content?

Questions that reflect the strength of operationalizing results:

— Who can be affected (positively or negatively) by the DSP in addition to the students and staff, is there a contribution to the business or research world?
— Are external stakeholders aware of the DSP?
— How can external stakeholders influence the DSP?

A low rating on operationalization indicates that the DSP might have academic value but, in fact, has no practical impact.

3.8. *Communication*

Effective communication of the course content and its usefulness directly impacts InfoQ. There are plenty of examples where miscommunication disenchants students or causes disasters in terms of lost opportunity and wasted resources. This is the dimension that typically sees the most discrimination between DSPs. Questions related to this dimension include:

— Is the exposition of the goal, content and methods clear?
— Is the exposition level appropriate for the students?
— Are there any confusing details or statements that might lead to confusion or misunderstanding?
— Is good communication taught and valued in the DSP?

A low rating on communication can be indicative that poor communication might cover the true value of the DSP and, thereby, lower the value of the course.

4. InfoQ Assessment of DSPs

In this section, we provide an InfoQ assessment of 14 DSPs delivered in Europe. As mentioned, we rely in this assessment only on publicly available information available through the world wide web. In carrying out the assessment, we combined two perspectives of data integration. One perspective was to assess if the DSP covers data integration, the other one was to consider whether different inputs to the DSP are integrated. The programs were chosen to cover a range of delivery characteristics. Some programs are designed as full time and some are suitable for part time students who presumably combine work with studies. Some programs are delivered by a collaborative effort of several universities across Europe and some are delivered by a single university or private education organization. The DSPs are from a list provided in www.kdnuggets.com/education/europe.html.

The programs we covered are:

(1) Erasmus Mundus Master Course in Data Mining and Knowledge Management (DMKM), based in six universities in four countries: France (University Pierre et Marie Curie, Paris 6, University Lumiere Lyon 2, Polytech'Nantes — Polytechnic Graduate School of Nantes University), Romania (Technical University of Bucharest), Italy (University of Eastern Piedmont and Spain (Technical University of Catalonia),

(2) EIT ICT Data Science Master's Program, at TU/e Eindhoven, UNS Nice Sophia-Antipolis, UPM Madrid, KTH Stockholm, TUB Berlin, and Polytechnic of Milan.

(3) ESSEC Business School MSc in Data Science and Business Analytics with Ecole Centrale Paris.

(4) Mannheim Master in Data Science, a two year full-time on campus program, covering Data Management, Data Mining and Text Mining, Predictive Analytics, Advanced Statistics.

(5) University of Hildesheim International MSc in Data Analytics (in English) — become a Data Scientist. Hildesheim, Germany.

(6) Athens University of Economics and Business MS in Business Analytics.

(7) University College Cork, MSc Data Science & Analytics.

(8) MADAS: Master in Data Science for complex economic systems, at University of Torino, Italy.

(9) Novosibirsk State University MS in Big Data Analytics, Russia.

(10) De Montfort University MSc in Business Intelligence Systems and Data Mining, Leicester, UK.

(11) Imperial College Business School MSc Business Analytics, London, UK.

(12) University of Edinburgh — Informatics: Centre for Doctoral Training in Data Science, offering MSc and Ph.D. in Data Science, Edinburgh, Scotland.

(13) University of Glasgow MS in Data Science provides a 12-month full time program and also a 24-month part time program. Glasgow, Scotland.

(14) University of Sheffield MSc Data Science. Sheffield, UK.

For each of these programs, we provide a link to the source of information and highlights of the InfoQ assessment. We conclude the section with a summary of our findings.

4.1. *Erasmus mundus master course in data mining and knowledge management*

The Master in DMKM is aimed at students from all over the world. Candidates must have a Bachelor's degree (or equivalent) in one of the fields of computer science, mathematics or statistics, as well as a good level of English.

Data Resolution
The first semester is devoted to basic training, and includes subjects in mathematics, statistics, databases, etc., whereas the two following ones are devoted to acquire two specialties among five ones, such as E-Science, Digital Humanities. This structure appears to properly address data resolution in the context of specific goals.

Data Structure
The course contains aspects of large database management with various data types including semantic analysis. This provides a solid exposure to issues of data structure.

Data Integration
The program is designed to deploy knowledge in decision support systems or intelligent systems, both in academic and in industrial environments. No indication is provided on how this integration takes place.

Temporal Relevance
Since around 50% of the program is devoted to applications in the field, solving real data mining problems the program appears to be of high temporal relevance.

Chronology of Data and Goal
The emphasis on the deployment of decision support systems in academic and in industrial environments facilitates the learning of chronology of data and goal.

Generalizability

The teaching staff includes academics and professionals from industry. The program provides exposure to a wide range of problems and thereby facilitates the learning of generalization.

Operationalization

During their obligatory stage in Semester 4, students can integrate research laboratories in Data Mining and/or Knowledge Management for academic research work or join a company that develops solutions and/or applications in DMKM. This ensures that students are immersed in an environment where operationalization of findings is a critical phase in the research life cycle.

Communication

This dimension is only indirectly addressed in the program. It is assumed however that communication skills are integrated in the program. The program offers several options based on local complementary areas of expertise that are not clearly integrated.

4.2. *EIT ICT data science master's program*

The Data Science Master's offers an academic program combining data science, innovation, and entrepreneurship. Students will learn about scalable data collection techniques, data analysis methods, and a suite of tools and technologies that address data capture, processing, storage, transfer, analysis, and visualization, and related concepts (e.g., data access, pricing data, and data privacy).

Data Resolution

The DSP emphasis on entrepreneurship and business application seems to provide the right context for properly addressing data resolution.

Data Structure

The DSP description does not provide specific information on how the program addresses different types of data structures.

Data Integration

The program includes courses such as data handling, data analysis, advanced data analysis and data management, visualization, and applications. This addresses data integration well.

Temporal Relevance

The emphasis on large data bases and online analytics provides some indication that the DSP addresses temporal relevance.

Chronology of Data and Goal

The DSP does not provide specific details on projects or application tasks required from students.

Generalizability

The DSP provides a diverse experience by combining courses in different application areas. Such combination supports the generalization dimension.

Operationalization

The specializations offered in the program are providing strong operationalization opportunities. These include

(i) Infrastructures for Large Scale Data Management and Analysis, (ii) Multimedia and Web Science for Big Data, (iii) Business Process Intelligence, (iv) Distributed Systems and Data Mining for Really Big Data and (v) Design, Implementation, and Usage of Data Science Instruments.

Communication

A course on visualization is part of the program. No information is provided on additional tasks for supporting training in effective communication. Except for stating that the DSP combines data science, innovation, and entrepreneurship, it is not clear how they are integrated.

4.3. *ESSEC business school*

This one year, full time program involves foundation courses, specialized courses in either business analytics or data sciences and courses on new topics in the field. The website includes several testimonials but relatively little information on the DSP itself.

Data Resolution

The course on signal processing covers methods of representation and inference, thus covering issues of data resolution

Data Structure

The DSP does not appear to cover data base design or topics covering unstructured data.

Data Integration

The course on business intelligence dealing with information systems & technologies and modeling techniques in decision-making probably deals with data integration.

Temporal Relevance

The program on massive data processing and business intelligence applications seems to address issues of temporal relevance.

Chronology of Data and Goal

The course on high performance and parallel computing is about distributed and parallel computing, covering theoretical foundation and practical applications related to chronology of data and goal.

Generalizability

The application of marketing analytics and econometric models are necessarily involving generalization of findings.

Operationalization

The application of case studies provides an opportunity to train in operationalization of findings. There are however no details on how practical projects are included in the DSP.

Communication

The DSP does not seem to involve visualization or specific communication techniques. The DSP goals and objectives themselves are poorly communicated.

4.4. *Mannheim master in data science*

The Mannheim Master in Data Science has a succinct front webpage with links to further details. Only the front page is considered in this brief review.

Data Resolution

The course is new and therefore likely to be up to date. It deals with a range of topics ensuring apparent proper treatment of matching data resolution with study objectives.

Data Structure

The course covers the main elements of data science needed to "gain operational insight from large and complex datasets". The interdisciplinary nature of the course implies good coverage. It runs as "a collaboration between University of Mannheim's Data and Web Science Group, Institute of Business Informatics, Department of Sociology, Department of Political Science, and Institute of Mathematics." This collaboration implies that there is likely to be a variety of teaching methods catering for different learning styles.

Data Integration

The collaboration between departments implies that there will be expert input for each part of the course. It is to be hoped that the input will be integrated although this aspect may take time to develop as the course is new.

Temporal Relevance

There is no explicit mention of orientation time put aside at the start of the course but it is of 24 months' duration so may be expected to have time for this. The entry requirements are broad and suggest a range of student abilities which will need to be catered for. A wide range of courses is offered which should help deal with diversity of entry status.

Chronology of Data and Goal

The DSP has strong practical elements: "The program provides both a solid theoretical foundation as well as practical skills for data management and data analytics" and "The students will carry out data science projects to apply the acquired knowledge in practice." This theoretical and practical approach is likely to make the students highly employable.

Generalizability

The DSP has input from different specialties and this is likely to raise awareness of a wide range of applications and make the students able to apply the ideas to new or different environments. This is extremely important in the fast moving world of data science.

Operationalization

The DSP focuses on data and statistics and is likely to be interesting for these subjects in themselves as well as being useful for practical purposes. There is no explicit mention of external business stakeholders and any feedback between academia and business.

Communication

In the brief summary webpage, there is no specific mention of communication skills although the involvement of the Departments of Sociology and Political Science make that more likely than when only Computer Science and Mathematics are involved.

4.5. *University of Hildesheim international MSc in data analytics*

A summary of the Hildesheim DSP is given in a single webpage and this source is the basis of the following observations:

Data Resolution

The DSP emphasizes that it is up to date referring to its "modern state-of-the-art Machine Learning methods." It is designed and taught by experts including those in selected application domains. This suggests that it is likely to be flexible to changes and evolution of data science applications.

Data Structure

The DSP includes a good range of subject matter. The entry requirements are for a Bachelor's degree in an analytical subject. There is no specific mention of provision to fill in any gaps in knowledge. There is a practical data analysis element but no other indication of variety in teaching and learning styles.

Data Integration

The DSP is intended to prepare students for careers in a variety of different jobs including

— Data Scientist
— Big Data Engineer
— Machine Learning Scientist
— Business Intelligence Analyst

There is a focus on interdisciplinary employment. Input to the course is from a range of experts as stated in "The program is designed and taught in close collaboration of experienced faculty and experts in machine learning and selected application domains." The implication is that the inputs from different specialists will be well integrated as they are involved in the design of the course. There is no specific detail of whether the course utilizes the vast range of teaching resources available, for example MOOCS, online material such as webinars and discussion forums.

Temporal Relevance

The DSP webpage does not go into details about how students will be oriented and brought to a similar starting level. There is clearly time for implementation and practice during the "hands on experience of handling large scale real-world data". The course appears to be aimed at students with Bachelor's degrees and does not explicitly mention suitability for different career or life stages.

Chronology of Data and Goal

The DSP puts great emphasis on preparing students for the job market by including relevant up to date analytical methods.

Generalizability

The DSP does not give much emphasis on how DSP methods can be tuned to different situations. There is a practical element but this is unlikely to be able to cover a wide range of applications.

Operationalization

The DSP addresses the needs of students who want to prepare for work in a wide range of data science applications. The implication is that there will be taught elements and some practical work. There is no explicit mention of how success will be measured. The content of the DSP is justified by being up to the minute and related to future jobs in business, computer and environmental science. There is no explicit mention of bringing in external business speakers or of facilitating their input to the design of the course.

Communication

The goal of the DSP is clearly stated and the webpage is clearly written with an appealing word cloud showing related concepts. The entry requirements and costs are detailed. There is no explicit mention of the importance of communicating the results of data analytics.

4.6. *Athens university of economics and business MS in business analytics*

The Athens University of Economics and Business MS in Business Analytics at University of Greece is succinctly described in its summary webpage.

Data Resolution

The DSP puts great emphasis on being up to date and inclusive: "Several factors have been taken into consideration to structure the content of the program:

- existing programs on business analytics and data science in business schools and engineering/CS departments at well-known universities worldwide,
- proposals and suggestions of members of the advisory committee of the program, consisting of university professors and industry experts in the US and Asia,
- evaluations, comments and feedback of the participants in AUEB's seminars and specialization programs on Big Data and Business Analytics during the last two years."

The input structure implies flexibility at least to consider adding new components to the DSP as seems appropriate. Actually carrying out the DSP, of course, depends upon having suitable lecturers available.

Data Structure

The DSP is careful to include all aspects of data science and the course content covers "in detail theoretical concepts on business, statistics and data management," These concepts are in four broad thematic areas:

- Business Environment and Processes (Information Systems & Business Process Management, Enterprise Information Systems, Innovation and Entrepreneurship, Privacy and Data Protection)
- Statistics for Business Analytics
- Data Management (Data Management & Business Intelligence, Big Data Systems)

- Optimization and Knowledge Discovery (Large-scale Optimization, Mining Big Datasets, Social Network Analysis & Social Media Analytics)

The course includes theoretical and practical work "The result is a well-balanced program between theory and practice. Theoretical concepts account for 50% of the program, systems and tools account for 25% of the program and the "breadth requirement" accounts for another 25% of the program."

There is no mention of teaching styles except that there will evidently be practical work. The range of subject areas is broad and it may be difficult to go into very deeply. There is no mention of flexibility for students to focus more on some subject areas than others.

Data Integration

The DSP aims to incorporate input from business and academic sources. As external business people have been instrumental in designing the course, it seems reasonable to expect that the input is integrated at least to the extent that there will be close adherence to the needs of practical applications. In an attempt to avoid exclusivity, "case studies will be presented in the context of finance, marketing, health, energy, human resources, transportation, supply chain analytics."

Temporal Relevance

The DSP summary webpage does not explicitly discuss entry requirements or suitability for people at different careers or life stages.

Chronology of Data and Goal

The involvement of a wide range of stakeholders in the design of the course implies suitability for future employment in the workplace. The intention is to expose students to a useful range of IT as it states: "Practical training on system and tools involve the following platforms: IBM, SAS, R, Hadoop and related projects, Spark, MongoDB, Redis, Neo4j, Python (tentatively)."

Generalizability

The DSP refers to case studies in a wide range of contexts. It is likely that these case studies will help students to be able to adapt the learning to new or different situations, environments and circumstances.

Operationalization

External stakeholders have clearly influenced the course. The feedback and influence of the course on business thinking is less clearly stated.

Communication

The course rationale and the methods behind its construction are clearly stated. There is no explicit consideration of the importance of communicating data science results to different audiences.

4.7. *University College Cork, MSc data science & analytics*

This DSP provides full time and part time options and includes core modules, elective modules and a dissertation.

Data Resolution

The course on Information Storage and Retrieval, from its title, seems to address aspects of data resolution.

Data Structure

Although the DSP does not seem to treat unstructured data as a topic, the courses on Database Technology, Relational Databases and Database Design and Administration apparently cover the data structure dimension.

Data Integration

There does not seem to be a course covering data integration such as ETL methods and tools.

Temporal Relevance

The course on Information Storage and Retrieval, from its title, seems to address aspects of temporal relevance.

Chronology of Data and Goal

The course on Information Storage and Retrieval, from its title, seems to address aspects of chronology of data and goal.

Generalizability

The DSP does not provide strong exposure to various application areas and seems therefore weak in terms of generalizability.

Operationalization

The dissertation appears as an academic task without specific focus on operationalization of findings.

Communication

This seems another weak aspect of the DSP which does not include courses on visualization and does not state how students get experience in the communication of findings.

4.8. *MADAS: Master in data science for complex economic systems, at university of Torino*

This DSP is a one year full-time postgraduate program emphasizing economic applications. The first part of the year is spent on a theoretical basis for understanding economic system and developing tools to model its complexity. Students gain competencies in statistics and informatics for advanced empirical analysis.

Data Resolution

There are no courses on data base design but the courses on microeconomics included micro-founded modeling tools. This probably covers issues of data resolution.

Data Structure

Topics such as semantic data, text analysis, image processing, GIS applications, etc. are not treated on the DSP.

Data Integration

The DSP does not seem to cover this dimension.

Temporal Relevance

Given the large emphasis on economic models, the DSP must deal with temporal relevance issues.

Chronology of Data and Goal

This aspect is reflected in applications to different problems in economics and business intelligence, for example, in "Simulation of urban systems".

Generalizability

The DSP is mostly focused on economic applications at various levels of generalization.

Operationalization

The list of applications mentioned in the program indirectly implies the treatment of operationalization.

Communication

The DSP does not seem to include courses or techniques for communicating and visualizing data and research insights.

4.9. *Novosibirsk state university MS in big data analytics*

The Novosibirsk State University MS in Big Data Analytics, Russia has an extensive front webpage including some excellent graphics of data analytics applications and biopics of staff members.

Data Resolution

The DSP gives a succinct, appealing overview of the role of the data scientist as one who "solves the problem by combining the hardcore science and breakthrough data mining technologies with inexplicable art of human understanding." The wide range of industrial and business partners involved in the DSP suggest that the course is kept up to date and can be flexible to accommodate the changing world of data science by refreshing the companies involved.

Data Structure

The range of modules taught in the DSP cover data science subjects focusing more on practicalities than on deeper mathematics or statistics in the first year. There are no details of the teaching methods or learning styles catered for but there are team building and elective elements.

Data Integration

The different specialist areas are led by experts in the field, for example, in physiology and natural language. Provided the students have opportunities to interact with each other and work in different groups there should be good integration.

Temporal Relevance

There is no explicit mention of coping with students with different entry levels but there is considerable flexibility to cater for students with different interests. Each student can select a domain and the courses specified for the domains are served by companies, which have a great experience in applying data analysis techniques to solve cutting edge problems. The domains include bioinformatics, healthcare, electronic, social networks and cognitive data science. There is an impressive range of partner companies.

Chronology of Data and Goal

The DSP offers a complementary mix of theory and practice. The great emphasis on practical problem solving suggests that successful students will be highly employable. A range of techniques is studied and aims to keep the DSP timely and relevant.

Generalizability

There are options to study some chosen area in greater depth. Provided students are encouraged to share their project work experiences the whole cohort will have valuable exposure to examples in a wide range of contexts. This will facilitate the students applying their knowledge to new situations, environments and circumstances.

Operationalization

The DSP puts great emphasis on real life problem solving. "As a student you will take part in real projects, working with the team through all the project stages to acquire deep knowledge and master your skills in analyzing the core problems of your customer, planning and managing project resources, engineering software, collecting and processing all sorts of data, and discovering the precious insights that put the whole data puzzle together."

It is unclear to what extent the data science subjects are studied for their own sake. There appears to be productive exchange between academics and businesses judging from the wide range of external supporting companies listed on the website.

Communication

The DSP webpage includes a list of courses studied and includes visualization tools and academic writing showing that communication is valued and taken seriously. The website has an automatic link to a "live chat" facility and is very encouraging for the browser to make contact and ask any questions for clarification of the course saying "Chat with us, we are online!.."

4.10. *De Montfort university MSc in business intelligence systems and data mining*

This DSP leads to an MSc or certificate and is focused on business intelligence systems, including predictive statistics and mathematical modeling. It is offered as either full time or two to six years part time and includes distance learning and a practical project.

Data Resolution

The DSP covers a range of business applications and includes a course on Data Warehouse Design and OLAP. As such, students are necessarily exposed to data resolution issues.

Data Structure

The DSP includes a course on Data Warehouse Design. What seems missing is the treatment of text analysis, social networks and image processing.

Data Integration

Even though not stated explicitly, the course on Business Intelligence Systems Application and Development probably covers data integration methods.

Temporal Relevance

Given the type of business applications addressed by the DSP, temporal relevance is treated in the DSP.

Chronology of Data and Goal

The course on Business Intelligence Systems Application and Development probably treats this aspect.

Generalizability

The DSP is focused on business applications. The course on Fundamentals of Business Intelligence Systems presumably deals with generalization of findings.

Operationalization

The course on Management of Information Systems must deal with this dimension.

Communication

This dimension is covered in the course on Human Factors in Systems Design.

4.11. *Imperial college business school MSc business analytics*

This DSP is a one year graduate program designed to equip graduates to derive business advantage using key analytical methods and tools. It includes online course pre-study modules, core modules, electives and a summer project.

Data Resolution

The DSP core modules seem to cover implicitly this dimension.

Data Structure

The data structure course appears as a focused approach to address this dimension.

Data Integration

The DSP core courses probably address this but no information on such methods is available on the web site.

Temporal Relevance

Given the business applications included in the DSP, this dimension is widely covered.

Chronology of Data and Goal

The type of business applications and electives, and the summer projects cover this dimension.

Generalizability

Given the wide range of electives, students are exposed to solid generalizability opportunities.

Operationalization

The summer projects provide ample opportunities to apply operationalization principles and tools.

Communication

The visualization course addresses this dimension quite extensively.

4.12. *University of Edinburgh — Informatics: Centre for doctoral training in data science*

University of Edinburgh — Informatics: Centre for Doctoral Training in Data Science includes a one year MSc by Research in Data Science Information which may then be followed by three years of PhD study. The DSP front page gives an overview with links to more details. The front page only is used for this brief review.

Data Resolution

The DSP is new and likely to be up to date and flexible to ongoing changes in the world of data science.

Data Structure

The DSP webpage gives a good description of data science:

"Data science is the study of computational principals, methods, and systems for extracting knowledge from data. Although this is a new term, there is a sense in which this is not a new field, because it is the intersection of many existing areas, including: machine learning, databases, statistics, numerical optimization, algorithms, natural language processing, computer vision, and speech processing." The DSP is attached to the centre for doctoral training and is therefore more of a foundation to ongoing PhD study than a self-contained employment oriented program. The teaching and learning will be tuned to the requirements of high academic achieving research students. The formal components of the course are supplemented by seminars, reading groups and workshops.

Data Integration

The DSP is taught by a range of staff and is hosted by the School of Informatics; there is insufficient information to determine the extent of integration.

Temporal Relevance

As the DSP is part of a four year study package there is likely to be extensive orientation and activities to raise everyone to a good starting level.

Chronology of Data and Goal

As the DSP is part of a four year study package there is less focus on employability and readiness for the market place after the one year MSc. It could also mean that not all subjects and teaching experiences associated with practical data science will be covered in the first year.

Generalizability

Being part of a centre for doctoral training will give students good exposure to a wide range of data science research projects and applications once the new DSP has been running for a few years.

Operationalization

The methods studied in the DSP are likely to be of interest in themselves and as examples of deeper analytics as they are designed to lead on to further research in data science. There will be support from external businesses and institutions before setting up the CDT and this exchange of ideas is likely to continue as the CDT progresses.

Communication

The DSP front webpage does not explicitly mention communication.

4.13. *University of Glasgow MS in data science*

University of Glasgow MS in Data Science is hosted by the School of Computing Science. This brief review is based on the opening webpage only.

Data Resolution

The DSP webpage does not give any indication about how the course content is determined or its flexibility to change.

Data Structure

The DSP has a strong focus on data and using data for problem solving.

Data Integration

The DSP course content is mostly from Computing Science.

Temporal Relevance

There is no information to assess this dimension.

Chronology of Data and Goal

The methods taught in the DSP suggest that it will make successful students suitable for employment in the market place. Being located in Computing Science, the IT components are likely to be up to date. The webpage states: "As well as studying a range of taught courses reflecting the state-of-the-art and the expertise of our internationally respected academic staff, you will undertake a significant programming team project, and develop your own skills in creating a project proposal and in conducting a data science project."

Generalizability

The team project and expertise of staff suggests that students will be exposed to a wide range of contexts.

Operationalization

The DSP aims to provide a "thorough grounding in the analysis and use of large data sets, together with experience of conducting a development project, preparing you for responsible positions in the Big Data and IT industries." This suggests that there is considerable emphasis on dealing with the business and research worlds.

Communication

The inclusion of team projects necessitates a focus on communication skills.

4.14. *University of Sheffield MSc data science*

University of Sheffield MSc Data Science has a summary webpage with links to further details. The summary webpage is used for this brief review:

Data Resolution

The course content appears to be up to date. It provides a set of fundamental principles that support extraction of information and knowledge from data. Case studies are used to show the practical application of the principles to real life problems. The real life problems are likely to be refreshed to keep them responsive to changes in data science worldwide.

Data Structure

The DSP offers good coverage of data science including: (i) fundamental data-related principles, (ii) supporting infrastructures, and (iii) organizational context.

Data Integration

There is no specific mention of how input from multiple sources is integrated.

Temporal Relevance

The entry requirements for the DSP include a good honors degree and a broad range of applicants can be considered. Work experience is not essential and there is no need for a prior knowledge of statistics or data analysis and so it is to be expected that time will be spent bringing everyone to a similar starting level.

Chronology of Data and Goal

The DSP aims to develop skills so that successful students can work in the data science market place. It is therefore likely that the topics covered are timely and relevant. For example, the course focuses on dealing with unstructured data in response to this growing need. Throughout the program, there are opportunities to gain hands-on experience using a variety of tools, such as R and SPSS, Weka, and Tableau/Spotfire.

Generalizability

The DSP includes a dissertation based on deeper study in a particular chosen area. Examples throughout the course should equip the student with awareness of how to apply data science techniques in a wide range of contexts and give confidence to tackle different situations, environments and circumstances.

Operationalization

The DSP covers a full range of data science subjects and includes case studies and real life data examples showing how the methods are put into practice.

Communication

The webpage is very welcoming and offers browsers the opportunity to view the MSc Data Science webinar about the course. It also gives context for the DSP explaining why you should take this course, as follows:

"All organizations face the challenge of how to analyze and use data, and the most successful are those that handle and exploit it effectively. More and more organizations therefore want Data Scientists." The course is described in good operational detail and makes very clear the outcomes which are that "You will gain the skills of a "data manager" who understands what the algorithms (e.g., for data mining or handling "Big Data") can do and when to use them for the benefit of the organization."

4.15. *Summary observations from the InfoQ appraisal of data science programs*

The exercise of appraising DSPs brings out important features to be considered when choosing a DSP as an exemplar.

In a new, dynamic subject such as data science, there needs to be flexibility of course content to deal with new topics as they emerge. Employability needs to be addressed regardless of the intellectual level of the course so that both theoretical and practical elements must be included.

DSPs differ in their apparent approach to communication and this can be a differentiating factor. DSPs should include courses on visualization and graphics; team work and projects can facilitate learning communication skills if they are handled carefully. A softer aspect but one which is nevertheless critical is the use of different teaching styles and the accommodation of students with different life experiences, situations and aims.

Integration implied by input from staff from a range of faculties is desirable but this input needs to be well planned and coordinated. Advice from business and an exchange of ideas both into and out of the DSP is valuable.

5. Designing a DSP with InfoQ

With the growth in popularity of analytics courses, faculty — both research faculty and teaching faculty — are engaged in the design of new analytics courses and redesign of existing ones in order to expand education programs with new topics, new audiences, and new programs.

Re-designing an existing course for a new audience — for example, modifying an existing graduate-level data mining course for an undergraduate audience — requires considering the background, the needs, and attitudes of the new audience. The important question is what parts should be modified and which components can remain as-is. Using the InfoQ framework helps maintain the key structure of the course: there is always a need to focus on goal, data, analysis methods, and utility metrics. In this context, the instructor can ask in preparation for his course:

Goal: How do I explain the main business goals to the new audience? How will the new audience be able to learn about goals of interest in practice? How will students learn to connect an analytics goal to a domain goal?

Data: What types of datasets will the new audience be enthusiastic about? What can they handle technically?

Analysis: Which sets of analysis methods are most needed for the new audience? What related methods have they already learned? What type of software can be used by these students?

Utility: What types of utility metrics must students learn? How will they learn to connect the overall utility of the analysis with the utility metrics taught?

InfoQ: How will students learn to integrate the four components? Is this new audience comfortable working in groups? How will they communicate their integrative ability?

Based on these answers, the instructor can re-design the learning materials and the evaluation activities and testing criteria. In some cases, instructors might find interest in the addition of formative assessment methods, such as MERLO, for assessing the conceptual understanding levels of students (Ref. 9). Designing a new course requires making further decisions about which topics to cover, what textbook and software to use, and what teaching style to use. While many instructors make choices based on a popular textbook, it can be useful to evaluate their options by considering the four InfoQ components and their integration:

Goal: What types of analysis and business or other domain goals are covered by the textbook?

Data: What datasets are provided by the textbook and/or software? What other sources of data can be used for this audience?

Analysis: Which analysis methods are covered by the textbook, and is the level of technicality (mathematical, computational, etc.) appropriate for the audience?

Utility: Which utility measures are presented in the textbook? Are they tied to the domain utility?

Following such an analysis, the instructor can map the methods and examples used in the textbook to the eight InfoQ dimensions: (i) Data Resolution, (ii) Data Structure, (iii) Data Integration, (iv) Temporal Relevance, (v) Generalizability, (vi) Chronology of Data and Goal, (vii) Operationalization, and (viii) Communication. As an example, the instructor can evaluate any reference to semantic data under Data Structure, integration methods like ETL under Data Integration, studies designed to consider applicability of findings in different contexts as Generalizability and the approach to the visualization of results as Communication. In redesigning a course, the instructor can add a session on InfoQ early in the course. Find a paper or case study relevant to the material taught in the course (perhaps one that is already used in the course), and analyze it using the InfoQ framework. In following sessions, the instructor can start with an overview of the method or case to be taught using the InfoQ terminology. This requires minimal adjustment to existing materials — a couple of slides at the beginning and slightly reorganizing or highlighting the four InfoQ components and eight InfoQ dimensions in the existing materials. For example, in a course on time series forecasting, before moving into teaching forecasting methods, the instructor can highlight:

Goal: Forecasting of future values of a series for different purposes (e.g., weekly demand forecasting for stocking decisions; daily air quality forecasting for issuing health advisory warnings; daily emergency department traffic for scheduling staff, minute-by-minute web server traffic forecasting for detecting cyber-attacks)

Data: Time series (typically treated in univariate mode; but possibly multivariate) and how it differs from cross-sectional data.

Analysis methods: An overview of the methods to be learned in the course (e.g., extrapolation methods, regression-based methods, etc.)

Utility: The type of performance metrics and performance evaluation approaches to be used, such as partitioning the series into training and holdout period and evaluating out-of-sample forecasts.

6. Summary

This chapter discusses the application of the InfoQ framework in assessing Data Science academic programs. It shows how such programs can be designed or redesigned with InfoQ as a unifying theme supporting a life cycle view of Statistics

(Ref. 10). Designing an InfoQ-based integrating approach can make the difference between successful programs that provide participants with both the theoretical and practical exposure necessary for effective and efficient analytic work. Specifically, consideration of the eight InfoQ dimensions (data resolution, data structure, data integration, temporal relevance, generalizability, chronology of data and goal, operationalization, and communication) provides a skeleton for assessing DSPs. To demonstrate the approach, we focus on 14 programs of mixed characteristics delivered in Europe. An application of InfoQ to assessing graduate students research proposals is presented in Ref. 11. An extension to this approach is to evaluate MOOC offerings of DSPs using similar dimensions. In that context, a MOOC can be assessed by also accounting for the profile of its participants (Ref. 5). A curriculum for a masters program in the related IT information quality domain is presented in Ref. 12.

References

[1] R. S. Kenett and G. Shmueli, On information quality, *J. R. Stat. Soc. Ser. A* **177**(1), 3 (2014).

[2] R. S. Kenett and P. Thyregod, Aspects of statistical consulting not taught by academia, *Stat. Neerl.* **60**(3), 396 (2006).

[3] R. S. Kenett and G. Shmueli, Helping authors and reviewers ask the right questions: The InfoQ framework for reviewing applied research, *J. Int. Assoc. Off. Stat. with Discussion* **32**, 11 (2016).

[4] R. S. Kenett and G. Shmueli, *Information Quality: The Potential of Data and Analytics to Generate Knowledge* (John Wiley and Sons, Chichester, UK, 2016).

[5] A. Bar-He, N. Villa-Vialaneix and H. Javaux, Analyse statistique des profils et de l'activité des participants d'un MOOC. *Rev. Int. Technol. Pédag. Univ.* **12**:(1–2), 11 (2015).

[6] J. Pearl, Transportability across studies: A formal approach, Working Paper R-372, UCLA Cognitive Science Laboratory (2013).

[7] G. Rasch, On specific objectivity: An attempt at formalizing the request for generality and validity of scientific statements, *Danish Yearbook of Philosophy*, 14 (1977), pp. 58–93.

[8] W. E. Deming, *Quality, Productivity, and Competitive Position*, (Massachusetts Institute of Technology, MA, 1982).

[9] M. Etkind, R. S. Kenett and U. Shafrir, The evidence based management of learning: Diagnosis and development of conceptual thinking with meaning equivalence reusable learning objects (MERLO). *Proc. 8th Int. Conf. Teaching Statistics (ICOTS)*, Ljubljana, Slovenia (2010).

[10] R. S. Kenett, Statistics: A life cycle view, *Qual. Eng. (with Discussion)* **27**(1), 111 (2015).

[11] R. S. Kenett, S. Coleman and I. Ograjenek, On quality research: An application of InfoQ to the phd research process, in *Proc. European Network for Business and Industrial Statistics (ENBIS) Tenth Annual Conf. Business and Industrial Statistics* (Antwerp, Belgium, 2010).

[12] Y. Lee, E. Pierce, J. Talburt, R. Wang and H. Zu, A curriculum for a master of science in information quality, *J. Inform. Syst. Edu.* **18**(2), 233 (2007).

Part 3

Data Integration

Enriching semantic search with preference and quality scores

Michele Missikoff[*,‡], Anna Formica[†,§], Elaheh Pourabbas[†,¶] and Francesco Taglino[†,||]

Istituto di Scienze e Tecnologie della Cognizione
National Research Council, Via San Martino della Battaglia 44 Rome 00185, Italy

†*Istituto di Analisi dei Sistemi ed Informatica "Antonio Ruberti"*
National Research Council, Via dei Taurini 19 Rome 00185, Italy

‡michele.missikoff@cnr.it
§anna.formica@iasi.cnr.it
¶elaheh.pourabbas@iasi.cnr.it
||francesco.taglino@iasi.cnr.it

This paper proposes an advanced searching method, aimed at improving Web Information Systems by adopting semantic technology solutions. In particular, it first illustrates the main solutions for semantic search and then proposes the semantic search method *SemSim+* that represents an evolution of the original *SemSim* method. The latter is based on the annotation of the resources in a given search space by means of Ontology Feature Vectors (*OFV*), built starting from a reference ontology. Analogously, a user request is expressed as a set of keywords (concepts) selected from the reference ontology, that represent the desired characteristics of the searched resources. Then, the searching method consists in extracting the resources having the *OFV* that exhibit the highest conceptual similarity to the user request. The new method, *SemSim+*, improves the above mechanism by enriching the *OFV* with scores. In the user request, a score (*High, Medium, Low*) is associated with a concept and indicates the preference (i.e., the priority) that the user assigns to the different concepts in searching for resources. In the resource annotation, the score indicates the level of quality of the concept used to characterize the resource. The *SemSim+* method has been experimented and the results show that it outperforms the *SemSim* method and, therefore, also the most representative similarity methods proposed in the literature, as already shown in previous works of the authors.

Keywords: Semantic search; semantic annotation; similarity reasoning; domain ontology.

1. Introduction

Information Systems (IS) are constantly evolving to meet the growing information needs of end users and, at the same time, improving their functionalities by including innovative solutions that the constant evolution of ICT proposes. Among the most important IS evolutions of recent years, we may cite the Web IS and the use of mobile devices (such as smartphones and tablets) to achieve the Ubiquitous IS.[1] The next promising evolution is the integration of IS and the Semantic Web. The Semantic Web is able to innovate the IS technology along both the structural and functional dimensions. The innovation along the structural dimension is mainly represented by the Linked Data approach[2] that allows the seamlessly expansion of the knowledge asset of the IS beyond its traditional boundaries. A second important structural element is represented by the adoption of shared vocabularies and ontologies[3] that empower the modeling of the reality managed by existing IS, enriching the "traditional" fact-centered view with a conceptual view of the reality. From the functional point of view, the most significant improvement proposed by the Semantic Web concerns the reasoning and searching capabilities, in particular, the semantic search services. The objective of this paper is to illustrate an advancement in semantic search techniques based on semantic

similarity. Semantic similarity reasoning is an emerging technique, different from the well known deductive reasoning (based on inference rules, e.g., in expert systems and prolog systems), relying on the availability of a reference ontology and a method for evaluating the semantic similarity between concepts of the ontology. A traditional approach to semantic similarity evaluation considers the nodes associated with the concepts of the ontology, and computes the length of the path connecting them in the concept hierarchy.[4] A different approach is based on the information content of concepts[5] (a notion tightly connected to the information entropy[6]). In a previous work, we proposed a method referred to as *SemSim*,[7] based on such an approach. In particular, we adopted a weighted ontology, where concepts are associated with weights, which enable us to compute their information content. Intuitively, the information content of a more abstract concept is lower than the information content of a more specialized concept in a taxonomy. For instance, according to the weighted ontology addressed in this paper in the tourism domain (see Fig. 1), the concept *Accommodation* carries a lower information content than the concept *InternationalHotel* and therefore, in a query, the latter will return a more precise result set than the former. In essence, semantic similarity search represents a new powerful service for users who need to search through a large base of (information) resources. In *SemSim*, each resource is semantically annotated with a set of concepts (features) from the weighted ontology, referred to as *Ontology Feature Vector* (*OFV*). When starting a search, the user specifies a request in the form of an *OFV*. Successively, the search engine activates a mechanism to contrast the request against the *OFV* associated with the resources in the search space, in order to extract and rank the resources exhibiting the highest similarity to the user request.

In this paper, we expand the *SemSim* method by introducing the scores *High* (*H*), *Medium* (*M*), *Low* (*L*) in the *OFV* at both request and resource sides. At the request side, scores denote the level of priority that the user gives to the features in the query. At the resource side, scores indicate the level of quality of the features describing the resource. For instance, if the user is looking for a holiday resource and specifies the features *Farmhouse* (*H*), *OpenAirActivity* (*H*), *CulturalActivity* (*M*), and *EthnicMeal* (*L*), he/she gives a marked preference for a resort which is a farmhouse offering open air activities, and less priority for the remaining features. Symmetrically, if a holiday resource is annotated with *Boating* (*H*), *Concert* (*L*), and *IndianMeal* (*M*), it means that it is characterized by the given features with different levels of quality.

In this paper, we propose the *SemSim*+ method, in which these scores are used in order to enhance the *SemSim* reasoning method. Such a new method has been implemented and integrated in the semantic similarity search engine *SemSim*+. It has been experimented in the same tourism domain where the previous method has been evaluated. The experiment shows that *SemSim*+ improves the performance of *SemSim*. Note that in Ref. 7, we have already shown that *SemSim* outperforms the most representative similarity methods proposed in the literature.

The rest of the paper is organized as follows. In Sec. 2, the related work is presented. In Sec. 3, the *SemSim*+ method is illustrated by recalling first the *SemSim*. In Sec. 4, the evaluation and discussion about the enhanced method are presented. Finally, in Sec. 5, the conclusion and future work are given.

2. Related Work

In the vast literature available (see for instance, Refs. 8–12), we restrict our focus on the proposals tightly related to our approach and, in particular, on the methods to compute the similarity between concept vectors.

Our work proposes a two stages method, firstly computing the pair-wise concept similarity (*consim*) and then deriving the similarity between vectors of concepts (*semsim*). As anticipated, the pair-wise concept similarity is performed according to the information content approach, originally proposed by Resnik[13] and successively refined by Lin.[5] The Lin's approach shows a higher correlation with human judgement than other methods, such as the edge-counting approach.[14,15] With regard to the second stage, the concept vector similarity, we adopted a solution inspired by the

maximum weighted matching problem in bipartite graphs.[16] In the literature, the Dice, Jaccard and Cosine[17] methods are often adopted in order to compare vectors of concepts. However, in these proposals the matchmaking method of two concept vectors is based on their intersection, without considering the position of the concepts in the ontology and their information contents. According to the Weighted Sum[18] approach, a fixed value (i.e., 0.5) is assigned to each pair of hierarchically related concepts. Our proposal is based on a more refined semantic matchmaking, since the matching of two concepts is performed according to their shared information content, and the vector similarity is based on the optimal concept coupling.

In Ref. 19, two algorithms for computing the semantic distance/similarity between sets of concepts belonging to the same ontology are introduced. They are based on an extension of the Dijkstra algorithm[20] to search for the shortest path in a graph. With respect to our approach, in the mentioned paper, the similarity is based on the distance between concepts rather than the information content of each concept.

In Ref. 21, in order to represent user preferences, the construction and exploitation of user profiles by means of an ontology-based model is discussed. A reference ontology has been defined for items in order to establish a relationship between user profiles and item features. Then, a semantic model is proposed that adjusts the level of interest of the user for a specific item by considering both item features and historical data about items.

In Ref. 22, the authors present an ontology-based approach that determines the similarity between classes using the traditional feature-based similarity measures, where features are replaced by attributes. The underlying idea of this paper is that if a given class shares all the attributes with another class in the reference ontology, then these classes are equivalent. This implies that the more attributes two classes share, the more similar they are.

In Ref. 23, a way of computing the similarity of users on the basis of their preference models in collaborative filtering is proposed. The main idea behind collaborative filtering is to find similar users rating a given set of items (or objects), and to analyze the ratings associated with these users. This technique is useful in the presence of a lot of users and ratings. Whereas, the approach proposed in the mentioned paper is conceived for a low number of users and ratings.

Overall, according to the mentioned proposals, it emerges that the *SemSim*+ method is substantially a novel approach with respect to the existing works because none of them extends the methods with semantic annotations of both resources and requests by using quality/preference scores.

3. The Semantic Similarity Method

As anticipated, the *SemSim*+ method derives from the *SemSim*,[7,24] which is here briefly recalled. The *SemSim* method is based on the information content carried by concepts organized as an ontology.[5] In the ontology, each concept has an associated weight such that, as the weight of a concept increases its information content decreases. Hence, the more abstract a concept, the lower its information content. Such an ontology is here referred to as a *Weighted Reference Ontology* (*WRO*) and is defined as follows:

$$WRO = \langle Ont, \; w \rangle$$

where:

- *Ont* $= \langle C, \; H \rangle$, in which C represents a set of concepts and H denotes the set of pairs of concepts of C that are in subsumption relationship. Essentially, *Ont* is a simplified notion of ontology, consisting of a set of concepts organized according to a specialization hierarchy;
- w is a concept *weight*, defined as a function on C, such that given $c \in C$, $w(c)$ is a rational number in the interval $[0, \ldots, 1]$.

The *WRO* that will be used in the running example of this paper is given in Fig. 1, where the weights have been defined according to the probabilistic approach defined in Ref. 25.

Then, the information content, ic, of a concept c in the *WRO* is defined as follows:

$$ic(c) = -\log w(c).$$

The *Universe of Digital Resources* (*UDR*) represents the totality of the available and searchable digital resources. Each resource in the *UDR* is annotated with an *OFV*[a], which is a structure that gathers a set of concepts of the ontology, aimed at capturing its semantic content. The same also holds for a user request. It is represented as follows:

$$ofv = (c_1, \ldots, c_n), \quad \text{where } c_i \in C, \; i = 1, \ldots, n.$$

When an *OFV* is used to represent the semantics of a user request, it is referred to as semantic *Request Vector* (*RV*), whereas, if it represents the semantics of a resource, it is referred to as semantic *Annotation Vector* (*AV*).

The *SemSim* method has been conceived to search for the resources in the *UDR* that best match the *RV*, by contrasting it with the various *AV*, associated with the searchable digital resources. This is achieved by applying the *semsim* function, which has been conceived to compute the semantic similarity between *OFV*. In particular, the *semsim* function is based on the notion of similarity between concepts (features), referred to as *consim*. Given two concepts c_i, c_j, it is defined as follows:

$$consim(c_i, c_j) = \frac{2 \times ic(lca(c_i, c_j))}{ic(c_i) + ic(c_j)}, \quad (1)$$

where *lowest common ancestor* (*lca*) represents the least abstract concept of the ontology that subsumes both c_i and c_j. Given an instance of *RV* and an instance of *AV*, say *rv* and *av* respectively, the *semsim* function starts by computing the *consim* for each pair of concepts of the Cartesian product of *rv*, and *av*.

However, we restrict our analysis to the pairs that exhibit high affinity. In particular, we adopt the exclusive match philosophy, where the elements of each pair of the concepts do not participate in any other pair of concepts. The method aims to identify the set of pairs of concepts of the *rv* and *av* that maximizes the sum of the *consim* similarity values (*maximum weighted matching problem in bipartite graphs*[16]). In particular, given:

$$rv = \{c_1^r, \ldots, c_m^r\}$$
$$av = \{c_1^a, \ldots, c_n^a\}$$

where $\{c_1^r, \ldots, c_m^r\} \cup \{c_1^a, \ldots, c_n^a\} \subseteq C$, we define S as the Cartesian product of *rv* and *av*:

$$S = rv \times av$$

and $\mathcal{P}(rv, av)$, which identifies the set of all possible marriages, as follows:

$$\mathcal{P}(rv, av) = \{P \subset S : \forall \; (c_i^r, c_j^a), (c_h^r, c_k^a) \in P,$$
$$c_i^r \neq c_h^r, c_j^a \neq c_k^a, |P| = \min\{n, m\}\}.$$

Therefore, on the basis of the maximum weighted matching problem in bipartite graphs, *semsim(rv, av)* is given below:

$$semsim(rv, av) = \frac{\max_{P \in \mathcal{P}(rv,av)} \left\{ \sum_{(c_i^r, c_j^a) \in P} consim(c_i^r, c_j^a) \right\}}{\max\{n, m\}}.$$

$$(2)$$

3.1. *SemSim*$^+$

With respect to the *SemSim*, the *SemSim*$^+$ method allows for the management of a richer representation of an *OFV*, in which a score is associated with each concept. In this case, an *OFV* is referred to as an *OFV*$^+$ and according to the previous section, we have *RV*$^+$ and *AV*$^+$ as well. A score is not an intrinsic property of a concept, but it is a value associated with a concept in an *OFV*$^+$. Consequently, a given concept c can appear in different *OFV*$^+$ with different scores.

The meaning of the score is different depending on the fact that it appears in a *AV*$^+$, which denotes the enriched annotation of a resource in the *UDR*, or in a *RV*$^+$, which represents an enriched request vector. In the former, the score, indicated as s^a, represents the level of quality of the feature describing the resource, whereas in the latter, indicated as s^r, it represents the level of priority given by the user to the requested feature. In this paper, we suppose that both these scores can assume the values H (*High*), M (*Medium*), or L (*Low*). Accordingly, a given *OFV*$^+$, say *ofv*$^+$, is

---

[a]The proposed *OFV* approach is an evolution of the *Term Vector* (or *Vector Space*) Model approach, where terms are substituted by concepts.[26] Accordingly, we avoid using *cosine* similarity in favor of the more suitable semantic similarity.[17]

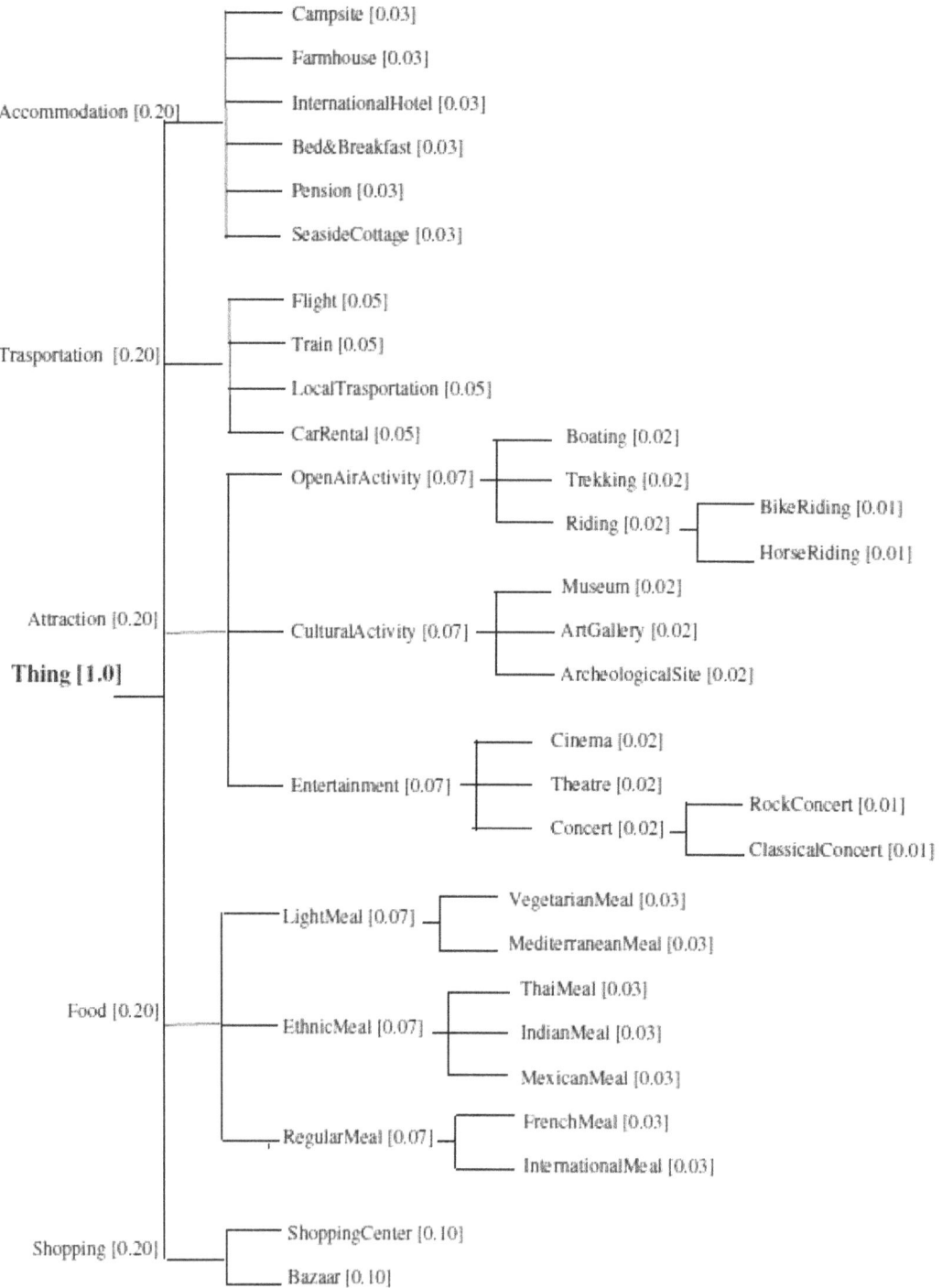

Fig. 1. *WRO* in the tourism domain.

represented as follows:

$$ofv^+ = \{(c_1, s_1), \ldots, (c_n, s_n)\},$$

where s_i is s_i^a or s_i^r, c_i is a c_i^a or c_i^r, $i = 1, \ldots, n$, according to the cases.

Similar to the *semsim*, the *semsim*$^+$ (defined below) computes the similarity between an instance of AV^+ and an instance of RV^+, represented as av^+ and a rv^+, respectively,

by pairing their concepts. However, the value computed by the *semsim*$^+$ function is obtained by multiplying the value of the *consim* function by the *score matching* value, indicated as *sm*, shown in Table 1, which takes into account both the s^a and s^r scores. In particular, given the following av^+ and rv^+:

$$rv^+ = \{(c_1^r, s_1^r), \ldots, (c_m^r, s_m^r)\}$$
$$av^+ = \{(c_1^a, s_1^a), \ldots, (c_n^a, s_n^a)\}$$

Table 1. The score matching function *sm*.

		s^r		
		H	M	L
	H	1.0	0.8	0.5
s^a	M	0.8	1.0	0.8
	L	0.5	0.8	1.0

Table 2. Tourist packages.

Packages	AV^+
P1	(*Campsite* (H), *LocalTransportation* (H), *Concert* (M), *Flight* (M), *ArcheologicalSite* (H), *Food* (L))
P2	(*FarmHouse* (H), *Trekking* (M), *HorseRiding* (H), *MediterraneanMeal* (H))
P3	(*InternationalHotel* (M), *LocalTransportation* (M), *ArcheologicalSite* (H), *Flight* (H), *RegularMeal* (M))
P4	(*InternationalHotel* (H), *CarRental* (H), *Museum* (H), *Cinema* (L), *Flight* (H), *InternationalMeal* (L), *ArtGallery* (H), *ShoppingCenter* (L))
P5	(*Bed&Breakfast* (M), *LocalTransportation* (H), *Train* (H), *RockConcert* (H), *Cinema* (M), *BikeRiding* (L))
P6	(*Bed&Breakfast* (H), *Bazaar* (H), *Museum* (M), *Theater* (M), *OpenAirActivity* (L))
P7	(*SeasideCottage* (M), *Riding* (H), *Boating* (H), *Train* (M), *VegetarianMeal* (H))
P8	(*Pension* (M), *CarRental* (H), *Shopping* (L), *CulturalActivity* (H), *LightMeal* (L))
P9	(*Campsite* (H), *LocalTransportation* (M), *OpenAirActivity* (H), *Train* (M), *VegetarianMeal* (H))
P10	(*Pension* (M), *ArtGallery* (H), *EthnicMeal* (H), *ClassicalConcert* (H), *LocalTransportation* (L), *Entertainment* (L))

the following holds:

$$semsim^+(rv^+, av^+)$$

$$= \frac{\sum_{(c_i^r, c_j^a) \in P_M} consim(c_i^r, c_j^a) \times sm(s_i^r, s_j^a)}{\max\{n, m\}}, \quad (3)$$

where $(c_i^r, s_i^r) \in rv^+$, $(c_j^a, s_j^a) \in av^+$, and P_M is the selected set of pairs belonging to $\mathcal{P}(rv, av)$ that is used to compute the *semsim* value between *rv* and *av*, obtained by removing the scores from rv^+ and av^+, respectively.

4. SemSim⁺ Evaluation

In our experiment, we asked a group formed by 13 colleagues of our Institute to provide their preferred tourist packages (request vector, *rv*) by selecting 4, at most 5, concepts of the taxonomy shown in Fig. 1. For instance, suppose the user wants to stay in a campsite easily connected by train, with local transportation services, and with the possibility of having ethnic meals. The corresponding request vector is defined as follows:

$$rv = (\text{Campsite, Train, LocalTransportation, EthnicMeal})$$

In the case, the user wants to reach the destination by using his/her car, it is sufficient he/she does not specify any transportation concept of the taxonomy. The user has also to associate a preference among *H*, *M*, and *L* with each concept in the selected request vector, indicating how much that concept in the package is relevant to him/her. Therefore, for instance, the user can refine his/her preferences in the above request vector as follows:

$$rv^+ = (\text{Campsite } (H), \text{ Train } (M), \\ \text{LocalTransportation } (M), \text{ EthnicMeal } (L))$$

Successively, we asked our colleagues to analyze the 10 tourist packages shown in Table 2, where the scores *H*, *M*, and *L* have been associated with the concepts describing the packages according to the level of quality of the offered resources (as for instance, in *TripAdvisor*), and to select five of them, which better approximate their request vectors, starting from the most similar tourist packages.

Furthermore, we asked to associate a value with each selected tourist package, representing the similarity degree of the package with the request vector (Human Judgment, *HJ*).

In Table 3, the request vectors specified by the 13 colleagues are shown. For instance, let us consider the request vector specified by the user *U8*. This user would like to reach the destination by flight, stay in an international hotel, use local transportation, and enjoy cultural activities and entertainments as attractions. Furthermore, the user *U8* assigns the high score to *Flight*, *InternationalHotel*, and *CulturalActivity*, whereas assigns the medium score to *LocalTransportation* and the low score to *Entertainment*. In Table 4, the results related to the user *U8* are shown. In particular, in the first column the packages selected by the user are given, that are *P3, P4, P10, P8, P6*, with similarity values 0.95, 0.8, 0.5, 0.4, 0.2, respectively. In the second and third columns, all the 10 packages ranked according to *SemSim* and *SemSim⁺* methods are shown, respectively, with the related similarity values with respect to the request vector *U8* given in Table 3. In order to evaluate the precision and recall of both the methods, we fixed a threshold to 0.5, as indicated in Table 4.

In the case of *U8*, as shown in Table 5, the precision increases (0.60 versus 0.75), while the recall remains invariant (i.e., 1). The precision increases because, as we observe in Table 4, *SemSim⁺* does not retrieve the package *P5*, which is not relevant to the user, that is indeed retrieved by *SemSim*. In fact, according to *SemSim*, the features of the vectors *U8* (see Table 3) and *P5* (see Table 2) are paired as follows: (*InternationalHotel*, *Bed&Breakfast*), (*LocalTransportation*, *LocalTransportation*), (*Flight*, *Train*), (*Entertainment*, *Cinema*), (*CulturalActivity*, *BikeRiding*), leading to the overall similarity value 0.52. In *SemSim⁺*, the same

Table 3. Request vectors.

Users	RV^+
$U1$	(*Bed&Breakfast* (*M*), *Train* (*H*), *RockConcert* (*H*), *ShoppingCenter* (*L*))
$U2$	(*InternationalHotel* (*M*), *Train* (*M*), *ArcheologicalSite* (*H*), *MediterraneanMeal* (*H*))
$U3$	(*Campsite* (*H*), *BikeRiding* (*M*), *Trekking* (*H*), *MediterraneanMeal* (*M*))
$U4$	(*InternationalHotel* (*H*), *Flight* (*M*), *LocalTransportation* (*H*), *InternationalMeal* (*H*), *Attraction* (*H*))
$U5$	(*Bed&Breakfast* (*M*), *Flight* (*H*), *Museum* (*M*), *EthnicMeal* (*L*))
$U6$	(*Bed&Breakfast* (*M*), *Riding* (*H*), *Boating* (*M*), *VegetarianMeal* (*H*), *Shopping* (*L*))
$U7$	(*InternationalHotel* (*M*), *Flight* (*M*), *Trekking* (*H*), *MediterraneanMeal* (*H*), *ShoppingCenter* (*L*))
$U8$	(*InternationalHotel* (*H*), *LocalTransportation* (*M*), *CulturalActivity* (*H*), *Entertainment* (*L*), *Flight* (*H*))
$U9$	(*Farmhouse* (*H*), *Train* (*H*), *Boating* (*H*), *MediterraneanMeal* (*M*))
$U10$	(*Bed&Breakfast* (*H*), *Train* (*H*), *LocalTransportation* (*H*), *OpenAirActivity* (*M*), *EthnicMeal* (*M*), *RockConcert* (*M*))
$U11$	(*Bed&Breakfast* (*H*), *Museum* (*M*), *MediterraneanMeal* (*H*), *Bazaar* (*H*))
$U12$	(*Bed&Breakfast* (*M*), *Car Rental* (*H*), *ArcheologicalSite* (*H*), *MediterraneanMeal* (*H*), *ShoppingCenter* (*M*))
$U13$	(*InternationalHotel* (*L*), *Flight* (*M*), *ArcheologicalSite* (*H*), *EthnicMeal* (*M*))

pairs are considered, but the similarity measure (0.41) is evaluated by taking into account the scores associated with the features. Since this value is less than the threshold (0.5), $P5$ is not retrieved by $SemSim^+$.

Note that in *SemSim*, pairing *CulturalActivity* with *BikeRiding* or *RockConcert* leads to the same value (0.52) because *BikeRiding* and *RockConcert* have the same weight (0.01). This does not hold in the case of $SemSim^+$, for which pairing *CulturalActivity* with *RockConcert* would lead to a higher value of similarity between the request vector of $U8$

Table 4. User $U8$.

	HJ		SemSim		SemSim$^+$
$P3$	0.95	$P3$	0.6757	$P3$	0.6357
$P4$	0.8	$P1$	0.6112	$P10$	0.5343
$P10$	0.5	$P10$	0.5913	$P1$	0.5157
$P8$	0.4	$P4$	0.5220	$P4$	0.5101
$P6$	0.2	$P5$	0.5206	$P9$	0.4508
		$P9$	0.4697	$P5$	0.4141
		$P8$	0.4369	$P8$	0.4084
		$P6$	0.3483	$P7$	0.2837
		$P7$	0.3407	$P6$	0.2684
		$P2$	0.2352	$P2$	0.1834

Table 5. Precision and recall.

	Precision		Recall	
User	SemSim	SemSim$^+$	SemSim	SemSim$^+$
$U1$	1.00	1.00	0.33	0.33
$U2$	0.33	0.33	0.33	0.33
$U3$	1.00	1.00	1.00	1.00
$U4$	0.67	0.67	0.67	0.67
$U5$	0.75	1.00	1.00	0.67
$U6$	0.60	1.00	1.00	0.67
$U7$	0.33	0.50	0.33	0.33
$U8$	0.60	0.75	1.00	1.00
$U9$	1.00	1.00	0.75	0.75
$U10$	0.40	0.67	0.67	0.67
$U11$	0.67	0.50	0.50	0.25
$U12$	1.00	1.00	0.33	0.33
$U13$	1.00	1.00	0.67	0.33

and $P5$ (in particular equal to 0.44) because these concepts are both associated with the score H (whereas in the case of the pair *CulturalActivity*, *BikeRiding* they are H and L, respectively). However, also in this case $P5$ would not be retrieved because the associated similarity value is less than the threshold (0.5).

It is worth noting that the $SemSim^+$ similarity values never increase with respect to *SemSim* because they are affected by the quality/preference scores. For this reason, with respect to *SemSim*, the recall of $SemSim^+$ necessarily is invariant or decreases (in the case of $U8$ it is still equal to 1).

In Table 5, the precision, and recall for all users are given. Note that the precision increases in five cases, decreases in one case, and is invariant in the remaining cases. In Table 6, the correlations of *SemSim* and $SemSim^+$ methods with *HJ* are shown. Note that $SemSim^+$ exhibits higher values in the 77% of the cases.

Overall, the results of the experiment show an improved performance of $SemSim^+$ with respect to *SemSim*, providing

Table 6. Correlation.

	Correlation	
User	SemSim	SemSim$^+$
$U1$	0.86	0.95
$U2$	0.51	0.52
$U3$	0.71	0.76
$U4$	0.80	0.85
$U5$	0.95	0.93
$U6$	0.81	0.85
$U7$	0.73	0.89
$U8$	0.85	0.90
$U9$	0.89	0.84
$U10$	0.49	0.72
$U11$	0.76	0.86
$U12$	0.87	0.82
$U13$	0.66	0.70

responses closer to those of user. These results are somehow expected, thanks to the presence of additional knowledge, i.e., the quality/preference scores, in *SemSim*$^+$. However, we do not intend to dismiss the original *SemSim* method since there are cases where it is more practical to use it than the new one. In fact, requiring the addition of scores for all the *AV* and, on the demand side, for the *RV*, may not be easy to be achieved or simply unpractical. Furthermore, another problem concerns the reliability of the scores associated with the resources in the search space. In the tourism domain, there are various options, such as the self-assessment of the tourism enterprise, the customer assessment (e.g., via *TripAdvisor*), and the assessment process delegated to a third entity (e.g., the local tourist office).

5. Conclusion and Future Work

In this paper, we presented the *SemSim*$^+$ method for semantic similarity reasoning. This work started from a previous method, *SemSim*, here extended by introducing the notion of a score. Scores are applied to both the semantic request vector, generated on the basis of the user request, and the semantic annotation vectors, associated with the resources in the search space, on the basis of their characteristics. The *SemSim*$^+$ has been experimented in the tourism domain and contrasted with the original method *SemSim*, according to human judgment evaluations. The experiment reveals that *SemSim*$^+$ outperforms *SemSim* on different perspectives, in particular with regard to the precision and the correlation with human judgment.

As a future work, we intend to propose a suite of methods to be used in a combined perspective, where none of the provided solutions will be dismissed and each might be useful for specific cases. Furthermore, we will address the problem of the generalization of the current tree-based structure of the reference ontology, by adopting a more flexible lattice organization. To this end, we need to investigate how multiple inheritance impacts on the weighting of the ontology.

References

[1] P. Dourish, The culture of information: Ubiquitous computing and representations of reality, *Designing Ubiquitous Information Environments: Socio-Technical Issues and Challenges*, (eds.) C. Corensen, Y. Yoo, K. Lyytinen and J. I. DeGross, IFIP, Vol. 185, pp. 23–26.

[2] T. Heath and C. Bizer, *Linked Data: Evolving the Web into a Global Data Space*, 1st edn., Synthesis Lectures on the Semantic Web: Theory and Technology, Vol. 1 (2011), pp. 1–136.

[3] T. R. Gruber, A translation approach to portable ontologies, *Knowl. Acquis.* **5**(2), 199 (1993).

[4] L. Rada, V. Mili, E. Bicknell and M. Bletter, Development and application of a metric on semantic nets, *IEEE Trans. Syst. Man, Cybern.* **19**(1), 17 (1989).

[5] D. Lin, An information-theoretic definition of similarity, *Proc. of the 15th Int. Conf. Machine Learning*, (ed.) J. W. Shavlik, Madison, Wisconsin, USA, Morgan Kaufmann (1998), pp. 296–304.

[6] C. E. Shannon, A mathematical theory of communication, *Bell Syst. Tech. J.* **27**(3), 379 (1948).

[7] A. Formica, M. Missikoff, E. Pourabbas and F. Taglino, Semantic search for matching user requests with profiled enterprises, *Comput. Ind.* **64**(3), 191 (2013).

[8] H. Alani and C. Brewster, Ontology ranking based on the analysis of concept structures, *K-CAP '05 Proc. of the 3rd Int. Conf. Knowledge Capture*, Banff, Alberta, Canada, October (2005), pp. 51–58.

[9] J. Euzenat and P. Shvaiko, *Ontology Matching* (Springer-Verlag, New York, 2007).

[10] W.-D. Fang, L. Zhang, Y.-X. Wang and S.-B. Dong, Towards a semantic search engine based on ontologies, *Proc. of 4th Int. Conf. Machine Learning and Cybernetics*, Guangzhou, August (2005), pp. 1913–1918.

[11] J. Madhavan and A. Y. Halevy, Composing mappings among data sources, *Proc. VLDB'03 — Int. Conf. Very Large Databases* (2003), pp. 572–583.

[12] A. G. Maguitman, F. Menczer, H. Roinestad and A. Vespignani, Algorithmic detection of semantic similarity, *Proc. of WWW'05 — World Wide Web Conf.*, Chiba, Japan, May (2005), pp. 107–116.

[13] P. Resnik, Using information content to evaluate semantic similarity in a taxonomy, *Proc. of IJCAI'95 — the 14th Int. Joint Conf. Artificial Intelligence*, Montreal, Quebec, Canada, August (1995), pp. 448–453.

[14] E. Pourabbas and F. Taglino, A semantic platform for enterprise knowledge interoperability, *Proc. I-ESA'12 — Enterprise Interoperability V, Shaping Enterprise Interoperability in the Future Internet 5*, (eds.) R. Poler, G. Doumeingts, B. Katzy and R. Chalmeta, March (2012), pp. 119–128.

[15] Z. Wu and M. Palmer, Verb semantics and lexicon selection, *Proc. 32nd Annual Meeting of the Association for Computational Linguistics*, Las Cruces, New Mexico, June (1994), pp. 133–138.

[16] A. L. Dulmage and N. S. Mendelsohn, Coverings of bipartite graphs, *Can. J. Math.* **10**, 517 (1958).

[17] Y. S. Maarek, D. M. Berry and G. E. Kaiser, An information retrieval approach for automatically constructing software libraries, *IEEE Trans. Softw. Eng.* **17**(8), 800 (1991).

[18] S. Castano, V. De Antonellis, M. G. Fugini and B. Pernici, Conceptual schema analysis: Techniques and applications, *ACM Trans. Databases Syst.* **23**(3), 286 (1998).

[19] V. Cordi, P. Lombardi, M. Martelli and V. Mascardi, An ontology-based similarity between sets of concepts, *Proc. of WOA'05* (2005), pp. 16–21.

[20] E. W. Dijkstra, A note on two problems in connexion with graphs, *Num. Math.* **1** 269 (1959).

[21] G. Ali and A. Korany, Semantic-based collaborative filtering for enhancing recommendation, *Proc. of KEOD'14 — Int. Conf. Knowledge Engineering and Ontology Development*, October (2014), pp. 176–185.

[22] S. Akmala, L. H. Shih and R. Batres, Ontology-based similarity for product information retrieval, *Comput. Ind.* **65**(1), 91 (2014).

[23] A. Eckhardt, Similarity of users' (content-based) preference models for Collaborative filtering in few ratings scenario, *Expert Syst. Appl.* **39**(14), 11511 (2012).

[24] A. Formica, M. Missikoff, E. Pourabbas and F. Taglino, Semantic search for enterprises competencies management, *Proc. of KEOD'10 — Int. Conf. Knowledge Engineering and Ontology Development*, Valencia, Spain, October (2010), pp. 183–192.

[25] A. Formica, M. Missikoff, E. Pourabbas and F. Taglino, *Weighted Ontology for Semantic Search*, Lecture Notes in Computer Science, Vol. 5332 (Springer Berlin/Heidelberg, Mexico, 2008), pp. 1289–1303.

[26] G. Salton, A. Wong and C. S. Yang, A vector space model for automatic indexing, *Commun. ACM* **18**(11), 613 (1975).

[27] WordNet 2010: http://wordnet.princeton.edu.

Multilingual semantic dictionaries for natural language processing: The case of BabelNet

Claudio Delli Bovi* and Roberto Navigli[†]

Department of Computer Science, Sapienza University of Rome
Viale Regina Elena 295, 00161 Roma, Italy
*dellibovi@di.uniroma1.it
[†]navigli@di.uniroma1.it

Accurate semantic modeling lies at the very core of today's Natural Language Processing (NLP). Getting a handle on the various phenomena that regulate the meaning of linguistic utterances can pave the way for solving many compelling and ambitious tasks in the field, from Machine Translation to Question Answering and Information Retrieval. A complete semantic model of language, however, needs first of all reliable building blocks. In the last two decades, research in lexical semantics (which focuses on the meaning of individual linguistic elements, i.e., words and expressions), has produced increasingly comprehensive and effective machine-readable dictionaries in multiple languages: like humans, NLP systems can now leverage these sources of lexical knowledge to discriminate among various senses of a given lexeme, thereby improving their performances on downstream tasks and applications. In this paper, we focus on the case study of BabelNet, a large multilingual encyclopedic dictionary and semantic network, to describe in detail how such knowledge resources are built, improved and exploited for crucial NLP tasks such as Word Sense Disambiguation, Entity Linking and Semantic Similarity.

Keywords: Lexical semantics; knowledge acquisition; multilinguality; word sense disambiguation; semantic similarity.

1. Introduction

One of the greatest challenges of a semantic model of language is lexical ambiguity. For instance, given the sentence:

Spring water can be found at different altitudes.

an intelligent system should be able to identify the intended meanings of *spring* (the geological versus the season sense) and *altitude* (the geographical versus the geometrical sense). The task of computationally determining the meaning of a word in context is named *Word Sense Disambiguation* (WSD).[1,2]

To date, many successful WSD approaches are based on supervised learning,[3–6] where the task is formulated as a classification problem for each target word. The sense inventory is provided by a reference computational lexicon (e.g. WordNet,[7] by far the most widespread), while training data have to be hand-labeled by expert annotators. This is a major issue, since obtaining annotations is extremely expensive and time-consuming, and supervised methods require large training datasets to attain state-of-the-art performance. To overcome such demanding requirements, approaches to unsupervised WSD, known as *Word Sense Induction*, have been proposed in the literature[8–10]: these methods do not require annotated data, as they dynamically induce groups of synonymous words (clusters) based on their occurrences in similar contexts. This however makes both comparison and evaluation quite hard, and lexico-semantic relationships between the clusters/word senses (typically provided by the lexicon) have to be established in a later phase, either automatically or by manually mapping the clusters to a reference sense inventory.

1.1. *Knowledge resources to the rescue*

A middle ground for dealing with the above issues consists in leveraging wide-coverage lexical resources to develop *knowledge-based* models for WSD. These models rely on existing sense inventories, but do not require training on hand-labeled data: instead, they leverage a reference lexical resource and exploit a graph-based representation of knowledge with word senses as vertices, and lexico-semantic relations as edges. The WSD problem is then solved using graph-based algorithms.[11,12] Knowledge-based approaches have shown comparable performances to their supervised counterparts in domain-independent settings,[11,12] and even superior results on specific domains.[13,14] Crucially, these performances depend strongly on the richness of the knowledge resource.[15,16]

WSD aside, this use of lexical resources encompasses all those Natural Language Processing (NLP) tasks in which modeling lexical semantics is crucial. Notable examples are *Entity Linking*[17] (as entity mentions can be ambiguous) and *Semantic Similarity*[18,19] (where word-based models conflate different meanings of an ambiguous word into the same semantic representation). Broadly speaking, the knowledge-based paradigm has always played a key role in NLP since the earliest years; despite the recent overwhelming success of corpus-based approaches,[20] purely data-driven models, whether supervised or unsupervised, still have limitations in terms of scalability and noise, particularly when it comes to fine-grained lexical distinctions. This is why, even today, the development and widespread application of lexical knowledge resources continues to be a major research thread.

1.2. *The problem of knowledge acquisition*

Nowadays, the main obstacle to developing knowledge resources with high quality and coverage (and, from there, high-performing knowledge-based models for NLP) lies in the so-called *knowledge acquisition bottleneck.*[21] In fact, even though WordNet already encodes a wide variety of lexical and semantic relations (Sec. 2.1.1), knowledge-based algorithms need larger amounts of nontaxonomic relations to achieve state-of-the-art results. These relations are mostly syntagmatic (e.g., car related-to driver, or play related-to game) and have to be acquired and encoded effectively in order for knowledge-based models to exploit them.

The challenging task of knowledge acquisition, i.e., building and enriching knowledge resources on a large scale, has been addressed by a very broad spectrum of approaches. A popular strategy consists in starting from existing knowledge and then applying some algorithms to collect new information associated with the concepts already known (for instance, disambiguating the textual definitions associated with those concepts;[11,22]) other approaches are instead based on the automatic extraction of relation triples with various techniques and degrees of supervision[23,24] (see Sec. 4.3).

Apart from the strategy used, a key issue for all these systems is that they should keep pace with the increasingly wide scope of human knowledge: new specialized terms are coined every day as new concepts are discovered or formalized, not to mention all knowledge about people, history and society which is continuously changing and evolving. Another crucial point to be addressed is *multilinguality*: the bulk of research on knowledge acquisition to date still focuses on English, and even though lexical resources do exist for other languages, in most cases they do not have enough coverage to enable accurate NLP models. This, in turn, prevents effective knowledge acquisition approaches to be implemented, especially for under-resourced languages.

1.3. *Collaborative semi-structured resources*

Fortunately, the stalemate caused by the knowledge acquisition bottleneck has recently begun to loosen up. A possible way of scaling up semantic knowledge effectively, both in terms of scope and languages, lies in the so-called *semi-structured resources,*[25] i.e., large-scale (typically collaborative) knowledge repositories that provide a convenient middle ground between fully-structured resources and raw textual corpora. These two extremes are indeed complementary: the former consists of manually-assembled lexicons, thesauri or ontologies which have the highest quality, but require strenuous

creation and maintenance effort and hence tend to suffer from coverage problems (Sec. 1.2); the latter consist instead of raw textual corpora, much easier to harvest on a large scale but usually noisy and lacking proper ontological structure. Semi-structured resources seem to take the best of both worlds, insofar as they are kept up to date and multilingual and, at the same time, relying on human-curated semantic information. Although quality should be intuitively lower when nonexperts are involved in the process, it has been shown that the collaborative editing and error correction process (*"wisdom of the crowd"*) leads to results of remarkable quality.[26]

The most prominent example of this kind is certainly Wikipedia, the largest and most popular collaborative multilingual encyclopedia of world and linguistic knowledge. Wikipedia features articles in over 250 languages, partially structured with hyperlink connections and categories, and constitutes nowadays an extraordinary resource for innumerable tasks in NLP.[27–29] Furthermore, machine-readable resources drawing upon Wikipedia have been continuously developed, including Wikidata,[30] YAGO,[31] and DBpedia.[32]

The crucial limitation of semi-structured resources, however, is that they tend to focus only on encyclopedic aspects of knowledge and neglect lexicographic ones (namely the knowledge encoded within dictionaries). In some cases this is intentional, since collaborative resources are first of all designed for humans to read. Wikipedia, for instance, provides style guidelines[a] suggesting users to hyperlink a certain concept or entity only when relevant and helpful in the context of the page: this avoids cluttered and less-readable papers, but prevents a lot of common-sense knowledge and basic word senses to be modeled within the Wikipedia structure.

1.4. *Linking knowledge sources together*

Given the advantages and limitations of both structured (Sec. 1.1) and semi-structured resources (Sec. 1.3), devising a way of bringing together the fully-structured information on general concepts (from WordNet-like resources) and the up-to-date, wide-ranging world knowledge (from semi-structured resources like Wikipedia) appears to be the key step towards the ambitious objective of creating a comprehensive lexical resource, capable of covering both encyclopedic and lexicographic information for as many languages as possible. Such a resource would enable NLP applications to integrate information otherwise available only in a multitude of heterogeneous lexical resources. For instance, let us consider a question answering scenario, where an intelligent system needs to know (or infer) that Pink Floyd was a group of people: although Wikipedia can be used to discover that Pink Floyd was indeed a band, having a link from band to its correct sense in WordNet would allow the system to immediately follow a hypernymy chain to organization, whose definition includes *"a group of people"*.

---

[a]https://en.wikipedia.org/wiki/Wikipedia:Manual_of_Style.

Apart from question answering, the landscape of NLP applications that a comprehensive, multilingual lexico-semantic resource can potentially enable varies widely, ranging from joint WSD and Entity Linking in multiple languages, to multilingual and cross-lingual sense-aware Semantic Similarity. The effectiveness of any downstream application, however, strictly depends on the quality of the resource: seamless integration of heterogeneous knowledge requires accurate methods for linking, or *aligning*, the entities and concepts across the individual inventories.

In this paper, our aim is to describe how such a knowledge resource is automatically built and exploited for various NLP applications. While doing this, and after a brief survey of the families of lexical resources currently available in the research community (Sec. 2), our main focus and case study will be **BabelNet**, a multilingual encyclopedic dictionary and semantic network originally designed as the seamless integration of WordNet and Wikipedia (Sec. 3). Finally, we will look at some application scenarios where such a resource proved to be effective (Sec. 4).

2. The Zoo of Knowledge Resources

Lexical Knowledge Resources (LKRs) exist in many flavors and with different features. To our aim, we can define a LKR as a resource that contains information on *lexical units* (words and multi-word expressions) of a particular language or set of languages. This information is expressed with respect to canonical word forms, usually *lemmas* or *lexemes* (i.e., lemmas in combination with parts of speech), and encoded as a set of pairings of lemma and meaning (*word senses*), which constitute the *sense inventory* of the LKR. Each sense is associated with a unique sense identifier, to deal with cases where a lemma can have more than one meaning (*polysemy*). Depending on its specific focus, each LKR contains a variety of lexical information (e.g., morphological, syntactic, semantic) and a particular internal structure.

2.1. Expert-built knowledge resources

Expert-built LKR are designed, created and edited by a group of designated experts (e.g., lexicographers, linguists or psycho-linguists). Despite their lower coverage, due to their slow and expensive production cycles, they have the highest quality, often including very specialized aspects of language.

2.1.1. WordNet

The Princeton WordNet of English[7] is a computational lexicon based on psycholinguistic principles. A concept in WordNet is represented as a synonym set (*synset*), i.e., a set of words that share the same meaning. For instance, the concept of play as a dramatic work is expressed by the following synset: $\{play_n^1, drama_n^1, dramatic\ play_n^1\}$, where

subscript and superscript of each word denote its part of speech and sense number, respectively. Hence, e.g., $play_n^1$ represents the first nominal sense of the word play. Being polysemous, the word play might appear in other synsets, e.g. the concept of play as children's activity: $\{play_n^8, child's\ play_n^2\}$.

Similarly to traditional dictionaries, WordNet provides a textual definition (*gloss*) and small usage examples for each synset. WordNet synsets are also connected with lexico-semantic relations, including *is-a* relations such as *hypernymy* (e.g., $play_n^1$ *is-a* dramatic composition$_n^1$) and *hyponymy*, which structure the concepts expressed by synsets into a lexicalized taxonomy, or *part-of* relations expressing the elements of a partition by means of *meronymy* (e.g., stage direction$_n^1$ is a meronym of $play_n^1$) and *holonymy* (e.g., $play_n^1$ is a holonym of stage direction$_n^1$). Various research projects stem from the Princeton WordNet,[22,33,34] including the creation of wordnets in other languages.[35–37]

2.1.2. FrameNet and VerbNet

The English FrameNet[38] is a LKR based on the theory of *frame semantics*[39] and focuses on modeling certain prototypical scenes or situations (*frames*) which are evoked by specific lexical clues in a text. For instance, the KILLING frame specifies a scene where "a KILLER or CAUSE causes the death of the VICTIM" and is evoked by verbs such as assassinate, or nouns such as liquidation or massacre. The participants of these scenes (e.g., KILLER and VICTIM in the KILLING frame) as well as other important elements (e.g., the INSTRUMENT or LOCATION of the KILLING) represent the semantic roles (*frame elements*) of the frame and are also realized in a sentence along with the frame-evoking elements (*lexical units*). Frames constitute the basic elements inside FrameNet, and each frame is associated with a set of *lexical units*: in fact, a word sense in FrameNet is identified by a pairing of lexical unit and frame (e.g., the verbal lemma assassinate in the KILLING frame).

Although predicate-argument structures are naturally modeled in the context of a frame, FrameNet lacks explicit information on the syntactic behavior of word senses. In this respect, an alternative model is represented by the English VerbNet,[40] a broad-coverage verb lexicon modeled on Levin's theory[41] and comprising hierarchically-structured verb classes based on syntactic alternations. In contrast to other LKRs, VerbNet defines word senses extensionally through the set of verbs forming a class (which share semantic roles and selectional preferences of their arguments).

2.2. Collaboratively-built knowledge resources

As mentioned in Sec. 1.3, a "crowd" of users can substitute a small group of experts in gathering and editing lexical information. This open approach can handle the otherwise enormous effort of building large-scale LKRs which quickly adapt to new information, and yet maintain a high quality, thanks to a continuous revision process.[26]

2.2.1. *Wikipedia*

Although Wikipedia is not a sense inventory strictly speaking, the pairing of an article and the concept it describes can be interpreted as a word sense. This interpretation complies with the *bracketed disambiguation* policy of Wikipedia, which associates ambiguous word in the title of a page with a parenthesized label specifying its meaning (e.g., JAVA (PROGRAMMING LANGUAGE) and JAVA (TOWN)). Due to its focus on encyclopedic knowledge, Wikipedia contains almost exclusively nominal senses. However, thanks to its partially structured text, it represents an important source of knowledge from which structured information can be harvested.[25] Apart from *infoboxes* (tables summarizing the most important attributes of an entity), articles are connected by means of a number of relations, including *redirections* (which can be seen as modeling synonymy), *internal hyperlinks* (which represent generic or unspecified semantic relatedness), *interlanguage links* (connections between concepts and their counterparts in other languages) and *categories* (used to encode common topics or features among related concepts).

2.2.2. *Wiktionary*

Wiktionary is a Wikimedia project designed to represent lexicographic knowledge that would not be well suited for an encyclopedia (e.g., verbal and adverbial senses). It is available for over 500 languages typically with a very high coverage, including domain-specific terms and descriptions that are not found in WordNet. For each lexeme, multiple Wiktionary senses can be encoded, and these are usually described by glosses. Moreover, a lexeme contains hyperlinks leading to semantically related lexemes and a variety of additional information (such as etymology or translations to other languages). Crucially, however, hyperlinks are not

disambiguated: they merely lead to the Wiktionary entry for the ambiguous lexeme. This is due to the human-oriented design of Wiktionary, which replicates the structure of a classical dictionary with word senses grouped by lemma. Nonetheless, structured lexical information can still be inferred from the wiki markup[43] and efforts have been made to ontologize Wiktionary and turn it into a machine-readable format.[44]

2.2.3. *Wikidata, freebase and DBpedia*

Among various approaches for turning Wikipedia into a fully structured resource, the Wikidata project[30] is the most prominent one. Wikidata is operated directly by the Wikimedia Foundation with the goal of providing a common source of data that can be used by other Wikimedia projects. It is designed as a document-oriented semantic database based on *items*, each representing a topic and identified by a unique identifier (e.g., the item for Politics is Q7163). Knowledge is encoded with the *statements* in the form of property-value pairs.

Part of the information currently in Wikidata comes from another large-scale collaborative knowledge base, Freebase.[45] Freebase was an online collection of structured data harvested from many sources, including individual Wikipedia contributions. In contrast to Wikidata, Freebase used a nonhierarchical graph model where tables and keys were replaced by a set of nodes and a set of links expressing semantic relationships. As of today, the project has been officially discontinued, and most of its data moved into Wikidata. Another popular Wikipedia-based project is DBpedia,[32] a crowdsourced community effort to extract structured information from Wikipedia and make it available on the Web by means of an RDF database and ontology accessible through SPARQL queries. Similarly to Wikidata, DBpedia exploits infoboxes as one of the richest sources of information.

Despite the plethora of LKRs available nowadays, it is arguable that no single resource works at best for all application scenarios or purposes: different LKRs cover not only

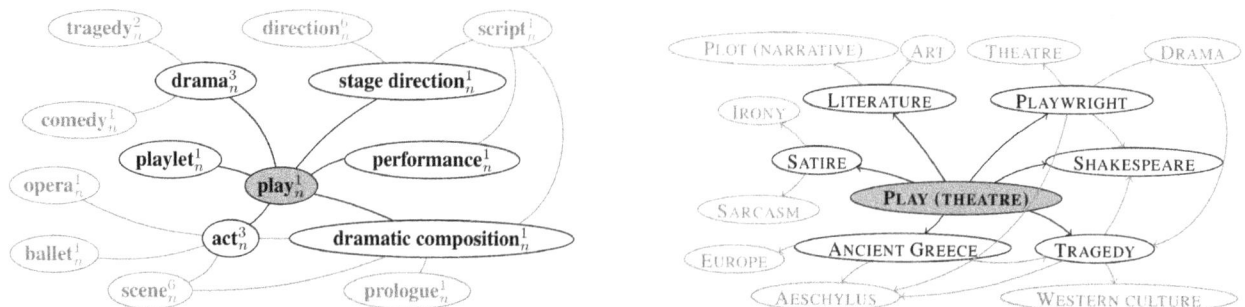

(a) Excerpt of the WordNet graph centered on the synset $play_n^1$ (b) Excerpt of the Wikipedia graph centered on the page PLAY (THEATRE)

Fig. 1. Excerpts of the WordNet (a) and Wikipedia (b) graphs drawn from the original article of BabelNet.[42] Both resources can be viewed as directed graphs with synsets (Wikipedia pages) as nodes and relations (internal hyperlinks) as edges.

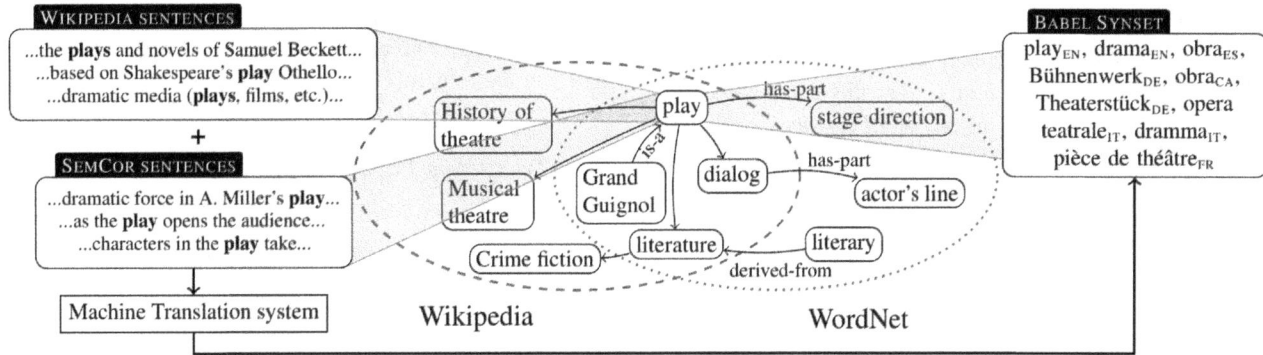

Fig. 2. An illustrative overview of BabelNet drawn from the original article.[42] Unlabeled edges come from hyperlinks inside Wikipedia articles (e.g., PLAY (THEATRE) links to MUSICAL (THEATRE)), while labeled edges are drawn from WordNet (e.g., $play_n^1$ *has-part* $stage\ direction_n^1$).

different words and senses, but sometimes completely different information types. Hence, the optimal way of making use of the available knowledge appears to be the orchestrated exploitation of multiple, heterogeneous LKRs[46] (Sec. 1.4). In our case study, BabelNet, the core idea is indeed integrating the lexicographic information of WordNet with the encyclopedic knowledge of Wikipedia. Despite their structural and conceptual differences, WordNet and Wikipedia can both be viewed as graphs. An excerpt of such graphs centered on the synset $play_n^1$ and the Wikipedia page PLAY (THEATRE) is given in Figs. 1(a) and 1(b), respectively. While there are nodes corresponding to the same concept (e.g., $tragedy_n^2$ and TRAGEDY), each resource also contains specific knowledge which is missing in the other, both general concepts (for instance no Wikipedia entry corresponding to $direction_n^6$) and named entities (like ANCIENT GREECE missing in WordNet).

3. BabelNet

The high degree of complementarity between WordNet and Wikipedia, together with the similarity between their internal structures (Fig. 1), opened the way for an integration that brought together seamlessly lexicographic information organized in a high-quality taxonomy (from WordNet) and specialized, up-to-date world knowledge in hundreds of languages (from Wikipedia). The result of this integration is BabelNet,[42,b] a large-scale, multilingual *encyclopedic dictionary* (i.e., a resource where both lexicographic and encyclopedic knowledge is available in multiple languages) and at the same time a *semantic network* where all this knowledge is interconnected with several million semantic relations.

BabelNet is structured as a labeled directed graph $G = (V, E)$ where V is the set of *nodes* — i.e., *concepts* such as play and *named entities* such as Shakespeare — and $E \subseteq V \times R \times V$ is the set of *edges* connecting pairs of concepts (e.g., play*is-a* dramatic composition). Each edge is labeled

with a *semantic relation* from R, e.g., {*is-a, part-of, . . . , ϵ* }, with ϵ denoting an unspecified semantic relation. Importantly, each node $v \in V$ contains a set of lexicalizations of the concept for different languages, e.g., {$play_{EN}$, $Theaterstück_{DE}$, $dramma_{it}$, $obra_{ES}$, . . . , $pièce\ de\ théâtre_{FR}$ }. Such multilingually lexicalized concepts are called *Babel synsets*.

Concepts and relations in BabelNet were harvested from both WordNet (Sec. 2.1.1) and Wikipedia (Sec. 2.2.1). In order to construct the BabelNet graph, extraction took place at different stages: from WordNet, all available word senses (as *concepts*) and all the lexical and semantic pointers between synsets (as *relations*); from Wikipedia, all the Wikipages (as *concepts*) and semantically unspecified *relations* from their internal hyperlinks. A graphical overview of BabelNet is given in Fig. 2. Crucially, the overlap between WordNet and Wikipedia (both in terms of concepts and relations) made the merging between the two resources possible and enabled the creation of a *unified knowledge resource*. After establishing this first Wikipedia-WordNet mapping, multilinguality was achieved by collecting lexical realizations of the available concepts in different languages. Finally, multilingual Babel synsets were connected by establishing semantic relations between them. To summarize, the construction of BabelNet consisted of three main steps:

- The **integration of WordNet and Wikipedia** via an automatic mapping between WordNet senses and Wikipedia pages (Sec. 3.1). This avoided duplicate concepts and allowed heterogeneous sense inventories of concepts to complement each other;
- The **collection of multilingual lexicalizations** of the newly-created concepts (*Babel synsets*) by means of (a) the human-generated translations provided by Wikipedia (i.e., the inter-language links), as well as (b) a machine translation system to translate occurrences of the concepts within sense-tagged corpora (Sec. 3.2);
- The **interconnection of Babel synsets** by harvesting all the relations in WordNet and in the Wikipedias in the languages of interest (Sec. 3.3).

[b]http://babelnet.org.

3.1. Mapping Wikipedia and WordNet

The Wikipedia-WordNet mapping task was formulated as the problem of defining a function μ over the *Wikipedia sense inventory* S_{Wiki} with values in the *WordNet sense inventory* S_{WN} such that, for each $w \in S_{\text{Wiki}}$:

$$\mu(w) = \begin{cases} s \in S_{\text{WN}}(w) & \text{if a link can} \\ & \text{be established,} \\ \epsilon & \text{otherwise,} \end{cases}$$

where $S_{\text{WN}}(w)$ is the set of WordNet candidate senses for the lemma of w. Given the disambiguation policy of Wikipedia (Sec. 2.2.1), the lemma for a Wikipedia page w is either the title itself (e.g., tragedy for TRAGEDY) or the main token if the title is sense-labeled (e.g., play for PLAY (THEATRE)).

In order to construct μ automatically, the core mapping algorithm of BabelNet[42] was based on maximizing the conditional probability $p(s|w)$ of selecting the WordNet sense $s \in S_{\text{WN}}(w)$ given the Wikipedia page w:

$$\mu(w) = \underset{s \in S_{\text{WN}}(w)}{\arg\max}\, p(s|w) = \arg\max_s \frac{p(s,w)}{p(w)}$$
$$= \arg\max_s p(s,w). \quad (1)$$

The most appropriate sense was then obtained by maximizing the joint probability $p(s,w)$ of sense s and page p. Excluding the trivial case in which w is monosemous in S_{WN} (that is, when $|S_{\text{WN}}(w)| = 1$), the joint probability $p(s,w)$ was estimated using a WSD approach that relies on a *disambiguation context Ctx* defined for both w and s.

Given a concept c, either page or sense, $Ctx(c)$ is a set of words, obtained from the corresponding resource (Wikipedia or Wordnet), whose senses are associated with c. The sources of information from which related words are extracted depend upon the resource: for instance, if c is a Wikipedia page, $Ctx(c)$ draws from sense labels in the title of c, internal hyperlinks, redirections to c and Wikipedia categories (e.g., Ctx(Play (theatre))={THEATRE, literature, comedy, ..., drama, character}). If c is a WordNet sense, $Ctx(c)$ comprises all synonyms of c (i.e., all senses that are part of the same synset C), all hypernym and hyponym senses of c, and the set of lemmatized content words occurring within the gloss of c (e.g., $Ctx(\text{play}_n^1)$={drama, dramatic play, performance, ..., actor, stage}).

Once disambiguation contexts had been determined, the joint probability in Eq. (1) was computed as:

$$p(s,w) = \frac{\text{score}(s,w)}{\displaystyle\sum_{\substack{s' \in S_{\text{WN}}(w), \\ w' \in S_{\text{Wiki}}(w)}} \text{score}(s',w')}, \quad (2)$$

where $\text{score}(s,w)$ was defined in two alternative ways: (1) as *bag-of-words*, i.e., the (smoothed) intersection $|Ctx(s) \cap Ctx(w)| + 1$ of the disambiguation contexts of s and w; (2) with a *graph-based method* that works on a disambiguation graph G, i.e., the WordNet subgraph with all the senses of w

and all edges and intermediate senses found along all paths of maximal length that connect them. Both procedures are detailed in the reference paper of BabelNet.[42]

3.2. Translating Babel synsets

With a Wikipedia-WordNet mapping finally established, the Babel synset for a given Wikipedia page w and its corresponding WordNet sense $s = \mu(w)$ was created as $S \cup W$, where S is the WordNet synset to which sense s belongs, and W includes: (1) w; (2) the set of *redirections* to w; (3) all pages connected to w via *inter-language links*; (iv) redirections to the Wikipedia pages pointed by inter-language links in the target language. For example, given $\mu(\text{PLAY (THEATRE)})$ = play$_n^1$, the following Babel synset was created: {play$_{\text{EN}}$, Bühnenwerk$_{\text{DE}}$, pièce de théâtre$_{\text{FR}}$, ..., opera teatrale$_{\text{IT}}$}. The inclusion of redirections additionally enlarged the Babel synset with {Theaterstück$_{\text{DE}}$, texte dramatique$_{\text{FR}}$}.

However, not in every case a link could be established, even when a given concept is present in both resources. To bridge this gap and maintain high coverage, English senses of each Babel synset were translated automatically into missing languages using state-of-the-art Machine Translation. First of all, given a specific Babel synset B, sentences annotated either with the corresponding Wikipedia page w_B or with the mapped WordNet sense $s_B = \mu(w_B)$ were collected: the former obtained from Wikipedia itself by identifying those pages where w_B is hyperlinked, while the latter drawn from SEMCOR,[47] a corpus annotated manually with WordNet senses.

After sense-annotated sentences for B had been obtained and translated, B was enriched with its *most frequent translation* in each language. For instance, in the example of PLAY (THEATRE) and its corresponding WordNet sense play$_n^1$, automatic translation augmented the initial Babel synset with, e.g., obra$_{\text{CA}}$ and obra$_{\text{ES}}$ (not captured by the mapping algorithm because of a missing inter-language link) but also with drama$_{\text{FR}}$ and dramma$_{\text{IT}}$.

3.3. Harvesting semantic relations

In order to generate the semantic network of concepts that constitutes BabelNet's underlying graph structure, newly created Babel synsets (Sec. 3.2) had to be connected with each other. In fact, the last step in the construction of BabelNet consisted in collecting semantic relations directly from WordNet and Wikipedia, and weighting them by means of a relatedness measure based on the Dice coefficient.

The weight of a BabelNet edge quantifies the strength of associations between the source and target Babel synsets. Different weighting strategies were used depending on whether the edge was drawn from WordNet or Wikipedia: in the case of WordNet, given a semantic relation between two synsets s and s', the corresponding weight was calculated using a bag-of-words method based on Extended Gloss

Overlap,[48] in the case of Wikipedia, instead, the weight was proportional to the degree of correlation between the two pages, according to co-occurrences within large amounts of hyperlinked text.[42]

Even with all the edges in WordNet and Wikipedia, however, the process of connecting concepts in BabelNet with high quality and coverage is today far from complete, and still subject to continuous research effort. In fact, when considering only WordNet and Wikipedia, the vast majority of edges comes from the latter resource, with no label or specification and only conveying a generic "semantic relatedness". Labeled edges, such as hypernyms and hyponymys, are limited to the (much smaller) lexicographic portion of WordNet. The case of taxonomic information, indeed, is of paramount importance: the huge amount of specialized knowledge from Wikipedia pages still lacks a proper integration with general concepts and semantic classes that populate WordNet. This is crucial for downstream applications: in the illustrative example of Sec. 1.4, the word band is not hyperlinked in the Wikipedia page PINK FLOYD: thus, even if the corresponding Wikipedia concept MUSICAL ENSEMBLE is correctly mapped to WordNet, there is no mean of establishing the connection with PINK FLOYD and MUSICAL ENSEMBLE in the first place (and hence, no hypernymy chain to follow). This shortcoming has motivated, among other efforts, the development of a Wikipedia Bitaxonomy,[49] i.e., an integrated taxonomy of both Wikipedia pages and categories. Constructing the bitaxonomy involves an iterative process of mutual reinforcement in which complementary information coming from either one of the individual taxonomies is propagated in the other. As in the construction of BabelNet, this method exploits at best the graph structure of Wikipedia, not only to extend coverage to as many Wikipedia concepts as possible, but also to project the obtained taxonomies from English (used as pivot language) to an arbitrary language, thereby achieving full multilinguality.[50]

Integrating the Wikipedia Bitaxonomy into BabelNet has been a major step towards characterizing the deluge of unlabeled semantic relations from Wikipedia, followed up by the integration of Wikidata (Sec. 2.2.3). A lot of work still remains to be done, and approaches based on extracting semantic relations from open text are currently under investigation (Sec. 4.3).

3.4. *Storyboard*

Since its earliest versions, BabelNet has been continuously developed and improved, pursuing the vision of a unified lexico-semantic resource capable of covering as many languages and areas of knowledge as possible. Table 1 reports some general coverage statistics.[c] across all BabelNet versions to date. Starting from version 1.1, limited to six European languages and four resources, the latest version

[c]Detailed statistics can be found at: http://babelnet.org/stats.

Table 1. General statistics on the various versions of BabelNet.

Version	Release	Languages	Sources	Babel synsets	Relations
1.1	2013/01	6	4	5 581 954	141 697 438
2.0.1	2014/03	50	5	9 348 287	262 687 848
2.5.1	2014/11	50	7	9 347 143	262 687 848
3.0	2014/12	271	7	13 789 332	354 538 633
3.5	2015/09	272	13	13 801 844	380 239 084
3.6	2016/01	271	13	13 801 844	380 239 084
3.7	2016/08	271	14	13 801 844	380 239 084

available (3.7) has reached 271 languages covered and 14 different resources integrated. The total number of concepts and entities, as well as the number of lexico-semantic relations, increased accordingly from 5.5 M to almost 14 M synsets, and from 141 M to 380 M relations, respectively. This extraordinary result is the outcome of a gradual development process which went through various milestones:

- **BabelNet 1.1** followed the first official release of the "encyclopedic dictionary" obtained from the integration of WordNet and Wikipedia (Secs. 3.1–3.3). This version was accompanied by a Web interface and a programmatic Java API, and featured millions of pictures associated with Babel synsets (drawn from the corresponding Wikipedia pages) as well as Wikipedia categories and external links to DBpedia;

- **BabelNet 2.0** improved over the first version by extending the coverage to 50 languages and five resources, including Open Multilingual WordNet[51] and OmegaWiki.[d] This version of BabelNet was the first to be integrated in the so-called Linguistic Linked Open Data (LLOD) cloud, a part of the Linked Open Data cloud made up of interlinked linguistic resources.[52] Integration was achieved by encoding the knowledge in BabelNet using the Lemon RDF model,[53] and then providing a public SPARQL endpoint;[e]

- **BabelNet 2.5** integrated Wikidata and Wiktionary (see Secs. 2.2.2 and 2.2.3) and marked the development of Babelfy,[54] a unified approach for multilingual WSD and Entity Linking fully powered by BabelNet (Sec. 4.1);

- **BabelNet 3.0** extended its coverage to all 271 languages available in Wikipedia and integrated the Wikipedia Bitaxonomy,[49] adding 92 M taxonomic relations for Wikipedia entities. This version was also accompanied by the first release of the RESTful API for both BabelNet and Babelfy, and it was awarded the prestigious META prize;[f]

- **BabelNet 3.5**, apart from extending the mapping to six very heterogeneous resources (from VerbNet[40] to Wikiquote,[g] GeoNames[h] and ImageNet,[55]) introduced

[d]http://www.omegawiki.org.
[e]http://babelnet.org/sparql.
[f]http://www.meta-net.eu/meta-prize.
[g]https://en.wikiquote.org.
[h]http://www.geonames.org.

Table 2. Statistics for the top seven languages covered by BabelNet.

Language	Lemmas	Synsets	Word senses	Avg. synonyms
English	11 769 205	6 667 855	17 265 977	2.59
French	5 301 989	4 141 338	7 145 031	1.73
German	5 109 948	4 03 9816	6 864 767	1.70
Spanish	5 022 610	3 722 927	6 490 447	1.74
Russian	4 645 114	3 497 327	6 046 022	1.73
Dutch	4 415 028	3 817 696	6 456 175	1.69
Swedish	4 265 069	3 011 458	6 412 872	2.13

various features, such as *domain labels* associated with 1.5 M synsets using a distributional representation of concepts (Sec. 4.2.2) and *compounds* also associated with Babel synsets. The key novelty of this version, however, was the integration of semantic relations (*properties*) from Wikidata, which turned BabelNet into an actual knowledge base with 58 M labeled relations and 2655 distinct relation types.

As of today, BabelNet integrates 14 different knowledge resources and comprises 13,801,844 entries in 271 languages, interconnected in a semantic network of 380,239,084 lexico-semantic relations. From a lexicographic perspective, BabelNet has been sometimes referred to as *the dictionary of the future*,[56] because of its encyclopedic breadth and scope, its organizational structure that favors semantic relatedness (instead of the mere alphabetical order of traditional dictionaries) and its richness of information which comprises, among other features, over 40 M textual definitions, 10 M images and 2.6 M domain labels.

Table 2 shows some coverage figures for the top seven languages available in BabelNet: total number of lemmas, total number of Babel synsets and word senses, and average number of synonyms per Babel synset. As expected, English is the language with the largest amount of entries. Out of all concepts and entities inside BabelNet, however, more than half (51.7%) are covered only by nonEnglish sources. This shows the crucial role of *multilinguality* in BabelNet: even if these concepts or entities lack an English counterpart (e.g., because they are tied to specific social or cultural aspects of a given language) they can still be connected across the network, and seamlessly exploited by downstream NLP applications.

4. BabelNet and Friends

As discussed in Sec. 3.1, the construction and continuous development of a resource like BabelNet, where both lexicographic and encyclopedic knowledge is available and interconnected in multiple languages, has a great impact on a variety of downstream tasks and applications. Throughout this section, we will examine some crucial examples of NLP approaches directly powered by BabelNet, where the advantage of using such a powerful resource is always two-fold: on the one hand, the unification of lexicographic and encyclopedic

information enables NLP systems to perform *jointly*, and hence with mutual benefit from one another, tasks that were previously conceived as separated; on the other, having language-independent information creates a direct bridge towards multilingual and "language-agnostic" methods, enabling English-centered models to be directly projected to other languages without modifying their basic structure.

This section does not present a collection of individual contributions *per se*, but rather a series of research efforts revolving around the common vision of the **MultiJEDI**[i] project, a 5-year ERC Starting Grant (2011–2016) with the objective of enabling *multilingual text understanding*. MultiJEDI led to the development of BabelNet in the first place, and defined the common thread that bundles together all knowledge-based approaches that rely on it.

4.1. Multilingual joint word sense disambiguation and entity linking

Across the NLP literature, an important task that is usually considered very related to WSD is *Entity Linking*[17] (EL). The goal of EL is to identify mentions of entities within a text, and then link (disambiguate) them with the most suitable entry in a reference knowledge base. The increasing popularity of EL is connected to the availability of semi-structured resources (Sec. 2.2), especially Wikipedia–to the extent that Wikipedia-based EL is sometimes known as *Wikification*.[57]

WSD and EL are undoubtedly similar, as in both cases text fragments have to be disambiguated according to a reference inventory. However, there are two important differences between them: the nature of sense inventory (dictionaries for WSD, encyclopedias for EL), and the fact that in EL mentions in context are not guaranteed to be complete but can be (and often are) *partial*, e.g., only the first or last name of a certain person. As a result of these and other discrepancies, the research community has spent a lot of time tackling WSD and EL separately, not only leading to duplicated efforts and results, but also failing to exploit the fact that these two tasks are deeply intertwined. Consider the following example

He loves driving around with his Mercedes.

where the ambiguous verb *driving* should be associated by a WSD system with the 'operating vehicles' sense, and the partial and ambiguous mention *Mercedes* should be recognized by an EL system and linked it to the automobile brand (Mercedes-Benz). Clearly, the former system would benefit from knowing that a brand of vehicles is mentioned in the local context of *driving*, and at the same time the latter could easily take advantage of the WSD information about *driving* referring to vehicles when linking *Mercedes*.

This is where BabelNet plays a role: by providing a large-scale encyclopedic dictionary as common ground for WSD

---

[i]http://multijedi.org.

and EL, it enables the design and development of unified WSD/EL algorithms. The first of this kind is **Babelfy**,[54] a graph-based approach to joint WSD and EL based on a loose identification of candidate meanings, and on a densest-subgraph algorithm to select high-coherence semantic interpretations. Babelfy disambiguates as follows:

- Given a lexicalized semantic network, such as BabelNet, a *semantic signature* is computed for each concept or entity. A semantic signature is a set of highly related vertices obtained by performing Random Walks with Restart (RWR)[58] for each vertex v of the semantic network. RWR models the conditional probability $P(v'|v)$ associated with an edge (v, v'):

$$P(v'|v) = \frac{\text{weight}(v, v')}{\sum_{v'' \in V} \text{weight}(v, v'')} \qquad (3)$$

where V is the set of vertices in the semantic network and weight(v, v') is the weight associated with (v, v'). This is a preliminary step that needs to be performed once and for all, independently of the input text;

- Given an input text, Babelfy extracts all the linkable fragments and, for each of them, lists all the possible meanings according to the sense inventory. Candidate extraction is a high-coverage procedure based on super-string (instead of exact) matching, hence it is able to handle partial mentions and overlapping fragments (e.g., given the mention *major league*, both *league* and *major league* are valid candidates);

- A graph-based semantic interpretation of the input text is generated using the semantic signatures of all candidate meanings. Then, Babelfy extracts a *dense subgraph* of this representation in order to select a coherent set of best candidate meanings for the target mentions. An example of semantic interpretation graph is shown in Fig. 3. Each candidate in the graph is weighted with a measure that takes into account both semantic and lexical coherence, exploiting graph centrality among the candidates as well as the number of connected fragments. This measure is used in the dense-subgraph algorithm to iteratively remove low-coherence vertices from the semantic graph until convergence.

One of the greatest advantages of Babelfy is flexibility: it can be used seamlessly for WSD, EL or even both at the same time. Furthermore, the whole procedure is language-independent,

and can be easily extended to any language for which lexicalizations are available inside the semantic network without relying on language-specific annotated corpora. In fact, Babelfy can even handle mixed text in which multiple languages are used at the same time, or work without knowing which languages the input text contains ("*language-agnostic*" setting). On the other hand, as in any knowledge-based approach (Sec. 1.1), the quality of disambiguation depends crucially on the quality of the underlying resource.

BabelNet and Babelfy have inaugurated a new, broader way of looking at disambiguation in lexical semantics, which has been further pursued by the research community[59,60] and has led to the organization of novel tasks focused on multilingual WSD and EL as part of the SemEval (Semantic Evaluation) competition series:

- The *SemEval*-2013 *task* 12 *on Multilingual Word Sense Disambiguation*,[61] which required participating systems to annotate nouns in a test corpus with the most appropriate sense from the BabelNet sense inventory (or, alternatively, from those of WordNet or Wikipedia). The corpus consisted of 13 articles covering different domains, from sports to financial news, and available in five different languages (English, French, German, Spanish and Italian). The number of sense-annotated words in each article varied from 1400 to 1900 (depending upon the language), totaling more than 8000 annotations;

- The *SemEval*-2015 *task* 13 *on Multilingual All-words WSD and Entity Linking*,[62] similar to the Semeval-2013 task, where the setup consisted of annotating four tokenized and part-of-speech tagged documents in three languages (English, Italian and Spanish) with information in the biomedical, computer science, and society domains. The total number of sense annotations was around 1200 for each language (more than 3700 overall). This was the first disambiguation task explicitly oriented to joint WSD and EL, including features of a typical WSD task (i.e., sense annotations for all open-class parts of speech) as well as features of a typical EL task (i.e., annotated named entities and nonspecified mention boundaries).

4.2. *Sense-aware representation of entities and concepts for semantic similarity*

One of the long-standing challenges of NLP, since its earliest days, has been that of representing the semantics of linguistic

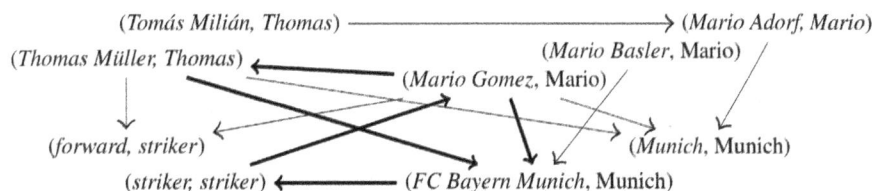

Fig. 3. Excerpt of the semantic interpretation graph for the example sentence *Thomas and Mario are strikers playing in Munich*, drawn from the original article.[54] The edges connecting the correct meanings (e.g., Thomas Muller for *Thomas* and Mario Gomez for *Mario*) are in bold.

items (mostly words) in a machine-interpretable form. Stemming from the well-known *distributional hypothesis*,[64] i.e., the fundamental idea that words occurring in the same contexts tend to have similar meanings, the paradigm of vector space models[19] took the lead, providing both a theoretical and practical framework in which a word is represented as a vector of numbers in a continuous metric space. Within this framework, linguistic phenomena are framed in terms of mathematical operations and, in particular, semantic similarity and relatedness between two words can be directly expressed in terms of proximity between the corresponding vectors, and computed in a quantifiable way (e.g., using cosine similarity). In recent times, the great success of neural networks and deep learning led to the development of *embedded* vector spaces,[65] which are compact and fast to compute from unstructured corpora, and at the same time capable of preserving semantic regularities between linguistic items.

Word representations, however, have a crucial limitation: they tend to conflate different meanings of a word into a single vector. A potential way of overcoming this limitation is to move to the *sense level* and generate representations of word senses, where each distinct meaning of a given word is associated with a distinct vector. Figure 4 shows an illustrative example with the word bank: in a word-level space, the vector for bank lies exactly in between two regions that relate to the geographical and financial meanings of bank, respectively; this shows that components pertaining to two different semantic areas are inherently mixed up when the word is ambiguous. Instead, in the sense-level space, the two regions are neatly separated and the previously conflated meanings of bank have their own vectors in the proper semantic areas.

In fact, the representation of individual word senses and concepts has recently become very popular, thanks to several experimental results showing significant performance improvements with respect to word representations. In this respect, LKRs can (and have been) be used to construct state-of-the-art models, including WordNet, Wikipedia and BabelNet. Compared to corpus-based approaches, where senses are typically not fine-grained, difficult to evaluate and statistically biased towards frequent meanings, a key advantage of knowledge-based representations is that they are directly linked to existing sense inventories, which makes them readily usable in downstream applications (e.g., disambiguation, clustering or information extraction).

4.2.1. *SensEmbed*

A possible way of constructing semantic representations of word senses is to leverage existing architectures that already proved effective for word representations,[65] such as the *Continuous Bag Of Words* (CBOW). CBOW architectures are used to produce continuous vector representations (*embeddings*) for words based on distributional information from a textual corpus: in particular, they learn to predict a token given its context, which is typically defined by a fixed-size sliding window around the token itself. In order to work at the sense level, the CBOW has to be trained on a *sense-annotated corpus*, where sense-level information is explicitly attached to words and multi-word expressions; this will tell the CBOW that two distinct meanings of the same ambiguous term (e.g., bank) have to be treated as distinct tokens (e.g., $bank_n^1$ and $bank_n^2$) and hence modeled with distinct embeddings. This is the core idea behind SensEmbed,[66] a technique to obtain continuous representations of word senses (*sense embeddings*) and use them effectively for word and relational similarity.[67] SensEmbed relied on a dump of the English Wikipedia automatically disambiguated with Babelfy (Sec. 4.1) in order to train a CBOW architecture, obtaining as a result latent representation of word senses linked to the sense inventory of BabelNet. By leveraging both distributional knowledge and structured knowledge coming from the semantic network,

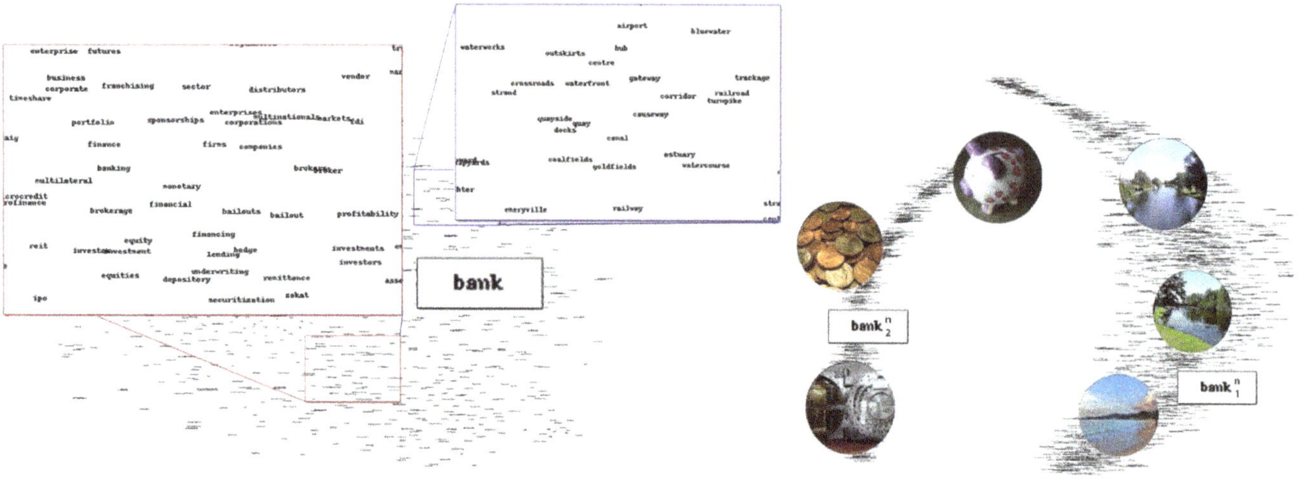

Fig. 4. Portions of a word-level vector space centered on the word bank (*left*) and a sense-level vector space where two different meanings of bank have distinct representations (*right*).[63]

SENSEMBED consistently achieved state-of-the-art performances on various similarity benchmark, proving the effectiveness of embeddings at the sense level.

4.2.2. *NASARI*

A major drawback of continuous models, such as WORD2VEC[65] and SENSEMBED,[66] is the lack of interpretability: embeddings are compact representations where meaning is latent, with no human-readable feature that describes their shape and structure. Also, being a corpus-based technique, the quality of a sense vector depends crucially on the frequency of the corresponding word sense inside the training corpus.

To address both issues, an alternative vector representation based on BabelNet was developed, named **NASARI**.[68] Instead of using a sense-annotated corpus, NASARI relies entirely on the BabelNet semantic network to construct a vector representation for each concept or entity (i.e., synset) in BabelNet: whereas SENSEMBED learns representations for word senses (hence two synonyms get two different embeddings), NASARI computes a single vector representing a whole Babel synset. This feature, thanks to the multilingual nature of BabelNet, directly translates into comparability across languages and linguistic levels (words, senses and concepts).

The NASARI representation of a given synset s is computed by first gathering a sub-corpus of contextual information relative to s: by exploiting BabelNet's inter-resource mappings, NASARI considers the Wikipedia page of s, all Wikipedia pages with an outgoing link to that page, and the Wikipedia pages of all the synsets connected to s via taxonomic relations in BabelNet. All content words inside this sub-corpus are then tokenized, lemmatized and weighted according to the source and type of semantic connections to s; finally the sub-corpus is turned into a vector using three different techniques that give rise to three different types of representations:

- A *lexical* representation, i.e., a vector defined in the space of individual words. In this lexical space, dimensions are explicitly associated with words, and the sub-corpus is represented in terms of the relevance of each word inside the text, estimated using *lexical specificity*[69] (a statistical measure based on the hypergeometric distribution);
- An *embedded* representation, i.e., a sense embedding in a continuous vector space obtained from the lexical vector with a two-steps procedure: (1) each dimension (i.e., word) is mapped to its embedded representation learnt from a textual corpus (e.g., using the CBOW architecture); and (2) these word representations are then combined using a weighted average. The resulting vector is still defined at the sense level, but lies in the same semantic space of word embeddings, thus enabling a direct comparison between words and synsets;
- A *unified* representation, i.e., a vector defined in the space of Babel synsets. This vector is obtained by clustering the

word dimensions of the lexical vector based on whether they have a sense sharing the same hypernym in the BabelNet taxonomy. Clustering sibling words turns a lexical space into a semantic space with multilingual Babel synsets as dimensions: not only does this process provide an implicit disambiguation of ambiguous word dimensions, but it also makes the obtained unified representation language-independent, and hence suitable for cross-lingual applications.

The flexibility of this approach allowed experimental evaluations on different benchmarks (monolingual and cross-lingual word similarity, sense clustering, WSD), for each of which NASARI reported state-of-the-art performance. Moreover, NASARI's technique has been used to label 1.5 M Babel synsets with *domain information*, by first constructing lexical vectors for a selected set of domains drawn from Wikipedia (and associated featured articles[j] used as seeds) and then selecting, for each synset and corresponding NASARI vector, the domain with the closest vector in the lexical space.

4.3. *Semantically-augmented open information extraction*

Inspired by the long-standing challenge of Machine Reading,[70] Information Extraction is a popular branch of NLP where the goal is the automatic extraction of knowledge from large-scale (often Web-scale) unstructured text and its formalization in terms of *relation triples*, i.e., triples in the form ⟨subject, predicate, object⟩.

When carried out in a completely unsupervised way, i.e., without relying on predefined entity or relation inventories, the process is known as Open Information Extraction (OIE). OIE is typically performed in a single pass over massive amounts of raw text, with no human input at all, in order to produce millions of relation instances that connect pairs of entity mentions with textual relation phrases (e.g., *is a city in*, *is married to*). While earlier approaches[23] paid little or no attention in making explicit the semantics of such extracted information, more recent work[71,72] leveraged deeper semantic analysis, as well as the availability of semi-structured resources (Sec. 2.2), in order to, on the one hand, link and disambiguate argument pairs with entities inside a knowledge base, and, on the other, cluster together synonymous relation phrases (e.g., *is a field of* and *is an area of*) or arrange them hierarchically in a relation taxonomy.

Throughout this section, we will show how the development of wide-coverage resources like BabelNet, along with joint approaches to WSD and EL (Sec. 4.1) and semantic representations of concepts and entities (Sec. 4.2), can greatly empower OIE by (1) enforcing an even broader semantic analysis to extract as much information as possible from text

---

[j]https://en.wikipedia.org/wiki/Wikipedia:Featured articles.

(Sec. 4.3.1), and (2) enabling the semantic alignment and unification of heterogeneous OIE-derived knowledge (Sec. 4.3.2).

4.3.1. *DefIE*

The intuition of exploiting at best joint WSD and EL for OIE is one of the underlying ideas behind DEFIE,[73] a full-fledged OIE pipeline based on BabelNet and designed to target textual definitions instead of massive (but noisy) Web-scale corpora. In DEFIE exploiting definitional knowledge is key to effectively harvest fully disambiguated relation instances on a large scale, and arrange them automatically in a high-quality taxonomy of semantic relations. DEFIE works by parsing a target definition with a dependency parser and disambiguating it with Babelfy; then it creates a graph-based representation of the text (*syntactic-semantic graph*) from which relation instances are extracted as shortest paths between pairs of disambiguated mentions.

Thanks to fully disambiguated argument pairs, DEFIE is capable of typifying relation patterns and ranking them by quality; at the same time, explicitly disambiguated relation phrases are exploited to integrate taxonomic information from BabelNet, and from there construct a high-quality relation taxonomy. A comprehensive experimental evaluation, carried out after running DEFIE on the set of English definitions in BabelNet 2.5.1, showed the effectiveness of coupling dense definitional knowledge with joint WSD and EL, and led DEFIE to state-of-the-art results against OIE approaches based on much larger corpora (such as entire Wikipedia dumps, or portions of the Web).

Table 3 shows some examples of semantic relations computed by DEFIE. Each relation pattern is accompanied by subject and object *semantic types*, obtained after integrating the disambiguated argument pairs (extracted from the definitions) into the BabelNet taxonomy and retrieving their hypernym senses. Relation patterns also contain disambiguated fragments (e.g., $research_n^1$ in the pattern '*covers* $research_n^1$ *in*'), a crucial feature for the DEFIE pipeline to taxonomize relations efficiently.

4.3.2. *KB-Unify*

Another way of leveraging semantic analysis is that of focusing on the *outputs* (rather than the inputs) of the various OIE systems developed by the research community. Indeed, these systems can be very different in nature and hence formalize the knowledge they extract in many different ways, which are typically not comparable one to the other. As a result, every new OIE system that enters the stage might end up discovering knowledge already formalized by other systems, with no means of recognizing and taking advantage of it.

This issue motivated the development of KB-UNIFY,[74] an approach for integrating OIE-derived knowledge from an arbitrary number of resources and systems into a single, unified and fully disambiguated knowledge repository. The unification algorithm of KB-UNIFY is based on BabelNet and comprises two subsequent stages:

- A *disambiguation* stage, where each individual resource, modeled as set of triples, is linked to BabelNet by means of its argument pairs (either by explicit disambiguation or by exploiting BabelNet's inter-resource mappings);
- An *alignment* stage, where equivalent relations across different resources are merged together into *relation synsets*. This step is based on representing a given relation in terms of its argument pairs within the continuous vector space of SENSEMBED (Sec. 4.2.1).

Throughout the whole unification process, BabelNet serves as backbone for KB-UNIFY by providing a *unified sense inventory*, with respect to which every individual resource is redefined. Once this crucial step is done, relations coming from very heterogeneous resources can be represented in the same semantic space, thanks to the sense-level vector representations of SENSEMBED, and compared accordingly.

5. Conclusion and Future Directions

In this paper, we looked at the intersection between machine-readable knowledge and NLP, focusing on how lexical resources can be exploited for building an effective computational model of lexical semantics. One of the major challenges for such a model is *lexical ambiguity*, and we argued that using wisely the vast amount of available machine-readable knowledge can pave the way for overcoming it. However, handling all this knowledge at best is far from easy: the nature, structure and scope of knowledge resources vary widely, ranging from expert-built lexicographic dictionaries (such as WordNet) to huge, collaborative encyclopedias (Wikipedia) and semantic databases (Wikidata) available in many languages. When considered in isolation, none of these can serve as the ultimate resource for all scenarios and applications: instead, the optimal solution seems to be the integration of multiple, heterogeneous knowledge repositories that can complement each other and fill each other's gaps.

Among other successful approaches for linking together heterogeneous resources, such as MENTA,[75] UBY[76] or YAGO,[31] we chose **BabelNet** as representative case study; we described it in detail, from the original mapping algorithm to the

Table 3. Examples of semantic relations from DEFIE.

Subject type	Relation pattern	Object type
$enzyme_n^1$	*catalyze* $reaction_n^1$ *of*	$chemical_n^1$
$album_n^1$	*record by*	$rock\ group_n^1$
$officer_n^1$	*command* $brigade_n^1$ *of*	$army\ unit_n^1$
$bridge_n^1$	*cross over*	$river_n^1$
$academic\ journal_n^1$	*cover* $research_n^1$ *in*	$science_n^1$
$organization_n^1$	*have* $headquarter_n^1$ *in*	$city_n^1$

continuous development that has turned it into the prototype for a *"dictionary of the future"*. At its very core, the rationale of BabelNet lies in the idea of a multilingual *encyclopedic dictionary*, where lexicographic and encyclopedic knowledge is seamlessly connected through a language-independent semantic network of concepts and entities (Babel synsets). As of today, BabelNet has become the largest resource of its kind: 13 million synsets, 380 million semantic relations and 271 languages covered. We showed that the availability of BabelNet has fueled the development of novel knowledge-based approaches capable of reaching the state of the art in various NLP areas: in each case, flexibility (especially in terms of language and scope) turned out to be a distinctive feature coming directly from the nature of BabelNet.

Notwithstanding its legacy within NLP and related fields, BabelNet by itself is not enough to solve lexical semantics. The encyclopedic dictionary is continuously growing and, as it grows, room for improvement increases accordingly. Among the many possible advancements that are subject of ongoing research, a prominent idea is that of real-time integration of new information that, especially in collaborative resources, is added or modified every day. This is not only due to the fundamental ever-changing nature of knowledge, but also to the continuous development of new knowledge resources, with their own features and advantages. All these efforts foster the vision of a universal "linking machine", where the more new knowledge is integrated, the more confirmation is obtained that current knowledge is appropriate (or not). Finally, on the application side, it is also arguable that knowledge-based NLP ultimately needs corpus-based learning approaches to attain outstanding results, as some contributions have already shown.[77,78] Once more, albeit in a different perspective, we argue that joining forces will pay off.

References

[1] R. Navigli, Word sense disambiguation: A survey, *ACM Comput. Surv.* **41**, 1 (2009).

[2] R. Navigli, A quick tour of word sense disambiguation, induction and related approaches, *Proc. of SOFSEM* (2012), pp. 115–129.

[3] B. Decadt, V. Hoste, W. Daelemans and A. van den Bosch, Gambl, genetic algorithm optimization of memory-based WSD, *Proc. of SensEval-3* (2004), pp. 108–112.

[4] J. F. Cai, W. S. Lee and Y. W. Teh, NUS-ML: Improving word sense disambiguation using topic features, *Proc. of SemEval-2007* (2007), pp. 249–252.

[5] Z. Zhong and H. T. Ng, It makes sense: A wide-coverage word sense disambiguation system for free text, *Proc. of ACL* (2010), pp. 78–83.

[6] K. Taghipour and H. T. Ng, Semi-supervised word sense disambiguation using word embeddings in general and specific domains, *Proc. of NAACL-HLT* (2015), pp. 314–323.

[7] G. A. Miller, R. Beckwith, C. D. Fellbaum, D. Gross and K. Miller, WordNet: An online lexical database, *Int. J. Lexicogr.* **3**, 235 (1990).

[8] H. Schütze, Automatic word sense discrimination, *Comput. Linguis.* **24**, 97 (1998).

[9] S. Brody and M. Lapata, Bayesian word sense induction, *Proc. of EACL* (2009), pp. 103–111.

[10] A. D. Marco and R. Navigli, Clustering and diversifying web search results with graph-based word sense induction, *Comput. Linguis.* **39**, 709 (2013).

[11] R. Navigli and P. Velardi, Structural semantic interconnections: A knowledge-based approach to word sense disambiguation, *IEEE Trans. Pattern Anal. Mach. Intell.* **27**, 1075 (2005).

[12] R. Navigli and S. P. Ponzetto, Joining forces pays off: Multilingual joint word sense disambiguation, *Proc. of EMNLP-CoNLL* (2012), pp. 1399–1410.

[13] E. Agirre, O. L. de Lacalle and A. Soroa, Knowledge-based WSD on specific domains: Performing better than generic supervised WSD, *Proc. of IJCAI* (2009), pp. 1501–1506.

[14] R. Navigli, S. Faralli, A. Soroa, O. L. de Lacalle and E. Agirre, Two birds with one stone: Learning semantic models for text categorization and word sense disambiguation, *Proc. of CIKM* (2011), pp. 2317–2320.

[15] M. Cuadros and G. Rigau, Quality assessment of large scale knowledge resources, *Proc. of EMNLP* (2006), pp. 534–541.

[16] R. Navigli and M. Lapata, An experimental study on graph connectivity for unsupervised word sense disambiguation, *IEEE Trans. Pattern Anal. Mach. Intell.* **32**, 678 (2010).

[17] D. Rao, P. McNamee and M. Dredze, Entity linking: Finding extracted entities in a knowledge base, *Multi-Source, Multilingual Information Extraction and Summarization* Vol. 11 (2013), p. 93.

[18] A. Budanitsky and G. Hirst, Evaluating WordNet-Based measures of lexical semantic relatedness, *Comput. Linguis.* **32**, 13 (2006).

[19] P. D. Turney and P. Pantel, From frequency to meaning: Vector space models of semantics, *J. Artif. Intell. Res.* **37**, 141 (2010).

[20] R. Collobert, J. Weston, L. Bottou, M. Karlen, K. Kavukcuoglu and P. Kuksa, Natural language processing (Almost) from scratch, *J. Mach. Learn. Res.* **12**, 2493 (2011).

[21] W. A. Gale, K. Church and D. Yarowsky, A method for disambiguating word senses in a corpus, *Comput. Humanit.* **26**, 415 (1992).

[22] R. Mihalcea and D. Moldovan, eXtended WordNet: Progress report, *Proc. of the NAACL Workshop on WordNet and Other Lexical Resources* (2001), pp. 95–100.

[23] M. Banko, M. J. Cafarella, S. Soderland, M. Broadhead and O. Etzioni, Open information extraction from the Web, *Proc. of IJCAI* (2007), pp. 2670–2676.

[24] A. Carlson, J. Betteridge, B. Kisiel, B. Settles, E. R. H. Jr. and T. M. Mitchell, Toward an architecture for never-ending language learning, *Proc. of AAAI* (2010), pp. 1306–1313.

[25] E. Hovy, R. Navigli and S. P. Ponzetto, Collaboratively built semi-structured content and artificial intelligence: The story so far, *Artif. Intell.* **194**, 2 (2013).

[26] J. Giles, Internet encyclopaedias go head to head, *Nature* **438**, 900 (2005).

[27] S. Cucerzan, Large-scale named entity disambiguation based on Wikipedia data, *Proc. of EMNLP-CoNLL* (2007), pp. 708–716.

[28] E. Gabrilovich and S. Markovitch, Computing semantic relatedness using Wikipedia-based explicit semantic analysis, *Proc. of IJCAI* (2007), pp. 1606–1611.

[29] F. Wu and D. S. Weld, Open information extraction using Wikipedia, *Proc. of ACL* (2010), pp. 118–127.

[30]D. Vrandečić, Wikidata: A new platform for collaborative data collection, *Proc. of WWW* (2012), pp. 1063–1064.

[31]F. Mahdisoltani, J. Biega and F. M. Suchanek, YAGO3: A knowledge base from multilingual Wikipedias, *Proc. of CIDR* (2015).

[32]J. Lehmann, R. Isele, M. Jakob, A. Jentzsch, D. Kontokostas, P. N. Mendes, S. Hellmann, M. Morsey, P. van Kleef, S. Auer and C. Bizer, DBpedia - A large-scale, multilingual knowledge base extracted from Wikipedia, *Seman. Web J.* 1 (2014).

[33]L. Bentivogli, P. Forner, B. Magnini and E. Pianta, Revising the Wordnet domains hierarchy: Semantics, coverage and balancing, *Proc. of MLR* (2004), pp. 101–108.

[34]S. Baccianella, A. Esuli and F. Sebastiani, Sentiwordnet 3.0: An enhanced lexical resource for sentiment analysis and opinion mining, *Proc. of LREC* (2010), pp. 2200–2204.

[35]A. Toral, S. Brancale, M. Monachini and C. Soria, Rejuvenating the italian WordNet: Upgrading, standarising, extending, *Proc. of GWC* (2010).

[36]H. Isahara, F. Bond, K. Uchimoto, M. Utiyama and K. Kanzaki, Development of the japanese wordnet, *Proc. of LREC* (2008), pp. 2420–2420.

[37]B. Hamp and H. Feldweg, Germanet – a lexical-semantic net for german, *Proc. of ACL workshop on Automatic Information Extraction and Building of lexical Semantic Resources for NLP Applications* (1997), pp. 9–15.

[38]C. F. Baker, C. J. Fillmore and J. B. Lowe, The berkeley framenet project, *Proc. of ACL* (1998), pp. 86–90.

[39]C. J. Fillmore, Frame semantics, *Linguistics in the Morning Calm* (1982), pp. 111–137.

[40]K. K. Schuler, Verbnet: A broad-coverage, comprehensive verb lexicon, Ph.D. thesis, University of Pennsylvania, Philadelphia, PA, USA (2005).

[41]B. Levin, *English Verb Classes and Alternations: A preliminary investigation* (University of Chicago press, 1993).

[42]R. Navigli and S. P. Ponzetto, BabelNet: The automatic construction, evaluation and application of a wide-coverage multilingual semantic network, *Artif. Intell.* 193, 217 (2012).

[43]T. Zesch, C. Müller and I. Gurevych, Extracting lexical semantic knowledge from Wikipedia and wiktionary., *Proc. of LREC* (2008), pp. 1646–1652.

[44]C. M. Meyer and I. Gurevych, Wiktionary: A new rival for expert-built lexicons? exploring the possibilities of collaborative lexicography, *Electronic Lexicography* (Oxford University Press, 2012), pp. 259–291.

[45]K. Bollacker, C. Evans, P. Paritosh, T. Sturge and J. Taylor, Freebase: A collaboratively created graph database for structuring human knowledge, *Proc. of SIGMOD* (2008), pp. 1247–1250.

[46]I. Gurevych, J. Eckle-Kohler and M. Matuschek, Linked lexical knowledge bases: Foundations and applications, *Synth. Lect. Hum. Lang. Technol.* 9, 1 (2016).

[47]G. A. Miller, C. Leacock, R. Tengi and R. T. Bunker, A semantic concordance, *Proc. of HLT* (1993), pp. 303–308.

[48]S. Banerjee and T. Pedersen, Extended gloss overlap as a measure of semantic relatedness, *Proc. of IJCAI* (2003), pp. 805–810.

[49]T. Flati, D. Vannella, T. Pasini and R. Navigli, Two is bigger (and better) than one: The Wikipedia bitaxonomy project, *Proc. of ACL* (2014), pp. 945–955.

[50]T. Flati, D. Vannella, T. Pasini and R. Navigli, MultiWiBi: The multilingual Wikipedia bitaxonomy project, *Artif. Intell.* 241, 66 (2016).

[51]F. Bond and R. Foster, Linking and extending an open multilingual Wordnet, *Proc. of ACL* (2013), pp. 1352–1362.

[52]C. Chiarcos, S. Hellmann and S. Nordhoff, Towards a linguistic linked open data Cloud: The open linguistics working group, *TAL* 52, 245 (2011).

[53]J. McCrae, D. Spohr and P. Cimiano, Linking lexical resources and ontologies on the semantic web with lemon, *Proc. of ESWC* (2011), pp. 245–259.

[54]A. Moro, A. Raganato and R. Navigli, Entity linking meets word sense disambiguation: A unified approach, *TACL* 2, 231 (2014).

[55]J. Deng, W. Dong, R. Socher, L.-J. Li, K. Li and L. Fei-Fei, ImageNet: A large-scale hierarchical image database, *Proc. of CVPR* (2009), pp. 248–255.

[56]K. Steinmetz, Redefining the modern dictionary, *TIME*, 20 (May 23rd 2016).

[57]R. Mihalcea and A. Csomai, Wikify!: Linking documents to encyclopedic knowledge, *Proc. of CIKM* (2007), pp. 233–242.

[58]H. Tong, C. Faloutsos and J.-Y. Pan, Random walk with restart: Fast solutions and applications, *Knowl. Inf. Syst.* 14, 327 (2008).

[59]P. Basile, A. Caputo and G. Semeraro, UNIBA: Combining distributional semantic models and sense distribution for multilingual all-words sense disambiguation and entity linking, *Proc. of SemEval-2015* (2015), pp. 360–364.

[60]D. Weissenborn, L. Hennig, F. Xu and H. Uszkoreit, Multi-objective optimization for the joint disambiguation of nouns and named entities, *Proc. of ACL-IJCNLP* (2015), pp. 596–605.

[61]R. Navigli, D. Jurgens and D. Vannella, SemEval-2013 Task 12: Multilingual word sense disambiguation, *Proc. of SemEval* (2013), pp. 222–231.

[62]A. Moro and R. Navigli, SemEval-2015 task 13: Multilingual all-words sense disambiguation and entity linking, *Proc. of SemEval* (2015), pp. 288–297.

[63]J. Camacho Collados, I. Iacobacci, M. T. Pilehvar and R. Navigli, Semantic representations of word senses and concepts ACL tutorial (2016).

[64]J. R. Firth, A synopsis of linguistic theory 1930–55, **1952–59**, 1 (1957).

[65]T. Mikolov, K. Chen, G. Corrado and J. Dean, Efficient estimation of word representations in vector space, *ICLR Workshop* (2013).

[66]I. Iacobacci, M. T. Pilehvar and R. Navigli, SensEmbed: Learning sense embeddings for word and relational similarity, *Proc. of ACL* (2015), pp. 95–105.

[67]D. L. Medin, R. L. Goldstone and D. Gentner, Similarity involving attributes and relations: Judgments of similarity and difference are not inverses, *Psychol. Sci.* 1, 54 (1990).

[68]J. C. Collados, M. T. Pilehvar and R. Navigli, Nasari: Integrating explicit knowledge and corpus statistics for a multilingual representation of concepts and entities, *Artif. Intell.* 240, 36 (2016).

[69]P. Lafon, Sur la variabilité de la fréquence des formes dans un corpus, *Mots* 1, 127 (1980).

[70]T. M. Mitchell, Reading the web: A breakthrough goal for AI, *AI Magazine* (2005).

[71]N. Nakashole, G. Weikum and F. M. Suchanek, PATTY: A taxonomy of relational patterns with semantic types, *Proc. of EMNLP-CoNLL* (2012), pp. 1135–1145.

[72]A. Moro and R. Navigli, Integrating syntactic and semantic analysis into the open information extraction paradigm, *Proc. of IJCAI* (2013), pp. 2148–2154.

[73]C. Delli Bovi, L. Espinosa Anke and R. Navigli, Knowledge base unification via sense embeddings and disambiguation, *Proc. of EMNLP* (2015), pp. 726–736.

[74]C. Delli Bovi, L. Telesca and R. Navigli, Large-scale information extraction from textual definitions through deep syntactic and semantic analysis, *Trans. Assoc. Comput. Linguis.* **3**, 529 (2015).

[75]G. de Melo and G. Weikum, MENTA: Inducing multilingual taxonomies from Wikipedia, *Proc. of CIKM* (2010), pp. 1099–1108.

[76]I. Gurevych, J. Eckle-Kohler, S. Hartmann, M. Matuschek, C. M. Meyer and C. Wirth, Uby: A Large-scale unified lexical-semantic resource based on LMF, *Proc. of EACL* (2012), pp. 580–590.

[77]M. T. Pilehvar and R. Navigli, A Large-scale pseudoword-based evaluation framework for state-of-the-art word sense disambiguation, *Comput. Linguis.* **40**, 837 (2014).

[78]K. Toutanova, D. Chen, P. Pantel, H. Poon, P. Choudhury and M. Gamon, Representing text for joint embedding of text and knowledge bases, *Proc. of EMNLP* (2015), pp. 1499–1509.

Model-based documentation

Feroz Farazi*, Craig Chapman[†], Pathmeswaran Raju[‡]
and William Byrne[§]

Knowledge Based Engineering Lab, Birmingham City University
Millennium Point, Birmingham, B4 7XG, UK
*mohammad.farazi@bcu.ac.uk
[†]craig.chapman@bcu.ac.uk
[‡]path.raju@bcu.ac.uk
[§]william.byrne@bcu.ac.uk

Knowledge acquisition is becoming an integral part of the manufacturing industries, which rely on domain experts in various phases of product life cycle including design, analysis, manufacturing, operation and maintenance. It has the potential to enable knowledge reuse, however, poorly managed knowledge can cause information loss and inefficiency. If technical documentation is managed well in the manufacturing industries, intended piece of knowledge can easily be located, used and reused for purpose and as a result, the corresponding industry can be benefited. Some examples of technical documentation are design specification, operating manual and maintenance manual. Model-based Documentation (MBD) is a documentation approach that uses model to provide structure to the data of the documents. MBD can be thought of as a way to better organize knowledge thereby knowledge identification and retrieval become easier, faster and efficient. In this paper, we propose MBD and its extension as a potential solution to overcome the issues involved in the typical technical documentation approaches.

Keywords: Semantic technology; ontology; engineering design knowledge; knowledge modeling; model-based documentation.

1. The Problem

Manufacturing industries all over the world are going through a difficult time mainly because of the high production cost. The production time influences the production cost and usually the former is proportional to the latter. Therefore, there is a pressing need for reducing the production time in order to survive in the highly competitive global market. In this ever-changing world, products also evolve continuously. Complex products which keep evolving and which require deep knowledge and detailed instruction to operate and maintain are necessarily released with the operating and maintenance manual. An aero-engine is an example of a complex product. The production time reasonably includes the product manual development time. Writing manuals is an onerous and time consuming job and performing this job after the manufacturing will delay the product release that might make manufacturing companies losing customers and profit. To reduce the total duration of the product release, documentation and manufacturing can proceed concurrently.[1] But the efforts required and the total man-months needed for the documentation remain unchanged.

Problem 1. *Therefore, the challenge is how to minimize the efforts and man-months in authoring and producing documentation?*

Design specification is a documentation used in the design phase of a product. It contains engineering design choices, rules and rationales. The choices, which were made, the rules, which were defined by the expert engineers in producing an earlier version of the product and the rationales behind both the choices and rules, are of the utmost importance for the engineers who have replaced them. The rules included in the design specification are identifiable by humans, however reading hundreds of or thousands of pages for detecting the rules lowers the efficiency of the design engineers. Tools developed using Natural Language Processing (NLP) techniques would be helpful in automating, for example, the rule detection process, unfortunately, these tools still underperform and sometimes the accuracy that they demonstrate is unacceptable. Automatic identification is crucial as it creates the environment for programmatic import of the rules to the engineering design automation tools such as Technosoft's AML,[a] Siemens NX[b] and CATIA.[c]

Problem 2. *The challenge, therefore, to overcome here is how to remove the barrier that hinders automatic identification of the rules?*

These rules are often a set of statements written in natural language. For making them actionable, in the current practice, the engineering workforce codifies them manually into the native platform of the design automation tools.

Problem 3. *The challenge to address here is how to automatically integrate the rules retrieved from the technical documentation with the design automations tools?*

---

[a]http://www.technosoft.com/application-software/adaptive-modeling-language/.
[b]https://www.plm.automation.siemens.com/en_gb/products/nx/.
[c]http://www.3ds.com/products-services/catia/.

The 2012 workshop on technical documentation challenges in aviation maintenance discussed the problems that have been identified and that lead to errors in maintenance, rework and maintenance delays. The participants of the workshop were mainly from the aero-engine producing companies (e.g., GE Aviation and Pratt & Whitney), airlines companies (e.g., US Airways and Delta) and airframe industries (e.g., Airbus and Boeing). In the workshop, they also discussed that while producing maintenance documents relying on low cost resources such as Microsoft Word for authoring and Adobe pdf for delivery prohibits to be cost-effective in the long term as the produced content lacks structure and makes the information management and search difficult.[2]

Problem 4. *The challenge is how to provide structure to the information codified in the technical documentation in order to make the management and search activities easier?*

2. State-of-the-Art

This section is divided into the following two parts: documentation approaches and documentation specifications. In the former part, a brief description of a number of document generation techniques with a focus on knowledge capturing and knowledge modeling is provided (Sec. 2.1) and in the latter part, DITA, DocBook and S1000D are briefly discussed (Sec. 2.2).

2.1. *Documentation approaches*

2.1.1. *Active document system*

Active Document System (ADS)[3] is an approach devised for capturing, indexing and managing engineering design knowledge (e.g., engineering drawings, prototype evaluations, analysis reports, engineering formulae and informal notes on specific design problems) in a way that makes search, identification and extraction of such knowledge easier. ADS is developed to capture the design knowledge that usually comes in unstructured format (e.g., free text) and that originates from the formal and informal design descriptions. It follows a technique called part or function relation for adding structure to the unstructured design knowledge of a product. Through this relational perspective (or aspect), structural design knowledge as well as part or function relational knowledge can be swiftly browsed, navigated and located. It allows the creation, maintenance and exploitation of customized facets on-demand to cover other aspects of design knowledge such as cost analysis.

ADS is applied to the creation of a knowledge management system for managing information about refrigerator design process. ADS engineering design knowledge management infrastructure consists of three different but correlated modules which are knowledge acquisition module, knowledge structuring module and knowledge retrieval module.

The knowledge acquisition module has provided the means for capturing both informal and formal design knowledge. An individual design engineer or a group of design engineers can write an informal design memo while product design activity is running in an engineering work environment. To capture this informal design knowledge, ADS has deployed an authoring web application with the necessary editing tools. Capturing formal knowledge including engineering drawings and mathematical formulae is on the other hand done through the use of templates, which are specific to design task and process users have at hand.

When the unstructured design knowledge flows from the acquisition module to the structuring module, it is passed through the Knowledge Perspective (KP) filter to link the slices of design knowledge to produce structured knowledge that is finally represented in the ADS knowledge base. A KP can be defined by following either top-down or bottom-up approach. In the top-down approach, a KP is defined first and then the ADS knowledge base is processed to produce relevant link between the pieces of relevant knowledge. In the bottom-up approach, the knowledge base is processed first to recognize the potential perspectives according to the relations between the pieces of knowledge.

The knowledge retrieval module works with the help of KPs created in the knowledge-structuring module on top of the design knowledge available in the ADS knowledge base. As like as the authoring application of the knowledge acquisition model, the KPs are also deployed on the Web to allow users browse the design knowledge. By choosing the right KP, a user can browse to find knowledge about a specific design.

2.1.2. *High value document generation*

Customized high-value document generation[4] requires synchronization of the inputs given by different experts to the process planning in the engineering product development. The goal of this work is to generate a value added document, e.g., experts supported semi-automatic generation of a Computer-Aided Manufacturing (CAM) document from the original Computer-Aided Design (CAD) document. The execution of the following macro-steps — project infrastructure definition, project architecture construction and document generation — can assist to achieve this goal.

The infrastructure definition includes the identification of standard concepts about processes, products, resources and external effects needed for the specification of the functional, behavioral and structural characteristics of the engineered objects. The architecture construction includes the analysis of the concepts to understand and build the relationships between them. At this step, duplicate and unnecessary concepts and instances are removed. Document generation relies on the refined and matured architecture of the project and as a result, becomes more optimized.

2.1.3. *Concurrent execution of manufacturing and documentation*

3DVIA Composer[1] is an authoring tool that can render 3D CAD models created in the engineering design phase and that can generate product documentation using these models for downstream phases such as manufacturing, assembly, operating and maintenance. As this composer can be integrated with the 3D CAD tool design environment, it offers the crucial advantage of executing the design and the documentation processes concurrently. Other advantages are automatic updating of the documentation when some changes are made in the CAD models, the facility to create animated visuals from the models to clearly show how to assemble and disassemble the product parts and capability to produce documentation in MS Word, MS PowerPoint and HTML formats.

2.1.4. *Model-based document and report generation*

Model-based document and report generation[5] is an approach relying on Model-Based Systems Engineering (MBSE) platform to produce documents from product or system models. It is one of the document generation initiatives taken at Jet Propulsion Laboratory (JPL). Systems Modeling Language (SysML) provides a firm underpinning for all of these initiatives.

This document generation approach leverages SysML's concepts Viewpoint and View to meet the requirements of different stakeholders, which might look at a product or a system from their own perspectives. With the help of these concepts, multiple views of the same (product or system) model can be created. A viewpoint captures the point of view of a stakeholder about a model using certain properties (e.g., purpose and stakeholder), constraints (e.g., view format and modeling language) and method. A view keeps it aligned with the constraints defined in the viewpoint to generate a view covering an aspect of the model. The method is responsible for running the process to create the view from the model. A viewpoint consists of a number of subordinate viewpoints. For example, a document viewpoint might contain section and subsection viewpoints.

2.1.5. *Model-based virtual document generation*

Device Modeling Environment (DME)[6] provides a modeling and simulation environment for engineered systems and supports the generation of virtual documents, which are answers to the questions about various aspects of such systems. The document generation relies on the inference performed over the mathematical and symbolic model of the systems.

DME made available a Web-based model library so that users can build their customized systems online combining various components. It allows users to predict the behavior of the systems being built by performing simulations. Users can pose questions about the physical structure and dynamic behavior of the systems and the answers are published in text and graphics in the form of explanations.

2.1.6. *Model-based requirement generation*

Model-based textual requirement generation[7] is an automatic documentation approach based on SysML structure and behavior diagrams. In the requirement generation, information from SysML's constructs such as blocks, states and activities are extracted and then represented in requirement constructs such as allocations, control flows and object flows.

2.1.7. *Rule-centric document generation*

Rule-centric object oriented approach[8] uses data and document template as the basic components for generating technical document. In this approach, the data component consists of a set of data objects. Similarly, the document template component is built with a set of document template objects. The data component and the document component are independent of each other. There are objects, which have many-to-many relations with the document template objects. The data objects are connected to the document template objects via a mapping. The objects have properties and methods. The rule that is defined by the user selects the document template object, which contains input parameters that help decide the right object and method and the corresponding data objects to populate the document template object.

2.2. *Documentation specifications*

2.2.1. *DITA*

Darwin Information Type Architecture (DITA)[9] is a documentation architecture, based on XML, created to provide an end-to-end support, from semi-automatic authoring all the way through to automatic delivery of technical documentation. It was developed in IBM[d] and is currently managed by OASIS.[e] It follows a set of principles for creating documentation in a specific way that can make the retrieval of information easier and that can meet the needs of product consumers. The principles are topic orientation, information typing, specialization and process inheritance. Topic orientation is about creating the topic as the smallest possible unit of information that can be reused and that can cover a subject or answer a question. Information typing deals with the creation of information of a specific type such as concept, task and reference topic. Specialization covers creating more specific information type depending upon the need. Process inheritance focuses on propagating processes of more generic information type to the more specific information type.

[d]https://www.ibm.com.
[e]https://www.oasis-open.org.

2.2.2. *DocBook*

DocBook[10] is a documentation system developed to facilitate the production of computer hardware and software related publications such as books and articles. Currently, it can be used for publishing almost everything that requires the structure of a set of books, chapters or papers. DocBook started as a collaborative project between partners HaL Computer Systems and O'Reilly. Since 1998, OASIS is responsible for its subsequent development and maintenance. XML is used for representing DocBook content. DocBook DTDs and schema languages such as XML Schema are employed to provide structure to the resulting documentation.

2.2.3. *S1000D*

S1000D[11] is a specification originally designed for aerospace and defense industry for the preparation and production of technical documentation. Its scope has subsequently been expanded to the domains of land and water vehicles and various equipment of both military and civilian markets. After S1000D's development by the AeroSpace and Defence Industries Association of Europe (ASD), a steering committee, formed with the ASD, the Air Industries Association (AIA) and the Air Transportation Association (ATA) of the USA, together with the industry and defense partners from the countries, which have user communities, has been maintaining the specification. At its core, there is the principle of information reuse that is facilitated by Data Modules. The Data Modules in version 4.0 of S1000D are represented in XML. S1000D is suitable for publishing in both printed and electronic form. The S1000D document generation architecture includes a data storage component, which is called Common Source Database (CSDB).

2.3. *Documentation summary*

In this section, we have summarized the documentation approaches and specifications from the design, modeling and representation technology perspectives. In Table 1, DITA, DocBook and S1000D are documentation specifications and the rest are documentation approaches. CAD is a design technology used both in Concurrent Execution of Manufacturing and Documentation and Model-Based Virtual Document Generation. SysML is a modeling technology (language) developed for systems engineering applications applied to Model-Based Document and Report Generation and Model-Based Requirement Generation. All three documentation specifications included XML as the data representation technology (language). XML is also included in the infrastructure of Model-Based Document and Report Generation and Rule-Centric Document Generation. Database and Knowledge Base are employed for representing (storing) data and knowledge, respectively. Ontology is used as a knowledge modeling and representation technology.

As shown in Table 1, among the modeling and representation technologies, Knowledge Base and Ontology are semantic technologies. In ADS and High Value Document Generation documentation approaches, semantic technologies are applied.

2.4. *Solution approach*

Research and development attempts have been taken both in the industry and academia to cover various aspects of technical documentation including ease of identification, machine readability and publishing format of information stored in the document databases of organizations.

Model-based Documentation (MBD) is a documentation approach that uses models of different kinds such as ontological model and template-based model to provide structure to the data of the documents. It can be thought of as a way to better organize knowledge thereby knowledge identification and retrieval become easier, faster and efficient. One size does not fit all. Similarly, one model does not capture all kinds of data. In MBD, therefore, the model needs to be created or updated according to the data.

For achieving interoperability, we follow the best practices of the engineering community. The International Council on Systems Engineering (INCOSE) fosters MBSE approach along with SysML for specification, design, analysis, verification and validation of engineering systems. The aerospace

Table 1. Knowledge representation technologies used by the documentation approaches and standards.

Documentation approach/specification	Design/modeling/representation technology	Semantic technology
ADS	Knowledge Base	Knowledge Base
High value document generation	Knowledge Base, Ontology	Knowledge Base, Ontology
Concurrent execution of manufacturing and documentation	CAD	Not used
Model-based document and report generation	SysML, XML	Not used
Model-based virtual document generation	CAD	Not used
Model-based requirement generation	SysML	Not used
Rule-centric document generation	XML, Database	Not used
DITA	XML	Not used
DocBook	XML	Not used
S1000D	XML, Database	Not used

and defense industries association recommended the use of S1000D for technical documentation. The documentation approaches other than the MBSE ones and the documentation specification other than S1000D out of the ones described in Sec. 2, to the best of our knowledge, lack connection with the recommendations of the engineering community. For interoperability and to avoid reinventing the wheel, our solution approaches include the latest documentation developments that include MBSE and S1000D. MBSE and S1000D-based MBD is described in the following sections with a potential direction on how the problems identified in this paper can be addressed.

2.5. *MBSE-based MBD*

MBSE uses models to capture the system requirements and enables system design and documentation process.[16] In MBSE, the system description can be given in a data model, which then can be used to generate documentation of different granularity and needs.[17] As the integration of MBD with MBSE ensures alongside existence of both documentation and system models, data consistency can be maintained, document production and reproduction can be automated[18,19] and in turn documentation as well as production time and cost can be reduced.

2.6. *S1000D-based MBD*

As S1000D is a specification for technical documentation and offers advantages including data management, it is currently in use in several organizations for the production of operating and maintenance manual.[12] In fact, many companies and organizations have converted their documentation into S1000D.[12] The key to S1000D's data management, search and retrieval is the CSDB database. S1000D allows data representation in various publishing format like HTML and PDF. By creating business rules (BRs), the intended piece of knowledge from the documents can automatically be identified. As a result, knowledge reuse can be enabled and manual efforts and man-months in generating documentation can be reduced.

2.7. *MBSE versus S1000D*

With the capabilities described in Secs. 3.1 and 3.2, MBSE and S1000D-based MBD can partially address Problems 1, 2 and 4. With respect to Problem 1, both the MBSE implementation using SysML and the S1000D implementation lack the support for creating engineering (product) design models with CAD design tools. Without the inclusion of engineering design models, documentation often remains incomprehensible and incomplete. To overcome this issue, a CAD design tool can be integrated with these implementations. In connection with Problems 2 and 4, search on the content of these implementations is limited to the keyword

matching only without taking into account the meaning of the data. In addition to this, inference capability is missing in these implementations. To enable meaning and inference dependent search, domain ontology can be used.[20]

As S1000D by design allows the use of Simplified Technical English (or Controlled Natural Language),[15] it is capable of overcoming the issue pointed out in Problem 3. According to the problem solving capability of both the implementations, S1000D can offer more benefits. Our solution proposal for various types of documentation described in the following sections, therefore, includes S1000D.

2.7.1. *Creating requirements document using S1000D*

Requirements of different stakeholders such as client, regulatory authorities and corporate standards are compiled in the product requirements document.[13] S1000D has been expanding its scope to produce various types of technical documentation. With the inclusion of business rules, it is now possible not only to create any types of documentation (e.g., requirements document) but also to identify and retrieve any types of information (e.g., weight and length). As shown in Fig. 1, some data modules are created in S1000D to represent physical requirements such as weight and length of an aeroengine. In the creation of the data modules, a business rule is used that includes component name (e.g., engine), component id, attribute name (e.g., weight) and attribute code value for the codification and automatic identification and retrieval of physical requirements. By using XML as the means of representation and unique id both for the component and attribute, the requirements are made machine-readable.

2.7.2. *Creating maintenance manual using S1000D and 3DVIA composer*

A maintenance manual depicts the procedures for fixing issues that might arise with a product in the course of use. Integration of the 3DVIA Composer authoring tool with the S1000D documentation environment will enable the creation

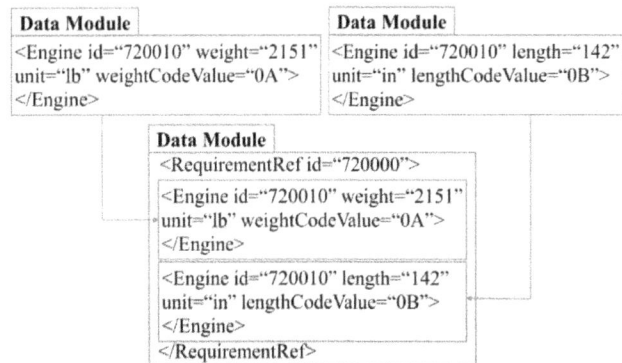

Fig. 1. Requirements codified in S1000D.

of animated visuals that can be put together with textual instructions to produce better understandable time saving maintenance manual.

It can be foreseen that the future will be more and more automated and the engineering tasks that are done today by humans alone or semi-automatically will be better supported by (software and physical) artifacts. Complete automation offers advantages such as getting rid of human errors. Product engineering world is heading towards complete automation. However, some areas are still behind, for example, the generation and exploitation of documentation, especially requirements document and product definition document. Improving machine readability of such documents is challenging, but has the potential to offer the crucial advantage of achieving better automation.

2.7.3.   *Semi-automatic generation of product definition document from requirements document*

Requirements document is discussed with the client as many times as it necessitates eliciting a concrete description of the product, which goes to the product definition document.[14] As the product definition document contains all possible details about a product, it is also called as detailed specification. To the best of our knowledge to date the product definition document is created manually. Industries, which make domain specific products, could use domain ontology guided template for requirements elicitation as well as representation to allow semi-automatic generation of the production definition document from the product requirements document.

2.7.4.   *Automatic generation of design model from product definition document*

Controlled natural languages, also supported by S1000D, offer the potential to produce unambiguous and machine-readable technical documentation.[15] It could be presumed that ontology guided semi-automatically generated product definition document could be given a structure that would be suitable for machines to convert into a controlled natural language developed for domain specific engineering design. The controlled natural language representation of a product definition document could be parsed to automatically generate the design model of the product. It can be used to identify and extract rules and also to codify them automatically in the design automation tools, thanks to its unambiguous nature.

References

[1]Streamlining Product Documentation across the Manufacturing Enterprise with 3DVIA Composer, White Paper, http://www.solidworks.com/sw/docs/3dvia_2010_eng_final.pdf.

[2]K. Avers, B. Johnson, J. Banks and B. Wenzel, Technical Documentation Challenges in Aviation Maintenance Workshop, *A Proc. Report* (2012).

[3]S. Ha, G. Pahng, M. Chang, S. Park and H. M. Rho, Managing design knowledge: Active document system, *Ann. CIRP* **48**(1), 89 (1999).

[4]N. du Preez, N. Perry, A. Candlot, A. Bernard, W. Uys and L. Lou, Customised high-value document generation, *CIRP Ann.* **54**(1), 123 (2005).

[5]C. Delp, D. Lam, E. Fosse and C. Y. Lee, Model based document and report generation for systems engineering, *IEEE Aerospace Conf.* (2013).

[6]T. R. Gruber, S. Vemuri and J. Rice, Model-based virtual document generation, *Int. J. Hum. Comput. Stud.* **46**, 687 (1997).

[7]B. London and P. Miotto, Model-based requirement generation, *2014 IEEE Aerospace Conf.* (2014).

[8]K. Rajbabu and S. Sudha, A novel rule-centric object oriented approach for document generation, *Comput. Ind.* **65**(2), 235 (2014).

[9]M. Priestley, DITA XML: A reuse by reference architecture for technical documentation, *Annual ACM Conf. Systems Documentation* (ACM Press, 2001), pp. 152–156.

[10]N. Walsh, L. Muellner and B. Stayton, *DocBook: The Definitive Guide* (O'Reilly & Associates, 1999).

[11]Inmedius Understanding and Implementing S1000D Issue 4.0, Now and in the Future, White Paper.

[12]Business Rules in S1000D™, All You Need to Know, *Produced by CDG, A Boeing Company*.

[13]R. Roy, C. Kerr, C. Makri and D. Kritsilis, Documenting Technical Specifications During The Conceptualisation Stages of Aeroengine Product Development.

[14]G. Cabral and A. Sampaio, Automated formal specification generation and refinement from requirement documents, *J. Braz. Comput. Soc.* **14**(1), 87 (2008).

[15]T. Kuhn, A survey and classification of controlled natural languages, *Comput. Linguist.* **40**(1), 121 (2014).

[16]J. S. Topper and N. C. Horner, Model-based systems engineering in support of complex systems development, *Johns Hopkins APL Tech. Dig.* **32**(1), (2013).

[17]P. Logan, D. Harvey and D. Spencer, Documents are an Essential Part of Model Based Systems Engineering, *INCOSE Int. Symp.*, Vol. 22. No. 1. (2012).

[18]R. Karban, M. Zamparelli, B. Bauvier and G. Chiozzi, Three years of MBSE for a large scientific programme: Report from the Trenches of Telescope Modelling, *Proc. 22nd Annual INCOSE Int. Symp.* (2012).

[19]R. Karban *et al.*, Model based systems engineering for astronomical projects, *In SPIE Astronomical Telescopes + Instrumentation*, (2014), pp. 91500L–91500L.

[20]F. Farazi, C. Chapman, P. Raju and L. Melville, WordNet Powered Faceted Semantic Search With Automatic Sense Disambiguation For Bioenergy Domain, *IEEE Tenth Int. Conf. Semantic Computing*, (2016), pp. 112–115.

Entity linking for tweets

Pierpaolo Basile*,‡ and Annalina Caputo†,§

*Department of Computer Science, University of Bari Aldo Moro
Via E. Orabona 4, Bari, 70125, Italy

†ADAPT Centre, Trinity College Dublin, Dublin, Ireland
‡pierpaolo.basile@uniba.it
§annalina.caputo@adaptcentre.ie

Named Entity Linking (NEL) is the task of semantically annotating entity mentions in a portion of text with links to a knowledge base. The automatic annotation, which requires the recognition and disambiguation of the entity mention, usually exploits contextual clues like the context of usage and the coherence with respect to other entities. In Twitter, the limits of 140 characters originates very short and noisy text messages that pose new challenges to the entity linking task. We propose an overview of NEL methods focusing on approaches specifically developed to deal with short messages, like tweets. NEL is a fundamental task for the extraction and annotation of concepts in tweets, which is necessary for making the Twitter's huge amount of interconnected user-generated contents machine readable and enable the intelligent information access.

Keywords: Entity linking; Twitter.

1. Introduction

An average of 500 billion messages is being posted every day on Twitter making this social networking highly valuable for this huge amount of interconnected user-generated content. This information comes as unstructured short messages often characterized by noise, like misspelling, grammatical errors, jargon, implicit references to other messages, etc. In order to make such information machine readable and enable the intelligent information access, tools for the extraction and annotation of concepts in tweets are required.

Named Entity Linking (NEL) is the task of semantically annotating entity mentions in a portion of text with links to a knowledge base (KB) (e.g., Wikipedia or DBpedia). This task comprises two steps. The former spots in the text all possible mentions to named entities, while the latter links each mention to the proper KB. This last phase often implies the disambiguation of named entities, i.e., selecting the proper concept from a restricted set of candidates (e.g., Java ⟨*programming language*⟩ or Java ⟨*place*⟩), since more than one concept can be referred to by the same textual form. Figure 1 shows a typical example of an ambiguous mention that can refer to different named entities. Here, from the context (*package, MineCraft, #gameDev*), it is possible to infer that the right named entity is *Java programming language*.

NEL, together with Word Sense Disambiguation, i.e. the task of associating each word occurrence with its proper meaning given a sense inventory, is critical to enable automatic systems to make sense of this unstructured text. Usually, the disambiguation of named entities is harder than the general word sense disambiguation due to their high ambiguity. Indeed, Hoffart *et al.*[1] report an average of 27 possible candidates per mention on CoNLL-YAGO dataset and an impressive average of 631 candidates per mention on KORE50. This is a remarkable figure if compared, for example, to 2.79, which is the average number of synsets associated to nouns in WordNet.[2] The mention context and the coherence with respect to other entity mentions play then a key role in the named entity disambiguation process since they provide useful evidence to discriminate among the many different concepts that a mention can take on.

NEL techniques were initially developed for textual documents, such as news articles,[1,3] where the usually lengthy and well-curated text provides enough context, in terms of surrounding words and co-occurring entities, in order to successfully disambiguate an ambiguous entity. The noise, shortness and poor language that characterize messages on microblogs like Twitter, however, severely hinder the performances of NEL techniques.[4,5]

The lack of context is one of the main factors that hampers Twitter-based NEL algorithms. Since the length of a Twitter message cannot exceed the 140 characters, these messages are often hard to disambiguate even for a human reader who does not know the context (background information on the user, tweet history, similar tweets with same mentions/hashtags, etc.) in which the tweet has been posted.

For example, in the following tweet, the lack of knowledge about the author or previously posted tweets makes impossible to assign the mention *Demi* with one of its possible six named entities listed in Wikipedia (Demi

171

Tweet

Candidate entities
(Wikipedia)

Having said
that, make a
game in
whatever
package that
suits you.
MineCraft was
made in
Java.
No reason you
can't be a
superstar.
#gameDev

Java \<Indonesia\>
Java Island
...

Java \<United States\>
Java, Alabama
...

Java \<Computing\>
Java programming language
...

Java \<Fictional Characters\>
Java (DC Comics)
...

...

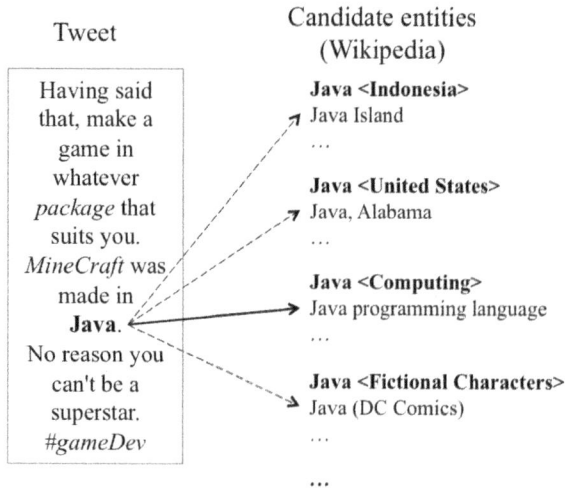

Fig. 1. An example of ambiguous mention (Java) that can refer to different named entities (dashed arrows). The correct named entity for the given mention is pointed by a continuous arrow.

⟨*author*⟩, Demi ⟨*singer*⟩, Demi Lovato, Demi Moore, Demi Orimoloye):

> *[Demi]'s been through enough and the fact that you would wish someone else's struggles on someone is sick.*

However, by expanding the analysis of just a few tweets, other mentions appear, like @*ddlovato*, @*nickjonas*, *Selena Gomez*, that can help disambiguating *Demi* as *Demi Lovato*.

Our contribution aims to provide an overview of the NEL task in Twitter and it is organized as follows: Section 2 describes the historical background, while Sec. 3 reports more details about the methodologies and techniques adopted to solve the problem of entity linking in tweets, with an emphasis on the techniques and methods adopted to overcome the noisy and short nature of this kind of messages. Section 4 describes the evaluation methodologies adopted for entity linking (dataset, protocols, and main outcomes) in the specific context of Twitter. Finally, Sec. 5 provides some scenarios of key applications and future directions.

2. Historical Background

Historically, the NEL task has been performed on regular documents, such as news, and has its roots in the Information Extraction (IE) research area. IE aims to automatically extract structured information from unstructured documents. Generally, IE involves the processing of texts by means of Natural Language Processing (NLP) techniques. One of the most relevant IE task related to NEL is the Named Entity Recognition (NER).[6–8] NER concerns the identification of names of entities, such as *organizations*, *locations*, *peoples*. Generally, it consists of two steps: (1) the recognition of entity span in the text and (2) the identification of the type of entity. NEL task can include NER, with the addition of the linking phase.

For example,[a] in the following text there are three text spans that should be annotated as named entities:

$$[U.N.]_{ORG} \text{ official } [Ekeus]_{PER} \text{ heads for } [Baghdad]_{LOC}$$

More recently, many research efforts have focused on IE for microblogs[9,7,8,10] showing how extremely challenging for state-of-the-art methods is to achieve good performance in this context. Ritter *et al.*[8] and Liu *et al.*[10] report that the NER accuracy on Twitter is about 30–50%, while NER methods achieve about 85–90% on regular text; these figures point out the extent of such a challenge on IE tasks applied at Twitter. The reasons behind such a low performance are to ascribe to the shortness of text, with its implication in terms of lack of context, in addition to phenomena like the use of slang, unusual spelling, irregular capitalization, emoticons and idiosyncratic abbreviation as reported in Ref. 5. Notwithstanding the difficulties, the upsurge of interest in this domain has its roots in the vast amount of user generated content that is published on these kinds of platforms, such as Twitter, and which allows the access to the learning and investigation of user and social behavior studies.[11]

Before delving deeply into discussing NEL methods for tweets in Sec. 3, we provide here background details about the NEL task. The NEL task is composed of four main stages:

(1) **Named Entity Identification.** During this step, sequences of words that could refer to a named entity are identified in the text. The beginning and the end offset of each named entity are automatically extracted from the text. The portion of text identified as entity is usually referred to as entity mention, spot or surface form. This step is very close to NER, in fact, NER systems could be exploited during this stage.

(2) **Candidate Entity Generation.** For each entity mention, a list of candidate entities in the KB is retrieved. In this step, it is possible to filter some nonrelevant entities or expand entities using dictionaries, surface form expansion from the document or other methods based on external search engines.

(3) **Candidate Entity Ranking.** The list of candidate entities for each mention usually contains more than one element. This means that the entity mention is ambiguous and a method to rank candidate entities in order to find the most likely link is needed. This step is similar to what happens in Word Sense Disambiguation when a meaning is assigned to each word occurrence by selecting it from a predefined set of meanings coming from a sense inventory.

(4) **Unlinkable Mention Prediction.** In some cases, it is not possible to link the mention or there is not enough evidence for choosing the correct link. In this case, a NIL value is assigned to the entity mention.

[a]http://www.cnts.ua.ac.be/conll2003/ner/.

A key component in NEL is the KB where entity mentions are linked. During the past years, several KBs have been built and many of them are related to Wikipedia. The most popular KB is certainly Wikipedia,[b] which is a free multilingual encyclopedia available online and developed by volunteers in a collaborative way. Each article in Wikipedia describes an entity and it is referenced by a unique identifier. Moreover, Wikipedia provides additional information such as categories, redirect pages, disambiguation pages and hyperlinks between Wikipedia articles. YAGO[12] is an open-domain KB built by combining Wikipedia and WordNet.[13] YAGO combines the large number of entities in Wikipedia with the clean and clear taxonomy of concepts proposed by WordNet. Similar to YAGO, BabelNet,[14] is a multilingual encyclopedic dictionary, with lexicographic and encyclopedic coverage of terms obtained by combining WordNet with several other resources such as Wikipedia, Open Multilingual WordNet, Wikidata, Wiktionary. Moreover, BabelNet is also a semantic network where concepts and named entities are connected in a very large network of semantic relations. Recently, one of the most used KB is DBpedia,[15] i.e., the structured version of Wikipedia. DBpedia is a multilingual KB that contains millions of RDF statements obtained by extracting structured information from Wikipedia info boxes, templates, categories and hyperlinks. Freebase[16] is a structured KB collaboratively built by its own community. It provides an interface in which the structured data represented in the KB can be either edited by non-expert users or harvested from several other sources. Freebase, which was acquired by Google in 2010, is part of the Google's Knowledge Graph. Nowadays, Freebase is not publicly available and its content has been moved to Wikidata[c].

For each step involved in NEL, we now provide a brief overview, while a wider analysis can be found in Ref. 17.

The named entity identification can be performed by using several NER tools such as Stanford NER,[d] OpenNLP,[e] LingPipe[f] and GATE.[g] Generally, when NER tools perform poorly (e.g., in tweets) the recognition step is jointly performed with the linking. We explain better this kind of approaches in Sec. 3.

The candidate entity generation is mainly performed by exploiting a dictionary. This dictionary is built by using Wikipedia or other KBs. Each entry in the dictionary corresponds to an entity mention (name) and a list of possible entities (links) is assigned to it. For example, the mention *Paris* has two possible entities: *Paris* ⟨*city*⟩ or *Paris Hilton*. When the dictionary is based on Wikipedia, it is usually built by leveraging some of its features like: to treat each page in Wikipedia as an entity and consider the page title as one of the possible mentions; to exploit redirect pages as alternative mentions that refer to the same entity; to compute the probability of an entity given a mention by using the disambiguation pages, which provide the list of entities that share the same mention; to define the list of all the possible alternative mentions for an entity by collecting the anchor text associated to the hyperlinks to a given entity page. Other techniques try to expand the surface forms in order to find new possible mentions. These approaches are based on rules or supervised methods,[18] while other heuristics try to expand text in parenthesis (e.g., *Hewlett-Packard* (*HP*)) or the other way round (e.g., *University of Bari* (*UNIBA*)). Finally, some approaches to the candidate generation use search engines, for example by querying a Web search engine in order to retrieve alternative mentions.[19,20] while in Ref. 21 the Wikipedia search engine is used to build infrequently mentions.

The key component of an entity linking system is the candidate ranking module. This module ranks the list of candidate entities for each mention and selects the most appropriate entity. We can identify two main approaches: (1) **supervised methods**, which require annotated examples to learn how to rank entities by using machine learning methods, such as binary classification, learning to rank, probabilistic and graph-based approaches; (2) **unsupervised methods**, which rely on unlabeled data and generally use approaches based on Vector Space Model or other information retrieval strategies. Moreover, it is possible to categorize the entity ranking strategies:

(1) **Independent:** These approaches consider each mention independently. They do not exploit the relations between entities occurring in the same document, but they try to rank the entities by exploiting the context in which the mention occur, for example the surrounding text;
(2) **Collective:** These approaches are based on the idea that a document is focused on few related topics and then each entity is related to the other entities occurring in the same text;
(3) **Collaborative:** The idea behind these approaches is to exploit cross-document contextual information. For each entity mention, these approaches try to find similar mentions occurring in similar contexts in other documents.

Several features can be taken into account in order to collect pieces of evidence useful for ranking candidate entities. Some of these features are context-independent, such as *name string comparison* between the mention and the entity name; *entity popularity*, which provides a prior probability of the candidate entity given the entity mention; *entity type*, which measures the consistency between the type of the entity mention and that of the candidate in the KB. The Entity popularity is one of the most used feature and can be easily computed by exploiting the anchor text of Wikipedia links. Other approaches[22,23] exploit Wikipedia page view statistics in order to estimate the popularity of each candidate entity or ranked entities through the Wikipedia graph structure.[20]

[b]www.wikipedia.org.
[c]https://www.wikidata.org.
[d]http://nlp.stanford.edu/software/CRF-NER.shtml.
[e]https://opennlp.apache.org/.
[f]http://alias-i.com/lingpipe/.
[g]https://gate.ac.uk/.

Another kind of features is called context-dependent: in this case, the context is not only the text around the mention but also the other entities in the documents. Some of these features are based on the textual content and try to measure the similarity between the description of each candidate entity and the text around the mention or the whole document. Both the description and the context can be represented using a simple bag-of-word approach or other conceptual vectors containing information like key-phrases automatically extracted from the text, categories, tags, anchor texts or other Wikipedia concepts. An important, and widely exploited, ranking feature is the *coherence* between entities that occur in the same document. Many state-of-the-art NEL approaches are based on this idea. For example, Cucerzan[24] exploits the agreement between categories of two candidate entities, while Milne and Witten[25,26] define the Wikipedia Link-based Measure (WLM), a measure based on the Google Distance[27] that computes the coherence between two entities according to the number of Wikipedia articles that link to both. This idea is used also by other authors to derive new coherence measures. For example, Ratinov *et al.*[28] propose a variation of the Google Distance based on the Point-wise Mutual Information, while Guo *et al.*[22] adopt the Jaccard index. These measures work well for popular entities but they provide poor results for newly emerging entities that have few associated links. The system described in Ref. 1 tries to overcome this problem by exploiting a measure of semantic relatedness between entities which are represented as sets of weighted (multi-word) key-phrases, this similarity takes into consideration also partially overlapping phrases. Ceccarelli *et al.*[29] combine 27 different measures through a learning to rank algorithm. Following this approach, the method in Ref. 30 extends the set of 27 features adding further features based on word-embeddings.

The large number of different features prove the existence of several aspects that should be taken into account during the development of a NEL system. It is impossible to absolutely identify the best set of features since it depends on the applicative context and the nature of documents.

Regarding the supervised methods adopted to solve the candidate entity ranking problem, the most simple approach is based on the binary classification. Given a pair of entity mention and a candidate entity, the classifier predicts whether the entity mention refers to the candidate entity. Since the classifier can positively predict more than one entity for a single mention, a further strategy is used to select the best candidate, for example by exploiting the classifier confidence. These systems require a large pairs of annotated entities during the training phase. Other supervised approaches rely on learning to rank techniques, which are able to directly learn the rank of a list of items. In this case, for each mention the algorithm exploit the list of items represented by candidate entities.

Coherence measures can be used also to build a graph where the edges between the entities are weighted according to the coherence. For example, in Ref. 31, a *Referent Graph* is built by exploiting both the textual context similarity and the coherence between entities. A collective inference algorithm over the graph is used to infer the mapping between entities and mentions. This approach is similar to the topic-sensitive PageRank proposed in Ref. 32. In other cases, the structure of the KB can be exploited. For example, Moro[33] proposes a graph-based method able to identify candidate meanings coupled with a sub-graph heuristic that selects semantic interpretations with high-coherence. The graph is built by exploiting semantic relations in Babelnet,

Recently, supervised methods based on deep learning have been developed.[34–36] Generally, these approaches do not rely on hand-crafted features but encode mention, context and entity in a continuous vector space. The method proposed in Ref. 36 tries to encode the KB structure by exploiting a deep learning approach. The idea is to map heterogeneous types of knowledge associated with an entity to numerical feature vectors in a latent space where the distance between semantically-related entities is minimized. In Ref. 37 a new measure of entities relatedness computed by a convolution network is proposed. The proposed network operates at multiple granularities to exploit different kinds of topic information.

3. Entity Linking in Tweets

In the previous section, we reported an overview of NEL methods, while in this section we describe how NEL approaches are modified or extended in order to deal with microblog texts, in particular tweets.

Two main challenges affect tweets: their noisy lexical nature and the lack of context. Tweets are very short (only 140 characters) and context-dependent features can reduce their effectiveness. The use of no regular language makes hard to identify mentions, for example the hashtag *#Barack Obama* contains the valid mention *BarackObama* that should be linked to the entity *Barack Obama*. This means that a correct pre-processing of the text is needed in order to correctly identify mentions. On the other side, the social nature of Twitter can provide further sources of context, such us the user profile, tweets posted by the same authors, or other tweets in the same stream or topic that can fill the gap of the lack of context.

Some first attempts to NEL in tweets are adaptation of existing NEL tools to the context of Twitter. For example, in Ref. 38, the authors describe an adaptation of the AIDA[39] tool by improving the NER and the entity candidate lookup. While in Ref. 40 an evolution of TAGME[41] is described. The proposed approach maintains the core algorithm of TAGME, but adds functionality and several improvements in terms of pre-processing for cleaning the input text and identifying mentions. The system proposed in Ref. 42 adapts several existing tools to the context of Twitter by using supervised algorithms, such as Support Vector Machine (SVM) and Conditional Random Field (CRF) for the disambiguation;

while REL-RW[43] is a RandomWalk approach based on the entity graph built from the KB to compute semantic relatedness between entities and it is used in Ref. 44. In Ref. 45 a supervised approach is boosted by the integration of a semantic search engine[46] in order to improve the mention detection. The system proposed in Ref. 47 is an adaptation of the method described in Ref. 48 that exploits several features, both context-independent and context-dependent, to which the authors added a new tokenizer and stop word removal specifically developed for tweets. Moreover, cut-off and threshold values are adapted to the context of tweets. This system achieves the best performance in the #Micropost 2016 NEEL challenge.[49]

An unsupervised approach for linking is proposed in Ref. 50 where a distributional semantic model is used to compute the semantic relatedness between the entity description and the textual context in which the entity mention occurs. Conversely in Ref. 51 three different learning models that rely on different sets of features are used to perform the linking, the NIL detection and the type prediction.

An interesting approach is proposed in Ref. 52 where a step called "Candidates Filtering" is added after the entity recognition and linking. A SVM classifier is used to predict which candidates are true positives and which ones are not by relying on several features: shape features related to the mention, the entity popularity and other features related to the KBs (WordNet and DBpedia). Mentions are identified using the algorithm described in Ref. 53 specifically developed for tweets. Also, in Ref. 54 a specific algorithm[8] for tweets is used to extract mentions, while the linking step is performed by exploiting several feature in a learning to rank approach based on LambdaMART.[55]

Differently from the previous approaches, the one proposed in Ref. 56 treats entity recognition and disambiguation as a single task by jointly optimizing them. The optimization is performed using a supervised approach and several features based on textual context and semantic cohesiveness between the entity–entity and entity-mention pairs. Since this approach generates overlapped linked mentions, a dynamic programming resolves these conflicts by choosing the best-scoring set of nonoverlapping mention-entity mappings. This system achieves the best performance in the named entity extraction and linking challenge[57] organized within the workshop of Making Sense of Microposts (#Microposts) 2014. We will provide more details about this challenge in Sec. 4. Also in Ref. 58, a collective inference method able to simultaneously resolve a set of mentions is proposed. This system exploits three kinds of similarities: mention–entity similarity, entity–entity similarity, and mention–mention similarity, to enrich the context for entity linking. The system proposed in Ref. 22 focuses on the mention detection task, which the authors consider as a performance bottleneck. In this work, the authors describe a supervised algorithm based on SVM that jointly optimizes mention detection and entity

disambiguation as a single end-to-end task. The learning step combines a variety of first-order, second-order, and context-sensitive features.

The supervised method proposed in Ref. 59 exploits a non-linear learning model based on trees. Nonlinear models are able to capture the relationships between features, this is useful when dense features such as statistical and embedding features are used. The Structured Multiple Additive Regression Trees (S-MART) proposed by the authors is able to capture high order relationships between features by exploiting non-linear regression trees.

One of the main challenge that affects tweet is the lack of context, in Ref. 60 the authors propose a graph-based framework to collectively link all the named entity mentions in all tweets posted by modeling the user's topics of interest. The main idea behind this approach is that each user has an underlying topic interest distribution over various named entities. The method integrates the intra-tweet local information with the inter-tweet user interest information into a unified graph-based framework. Another approach proposed in Ref. 23 collects several "social signals" to improve the NEL accuracy in the context of social media such as Twitter. For example, the content of a cited URL is retrieved, the most recent tweets about any hashtags are included, and the last tweets posted by a mentioned user are extracted. The approach proposed in Ref. 61 tries to extend the context by collecting additional tweets that are similar to the target one. The authors indexed a collection of tweets that is subsequently exploited to retrieve similar tweets by using the target as a query. The system described in Ref. 62 extends the context by analyzing both the user interest and the content of news. In particular, the system exploits other tweets containing the mention under analysis published by the user and the content of news that cite the mention.

An interesting approach proposed in Ref. 63 tries to include spatio-temporal information during the linking. The idea is that the prior probability of an entity of being assigned to the mention depends by spatio-temporal signals. As reported by the authors, for example, the mention "spurs" can refer to two distinct sport teams (San Antonio Spurs, which is a basketball team in the US, and Tottenham Hotspur F.C., which is a soccer team in the UK). In this case, the information about the location is crucial. The proposed method incorporates spatio-temporal signals through a weakly supervised process. In particular, the timestamps and the location (if available) are exploited as further features.

In conclusion, we can split the NEL methods for tweets in two macro categories: (1) systems that tries to improve existing NEL tools by adding specific pre-processing operations or typical features related to Twitter; (2) methods that extend the context by analyzing the stream or the user profile. Sometime, these two approaches can be combined to improve the performance.

4.   Evaluation

Entity Linking algorithms are evaluated using typical metrics such as precision (P), recall (R) and F1-measure (F). However, the linking task can involve several steps: entity recognition, entity typing, linking and NIL instances identification. This opens the possibility to several evaluation metrics which combine some or all the involved aspects.

Following the guidelines of the #Microposts2015 NEEL challenge[64] and the KB Population (KBP2014) Entity Linking Track,[h] we can identify three measures used in the context of NEL in tweets:

(1) *strong_typed_mention_match*: it is the micro average F1 for all annotations considering the mention boundaries and their types. An annotation is correct if both its boundaries and type correspond to those in the gold standard;
(2) *strong_link_match*: it is the micro average F1 for annotations obtained by considering the correct link for each mention;
(3) *mention_ceaf*: the Constrained Entity-Alignment F-measure (CEAF)[65] is a clustering metric that evaluates clusters of annotations. It measures the F1 score for both NIL and non-NIL annotations in a set of mentions. The CEAF measure was originally proposed to evaluate co-reference resolution systems. The metric is computed by aligning gold standard annotations and system annotations with the constraint that a gold annotation is aligned with at most one system annotation. Finding the best alignment is a maximum bipartite matching problem which can be solved by the Kuhn–Munkres algorithm. More details about this metric are reported in Ref. 65.

In order to produce a unique evaluation score, Rizzo *et al.* [64] propose a weighted linear combination of the three aforementioned measures. Moreover, for the first time in this kind of challenge, the organizers also considered a *latency* measure. The *latency* computes the time, in seconds, required to produce a tweet annotation. However, the *latency* is used only in case of a tie and it is not included in the final score.

Results reported in several Micrposts NEEL challenges show that some remarkable results can be achieved. For example, in #Microposts2015, the winning system[51] achieves a final score of 0.8067 during the challenge, while the other participants obtain very low performance. For instance, the second system has a final score of 0.4756. It is important to underline that this system[51] is an extension of the winner system during the #Microposts2014 challenge. This proves that an end-to-end approach for both candidate selection and mention typing is effective, moreover this approach exploits two supervised learning models for NIL and type prediction.

When the type of the entity is not involved, generally the micro average F1 is computed taking into account both the entity boundaries and the link. In this case, a pair is correct only if both the entity mention and the link match the corresponding set in the gold standard. This is the case of the #Microposts2014 NEEL challenge[57] and the Entity Recognition and Disambiguation Challenge (ERD 2014).[66] It is important to underline that the ERD challenge is not focused on tweets but the short text track is performed in the context of search engine queries.

Another resource for the evaluation of NEL in Twitter is the dataset[i] exploited by[59] and developed by Microsoft. In this case, the evaluation schema is the same adopted in #Microposts2014, since entity type and NIL instances are not used.

All the previous datasets are developed for the English, however a first attempt to provide a dataset for the Italian language is reported in Ref. 67. Moreover, a preliminary evaluation of NEL systems for the Italian is provided. The reported results prove that the task is quite difficult, as pointed out by the very low performance of all the systems employed.

In conclusion, a valuable effort to provide a standard framework for the evaluation of NEEL in tweets has been conducted during #Microposts NEEL challenges since 2013. Additional data for training and testing can be found in the dataset developed by Microsoft. All these datasets are for English, and currently only one resource[67] is available for a language different from English, in this instance for the Italian language.

5.   Key Applications and Future Directions

NEL is a fundamental task for the extraction and annotation of concepts in tweets, which is necessary for making the Twitter's user-generated content machine readable and enable the intelligent information access. Linking mentions in tweets allows to connect these very short messages to the Linked Open Data (LOD)[68] cloud thorough DBpedia or other KBs published in the LOD. This allows data from different sources, tweets included, to be connected and queried.

From an applicative perspective, microposts comprise an invaluable wealth of data, ready to be mined for training predictive models. Analyzing the sentiment conveyed by microposts can yield a competitive advantage for businesses[69] and mining opinions about specific aspects of entities[70] being discussed is of paramount importance in this sense. Beyond the pure commercial application domain, the analysis of microposts can serve to gain crucial insights about political sentiment and election results,[71] political movements,[72] and health issues.[73] Due to the pervasiveness of mobile devices and the ubiquitous diffusion of social media platforms, the information analysis of microposts is now being exploited to forecast real-world market outcomes.[74]

---

[h]http://nlp.cs.rpi.edu/kbp/2014/.

[i]https://www.microsoft.com/en-us/download/details.aspx?id=52530□.

The availability of a constant flow of information makes possible to collect real time information about several events that are being written about. The attractiveness of this is evident, and so is its potential social utility. Entity Linking is a fundamental step to add semantics and this can boost and improve any tools for the analysis of microposts.

Many challenges still remain open: (1) it is necessary to improve the pre-processing steps in order to tackle the noisy language of tweets; (2) a deep analysis of the effectiveness of different methods for extending the context is needed, in particular about the user profile and the social relations between users; (3) how to deal with emerging and popular entities mentioned in tweets that are not in the KB.

Furthermore, many few supervised approaches exploit Deep Learning techniques, which have shown to improve the performance in different NLP tasks.

Another point to take into account is the computational complexity that is crucial in the case of social media. Currently, most work on NEL lacks an analysis of computational complexity, and they usually do not evaluate the scalability and efficiency of their systems. However, for real-time and large-scale applications such as social media analysis, efficiency and scalability are significantly important and essential. Therefore, a promising direction for future research is to design methods that can improve the efficiency and scalability while aiming at, or preserving, high accuracy.

Acknowledgments

This work is supported by the project "Multilingual Entity Liking" funded by the Apulia Region under the program FutureInResearch and by the ADAPT Centre for Digital Content Technology, which is funded under the Science Foundation Ireland Research Centres Programme (Grant 13/RC/2106) and is co-funded under the European Regional Development Fund.

References

[1] J. Hoffart, S. Seufert, D. B. Nguyen, M. Theobald and G. Weikum, Kore: Keyphrase overlap relatedness for entity disambiguation, *Proc. 21st ACM Int. Conf. Information and Knowledge Management* (2012), pp. 545–554.

[2] D. Weissenborn, L. Hennig, F. Xu and H. Uszkoreit, Multi-objective optimization for the joint disambiguation of nouns and named entities, *Proc. 53rd Annual Meeting of the Association for Computational Linguistics and the 7th Int. Joint Conf. Natural Language Processing (Volume 1: Long Papers)* (Association for Computational Linguistics, Beijing, China, July 2015), pp. 596–605.

[3] J. Hoffart, M. A. Yosef, I. Bordino, H. Fürstenau, M. Pinkal, M. Spaniol, B. Taneva, S. Thater and G. Weikum, Robust disambiguation of named entities in text, *Proc. Conf. on Empirical Methods in Natural Language Processing* (2011), pp. 782–792.

[4] E. Meij, W. Weerkamp and M. de Rijke, Adding semantics to microblog posts, *Proc. Fifth ACM Int. Conf. Web Search and Data Mining* (2012), pp. 563–572.

[5] L. Derczynski, D. Maynard, G. Rizzo, M. van Erp, G. Gorrell, R. Troncy, J. Petrak and K. Bontcheva, Analysis of named entity recognition and linking for tweets, *Inf. Process. Manage.* **51**, 32 (2015).

[6] E. F. Tjong Kim Sang and F. De Meulder, Introduction to the conll-2003 shared task: Language-independent named entity recognition, *Proc. CoNLL-2003*, eds. W. Daelemans and M. Osborne (Edmonton, Canada, 2003), pp. 142–147.

[7] T. Finin, W. Murnane, A. Karandikar, N. Keller, J. Martineau and M. Dredze, Annotating named entities in twitter data with crowdsourcing, *Proc. NAACL HLT 2010 Workshop on Creating Speech and Language Data with Amazon's Mechanical Turk, CSLDAMT'10* (Association for Computational Linguistics, Stroudsburg, PA, USA, 2010), pp. 80–88.

[8] A. Ritter, S. Clark, O. Etzioni *et al.*, Named entity recognition in tweets: An experimental study, *Proc. Conf. Empirical Methods in Natural Language Processing* (2011), pp. 1524–1534.

[9] A. E. Cano, M. Rowe, M. Stankovic and A. Dadzie (eds.), *Proc. Concept Extraction Challenge at the Workshop on 'Making Sense of Microposts'*, Rio de Janeiro, Brazil, May 13, 2013, *CEUR Workshop Proc.* Vol. 1019 (CEUR-WS.org, 2013).

[10] X. Liu, M. Zhou, F. Wei, Z. Fu and X. Zhou, Joint inference of named entity recognition and normalization for tweets, *Proc. 50th Annual Meeting of the Association for Computational Linguistics: Long Papers-Volume 1* (2012), pp. 526–535.

[11] K. Bontcheva and D. Rout, Making sense of social media streams through semantics: A survey, *Sem. Web* **5**, 373 (2014).

[12] G. K. Fabian, M. Suchanek and G. Weikum, Yago: A core of semantic knowledge unifying wordnet and wikipedia, *16th Int. World Wide Web Conf. (WWW 2007)* (2007), pp. 697–706.

[13] G. A. Miller, Wordnet: A lexical database for english, *Commun. ACM* **38**, 39 (1995).

[14] R. Navigli and S. P. Ponzetto, BabelNet: The automatic construction, evaluation and application of a wide-coverage multilingual semantic network, *Artif. Intell.* **193**, 217 (2012).

[15] S. Auer, C. Bizer, G. Kobilarov, J. Lehmann, R. Cyganiak and Z. Ives, Dbpedia: A nucleus for a web of open data, *6th Int. Semantic Web Conf. (ISWC 2007)* (Springer, 2007), pp. 722–735.

[16] K. Bollacker, C. Evans, P. Paritosh, T. Sturge and J. Taylor, Freebase: A collaboratively created graph database for structuring human knowledge, *Proc. 2008 ACM SIGMOD Int. Conf. Management of data* (2008), pp. 1247–1250.

[17] W. Shen, J. Wang and J. Han, Entity linking with a knowledge base: Issues, techniques, and solutions, *IEEE Trans. Knowl. Data Eng.* **27**, 443 (2015).

[18] W. Zhang, Y. C. Sim, J. Su and C. L. Tan, Entity linking with effective acronym expansion, instance selection, and topic modeling., *IJCAI* (2011), pp. 1909–1914.

[19] X. Han and J. Zhao, Nlpr_kbp in tac 2009 kbp track: A two-stage method to entity linking, *Proc. Test Analysis Conf. 2009 (TAC 09)* (2009).

[20] M. Dredze, P. McNamee, D. Rao, A. Gerber and T. Finin, Entity disambiguation for knowledge base population, *Proc. 23rd Int. Conf. Computational Linguistics* (2010), pp. 277–285.

[21] W. Zhang, J. Su, C. L. Tan and W. T. Wang, Entity linking leveraging: Automatically generated annotation, *Proc. 23rd Int. Conf. Computational Linguistics* (2010), pp. 1290–1298.

[22] S. Guo, M.-W. Chang and E. Kiciman, To link or not to link? a study on end-to-end tweet entity linking, *HLT-NAACL* (2013), pp. 1020–1030.

[23] A. Gattani, D. S. Lamba, N. Garera, M. Tiwari, X. Chai, S. Das, S. Subramaniam, A. Rajaraman, V. Harinarayan and A. Doan, Entity extraction, linking, classification, and tagging for social media: A wikipedia-based approach, *Proc. VLDB Endowment* **6**, 1126 (2013).

[24] S. Cucerzan, Large-scale named entity disambiguation based on wikipedia data, *EMNLP-CoNLL* (2007), pp. 708–716.

[25] D. Milne and I. H. Witten, Learning to link with wikipedia, *Proc. 17th ACM Conf. Information and Knowledge Management* (2008), pp. 509–518.

[26] D. Milne and I. H. Witten, An open-source toolkit for mining wikipedia, *Artif. Intell.* **194**, 222 (2013).

[27] R. L. Cilibrasi and P. M. Vitanyi, The google similarity distance, *IEEE Trans. Knowl. Data Eng.* **19**, 370 (2007).

[28] L. Ratinov, D. Roth, D. Downey and M. Anderson, Local and global algorithms for disambiguation to wikipedia, *Proc. 49th Annual Meeting of the Association for Computational Linguistics: Human Language Technologies-Volume 1* (2011), pp. 1375–1384.

[29] D. Ceccarelli, C. Lucchese, S. Orlando, R. Perego and S. Trani, Learning relatedness measures for entity linking, *Proc. 22nd ACM Int. Conf. Information & Knowledge Management* (2013), pp. 139–148.

[30] P. Basile, A. Caputo, G. Rossiello and G. Semeraro, Learning to rank entity relatedness through embedding-based features, *Int. Conf. Applications of Natural Language to Information Systems* (2016), pp. 471–477.

[31] X. Han, L. Sun and J. Zhao, Collective entity linking in web text: A graph-based method, *Proc. 34th Int. ACM SIGIR Conf. Research and Development in Information Retrieval* (2011), pp. 765–774.

[32] T. H. Haveliwala, Topic-sensitive pagerank, *Proc. 11th Int. Conf. World Wide Web* (2002), pp. 517–526.

[33] A. Moro, A. Raganato and R. Navigli, Entity linking meets word sense disambiguation: A unified approach, *Trans. Assoc. Comput. Linguist. (TACL)* **2**, 231 (2014).

[34] Y. Sun, L. Lin, D. Tang, N. Yang, Z. Ji and X. Wang, Modeling mention, context and entity with neural networks for entity disambiguation, *Proc. Int. Joint Conf. Artificial Intelligence (IJCAI)* (2015), pp. 1333–1339.

[35] Z. He, S. Liu, M. Li, M. Zhou, L. Zhang and H. Wang, Learning entity representation for entity disambiguation., *51st Annual Meeting of the Association for Computational Linguistics* (2013), pp. 30–34.

[36] H. Huang, L. Heck and H. Ji, Leveraging deep neural networks and knowledge graphs for entity disambiguation, arXiv: 1504.07678.

[37] M. Francis-Landau, G. Durrett and D. Klein, Capturing semantic similarity for entity linking with convolutional neural networks, arXiv:1604.00734.

[38] M. A. Yosef, J. Hoffart, Y. Ibrahim, A. Boldyrev and G. Weikum, Adapting aida for tweets, *Making Sense of Microposts (# Microposts2014)* (2014).

[39] M. A. Yosef, J. Hoffart, I. Bordino, M. Spaniol and G. Weikum, Aida: An online tool for accurate disambiguation of named entities in text and tables, *Proc. VLDB Endowment* **4**, 1450 (2011).

[40] U. Scaiella, M. Barbera, S. Parmesan, G. Prestia, E. Del Tessandoro and M. Veri, Datatxt at# microposts2014 challenge, *Making Sense of Microposts (# Microposts2014)* (2014), pp. 1–15.

[41] P. Ferragina and U. Scaiella, Fast and accurate annotation of short texts with wikipedia pages, *IEEE Softw.* **1**, 70 (2012).

[42] H. Barathi Ganesh, N. Abinaya, M. Anand Kumar, R. Vinayakumar and K. Soman, Amrita-cen@ neel: Identification and linking of twitter entities, *Making Sense of Microposts (# Microposts2015)* (2015).

[43] Z. Guo and D. Barbosa, Robust entity linking via random walks, *Proc. 23rd ACM Int. Conf. Conf. Information and Knowledge Management* (2014), pp. 499–508.

[44] Z. Guo and D. Barbosa, Entity recognition and linking on tweets with random walks, *Making Sense of Microposts (# Microposts2015)* (2015).

[45] C. Gârbacea, D. Odijk, D. Graus, I. Sijaranamual and M. de Rijke, Combining multiple signals for semanticizing tweets: University of amsterdam at# microposts2015, *Making Sense of Microposts (# Microposts2015)* (2015), pp. 59–60.

[46] D. Graus, D. Odijk, M. Tsagkias, W. Weerkamp and M. De Rijke, Semanticizing search engine queries: The university of amsterdam at the erd 2014 challenge, *Proc. first Int. Workshop on Entity Recognition & Disambiguation* (2014), pp. 69–74.

[47] J. Waitelonis and H. Sack, Named entity linking in# tweets with kea.

[48] H. Sack, The journey is the reward-towards new paradigms in web search, *Int. Conf. Business Information Systems* (2015), pp. 15–26.

[49] D. R. K. W. Amparo E. Cano, Daniel PreoÂÿtiuc-Pietro and A.-S. Dadzie, *6th Workshop on Making Sense of Microposts (# microposts2016), Word Wide Web Conf. (WWWâÄŹ16) Companion* (ACM).

[50] P. Basile, A. Caputo, G. Semeraro and F. Narducci, Uniba: Exploiting a distributional semantic model for disambiguating and linking entities in tweets *Making Sense of Microposts (# Microposts2015)* (2015).

[51] I. Yamada, H. Takeda and Y. Takefuji, An end-to-end entity linking approach for tweets, *Making Sense of Microposts (# Microposts2015)* (2015).

[52] M. B. Habib, M. Van Keulen and Z. Zhu, Named entity extraction and linking challenge: University of twente at# microposts2014, *Making Sense of Microposts (# Microposts2014)*, (2014).

[53] C. Li, J. Weng, Q. He, Y. Yao, A. Datta, A. Sun and B.-S. Lee, Twiner: named entity recognition in targeted twitter stream, *Proc. 35th Int. ACM SIGIR Conf. Research and Development in Information Retrieval* (2012), pp. 721–730.

[54] R. Bansal, S. Panem, P. Radhakrishnan, M. Gupta and V. Varma, Linking entities in# microposts, *Making Sense of Microposts (# Microposts2014)* (2014).

[55] Q. Wu, C. J. Burges, K. M. Svore and J. Gao, Adapting boosting for information retrieval measures, *Inf. Ret.* **13**, 254 (2010).

[56] M.-W. Chang, B.-J. Hsu, H. Ma, R. Loynd and K. Wang, E2e: An end-to-end entity linking system for short and noisy text, *Making Sense of Microposts (# Microposts2014)* (2014).

[57] A. E. Cano, G. Rizzo, A. Varga, M. Rowe, M. Stankovic and A.-S. Dadzie, Making sense of microposts:(# microposts2014) named entity extraction & linking challenge, *CEUR Workshop Proc* (2014), pp. 54–60.

[58] X. Liu, Y. Li, H. Wu, M. Zhou, F. Wei and Y. Lu, Entity linking for tweets, *51st Annual Meeting of the Association for Computational Linguistics* (ACL, 2013), pp. 1304–1311.

[59] Y. Yang and M.-W. Chang, S-mart: Novel tree-based structured learning algorithms applied to tweet entity linking, *Proc. Association for Computational Linguistics* (2015), pp. 504–513.

[60] W. Shen, J. Wang, P. Luo and M. Wang, Linking named entities in tweets with knowledge base via user interest modeling, *Proc. 19th*

ACM SIGKDD Int. Conf. Knowledge Discovery and Data Mining (2013), pp. 68–76.

[61]Y. Guo, B. Qin, T. Liu and S. Li, Microblog entity linking by leveraging extra posts, *Proc. 2013 Conf. Empirical Methods in Natural Language Processing* (2013), pp. 863–868.

[62]S. Jeong, Y. Park, S. Kang and J. Seo, Improved entity linking with user history and news articles, *9th Pacific Asia Conf. on Language, Information and Computation* (2015), pp. 19–26.

[63]Y. Fang and M.-W. Chang, Entity linking on microblogs with spatial and temporal signals, *Trans. Assoc. Comput. Linguist.* **2**, 259 (2014).

[64]G. Rizzo, A. C. Basave, B. Pereira, A. Varga, M. Rowe, M. Stankovic and A. Dadzie, Making sense of microposts (# microposts2015) named entity recognition and linking (neel) challenge, *5th Workshop on Making Sense of Microposts (# Microposts2015)* (2015), pp. 44–53.

[65]X. Luo, On coreference resolution performance metrics, *Proc. Conf. Human Language Technology and Empirical Methods in Natural Language Processing* (2005), pp. 25–32.

[66]D. Carmel, M.-W. Chang, E. Gabrilovich, B.-J. P. Hsu and K. Wang, Erd'14: entity recognition and disambiguation challenge, *ACM SIGIR Forum* (2), 63 (2014).

[67]P. Basile, A. Caputo and G. Semeraro, Entity linking for italian tweets, *Proc. Second Italian Conf. Computational Linguistics CLiC-it 2015*, eds. C. Bosco, S. Tonelli and F. M. Zanzotto (Accademia University Press, 2015), pp. 36–40.

[68]C. Bizer, T. Heath and T. Berners-Lee, Linked data-the story so far, *Semantic Services, Interoperability and Web Applications: Emerging Concepts*, 205 (2009).

[69]B. J. Jansen, M. Zhang, K. Sobel and A. Chowdury, Twitter power: Tweets as electronic word of mouth, *J. Am. Soc. Inf. Sci. Technol.* **60**, 2169 (2009).

[70]S. Batra and D. Rao, Entity based sentiment analysis on twitter, *Science* **9**, 1 (2010).

[71]A. Tumasjan, T. Sprenger, P. Sandner and I. Welpe, Predicting elections with twitter: What 140 characters reveal about political sentiment (2010).

[72]K. Starbird and L. Palen, (how) will the revolution be retweeted?: Information diffusion and the 2011 egyptian uprising, *Proc. ACM 2012 Conf. Computer Supported Cooperative Work, CSCW '12* (ACM, New York, NY, USA, 2012), pp. 7–16.

[73]M. D. Michael and J. Paul, You are what you tweet: Analyzing twitter for public health, *Proc. Fifth Int. AAAI Conf. Weblogs and Social Media* (2011), pp. 265–272.

[74]S. Asur and B. A. Huberman, Predicting the future with social media, *Proc. 2010 IEEE/WIC/ACM Int. Conf. Web Intelligence and Intelligent Agent Technology — Volume 01, WI-IAT '10* (IEEE Computer Society, Washington, DC, USA, 2010), pp. 492–499.

Enabling semantic technologies using multimedia ontology

Antonio M. Rinaldi

Dipartimento di Ingegneria Elettrica e delle Tecnologie dell'Informazione
Università di Napoli Federico II, 80125 Via Claudio, 21, Napoli, Italy

IKNOS-LAB - Intelligent and Knowledge Systems - LUPT
Università di Napoli Federico II, 80134 Via Toledo, 402, Napoli, Italy
antoniomaria.rinaldi@unina.it

The new vision of the Web as a global intelligent repository needs advanced knowledge structure to manage complex data and services. From this perspective, the use of formal models to represent information on the web is a suitable way to allow the cooperation of users and services. This paper describes a general ontological approach to represent knowledge using multimedia data and linguistic properties to bridge the gap between the target semantic classes and the available low-level multimedia descriptors. We choose to implement our approach in a system to edit, manage and share multimedia ontology in the WEB. The system provides tools to add multimedia objects by means of user interaction. The multimedia features are automatically extracted using algorithms based on standard MPEG-7 descriptors.

Keywords: Multimedia ontology; OWL; WordNet; semantic network; P2P.

1. Problem Description

The task of representing knowledge is one of the most important activity in the field of advanced data management. In this context, the exponential growth of informative contents needs intelligent information systems able to use data to create information. In this way, complex data can be managed and used to perform new tasks and implement innovative functionalities. In the semantic web context, multimedia contents have to be semantically described in order to be discovered and exploited by services, agents and applications. Moreover, bridging the gap between semantics and low-level multimedia descriptors is an unsolved problem. Hence, it is crucial to select an appropriate set of low-level multimedia descriptors and to combine them, so that the results obtained with individual descriptors are improved together with high level concepts annotation. In this perspective, a significant progress has been made on automatic segmentation or structuring of multimedia content and the recognition of low-level features. However, the generation of multimedia content descriptions is highly problematic due to the number and complexity of data and the subjectivity of human-generated descriptions. From this point of view, efficient techniques have been developed to solve those problems. Some of them are based on ontologies to delete or at least smooth conceptual or terminological messes and to have a common view of the same information.

In the author's opinion a formalization of an ontology based model to represent multimedia knowledge can be a unified approach taking into account both high level semantic meanings and low-level features. In this way, we can use multimodal *"signs"* defined as "something that stands for something, to someone in some capacity"[1] including words, images, gestures, scents, tastes, textures, sounds, essentially all of the ways in which information can be communicated as a message by any sentient, reasoning mind to another. We use linguistic properties in order to relate *"signs"* (text and audio-visual features) and *"signifiers"* (concepts). In our work we show a complete case study to describe a system to edit, manage and share multimedia ontologies in the WEB using our approach.

We can address our context of interest presenting different dimensions of knowledge representation (KR) using formal models and languages with a discussion on the use of high and low features to interpret and analyze multimedia objects.

Our approach starts from the *modeling view* of knowledge acquisition,[2] where the modeling activity must establish a correspondence between a knowledge base and two separate subsystems: the agents behavior (i.e., the problem-solving expertise) and its own environment (the problem domain) (see also Refs. 3 and 4). This vision is in contrast with the *transfer view*, wherein a knowledge base is a repository of knowledge extracted from one expert's mind. Using the modeling view approach, knowledge is much more related to the classical notion of truth as correspondence to the real world, and it is less dependent on the particular way an intelligent agent pursues its goals. Although knowledge representation is a basic step in the whole process of knowledge engineering, a part of the AI research community seems to have been much more interested in the nature of reasoning than in the nature of "real world" representation. The dichotomy between reasoning and representation is comparable with the philosophical distinction between epistemology and ontology, and this distinction allows us to better understand our research aim and the proposed approach. Epistemology can be defined as "the field of philosophy which deals with the nature and sources of knowledge".[5] According to the usual logistic interpretation, knowledge consists of propositions, whose formal structure is the source of new knowledge. The inferential aspect seems to be essential to epistemology (at least in the sense that this term has in AI): the study of the "nature" of knowledge is limited to its superficial meaning (i.e., the form), since it is mainly motivated by the study of the inference process. Ontology, on the other hand, can be seen as the study of the organization and the nature of the world is independent of the form of our knowledge about it.

A basic step in the knowledge engineering process is the use of "tools" to represent knowledge, for both inferring and organizing it. From this point of view, one of the most important enhancements in the KR applications is derived from proposing,[6] studying[7,8] and developing[9–11] languages based on the specification of objects (concepts) and the relationships among them.

The main features of all KR languages are the following:

(i) *object-orientedness*, for which all the information about a specific concept is stored in the concept itself (in contrast, for example, to rule-based systems;
(ii) *generalization/specialization*, are basic aspects of the human cognition process,[25] the KR languages have mechanisms to cluster concepts into hierarchies where higher-level concepts represent more general attributes than the lower-level ones, which inherit the general concept attributes but are more specific, presenting additional features of their own;
(iii) *reasoning*, is the capability to infer the existence of information not explicitly declared by the existence of a given statement;
(iv) *classification*, in which given an abstract description of a concept, there are mechanisms to determine whether a concept can have this description; this feature is a special form of reasoning.

Their features as object orientation and generalization/specialization help human users in understanding the represented knowledge; reasoning and classification guide an automatic system in building a KR, as the system knows what it is going to represent.

The proposed approach arises from the above considerations and it is also suggested by the work of Guarino.[12] When a KR formalism is constrained so as its intended models are made explicit, it can be classified as belonging to the ontological level[12] introduced in the distinctions proposed in Ref. 8, where KR languages are classified according to the kinds of primitives offered to the user. At the (first-order) *logical level*, the basic primitives are predicates and functions, which are given formal semantics in terms of relations among objects of a domain. However, no particular assumption is made regarding the nature of such relations, which are completely general and content-independent. The *epistemological level* was introduced by Brachman in order to fill the gap between the logical level, where primitives are extremely general, and the conceptual level, where they acquire a specific intended meaning that must be taken as a whole, without any consideration of its internal structure. At the *ontological level*, the ontological commitments associated with the language primitives are specified explicitly. Such a specification can be made in two ways: either by suitably restricting the semantics of the primitives or by introducing meaning postulates expressed in the language itself. In both cases, the goal is to restrict the number of possible interpretations, characterizing the meaning of the basic ontological categories used to describe the domain: the ontological level is therefore the level of meaning. At the *conceptual level*, primitives have a definite cognitive interpretation, corresponding to language-independent concepts such as elementary actions or thematic roles. The skeleton of the domain structure is already given, independently of an explicit account of the underlying ontological assumptions. Finally, primitives at the *linguistic level* refer directly to lexical categories.

In the last few years, a huge number of methodologies and tools to create, manage, represent, and match ontologies have been proposed and implemented in several contexts, often for ad hoc purposes (e.g., to map well-known knowledge bases or represent specific knowledge domains). A complete discussion of these does not concern with our work, but useful books, surveys and ad hoc models are available in literature (e.g., Refs. 13–17). From a conceptual point of view, human beings tend to use high-level features (concepts), such as keywords and text descriptors, to interpret and analyze multimedia objects.

For example, in literature there are a lot of algorithms designed to describe color, shape, and texture features. In our case they are far to adequately model multimedia semantics and have many limitations when dealing with broad multimedia databases.

More specifically, the discrepancy between the limited descriptive power of low-level multimedia features and the richness of user semantics, is referred to as the semantic gap.[18,19] In this context, several approaches and techniques for attempting to bridge the semantic gap in multimedia data mining and retrieval have been presented.[20,21] Moreover, interesting surveys on low-level features and high-level semantics for multimedia analysis and retrieval are respectively in Refs. 22 and 23.

In addition, some standards have been defined and implemented to manage multimedia information content; in the following an overview on MPEG-7 standardized in ISO/IEC 15938 is presented and an extended overview about it is in Ref. 24. MPEG-7 is formally called Multimedia Content Description Interface. Thus, it is not a standard which deals with the actual encoding of moving pictures and audio, like MPEG-1, MPEG-2 and MPEG-4. It uses XML to store metadata, and it can be attached to timecode in order to tag particular events, or synchronize lyrics to a song. MPEG-7 is intended to provide complementary functionality to the previous MPEG standards, representing information about the content, not the content itself. This functionality is the standardization of multimedia content descriptions. MPEG-7 can be used independently of the other MPEG standards — the description might even be attached to an analogue movie. This representation is basic to the process of categorization. In addition, MPEG-7 descriptions could be used to improve the functionality of previous MPEG standards.

Neither automatic nor semiautomatic feature extraction algorithms are inside the scope of the standard because their standardization is not required to allow interoperability.

The MPEG-7 consists of different parts which cover a certain aspect of the whole specification.

An MPEG-7 architecture requirement is that description must be separated from the audio-visual (AV) content. On the other hand there must be a relation between the content and its description. Thus the description is multiplexed with the content itself.

MPEG-7 uses the following tools:

Descriptor (D): it is a representation of a feature defined syntactically and semantically. It could be that a unique object was described by several descriptors.

Description Schemes (DS): they specify the structure and semantics of the relations between its components, these components can be descriptors or description schemes.

Description Definition Language (DDL): it is based on XML language used to define the structural relations between descriptors. It allows the creation and modification of description schemes and also the creation of new descriptors.

System tools: these tools deal with binarization, synchronization, transport and storage of descriptors. It also deals with Intellectual Property protection.

2. Method

In this section, we describe a possible solution to the issues listed above. Starting from a definition of ontology[4] and the way to proceed in order to construct it, we consider also multimedia data to represent a concept; this data is represented using multimedia low-level features defined in MPEG-7 standard. We describe an implementation of this model in a prototype system to create and share multimedia ontology in the semantic web.

2.1. *Multimedia ontology model*

Thus an ontology can be seen as a set of "signs" and "relations" among them, denoting the concepts that are used in a specific domain. The proposed knowledge structure is composed of a triple $\langle S, P, C \rangle$ where:

S is a set of signs;

P is a set of properties used to link the signs in S;

C is a set of constraints on P.

In this context, signs are words and multimedia data. The properties are linguistic relations, and the constraints are validity rules applied to linguistic properties with respect to the multimedia category considered. In our approach, knowledge is represented by an ontology implemented by a semantic network (SN). A SN can be seen as a graph where the nodes are concepts and the edges are relations among concepts. A concept is a set of multimedia data representing an abstract idea. In this paper, we focus on visual descriptors but our approach can be generalized using other multimedia data types (e.g., audio).

Several languages to represent ontologies have been proposed during years. It is our opinion that OWL[25] is the best language for the purpose of the proposed approach due to its expressive power and because of some relevant remarks found in previous author' works.[26,27] The SN — which implements the ontology — is described in DL OWL because it is sufficiently effective to describe the ontology. The DL version allows the declaration of disjoint classes, which may be exploited to assert that a word belongs to a syntactic category. Moreover, it allows the declaration of union classes used to specify domains and property ranges used to relate concepts and words belonging to different lexical categories. Every node (both concept and multimedia) is an OWL individual. The connecting edges in the SN are represented as *ObjectProperties*. These properties have constraints that depend on the syntactic category or type of property (semantic or lexical). For example, the hyponymy property can only relate nouns to nouns or verbs to verbs. In contrast, a semantic property links concepts to concepts, and a syntactic property relates word forms to word forms. Concept and multimedia are considered with *DatatypeProperties*, which relate individuals to pre-defined data types. Each multimedia is related to the concept that represents by means the ObjectProperty *hasConcept*, whereas a concept is related to multimedia that represent it using the ObjectProperty *hasMM*. These are the only properties that can relate words to multimedia and vice versa; all of the other properties relate multimedia to multimedia and concepts to concepts. Concepts, multimedia and properties are arranged in a class hierarchy resulting from the syntactic category for concepts and words, data type for multimedia and semantic or lexical for the properties. From a logical point of view, a multimedia representation can be related to all kinds of concepts.

In Table 1, the model features used to represent the objects of interest in our model are shown. The two main classes are Concept, in which all objects are defined as individuals, and MM, which represents all the "signs" in the ontology. These classes are not supposed to have common elements; therefore we define them as disjoint. The class MM defines the logical model of the multimedia forms used to express a concept. On the other hand, the class concept represents the meaning related to a multimedia form; the subclasses have been derived from related categories. There are some union classes that are useful for defining the properties of domain and codomain.

Table 1. Model features.

Schema component	Features	Classes
Concept	ID, Name, Description	NounConcept, VerbConcept, AdjectiveConcept, AdverbConcept
MM	ID, Name	Visual Features, NounWord, VerbWord, AdjectiveWord, AdverbWord
Lexical property		Synonym, Antonym, Partanym, Nominalization, Also see, Derived from adjective, Participle of verb
Semantic property		Hyperonym, Hyponym, Meronym, Entail, Entailed by, Cause, Similar, Attribute, Member of usage domain, Member of region domain, Member of category domain, Usage domain, Region domain, Category domain, Similar, Verb group

We also define attributes for Concept and MM respectively; Concept has: *Name* that represents the concept name; *Description* that gives a short description of concept. On the other hand, MM has an attribute *Name* representing the MM name and a set of features which depends on the multimedia data type described in Table 2. All elements have an *ID* within a unique identification number.

The multimedia features are the low-level descriptors in MPEG-7 standard. The *semantic* and *lexical properties* are shown in Table 1. Table 3 shows some of the properties considered and their domains and ranges of definition. The use of domain and codomain reduces the property range application; however, the model as described so far does not exhibit perfect behavior in some cases. For example, the model does not know that a hyponymy property defined on sets of nouns and verbs would have (1) a range of nouns when applied to a set of nouns and (2) a range of verbs when applied to a set of verbs. Therefore, it is necessary to define

Table 2. Visual features.

Data type	Features
Visual	Dominant Color, Color Structure, Color Layout, Homogeneous Texture, Edge Histogram, Region-based Shape, Contour-based Shape

Table 3. Properties.

Property	Domain	Range
hasMM	Concept	MM
hasConcept	MM	Concept
hypernym	NounsAnd VerbsConcept	NounsAnd VerbsConcept
holonym	NounConcept	NounConcept
entailment	VerbWord	VerbWord
similar	AdjectiveConcept	AdjectiveConcept

Table 4. Model constraints.

Costraint	Class	Property	Constraint range
AllValuesFrom	NounConcept	hyponym	NounConcept
AllValuesFrom	AdjectiveConcept	attribute	NounConcept
AllValuesFrom	NounWord	synonym	NounWord
AllValuesFrom	VerbWord	also_see	VerbWord

several *constraints* to express the ways that the linguistic properties are used to relate concepts and/or MM. Table 4 shows some of the defined constraints specifying the classes to which they have been applied with respect to the considered properties. The table also shows the matching range. Sometimes, the existence of a property between two or more individuals entails the existence of other properties. For example, since the concept "dog" is a hyponym of "animal", animal is a hypernym of dog. These characteristics are represented in OWL by means of property features. Table 5 shows several of those properties and their features. The use of a linguistic approach allows an extension of linguistic properties also to multimedia data; e.g., different multimedia information related to the same concept are synonyms and in the same way hyperonym/hyponym or meronym properties entail a semantic relation among the multimedia representation of concepts. Some examples about the implementation of the model in an ontology management system will be shown in next subsections. The proposed model allows a high-level conceptual matching using different types of low-level representations. Moreover, an ontology built using this model can be used to infer information by means of formal representation of properties among multimedia data and concepts.

2.2. *Implementation*

The proposed model has been implemented in a system to create, populate and share multimedia ontologies in a peer to peer envirorment.

The system has a common model for defining ontologies. In this way all peers have a common view of distributed knowledge and they can share it in a simple way. The adoption of this model can help external agents (outside the P2P network) to use the ontologies for their purposes. In the proposed approach the knowledge is represented by an ontology implemented using a semantic network. The system

Table 5. Property features.

Property	Features
hasMM	*inverse* of hasConcept
hasConcept	*inverse* of hasMM
hyponym	*inverse* of hypernym; *transitivity*
hypernym	*inverse* of hyponym; *transitivity*
cause	*transitivity*
verbGroup	*symmetry* and *transitivity*

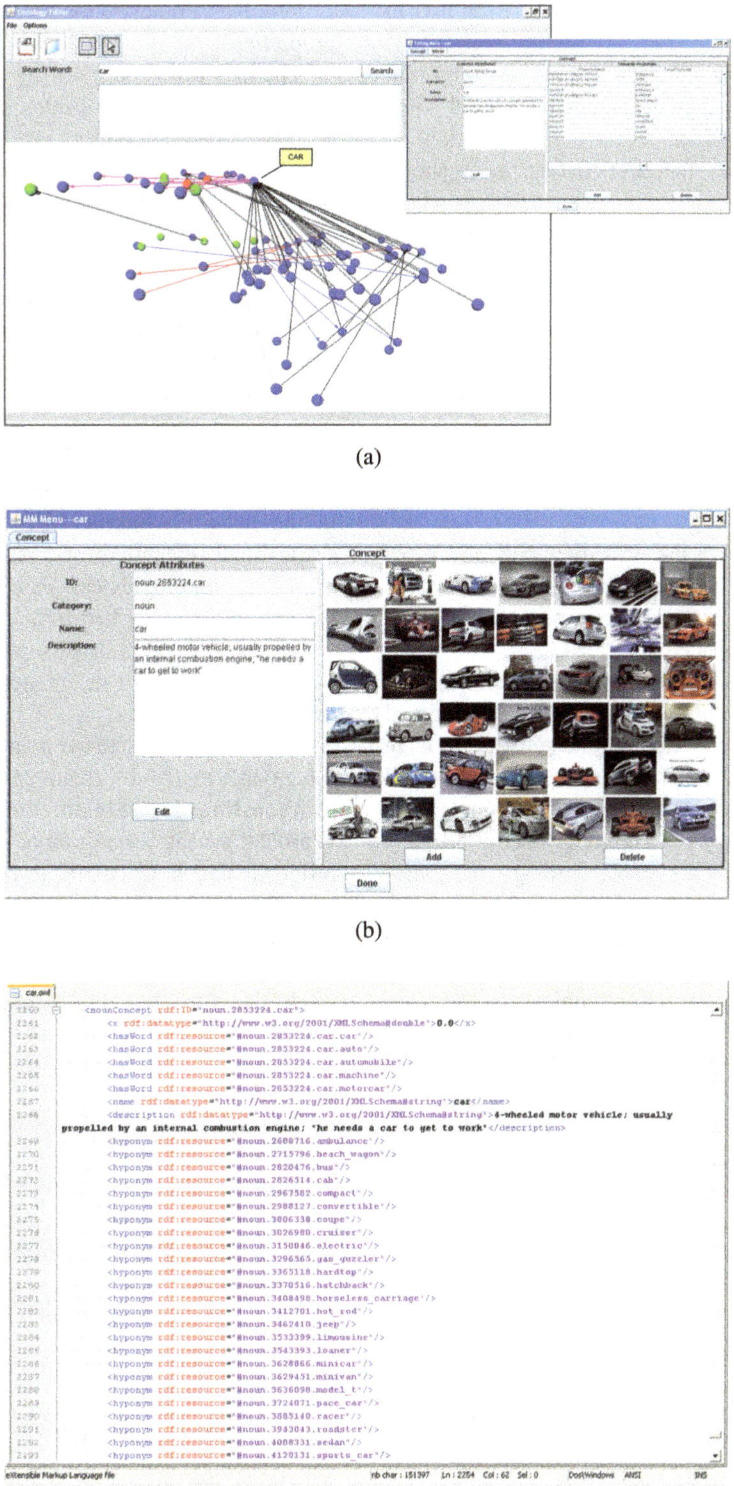

(a)

(b)

(c)

Fig. 1. System interface.

uses WordNet[24] as a general knowledge base to assist user in the ontology creation task.

The proposed system has several software modules and, from a top-level view, they can be organized around some entities and macro-functionalities.

The main system entities are: **Peer:** it is the agent in charge of editing and managing ontologies; each user which takes part in the network is a peer; **Rendez-Vous Peer:** its task is to build the P2P network and manage a list of sharing ontologies between peers and Web Service; **Web Service:** it exposes the ontologies out of the P2P network.

The general architecture of the system is hereinafter described and it is drawn in Fig. 1, together with an example of each single macro-module.

A peer has two main tasks: (i) managing and editing local ontologies and (ii) putting in share local ontologies as shown in Fig. 1.

A Rendez-Vous peer has a list of active peers and a description of their contents. It uses these information in the knowledge discovery step both between peers and in the sharing phase with Web Service.

In each single peer a system interface shows the catalog of the ontology stored in the ontology repository (i.e. a relational DB) to the user by means of an appropriate software module called OntoSearcher; OntoSearcher performs a syntactic search or a browsing in a directory structure arranged by arguments to the aim of finding an ontology relevant to the user interest.

When OntoSearcher finds a suitable ontology, the Onto-Viewer builds a graph (a semantic network) to represent the ontology. A user can modify the semantic network or build a new one with the peer editing functionalities.

On the other hand a peer must communicate to the other peer and with the Rendez-Vous one for sharing ontologies. JXTA is the framework used to build the P2P network; it uses advertisements in the communication steps. In the following subsections are described into details both the remaining modules drawn in Fig. 1 and the algorithm used to build dynamically the semantic network.

Many information systems use a knowledge base to represent data in order to satisfy information requests and in the author's vision it is a good choice for having a common view of the same general and specific knowledge domain.

In the proposed framework we use WordNet[24] as a "starting point" for users because they can extract an initial general ontology from this knowledge base and expand it to have a specialized one; these tasks are explained in the following of this section.

The ontology is implemented by means of a semantic network. This structure is often used as a form of knowledge representation: it is a graph consisting of nodes which represent concepts and edges which represent semantic relations between concepts.

The semantic network is dynamically built using an ad hoc algorithm which takes into account the WordNet structure.

WordNet organizes the several terms using their linguistic properties.

The network is built starting from a domain keyword that represents the context of interest for the user. After this step all the component synsets are considered to construct a hierarchy, only based on the hyponymy property; the last level of this hierarchy corresponds to the last level of WordNet one.

Afterwards the hierarchy is enriched considering all the other kinds of relationships in WordNet (see Table 3). According to these relations other terms are added in the hierarchy obtaining a highly connected semantic network.

In addition a user can associate multimedia representations to concepts.

Using the OntoEditor functionalities a user can modify the ontology structure as a whole adding new MM and Concepts in the network, linking MM and Concepts using arrows (lexical and semantic properties), deleting nodes and arcs.

All the ontologies can be exported in OWL following a schema model described in Sec. 2.1.

At present the system implements low-level image features extraction with the related multimedia ontology management tool.

The images are fetched using a search engine image tool (i.e. google image) by means of a query with the synset name in WordNet. In addition, the user can use words from WordNet synset description or other ones manually added to refine his search. Once images have been fetched, they can be added to the consider concept using an ad hoc interface.

The system extracts multimedia features in according to MPEG-7 standard descriptions included in the proposed model. This functionality is based on MPEG-7 XM software and MPEG-7 Visual Standard.[30]

3. The Case Study

At this step of our research, we are interested in showing a real implementation of our model. Therefore, the proposed methods and techniques are described and tested by means of a complete use case in order to put in evidence the several features of the proposed model and implemented system. The system has been completely developed using Java and the P2P network is based on JXTA libraries while the Web Service uses the AXIS framework. The process of extracting an ontology from WordNet begins with an interaction in which the user inserts a specific term (e.g., car) by means of the user interface and chooses the proper sense by reading the description of the related concepts. The system retrieves the correct sense and builds the ontology by following the steps described in the previous section. An example of system interfaces is shown in Fig. 1(a) where the SN of car is drawn together with some properties among the related concepts (e.g., coupe, cruiser, alternator, rental,...); moreover a user

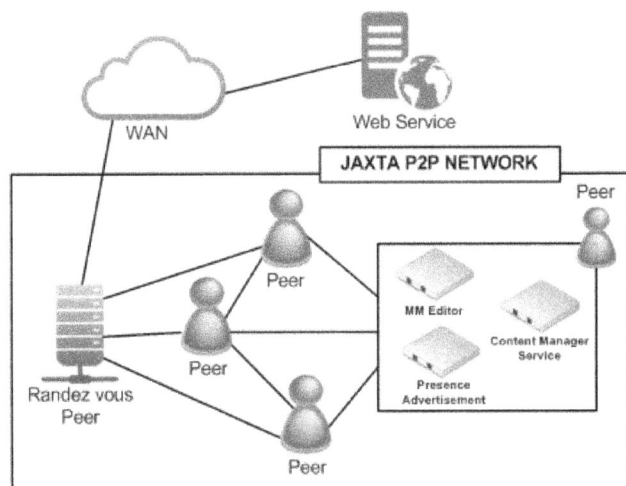

Fig. 2.

can interact with the system editing tools using an ad hoc interface shown in the same figure.

A user can add multimedia objects after the fetching strategy described before. The MM objects interfaces is shown in Fig. 1(b). The ontology OWL representation is shown in Fig. 1(c).

4. Conclusions and Future Works

The design, implementation, and reuse of existing ontologies is a nontrivial task. When users want to interact with different ontologies, they must be combined in some way. This task is performed either via ontology integration or by leaving the ontologies separated. In both cases, the ontologies must be aligned so that they are in a condition of mutual compatibility; the proposed formal model lets to have this compatibility. A P2P approach allows the creation of knowledge communities in which information can be shared and reused in an effective way. Moreover the specialized knowledge in the local communities should be used by other sentient agents to perform their tasks in a more accurate way. In this paper, a global framework to define and develop multimedia ontologies has been presented. The whole ontology management process has been implemented in a system in order to share and create ontologies in a P2P network; the network knowledge is exposed out using a Web Service. The distinctive features of our framework is to use a simple and general formal model for multimedia KR taking into account a linguistic approach considered as the natural communication way between human agents integrating standard descriptions for multimedia data. The ontologies are represented using OWL to represent multimedia ontologies in a machine-processable language. In this way, we have been able to generate an unambiguous machine-understandable formal representation of the semantics associated with multimedia description. A complete case study shows the real use

of our model and its expressive power. The proposed model can be used in crucial knowledge based applications to improve the data mining process and information representation using multimedia features.[30–33]

References

[1] M. Danesi and P. Perron, *Analyzing Cultures*, Indiana University Press, Bloomington, Indiana, USA (1999).

[2] W. Clancey, The knowledge level reinterpreted: Modelling sociotechnical systems, *Int. J. Intell. Syst.* **8**, 33 (1993).

[3] B. Gaines, Modeling as framework for knowledge acquisition methodologies and tools, *Int. J. Intell. Syst.* **8**, 155 (1993).

[4] T. R. Gruber, A translation approach to portable ontology specifications, *Knowl. Acquis.* **5**(2), 199 (1993).

[5] J. T. Nutter, Epistemology, *Encyclopedia of Artificial Intelligence*, S. Shapiro (ed.) (John WyleyS, 1998).

[6] M. Minsky, A framework for representing knowledge, Technical Report, Massachusetts Institute of Technology, Cambridge, MA, USA (1974).

[7] W. A. Woods, What's in a link: Foundations for semantic networks, *Representation and Understanding*, D. G. Bobrow, and A. Collins (eds.) (Academic Press, New York, 1975), pp. 35–82.

[8] R. J. Brachman, On the epistemological status of semantic networks, *Associative Networks: Representation and Use of Knowledge by Computers*, N. V. Findler (ed.) (Academic Press, Orlando, 1979), pp. 3–50.

[9] R. J. Brachman and J. Schmolze, An overview of the kl-one knowledge representation system, *Cogn. Sci.* **9**(2), 171 (1985).

[10] D. G. Bobrow and T. A. Winograd, An overview of krl, a knowledge representation language, Technical Report, Stanford University, Stanford, CA, USA (1976).

[11] A. Mallik, H. Ghosh, S. Chaudhury and G. Harit, MOWL: An ontology representation language for web-based multimedia applications, ACM Transactions on Multimedia Computing, *Commun. Appl. (TOMM)* **10**(1), 8 (2013).

[12] N. Guarino, The ontological level, in *Philosophy and the Cognitive Sciences*, R. Casati, B. B. Smith and G. White (eds.) (Holder-Pichler-Tempsky, Vienna, 1994).

[13] M. Cristani and R. Cuel, A survey on ontology creation methodologies, *Int. J. Semant. Web Inf. Syst.* **1**(2), 49 (2005).

[14] J. Euzenat and P. Shvaiko, *Ontology Matching* (Springer-Verlag, Berlin Heidelberg, DE, 2007).

[15] M. Denny, Ontology tools survey, revisited, XML.com (2004), URL http://www.xml.com/pub/a/2004/07/14/onto.html.

[16] M. van Assem, A. Gangemi and G. Schreiber, RDF/OWL Representation of WordNet, W3C Working Draft (2006), URL http://www.w3.org/TR/wordnet-rdf/.

[17] X.-X. Huang and C.-L. Zhou, An OWL-based wordnet lexical ontology, *J. Zhejiang Univ. - Sci. A* **8**(6), 864 (2007).

[18] Y. Chen, J. Wang and R. Krovetz, An unsupervised learning approach to content-based image retrieval, *Proc. Seventh Int. Symp. Signal Processing and its Applications* (2003).

[19] A. W. M. Smeulders, M. Worring, S. Santini, A. Gupta and R. Jain, Content-based image retrieval at the end of the early years, *IEEE Trans. Pattern Anal. Mach. Intell.* **22**(12), 1349 (2000).

[20] M. S. Lew, N. Sebe, C. Djeraba and R. Jain, Content-based multimedia information retrieval: State of the art and challenges, *ACM Trans. Multimedia Comput. Commun. Appl.* **2**(1), 1 (2006).

[21] J. S. Hare, P. A. S. Sinclair, P. H. Lewis, K. Martinez, P. G. B. Enser and C. J. S, Bridging the semantic gap in multimedia information retrieval: Top-down and bottom-up approaches, *Proc. 3rd European Semantic Web Conf. (ESWC'06)*, LNCS4011, Springer Verlag (2006).

[22] Y. Rui, T. S. Huang and S. fu Chang, Image retrieval: Current techniques, promising directions and open issues, *J. Vis. Commun. Image Represent.* **10**, 39 (1999).

[23] Y. Liu, D. Zhang, G. Lu and W.-Y. Ma, A survey of content-based image retrieval with high-level semantics, *Pattern Recogn.* **40**(1), 262 (2007).

[24] S. F. Chang, T. Sikora and A. Puri, Overview of the MPEG-7 standard, *IEEE Trans. Circuits Syst. Video Technol.* **11**(6), 688 (2001).

[25] M. Dean and G. Schreiber, OWL Web Ontology Language Reference, Technical Report http://www.w3.org/TR/2004/REC-owl-ref-20040210/, W3C (February 2004).

[26] M. Albanese, P. Maresca, A. Picariello and A. M. Rinaldi, Towards a multimedia ontology system: An approach using tao_xml, *Proc. 11th Int. Conf. Distributed Multimedia Systems (DMS'05)* (2005).

[27] A. Cataldo and A. M. Rinaldi, An ontological approach to represent knowledge in territorial planning science, *Comput. Environ. Urban Syst.* **34**(2), 117 (2010).

[28] G. A. Miller, Wordnet: A lexical database for english, *Commun. ACM* **38**(11), 39 (1995).

[29] T. Sikora, The MPEG-7 visual standard for content description-an overview, *IEEE Trans. Circuits Syst. Video Techn.* **11**(6), 696 (2001).

[30] M. Albanese, P. Capasso, A. Picariello and A. M. Rinaldi, Information retrieval from the web: An interactive paradigm, *Int. Workshop on Multimedia Information Systems*, Springer (2005).

[31] V. Moscato, A. Picariello and A. M. Rinaldi, A recommendation strategy based on user behavior in digital ecosystems, *Proc. Int. Conf. Management of Emergent Digital EcoSystems*, ACM (2010).

[32] A. M. Rinaldi, Document summarization using semantic clouds, *Semantic Computing (ICSC), 2013 IEEE Seventh Int. Conf.* (IEEE, 2013).

[33] E. G. Caldarola, A. Picariello and A. M. Rinaldi, An approach to ontology integration for ontology reuse in knowledge based digital ecosystems, *Proc. 7th Int. Conf. Management of Computational and Collective intElligence in Digital EcoSystems*, ACM (2015).

Part 4

Applications

Semantic software engineering*

Taehyung Wang[†], Astushi Kitazawa[‡] and Phillip Sheu[§,¶]

[†]*Department of Computer Science, California State University Northridge*
Northridge, California 91330, USA

[‡]*NEC Soft, Japan*

[§]*Department of EECS, University of California Irvine*
Irvine, California 92697, USA

[¶]psheu@uci.edu

One of the most challenging task in software development is developing software requirements. There are two types of software requirements — user requirement (mostly described by natural language) and system requirements (also called as system specifications and described by formal or semi-formal methods). Therefore, there is a gap between these two types of requirements because of inherently unique features between natural language and formal or semi-formal methods. We describe a semantic software engineering methodology using the design principles of SemanticObjects for object-relational software development with an example. We also survey other semantic approaches and methods for software and Web application development.

Keywords: Semantic software engineering; user requirements; system requirement and specification; object-relational software development; SemanticObjects.

1. Introduction

Although there have been a lot of efforts trying to bridge the gap between informal requirements (especially requirements specifications in natural language) and formal specification methods, the task is far from over. The inherently distinctive characteristics between informality and formality make the task inherently difficult.

The design principles of SemanticObjects[1] essentially back the Semantic Software Engineering (SSE) Methodology that supports the entire life cycle for object:

A semantic system is built by transforming fundamental user requirements (REQUIREMENTS) into an object relational model (DESIGN), and SemanticObjects implements the design (IMPLEMENTATION). Additional building blocks can be added incrementally as the system evolves (MAINTENANCE).

The SSE paradigm is summarized in Fig. 1.

(i) The object model: An object type consists of the type name, a set of attributes whose types can be primitive data types or compound data types, and a set of methods associated with the object type.

(ii) The command model: A command is a method that does not belong to any object class. Example commands are "retrieve" and "list".

(iii) The data-trigger rule base: A data-trigger rule base is a set of data-trigger rules.

(iv) The action-trigger rule base: An action-trigger rule is triggered by a database action.

Amoroso[2] listed five general steps in creating formal specifications from informal requirements: Requirements Categorization, Initial Specification, Requirements Restatement, Evolutionary Refinement, and Target Language Specification. Here, we will follow similar but different steps.

2. Requirements Categorization

In this step, requirements specifications in natural language are relational software development categorized into three categories:

(i) Object Model Requirements: Object model requirements describe the details of the types of objects that should appear in the object-relational model. The details include the name of the object type, a set of attributes, and a set of methods this object type may invoke.

(ii) Query Requirements: The query model requirements describe a set of queries that is not covered by the relational algebra. Each sentence should describe one type of queries, unless the query is too complicated to be stated in a single sentence.

(iii) Rule Requirements: There are two types of rules. Data-trigger rules follow the format: If A then B, where A is a

*This paper is revised from an earlier paper "From SemanticObjects to Semantic Software Engineering, *International Journal of Semantic Computing* 1(1) (2007) 11–28.

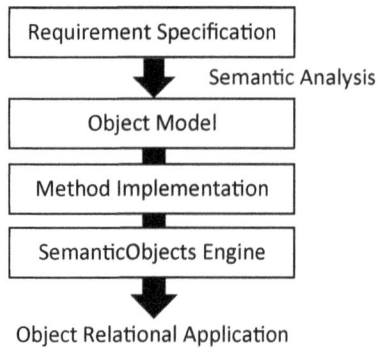

Fig. 1. The SSE software development process.

condition and B is some action to be performed. Action-trigger rules follow the format: When action A is performed then B.

3. Specification Transformation

In this step, the categorized requirements are translated into our choice of the specification language:

(i) Object Model Requirements: The object model requirements are specified using UML class diagrams. In general, the subject of each sentence shall be modeled as an object type. Each subsequent sentence either describes some primitive attributes, some compound attributes related to the subject through the Whole-Part relation or other types of relations, or some action methods the subject may perform. An action method here should be a method that changes the contents of the database.

(ii) Query Requirements: The query requirements are specified using natural language. An important step in this stage is to identify command methods, logical methods and general methods. Typically, an operative verb of a query requirement sentence is identified as a command method or a general method. The objects it operates on are either attributes of some objects or some object types. Any adjective phrase constraining an object is identified as a logical method of that object type. Aggregation functions usually operate on multiple object instances or different object types.

(iii) Rule Requirements: The rule requirements are specified in a similar way. We will show in an example later how this can be done.

4. Consistency Analysis

In this step, we check the consistency of the object-relational model constructed from the natural langue requirements.

(i) Check to see whether there are any "dangling methods". Dangling methods are methods that do not belong to any part of the constructed model in the previous step. A careful analysis should be carried out to see if these are useless methods or methods that actually should belong somewhere.

(ii) Check if any object types that appear in the query requirements and the rule requirements do not have a place in the UML class diagram constructed.

(iii) Check if there are any primitive or compound types used as the input parameters into any methods that cannot be found in the UML class diagram.

(iv) Check the consistency of the rules.

5. An Example

We now illustrate our approach using an example scenario that involves hospital patients.

Data Model Requirements: A patient pays a visit to the hospital when he/she has some symptoms. A patient pays multiple visits to the hospital. Each patient has his/her own PatientInfo record. A PatientInfo record has the following contents: Last Name, First Name, Date of Birth, PhoneNumber, BloodType, Alcoholic, Smoking, and Occupation. A doctor diagnoses the causes of the symptoms and prescribes treatments to that patient at each visit. A doctor gives one prescription to one patient at each visit. Each prescription shall list the medication name and its dose. Each visit date shall be recorded as well. At each visit, the patient shall give a review score for his/her doctor. The score runs from 1(worst) to 10 (best).

Query Requirements: List all the frequent patients. Definition: A patient is a frequent patient if he/she has visited the hospital more than five times during the past month. Ordering Criteria: List the patients in alphabetical order.

List all the patients who show signs of the serious disease "S1". Definition: Patients who show signs of the serious decease "S1" have the following symptoms in sequence: symptom "A", symptom "B", symptom "C". Ordering criteria: List patients in alphabetical order.

Some Rules:

- R1: If a patient shows signs of the serious disease "S1", then prescribe medicine "S1 Cure" to that patient.
- R2: When a patient whose last visit was prescribed the medicine "S1 Cure" pays a new visit to the hospital, notify the doctor of that patient's last visit.

5.1. *Requirements categorization*

In this step, we categorize the requirements and translate them into some natural language form with a preferred style.

Data Model Requirements:

- Patient pays multiple visits to the hospital.
- Each patient has a PatientInfo.
- Each PatientInfo records: Last Name, First Name, Date of Birth, PhoneNumber, BloodType, Alcoholic, Smoking, and Occupation.

- Each visit is associated with a symptom of the patient, a doctor, a diagnosis record, a set of prescription records, and a review score for the doctor.
- Each symptom has a symptom name.
- Each symptom is associated with a symptom description.
- Each doctor has a last name, a first name, and an expertise.
- Each diagnosis has a diagnosis name.
- Each prescription has a medication name and a medication dose.

Query Requirements: The query requirements stated earlier are used.

Rule Requirements: The query requirements stated earlier are used.

5.2. *Specification transformation*

We first extract the subject phrases from the data model requirements. They are: Patients, PatientInfo, Visit, Symptom, Doctor, Diagnosis, and Prescription. For our example, these six objects sufficiently describe our data model. The rationale is that each noun that is a subject should be modeled as an object since it is complex enough to have at least a whole sentence to describe this noun. For this example, we do not have any complex clause structure in the sentences. However, if there is a clause within a sentence that has its own subjects, then each of these subjects within the clause may well be modeled as an object.

For each noun phrase in a sentence, unless modeled as an object, it is treated as a primitive attribute name. The types of these attributes should be determined as String, unless it obviously belongs to another type. The resulting UML class diagram (simplified) is shown in Fig. 2.

It would be nice if every requirement sentence can be transformed into a UML class diagram mechanically. Unfortunately, there are always situations that this is difficult to be achieved. For instance, for the sentence "patient pays multiple visits to the hospital", should the noun phrase "hospital" in the propositional phrase be treated as an attribute name or an object? In this case, the word "hospital" seems to have a value in the context, but does not play a role in the actual database model.

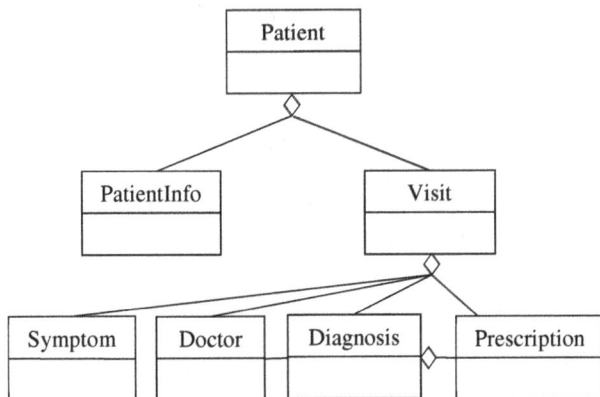

Fig. 2. UML class diagram for the example.

In the next step, we transform the query requirements into COMPOSE:

Q1: List Patient who visit frequently

COMPOSE:
range p is Patient : Patient
list(p) where p.frequentVisit ()

In this case, "List" is a command method in SemanticObjects that does not belong to any class. It takes no arguments and returns a set of Patient objects. The method frequentVisit() is a logical method of Patient. It returns True if the patient object satisfies the definition of "frequent", and returns False otherwise. The implementation detail of the method is left to the programmers. We only care about "what" should be done instead of "how" it should be done, which well coincides with the basic principle of requirements.

Q2: List Patient who show signs of serious disease "S1"

COMPOSE:
range of p is Patient:Patient
listc (p) where p.showSignOfSeriousDisease ("S1")

Again, the implementation detail of the method showSignOfSeriousDisease() is not given. Only the definition and guideline are given in the requirement. The implementation should follow the definitions and ordering criteria.

Subsequently, we transform the rule description into COMPOSE:

R1: If Patients who show signs of serious disease "S1" then Patients is prescribed "SI Cure"

COMPOSE:
var p is INPUT patient
modifyObject(p)
when p. showSignOfSeriousDisease("S1") and
p.prescribe("SI Cure")

To satisfy R1, we need to add another SemanticObjects method "p.prescribe()". This method should add the prescription "SI CURE" to patient p.

R2: When a patient whose last visit was prescribed the medicine "S1 Cure" pays a new visit to the hospital, notify the doctor of that patient's last visit. To make rule 2 simpler, we assume that the object type Visit has its corresponding Patient as one of its attributes. This is a reasonable assumption because we can simply enforce that each object type should have a reference to each object that it is associated with.

On Insert Visit Whose Patients p who show signs of serious disease "S1". Then Notify Doctor who last time diagnosed p.

Here, p is a variable that represents an instance of the object type Patient. The corresponding COMPOSE query is:

var v is Visit:Visit
range of d is Doctor:Doctor
OnInsert(v) where

v.p. showSignOfSeriousDisease("S1")
then (Notify(d) Where d.lastDiagnose(p))

Here, the new method d.lastDiagnoses(p) is a method of the object type Doctor. It returns True when the instance of Doctor is the one who last diagnosed Patient p.

5.3. *Consistency analysis*

In this example, there is no need to check the inconsistency of the object-relational data model constructed. However, for larger and more complex requirements specifications, inconsistency will likely to occur.

6. Related Work

Witte *et al.*[3] presents a "complete environment" for implanting natural language processing into software development through their research and plug-in for Eclipse. They argue that software engineering is a knowledge-based discipline and a large chunk of that knowledge resides in natural language artifacts. Information pertaining to both functional and nonfunctional requirements for example would reside in the artifacts in natural language. This same information would be a trial or even unfeasible to recreate using source code. Tools developers commonly use help with syntactical issues, but do not process unstructured natural language. Natural language support has been scare overall. Their research proposes the use of NLP techniques to assist with the workload. They argue that a seamless, generic implementation of these techniques will produce the highest rate of success as software engineers are end users of computational linguistics. The paper makes the argument that in order to be widely adopted, the NLP process must function as a tool in the overall process. To that point, the researchers have developed a process to analyze source code comment quality automatically. Their reasoning is due to the shift from document-intense development methods towards agile development, there are situations where important documentation is only available as comments, and the manual task of verifying comments for each component is arduous. The exact quality of the comments is influential in further development processes and the automation is of benefit to the developer.

Schugerl *et al.*[4] address assessing nonfunctional requirements (in particular evolvability) through semantic modeling of software artifacts. Nonfunctional requirements are a large factor of acceptability. However, the ability to assess whether NFRs are met are still not well-developed in existing processes. The importance of this is substantiated by the fact that software development has become highly collaborative since the widespread adoption of the internet because collaborators are no longer necessarily working at the same location. As a result, managing distributed workspaces, processes, and knowledge of resources (including various artifacts, formats,

and abstraction levels) is very important to organizations. Their research produces a unified ontological representation to support the consolidation of information from different locations. They use this unified representation to then analyze and evaluate nonfunctional requirement of evolvability, but also other NFRs. They advocate the use of ontologies because they support "semantic modeling for quality information representation and communication" (in addition to encouraging and assisting "the conceptual representation of a software ecosystem"). They break down non-functional requirements into two categories: execution qualities (performance, usability, etc.) and evolution qualities (testability, maintainability, extensibility, scalability, etc.). They advocate the use of ontologies because they support "semantic modeling for quality information representation and communication" (in addition to encouraging and assisting "the conceptual representation of a software ecosystem"). They break down non-functional requirements into two categories: execution qualities (performance, usability, etc.) and evolution qualities (testability, maintainability, extensibility, scalability, etc.).

Rilling *et al.*[5] present a formal representation of an existing process model to support the evolution of software systems. It uses ontologies and description logics in its representation of knowledge resources and the process model through a shared model. The formal representation promotes the discovery of direct and indirect relationships among various resources, supporting the use of reasoning services. The research focuses on the relationships between the maintainers, process model, and appropriate knowledge resources. They introduce a software evolution ontology that models aspects of the process as well as the knowledge resources of software evolution. That is, it models and combines information pertaining to the process with software and the knowledge resources. The desired result is to reduce disconnect created by abstraction and the language used in the artifacts. This directly helps maintainers discover information relevant to their particular task from the resources more easily, a major challenge that maintainers face. Relationships can be established to show traceability between software processes and knowledge resources. Ontology reasoners are also able to find implicit relationships between the two through the formal ontological representation via automated reasoning services.

Khamis *et al.*[6] discuss the assessment of natural language to help maintainers perform their tasks more efficiently. The researchers propose an automated method to evaluate the quality of inline documentation using a set of heuristics (aimed at evaluating language used and consistency between code and comments). They are focusing on analyzing the quality of comments that was not possible beforehand. A lot of the knowledge that maintainers need is kept as inline documentation (such as comments written in natural language). The state of the inline documentation has a tremendous and resounding effect on the product during its lifecycle. The quality of the documentation, which needs to be verified manually, is very time intensive task. The researchers chose to make a Javadoc tool because Javadoc is an already existing tool for developers to produce documentation from comments (using special comments or tags). The tool has two functions, analyze the comments in the code and return the results of the analysis to an ontology. The analysis came down to two well-defined metrics as well: the overall grade of natural language and the consistency of code and comments.

Zhang *et al.*[7] focus on recreating traceability links between source code and documentation in order to assist with software maintenance. Using an ontological representation, they sift through documentation and source code artifacts (two of the artifacts that impact understanding greatly) to rediscover traceability at the semantic level. This process is assisted by ontology reasoners to find the relationships between software artifacts. The problem of sifting through various knowledge resources is repeated here, but with the condition that even for well-documented processes the task of maintaining software remains burdensome because the links are difficult to form. Their procedure in implementing differs from existing ones that focus on information retrieval, which ignore information about structure and semantics. They employ a "Text Mining system" to semantically analyze documents and source code in order to find traceability links. Again, the ontological representation provides them the ability to use automated services from ontology reasoners. They first create ontologies for the artifacts and then populate them from code and documentation. After that, they establish traceability relations between the models so that ontology reasoners can be run. This ontological method for natural language processing can add further knowledge not accessible due to semantic language. The shared representation of code and documentation also helps with the integration of common ideas via traceability links. Using the traceability links and existing ontological knowledge representation techniques, this research provides the user with the ability to discover new concepts and types of relationships between artifacts.

Khami *et al.*[8] describe about generating a corpus from information in the source code and inline documentation via a doclet for Javadoc. The corpus is compatible with natural language processing applications so that extra energy can be put into text analysis. The research was aimed in producing a tool that converts information found in source code and documentation to XML, a language that is very complementary to natural language processing applications. Other NLP tools have trouble sifting through artifacts and differentiating inline documentation and code, or they lose some information in their processing technique.

Bauer and Roser[9] address software industrialization arguing that the current state of development – software being developed from the ground up — is not a cost-effective and that the process can be improved to be automated and therefore "industrialized". They make use of model-driven software development and the Semantic Web to realize this. They refer the Object Management Group's model-driven architecture as noteworthy progress made towards the goal of automation and then generalize it through model-driven software development. They state the issues holding back the automation of development are "reuse of standardized components and processes, and vertical integration." They then show that the ontological operations offered by the Semantic Web, combined with model-driven software development, can resolve these issues so that software development can be industrialized.

References

[1] P. C.-Y. Sheu and A. Kitazawa, *Int. J. Seman. Comput.* **1**(1), 11, (2007).

[2] E. G. Amoroso, Creating formal specifications from requirements documents, *ACM SIGSOFT Softw. Eng. Notes* **20**(1), 67, (1995).

[3] R. Witte, B. Sateli, N. Khamis and J. Rilling, Intelligent software development environments: Integrating natural language processing with the eclipse platform, *24th Canadian Conf. Artificial Intelligence*, LNCS 6657 (2011), pp. 408–419.

[4] P. Schugerl, J. Rilling, R. Witte and P. Charland, A quality perspective of evolvability using semantic analysis, *Third IEEE Int. Conf. Semantic Computing* (2009), pp. 420–427.

[5] J. Rilling, W. Meng, R. Witte and P. Charland, Story driven approach to software evolution, *IET Softw. Spec. Sec. Softw. Evolv.* **2**(4), 304, (2008).

[6] N. Khamis, R. Witte and J. Rilling, Automatic quality assessment of source code comments: The JavadocMiner, *15th Int. Conf. Applications of Natural Language to Information Systems* (2010), pp. 68–79.

[7] Y. Zhang, R. Witte, J. Rilling and V. Haarslev, Ontological approach for the semantic recovery of traceability links between software artifacts, *IET Softw. Spec. Issue on Lang. Eng.* **2**(3), 185, (2008).

[8] N. Khamis, J. Rilling and R. Witte, Generating an NLP corpus from java source code: The SSL Javadoc Doclet, *New Challenges for NLP Frameworks, Workshop at LRE* (2010), pp. 41–45.

[9] B. Bauer and S. Roser, Semantic-enabled software engineering and development, *INFORMATIK 2006 — Informatik für Menschen Band 2, 1st Int. Workshop on Applications of Semantic Technologies*, (2006), 94 of Lecture Notes in Informatics, pp. 293–296.

A multimedia semantic framework for image understanding and retrieval

Antonio Penta

United Technology Research Center Ireland (UTRC-I)

pentaa@utrc.utc.com

On the grounds, ontologies have been shown to be a powerful resource for the interpretation and translation of the terminological and semantic relationships within domains of interest but it is still unclear how they can be applied in the context of multimedia data. In this paper, we describe a framework which can capture and manage semantic information related to the multimedia data by modeling in the ontology their features. In particular, the proposed ontology-based framework is organized in the following way: at the lower levels, spatial objects, colors, shapes are represented, and semantic relationships can be established among them; at the higher levels, objects with semantic properties are put into relationship among themselves as well as with the corresponding low-level objects. On this basis, we have designed an ontological system particularly suitable for image retrieval. We have also taken into account the inherent uncertainty related to the representation and detection of multimedia properties in this complex domain. Along this work, we have provided examples from the image domain; moreover, since ontologies provide a semantic means for the semantic comparison of objects and relationships across different formats, the system is easily extensible to other, heterogeneous data sources.

Keywords: Multimedia semantic; multimedia ontology; image retrieval.

1. Introduction

In the last few years, we have assisted to a tremendous growth of multimedia data in all the aspects of everyday life, mixed with all the modern consumer technologies. However, despite the great efforts of the research community in multimedia processing, in both the academic and industrial contexts, representing, organizing and managing multimedia data and the related semantics by means of a formal framework still remains a challenge. Some sample scenarios from common real life situations can help understand our vision.

Example 1: Criminal Investigation. Let us consider a secret service investigation of a large scale anti-terroristic operation. In order to carry out the investigation successfully and to avoid dramatic events, the agents use a large number of electronic devices to conduct surveillance of places and people involved or suspected to be involved in activities of terroristic organizations. In particular, they may use the following devices in order to gather data and information:

- CCTV video cameras may be distributed at crucial places to record activities of suspected persons.
- In addition, the officers may have (hopefully) legally authorized telephone wiretaps, collecting audio conversations involving suspects.
- The agents may also have a number of photographs taken, containing faces of suspected people and/or a number of illegal activities.
- The officers may have a great number of textual documents, containing a description of all the previous investigations, judge-court sentences about such people, and so on.

- Possibly, a relational data base may contain several structured information, i.e., bank account transactions, credit card and so on.

Example 2: Horse Racing. Consider the production of sport-news about horse racing. In order to produce interesting reports, the reporters would like to have information and succinct stories about the horses, the jokers, videos and pictures of prizes and awards, the story of the horse families, newspapers and video news about previous races, etc. In particular, they may have gathered data and information from:

- audio records from a radio digital library;
- video news from a video digital library of their broadcasts;
- newspapers collected from the internet or pictures related to horses, jokers and the games in general.

In both cases, it is clear that the core aspect is the idea of having multimedia documents containing a variety of formats (textual, pictorial, video, audio) and a variety of metadata, sometimes manually added to the multimedia sources and sometimes automatically extracted. Note that, in real cases, the number of multimedia data is very huge, and the only way to process such a large amount of data is to use automatic tools that can extract information and represent them in a suitable way. In this framework, it is mandatory to provide novel techniques and methodologies for storing and accessing multimedia data based on their semantic contents and to consider both the variety of data sources and the associated uncertainty of the automatic analysis and recognition systems.

In particular, we need a framework that allows specifications for: *Special Relationships* that exist between the different media entities characterizing a media object or an event — for example, geometrical, spatial, temporal relationships and so on; *Uncertainty*, that is produced by Computer Vision systems when they are processing and recognizing multimedia contents — for example, object detection in an image or a video is always associated to a certain membership degree; *Associations between the low-level properties and semantic properties of images* — for example, the semantics of an image can be enriched/learned/guessed by observing the relationships of its color and shape with real-world concepts; An *associated reasoning service* which can use the available feature observations and concept descriptions to infer other probable concepts in the presence of uncertain relationships — for example, some shape, texture and color properties might be used to infer that a certain media object is an instance of a given concept: e.g., *color = yellow* with a grade μ_y, *shape = circle* with a grade μ_c may be associated with the concept of the *sun* with a grade $\min\{\mu_y, \mu_c\}$. In the data and knowledge engineering community, the formal representation of domain knowledge is systematically treated by using ontologies. Especially, in the semantic web field, several models and languages have been proposed in order to define the concept of ontology and to design suitable and efficient systems that really use the ontological framework for real problems. In the multimedia community, great emphasis has been given to the *extensional aspects* of multimedia ontologies: it is easy to find ontologies about images, videos and audios that contain relevant information about technical aspects related to multimedia data, its format along with a variety of ways used for annotating complex and rough data.[1] Unfortunately, the same is not true as far as the *intensional aspects* of the multimedia ontologies. Indeed, starting from the very beginning, it is still not at all clear whether a multimedia ontology is simply a taxonomy, or a semantic network, whether it is a simple organization of metadata or there is a role also for concrete data, and which. In addition, the semantics of multimedia data itself are very hard to define and to capture: for example, in the image domain, the information carried by an image is inherently both complex and uncertain, therefore its semantics has a fuzzy nature. In this paper, we describe a novel formal framework for multimedia ontologies and in order to make our theory understandable, we will concentrate in particular on image data. The proposed framework is based on a constructivist vision of the multimedia data processing and representation phases. In other words, we provide a suitable knowledge base that can accommodate and manage different levels of multimedia data in terms of rough data, intermediate and high level concepts, as well as some abstractions that can be observed over them. In this way, we provide a comprehensive framework that can be used for a variety of purposes: e.g., information storing and management, information extraction, information retrieval and automatic annotations. Throughout, the rest of the paper, we try to answer the following questions:

(a) Do we really need yet another knowledge framework for images?

(b) What is a multimedia ontology?

(c) Is this kind of ontology suitable for representing both intensional and extensional aspects of multimedia data? What kind of advantages do we get from image annotation?

More technically speaking, in this paper, we contribute details concerning: (i) how we represent and manage the multimedia information; (ii) how we derive high level concepts, considering the discovered features, objects and elementary concepts.

The paper is organized as follows. In Sec. 2, we provide an introduction on the logic language used in our framework. In Sec. 3, we describe at a glance the underlying vision theory that is at the basis of our ontological framework, and we provide a theory for the multimedia knowledge-base and multimedia ontology foundations. Section 4 describes the data model used in our frameworking along with the query processing algorithm, and in Sec. 5 we provide the experiments that have been realized. A related work section and some conclusions are outlined in Secs. 6 and 7, respectively.

2. Theoretical Background: Description Logic

Let us now provide some basic concepts on ontologies. Informally, an ontology consists of a hierarchical description of important concepts in a particular domain, along with the description of the properties (of the instances) of each concept. Description Logics (DL) are a formalism for representing knowledge, and they play an important role in this context, as they are essentially the theoretical counterpart of the Web Ontology Language (OWL), the state-of-the-art language to specify ontologies. It is a family of different languages, distinguished by the set of constructors they provide, each one derived from the composition of different properties and operators, and constitute the core of most current knowledge representation systems, considering both the structure of a DL knowledge base and its associated reasoning services. A machine, in order to understand the true content of an image, must have knowledge about the domain the image belongs to, and be capable to derive some concepts or relations that describe the multimedia objects inside the image. DLs offer a useful contribution to content-based image retrieval, while allowing a powerful logical language able to describe and to reason about the semantic contents derived from the image. DL-based representation is at the predicate level: no variables are present in the formalism. A DL theory has two parts: the definition of predicates is the Terminological Box (TBox), and the assertion over constants is the Assertion Box (Abox). The terminological part describes the structural properties of the terms of the domain, while the assertional part depicts a particular configuration of a domain by introducing individuals and asserting their properties. Thus, statements in the TBox and in the ABox represent first-order logic formulae with, possibly, some extension. A DL system not only stores terminologies and assertions, but also offers services that reason about them. The foundations of the DL languages are *concepts* and *roles*: a concept represents a class of objects sharing some common characteristics, while a role represents a binary relation between objects or attributes attached to objects. In addition to atomic concepts and roles, all DL systems allow their users to build complex descriptions of new ones. There are different versions of DL, having different expressivities and complexities. $\mathcal{SHOIN}(D)$ is one of the first DLs used in the context of the semantic web, for the ontology description language known as OWL-DL,[a] and is supported by the most popular ontology editors, such as Protege.[b] It allows the use of concrete domains in its syntax and semantic rules. There are also some interesting extensions of the DL, such as the Fuzzy DL[2] and Probabilistic DL[3] or more in general DL and Rule programs that are able to handle both uncertainty and vagueness.[4] Let us introduce the formalism for the very basic DL language denoted by the prefix $\mathcal{AL}$ (Attribute Language), which is close to the expressivity of frame-based representation systems. Concept descriptions in $\mathcal{AL}$ are formed according to the following syntactic rules:

$$
\begin{array}{llll}
C, D & \rightarrow & A| & \text{(atomic concept)} \\
& & \top| & \text{(universal concept)} \\
& & \bot\,| & \text{(bottom concept)} \\
& & \neg A| & \text{(atomic negation)} \\
& & C \sqcap D| & \text{(intersection)} \\
& & \forall R.C| & \text{(value restriction)} \\
& & \exists R.\top & \text{(limited existential quantification)}
\end{array}
$$

In the most of general case, the terminological axioms have the form:

$$C \sqsubseteq D \quad \text{or} \quad C \equiv D$$

C, D being concepts. The first are the *inclusion* axioms, the second are the *equivalence* axioms. In Example 1, we describe a simple knowledge base, where we have the information written in natural language followed by the respective expressions of the T-Box and the A-Box.

Example 1. An example of Knowledge Base expressed in $\mathcal{AL}$.

Terminological Axioms:

A Person that rides on a RaceHorse is a Jockey.
Person $\sqcap$ $\exists$ride_on.(RaceHorse) $\sqsubseteq$ Jockey
A Horse that runs on a RaceHorseTrack is a RaceHorse.
Horse $\sqcap$ $\exists$run_on.HorseRacerTrack $\sqsubseteq$ RaceHorse
A Track that is surrounded by Grass is-a HorseRaceTrack.
Track $\sqcap$ $\exists$surrounded_by.Grass $\sqsubseteq$ HorseRacerTrack

---

[a]http://www.w3.org/TR/owl-features/.
[b]http://protege.stanford.edu/.

A Quadruped is an Animal.
Quadruped $\sqsubseteq$ Animal.
A Elephant is a Quadruped and it has the trunk.
Elephant $\sqsubseteq$ Quadruped $\sqcap$ $\exists$has.Trunk.
A Horse is a Quadruped and it not has the trunk.
Horse $\sqsubseteq$ Quadruped $\sqcap$ $\neg$($\exists$has.Trunk).

Assertional Axioms:

"furia" is a Horse.
Horse(*furia*).
"dumbo" is an Elephant.
Elephant(*dumbo*)

---

3. The Multimedia Semantic Framework

In this section, we describe a novel model for representing and managing multimedia data. In particular, we first start from several considerations about how a human vision system is able to store and manage multimedia information for high-level image-understanding purposes. Furthermore, a formal representation of the processed data will be given, having the aim of designing an automatic, content-based multimedia query engine. Let us consider the picture in Fig. 1. Using an image processing and analysis system, it is possible to obtain a description of the content of this image, for example in terms of color, shape and texture together with the grade of uncertainty that we expect each image processing algorithm to produce. Then, a domain-trained classifier can associate some elementary concepts to the extracted multimedia feature, e.g., {⟨*person, horse, grass, sand*⟩}. Our proposed framework will provide primitives to store all these information in order to enhance the semantic of the detected objects. In particular, it will provide utilities

Fig. 1. Running example.

for: (i) representing spatial relationships, such as: a person is positioned on the top of a horse; (ii) managing the uncertainty that is related to all the detected objects, in our case the person and the horse; (iii) representing suitable features (color, shape and texture) for each detected object, i.e., the person and the horse; (iv) providing an appropriate reasoning service that could infer that in the image there is indeed a *jockey riding a racing horse*. With this framework, we can overcome the limitation in representing and manipulating this kind of knowledge by means of classical data models, such as the relational one. Thus, in our view, the proposed model is able to express and elicit the semantics of multimedia data.

3.1. *The human vision system*

Given an image *I*, a human decodes its knowledge content after different cognitive steps, as described in Fig. 2(a). Each step is related to a human perceptive process and some of these steps are iterated in order to derive more complex concepts. Several steps are image processing blocks that approximate the human vision process on the whole image or on parts of an image. Psychological theories propose two different approaches for recognizing concepts related to an image: the holistic and the constructive one.[5] According to the holistic theory, an image is processed and recognized by humans considering the whole representation. In contrast,

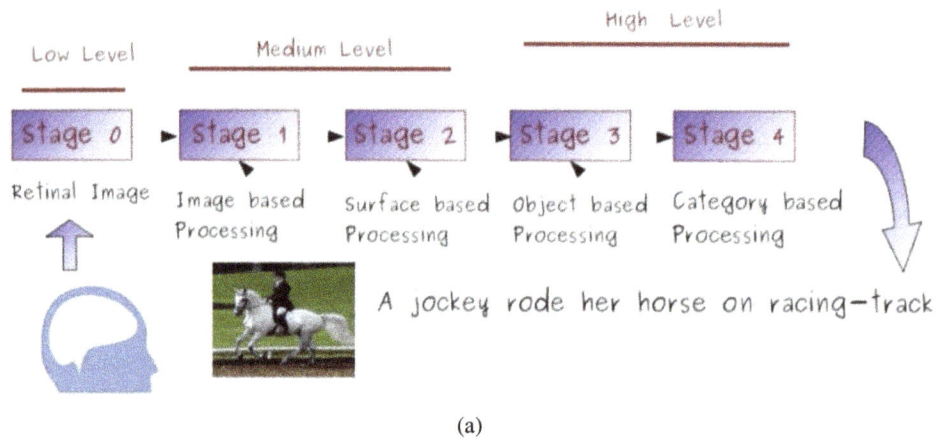

(a)

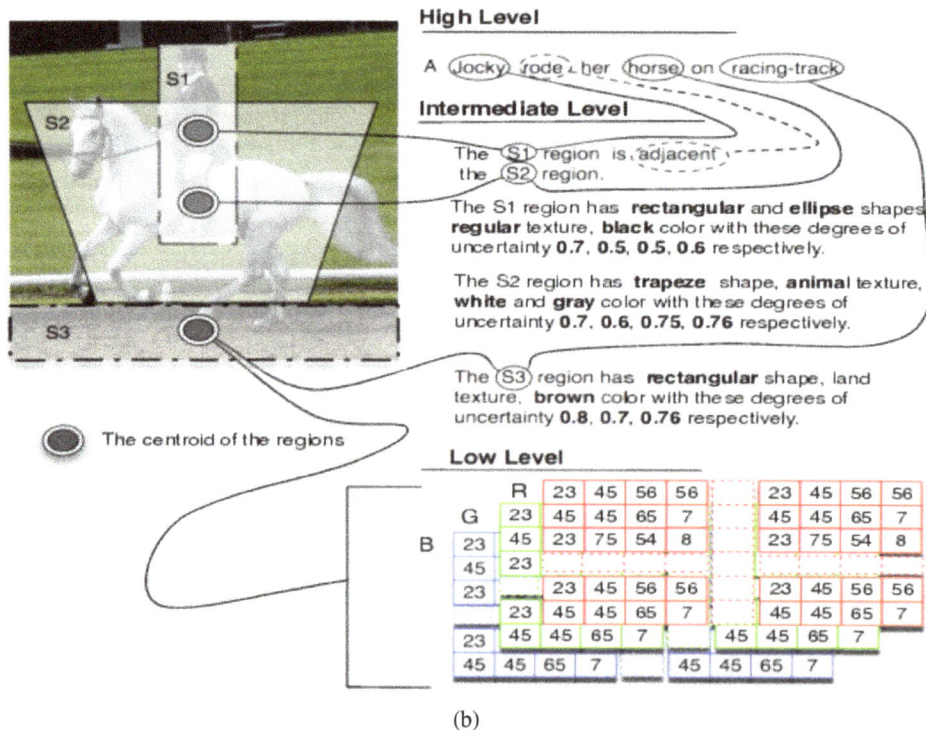

(b)

Fig. 2. (a) The process of visual perception, (b) the level-based description of our sample image.

the constructive theory considers image understanding as a progressive process: a human first recognizes an interesting part of an image, then he/she infers the knowledge of the whole image from the knowledge of its parts, in a recursive fashion. We follow the latter approach. In addition, according to the classical "meaning triangle",[6] in a given media we must be able to detect symbols, objects and concepts; in a certain image we have a region of pixels (*symbol*) related to a portion of multimedia data and this region is an instance (*object*) of a certain *concept*. Note that we can detect concepts but we are not able to disambiguate among the instances without further, specific knowledge.

In a simplified version of the constructive vision process will consider only three main levels: *Low, Medium and High*, as depicted in Fig. 2(b). The knowledge associated to an image is described at three different levels: *Low level*: raw images, computationally and abstractly thought of as discrete functions of two variables defined on some bounded and usually regular regions of a plane, i.e., a pixel map used to structure the image perceptual organization and additional maps obtained by filtering processes; *Intermediate level*: an aggregation of data related to the use of spatial features — including points, lines, rectangles, regions, surfaces, volumes — color features, textures and shape features, for example colors are usually described by means of *color histograms* and several features have been proposed for texture and shapes, all exploiting spatial relations among a number of low level features (pixels) in a certain region; *High level*: this layer is related to axioms that involve concepts conveyed by an image, along with their relations; looking at Fig. 1, we could use these sentences to define the high level description: "A jockey rides a horse on a racing-track". Due to the inherent uncertainty of the image domain, the features associated to these layers should be characterized in terms of a *fuzzy value*. These *fuzzy values* represent the *degree of uncertainty* that each image processing algorithm produces, i.e., we might say the shape is "highly" trapezoid, or that it is "a little bit" rectangular. Expressions such as *highly, a little bit*, and so on, recall this notion of fuzziness implicitly related to the *similarity of visual stimuli*. We can associate this fuzziness to some regions inside the image related to colors, shapes and textures. Considering the running example image, some derived image attributes are depicted in Example 2.

Example 2. Colors:$\{\langle Green, 0.8 \rangle, \langle White, 0.89 \langle Black, 0.7 \rangle, \langle Brown, 0.75 \rangle\}$. Shapes: $\{\langle Rectangle, 0.6 \rangle, \langle Trapeze, 0.9 \rangle\}$. Textures: $\{\langle Animal, 0.8 \rangle, \langle Nature, 0.6 \rangle\}$.

3.2. *Multimedia ontology-based model*

We define a multimedia semantic framework that takes into account the specificity of multimedia data — and in particular of images —, providing the means to link this extracted knowledge with that designed by a domain expert. Our aim is thus to build a multimedia ontology that "mediates" the

domain ontology with the multimedia nature of some concepts and with the fuzzy nature of the computer vision results. As described in the previous sections, each image may be decomposed into a set of regions that are characterized in terms of texture, color and shape. By applying appropriate image analysis algorithms, some of these regions can be associated to the instances of some concepts and in some cases, the semantic nature of these concepts can be entirely described by their multimedia representation. While for other concepts, we need to infer their semantic by exploring the different relationships among the intermediate image features extracted from the image processing and analysis algorithms. First, let us explain, using the running example, how some domain concepts can be visually re-defined in terms of some spatial relationships that can be defined in our framework. If we consider the knowledge-based depicted in Example 1, we have different concepts that are linked using the domain knowledge about the horse-races' application domain. Then, the left-hand-side concepts of the terminological axioms can be also detected from a computer vision analysis process, for example *Track* and *Horse* could be recognized by training a classifier through their image features, while concept "Jockey" "HorseRacerTrack", "RacerHorse" can be inferred over the previous concepts. In particular, the relations in the definitions can be translated into spatial constraints among the image regions that are recognized as instances of the given concepts; for example, the *ride* role can be translated as the spatial relation *on_the_top_of* between the regions that are the image representations of the concepts *Person* and *Race-Horse*. These definitions can also be specialized in the image domain, by adding some multimedia properties over the terminological axioms. In fact, we can add some intermediate concepts that describe the spatial relationships among regions, the kind of shapes and textures and other intermediate features as follows:

$$\exists \text{ has\_geometry.}\{\text{pathRegion}\} \sqcap \text{Sand} \sqsubseteq \text{Track}$$
$$\text{BayHorse} \equiv \text{Horse} \sqcap \exists \text{ has\_color.}\{\text{dark\_brown}\}$$

Thus, the *Track* concept can be visually redefined by the *pathRegion* value of the *has_geometry* concrete role. In particular, this can be assigned to a region that has the spatial property that a path line can always be drawn across the whole geometry. Moreover, the instances of *Track* have to be also instances of the *Sand* concept. In the second axioms, we can specialize the *Horse* concept into the *BayHorse*, associating it to the color *dark_brown*, which is an instance of the concrete predicate *has_color*.

Now, we are in position to formally define our multimedia ontology-based framework. Let Δ_{IM} be our reference domain of IMages. We informally define $C_{Ag}, C_{HM}, C_{IM}, Image, Sub Image$ as follows:

- C_{IM} (*Intermediate Media concepts*) is the set of auxiliary concepts describing the shape, texture, color properties of objects belonging to the reference domain of IMages (Δ_{IM}), with a certain *degree of fuzziness*.

- C_{MR} (*Media Representation concept*) is an auxiliary concept used to express the multimedia representation with a certain *degree of fuzziness* of the domain concepts using a multimedia domain such as the reference domain of IMages (Δ_{IM}).

- C_{HM} (*High Media concepts*) is the set of concepts whose semantics is completely and automatically inferred, by means of their multimedia features, through computer vision techniques. Between objects of C_{HM} and objects of C_{IM} there may be relations; moreover, objects of C_{HM} can also be in relation with objects of Δ_{IM}. These relations also have a certain *degree of fuzziness*.

- C_{Ag} (*Aggregate concepts*) is the set of concepts belonging to a general domain defined through the axioms over high media concepts and/or aggregate concepts and/or some relations over them. These axioms may also relate the concepts of C_{Ag} with the objects of Δ_{IM}.

- *Image* and *SubImage* are two concepts whose individuals belong to Δ_{IM}.

Examples of C_{HM} are water, sand, elephant, grass, horse, while examples of C_{Ag} are jockey, racing-track. Through the use of the *reification pattern*,[c] between the individuals in $C_{HM} \bigcup C_{IM}$ and in *SubImage* and/or *Image*, we are able to associate a value belonging to the concrete domain (i.e., xsd: float). This value is used as measures of the uncertainty produced by the vision engines. These values are interpreted as fuzzy values and they are used at query time to formulate the output ranking. We also add to our knowledge base some useful axioms that take into account intuitive relations within the image domain, modeled through the concepts of *Image* and *SubImage*. For instance, the axiom *SubImage* $\sqsubseteq$ $\exists part\_of.Image$ captures the idea that each image may be formed by sub-images, while $\exists hasimage.(SubImage \sqcap \exists has\_fuzzy\_value.xsd : float) \sqsubseteq C_{HM}$ means that each C_{HM} has a vision content depicted by a region of image and the quality of this association is described by a degree of fuzziness. Moreover, some spatial relations among elements of *SubImage* exist, by means of which we represent how the *SubImage* elements are related to each other in a spatial way: *on_the_top_of*, *on_the_left_of*, *on_the_right_of*, *on_the_bottom_of*, *spatialDisjoint*, *close_to*, *full_intersected_with*. With respect to our running example, the table below illustrates the spatial conversion of roles into binary spatial predicates among image regions, along with the objects that satisfy the related predicates. The spatial predicates are derived from the analysis of the relationship between the centers of the shape and their corners.

More details about the axioms used in this framework can be found in Refs. 7 and 8, where also the semantics of all these roles and concepts has been described in terms of the

[c]https://www.w3.org/TR/swbp-n-aryRelations/.

Table 1. Example of spatial conversion of roles in binary spatial predicates among regions in image and some example that satisfy the related predicates. The spatial predicates are derived from the analysis of the relationship among the centers of the shape and the their corners.

Role	Spatial predicate	Examples
ride_on, run_on	on_the_top_of	
surrounded_by	full_intersected_with	

classical Tarsky-style semantic.[9] In particular, we note that its core consists in the introduction of the new multimedia domain Δ_{IM}, which is used to assign a multimedia representation (i.e., raw image data) to the concepts of *SubImage* and *Image*. Do notice that, since our query system only allows the expression of conjunctive queries, we only use a sub-set of the expressivity rules of $\mathcal{SHOIN}(D_n)$ for representing the above knowledge.[7]

3.3. *An example of multimedia ontology-based model*

In order to best understand the intensional and extensional levels of our proposed ontology-based framework, let us consider how the framework introduced in the previous section is applied in the "jocker" running example. As regard to the *intensional* aspect described in first three assertions of Example 1, we can define those concepts as specialization of C_{IM}, C_{HM} and C_{Ag}. Then, with respect to C_{IM} and C_{HM}, concepts such as *Person*, *Horse*, *Grass* and *Sand* are also associated to *SubImage*s of an *Image* with a related fuzziness value. Then, those *SubImage*s have also their own *Shape*, *Texture*, *Color* and *Geometry* with their related fuzziness values. In the table above, we have reported an example of how these abstract concepts introduced in our framework are associated to the concepts used in the knowledge base of Example 1.

As regard to the *extensional* aspect, let us consider the table below which contains the part of images obtained by applying an image segmentation algorithm[10] to the image

Table 2. Example of concepts of type Intermediate Media, High Media, Aggregate.

C_{IM}	C_{HM}	C_{Ag}
Texture	Person	Jockey
Color	Grass	Racehorse
Shape	Horse	Horse-race-track
Geometry	Sand	Track

Table 3. Images and SubImage instances.

1	2	3	4

depicted in Fig. 1. Now, these images can be considered as instances of the *SubImage* concept and they are also part of the image in Fig. 1, which can be considered as an instance of the concept *Image*. Now, in order to explain how these image are represented in our framework, let us label them as 1–4 as depicted in the table below, and let also use the label 5 for the image in Fig. 1.

Now, we can assume that our computer vision system have extracted a set of associations that can be used to create our multimedia knowledge as follows:

- An instance of *Person* is associated to the image 1 with a degree of fuzziness 0.58; the image 1 is also linked to an instance of the concept *Color* that is in turn associated to the concrete value "*black*" with a degree of fuzziness 0.7

and to the value "*gray*" with a degree of fuzziness 0.3. Then, the same image 1 is linked to the *Shape* instance, named *shape_p*1, which is associated to value "*rectangular*" with a degree of fuzziness 0.6, and to "*ellipse*" value with a degree of fuzziness 0.4; the image 1 is also associated to the value "*fine*", with a a degree of fuzziness 0.35 using an instance of the concept *Texture*.

- An instance of *Grass* is associated to the image 2, with a degree of fuzziness 0.9; the image 2 has as *Color* an instance "*green*" with degree of fuzziness 0.8; and as *Shape* an instance, named *shape_g*1, which is linked to the concrete value "*rectangular*" with degree of fuzziness 0.7; and as *Texture* an instance linked to the concrete value "*nature*" with a degree of fuzziness 0.6.

- An instance of *Horse* is associated to the image 3, with a degree of fuzziness 0.7; the image 3 is linked to a *Color* instance which is in turn linked to the concrete data "*white*" with a degree of fuzziness 0.75 and "*gray*" with a degree of fuzziness 0.3; and to a *Shape* instance, named *shape_h*1, associated to the concrete value "*trapeze*" with a degree of fuzziness 0.9; and as *Texture* it is linked to an instance associated to the concrete data "*animal*" with a degree of fuzziness 0.8.

- An instance of *Sand* is associated to the image 4 with a degree of fuzziness 0.6; the image 4 has also as *Color* an instance associated to the concrete value "*brown*" with a degree of fuzziness 0.75; and as *Shape* an instance, named *shape_s*1, associated to the concrete data "*rectangular*",

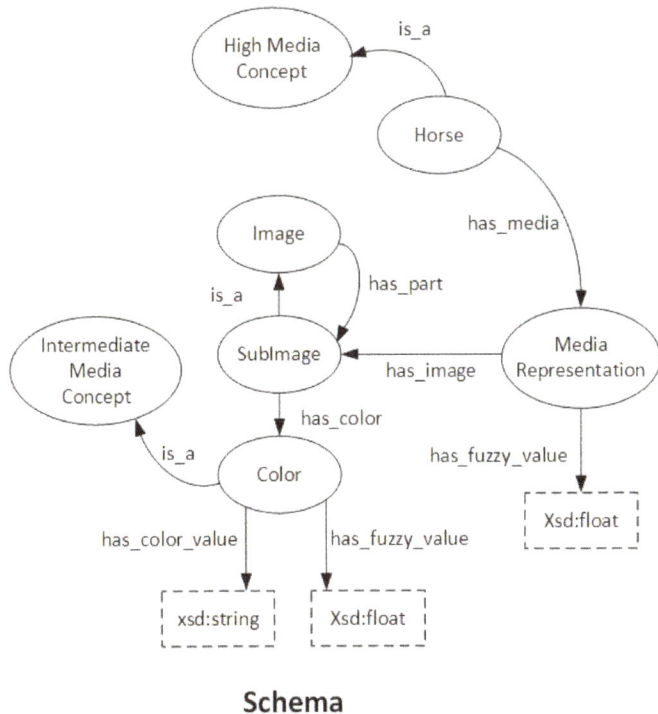

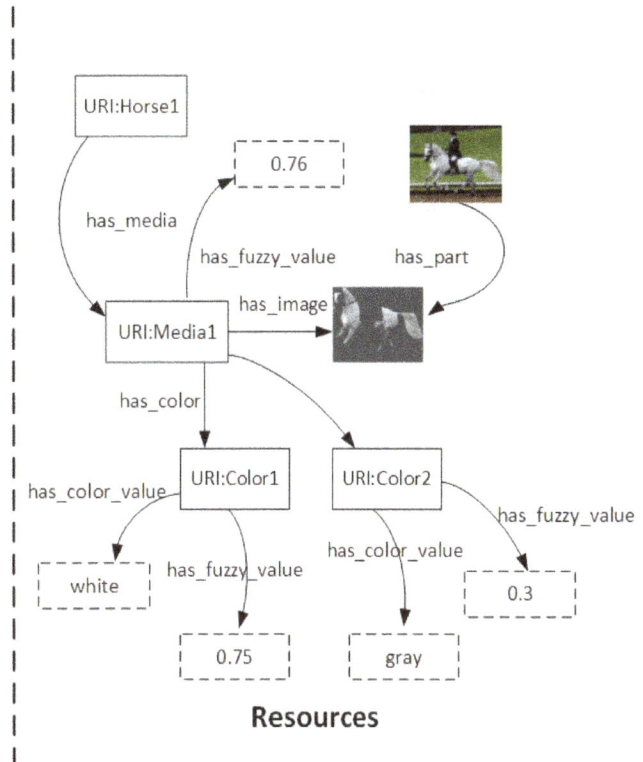

Fig. 3. A snapshot of the graph representation of our ontology-based model for the running example.

Table 4. Mapping between the concepts and resources in the schema and resource layers rispectivlty.

Schema layer	Resources layer
SubImage	
Image	
Color	URI:Color1,URI:Color2
MediaRepresentation	URI:Media1
Horse	URI:Horse1

with a degree of fuzziness 0.65; and as *Texture* an instance associated to the concrete data *"organic"* with its related degree of fuzziness 0.55.

• Now, we can also deduce from the image analysis algorithm that the image instance 4 is linked to the *Geometry* concept with a concrete data value of *"pathRegion"*. The image 1 is *on_the_top_of* the image 3, the image 3 is *on_the_top_of* of the instance 4 and the image 2 of *SubImage* is *full_intersected_with* of the image 4 of *SubImage*.

In particular, we have used in the above descriptions that an image and its sub-image are instances of our ontology, then we have represented their multimedia attributes by applying the reification pattern such as for color, texture, shape concepts. We have also used concrete domains (i.e., fined set of values) for the value domains of these attributes. The reification is also used to associate the uncertainty related to the detection, which is in the above example interpreted as fuzziness. From the above example, we also explicitly note that in our theory we have *a full integration of both data and knowledge level*. We also note that, although we have described only a few spatial relations such as *on_the_top_of*, our model is sufficiently general to implement different spatial and geometrical relations (for example, direction, orientation and so on). A description of the portion of the our ontology related to this example is described in terms of RDF/OWL graphs in Fig. 3. In particular, the mapping between the concept in the Schema layer and the instances in the Resource layer in Fig. 3 is defined in the table below.

4. Multimedia Knowledge Base: Data Models and Query Processing

In this section, we explain how the multimedia knowledge is stored according to the framework described in the previous section. We essentially have two choices: according to the first one, we may store the terminological and assertional information in an OWL file; otherwise, we can use an OWL file to describe the terminological knowledge and an object-relational data model for the assertional information. The main difference between these solutions is related to the development and performances of query processing and how the system should manage the uncertainty. Using a full OWL data model involves choosing a query language such as SPARQL[d]; instead, in the second solution, the OWL file is used only to build an intelligent query plan and a more common query language such as relational algebra is used at the leaf level of the query plan tree. At same time, if we are storing the uncertainty in the OWL/RDF file, we need to manage this information within the ontology, changing the expressivity and the reasoning procedures of the selected OWL dialect while in the second case we can apply the uncertainty only for aggregating the results coming from the different queries, for example using ranking algorithms.[11] In the first case, we could use an OWL reasoner also for the extensional level of the multimedia knowledge; this is actually the simplest way to create instances in the ontology as described above, but it is not the most scalable solution. In the second case, we can use several efficient query engines developed also to deal with fuzzy values and integrated with database indexes to enhance query performance, but the query process should involve two different languages and semantics: the ontology and of the database one. However, to satisfy the very important requirement of performance, we decided for the second option, adopting an object-relational model with its corresponding query algebra. In particular, our storage solution is provided by an NF^2 relational data model with an appropriate fuzzy algebra[12] implemented on top of an object-relation DBMS. An example of NF^2 relation related to the running example is reported in table below.

Table 5. An NF^2 relation representing color and shape features of the example.

SubImage	Color	HMConcept
1	{⟨black,0.7⟩, ⟨white,0.3⟩}	⟨person,0.58⟩
3	{⟨white,0.65 ⟩, ⟨gray,0.3⟩}	⟨horse,0.7⟩

The textual query may be a single concept or a conjunctive query written in Datalog.[13] As an example, let us consider the following DL queries that involve a general concept and some multimedia predicates:

1	$Q(x) \leftarrow Jockey(x), SQ(x)$
2	$SQ(x) \leftarrow ride(x,y), Horse(y)$ $,has\_color(y,z), z = \text{``white''}$

The query processing module builds a query plan using the knowledge expressed within our framework. The query plan is built by means of a rewriting technique[7,14] that permits to express an aggregate concept as a set of nested queries involving only high media or intermediate media concepts.

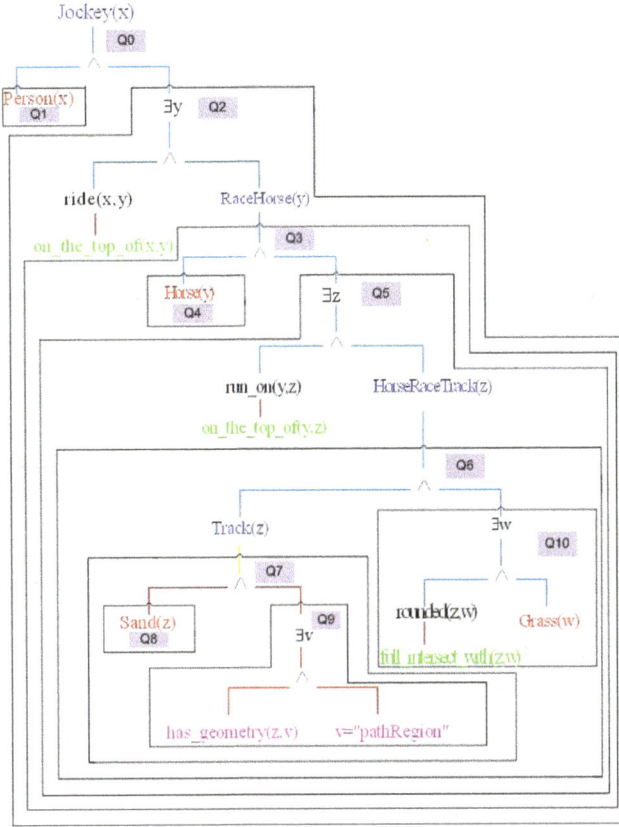

Fig. 4. (Color online) Query rewriting plan (QRP) for the concept *Jockey*, (better in color).

For example, for our running example, the query plan is described in Fig. 4, where we have depicted only the plan developed for the aggregate concept *Jockey* (Query 1), while Query 2 is translated into a simple relational join query because it does not require any decomposition of aggregate concepts and it involves only high concepts and multimedia relationships. To better understand the used technique, the nodes and edges in Fig. 4 have been given different colors: the blue edges are obtained using the domain external terminological knowledge; the red edges express the multimedia axioms and the multimedia predicate transformations of the predicates; all the aggregate concepts (depicted as blue nodes) are rewritten as sub-queries involving high media concepts (depicted as red nodes) which describes the content of the sub-image and/or intermediate media concepts (green nodes); finally, the magenta nodes refer to attributes and attribute values.

Let us consider the following set of tables used to store our annotations.

- $T1$: $\langle SubImage, Color, Geometry, C\rangle$, which is used to store the information about the sub-images extracted from the images with their multimedia relationships and the association with High Media Concepts (C).

- $T2$: $\langle Image, SubImage\rangle$, which is used to store the sub-images extracted from an image with a segmentation algorithm.
- $T3$: $\langle SubImageX, SubImageY\rangle$, which is used to store the relationships *on_the_top_of* between sub-images.
- $T4$: $\langle SubImageX, SubImageY\rangle$, which is used to store the relationships *full_intersect_with* between sub-images.

Note that table $T1$ is in NF^2 form, thus storing the fuzzy membership together with the content values; the remaining tables are just cross-relational tables. According to the query plan 4, and the above tables, we can rewrite the conceptual query plan in terms of relational expressions such that we can compute Queries 1 and 2 using a relational-based technology. The query plain depicted in 4 is described in terms of relational query as follows:

- $Q_{10} = \prod_{T1.SubImage, T1.C}(\sigma_{T1.C=\text{``grass''}}(T1))$
  $\bowtie_{T1.SubImage=T4.SubImageY}(T4))$
- $Q_9 = \prod_{T1.SubImage, T1.Geometry}(\sigma_{T1.Geometry=\text{``pathRegion''}}(T1))$
- $Q_8 = \prod_{T1.SubImage, T1.HMConcept}(\sigma_{T1.C=\text{``sand''}}(T1))$
- $Q_7 = (Q8)\bowtie_{Q8.SubImage=Q9.SubImage}(Q9)$
- $Q_6 = (Q7)\bowtie_{Q8.SubImage=Q9.SubImage}(Q10)$
- $Q_5 = (Q6)\bowtie_{Q6.SubImage=T3.SubImageY}(T3)$
- $Q_4 = \prod_{T1.SubImage, T1.C}(\sigma_{T1.C=\text{``horse''}}(T1))$
- $Q_3 = (Q4)\bowtie_{Q4.SubImage=Q5.SubImage}(Q5)$
- $Q_2 = (T3)\bowtie_{T3.SubImageY=Q3.SubImage}(Q3)$
- $Q_1 = \prod_{T1.SubImage, T1.C}(\sigma_{T1.C=\text{``person''}}(T1))$
- $Q0 = (Q1)\bowtie_{Q1.SubImage=Q2.SubImage}(Q2)$

In particular, the relational operators in the above queries can be interpreted based on a fuzzy semantic.[12] Then, in order to compute the query in 1, we need to also consider the next steps:

- $SQ = (T3)\bowtie_{T3.SubImageY=T6.SubImage}$
  $(\prod_{T1.SubImage, T6.C}(\sigma_{T1.C=\text{``horse''}\wedge T1.Color=\text{``white''}}(T1)))$
- $Q = (Q0)\bowtie_{Q0.SubImage=SQ.SubImage}(SQ)$
- $Q^* = Q\bowtie_{Q.SubImage=T2.SubImage}(T2)$

Note that all the queries $Q_0 \ldots Q_{10}$ are views and the the last query Q^* returns all the sub-Images that satisfy the previous views, together with the related images and multimedia attributes with their values and fuzziness. Then, we cross-combine the results of our views with table $T2$ in order to get the images whose sub-images are obtained by our query rewrting process. The final output ranking is obtained with a well-know Fagin algorithm.[15] Note that we can use in this query strategy the classical algebraic rules, such as push of selections, to optimize the query processing. In fact, using a unification procedure, we can push down Query 2 in the query plan tree adding a multimedia property to the high media concept *Horse*. In this way, we can exclude images during the execution of the query plan adding more selectivity to the high concept *Horse*.

5. Experiments

In order to describe the effectiveness of our approach, we have done a set of experiments. First, let us describe what kind of image processing techniques, we have used to extract the information from the images. In order to detect sub-images, we have used a graph-based segmentation algorithm with the settings suggested in the paper,[16] while for the extraction of high media concepts, we have used a Support Vector Machine classifier with RBF kernel and standard settings and as features, we have used a concatenation of color histograms and localy binary patterns.[17] For the intermediate media concepts, we have used a dictionary-based model for each concept. The final ranking is computed according to the well-known Fagin algorithm.[15] We note that we can adapt more advanced image segmentation and classification algorithms for our analysis, but the main goal of this work is to show how we can use the information coming from a computer vision system rather than increase the accuracy of the image processing algorithm, so we decide to use an analysis based on a very standard image-processing pipeline. We use a small database of about 800 images, 400 coming from a subset of the standard corel database (lite version) and 400 coming from google image engine. We have chosen those images that take into account one or a combination of the following high media concepts: sky, water, sun, savannah, grass, elephant, horse, sand and person. We have also developed a general domain ontology containing the previous concepts together with an additional 11 aggregate concepts (such as Track, Jockey, Racehorse, Horse-race-track, African-Elephant, Asian-Elephant, Island, Beach, SunSet, African-SunSet) and 20 axioms among those aggregate concepts. We have subdivided these images as follows: 100 images containing horse and/or grass and/or sky and/or sun and/or sand and/or person, 100 images containing sky and/or sun and/or person and/or water, 300 images containing horse and/or grass and/or sky and/or sand and/or savannah, 300 images containing elephant and/or grass and/or sky, and/or water and/or savanna and/or sun. About 40% of those images have been used to train the classifier. We have manually labeled an optimal ranking for five images belonging to the concepts Horse-race-track, and two images belonging to the African-Elephant. In the following table, we have reported the average results in terms of average precision:

Aggregate concepts	Top-5	Top-10	Top-15
Horse-race-track	92%	95%	98%
African-Elephant	87%	90%	92%

6. Related Works

In the last few years, several papers have been presented about multimedia systems based on knowledge models, image ontologies, fuzzy extension of ontology theories.[2,18–20] In almost all the previous works, multimedia ontologies are effectively used to perform *semantic annotation* of the media content by manually associating the terms of the ontology with the individual elements of the image or of the video,[21,22] thus demonstrating that the use of ontologies can enhance classification precision and image retrieval performance. Differently from us, they suppose that the images are annotated with metadata format and they do not address how the media knowledge are integrated with a general one. Other kinds of systems in literature use an initial label on the image combining classic vision-based techniques with the Natural Language Processing methodologies to derive more accurate knowledge.[23] These systems infer new kind of annotation looking at the text of the images that have similar visual content, but the humans annotated in a different way. Further interesting papers are Refs. 24, 25 and 26. All of them have the same purpose and they define DL framework to multimedia data following different approaches. Differently from the previous works, in both research fields, we propose a formal definition of multimedia ontology, particularly suitable for capturing the complex semantics of images during several steps of the image analysis process. We do not propose any extension of the usual ontology theory and languages, but manage uncertainty implementing ternary properties by means of a reification process, thus taking advantages of the several existing reasoning systems and using a optimized solution to store the extensional level. MPG7 has proposed an instrument to improve the current multimedia representation and applications, but is not currently suitable for describing the semantic about the top-level multimedia features. Some interesting works was done in order to define a multimedia ontology linked to this format.[27]

7. Conclusions

In this paper, we have described a semantic multimedia knowledge framework with the purpose to make a full integration between a general domain and media knowledge. Preliminary Experiments have demonstrated that the proposed approach achieves good performance. Future works will be devoted to apply this framework on domain applications where the semantic of the query is by far different from the results obtained by the computer vision system such as in the medical domain.

Acknowledgments

I would like to show my gratitude to Prof. Antonio Picariello and Prof. Letizia Tanca who provided insight and expertise that greatly assisted this research and for the comments that greatly improved this paper. This research was done before joining UTRC-I.

References

[1] O. Russakovsky, J. Deng, H. Su, J. Krause, S. Satheesh, S. Ma, Z. Huang, A. Karpathy, A. Khosla, M. Bernstein, A. C. Berg and Li Fei-Fei, ImageNet Large Scale Visual Recognition Challenge, in *Int. J. Comput. Vis.* **115**(3), 211 (2015).

[2] S. Umberto, *Foundations of Fuzzy Logic and Semantic Web Languages* (Chapman & Hall/CRC, 2013).

[3] T. Lukasiewicz, Probabilistic description logic programs, *Int. J. Approx. Reason.* **45**(2), 288 (2007).

[4] T. Lukasiewicz and U. Straccia, Description logic programs under probabilistic uncertainty and fuzzy vagueness, *Int. J. Approx. Reason.* **50**(6), 837 (2009).

[5] I. Biederman, Recognition-by-components: A theory of human image understanding, *Psycholol. Rev.* **94**(2), 115 (1987).

[6] J. F. Sowa, *Knowledge Representation: Logical, Philosophical, and Computational Foundations* (Brooks Cole Publishing Co., 2000).

[7] A. Penta, Multimedia Knoledge Management using ontology, Phd Thesis, University of Naples Federico II, Department of Computer Science (2008).

[8] A. Penta, A. Picariello and L. Tanca, Multimedia knowledge management using ontologies, *Proc. 2nd ACM Workshop on Multimedia semantics*, ACM (2008), pp. 24–31.

[9] S. Ceri, G. Gottlob and L. Tanca, *Logic Programming and Databases* (Springer-Verlag, New York, 1990).

[10] F. J. Estrada and A. D. Jepson, Benchmarking Image Segmentation Algorithms, *Int. J. Comput. Vis.* **85**(2), 167 (2009).

[11] L. Yiping, J. Chen and L. Feng, Dealing with uncertainty: A survey of theories and practices, *IEEE Trans. Knowl. Data Eng.* **25**(11), 2463 (2013).

[12] A. Chianese, A. Picariello, L. Sansone and M. L. Sapino, Managing uncertainties in image databases: A fuzzy approach, *J. Multimedia Tools Appl.* **23**(3), 237 (2004).

[13] S. Abiteboul, R. Hull and V. Vianu, *Foundations of Databases: The Logical Level*, (Addison-Wesley, Longman, 1995).

[14] D. Calvanese, G. De Giacomo, D. Lembo, M. Lenzerini and R. Rosati, *Data Complexity of Query Answering in Description Logics, Artif. Intell.* **195**, 335 (2013).

[15] R. Fagin, Combining Fuzzy information from multiple systems, *J. Comput. Syst. Sci.* **58**(1), 83 (1999).

[16] J. Shi and J. Malik, Normalized cuts and image segmentation, *IEEE Trans. Pattern Anal. Mach. Intell.* **22**(8), 888 (2000).

[17] R. C. Gonzalez and R. E. Woods, *Digital Image Processing* (Prentice-Hall, Inc., USA, 2008).

[18] J. Deng, K. Li, M. Do, H. Su and L. Fei-Fei, Construction and analysis of a large scale image ontology, *Vision Sciences Society (VSS)* (2009).

[19] M. Naphade, J. R. Smith, J. Tesic, S.-F. Chang, W. Hsu, L. Kennedy, A. Hauptmann and J. Curtis, Large-scale concept ontology for multimedia, *J. IEEE MultiMed.* **13**(3), 86 (2006).

[20] T. Raphael, B. Huet and S. Schenk, *Multimedia Semantics: Metadata, Analysis and Interaction* (John Wiley & Sons, 2011).

[21] K. Petridis *et al.*, Knowledge representation and semantic annotation of multimedia contentvision, *IEEE Proc. Image Signal Process.* **153**, 255 (2006).

[22] G. Stamou *et al.*, Multimedia annotations on the semantic web, *IEEE Multimed.* **13**, 86 (2006).

[23] J. Z. Wang and J. Li, Real-time computerized annotation of pictures, *IEEE Trans. PAMI* **30**, 985 (2008).

[24] B. Neumann and R. Maller, Ontology-based reasoning techniques for multimedia interpretation and retrieval, *Semantic Multimedia and Ontologies* (Springer, 2008), pp. 55–98.

[25] H. Wang *et al.*, Image retrieval with a multi-modality ontology, in *Multimedia System*, Vol. 13 (Springer, 2007).

[26] N. Simou *et al.*, Multimedia reasoning with f-shin, *2nd Int. Work. on SMAP* (2007).

[27] S. Figueroa, M. Carmen, G. A. Atemezing and O. Corcho, The landscape of multimedia ontologies in the last decade, *J. Multimed. Tools Appl.* **62**(2), 377 (2013).

[28] S. Manjunathan *et al.* Cortina: Searching a 10 milion + images database, Technicak Report, VRL, ECE, University of California (2007).

[29] R. Fagin, Fuzzy queries in multimedia database systems, in *PODS* (ACM Press, 1998), pp. 1–10.

[30] U. Straccia, A fuzzy description logic for the semantic web, in *Capturing Intelligence: Fuzzy Logic and the Semantic Web*, ed. Elie Sanchez (Elsevier, 2006).

[31] V. S. Subrahmanian, *Principles of Multimedia Database Systems* (Morgan Kaufmann, 1998).

Use of semantics in robotics — improving doctors' performance using a cricothyrotomy simulator

Daniela D'Auria[*,‡] and Fabio Persia[†,§]

*Department of Electrical Engineering and Information Technology
University of Naples, Federico II
Via Claudio 21, Naples, 80125, Italy
†Faculty of Computer Science, Free University of Bozen-Bolzano
Piazza Domenicani 3 Bozen-Bolzano, 39100, Italy
‡daniela.dauria4@unina.it
§fabio.persia@unibz.it

In the last years, the use of robotics and semantics in medical context has become more and more essential to improve medical doctors' performance. In this work, we present a framework which exploits reasoning and semantic techniques to assist medical doctors during the cricothyrotomy — a well-known life-saving procedure. More specifically, it first acquires data in real-time from a cricothyrotomy simulator, when used by medical doctors, then it stores the acquired data into a scientific database and finally it exploits an *Activity Detection Engine* for finding expected activities, in order to evaluate the medical doctors' performance in real-time, that is very essential for this kind of applications. In fact, an incorrect use of the simulator promptly detected can save the patient's life.

Keywords: Semantics in robotics; medical simulator; cricothyrotomy simulator; activity detection.

1. Problem Description

Robotic surgery, computer-assisted surgery, and robotically-assisted surgery are terms for technological developments that use robotic systems to aid in surgical procedures. Robotically-assisted surgery was developed to overcome the limitations of minimally-invasive surgery and to enhance the capabilities of surgeons performing open surgery.

In the case of robotically-assisted minimally-invasive surgery, instead of directly moving the instruments, the surgeon uses one of the five methods to control the instruments; either a direct telemanipulator or through computer control. A telemanipulator is a remote manipulator that allows the surgeon to perform the normal movements associated with the surgery whilst the robotic arms carry out those movements using end-effectors and manipulators to perform the actual surgery on the patient. In computer-controlled systems, the surgeon uses a computer to control the robotic arms and its end-effectors, though these systems can also still use tele-manipulators for their input. One advantage of using the computerized method is that the surgeon does not have to be present, but can be anywhere in the world, leading to the possibility for remote surgery.

In the case of enhanced open surgery, autonomous instruments (in familiar configurations) replace traditional steel tools, performing certain actions (such as rib spreading) with much smoother, feedback-controlled motions than could be achieved by a human hand. The main object of such smart instruments is to reduce or eliminate the tissue trauma traditionally associated with open surgery without requiring more than a few minutes' training on the part of surgeons. This approach seeks to improve open surgeries, particularly cardiothoracic, that have so far not benefited from minimally-invasive techniques.

Thus, it turns out that in the last years, the use of robotics and semantics in medical context has become more and more essential to improve medical doctors' performance. For instance, some *reasoning* techniques are more and more often applied in order to assist medical doctors in real-time during surgical operations. *Reasoning techniques* are very essential in many application domains, such as video surveillance, cyber security, fault detection, fraud detection and in clinical domain, as well. In all cases, *temporal information* is crucial. For instance, for what the clinical research concerns, investigating disease progression is practical only by definition of a time line; otherwise, possible causes of a clinical condition have to be found by referring to a patient's past clinical history. In Ref. 1, the basic concepts of temporal representation in medical domain have been described in order to include: category of time (natural, conventional, logical), structure of time (line, branch, circular, parallel), instant of time versus interval, and, absolute time versus relative time. Anyway, this is still a challenging and active subject of research. The main goal of Ref. 2 consists in creating a special purpose query language for clinical data analytics (ClinIDAL) to place in any clinical information system (CIS) and answer any answerable question from the CIS. More specifically, a category scheme of five classes of increasing complexity, including point-of-care retrieval queries, descriptive statistics, statistical hypothesis testing, complex hypotheses of scientific studies and semantic record retrieval have been designed to capture the scope encompassed by CliniDAL's objectives.[3] However, a review of temporal query languages reflects that the importance of time has led to the development of custom temporal management solutions, which are mostly built to extend relational database systems (for instance, T4SQL[4]). Many efforts in the relational database field have been conducted for developing expressive temporal query languages; nevertheless, they still suffer from two issues: firstly, they are only applicable to structural relational databases; secondly, it is difficult for hospital staff with poor IT skills to apply them. On the other hand, in most ontology-based approaches, composing queries can be difficult due to a complex underlying model representation and lack of expressivity.

In other contexts, such as video surveillance, cyber security and fault detection, the reasoning techniques using temporal information are broadly used for *activity detection*. Thus, several researchers have studied how to search for specifically defined patterns of normal/abnormal activities.[5] Vaswani *et al.*[6] study how HMMs can be used to recognize complex activities, while Brand *et al.*[7] and Oliver *et al.*[8] use coupled HMMs. Albanese *et al.*[9] developed a stochastic automaton-based language to detect activities in video, while Cuntoor *et al.*[10] presented an HMM-based algorithm. In contrast,[11,12] start with a set A of *activity models* (corresponding to innocuous/dangerous activities) and find observation sequences that are not sufficiently explained by the models in A. Such unexplained sequences reflect activity occurrences that differ from the application's expectations.

In this work, we present a framework designed and developed for activity detection in the medical context. The context of use is very concrete and relevant in the robotic surgery research area, as it is represented by a *cricothyrotomy simulator* built by the BioRobotics Laboratory of the University of Washington, Seattle (USA).[13–15] Such a simulator is very useful for helping both patients and medical doctors when a cricothyrotomy procedure is performed. Our main aim consists in making the medical doctors able to get a real-time feedback about their performance when using the simulator, that is very essential for this kind of applications. Moreover, this real-time feedback can even save the patient's life, as in this way, a serious error of the medical doctor during the procedure could be fixed by an immediate recovery procedure.

The remainder of the paper is organized as follows. Section 2 describes the context of use of our prototype architecture, which is the *cricothyrotomy simulator* designed by the University of Washington, Seattle, while Sec. 3 describes the architecture of the overall framework. Section 4 shows a simplified case study demonstrating the usefulness of the proposed framework. Eventually, Sec. 5 discusses some conclusions and future work.

2. Context of Use: A Cricothyrotomy Simulator

Modern airway protocols involve many techniques to restore ventilation including bag-mask-ventilation, placement of a laryngeal mask airway, and intubation with or without videolaryngoscope. In cases, where conservative measures fail or when contraindicated, the only methods remaining to re-establish ventilation may be surgical. In the developing world, where devices such as the videolaryngoscope may not be available, accurate knowledge and training in the creation of a surgical airway may have a significant impact on patient outcomes.

A *cricothyrotomy* is a life-saving procedure performed when an airway cannot be established through less invasive techniques: although performing such a procedure seems relatively straightforward, studies have shown that those performed in the pre-hospital setting were mostly unsuccessful.[16] A review of 54 emergency cricothyrotomies found that the majority of the procedures performed in the field were unsuccessful or resulted in complications.[17] A military team identified gap areas in the training of cricothyrotomy in emergency situations; these included lack of anatomical knowledge including *hands on* palpation exercises, poor anatomy in medical mannequins, and nonstandard techniques.[18]

Most of the unsuccessful attempts were due to inaccurate placement, and incorrectly identifying anatomy. If the anatomy is not properly identified, it is unlikely that the procedure will be successful. Further, a large review of emergency airway cases found that emergency cricothyrotomies performed by anesthesiologists were successful in only 36% of instances.[19] Although many reports suggest that the success rate of surgical airway placement is low, publications from advanced centers with extensive training for airway protocols including simulation show that pre-hospital cricothyrotomy success rates can be as high as 91%.[20] Studies such as this suggest that with adequate training, the success rate of cricothyrotomy can be dramatically improved. Thus, an improved method of training needs to be provided for this rare, but life-saving procedure.

For such reasons, the BioRobotics Laboratory of the University of Washington, Seattle (USA) developed a low-cost cricothyrotomy simulator[13–15] from readily available components that is equipped with inexpensive sensors. The simulator emphasizes the palpation and the correct identification of anterior cervical anatomy and has the ability to record in real time the contact location of instruments on the trachea model during the full duration of the simulated procedure.

3. The Proposed Implementation

For the reasons listed in the previous sections, we have the necessity to integrate semantic and reasoning techniques into the cricothyrotomy simulator described in Sec. 2. Thus, the overall structure of the system is based on a modular architecture, as shown in Fig. 1, which allows the medical doctors to get a real-time feedback about their performance when using the simulator.

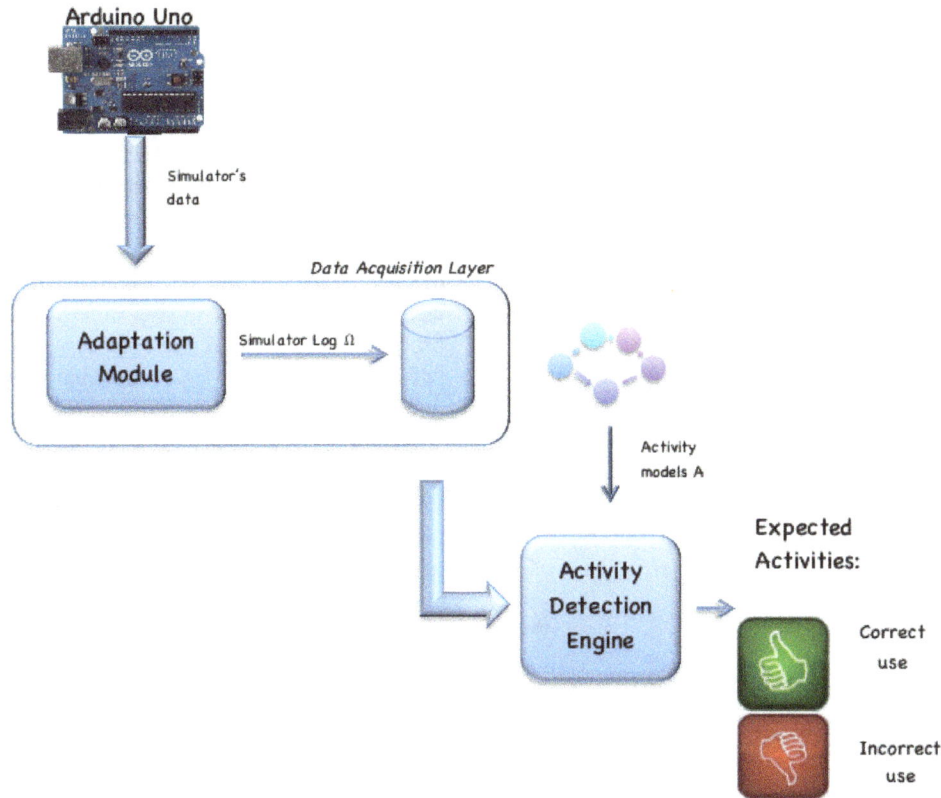

Fig. 1. System architecture.

The following sections describe the single components of the overall system architecture.

3.1. *The Arduino microcontroller board*

The *Arduino microcontroller board* allows us to capture in real-time the contact data of the instruments (scalpel, tracheal hook, and hemostat) from six different landmarks of the simulator. In such a way, this component records the series of time-stamped events, corresponding to the medical doctors' interactions with the simulator. More specifically, events are defined as the start and end times of contacts between specific instruments and surfaces on the anatomical model. Other types of events are defined in terms of readings from different sensor types. Thus, events are represented by a series of symbols (ASCII characters).

Data is encoded attaining to the semantics listed in the following:

- The first single digit number indicates the instrument (1 means *Scalpel*, 2 *Hemostat* and 3 *Tracheal Hook*).
- The (second) character indicates which foil patch is touched: upper-case for making contact and lower-case for breaking contact. More specifically, A means *Posterior tracheal wall*, B the *Right lateral trachea and cricothyroid membrane*, C the *Midline cricothyroid membrane*

(correct placement of incision), D the *Left lateral trachea and cricothyroid membrane*, E the *Cricoid cartilage* and F the *Cartilaginous ring of lower tracheal wall*.
- The last number is the time in milliseconds.

Then, the data captured in this way represents the input of the *Data Acquisition* component.

3.2. *The data acquisition component*

The *Data Acquisition* component includes an *Adaptation Module* that converts the data captured using the *Arduino* in a format suitable to the *Activity Detection Engine* (i.e., the *Simulator Log*): it also saves them into a scientific database, which is also able to store personal information about the medical doctors who are using the simulator.

3.3. *The activity detection engine*

The *Activity Detection Engine* takes as inputs time-stamped user data collected in the *Simulator Log* and a set of activity models representing our *knowledge base* to find the activity occurrences matching such models. These models have been previously defined by domain experts who have classified them in two different categories: the *good activities*, corresponding to a correct use of the simulator and the *bad*

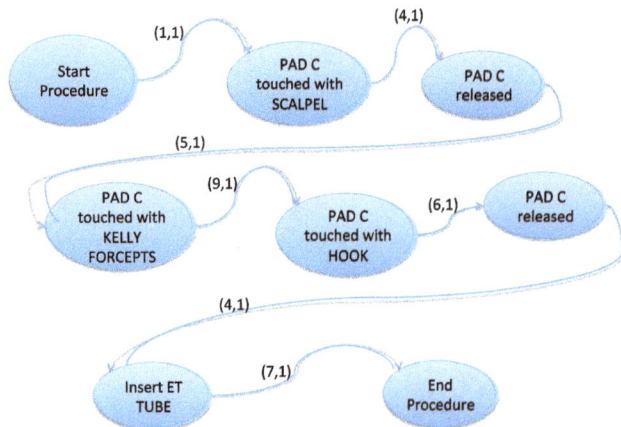

Fig. 2. Model of an excellent performance.

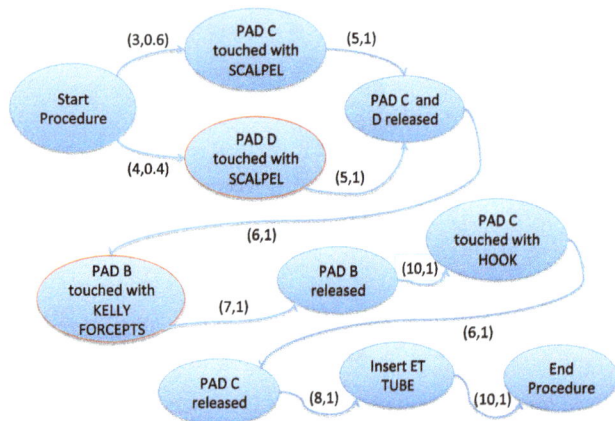

Fig. 3. Model of a bad performance.

activities, corresponding to an incorrect use of the simulator. Figures 2 and 3 show two model examples of a *good activity* (Fig. 2), corresponding to an excellent performance of the medical doctor and a *bad activity* (Fig. 3), corresponding to a very bad performance. Take into account that the two values on each edge (Figs. 2 and 3) respectively represent an upper bound of time that can elapse between the two connected nodes and a function that associates a probability distribution with the outgoing edges of each node.

Expected activity occurrences in a data stream are efficiently detected using *tMAGIC*,[21] which allows to solve the problem of finding occurrences of high-level activity model in an observed data stream. As a matter of fact, they propose a data structure called *temporal multiactivity graph* to store multiple activities that need to be concurrently monitored, corresponding to our knowledge base of *good* and *bad* activities. They, then define an index called *Temporal Multiactivity Graph Index Creation (tMAGIC)* that, based on this data structure, examines and links observations as they occur. Finally, they define an algorithm to

solve the *evidence problem* that tries to find all occurrences of an activity (with probability over a threshold) within a given sequence of observations.

The procedure for the identification of the *Expected Activities* follows an *event-driven approach*, as it is automatically invoked every time that a new action symbol is captured by the *Arduino microcontroller board*: in this way, if the *Activity Detection Engine* discovers a *bad activity* when the procedure has not been completed yet, it generates an alert inducing the medical doctor to immediately stop his procedure and to start the recovery process for saving the patient's life. In this way, we are able to evaluate the medical doctors' performances while using the simulator both during and after the procedure. Obviously, the *bad performances* identified during the procedure are definitely more dangerous than the ones detected after the procedure: in fact, the former ones could even cause the death of the patient and thus need to be stopped, while the latter ones are mostly slow or inaccurate procedures.

4. A Case Study

In order to better clarify what is the main goal of this work and our vision of *expected activities*, in what follows we will briefly describe a simple and usual example from a real case study. Let us informally consider an *expected activity* as an ordered sequence of actions describing the interactions of a medical doctor with the simulator. An example of such a sequence in a simulator log could be: ⟨Start Procedure, Pad C touched with SCALPEL, Pad C touched with KELLY FORCEPS, Pad C touched with HOOK, Pad C released, Pad B touched with KELLY FORCEPS, End Procedure⟩ (see Fig. 4). For the sake of simplicity, let us consider the graph in Fig. 5 as the only model representing our knowledge base, corresponding to an incorrect use of the simulator. In this example, we are overlooking the temporal constraints

Fig. 4. Example of log sequence.

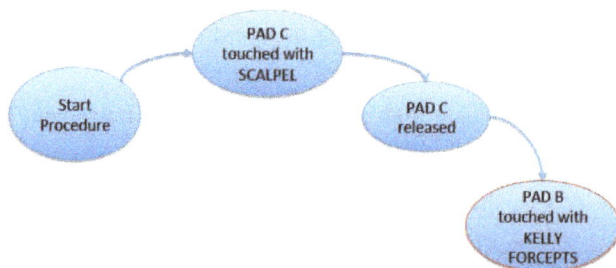

Fig. 5. Model of an expected (bad) activity.

fixed between an action and the following one within the activity model and also the transition probabilities specified on each edge.

At this point, we have to recall that the procedure for discovering expected activities follows an *event-driven* approach and is thus invoked every time that a new action is recorded by our system. In this example, the procedure is called for the first time when the *Start Procedure* action is detected — no occurrences of the only activity model is discovered — for the second time when the *Pad C touched with SCALPEL* action is detected — no occurrences found again — and so on. Then, when the *Pad B touched with KELLY FORCEPS* action is recorded, if all temporal constraints (that we are overlooking in this example) are satisfied, an occurrence of the expected activity model is found, then an alert is generated thus stopping the procedure, in order to immediately start an appropriate recovery process. This is a classic example of how important the acquisition of a real-time feedback from the simulator is: an incorrect use promptly detected can save the patient's life.

5. Conclusion and Future Work

This work presented a framework which exploits reasoning and semantic techniques to assist medical doctors during the cricothyrotomy, that is a well-known life-saving procedure. More specifically, it starts acquiring data from a *cricothyrotomy simulator*, when used by medical doctors and then it stores the captured data into a *scientific database*. Finally, it exploits some stable activity detection algorithms for discovering expected activities, corresponding to specific performances obtained by the medical doctors when using the simulator, that can be detected both during and after the procedure. Some experiments showed encouraging results concerning *efficiency*, *effectiveness* and *user satisfaction*.

Future work will be devoted to enlarge the experimentation and to plan to integrate the prototype in more complex and thorny applications by adding new functionalities and, if necessary, additional layers to the overall system architecture. For example, a potential application of this tool could consist in detecting potential safety hazard *in advance*, for instance, using machine learning techniques and observations learned during the training of medical personnel, or even in suggesting the correct recovery process to apply when a bad activity is discovered during the procedure. Moreover, data mining techniques could be used in an offline setting to analyze in detail the medical doctors' performance.

References

[1] L. Zhou and G. Hripcsak, Temporal reasoning with medical data — a review with emphasis on medical natural language processing, *J. Biomed. Inf.* **40**, 183–203 (2007).

[2] L. Safari and J. D. Patrick, A temporal model for clinical data analytics language, in *35th Annual Int. Conf. IEEE, Engineering in Medicine and Biology Society (EMBC)*, (2013), pp. 3218–3221.

[3] J. D. Patrick, L. Safari and Y. Cheng, Knowledge discovery and knowledge reuse in clinical information systems, in *Proc. 10th IASTED Int. Conf. Biomedical Engineering (BioMed 2013)*, Innsbruck, Austria (2013).

[4] C. Combi, A. Montanari and G. Pozzi, The t4sql temporal query language, *Sixteenth ACM Conf. Information and Knowledge Management, ACM*, Lisbon, Portugal, (2007), pp. 193–202.

[5] S. Hongeng and R. Nevatia, Multi-agent event recognition, *Proc. Int. Conf. Computer Vision (ICCV)*, (2001), pp. 84–93.

[6] N. Vaswani, A. K. R. Chowdhury and R. Chellappa, Shape activity: A continuous-state HMM for moving/deforming shapes with application to abnormal activity detection, *IEEE Trans. Image Process.* **14**(10) 1603 (2005).

[7] M. Brand, N. Oliver and A. Pentland, Coupled hidden Markov models for complex action recognition, *Proc. IEEECS Conf. Computer Vision and Pattern Recognition (CVPR)*, (1997), pp. 994–999.

[8] N. Oliver, E. Horvitz and A. Garg, Layered representations for human activity recognition, *Proc. IEEE Fourth Int. Conf. Multimodal Interfaces (ICMI)*, (2002), pp. 3–8.

[9] M. Albanese, V. Moscato, A. Picariello, V. S. Subrahmanian and O. Udrea, Detecting stochastically scheduled activities in video, *Proc. 20th Int. Joint Conf. Artificial Intelligence*, (2007), pp. 1802–1807.

[10] N. P. Cuntoor, B. Yegnanarayana and R. Chellappa, Activity modeling using event probability sequences, *IEEE Trans. Image Process.* **17**(4) 594 (2008).

[11] M. Albanese, C. Molinaro, F. Persia, A. Picariello and V. S. Subrahmanian, Discovering the Top-k unexplained sequences in time-stamped observation data, *IEEE Trans. Knowl. Data Eng.* **26**(3) 577 (2014).

[12] M. Albanese, C. Molinaro, F. Persia, A. Picariello and V. S. Subrahmanian, Finding unexplained activities in video, *Int. Joint Conf. Artificial Intelligence (IJCAI)*, (2011), pp. 1628–1634.

[13] L. White, R. Bly, D. D'Auria, N. Aghdasi, P. Bartell, L. Cheng and B. Hannaford, Cricothyrotomy simulator with computational skill assessment for procedural skill training in the developing world, *J. Otolaryngol. — Head and Neck Surg.* in press (2014).

[14] L. White, R. Bly, D. D'Auria, N. Aghdasi, P. Bartell, L. Cheng and B. Hannaford, Cricothyrotomy simulator with computational skill assessment for procedural skill training in the developing world, *AAO-HNSF Annual Meeting and OTO Expo*, Vancouver, BC (2013).

[15] L. White, D. D'Auria, R. Bly, P. Bartell, N. Aghdasi, C. Jones, B. Hannaford, Cricothyrotomy simulator training for the developing word, *2012 IEEE Global Humanitarian Technology*, Seattle, WA, (2012).

[16] H. Wang, N. Mann, G. Mears, K. Jacobson and D. Yealy, Out-of-hospital airway management in the united states, *Resuscitation* **82**(4), 378–385 (2011).

[17] D. King, M. Ogilvie, M. Michailidou, G. Velmahos, H. Alam, M. deMoya and K. Fikry, Fifty-four emergent cricothyroidotomies: Are surgeons reluctant teachers? *Scand. J. Surg.* **101**(1), 13 (2012).

[18] B. Bennett, B. Cailteux-Zevallos and J. Kotora, Cricothyroidotomy bottom-up training review: Battlefield lessons learned, *Mil. Med.* **176**(11), 1311 (2011).

[19] T. Cook, N. Woodall and C. Frerk, Major complications of airway management in the uk: Results of the fourth national audit project of

the royal college of anaesthetists and the difficult airway society. Part 1: Anaesthesia, Fourth National Audit Project **106**(5), 61731 (2011).

20. K. Warner, S. Sharar, M. Copass and E. Bulger, Prehospital management of the difficult airway: A prospective cohort study, *J. Emerg. Med.* **36**(3), 257 (2009).

21. M. Albanese, A. Pugliese and V. S. Subrahmanian, Fast activity detection: Indexing for temporal stochastic automaton based activity models, *IEEE Trans. Knowl. Data Eng.* **25**(2) 360 (2013).

22. R. T. Snodgrass, *The TSQL2 Temporal Query Language*, Vol. 330 (Springer, 1995).

23. J. Tappolet and A. Bernstein, Applied temporal RDF: Efficient temporal querying of RDF data with SPARQL, *The Semantic Web: Research and Applications* (2009), pp. 308–322.

24. M. J. O'Connor and A. Das, SQWRL: A Query language for OWL, *Proc. 6th OWL: Experiences and Directions Workshop (OWLED2009)* (2009).

25. C. Tao, W. Q. Wei, H. R. Solbrig, G. Savova and C. G. Chute, CNTRO: A semantic web ontology for temporal relation inferencing in clinical narratives, *Proc. AMIA Annual Symp. Proc. American Medical Informatics Association* (2010), pp. 787–792.

26. L. Zhou, C. Friedman, S. Parsons and G. Hripcsak, System architecture for temporal information extraction, representation and reasoning in clinical narrative reports, *Proc. AMIA Annual Symp. Proc., American Medical Informatics Association* (2005), pp. 869–873.

27. J. Hsiao and V. Pacheco-Fowler, Cricothyrotomy, *N. Engl. J. Med.* **358**, e25 (2008), doi: 10.1056/NEJMvcm0706755, http://www.nejm.org/doi/full/10.1056/NEJMvcm0706755.

28. BioRobotics Laboratory, University of Washington, Seattle, Global Simulation Training in Healthcare, http://brl.ee.washington.edu/laboratory/node/2768.

29. V. Moscato, A. Picariello, F. Persia and A. Penta, A system for automatic image categorization *3rd Int. Conf. Semantic Computing (ICSC'09)*, (IEEE, 2009), pp. 624–629.

30. V. Moscato, F. Persia, A. Picariello and A. Penta, Iwin: A summarizer system based on a semantic analysis of web documents in *6th Int. Conf. on Semantic Computing (ICSC'12)*, (IEEE, 2012), pp. 162–169.

Semantic localization

Shang Ma[*,‡] and Qiong Liu[†]

*Department of EECS, University of California Irvine,
Irvine, California 92612, USA*

and

[†]*FX Palo Alto Laboratory, Palo Alto, California 94304, USA*
[‡]shangm@uci.edu

Improvements in sensor and wireless network enable accurate, automated, instant determination and dissemination of a user's or objects position. The new enabler of location-based services (LBSs) apart from the current ubiquitous networking infrastructure is the enrichment of the different systems with semantics information, such as time, location, individual capability, preference and more. Such semantically enriched system-modeling aims at developing applications with enhanced functionality and advanced reasoning capabilities. These systems are able to deliver more personalized services to users by domain knowledge with advanced reasoning mechanisms, and provide solutions to problems that were otherwise infeasible. This approach also takes user's preference and place property into consideration that can be utilized to achieve a comprehensive range of personalized services, such as advertising, recommendations, or polling. This paper provides an overview of indoor localization technologies, popular models for extracting semantics from location data, approaches for associating semantic information and location data, and applications that may be enabled with location semantics. To make the presentation easy to understand, we will use a museum scenario to explain pros and cons of different technologies and models. More specifically, we will first explore users' needs in a museum scenario. Based on these needs, we will then discuss advantages and disadvantages of using different localization technologies to meet these needs. From these discussions, we can highlight gaps between real application requirements and existing technologies, and point out promising localization research directions. By identifying gaps between various models and real application requirements, we can draw a roadmap for future location semantics research.

Keywords: Location semantics; indoor localization; user model.

1. Introduction

With the rapid technology advances on mobile networks and radio communication, individual's demand to be "always connected" continuously increases. This revolution facilitates the vision for ubiquitous services, which aid users in their every-day life activities in an intelligent and unobtrusive way no matter the place or time. And this results in the location-dependent information access paradigm, known as location-based services (LBSs).

In LBS, applications persistently keep track of user's location in an unobtrusive manner and proactively offer them potentially useful information and services. The delivery of personalize services is built on three main pillars: continuous background position tracking, analysis of varieties of context information which should be related to users at this particular location, and user's personal preference. It is necessary for our applications to have not only accurate location information at this particular time but also more semantic information which may or may not derived from the location data to provide more reasonable services.

A museum scenario we will use throughout this study is an ideal environment which reveals an everyday yet complex interaction situation.[1] The factors within museum experiences can be cultural, historical, psychological, and social. From these studies, we learn that visitor's experience in a tour of a

museum cannot be assessed by a single factor. It can be influenced by previous knowledge of the visitor, visitor's leaning style, and the dynamics of other people around, such as friends, family, and even strangers. Of course, the way the artifacts and works are present can affect visitor's experience, which are determined by exhibition design, architecture, and institution history. Last but not the least, the time of day, stay-duration, room temperature and so on may all have an impact. Apparently, what visitor experience during a tour should not be universal, but adaptive based on user model, their location and interaction history. Assume that you plan to spend some time in the San Francisco Museum of Modern Art. Before starting your explorations, you launch an application on your mobile phone which is provided by the museum and ask for the recommendations. The application tells you that the most famous work in this museum is *Ocean Park #54* by *Richard Diebenkorn*. However, currently there are too many people standing right in front of it and it is very likely for you not to be able to enjoy the paintings at a good angle. So the application suggests that you can alternatively go check out the section of *Six Self-Portraits* by *Andy Warhol* first, which is also a popular place based on historical visiting data and you seem interested to them as well according to your preference. Besides this, it also shows the path from your current position to that section on your mobile screen. And once you get to the section, the application can also talk to you about the history and other information of each artwork.

In the next section, we will provide several typical scenarios of how semantics-enhanced indoor localization systems can be used in a way to provide seamless services. From these scenarios, we should be able to obtain what kinds of location semantics are most useful in indoor environment beyond spatial coordinates, and how they can be obtained from users' location data. In Sec. 3, related indoor positioning methods are surveyed, from which we can see why they are not sufficient for providing more personalized services. Following that, Sec. 4 then focuses specifically on user modeling with location semantics. We then conclude with future issues and research direction in Secs. 5 and 6.

2. Usage Scenarios of Indoor Location Data

Traditionally, a museum visit is limited to audio guides and interactive kiosks. While in fact, a museum experience can be social, cultural, and historical and visitors might have abundant information to deal with when they visit a museum. User's experience in a museum could be influenced by visitor's previous knowledge, the presence of the artifacts and collections, as well as the dynamics in the environment around them including friends, family, and strangers. Other factors such as the time of the day, room temperature, and duration of visit may all have an impact how visitors enjoy their visit.

In response to these issues, location semantics, by taking into account user's location, visit history, user's preference, as well as environmental dynamics, intends to predict user's behavior and make recommendation to them. In the setting of a museum, visitors will spend less time finding out which collections are desirable, thereby being able to go directly to the place of certain items they are looking for. Additionally, determining what information a visitor is trying to pull from an exhibit can be modeled by determining relationships between artifacts. If visitors examine multiple items in a certain period of time, we can use the information overlap to determine what information the visitors are trying to pull from the exhibit. This overlap can then be used to find collections with similar content and those collections will be recommended to visitors.

In this section, we create a number of use cases on how people interact with the context and other people, from which we intend to find the nature of context information and determine the design requirements for our context model and user model.

Number of people: Consider the following scenario. Visitors usually need some time to enjoy a painting, but the space around a specific item is limited and the time for visitors should be limited especially if the museum is crowed. If too many people are standing in front of a particular painting, other people might be blocked. This situation poses a challenge to a localization system, which needs to detect both the number of people in such areas and how much time they have stayed individually. And this information can be used to trigger a notification to visitors who have stayed too long to make room for other visitors.

Moving speed: Consider a scenario where an evacuation from a museum is needed and all the people in the building need to leave in a limited time. In order to be safe, all the people have to move at a minimum speed so that they can leave the building in time. And the localization should monitor people's movement and if it finds some abnormal situation, say one person is moving really slow, then it should notify security that there might be some emergency with this specific person.

Staying duration: People may spend different amounts of time at specific locations depending on what they would do there. This timing information can also be used for detecting abnormal behaviors in some scenarios, such as visitors who spend too much time in the restroom may have an emergency situation and need help.

Acceleration: Indoor localization with high refresh rate can be used to detect user's acceleration. A good application would be fall detection for people that need special care like the elderly or places where many people may stay together in a limited space, such as a museum. With high refresh rate, the system can analyze people's location data in real time and further classify events such as falls or other normal and abnormal events.

Usage time of a place: From the number of people staying at a particular place and how long the duration of stay is, the system can further reason how popular a place is. In the case of a museum, certain items usually attract a lot of people. And they tend to spend much time around these artifacts. It would not be a good idea to put two popular painting next to each other, or put a popular item in a tight space.

Group of people: In a typical party scenario, there are usually many people talking and laughing and the place can be very crowded. It would not be a trivial task to find a particular person even though he/she can be just nearby. A possible way to address this challenge is to estimate the relative positions of surrounding people and classify the crowd based on their group activity, such as "five persons walking from the middle to the corner" and "three persons talking at the corner". The underlying scheme is that in such situations, people tend to move together with others and form different groups. They might be grouped by friends, families and colleagues, or just strangers who are moving towards the same direction. This requires the localization system to detect the location of all the people in real time and analyze the similarity of their movement.

In spite of all the use cases we discuss above, we envision a system that could provide real-time location information for both human and objects in the environment, and it can provide customized navigation path for users by adapting its behavior to changes of user's location. Take the museum scenario as an example, the system is expected to create different tours based on visitor's interests, his current location, schedule, physical capabilities and environmental dynamics. Moreover, the system should also update the recommended tours as these conditions change.

3. Current Indoor Localization Technologies

The state-of-the-art indoor localization is quite sophisticated. A variety of methods has been investigated to estimate indoor location of human and objects and they can be grouped into four different techniques: (1) dead-reckoning, (2) proximity sensing, (3) triangulation, and (4) scene analysis, which will be discussed next separately.

3.1. *Dead-reckoning*

These systems estimate a user's location by keeping track of travel distance and direction of turns based on a previously estimated or known position. While a user is moving, the system obtains his current velocity from sensors on his body, and uses this information in conjunction with the amount of time that has elapsed since last update to derive user's current position. These sensors could be accelerometers,[2–4] magnetometers,[5] gyroscopes,[6] or a combination of some of those sensors.[7,8] Other sensors, such as EMG,[9] pressure sensors,[10] Ultrasonic,[11] have also been explored.

The major drawback of this approach is that the position estimation errors quickly accrue over time if external references are not available, since the estimation process is recursive. RFID tags,[12] ultrasound beacons,[13] and map-matching[14] are often used to correct this accumulated errors. Because of its cumulative error propagation and the need to combine it with other localization techniques for eliminating errors, this method might also introduce other drawbacks. If the system uses RFID for error correction, the system would have most of the disadvantages of the RFID localization such as change in the infrastructure and the need for users to carry a RFID reader. If map matching or landmarks are used for error correction, some previous knowledge of the environment is required. Also a starting point is also required, typically determined by the external references.

3.2. *Proximity sensing*

Proximity refers to a class of methods which determine the presence of human subjects or objects in the vicinity of sensors, which alone has limited sensing range and analysis capabilities. Common architecture of proximity sensing system is having a fixed number of sensing stations installed in the environment and determining the location of the user through receiving signals from identifiers or tags carried by users. Six different technologies to implement this kind of systems have been proposed:

Radio frequency identifier description (RFID) tags are used extensively in many indoor localization systems, where one or more reading devices can wirelessly obtain the ID of RFID tags present in the environment. The reader transmits a RF signal and the tags present in the environment reflect the signal, modulating it by adding a unique identification code. The tags can be active, powered by battery, or passive drawing energy from the incoming radio signal. Active tags usually have a larger range, which could reduce the number of tags that need to be installed in the environment. But the batteries they use would need replacement after 3–5 years. While passive tags are much less expensive, they have much shorter range. Therefore, more tags would be needed to cover a certain amount of area. The main drawback of this method is that even though RFID tags are relatively inexpensive, deploying enough of them to cover a large area can be costly. An alternative way is to embed them in the carpet,[15] which might reduce the cost.

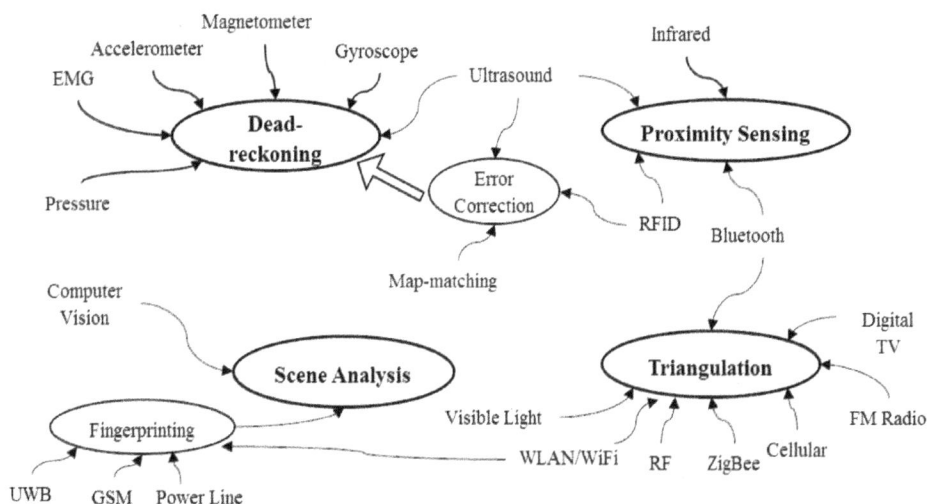

Fig. 1. Indoor localization technologies.

Infrared (IR) has been used in various ways for detection or tracking of objects or persons. One of its advantages is that its wavelengths are longer than that of visible light, but shorter than that of terahertz radiation. Therefore, it is invisible to the human eye under most conditions, making it less intrusive compared to indoor positioning based on visible light. There are three general methods of exploiting IR signals for localization.

- Active beacons approach, which is based on IR transmitters that are installed in known positions where each transmitter broadcasts a unique ID in a cone shaped region. The user carries an IR receiver that picks up data from IR transmitters in range. The system may include only one transmitter in each room for room-level localization[16,17] or several transmitters deployed in every room to disambiguate sectors of a room.
- IR imaging approach, where sensors operate in the long wavelength IR spectrum, known as the thermography region, to obtain a passive image of the environment from natural thermal emissions. The advantage of this approach is that there is no need to deploy active IR illuminators or any other dedicated thermal source, and the IR radiation can be used to determine the temperature of human body or other objects without wearing any tags or emitters.[18,19] As its main drawback, passive IR approaches are comprised by strong radiation from the sun.
- Artificial IR light approach can be a common alternative to indoor localization systems using visible light. It might be based on active IR light sources[20] or retro reflective targets.[21,22] Microsoft Kinect[23] used for video game console Xbox uses continuously projected IR structured light to capture 3D scene information with an IR camera. The 3D structure will be computed from the distortion of a pseudo random pattern of structure IR light dots. And people can be tracked simultaneously up to a distance of 3.5 m at a frame rate of 30 Hz. An accuracy of 1 cm at 2 m distance has been reported.

Ultrasound identification (USID) determines a user's position based on distance between ultrasound emitters carried by human users and static receivers installed in the environment.[24] Other systems may have the user carry the receivers and emitters are mounted at the ceilings or walls.[25] The relative distance between an emitter and a receiver can be estimated from time of arrival (TDA) measurements or time difference of arrival (TDOA) of ultrasound pulse. A disadvantage of ultrasound is that walls may reflect or block ultrasound signals, which result in less accurate localization. The other drawback of using ultrasound for localization is required line of sight between the receivers and emitters.

Bluetooth beacons have been designed as a short-range communication system with range of comparable size to a room,[26] making proximity-based location simple to implement and relatively reliable. Basically, a group of fixed beacons continually issue inquiry packets on each possible channel, and mobile devices need to be set "discoverable" to respond to these packets, identifying themselves. Since the location of these fixed beacons is known in the system, users or their mobile devices can be located although users will have to walk slower than with other techniques because of the device delay. One of the advantages of this design is that no custom code need to be deployed on the user's side, but is often considered as a privacy issue since anyone in the environment can track the devices by creating their own stations. Thus, more recent researches have concentrated on the user's side scanning for the fixed beacons. Although it is more secure since Bluetooth technology does not require scan packets to identify their source address, it does require custom application code on user's mobile device.

3.3. *Triangulation*

Different from most proximity sensing techniques which locate the user by sensing one unique identifier, a number of systems use the location of at least three known points and locate the user by triangulating the tags installed in known positions. These systems might use technologies of WLAN/WIFI,[27-34] RF,[35] ZigBee,[36] Cellular Network,[37] FM Radio,[38] Digital Television,[39] Bluetooth[40] and visible light.[41,42] Depending on the type of radio signal measurements, triangulation can be divided into angulation and multilateration method. In angulation systems, specific antenna designs or hardware equipment are needed and angle of arrival (AOA) measurements[43] are used for inferring the receiver's location from the angular measurements of at least three known points. In multilateration systems, TOA, TDOA, or received signal strength (RSS) measurements from multiple reference points (RPs) are used to estimate the receiver's location with the help of a radio propagation model. However, indoor environment can be harsh and characteristics of the wireless signal channel in such environments might be changeable and unpredictable, which makes multipath and nonline of propagation conditions common. Therefore, these systems cannot guarantee an adequate performance. A few hybrid systems have been developed as well, in order to compensate for the shortcomings of a single technology[44,45] and did show some progress on localization accuracy, coverage, or robustness. But as previous work[46] has presented, fusing several technologies requires reliable measurements and complex fusion techniques. It also increases the overall system complexity.

3.4. *Scene analysis*

Scene analysis based localization is a pattern recognition method which extracts features from data collected by one or more sensors carried or worn by users or installed in the environment and compares these features with a set of prior collected sensor data that has been coupled with a specific environment. The scene can be visual images, acoustic sound, and radio frequency waves. The advantage of using this method is that accurate physical quantities, such as distance, are not required for calculating a user's location. However, the observed features are usually specific and unique, and are subject to re-evaluation if the environment is changed.

Computer vision based localization techniques, which cover a wide field of applications at all levels of accuracy, provide a number of advantages. While users navigate in an environment, a camera captures images of the environment, and then by matching the images against a database of images with known location, users' position and orientation can be determined.[24,47] Recently, a number of researchers have also contributed to vision-based localization using smartphone cameras.[48,49] The main advantage of this method is that both the camera and computation power are inbuilt. This simplifies the process of deploying and using such a system. Besides, most of the state-of-the-art phones already have a variety of inertial sensors, such as accelerometer and gyroscope. Hybrid systems of camera and inertial sensors for localization have also been getting more popular.

Fingerprinting localization techniques fingerprint the unique signal measurement or its distribution over time from one or multiple sources at every location in the area of interests to build a map of prerecorded data. When the user is navigating, his location is estimated by mapping the currently received signal measurement against the map to find the closet match. Common metrics for fingerprinting include AOA, RSS, or time of flight (TOF) of the incoming radio signal.[50] Due to its increasing prevalence in indoor environments and the existing infrastructures, WLAN/WIFI[29–34] has been exploited extensively with fingerprinting schemes. Other technologies, such as Ultra wideband (UWB),[50] GSM,[51] PowerLine,[52] and LED[53,54] have been studied as well.

4. Location Semantics Modeling

Building context-aware applications to provide adaptive services is complicated. This situation can be remedied by creating a suitable user model which captures features such as user interests, user location, and other context information. Since we cannot find established models specifically defined for a museum scenario, we provide our own opinions based on state-of-the-art technologies. This section presents an object-based user model in which context information is structured around a set of entities, including human, object, and relations among them. These entities provide a formal basis for representing and reasoning about some of the properties of context information we discussed in Sec. 2.

4.1. *User model*

The core of a location semantics system is a user model that is dynamically updated as the user moves in the museum by considering user's current location and events occurring during user's visit. It is driven by the directional location tracking of users, their relative positions, as well as their interactions with the environment.

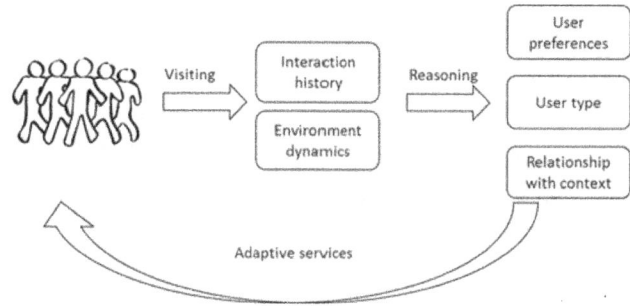

Fig. 2. User modeling in the museum scenario.

The user model also performs the functionality of a recommendation system. In our museum scenario, we will use the knowledge-based modeling techniques to recommend visiting routes and artwork collections to visitors. Knowledge-based recommendation systems usually require three types of knowledge: knowledge about the objects to be recommended, user knowledge, and functional knowledge of the mapping between user needs and object. In our case of adaptive services in a museum, the functional knowledge could include the knowledge of the environment, such as room temperature, time of the day, or number of visitors in the same exhibit.

Based on the above, the user model could be designed to contain two parts: one that tracks the user's location and maintains context data; the other one that infers user's preference, his relationship with all the objects in the environment and other users and that provides personalized information.

The detailed structure is given as follows:

(i) Data component, including information about users and environment

(a) Interaction history, which contains how the user interacts with the environment. Two types of data could be stored in the interaction history.

  (i) User location, which can be used to form the user's path through the museum.
  (ii) Usage data, such as how long the user has stayed in front of a specific painting, and how much time the user has listened to the description of certain artworks, by which user's favorite types of artifacts and preferences can be assessed.

(b) Environment dynamics

  (i) Physical factors, such as room temperature, time of the day, and the number of people within an area.
  (ii) Knowledge about all artworks, such as their location at the museum, author, chronology, material, and artwork category (e.g., sculpture, painting, and photo/picture).

(ii) Inference component, which will analyze stored data to infer

(a) User preferences, which is dynamic, evolving with user's interaction with the artifacts and environment. User model should be able to monitor user's behavior and make predictions about the user based on their interaction with various items in the environment.

(b) User type, which is related to user preference and knowledge. In the case of a museum, one may want to know and see as much as possible, and review almost every artifact on his path, and another user may be more selective and prefer to explore artifacts that have only certain concepts. Some visitors do not want to spend much time on a single artifact preferring to go through the museum in order to get a general idea of the exhibition.

(c) User's relationship with nearby objects and other people.

4.2. *Interaction model*

Based on all the potential applications we discussed in Sec. 2 for our museum scenario, we recognized several classes of interactions that exhibit different properties in accordance with their persistence and source. In this section, we formalize the analysis in a scheme for categorizing interaction based on the entities involved in the interaction.

4.2.1. *Human to object*

In a traditional museum setting, interaction between human and object, such as a specific painting, could be limited to audio guides and interactive kiosks. However, if both the location of visitors and artifacts are available, many customized services could be enabled:

- Multimedia presentation for different artworks could be dynamically generated and delivered to visitors taking into consideration their real-time location.
- A visitor's stay duration in front of certain artworks could be used as the indicator of user interest and the physical path covered by the user during his visit can be used to build a user model for delivery of personalized multimedia information to enhance interactivity in the museum.
- The system could recommend certain collections to visitors based on their preference which can be manually input beforehand or their previous interaction with the artworks in the museum and show the path to a specific collection.

4.2.2. *Human to human*

Social interaction among visitors is known to enhance the museum visit experience. By combining the location information of multiple users and integrating the communication channel among them, social interaction is possible:

- Visitors could attach virtual comments about certain artworks for other visitors who visit these artifacts later.
- Visitors could share their comments and experiences for certain artworks with their family or group members who are also in the museum at the same time.
- Visitors could see the nicknames of visitors who had already visited a specific artwork, so they would share similar interests at the museum or to keep in touch after the visit.
- Multiple visitors could be grouped together to play certain games in teams, such as treasure hunting, to learn the knowledge about the artworks based on observation, reflection and action, and improve their learning experience by challenging themselves.

4.2.3. *Object to object*

A major goal of location semantics is to reveal the rich semantic linkage connecting the artifacts with each other. The linkage can be obtained from the experts who have studied these artworks for years or inferred from visitors according to their inaction history. And this linkage can be used to provide adaptive services to the visitors and enhance their museum visit experience.

- From historical data, we can easily find which two or more collections visitors tend to interact with in the same visit. This implies that these collections should not be placed far away from each other.
- If two collections tend to attract many people, it is not wise to put them side by side, which might cause congestion.

5. Challenges and Future Directions

Indoor localization is becoming increasingly important. Although many positioning devices and services are currently available, some important problems remain unsolved and it is necessary to develop an integrated and seamless positioning platform to provide a uniform solution for different scenarios and applications. Directions for future research in this area can be summarized as follows:

- Fusion techniques: Both indoor and outdoor localization have been addressed separately. While for a number of mixed scenarios where both indoor and outdoor locations are needed, the transitions between indoor and outdoor areas need be managed seamlessly and exploited as a whole. Therefore, both system integration and data fusion techniques need to developed, but much work remains to be done in this area.
- Direct localization: Most indoor localization systems contain two steps for positioning: parameter measurement and position estimation. This method has the disadvantage of making a premature decision on intermediate parameters in their first step. This can be remedied by direct

localization employing the principle of least commitment; these algorithms preserve and propagate all intermediate information until the end of the process and make an informed decision as a very last step. Little work has been done on this problem to date.

- Unobtrusiveness: many systems require users to carry sensors attached to the body for location tracking and activity monitoring, and unobtrusiveness becomes a major challenge. Certain progress has been made in the integration of sensor devices in fabric, but the design and development of wearable sensors without violating unobtrusiveness is still a significant challenge.
- Security and Privacy: The fundamental security requirements of a localization system are privacy, confidentiality, accountability, and access control. Users should have autonomy and control over their data of any type. Researchers have identified many types of privacy leaks, even when the wireless communication channel in the system is encrypted.

6. Conclusion

In this paper, we provide a comprehensive overview of state of the art positioning techniques and how the system can be enriched semantically to provide adaptive services in a museum. The key feature of location semantics is the use of user model (1) to define a general and well-defined user/context model and this model should be independent of a particular positioning system, (2) to perform inference and reasoning to provide environment information and adaptive services at a semantic level. This enables the system to provide personalized services continuously and dynamically.

References

[1] S. Ma, Q. Liu and H. Tang, An overview of location semantics technologies and applications. *Int. J. Semant. Comput.* **9**(3), 373 (2015).

[2] P. Goyal, V. J. Ribeiro, H. Saran and A. Kumar, Strap-down Pedestrian Dead-Reckoning system, *Proc. 2011 Int. Conf. on Indoor Positioning and Indoor Navigation (IPIN)* (2011), pp. 1–7.

[3] A. Rai, K. K. Chintalapudi, V. N. Padmanabhan and R. Sen, Zee: zero-effort crowdsourcing for indoor localization, *Proc. 18th Int. Conf. on Mobile Computing and Networking (MobiCom)* (2012), pp. 293–304.

[4] R. M. Faragher, C. Sarno and M. Newman, Opportunistic radio SLAM for indoor navigation using smartphone sensors, *Position Location and Navigation Symp. (PLANS)* (2012), pp. 120–128.

[5] J. Chung, M. Donahoe, C. Schmandt, I. J. Kim, P. Razavai and M. Wiseman, Indoor location sensing using geo-magnetism, *Proc. 9th Int. Conf. on Mobile Systems, Applications, and Services* (2011), pp. 141–154.

[6] O. Woodman and R. Harle, Pedestrian localisation for indoor environments, *Proc. 10th Int. Conf. Ubiquitous Computing* (2008), pp. 114–123.

[7] A. R. Jimenez, F. Seco, C. Prieto and J. Guevara, A comparison of pedestrian dead-reckoning algorithms using a low-cost MEMS IMU, *IEEE Int. Symp. Intelligent Signal Processing (WISP'09)* (2009), pp. 37–42.

[8] N. Castaneda and S. Lamy-Perbal, An improved shoe-mounted inertial navigation system, *Proc. 2010 Int. Conf. Indoor Positioning and Indoor Navigation (IPIN)* (2010), pp. 1–6.

[9] Q. Wang, X. Zhang, X. Chen, R. Chen, W. Chen and Y. Chen, A novel pedestrian dead reckoning algorithm using wearable EMG sensors to measure walking strides, *Ubiquitous Positioning Indoor Navigation and Location Based Service (UPINLBS)* (2010), pp. 1–8.

[10] Y. S. Suh and S. S. Park, Pedestrian inertial navigation with gait phase detection assisted zero velocity updating, *Proc. 4th Int. Conf. Autonomous Robots and Agents (ICARA'09)* (2009) pp. 336–341.

[11] J. Saarinen, J. Suomela, S. Heikkila, M. Elomaa and A. Halme, Personal navigation system, *Proc. 2004 IEEE/RSJ Int. Conf. Intelligent Robots and Systems (IROS 2004)* (2004), pp. 212–217.

[12] S. Koide and M. Kato, 3-d human navigation system considering various transition preferences, *Proc. 2005 IEEE Int. Conf. on Systems, Man and Cybernetics* (2005), pp. 859–864.

[13] C. Fischer, K. Muthukrishnan, M. Hazas and H. Gellersen, Ultrasound-aided pedestrian dead reckoning for indoor navigation, *Proc. 1st ACM Int. Workshop on Mobile Entity Localization and Tracking in GPS-Less Environments* (2008), pp. 31–36.

[14] K. Nakamura, Y. Aono and Y. Tadokoro, A walking navigation system for the blind, *Syst. Comput.* **28**(13), 36 (1997).

[15] S. Ma and Y. Shi, A scalable passive RFID-based multi-user indoor location system, *Proc. 7th Int. Conf. Wireless Communications, Networking and Mobile Computing (WiCOM)* (2011), pp. 1–4.

[16] R. Want, A. Hopper, V. Falcao and J. Gibbons, The active badge location system, *ACM Tran. Inf. Sys. (TOIS)* **10**(1), 91 (1992).

[17] K. Atsuumi and M. Sano, Indoor IR azimuth sensor using a linear polarizer, *Int. Conf. Indoor Positioning and Indoor Navigation* (2010).

[18] D. Hauschildt and N. Kirchhof, Advances in thermal infrared localization: Challenges and solutions, *Proc. 2010 Int. Conf. Indoor Positioning and Indoor Navigation (IPIN)*, Zurich, Switzerland (2010), pp. 1–8.

[19] Ambiplex (2011), http://www.ambiplex.com/, last accessed March (2015).

[20] F. Boochs, R. Schutze, C. Simon, F. Marzani, H. Wirth and J Meier, Increasing the accuracy of untaught robot positions by means of a multi-camera system, *Proc. 2010 Int. Conf. Indoor Positioning and Indoor Navigation (IPIN)*, Zurich, Switzerland, (2010), pp. 1–9.

[21] AICON 3D Systems (2011), http://www.aicon.de, last accessed March (2015).

[22] Hagisonic (2008), User's Guide Localization System StarGazerTM for Intelligent Robots, http://www.hagisonic.com/, last accessed 17 March (2010).

[23] Microsoft Kinect (2015), http://www.xbox.com/en-US/xbox-one/accessories/kinect-for-xbox-one, last accessed March (2015).

[24] L. Ran, S. Helal and S. Moore, Drishti: An integrated indoor/outdoor blind navigation system and service, *Proc. 2nd IEEE Conf. Pervasive Computing and Communications (PerCom'04)*, (2004), pp. 23–30.

[25]N. B. Priyantha, A. Chakraborty and H. Balakrishnan, The cricket location-support system, *Proc. 6th Int. Conf. Mobile Computing and Networking* (2000), pp. 32–43.

[26]ZONITH (2011), http://www.zonith.com/products/ips/, last accessed March (2015).

[27]Q. Yang, S. J. Pan and V. W. Zheng, Estimating location using wi-fi, *IEEE Intelli. Syst.* **18** (2008).

[28]G. V. Zàruba, M. Huber, F. A. Kamangar and I. Chlamtac, Indoor location tracking using RSSI readings from a single Wi-Fi access point, *Wirel. Netw.* **13**(2) 221–235 (2007).

[29]R. Ban, K. Kaji, K. Hiroi and N. Kawaguchi, Indoor positioning method integrating pedestrian Dead Reckoning with magnetic field and WiFi fingerprints, *Proc. 8th Int. Conf. on Mobile Computing and Ubiquitous Networking (ICMU)*, (2015), pp. 167–172.

[30]I. Bisio, M. Cerruti, F. Lavagetto, M. Marchese, M. Pastorino, A. Randazzo and A. Sciarrone, A trainingless wifi fingerprint positioning approach over mobile devices, *Proc. Antennas and Wireless Propagation Letters, IEEE*, Vol. 13 (2014), pp. 832–835.

[31]J. Niu, B. Lu, L. Cheng, Y. Gu and L. Shu, Ziloc: Energy efficient wifi fingerprint-based localization with low-power radio, *Wireless Communications and Networking Conf. (WCNC)*, (2013), pp. 4558–4563.

[32]H. Liu, Y. Gan, J. Yang, S. Sidhom, Y. Wang, Y. Chen and F. Ye, Push the limit of wifi based localization for smartphones, *Proc. 10th Int. Conf. Mobile Computing and Networking* (2012), pp. 305–316.

[33]M. Azizyan, I. Constandache and R. Roy Choudhury, Surround-Sense: Mobile phone localization via ambience fingerprinting, *Proc. 15th Int. Conf. Mobile Computing and Networking* (2009), pp. 261–272.

[34]J. Rekimoto, T. Miyaki and T. Ishizawa, LifeTag: WiFi-based continuous location logging for life pattern analysis, LoCA, Vol. (2007), pp. 35–49.

[35]C. Xu, B. Firner, Y. Zhang, R. Howard, J. Li, and X. Lin, Improving rf-based device-free passive localization in cluttered indoor environments through probabilistic classification methods, *Proc. 11th Int. Conf. Information Processing in Sensor Networks* (2012), pp. 209–220.

[36]MyBodyguard (2011), http://www.my-bodyguard.eu, last accessed March (2015).

[37]Loctronix (2011), http://www.loctronix.com, last accessed March (2015).

[38]A. Popleteev, Indoor positioning using FM radio signals, Ph.D. Dissertation at the University of Trento, School in Information and Communication Technologies, (2011).

[39]D. Serant, O. Julien, L. Ries, P. Thevenon, M. Dervin and G. Hein, The digital TV case-Positioning using signals-of-opportunity based on OFDM modulation. Inside GNSS 6, No. 6 (2011), p. 54.

[40]L. Chen, L. Pei, H. Kuusniemi, Y. Chen, T. Kröger and R. Chen, Bayesian fusion for indoor positioning using bluetooth fingerprints, *Wirel. Pers. Commun.* **70**(4) 1735 (2013).

[41]L. Li, P. Hu, C. Peng, G. Shen and F. Zhao, Epsilon: A visible light based positioning system, *Proc. 11th USENIX Symp. Networked Systems Design and Implementation (NSDI'14)* (2014), pp. 331–344.

[42]M. Fan, Q. Liu, H. Tang and P. Chiu, HiFi: hi de and fi nd digital content associated with physical objects via coded light, *Proc. 15th Workshop Mobile Computing Systems and Applications*, (2014).

[43]Ubisense: http://www.ubisense.net/default.asp, last accessed March (2015).

[44]A. Baniukevic, C. S. Jensen and H. Lu, Hybrid indoor positioning with Wi-Fi and Bluetooth: Architecture and performance, *Proc. 14th Int. Conf. Mobile Data Management (MDM)*, (2013), pp. 207–216.

[45]Y. U. Lee and M. Kavehrad, Long-range indoor hybrid localization system design with visible light communications and wireless network, *Photonics Society Summer Topical Meeting Series* (2012), pp. 82–83.

[46]M. Laaraiedh, L. Yu, S. Avrillon and B. Uguen, Comparison of hybrid localization schemes using RSSI, TOA, and TDOA, *11th European, Wireless Conf. 2011-Sustainable Wireless Technologies (European Wireless)*, VDE (2011), pp. 1–5.

[47]O. Koch and S. Teller, A self-calibrating, vision-based navigation assistant, *Workshop on Computer Vision Applications for the Visually Impaired* (2008).

[48]A. Mulloni, D. Wagner, I. Barakonyi and D. Schmalstieg, Indoor positioning and navigation with camera phones, *IEEE Pervasive Comput.* **8**(2) 22 (2009).

[49]M. Werner, M. Kessel and C. Marouane, Indoor positioning using smartphone camera, *Proc. 2011 Int. Conf. Indoor Positioning and Indoor Navigation (IPIN)* (2011), pp. 1–6.

[50]K. Pahlavan, X. Li and J. P. Makela, Indoor geolocation science and technology, *IEEE Commun. Mag.* **40**(2) 112 (2002).

[51]V. Otsasson, A. Varshavsky, A. LaMarca and E. De Lara, Accurate GSM indoor localization, *UbiComp 2005: Ubiquitous Computing* (Springer Berlin Heidelberg, 2005), pp. 141–158.

[52]S. N. Patel, K. N. Truong and G. D. Abowd, Powerline positioning: A practical sub-room-level indoor location system for domestic use, *UbiComp 2006: Ubiquitous Computing* (Springer Berlin Heidelberg, 2006), pp. 441–458.

[53]S. Ma, Q. Liu and P. Sheu, On Hearing Your Position through Light for Mobile Robot Indoor Navigation, In *Proc. ICMEW* (2016).

[54]M. Fan, Q. Liu, S. Ma and P. Chiu, Smart Toy Car Localization and Navigation using Projected Light, *2015 IEEE Int. Symp. Multimedia* (2015), pp. 399–402.

Use of semantics in bio-informatics

Charles C. N. Wang* and Jeffrey J. P. Tsai

Department of Biomedical Informatics, Asia University
500, Lioufeng Rd., Wufeng, Taichung 41354, Taiwan
*chaoneng.wang@gmail.com

Bioinformatics conceptualizes biological processes in terms of genomics and applies computer science (derived from disciplines such as applied modeling, data mining, machine learning and statistics) to extract knowledge from biological data. This paper introduces the working definitions of bioinformatics and its applications and challenges. We also identify the bioinformatics resources that are popular among bioinformatics analysis, review some primary methods used to analyze bioinformatics problems, and review the data mining, semantic computing and deep learning technologies that may be applied in bioinformatics analysis.

Keywords: Bioinformatics; semantic computing; data mining; deep learning.

1. Overview of Bioinformatics

The field bioinformatics conceptualizes biological processes in terms of genomics and applies computer science (derived from disciplines such as applied modeling, data mining, machine learning and statistics) to extract knowledge from biological data. It includes the collection, storage, retrieval, manipulation and modeling of data for analysis, visualization or prediction through the development of algorithms and software.[1]

1.1. Applications

In recent years, the scientific world has witnessed the completion of the whole genome sequences of many organisms. The analysis of genomic data by the Human Genome Project was a landmark achievement for bioinformatics. Bioinformatics is also essential for management of data and prediction in biological science, which involves the application of tools of computation and analysis to capture and interpretation of biological data and analysis of genome sequence data. Its future contribution to functional understanding of the human genome, leading to enhanced discovery of drug targets and individualized therapy is expected.[2] Today bioinformatics is widely used in many practical applications such as the Basic Local Alignment Search Tool (BLAST), that finds regions of similarity between biological sequences,[3] and ArrayMining which is an online microarray data mining tool for gene expression.[4]

1.2. Challenges

The volume and diversity of biologic data is growing rapidly, presenting a number of challenges ranging from data management, data analysis and data mining. The analysis of biological data can generate new knowledge that needs to be captured. Developing bioinformatics methods is a formidable task which requires solutions for various challenges in data management, data analysis and resources integration.

2. Bioinformatics Resources

Some currently available bioinformatics resources are summarized in this section.

2.1. The national center for biotechnology information (NCBI)

NCBI (http://www.ncbi.nlm.nih.gov/) is a leader in the field of bioinformatics. It studies computational approaches to answer some fundamental questions in biology, and it provides online delivery of biomedical information and bioinformatics tools. As of now, NCBI hosts approximately 40 online literature and molecular biology databases including PubMed, PubMed Central, and GenBank that serve millions of users around the world.

2.2. Gene expression omnibus (GEO)

The GEO (https://www.ncbi.nlm.nih.gov/geo/) is an international public repository of high-throughput microarray and next-generation sequencing of functional genomic data sets submitted by the research community. It supports the archiving of raw data, processed data and metadata which are indexed, cross-linked and searchable. GEO also provides several web-based tools and strategies to assist users to query, analyze and visualize data.[5]

2.3. The protein data bank (PDB)

The PDB (http://www.rcsb.org/pdb/home/home.do) is the single worldwide repository of information about the three-dimensional (3D) structures of large biological molecules, including proteins and nucleic acids. These are the molecules of life that are found in all organisms including bacteria, yeast, plants, flies, and humans. Understanding the shape of a molecule can deduce a structure's role in a disease to facilitate drug development. The structures in the archive range from tiny proteins and bits of DNA to complex molecular machines like the ribosome.[6]

2.4. *The biological general repository for interaction datasets (BioGRID)*

The BioGRID (http://thebiogrid.org) is an open access database that houses genetic and protein interactions curated from the primary biomedical literature for all major model organism species and humans. As of 2016, the BioGRID contains 749,912 interactions drawn from 43,149 publications that represent 30 model organisms. BioGRID data are freely distributed through its partner model organism databases and meta-databases that are directly downloadable in a variety of formats.[7]

2.5. *Gene ontology (GO)*

GO (http://www.geneontology.org/) is a collaborative effort to develop and use ontologies to support biologically meaningful annotation of genes and their products in a wide variety of organisms. Several major model organism databases and other bioinformatics resource centers have contributed to the project.[8]

2.6. *GeneCards*

GeneCards (www.genecards.org) is a comprehensive, authoritative compendium of annotative information about human genes, widely used for nearly 15 years. Its gene-centric content is automatically mined and integrated from over 80 digital sources, resulting in a web-based deep-linked card for each of $> 73,000$ human gene entries that encompass the following categories: protein coding, pseudogene, RNA gene, genetic locus, cluster, and uncategorized.[9]

2.7. *The database for annotation, visualization and integration discovery (DAVID)*

DAVID (www.david.niaid.nih.gov) is a web-accessible program that integrates functional genomic annotations with intuitive graphical summaries. Lists of gene or protein identifiers are rapidly annotated and summarized according to shared categorical data for GO, protein domains, and biochemical pathway memberships. It has four analysis modules: (1) Annotation Tool, that rapidly appends descriptive data from several public databases to lists of genes; (2) GoCharts, that assigns genes to GO functional categories based on user selected classifications and term specificity

levels; (3) KeggCharts, that assigns genes to KEGG metabolic processes and enables users to view genes in the context of biochemical pathway maps; and (4) Domain Charts, that groups genes according to PFAM conserved protein domains.[10]

3. Bioinformatics Methods

The primary goal of bioinformatics is to increase the understanding of biological processes. What sets it apart from other approaches, however, is its focus on developing and applying computationally intensive techniques to achieve this goal. In this section, we review some basic bioinformatics problems and solution methods including data mining, machine learning, and visualization. Major research efforts in the field include sequence alignment, prediction of gene expression, protein structure prediction, protein–protein interaction, genome-wide association, and modeling of evolution and cell behavior. Bioinformatics can help to understand the evolutionary aspects of molecular biology. At a more integrative level, it can help to analyze biological pathways and networks that are important in systems biology. In structural biology, it aids in the simulation and modeling of proteins as well as biomolecular interactions.

3.1. *Sequence alignment*

Sequence alignment is a way of arranging a set of DNA, RNA or protein sequences to identify regions of similarity among the sequences. Altschul[3] proposed an approach to rapid sequence comparison in 1990, called the BLAST, that directly approximates the alignments that optimize a measure of local similarity, i.e., the maximal segment pair score. The basic algorithm is simple and robust; it can be implemented in a number of ways and be applied in a variety of contexts including the search of DNA, RNA and protein sequence database, searching motifs, searching gene identifications, and the analysis of multiple regions of similarity in long sequences. BLAST can be used for several purposes: (1) identifying species — BLAST can correctly identify a species or find homologous species; (2) locating domains — BLAST can help locate known domains within a sequence of interest; (3) DNA mapping when working with a known species, and it can sequence a gene at an unknown location. BLAST can compare the chromosomal position of a sequence of interest to relevant sequences in the species database.

To understand the sequence alignment problem, for example, assume the two sequences to be globally aligned are:

$$\begin{array}{ll} \texttt{GAATTCAGTTA} & \texttt{(sequence \#1)} \\ \texttt{GGATCGA} & \texttt{(sequence \#2)} \end{array}$$

So $M = 11$ and $N = 7$ (where M is the length of sequence #1 and N is the length of sequence #2).

In this case, global sequence alignment can be achieved using dynamical programming with three steps: (1) initialization, (2) matrix fill, and (3) traceback. The Initialization step in the global alignment dynamic programming approach is to create a matrix with $M + 1$ columns and $N + 1$ rows. The matrix fill step finds the maximum global alignment score by starting in the upper left corner in the matrix and finding the maximal score $M_{i,j}$ for each position in the matrix. The traceback step determines the actual alignment(s) that result in the maximum score. Repeating the traceback step can eventually get to a position which tells us that traceback is completed. Based on the algorithm, the two example sequences can be aligned as follows:

```
GAATTCAGTTA  (sequence  #1)
GGA − TC − G − −A  (sequence  #2)
```

The details of the algorithm may be found in Polyanovsky *et al.*[11]

3.2. *Gene expression*

Gene expression is the process by which information from a gene is used in the synthesis of a functional gene product. Microarrays can simultaneously measure the expression level of thousands of genes within a particular mRNA sample. They have been routinely used to study gene expressions and gene regulatory networks. They are also increasingly being used to identify biomarkers and to validate drug targets, as well as to study the gene and potential toxicological effects of compounds in a model. Microarray analysis is usually presented as a list of genes whose expressions are considered to change (and they are known as differentially expressed genes.) The identification of differential gene expressions, together with clustering and classification are the core of in depth microarray analysis.

For microarray analysis, clustering plays a growing role in the study of co-expressed genes for gene discovery. It is often the first step to be performed, which employs an unsupervised approach to classify the genes into groups with similar patterns. Classification is then performed with a supervised learning method; it is also known as class prediction or discriminant analysis. Data mining techniques have been proposed to address various issues specific to gene discovery problems such as consistent co-expression of genes over multiple microarray datasets.[12]

For example, consider a microarray dataset such as GEO database (GSE19188). It is the result of a genome-wide gene expression analysis that was performed on a cohort of 91 patients using 91 tumor- and 65 adjacent normal-lung tissue samples.[13] In this case, the first important step in microarray analysis is normalization, which involves weighted regression applied alternately in two different ways. The processed microarray data, after the normalization procedure, can then be represented in the form of a matrix, often called gene expression matrix, as exemplified in Table 1.

Table 1. Gene expression matrix that contains rows representing genes and columns representing particular conditions. Each case contains a value that reflects the expression level of a gene under a corresponding condition.

	Case 1	Case 2	Case 3
Gene 1	8.61	7.92	10.12
Gene 2	12.03	6.11	8.45
Gene 3	8.11	7.38	11.40
Gene 4	7.02	3.78	6.91

The second step is to identify differentially expressed genes, using a Bayesian model in the gene expression matrix. The third step is data mining that clusters the genes to make meaningful biological inference. Clustering methods can be hierarchical. The basic idea of hierarchical clustering is shown in Fig. 1.

Several statistical methods may be used to determine either the expression or relative expression of a gene from normalized microarray data, including *t*-tests,[14] F-statistic[15] and Bayesian models. Clustering is the most popular method currently used in the first step of gene expression data matrix analysis. It is used for finding co-regulated and functionally related groups. There are three common types of clustering methods: hierarchical clustering, *k*-means clustering and self-organizing maps. Hierarchical clustering is a commonly used unsupervised technique that builds clusters of genes with similar patterns of expression.[16] Classification is also known

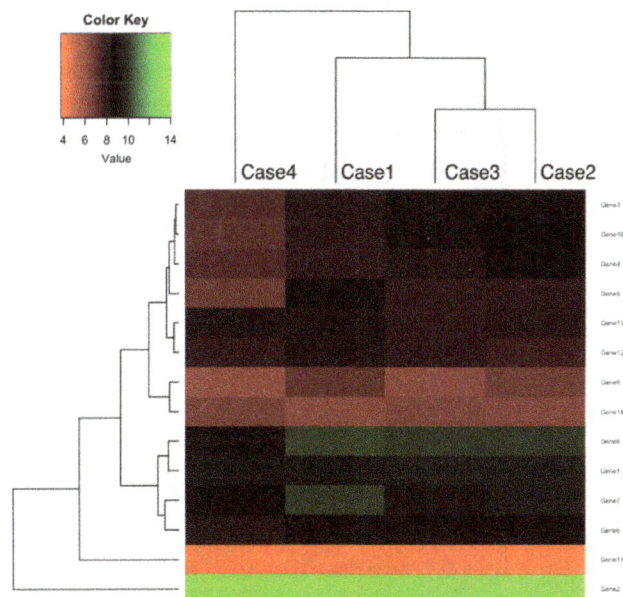

Fig. 1. (Color online) Example result of hierarchical clustering. The color code represents the log2 (expression ratio), where red represents upregulation, green represents downregulation, and black represents no change in expression.

as class prediction, discriminant analysis, or supervised learning. Given a set of pre-classified examples, (for example, different types of cell lines) a classifier finds a rule that assigns new samples to one of the above classes.[17] There are a wide range of algorithms that can be used for classification, including Artificial Neural Networks, and Support Vector Machines (SVMs).

Lu *et al.*[18] used the microarray analysis approach to evaluate the changes of gene expression profiles during the initiation and progression of squamous cell carcinoma of the esophagus. They examined gene expression profiles in different stages of the initiation and progression of esophageal cancer in order to identify the genes that were differentially expressed between these stages. Their results suggest that microarray technology is a useful tool to discover the genes frequently involved in esophageal neoplasia and it can provide novel clues to diagnosis, early detection and intervention of squamous cell carcinoma of esophagus. Frierson[19] used microarray analysis to study the expression of 8,920 different human genes in 15 Adenoid Cystic Carcinomas (ACCs), one ACC cell line and five normal major salivary glands. Other genes with altered expressions in ACC were those that encode the transcription factors SOX4 and AP-2 gamma, casein kinase 1 as well as epsilon and frizzled-7, both of which are members of the Wnt/beta-catenin signaling pathway.

3.3. *Protein structure prediction*

Protein structure refers to the three-dimensional arrangement of atoms in a protein molecule. Predicting protein 3D structures from the amino acid sequence still remains as an unsolved problem after five decades of efforts. They are important because structural features can shed some light on biological functions. De Brevern *et al.*[20] proposed a web server for protein fold recognition and structure prediction using evolutionary hybrid profiles. This is an improved method by adding solvent accessibility as a new structural feature, which improves template detection by more than 5% compared to the initial version.

As an example of protein structure predication, consider the following DNA sequence:

```
GATGGGATTGGGGTTTTCCCCTCCCATGTGCTCAAGACTGGCGCTA
AAAGTTTTGAGCTTCTCAAAAGTCTAGAGCCACCGTCCAGGGAGCA
GGTAGCTGCTGGGCTCCGGGGACACTTTGCGTTCGGGCTGGGAGCG
TGCTTTCCACGACGGTGACACGCTTCCCTGGATTGGGTAAGCTCCT
GACTGAACTTGATGAGTCCTCTCTGAGTCACGGGCTCTCGGCTCCG
TGTATTTTCAGCTCGGGAAAATCGCTGGGGCTGGGGGTGGGGCAGT
GGGGACTTAGCGAGTTTGGGGGTGAGTGGGATGGAAGCTTGGCTAG
AGGGATCATCATAGGAGTT    (DNA  sequence  #1)
```

The first step is to translate it into a protein sequence, which can be done using a translate tool (e.g., ExPASy: http://web.expasy.org/translate/). Below shows the result of translation:

```
MEEPQSDPSVEPPLSQETFSDLWKLLPENNVLSPLPSQAMDDLMLSP
DDIEQWFTEDPGPDEAPRMPEAAPPVAPAPAAPTPAAPAPAPSWPLS
SSVPSQKTYQGSYGFRLGFLHSGTAKSVTC
```
(Protein sequence #1)

The second step is sequence alignments, because those proteins having low percent sequence identities can be inaccurate. We can do sequence alignment by searching the Swiss-Prot sequence database using the BLAST search method, and then align the sequences with the multiple sequence alignment method. The result is shown in Fig. 2.

The third step is building a homology 3D structure model, shown in Fig. 3.

3.4. *Biological network and computational systems biology*

Biological networks include protein–protein interaction networks, gene regulatory networks and metabolic networks. Computational systems biology involves the use of computer simulations of gene regulatory networks to both analyze and visualize the complex connections of biological behaviors. The biological network and computational systems biology approaches are vital for developing and implementing effective strategies to deliver personalized therapies. Specifically, these approaches are important to select those patients who are most likely to benefit from targeted therapies and rational combinatorial therapies.[21] Breitkopf *et al.*[22] used a comparative PPI strategy to identify proteins surrounding the p85 regulatory subunit of Phosphoinositide-3-Kinase (PI3K), a

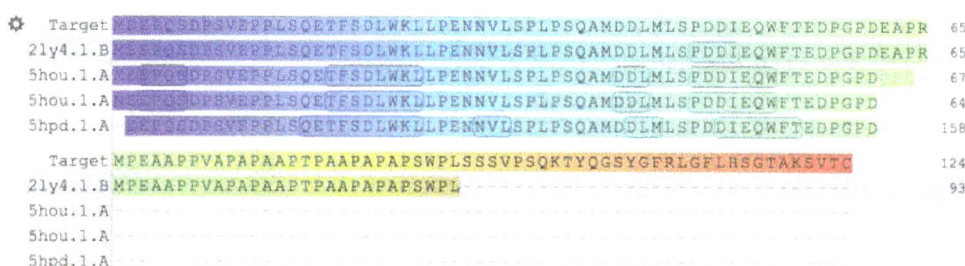

Fig. 2. The alignment results.

Fig. 4. A generic network with five dependent variables and two regulatory signals.

consider a generic branched network with four dependent variables and two regulatory signals (shown in Fig. 4) and a set of sample gene expression data (shown Table 2).

In this case, the first step in computational system biology is dynamic model maps, using the S-system model[24] to map the model and the branched network onto its parameters.

$$\dot{X}_i = \alpha_i \prod_{j=1}^{M} X_j^{g_{ij}} - \beta_i \prod_{j=1}^{M} X_j^{g_{ij}}, \qquad (1)$$

where X_i is the concentration of gene i measured at time t, whose change rate is the difference between the production and degradation terms, α_i and β_i are rate constants, g^{ij} and h^{ij} are kinetic orders accordingly. If $g^{ij} > 0$, X_j activates the production of X_i; if $g^{ij} < 0$ then X_j inhibits the production of X_i; and h^{ij} has the same effects but on degradation.

The S-systems model is listed in the following:

$$\begin{aligned}
\dot{X}_1 &= \alpha_1 X_4^{(1.4)} - \beta_1 X_1^{(1.1)}, \\
\dot{X}_2 &= \alpha_2 X_1^{(2.1)} - \beta_2 X_2^{(2.2)}, \\
\dot{X}_3 &= \alpha_3 X_2^{(3.2)} - \beta_3 X_3^{(3.3)}, \qquad (2) \\
\dot{X}_4 &= \alpha_4 X_3^{(4.3)} X_5^{(4.5)} - \beta_4 X_4^{(4.4)}, \\
\dot{X}_5 &= \alpha_5 X_2^{(5.2)} - \beta_5 X_5^{(5.5)}.
\end{aligned}$$

The second step is parameter estimation and structure identification which are arguably the most difficult steps of a biological systems analysis. The objective of parameter estimation is to adjust the parameter values of a dynamic model via an optimization procedure so that the predictions based on the model can closely express the observation data. Parameter estimation can be performed through global

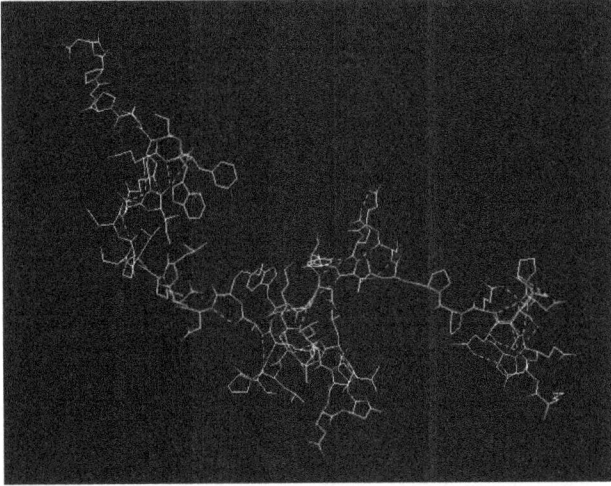

Fig. 3. A homodimer model for protein sequence #1based on a selected template, which is the second best hit according to our global quality estimation, where the amino acid variant was predicated by using Swiss-PdbViewer.

critical lipid kinase in cellular signaling events leading to cell proliferation and growth. Using this strategy, they could assess the core biology that was conserved through evolution and looked past nonspecific binding proteins that are common to proteomics PPI experiments. By analyzing and comparing protein complexes with shotgun LC-MS/MS in drosophila and mammalian cancer cells, the unusually strong binding of SHP2 (Csw) to p85 (Pi3k21B) was identified. The biology of PI3K showed that SHP2 plays a distinct role in a ternary complex with the GAB2 adaptor and the p85 regulatory component of PI3K in BCR-ABL positive H929 multiple myeloma cancer cells.

Wang *et al.*[23] compared three dynamical models to describe the gene regulation of the flowering transition process in Arabidopsis. Among the three, the Mass-action model is the simplest and uses the least parameters. It is therefore less computation-intensive with the smallest AIC value. The disadvantage, however, is that it assumes the system is simply a second-order reaction which is not the case in the study. The Michaelis–Menten model also assumes the system is homogeneous and ignores the intracellular protein transport process. The S-system model has the best performance and it does describe the diffusion effects. A disadvantage of the S-system is that it involves the most parameters. The largest AIC value also implies an over-fitting may occur in parameter estimation. The dynamical model can be used for any cellular process for which data is available and allows a scalable step-by-step approach to the practical construction of a gene regulation network. Specifically, it can treat integrated processes that need explicit accounting of genes and proteins, which allows simulation at the molecular level.

The inverse problem of identifying the biological networks from their time series responses is a cornerstone challenge in computational systems biology. For example,

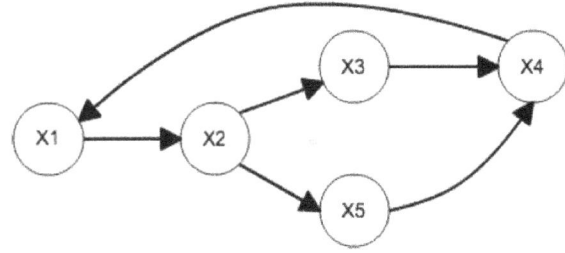

Table 2. Gene expression matrix that contains rows representing genes and columns representing time series. Each case contains a value, given in arbitrary units.

	Time1	Time2	Time3	Time4
X_1	8.61	9.12	7.92	10.12
X_2	12.03	5.91	6.11	8.45
X_3	8.11	4.23	7.38	11.40
X_4	3.41	5.01	6.01	6.21
X_5	11.20	10.22	8.45	9.55

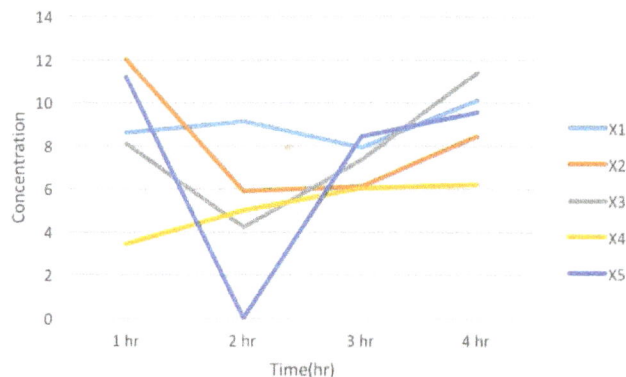

Fig. 5. Results of simulating the estimated S-system model (Eq. (2)).

methods or local methods. The third step is simulation. The simulation results for the example are shown in Fig. 5.

4. Other Methods

Other bioinformatics methods that may be employed to analyze biological data include: (1) semantic computation base on GO annotation ontology for biological relatedness of gene clusters, and (2) deep learning.

4.1. *Application of latent semantic analysis to gene ontology clusters*

Gene expression profiling from microarray experiments has produced a large amount of numerical tabular data. One strategy for the analysis of gene expression data is hierarchical clustering, which creates a binary tree of genes ordered by their similarity of regulations. The measure for similarity is usually a correlation coefficient that compares the regulation of one gene with the regulation of another one with various experimental conditions.

Clustering aims for the identification of regulated biological processes through the evaluation of co-regulated genes based on the assumption that a cellular response is mainly reflected in transcriptional levels. Unfortunately, assignment to a certain cluster, the genetic co-regulation and biological function do not necessarily coincide. The reasons for this are manifold and lie mainly in the biological response, e.g., cellular processes are affected by both up or down regulation. Therefore, genes involved in a common pathway can end up in completely different clusters.

Denaxas and Tjortjis[25] proposed to combine statistical natural language processing techniques with the GO annotation ontology for assessing the biological relatedness of gene products clusters. Their result suggested that a biological similarity figure of merit can assess gene expression cluster analysis results. Ovaska *et al.*[26] presented fast software for advanced gene annotation using semantic similarity for GO terms combined with clustering and heat map visualization.

The methodology allows rapid identification of genes sharing the same GO cluster.

4.2. *Deep learning in bioinformatics*

In the era of big data, transformation of large quantities of data into valuable knowledge has become increasingly important in various domains and bioinformatics is no exception.[27] Indeed transformation of biological data and medical data into valuable knowledge has been one of the most important challenges in bioinformatics.[28] Min[29] presented a deep learning method to infer the expression of target genes from the expression of landmark genes. Leung *et al.*[30] used a deep neural network model inferred from mouse RNA-Seq data to predict splicing patterns in individual tissues and differences in splicing patterns across tissues. Alipanahi *et al.*[31] suggested that sequence specificities can be ascertained from experimental data with deep learning, which offers a scalable, flexible and unified computational approach for pattern discovery. Using a diverse array of experimental data and evaluation metrics, they found deep learning outperforms other state-of-the-art methods.

References

[1] L. NM, G. D. and G. M, What is bioinformatics? A proposed definition and overview of the field, *Methods Inf. Med.* **40**, 346 (2001).

[2] A. Bayat, Bioinformatics. (Science, Medicine, and the Future), *Br. Med. J.* **324**, 1018 (2002).

[3] S. F. Altschul, W. Gish, W. Miller, E. W. Myers and D. J. Lipman, Basic local alignment search tool, *J. Mol. Biol.* **215**, 403 (1990).

[4] E. Glaab, J. M. Garibaldi and N. Krasnogor, ArrayMining: A modular web-application for microarray analysis combining ensemble and consensus methods with cross-study normalization, *BMC Bioinf.* **10**, 1 (2009).

[5] T. Barrett *et al.*, NCBI GEO: Archive for functional genomics data sets — update, *Nucleic Acids Res.* **41**, D991 (2013).

[6] H. M. Berman *et al.*, The protein data bank., *Nucleic Acids Res.* **28**, 235 (2000).

[7] A. Chatr-aryamontri *et al.*, The BioGRID interaction database: 2015 update, *Nucleic Acids Res.* **43**, D470 (2015).

[8] M. A. Harris *et al.*, The Gene Ontology project in 2008., *Nucleic Acids Res.* **36**, D440 (2008).

[9] M. Safran *et al.*, GeneCards version 3: The human gene integrator, *Database* **2010**, baq020 (2010).

[10] G. Dennis *et al.*, DAVID: Database for annotation, visualization, and integrated discovery, *Genome Biol.* **4**, 1 (2003).

[11] V. O. Polyanovsky, M. A. Roytberg and V. G. Tumanyan, Comparative analysis of the quality of a global algorithm and a local algorithm for alignment of two sequences, *Algorithms Mol. Biol.* **6**, 25 (2011).

[12] B. Abu-Jamous, R. Fa, D. J. Roberts and A. K. Nandi, paradigm of tunable clustering using Binarization of Consensus Partition Matrices (Bi-CoPaM) for gene discovery, *PLOS One* **8**, e56432 (2013).

[13] J. Hou *et al.*, Gene expression-based classification of non-small cell lung carcinomas and survival prediction, *PLOS One* **5**, e10312 (2010).

[14]O. G. Troyanskaya, M. E. Garber, P. O. Brown, D. Botstein and R. B. Altman, Nonparametric methods for identifying differentially expressed genes in microarray data, *Bioinformatics* **18**, 1454 (2002).

[15]X. Cui, J. T. G. Hwang, J. Qiu, N. J. Blades and G. A. Churchill, Improved statistical tests for differential gene expression by shrinking variance components estimates, *Biostatistics* **6**, 59 (2005).

[16]M. B. Eisen, P. T. Spellman, P. O. Brown and D. Botstein, Cluster analysis and display of genome-wide expression patterns, *Proc. Natl. Acad. Sci.* **95**, 14863 (1998).

[17]J. Quackenbush, Computational analysis of microarray data, *Nat. Rev. Genetics* **2**, 418 (2001).

[18]J. Lu *et al.*, Gene expression profile changes in initiation and progression of squamous cell carcinoma of esophagus, *Int. J. Cancer* **91**, 288 (2001).

[19]H. F. Frierson, A. K. El-Naggar and J. B. Welsh, Large scale molecular analysis identifies genes with altered expression in salivary adenoid cystic carcinoma, *Am. J. ...* (2002).

[20]A. G. De Brevern and J. C. Gelly, ORION: A web server for protein fold recognition and structure prediction using evolutionary hybrid profiles, *researchgate.net*.

[21]H. M. J. Werner, G. B. Mills and P. T. Ram, Cancer systems biology: A peek into the future of patient care?, *Nat. Rev. Clin. Oncol.* **11**, 167 (2014).

[22]S. B. Breitkopf *et al.*, A cross-species study of PI3K protein-protein interactions reveals the direct interaction of P85 and SHP2, *Sci. Rep.* **6**, 20471 (2016).

[23]C. C. N. Wang *et al.*, A model comparison study of the flowering time regulatory network in Arabidopsis, *BMC Syst. Biol.* **8**, 15 (2014).

[24]E. O. Voit, Recasting nonlinear models as S-systems, *Math. Comput. Model.* **11**, 140 (1988).

[25]S. C. Denaxas and C. Tjortjis, Quantifying the biological similarity between gene products using GO: An application of the vector space model, *Presented at: Information Technology in Biomedicine* (2006).

[26]K. Ovaska, M. Laakso and S. Hautaniemi, Fast gene ontology based clustering for microarray experiments, *BioData Mining* **1**, 1 (2008).

[27]J. Manyika *et al.*, Big data: The next frontier for innovation, competition, and productivity (2011).

[28]S. Min, B. Lee and S. Yoon, Deep learning in *Bioinformatics* (2016).

[29]Y. Chen, Y. Li, R. Narayan, A. Subramanian and X. Xie, Gene expression inference with deep learning, *Bioinformatics* **32**, btw074 (2016).

[30]M. K. K. Leung, H. Y. Xiong, L. J. Lee and B. J. Frey, Deep learning of the tissue-regulated splicing code, *Bioinformatics* **30**, i121 (2014).

[31]B. Alipanahi, A. Delong, M. T. Weirauch and B. J. Frey, Predicting the sequence specificities of DNA- and RNA-binding proteins by deep learning, *Nat. Biotechnol.* **33**, 831 (2015).

Actionable intelligence and online learning for semantic computing

Cem Tekin*,‡ and Mihaela van der Schaar†,§

*Electrical and Electronics Engineering Department
Bilkent University, Ankara, Turkey

†Electrical Engineering Department, University of California
Los Angeles, California, USA
‡cemtekin@ee.bilkent.edu.tr
§mihaela@ee.ucla.edu

As the world becomes more connected and instrumented, high dimensional, heterogeneous and time-varying data streams are collected and need to be analyzed on the fly to extract the actionable intelligence from the data streams and make timely decisions based on this knowledge. This requires that appropriate classifiers are invoked to process the incoming streams and find the relevant knowledge. Thus, a key challenge becomes choosing online, at run-time, which classifier should be deployed to make the best possible predictions on the incoming streams. In this paper, we survey a class of methods capable to perform online learning in stream-based semantic computing tasks: multi-armed bandits (MABs). Adopting MABs for stream mining poses, numerous new challenges requires many new innovations. Most importantly, the MABs will need to explicitly consider and track online the time-varying characteristics of the data streams and to learn fast what is the relevant information out of the vast, heterogeneous and possibly highly dimensional data streams. In this paper, we discuss contextual MAB methods, which use similarities in context (meta-data) information to make decisions, and discuss their advantages when applied to stream mining for semantic computing. These methods can be adapted to discover in real-time the relevant contexts guiding the stream mining decisions, and tract the best classifier in presence of concept drift. Moreover, we also discuss how stream mining of multiple data sources can be performed by deploying cooperative MAB solutions and ensemble learning. We conclude the paper by discussing the numerous other advantages of MABs that will benefit semantic computing applications.

Keywords: Stream mining; online learning; multi-armed bandits; semantic computing.

1. Introduction

Huge amounts of data streams are now being produced by more and more sources and in increasingly diverse formats: sensor readings, physiological measurements, GPS events, network traffic information, documents, emails, transactions, tweets, audio files, videos etc. These streams are then mined in real-time to assist numerous semantic computing applications (see Fig. 1): patient monitoring,[1] personalized diagnosis,[2,3] personalized treatment recommendation,[4,5] recommender systems,[6–8] social networks,[9] network security,[10] multimedia content aggregation,[11] personalized education[12,13] etc. Hence, online data mining systems have emerged that enable such applications to analyze, extract actionable intelligence and make decisions in real-time, based on the correlated, high-dimensional and dynamic data captured by multiple heterogeneous data sources. To mine the data streams, the following questions need to be answered continuously: Which classifiers should process the data? How many and in which order, configuration or topology? What are the costs (e.g., delay) and benefits (accuracy of predictions) in invoking a specific classifier?

In this paper, we formalize the real-time mining of data streams for the purpose of semantic computing as an online learning and sequential decision problem, where classifiers and their configurations are chosen online to make predictions based on the gathered data, and subsequently focus on multi-armed bandits (MABs) as an important class of solutions for solving this problem. In the considered systems, such as the example given in Fig. 2, data from multiple sources are processed by a learner which determines on-the-fly how to classify the different data streams and make decisions based on the predictions. For this, the learner uses one of its available classifiers (or an ensemble of classifiers or classifier chains) to make a prediction. Since the prediction accuracy of the classifiers changes dynamically, over time, based on the characteristics of the collected data streams, this needs to be learned online.[14] Hence, the learner needs to continuously learn while at the same time make accurate predictions and decisions, i.e., the learning and decision making are coupled and concurrent.

Such online learning and sequential decision making under uncertainty problems can be modeled as MAB.[15,16] In the MAB framework, the learner chooses actions (bandits' arms) at each time slot and, based on this, random rewards (feedback) are revealed. Previously, MAB methods are applied to solve problems in clinical trials,[15] multi-user communication networks[17] and recommender systems.[18,19] A key advantage of MABs as compared to other online learning

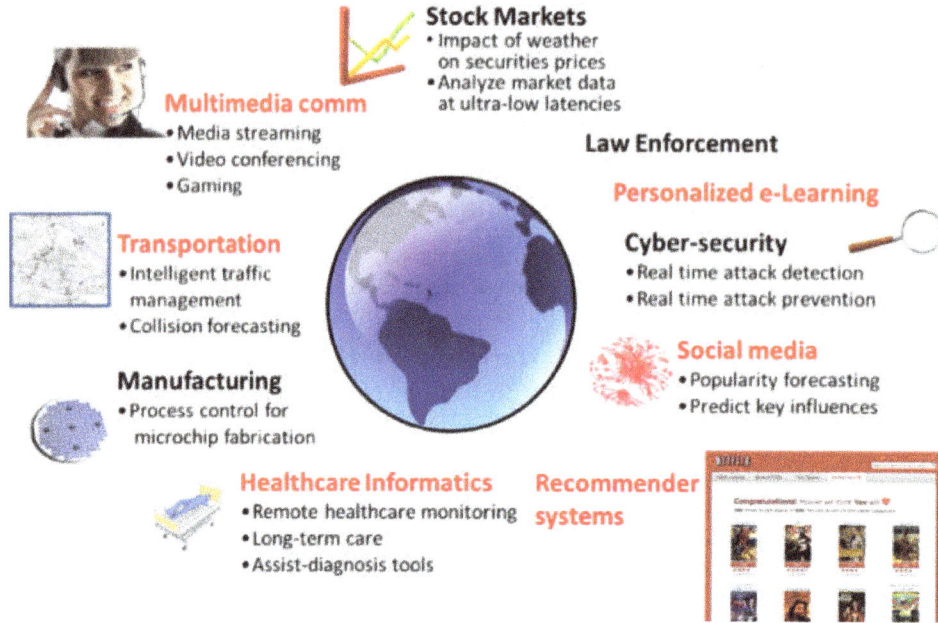

Fig. 1. Semantic computing applications.

methods (e.g., see Refs. 20 and 21) is that they can provide a bound on the convergence speed as well as a bound on the loss due to learning compared to an oracle solution which requires knowledge of the stochastic model of the system, which is named regret. In stream mining, regret of a learner's algorithm at time T is defined as the difference between the expected number of correct predictions minus costs of making a prediction using this algorithm and the expected number of correct predictions minus costs of the "oracle" algorithm which acts optimally by knowing the accuracies of all classifiers for all data and contexts. The regret, which is a non-decreasing function of T, is denoted by $\text{Reg}(T)$. Any algorithm whose regret grows sublinearly in T will acquire the same average reward with the "oracle" algorithm as $T \rightarrow \infty$.

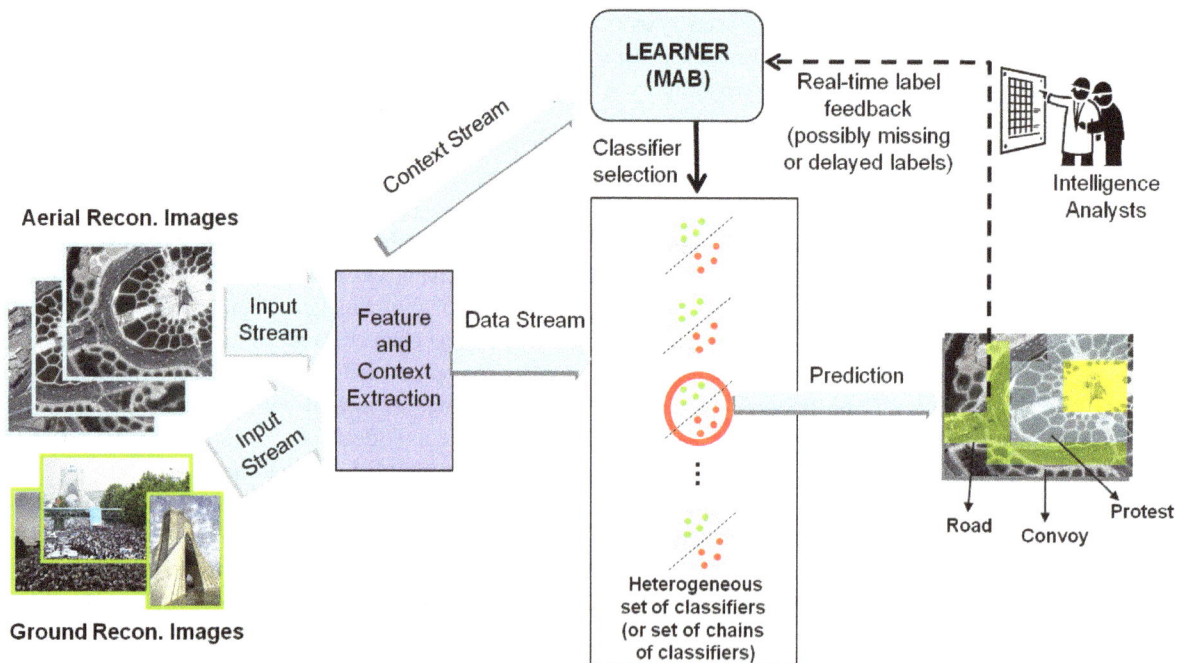

Fig. 2. Online learning of the best classifier (or the best chain of classifiers) to maximize the prediction accuracy, based on the data and context stream characteristics, through predictions and label feedback which can be delayed or missing.

Importantly, unlike many of the aforementioned MAB works, the focus in stream mining is on making decisions based on data streams ("data-in-motion") with different contexts, rather than based on channel or network states, user feedbacks or recommendations, etc. Therefore, applying MABs to formalize and solve stream mining problems presents numerous new challenges which will be discussed in the subsequent sections. To address these new and unique challenges, we will focus on a special class of MABs, referred to as contextual MABs,[22,23] which are especially suitable because they can exploit the (automatically) generated meta-data, i.e., the context, which is gathered or associated to the data streams in the process of capturing or pre-processing them (e.g., location, data modality etc.), or the features extracted directly from the data during a pre-processing phase. Since it is unknown *a priori* which contexts should be exploited at each moment in time to yield the best predictions based on the time-varying data characteristics, it becomes essential for the efficiency of contextual MABs when applied to stream mining to find the relevant contexts on the fly.[8]

2. Formalizing Real-Time Stream Mining Problems as MABs

In a stream mining system, the learner is equipped with a set of classifiers $\mathcal{F}$, each of which provides a prediction when called by the learner, based on the data. Time varying and heterogeneous characteristics of data streams makes it impossible to design a classifier which works well for any data. Usually, the classifiers are specialized on specific data streams, for which they can produce accurate predictions. Since the characteristics of the data stream is unknown *a priori*, the learner needs to learn which classifiers to choose online. Classifiers used by the learner can be pre-trained or they can even learn online based on the predictions they make on the data and the labels they receive. Choosing the right classifier for a given context is a highly nontrivial problem due to lack of *a priori* knowledge about performance of the classifiers on the dynamic and heterogeneous data as well as the lack of *a priori* knowledge about the relationships between the contexts and prediction accuracies.

An important goal in stream mining is to balance the short term and long term performance. Stream applications run indefinitely, and there is no predetermined final time T for which the learner can plan an optimal learning strategy. The learner's reward at time t is defined as the prediction accuracy of the classifier chosen at time t minus costs of prediction. Therefore, the learner should continuously balance exploration, i.e., trying different classifiers to estimate their accuracies, and exploitation, i.e., selecting the classifier with the highest estimated reward to maximize the instantaneous reward, to have high expected total reward at any time slot. Without loss of generality, in our discussion we

assume that costs of selecting classifiers is the same for each classifier, thus we focus on maximizing the number of correct predictions.

We first explain how the data, labels and contexts are generated. It is assumed that at each time slot $t = 1, 2, \ldots$, data $s(t)$, label $y(t)$ and context $\boldsymbol{x}(t)$ are drawn from an unknown joint distribution J over $\mathcal{S} \times \mathcal{Y} \times \mathcal{X}$, which is called the *stream distribution*, where $\mathcal{S}$ is the set of data instances, $\mathcal{Y}$ is the set of labels and $\mathcal{X}$ is the set/space of contexts. It is usually assumed that $\mathcal{X}$ is very large.[18,22] The conditional distribution of data and label given context $\boldsymbol{x}$ is $G_{\boldsymbol{x}}$ on $\mathcal{S} \times \mathcal{Y}$, and it depends on J. The accuracy of classifier f for context $\boldsymbol{x}$ is given by $\pi_f(\boldsymbol{x})$. Hence, the optimal classifier given context $\boldsymbol{x}$ is $f^*(\boldsymbol{x}) := \arg\max_{f \in \mathcal{F}} \pi_f(\boldsymbol{x})$. Classifier accuracies are unknown to the learner since J is unknown. Learning J from past observations and using the prediction rules of the classifiers to estimate the classifier accuracies is not feasible both because of the dimensionality of the data stream and computational issues related to the complexity of the classification rules. In order to overcome this issue, MAB methods directly learn the accuracy without estimating J.

Data streams usually have the *similarity property*,[22] which implies that the prediction accuracies of a classifier for two contexts $\boldsymbol{x}$ and $\boldsymbol{x}'$ are related to each other when the contexts are related to each other. There are many metrics to define similarity between contexts and similarity between classifier accuracies, and one of the most widely used metric is the Hölder continuity metric, which is defined as

$$|\pi_f(\boldsymbol{x}) - \pi_f(\boldsymbol{x})| \leq L||\boldsymbol{x} - \boldsymbol{x}'||^\gamma \tag{1}$$

for all $\boldsymbol{x}, \boldsymbol{x}' \in \mathcal{X}$, where $||\cdot||$ is the standard Euclidian metric, and $L > 0$ and $\gamma > 0$ are constants that define the structure of similarity. Some MAB methods learn independently for each context,[16] while some MAB methods exploit the similarity between classifier accuracies.[22]

While in the above formulation the stream distribution is static, numerous works considered time-varying distributions for classification rules,[11] which is also called *concept drift*.[24,25] A change in accuracy of a classifier can happen when the classifier updates its prediction rule. For example, online learning classifiers can update their prediction rule based on the past predictions and labels, and hence can improve their accuracy. In this case, the prediction rule of a classifier will be time varying. Therefore, a more systematic characterization of concept drift is *accuracy drift*, i.e., the change in classifier accuracies which can be the result of concept drift, prediction rule update or both. An important class of this is gradual accuracy drift, i.e., for each $t, t' \in \{1, 2, \ldots\}$ and $f \in \mathcal{F}$, there exists constants $\gamma > 0$ and $L > 0$ such that for all $\boldsymbol{x}, \boldsymbol{x}'$, we have

$$|\pi_{f,t}(\boldsymbol{x}) - \pi_{f,t'}(\boldsymbol{x}')|$$
$$\leq L(||\boldsymbol{x} - \boldsymbol{x}'||^2 + |t'/\tau - t/\tau|^2)^{\gamma/2} \tag{2}$$

where $\pi_{f,t}(\cdot)$ is the time-varying accuracy of classifier f, τ is the *stability of accuracy*, hence $1/\tau$ is the *speed of drift*. This equation limits how much the similarity between the accuracies of classifier f for two contexts can change with time. Knowing this, the learner can analytically determine the window of history of past predictions, labels and decisions it should take into account when estimating the current classifier accuracies.[11] Intuitively, as τ increases, the learner can rely on a larger window of history to estimate the classifier accuracies. MAB methods can also be used for the case when the accuracy drift is abrupt but infrequent, i.e., there can be a large change in a classifier's accuracy between two consecutive time slots, but the frequency of such changes is low so that the changes can be tracked.[26] Thus, the important design challenge is how to optimally combine the past observations to estimate classifier accuracies. In the following sections, we will review several methods for this.

3. Dealing with Heterogeneous and Dynamic Data: The Role of Contextual MABs

The idea behind contextual bandit algorithms is to form a partition of the context space consisting of sets of contexts such that the classifier accuracies are estimated independently for each set instead of being estimated independently for each context, based on the *mining history*.[19,22] The partition of the context space can be even generated on the fly, based on the past context arrivals and the similarity information in Eq. (1) given to the learner. The number of past contexts that lie in a set as well as the variation of classifier accuracies for contexts within that set, increases with the size (volume) of the set. From an estimation perspective, the first one can be seen as an increase in the sample size, and the second one can be seen as a decrease in the sample quality. An optimal contextual bandit algorithm should balance the tradeoff between these two. Since accuracy drift in Eq. (2) translates into an increase in the variation of classifier accuracies between past time slots and the current time slot, the partitioning idea of contextual bandits also works well in this setting.

To differentiate between different types of contexts, we write the context (vector) at time step t as $\boldsymbol{x}(t) = (x_1(t),\ldots,x_d(t))$, where d is the dimension of the context vector and $x_i(t)$ is a type-i context that lies in the set of type-i contexts $\mathcal{X}_i$, which can be either discrete or continuous. Hence, $\mathcal{X}$ is equal to the Cartesian product of type-i context sets. For a data stream, one type of context can be the packet size, while another one can be the location. Even a feature of the raw data, or the output of a preprocessor on data can be a type of context. There are two ways to partition the contexts. The first way, i.e., the *non-adaptive contexts* method, is to form a partition over $\mathcal{X}$ to estimate the classifier accuracies for each set in that partition without learning about the impact of different types of contexts in the context vector to the accuracy of classifier selection.[2,7,18,22] The second way, i.e., the *adaptive contexts* method, is to form partitions over the context space by learning the *relevant contexts*, i.e., the contexts whose values affect the prediction accuracy the most.[8] The adaptive contexts method learns the classifier accuracies much faster, especially when the number of relevant context types is small. However, it requires more processing power, since it must handle the task of identifying the relevant contexts in addition to choosing the best classifier. Nonadaptive contexts method has been successfully applied in numerous semantic computing applications including context-driven image stream mining[2] and item recommendation in social networks.[9] Similarly, adaptive contexts methods has been successfully applied in context-driven medical expertise discovery,[4] multimedia content aggregation[11] and recommender systems.[8]

In the presence of accuracy drift, the learner needs to choose classifiers to make predictions solely on the recent relevant history. An important challenge arises due to the fact the learner cannot trust on the entire mining history, because past predictions, labels and classifier selection may have become irrelevant due to the concept drift or change in classifiers. Thus, the learner should decide which parts of the mining history, it should use to estimate the classifier accuracies to balance the estimation errors due to small number of past samples and variations in the classifier accuracies over time. Hence, the number of past samples that should be used when estimating the accuracies should be optimized depending on the speed of the drift, i.e., $1/\tau$ in Eq. (2).

Approaches used in dealing with accuracy drift include using a sliding time window of mining history to estimate accuracies or combining time slots into rounds where a new MAB-based learning algorithm run for each round.[26] When using a sliding time window, creating the correct partition of the context space becomes complicated since the sets in the partition could also merge to form bigger sets when past mining histories are discarded in forming accuracy estimates. The second approach creates the problem of cold-start, which slows down learning and increases loss due to explorations, since mining history in the previous rounds is completely neglected when deciding how to choose classifiers in the initial slots of the current round. An alternative to both of these methods is to run different instances of the MAB algorithm with overlapping rounds, where each round is a time window.[11] In this method, time is divided into rounds with multiple decision epochs. Each round is further divided into two passive and active sub-rounds of equal lengths such that active sub-round of round $\rho-1$ overlaps with the passive sub-round of round ρ. At the beginning of round ρ a new instance of the MAB algorithm, denoted by MAB_ρ, is created. In the passive sub-round, MAB_ρ learn from the classifier selections made by $\text{MAB}_{\rho-1}$ but does not select any classifier. In the active sub-round, MAB_ρ both learn from the predictions and labels and also selects the classifier to produce the prediction.

4. Learning from Multiple Data Sources: Cooperative MABs and Ensemble of MABs

4.1. *Cooperative MABs*

Cooperative stream mining emerged as a result of applications running in geographically different locations such as security cameras, distributed databases of large companies, cloud servers, etc., as well as applications running under different software platforms and applications running by different entities/companies. In this section, we review decentralized and cooperative learning implementations named cooperative contextual bandits.[27] In these problems, the data stream of each source is locally processed by a learner which has its own set of classifiers. When data arrives along with the context, a learner can use one of its own classifiers to make a prediction, or it can call another learner and ask for a prediction. When calling another learner, the learner can send both its data and context (high cost, better prediction) or just its context (low cost, worse prediction). The goal of each learner is to maximize its total expected reward (correct predictions minus cost) by learning the best distributed context-dependent classification strategy.

Cooperation by learners not knowing other learners expertise (i.e., the classifiers used by other learners and their accuracies when processing a specific type of data) requires a novel 3-phase learning structure involving training, exploration and exploitation phases as compared to the conventional single-learner solutions. The additional training phase for learner i serves the purpose of helping other learners discover their best classifiers for learner i's contexts. Since the data and context arrivals to learners are different, without the training phase, learner j may not be able to learn its best action for learner i's contexts, hence learner i may not be able to assess the potential of learner j in making predictions about i's data.

Cooperative contextual bandits have been successfully applied in applications with decentralized learners. In one application, the problem of assigning patients to medical experts at different clinics is considered.[4] The system model for this application is given in Fig. 3. In this application, clinics, that act as decentralized entities, manage to learn to match each new patient with the best expert for that patient via cooperation. Experts in this application can be viewed as classifiers. It is assumed that a clinic knows its own experts but does not know the experts available at other clinics. However, clinics are not aware of the quality/accuracy of their own experts and of other clinics. Moreover, unlike the standard one-size-fits-all approach in which the new patient is matched with the best expert on average, the goal in this application is to provide personalized matching based on the context x of the new patient. For instance, some senior experts may be substantially better at diagnosing patients with complex co-morbidities than junior experts. In addition, the diagnostic accuracy of an expert may depend on family history, age, weight or genes of the patient. All of these

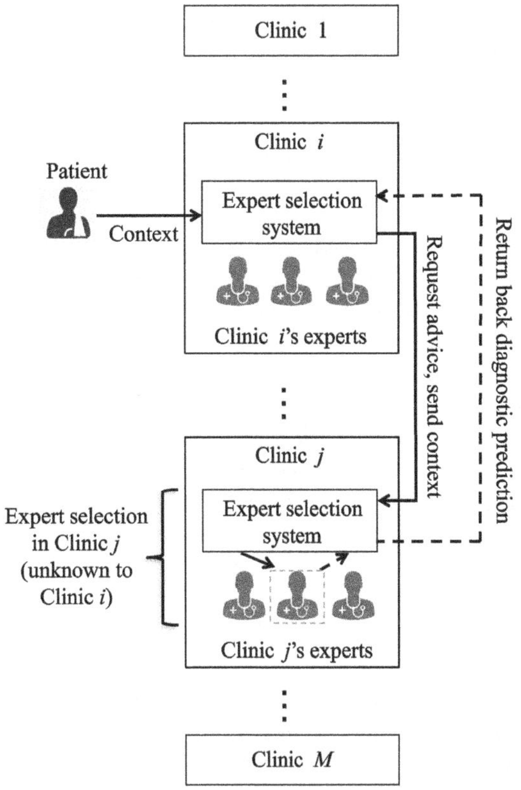

Fig. 3. Cooperative MABs for matching patients with experts.

features can be used as contexts to personalize the patient-expert matching. In such a setting, context-dependent quality of each expert must be learned through repeated interaction.

As an example, assume that there are M clinics, indexed by $i \in \mathcal{M} := \{1, 2, \ldots, M\}$, and E_i experts in clinic i indexed by $e \in \mathcal{E}_i := \{1, 2, \ldots, E_i\}$. Clinic i keeps an estimate of the quality/accuracy of its own experts $\hat{\pi}_e(x)$, $e \in \mathcal{E}_i$ and the quality/accuracy of the other clinics $\hat{\pi}_j(x)$, $j \in \mathcal{M} - \{i\}$ for each patient context $x \in \mathcal{X}$. Here, $\hat{\pi}_j(x)$ is an estimate of the quality/accuracy of the best expert of clinic j given x. The 3-phase learning structure proposed in Ref. 27 allows clinic i to form accurate estimates of this quantity without requiring it to know from which expert of clinic j the predictions come from.

Since learning and keeping separate quality estimates for each $x \in \mathcal{X}$ is inefficient, clinic i partitions $\mathcal{X}$ into finitely many sets $\{p_1, \ldots, p_J\}$ of identical size. This partition is denoted by $\mathcal{P}$. Quality estimates are kept and updated for each $p \in \mathcal{P}$. Hence, for any context $x \in p$, $\hat{\pi}_e(x) = \hat{\pi}_e(p)$ and $\hat{\pi}_j(x) = \hat{\pi}_j(p)$. The granularity of $\mathcal{P}$ determines the learning speed and accuracy. The estimates converge quickly when the number of elements in $\mathcal{P}$ is small. On the other hand, the approximation error of $\hat{\pi}_e(x)$ and $\hat{\pi}_j(x)$ is higher when $\mathcal{P}$ is coarse, since the estimation is done using contexts more dissimilar to x. The optimal way to set $\mathcal{P}$ is discussed in Ref. 27.

When a new patient arrives to clinic i, the learning algorithm first retrieves the context of the patient, which is denoted by $x_i(t)$. Then, it computes the set in the partition $\mathcal{P}$

that $x_i(t)$ belongs to, which is denoted by $p_i(t)$. Based on the accuracy of the estimates $\hat{\pi}_e(p_i(t))$, $e \in \mathcal{E}_i$ and $\hat{\pi}_j(p_i(t))$, $j \in \mathcal{M} - \{i\}$, clinic i will choose the clinic or expert to train, explore or exploit. The rule of thumb is to exploit only when the clinic is sufficiently confident about the quality of its own experts and the other clinics for the new patient. As seen in Fig. 3, this operation does not require clinic i to know the experts of the other clinics. All requests made by clinic i will be handled by the learning algorithm responsible for the expert selection system at clinic j. This allows the clinics to function autonomously, while also helping each other utilize their own resources when necessary.

In another application of cooperative contextual bandits, a network of multimedia content aggregators is considered.[11] These aggregators, each serving different types of users and having access to different types of multimedia content, learned to cooperate with each other in order to match their users with the right content.

4.2. *Ensemble of MABs*

In another strand of literature (See Refs. 28 and 29) ensemble learning methods are introduced to learn from multiple data sources. Data is processed locally by *local learners* (LLs) and the prediction of the LLs are sent to an *ensemble learner* (EL) which produces the final prediction. While majority of the related works treat LLs as black-box algorithms, in Ref. 3 a joint learning approach for LLs and the EL is developed. In this method, LLs implement a contextual MAB algorithm to learn their best classifier. On the other hand, the EL uses the dynamic meta-data provided about the LLs in order to combine their predictions.

An important application of this work is medical diagnosis,[30] in which predictions about the health condition of a patient are made by a set of distributed learners (or experts) that have access to different parts of the patient data. For instance, consider the situation described in Fig. 4, in which experts make local predictions based on different chunks of the patient's multi-modal medical data, which includes the *electronic health record* (EHR), mobile application data, lab test results and screening test results. This data is processed by multiple experts (some of which can be computerized diagnostic decision support systems) with different skills and different access rights to the data. First, each expert makes its own local diagnostic prediction. Then, these predictions are combined by an EL to produce a final prediction. Finally, after the true diagnosis (label) is revealed both the EL and the LLs update their prediction strategy.

The goal in this application is to maximize the expected number of correct predictions (over all patients arrived so far) by designing a decentralized learning algorithm, by which both the LLs and the EL update their prediction strategy on-the-fly. For instance, such an algorithm, which achieves the optimal learning rate is proposed in Ref. 3. The main idea behind this algorithm is to simultaneously enable LLs to learn

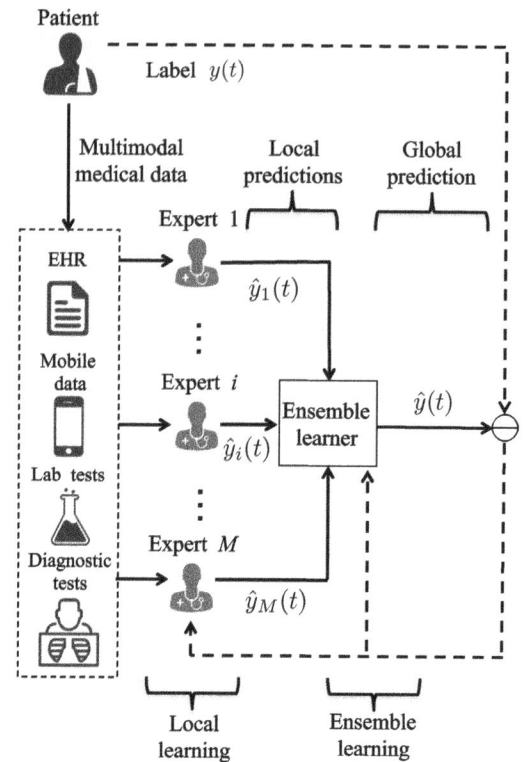

Fig. 4. Ensemble of MABs for medical diagnosis.

their best context-dependent prediction strategy by applying a contextual MAB learning algorithm and enable the EL to optimally fuse the predictions of the LLs by using a parameter-free ensemble learning algorithm.

It is shown in Ref. 3 that such a learning algorithm achieves prediction accuracy that is much higher than the prediction accuracy of the individual LLs or the prediction accuracy of an EL that works together with LLs that do not learn over time.

Apart from medical diagnosis, this method can also be used in big data stream mining. The benefit comes from both computation and memory savings as well as guaranteed performance bounds. Basically, it is shown in Ref. 3 that the memory requirement of the LLs in the proposed approach only increases sublinearly in the size of the dataset. On the other hand, the memory requirement for the EL is constant, since it only requires to learn the weights of the LLs.

5. Staged MABs

Apart from the task of selecting the right classifiers to maximize the prediction accuracy, in numerous semantic computing applications such as personalized education and clinical decision support, each decision step involves selecting multiple actions (e.g., selecting various materials to display or various tests to be performed) whose reward is only revealed after the entire action sequence is completed and a decision is made to stop the action sequence and (possibly) take a final action (e.g., take a final exam, perform a surgery or finalize a treatment decision). For instance, in personalized online education, a sequence of materials can be used to teach or remind students the key concepts of a course subject and the final exam is used as a benchmark to evaluate the overall effectiveness of the given sequence of teaching materials. In addition, a sequence of intermediate feedbacks like quiz and homework grades can be used to guide the teaching examples online. These feedbacks can be combined into a context. For instance, a student's context can include fixed features such as her CGPA, as well as dynamic features such as the percentage of questions about a subject that she answered correctly. Most of the prior works on contextual bandits do not take into account such dynamic features.

Since the order of actions taken in the above problem affects the reward, previously discussed methods are incapable of addressing this problem. Such learning problems can be efficiently solved using staged MAB methods.[12,13] In a staged MAB, the learning algorithm selects the next actions to take in each round based on the estimated marginal gain of that action, while also taking into account the estimation error due to finitely many past observations. It is shown that this type of greedy action selection results in sublinear regret with respect to an approximately optimal benchmark, when the reward function is adaptive submodular.[31]

6. MABs, Regret Bounds and Confidence Intervals

One major advantage of applying MAB methods for semantic computing applications is their strong theoretical performance guarantees both in terms of regret and confidence intervals. Upper bounds on the regrets (defined in the introduction section) of various MAB methods are given in Table 1. While all methods achieve sublinear in T regret, the convergence speed of the time averaged regret values differ for these methods. Specifically, when adaptive contexts method is used, the time order of the regret depends only on the number of relevant context dimensions d_{rel}, which is in general much smaller than d. While the regret bounds characterize the long-run performance of MAB methods, confidence intervals provide information about the trustworthiness of the selected classifier. Basically, the confidence interval of classifier f at time slot t is a range of values $[L_f(t), U_f(t)] \subset [0, 1]$ such that $\pi_f(\boldsymbol{x}(t))$ lies within $[L_f(t), U_f(t)]$ with a very high probability. Here, $L_f(t)$ is called the *lower confidence*

bound and $U_f(t)$ is called the *upper confidence bound*. Numerous works provided data-size dependent confidence intervals and confidence bounds for MAB methods.[3,11,32,33] As expected, the confidence interval shrinks as the number of past data instances increase, depending on the risk awareness of the semantic computing application, more confident classifiers can be preferred over classifiers that perform better on average.

References

[1] D. Simons, Consumer electronics opportunities in remote and home healthcare, *Philips Res.* (2008).

[2] C. Tekin and M. van der Schaar, Active learning in context-driven stream mining with an application to image mining, *IEEE Trans. Image Process.* **24**, 3666 (2015).

[3] C. Tekin, J. Yoon and M. van der Schaar, Adaptive ensemble learning with confidence bounds, to appear in *IEEE Trans. Signal Process* (2016).

[4] C. Tekin, O. Atan and M. van der Schaar, Discover the expert: Context-adaptive expert selection for medical diagnosis, *IEEE Trans. Emerg. Top. Comput.* **3**, 220 (2015).

[5] J. Yoon, C. Davtyan and M. van der Schaar, Discovery and clinical decision support for personalized healthcare, to appear in *IEEE J. Biomed. and Health Inform* (2016).

[6] Y. Cao and Y. Li, An intelligent fuzzy-based recommendation system for consumer electronic products, *Expert Syst. Appl.* **33**, 230 (2007).

[7] L. Song, C. Tekin and M. van der Schaar, Online learning in large-scale contextual recommender systems, *IEEE Trans. Serv. Comput.* **9**, 433 (2016).

[8] C. Tekin and M. van der Schaar, RELEAF: An algorithm for learning and exploiting relevance, *IEEE J. Sel. Top. Signal Process.* **9**, 716 (2015).

[9] C. Tekin, S. Zhang and M. van der Schaar, Distributed online learning in social recommender systems, *IEEE J. Sel. Top. Signal Process.* **8**, 638 (2014).

[10] A. M. Eskicioglu and E. J. Delp, An overview of multimedia content protection in consumer electronics devices, *Signal Process: Image Commun.* **16**, 681 (2001).

[11] C. Tekin and M. van der Schaar, Contextual online learning for multimedia content aggregation, *IEEE Trans. Multimedia* **17**, 549 (2015).

[12] J. Xu, T. Xiang and M. van der Schaar, Personalized course sequence recommendations, *IEEE Trans. Signal Process.* **64**, 5340 (2016).

[13] C. Tekin, J. Braun and M. van der Schaar, eTutor: Online learning for personalized education, *IEEE Int. Conf. Acoustics, Speech and Signal Processing (ICASSP)* (2015), pp. 5545–5549.

[14] G. Mateos, J. A. Bazerque and G. B. Giannakis, Distributed sparse linear regression, *IEEE Trans. Signal Process.* **58**, 5262 (2010).

[15] T. Lai and H. Robbins, Asymptotically efficient adaptive allocation rules, *Adv. Appl. Math.* **6**, 4 (1985).

[16] P. Auer, N. Cesa-Bianchi and P. Fischer, Finite-time analysis of the multiarmed bandit problem, *Mach. Learn.* **47**, 235 (2002).

[17] K. Liu and Q. Zhao, Distributed learning in multi-armed bandit with multiple players, *IEEE Trans. Signal Process.* **58**, 5667 (2010).

Table 1. Upper bounds on the regrets of various MAB methods.

Nonadaptive contexts Ref. 3	$O\left(T^{\frac{\gamma+d}{2\gamma+d}}\log T\right)$
Adaptive contexts Ref. 8 ($\gamma = 1$)	$O\left(T^{\frac{2+2d_{\text{rel}}+\sqrt{4d_{\text{rel}}^2+16d_{\text{rel}}+12}}{4+2d_{\text{rel}}+\sqrt{4d_{\text{rel}}^2+16d_{\text{rel}}+12}}}\log T\right)$
Cooperative contextual MAB Ref. 27	$O\left(T^{\frac{2\gamma+d}{3\gamma+d}}\log T\right)$

[18] T. Lu, D. Pál and M. Pál, Contextual multi-armed bandits, *Proc. Int. Conf. Artificial Intelligence and Statistics (AISTATS)* (2010), pp. 485–492.

[19] L. Li, W. Chu, J. Langford and R. E. Schapire, A contextual-bandit approach to personalized news article recommendation, *Proc. 19th Int. Conf. World Wide Web* (2010), pp. 661–670.

[20] C. J. Watkins and P. Dayan, Q-learning, *Mach. Learn.* **8**, 279 (1992).

[21] W. A. Gardner, Learning characteristics of stochastic-gradient-descent algorithms: A general study, analysis, and critique, *Signal Process.* **6**, 113 (1984).

[22] A. Slivkins, Contextual bandits with similarity information, *J. Mach. Learn. Res.* **15**, 2533 (2014).

[23] J. Langford and T. Zhang, The epoch-greedy algorithm for contextual multi-armed bandits, *Adv. Neural Inf. Process. Syst.* **20**, 1096 (2007).

[24] I. Zliobaite, Learning under Concept Drift: An Overview, Technical Report, Vilnius University, Faculty of Mathematics and Informatics (2010).

[25] J. Gao, W. Fan and J. Han, On appropriate assumptions to mine data streams: Analysis and practice, *Proc. IEEE ICDM* (2007), pp. 143–152.

[26] A. Garivier and E. Moulines, On upper-confidence bound policies for non-stationary bandit problems, arXiv:0805.3415.

[27] C. Tekin and M. van der Schaar, Distributed online learning via cooperative contextual bandits, *IEEE Trans. Signal Process.* **63**, 3700 (2015).

[28] N. Littlestone and M. K. Warmuth, The weighted majority algorithm, *30th Annual Symp. Foundations of Computer Science* (1989), pp. 256–261.

[29] Y. Freund and R. E. Schapire, A decision-theoretic generalization of on-line learning and an application to boosting, *Computational Learning Theory* (1995), pp. 23–37.

[30] C. Tekin, J. Yoon and M. van der Schaar, Adaptive ensemble learning with confidence bounds for personalized diagnosis, *AAAI Workshop on Expanding the Boundaries of Health Informatics using AI (HIAI '16)* (2016).

[31] V. Gabillon, B. Kveton, Z. Wen, B. Eriksson and S. Muthukrishnan, Adaptive submodular maximization in bandit setting, *Adv. Neural Inf. Process. Syst.* 2697 (2013).

[32] Y. Abbasi-Yadkori, D. Pál and C. Szepesvári, Improved algorithms for linear stochastic bandits, *Adv. Neural Inf. Process. Syst.* 2312 (2011).

[33] D. Russo and B. Van Roy, Learning to optimize via posterior sampling, *Math. Oper. Res.* **39**, 1221 (2014).

Subject Index

Activity Detection Engine, 211
additive model, 53
anomaly detection, 37
Artificial Intelligence (AI), 103
Artificial Neural Network (ANN), 88
Association rule learning, 89
automated even, 38

Bayesian networks, 63
big data, 73
bioinformatics, 223
bootstrap, 59
business processes, 117

Causality analysis, 64
Classification, 87, 88
clause-based approach, 6
Clustering, 88
community detection, 29
concept drift, 122
Conformance checking, 120
cosine similarity, 10
Cox proportional hazards model, 91
cricothyrotomy simulator, 210
cubic spline function, 52

Data mining, 225
Data Science programs (DSPs), 127
decision support systems, 130
deep learning, 103, 228
Deep Naural Networks (DNNs), 103
detection, 38

engineering design knowledge, 166
estimation, 112
event detection, 21
expert opinion, 63
exponential type, 77

Generalized additive models (GAMs), 92
Generalized linear models, 77
GLiM, 78
graphical model, 63

histogram, 46

image retrieval, 198
indoor localization, 217
Information Extraction, 3
information quality (InfoQ), 126
information retrieval, 9
Information Systems (IS), 141

jackknife, 58

kemel density, 48
knowledge acquisition, 150
knowledge modeling, 166
knowledge representation (KR), 181

lexical ambiguity, 149
Lexical Knowledge Resources (LKRs), 151
lexical semantics, 149
Link-based approaches, 31
local regression, 50, 51
location semantics, 216

Machine learning (ML), 85
Markov Chain Monte Carlo, 45
maximum likelihood estimator (MLE), 80
model goodness, 80
Model-based Documentation (MBD), 168
multi-armed bandits (MABs), 231
multilinguality, 150
multimedia ontology, 183, 201
Multimedia Semantic Framework, 199

Named Entity Linking (NEL), 171
Natural Language Processing, 4, 9

object-relational model, 191
On-Line Analytic Processing (OLAP), 85
online learning, 231
Ontology Feature Vector (OFV), 142
Ontology, 168, 183
Open IE, 3
Organizational mining, 120
OWL, 183

P2P network, 186
Precision, 112
process discovery technique, 118
Process mining, 117

Regression, 87
robotics, 209

semantic annotations, 142
semantic computing applications, 236
semantic network (SN), 183
semantic relatedness, 9
semantic search, 141
Semantic similarity reasoning, 141
Semantic Similarity, 149
Semantic Software Engineering (SSE), 191
Semantic technology, 168
SemanticObjects, 191
semantics, 209
sematic atoms, 17
SemSim+ method, 142
sequential decision making, 231
sequential sampling, 112
smoothing, 94

social networks, 21, 29
spline methods, 52
SPRT, 114
stream mining, 232
Summarization Algorithm, 17
summarization, 15, 16
Survival analysis, 91

text summarization, 16
topic detection and tracking, 21
topic modeling, 32
training, 105
Tweets, 174
Twitter, 171

user model, 219
user requirements, 191

verb phrases, 5
verb-phrase based relation extraction, 6
video surveillance system, 37

word sense, 152
World Sense Disambiguation (WSD), 149

Author Index

Amato, F.   15

Bagheri, E.   3, 9, 117, 21, 29
Bai, L.   91
Barr, J. R.   77
Basile, P.   171
Bovi, C. D.   149
Byrne, W.   165

Caputo, A.   171
Chapman, C.   165
Chatla, S. B.   45
Chen, C.-H.   45
Coleman, S. Y.   125

D'Acierno, A.   15
D'Auria, D.   37, 209

Fani, H.   29
Farazi, F.   165
Feng, Y.   9
Formica, A.   141

Gillen, D.   91

Hao, X.   103

Jin, J.   85

Kenett, R. S.   63, 125
Kitazawa, A.   191

Liu, Q.   215

Ma, S.   215
Missikoff, M.   141
Moscato, V.   15

Navigli, R.   149

Penta, A.   15, 197
Persia, F.   37, 209
Picariello, A.   15
Pourabbas, E.   141
Pourmasoumi, A.   117

Raju, P.   165
Rinaldi, A. M.   181

Sheu, P.   191
Shmueli, G.   45
Sperlí, G.   15

Taglino, F.   141
Tekin, C.   231
Tsai, J. J. P.   223

van der Schaar, M.   231
Vo, D.-T.   3

Wang, C. C. N.   223
Wang, T.   191

Zacks, S.   77, 111
Zarrinkalam, F.   21
Zhang, G.   103

www.ingramcontent.com/pod-product-compliance
Lightning Source LLC
Chambersburg PA
CBHW081344190326
41458CB00018B/6082